A Political Companion to Frederick Douglass

A POLITICAL COMPANION TO
Frederick Douglass

EDITED BY Neil Roberts

UNIVERSITY PRESS OF KENTUCKY

The University Press of Kentucky, scholarly publisher for the Commonwealth,
serving Bellarmine University, Berea College, Centre
College of Kentucky, Eastern Kentucky University,
The Filson Historical Society, Georgetown College,
Kentucky Historical Society, Kentucky State University,
Morehead State University, Murray State University,
Northern Kentucky University, Transylvania University,
University of Kentucky, University of Louisville,
and Western Kentucky University.
All rights reserved.

Editorial and Sales Offices: The University Press of Kentucky
663 South Limestone Street, Lexington, Kentucky 40508-4008
www.kentuckypress.com

Library of Congress Cataloging-in-Publication Data

Names: Roberts, Neil, 1976- editor.
Title: A political companion to Frederick Douglass / edited by Neil Roberts.
Description: Lexington, Ky. : University Press of Kentucky, 2018. | Includes
 bibliographical references and index.
Identifiers: LCCN 2017060706| ISBN 9780813175621 (hardcover : alk. paper) |
 ISBN 9780813175645 (pdf) | ISBN 9780813175638 (epub)
Subjects: LCSH: Douglass, Frederick, 1818–1895—Political and social views. |
 Douglass, Frederick, 1818–1895—Influence. | African American abolition-
 ists—Biography. | Antislavery movements—United States—History—19th
 century. | United States—Race relations—History—19th century.
Classification: LCC E449.D75 P65 2018 | DDC 973.8092—dc23 LC record
 available at https://lccn.loc.gov/2017060706

This book is printed on acid-free paper meeting
the requirements of the American National Standard
for Permanence in Paper for Printed Library Materials.

Manufactured in the United States of America.

Member of the Association of University Presses

For Santiago
and in loving memory of
Olive Gordon and Hyacinth Roberts

I, therefore, leave off where I began, with hope.
—Frederick Douglass, "What to the Slave Is the Fourth of July?"

Contents

Illustrations

Series Foreword

Those who undertake a study of American political thought must attend to the great theorists, philosophers, and essayists. Such a study is incomplete, however, if it neglects American literature, one of the greatest repositories of the nation's political thought and teachings.

America's literature is distinctive because it is, above all, intended for a democratic citizenry. In contrast to eras when an author would aim to inform or influence a select aristocratic audience, in democratic times public influence and education must resonate with a more expansive, less leisured, and diverse audience to be effective. The great works of America's literary tradition are the natural locus of democratic political teaching. Invoking the interest and attention of citizens through the pleasures afforded by the literary form, many of America's great thinkers sought to forge a democratic public philosophy with subtle and often challenging teachings that unfolded in narrative, plot, and character development. Perhaps more than any other nation's literary tradition, American literature is ineluctably political—shaped by democracy as much as it has in turn shaped democracy.

The Political Companions to Great American Authors series highlights the teachings of the great authors in America's literary and belletristic tradition. An astute political interpretation of America's literary tradition requires careful, patient, and attentive readers who approach the text with a view to understanding its underlying messages about citizenship and democracy. Essayists in this series approach the classic texts not with a "hermeneutics of suspicion" but with the curiosity of fellow citizens who believe that the great authors have something of value to teach their readers. The series brings together essays from varied approaches and viewpoints for the common purpose of elucidating the political teachings of the nation's greatest authors for those seeking a better understanding of American democracy.

Patrick J. Deneen
Series Editor

Introduction

Political Thought in the Shadow of Douglass

Neil Roberts

Our past was slavery. We cannot recur to it with any sense of complacency or composure. The history of it is a record of stripes, a revelation of agony. It is written in characters of blood. Its breath is a sigh, its voice a groan, and we turn from it with a shudder. The duty of to-day is to meet the questions that confront us with intelligence and courage.
—Frederick Douglass, "The Nation's Problem" (1889)

Intellectual Horizons

Interpreting the political thought of Frederick Douglass (1818–1895) requires close attention to time. Douglass was nearly fifty when the Civil War ended, and he lived another thirty years afterward. Although the division of years between the ante- and postbellum periods in Douglass's life wasn't as equally split as the years before (thirty-five) and after (thirty-four) the German émigré political theorist Hannah Arendt arrived in America,[1] the bloody intrastate struggle over slavery and the fate of the American republic was a critical marker for Douglass. Yet to situate Douglass's political thought in either an "antebellum" period or a "postbellum" period elides the major thematic areas that cut across Douglass's oeuvre, select changes in his positions within those eras notwithstanding.

Consider a series of critical junctures. Douglass was six years old when, as an enslaved being, chattel, a person reduced to the category of thing, he was brought to Colonel Edward Lloyd's plantation off the Wye River on Maryland's Eastern Shore; eight when sent to Baltimore to live under the mastery of Hugh and Sophia Auld; an unsweet sixteen when outsourced to the slave breaker Edward Covey; twenty when he escaped from Maryland as a fugitive, disguised as a sailor; twenty-three when he began speaking as a lecturer for the Massachusetts Anti-Slavery Society under the influence of Garrisonian abolitionists; twenty-seven when *Narrative of the Life of Frederick Douglass, an American Slave, Written by Himself* was published and he left for Great Britain for twenty-one months; twenty-nine when he launched the paper the *North Star* with Martin Robison Delany; thirty-three when the first printing of *Frederick Douglass' Paper* materialized; thirty-four at the time of delivering the oration "What to the Slave Is the Fourth of July?"; midthirties at the time of his increased focus on Caribbean and Central American politics; thirty-seven when his second autobiography, *My Bondage and My Freedom,* was published after his break with William Lloyd Garrison; thirty-nine when Chief Justice Roger B. Taney rendered his *Dred Scott v. Sanford* opinion that stated blacks "had no rights which the white man was bound to respect";[2] forty when his next newspaper, *Douglass' Monthly,* began circulation; forty-three when the Civil War started and Harriet Jacobs's account of the "loophole of retreat" in *Incidents in the Life of a Slave Girl, Written by Herself* appeared; forty-seven when the Civil War concluded; fifty-two at the launch of the *New National Era;* fifty-nine after appointment as the US marshal of the District of Columbia; sixty-three when the first edition of *Life and Times of Frederick Douglass* was published; sixty-eight when he returned to Europe; sixty-nine as his tour of North Africa commenced; seventy-one when he began duties as US consul general and minister resident to postrevolutionary Haiti; seventy-four when the expanded second edition of *Life and Times* was released; seventy-five when he collaborated with Ida B. Wells on *The Reason Why the Colored American Is Not in the World's Columbian Exposition;* and seventy-seven when he died.

Douglass was a multifaceted and versatile thinker: theorist and practitioner, autobiographer and editor, abolitionist and statesman, orator and phenomenologist, romantic and realist, feminist and masculinist, assimilationist and decolonialist, moral suasionist and violent-resistance defender, Christian and critic of slaveholding Christianity, liberal and republican, law-breaker and constitutionalist, particularist and universalist, historicist and poeticist, a Marylander, a New Englander, a Rochesterian, a communitarian, a self-made man, a black man, a slave, a fugitive, an antiracist, an exslave. These positions and categorizations, however compatible and contradictory, have fascinated and challenged his interpreters for nearly 180 years.

Douglass is now a canonical figure in many aspects of North American letters, be it in primary and secondary schools or fields of academia, including black studies, history, literature, geography, photography, American studies, cultural studies, public policy, rhetoric, education, and, increasingly, political theory. However, as Toni Morrison warns in "Unspeakable Things Unspoken," we must be careful not to forge a *canon* in the manner of a *cannon*, obliterating the prime content and intellectual impetuses behind thinkers and movements once excluded from a field's scholarly investigations merely to achieve canonization through a limiting form of the politics of recognition.[3] This is an obstacle we face when writing on Douglass.

At least two factors complicate our assessment of Douglass's political thought and its afterlives. First, there is the question of *what texts* to examine. Douglass's writings as an autobiographer are today considered pro forma for scholars to analyze. Elementary schools, high schools, colleges, and universities routinely teach Douglass's first autobiography.[4] *My Bondage and My Freedom* (1855) is the object of greater philosophical and social scientific study due to its accessible prose, argumentative precision, and development of the concept of "comparative freedom" absent from the *Narrative*.[5] Douglass writes in his memorable retelling of the fight with Covey: "Covey was a tyrant, and a cowardly one, withal. After resisting him, I felt as I had never felt before. It was resurrection from the dark and pestiferous tomb of slavery, to the heaven of comparative freedom. . . . I had reached the point, at which I was *not afraid to die.* This spirit made me a freeman in *fact,* while I remained a slave in *form.* When a slave cannot be flogged he is more than half free."[6]

Life and Times (1881, second edition 1892),[7] a central source of study for historians and literary critics, is slowly also becoming a basis for inquiry by political theorists. However, for a long time Douglass wasn't taken seriously as an autobiographer. Only *Bondage* and *Life and Times* were discussed, if at all, seventy-five years after Douglass's death.

Strikingly and to the surprise of many contemporary observers, Douglass's *Narrative,* published in 1845, was out of print from the early 1850s until 1960, when Douglass biographer Benjamin Quarles,[8] in partnership with Harvard University Press, issued a new edition of the work in the press's John Harvard Library series.[9] That's more than a century of textual irrelevance. Douglass the orator and by extension the speeches and lectures Douglass delivered long took precedence among scholars. Yet to analyze Douglass comprehensively requires examination of additional textual forms.

Visual texts are another important medium. The most photographed American of the nineteenth century,[10] ahead even of Abraham Lincoln, Douglass believed pictorial representations of the self and others are effective tools for the transmission of one's disposition and political principles. The centrality of the relationship between aesthetics and politics is especially salient in Douglass's lecture on photography "Pictures and Progress" (1864–1865). "Art," Douglass suggests, "is a special revelation of the higher powers of the human soul."[11] Humans have the capacity, through art, for "picture-making," an act uniting physical composition with the nonphysical imagination. "Poets, prophets, and reformers are all picture-makers—and this ability is the secret of their power and of their achievements. They see what ought to be by the reflection of what is, and endeavor to remove the contradiction." In Douglass's estimation, art grounds human aspirations for reform, revolution, and progress. None of this should obviate us from critique, for "where there is no criticism there is no progress."[12] Douglass facilitates inauguration of what bell hooks, Jacques Rancière, and commentators today describe as the "aesthetic turn" in modern political thought.[13]

Therefore, Douglass's speeches, lectures, journalism, autobiographies, and visual art commentaries *all* demand our attentiveness.

The second complication is that there is the question of *scope* underlying Douglass's epistemology and vision of politics. This issue is acute as pertains to geographic scope. Scholarship by philosophers and political theorists over the past two decades overwhelmingly advance readings of Douglass as a preeminent thinker of America and American political thought. These studies frame Douglass as a defender of Americanity, American exceptionalism, and the possibility of America perfecting itself and its territorial sovereignty within rigid demarcated boundaries despite plunder, the extermination of the indigenous communities, the original sin of slavery, ongoing cross-border exchanges between peoples as a consequence of its heterogeneous population, rampant inequality and unfreedom, and, as Charles Mills terms it, the "racial liberalism"[14] pervading the republic since its founding. Douglass, however, persistently rejected provincialism even during his brief contemplation of African Americans' immigration to the Caribbean and Central America before the Civil War.

The aforementioned studies separate out Douglass's views on the past, present, and future of the United States from his critical *hemispheric* world-view that inform those views. They don't engage substantively with works such as "The Claims of the Negro Ethnologically Considered" (1854) and "Our Composite Nationality" (1869), and they neglect or omit altogether Douglass's *relational* opinions on race, nation, slavery, resistance, creoliza-tion, fugitivity, constitutionalism, and sovereignty as well as their pertinence to identity formation, voting, transnationalism, political theology, freedom, democracy, law, rhetoric, judgment, citizenship, and the interactions of peoples within and across borders.[15] They ignore Douglass's views on the Mosquito Kingdom and Nicaragua. They also downplay the significance of Haiti to Douglass's political imagination,[16] which Douglass conveys in "A Trip to Haiti" (1861), the trenchant reflections on the postrevolutionary black republic in the second edition of *Life and Times* (1892), *Lecture on Haiti* (1893), and manuscript writings on Haitian revolutionary Toussaint L'Ouverture.[17] In the final sentence of *Life and Times*, Douglass states: "I have been the recipient of many honors, among which my unsought appoint-ment by President Benjamin Harrison to the office of Minister Resident and Consul-General to represent the United States at the capital of Haïti, and my equally unsought appointment by President Florvil Hyppolite to repre-sent Haïti among all the civilized nations of the globe at the World's Colum-bian Exposition, are crowning honors to my long career and a fitting and happy close to my whole public life."[18]

Douglass argued that Haiti occupied a unique role for blacks in the United States, who experienced, on the one hand, enslavement in slavehold-ing states and daily uncertainty in the other states as a consequence of the Fugitive Slave Act of 1850 and, on the other hand, the afterlives of racial slavery with the rise and fall of Reconstruction and consolidation of Jim Crow, which perpetuated white supremacy, inequality, and black unfree-dom. "Born a slave as we were, in this boasted land of liberty, tinged with a hated color, despised by the rulers of the State," Douglass writes, "we [black Americans], naturally, enough, desire to see, as we doubtless shall see, in the free, orderly and Independent Republic of Haiti, a refutation of the slanders and disparagements of our race. We want to experience the feeling of being under a Government which has been administered by a race denounced as mentally and morally incapable of self-government."[19] In addition, in his speech at the Haitian Pavilion dedication ceremony at the World's Fair in Chicago, he remarks:

> In just vindication of Haiti, I can go one step further. I can speak of her, not only words of admiration, but words of gratitude as well. She has grandly served the cause of universal human liberty. We should not forget that the freedom you and I enjoy today; that the freedom that eight hundred thousand colored people enjoy in the British West Indies; the freedom that has come to the colored race the world over, is largely due to the brave stand taken by the black sons of Haiti ninety years ago. . . . It is said of ancient nations, that each had its special mission in the world and that each taught the world some important lesson. . . . Haiti, anchored in the Caribbean Sea, has had her mission in the world, and a mission which the world had much need to learn. She has taught the world the danger of slavery and the value of liberty. In this respect she has been the greatest of all our modern teachers.[20]

Provincial scholarship fails to reconcile Douglass's rethinking of America with his repeated observations on postemancipation societies in the British Caribbean. "West India Emancipation" (1857), for example, is the speech in which Douglass explores the meanings of reform, struggle, freedom, and power, stating therein some of his most famous words. "The whole history of the progress of human liberty," he exhorts, "shows that all concessions yet made to her august claims, have been born of earnest struggle." "Power," Douglass argues, "concedes nothing without a demand. It never did and it never will."[21]

Moreover, we must note how, in a convergence of the textual and the geographic, contemporary philosophers and political theorists' narrow studies rarely focus on Douglass's journalism and his role as an editor, even though it becomes apparent in these mediums that his editorial work complements his other intellectual and political interventions. This neglect enables the submersion and disavowal of Douglass's hemispheric influence during his lifetime. Juliet Hooker's essay "'A Black Sister to Massachusetts': Latin America and the Fugitive Democratic Ethos of Frederick Douglass" and book *Theorizing Race in the Americas* are recent exceptions to this unfortunate pattern.[22]

We must rethink our approach to deciphering Douglass as a political thinker.

Robert Gooding-Williams contends that Afro-modern political thought is still in the shadow of the Great Barrington polymath W. E. B. Du Bois.[23] The trope of the shadow is powerful, but I suggest that we look earlier than Du Bois to discern its full utility; for Du Bois, Afro-modern political thought, American political thought, and modern political thought more broadly arguably remain in the shadow of Frederick Douglass. The contributions by thinkers including Angela Davis, Harold Cruse, Herbert Storing, Leslie Goldstein, David Blight, Deborah McDowell, Waldo Martin Jr., Saidiya Hartman, George Shulman, Peter Myers, Leigh Fought, and Michelle Alexander lend credence to this position,[24] as does Gooding-Williams implicitly, in chapter 5 of this volume, by presenting Douglass's views on the true nature of slavery, plantation politics, declarations of independence, the political system of white supremacy, and race consciousness as solutions to weaknesses in Du Bois's expressivist politics and attendant conceptions of leadership and rule. Furthermore, Du Bois explicitly admits writing in Douglass's shadow in two of his most enduring texts, *The Souls of Black Folk* (1903) and *Black Reconstruction in America* (1935),[25] as well as in his unsuccessful attempt to acquire rights to compose the authoritative biography of Douglass.[26]

While in the young Du Bois's estimation "the most striking thing in the history of the American Negro since 1876 is the ascendency of Mr. Booker T. Washington," Du Bois concludes nevertheless that "the great form of Frederick Douglass" is "the greatest of American Negro leaders."[27] Leadership and conceptions of rule, though, aren't Douglass's sole distinguishing marks. Du Bois argues in *Souls* that Douglass differentiates himself from Washington with regard to three vital issues in the nineteenth century, which Douglass's contemporaries Anna Julia Cooper and Joseph Anténor Firmin would articulate opinions on in their unique ways: the right to vote, or black suffrage; civic equality; and the education of black youth. In addition, in contrast to Washington, who separates the spheres of the political and the social in a presaging of Arendt's categorizations in *The Human Condition*,[28] Douglass neither brackets the social from the political nor asks blacks to accept exclusion from all facets of political power within the inegalitarian racial state.[29]

In *Black Reconstruction*, the mature Du Bois elaborates on principles whose examination is motivated by Douglass's shadow over the modern period. Du Bois cites Douglass's work more extensively and provides an economic basis to complement the philosophical underpinnings of Douglass's politics. Pace Douglass, Du Bois looks "back toward slavery" to come to grips with a Great Depression world split in two: the white world and the black world.[30] Slavery's effects haunt the black world. And yet "the attempt to make black men American citizens was in a certain sense all a failure, but a splendid failure. It did not fail where it was expected to fail."[31] Du Bois surmises that progress, measured by mitigation of the black world–white world division, can happen. He wants to know how.

Du Bois devotes sustained consideration to fugitivity and a figure Douglass embodied for a notable time: the fugitive slave. Du Bois calls the fugitive slave the "Safety Valve of Slavery." "Fugitive slaves, like Frederick Douglass," Du Bois opines, are integral to the realization of freedom, citizenship, and democracy. Masters simultaneously fear fugitives' flight and use the fear of potential fugitives' escape to reinforce the arduous vicissitudes of the slavery system. "The true significance of slavery in the United States to the whole social development of America lay in the ultimate relation of slaves to democracy."[32] Du Bois would apply the core findings of *Black Reconstruction* to his scholarship on regions outside the United States, especially Africa and South Asia, and Douglass was his inspiration.

Douglass's legacy in the late twentieth and early twenty-first centuries is as vibrant as it was in Du Bois's time. We explore that legacy in the pages of this book.

Précis

A Political Companion to Frederick Douglass is the first book to include in a single text both classic and new late-modern essays on Douglass's political thought. The volume contains fourteen chapters, divided into four thematic parts, and a select bibliography listing essential texts by, about, and pertaining to Douglass and his politics, political philosophy, and applied political theory.

Part I, "Slavery, Freedom, Agency," is the bulwark for the book's ensuing sections. Paul Gilroy, Bernard R. Boxill, Margaret Kohn, Angela Y. Davis, and Robert Gooding-Williams examine what Douglass argues is the inextricable relationship between slavery and freedom; Douglass's observations on the dynamic effects of this relationship following the onset of modernity; alternative conceptualizations of mastery and enslavement; and Douglass's contention that persons, irrespective of social and political condition, possess an intrinsic ability to act. According to Douglass, slaves and nonslaves alike have this capacity. Such a position contests Orlando Patterson's idea of slavery as a state of "social death" and the notion that slaves are beings lacking the inherent capacity for action. These chapters also interrogate the struggle for recognition, the meaning of resistance, the reasons why different renditions of the fight with the slave breaker Edward Covey are included in Douglass's three autobiographies, Douglass's shifting views on violence, and his definitions of liberation, independence, emancipation, and freedom, which, their connections notwithstanding, have their own distinct meanings. Moreover, these chapters detail central recurring figures and leitmotifs in a range of Douglass's writings and speeches. Through their explorations, we gain key insights, first, into the tensions between Enlightenment discourses on the free life and modern herrenvolk democracies legally sanctioning hierarchy, the slave trade, and slavery; second, into the strategies for denouncing and abolishing the latter; and, third, into the diagnostic elements of Douglass's thinking that ground his normative theory.

Jack Turner, Ange-Marie Hancock Alfaro, and Nicholas Buccola build on Douglass's foundational premises on slavery, freedom, and action to explore another set of integral concepts in his political thought. In part II, "Judgment, Intersectionality, Human Nature," chapter 6 illuminates the ramifications of Douglass's analyses of US Supreme Court civil rights cases after Reconstruction for the idea of political judgment. Whether the deployment of Douglass in the legal opinions of justices in the current John Roberts Court aligns with Douglass's argumentation is also a subject of inquiry. Chapters 7 and 8 describe Douglass's views on black men's lived experiences of restorative caring, the relationships among black men during racial slavery, and how the idea of human nature provides the terms for understanding free will and liberal politics. Taken together, these chapters rebut readings of Douglass that reduce him to a republican theorist of nondomination, a masculinist feminist concerned with care only vis-à-vis postemancipation white women suffragettes, and a static thinker whose ideas did not change over time.

The book turns in part III to an important concept in political theory with implications for human life and the divine: law. The study of law includes and exceeds jurisprudence. Whereas Peter C. Myers and

Vincent Lloyd interrogate natural law and God's law, respectively, Anne Norton delves into circumstances under which an agent intentionally violates the law of a state. Chapter 9 assesses *Life and Times* to explain Douglass's understanding of natural law and time and why Douglass embraced rational hopefulness rather than Afro-pessimism in spite of the geopolitical retrenchments of the third quarter of the nineteenth century. Chapter 10 emphasizes Douglass's speeches, the texts in which he most frequently invokes the language of God's law. It uses affect theory and political theology to describe Douglass's view on God's law, which includes discussions of natural law yet extends its intellectual genealogy beyond the Catholic theology of Thomas Aquinas to include the black natural-law tradition. In chapter 11, Maryland's Eastern Shore frames the opening and closing meditations on uncertainty. For Douglass, the Eastern Shore, where he was born and raised a slave, was a site of uncertainty and precariousness. The essay proffers an account of lawbreaking in the face of uncertainty and the ways in which Douglass's constitutional theory disrupts interpretations of representation, constitutionalism, and the rule of law, which are hallmarks of liberal democracy. The chapter considers if fugitive lawbreaking is not only justified but also necessary at times to refashion freedom, democracy, and the rule of law in a fractured polity.

In part IV, "Rhetoric, Citizenship, Democracy," Herbert Storing, Jason Frank, and Nick Bromell elucidate how the rhetoric and the associated usages of language, elocution, and performance function in Douglass's ideals of citizenship and democracy. Chapter 12 examines speeches spanning several decades and inquires into the content of Douglass's rhetoric. Specifically, the essay probes Douglass's word choices when addressing audiences, such as the oft-uttered phrase "Fellow-Citizens" used to begin speeches, and what we may learn from those selections regarding his notion of citizenship. Citizenship for Douglass isn't merely a person's legal status in a polity. The act of proclaiming one's citizenship to others matters. Chapter 13 returns us to the Fourth of July oration of 1852 and argues that the art of rhetoric embodied by the speech signifies a "constituent moment" of the people and a "staging of dissensus." The people in a democracy don't emerge from speaking in their name alone. In giving this speech, Douglass invoked the language of the people still to come in front of an audience whose views of Independence Day differed from the opinions held by other persons in the United States. He implored listeners to imagine another world in which the words "We the People" from the Constitution's preamble truly materialize out of the unsettling state of dissensus. Finally, chapter 14 explains Douglass's provocative theory of democratic citizenship through his "blending of opposite qualities"—that of an enslaved person and that of a free man. Douglass confronted a series of conundrums: reconciling higher law and history; formulating a model of citizenship that is decoupled from the wages of whiteness; and conceiving of a democratic citizenship in a democracy whose practices belie the characteristics of its political form. Democratic citizenship requires interaction and mutual exchanges between individuals and groups, and it involves accessing our sentiments. It also demands, for Douglass, political friendship. Bonds of political friendship can lead to transformations lasting generations. Douglass dreamed of such transformations as part of his legacy.

The afterlives of Douglass's political thought are discernable currently not only in this volume's essays but also in advocacy by liberal civil rights activists, jurisprudence of conservative judges, Straussian intellectuals, republican theorists of justice, death penalty and prison abolitionists, aspiring orators, teachers of elocution, prophetic political theologies, global immigration debates, discussions on human trafficking, and the black radical tradition to which the decentralized movement for black lives belongs.

Alicia Garza, Patrisse Cullors, and Opal Tometi started the #BlackLivesMatter (BLM) movement in the wake of the shooting of seventeen year-old Trayvon Martin in Sanford, Florida, on February 26, 2012. The deaths of Michael Brown, Renisha McBride, Eric Garner, Sandra Bland, and several other unarmed black youth and adults led to a rapid proliferation of BLM chapters. Widespread utterances of "I can't breathe" and "Hands up, don't shoot!" at marches and demonstrations—coupled with forums and hashtags in the print press and digital public sphere commenting on the import of these utterances for black death, black life, and the human— ensued. "Alright" by Kendrick Lamar became the movement's song, and its refrain "we gon' be alright" served as a reminder of how progress is possible through struggle and assertion even at the darkest hour.

BLM is a national, hemispheric, and international network, and it uses social media as a conduit to organize and mobilize.[33] "Find out just what any people will quietly submit to," Douglass cautions, "and you have found out the exact measure of injustice and wrong which will be imposed upon them."[34] BLM encourages the public identification of wrongs, resistance to

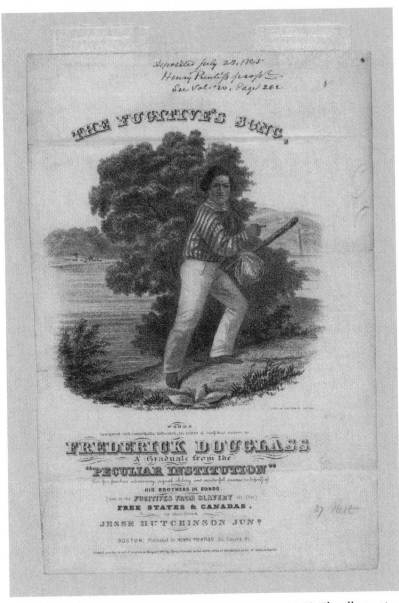

Figure 1. "The Fugitive's Song," sheet music cover, 1845. The illustration depicts Frederick Douglass, barefoot, on the run from two slave catchers and their dogs. It states that Douglass is dually a fugitive and "a graduate from the 'peculiar institution'" of slavery. A signpost shows Douglass headed in the direction of New England. (Published by Henry Prentiss. Reproduction number: LC-DIG-ppmsca-07616, Library of Congress.)

acts of antiblackness, and development of processes of rehumanization instead of silence, denigration of others, and inaction. Like Douglass, BLM doesn't espouse a genre of black nationalism, though it supports the cultivation of black life, dignity, respect, intersecting identities, and institutions that combat injustice and unfreedom. Also like Douglass, BLM believes that examining the conditions of enslavement, rights, law, the value of black lives, and the meaning of freedom should be a central focus of humanists.

"Stay woke" is a BLM adage, a clarion call to remember the past, contemplate the future, and imagine alterative future worlds. To "stay woke" is to be conscious of the philosophical and political terrain one encounters and inhabits. Stay woke beckons *hope*.

Frederick Douglass declared near the end of his Fourth of July oration delivered to the Ladies' Antislavery Society at Corinthian Hall in Rochester, New York, in 1852, "I, therefore, leave off where I began, with hope." "Oceans," he insisted, "no longer divide, but link nations together."[35] And in his address "The Nation's Problem," given in Washington, DC, in 1889, Douglass asserted, "The duty of to-day is to meet the questions that confront us with intelligence and courage."[36]

We live in the shadow of Douglass. May this volume challenge you to wrestle with Douglass's ideas intelligently and courageously whether you agree with them or not. The book aims for novelty, but it doesn't answer all the questions posed earlier concerning gaps in the literature. My heartfelt hope is that the book fosters commentaries on Douglass's political thought from a range of interlocutors and sparks scholars to fill in its apertures.

Notes

1. Richard H. King, *Arendt and America* (Chicago: University of Chicago Press, 2015); Neil Roberts, "Arendt: American Revolutionary?" *Society for U.S. Intellectual History* forum, June 28, 2016, at http://s-usih.org/2016/06/arendt-american-revolutionary.html.

2. Justice Roger B. Taney opinion, *Dred Scott v. Sanford*, 60 US 393, at 407.

3. Toni Morrison, "Unspeakable Things Unspoken: The Afro-American Presence in American Literature," Tanner Lectures on Human Values, October 7, 1988, at http://tannerlectures.utah.edu/_documents/a-to-z/m/morrison90.pdf. Jane Anna Gordon and I address Morrison's admonitions on canonization through the framework of *creolizing* theory in *Creolizing Rousseau* (London: Rowman and Littlefield International, 2015) and in our Rowman and Littlefield book series Creolizing the

Canon, described at http://www.rowmaninternational.com/our-publishing/series/
creolizing-the-canon/.

4. There are also late-modern books designed for educators on how to teach
the *Narrative*. An example is James C. Hall, ed., *Approaches to Teaching* Narrative of the Life of Frederick Douglass (New York: Modern Language Association
of America, 1999).

5. It is noteworthy, however, that various editions of *Narrative* and *Life and
Times* were on display and available for purchase in the bookstore when in the fall
of 2016 I visited Cedar Hill, Douglass's home in Anacostia, Washington, DC, during the final eighteen years of his life and maintained as a historic site by the US
National Park Service (https://www.nps.gov/frdo/index.htm). There weren't any
copies of *Bondage*, though.

6. Frederick Douglass, *My Bondage and My Freedom*, ed. John David Smith
(New York: Penguin, 2003), 181, original emphasis. Douglass inserts throughout
Bondage the adjectives *comparative* and *comparatively* before the word *freedom*
and other key nouns in the text that don't exist in similar passages of the *Narrative*.
I describe the *fact–form* distinction, the concept of *comparative freedom*, and
Douglass's revisions to his account of the fight with Covey in *Freedom as Marronage* (Chicago: University of Chicago Press, 2015).

7. Scholars invoke two different dates for the second edition of Douglass's *Life
and Times:* 1892 and 1893. Wolfe, Fiske, and Company published the revised edition in December 1892, but its title page lists 1893 as the release date. A way to
understand this is to imagine acquiring a book from a bookstore or online site in
late fall 2017 that lists its publication date as 2018. The book may be widely circulated and available for attainment via a range of distributors, yet its formal release
date would be January or February in the following calendar year. Although I use
the date 1892 in my work, contributors to this volume employ both dates.

8. Benjamin Quarles, *Frederick Douglass* (New York: Atheneum, 1968).

9. Robert Levine, *The Lives of Frederick Douglass* (Cambridge, MA: Harvard
University Press, 2016), 1–30.

10. John Stauffer, Zoe Trodd, and Celeste-Marie Bernier capture this point in
Picturing Frederick Douglass: An Illustrated Biography of the Nineteenth Century's Most Photographed American (New York: Liveright, 2015).

11. Frederick Douglass, "Pictures and Progress," in Stauffer, Todd, and Bernier,
Picturing Frederick Douglass, 169. Douglass wrote four lectures on photography:
"Lecture on Pictures" (1861), "Life of Pictures" (1861), "Age of Pictures" (1862),
and "Pictures and Progress" (1864–1865). "Pictures and Progress" develops to the
greatest extent his views on photography, aesthetics, and politics. Douglass's interest in the aesthetics–politics nexus occurred not only during the Civil War but also
throughout much of his adult life.

12. Douglass, "Pictures and Progress," 166, 171, 170.

13. bell hooks, *Black Looks: Race and Representation* (Boston: South End, 1992) and *Art on My Mind: Visual Politics* (New York: New Press, 1995); Jacques Rancière, *Aisthesis: Scenes from the Aesthetic Regime of Art* (London: Verso, 2013) and *Dissensus: On Politics and Aesthetics* (New York: Bloomsbury, 2015); Nikolas Kompridis, ed., *The Aesthetic Turn in Political Thought* (New York: Bloomsbury, 2014); David Panagia, *Ten Theses for an Aesthetics of Politics* (Minneapolis: University of Minnesota Press, 2016).

14. Charles W. Mills, *Black Rights/White Wrongs: The Critique of Racial Liberalism* (Oxford: Oxford University Press, 2017).

15. See Frederick Douglass, "Our Composite Nationality," in *The Frederick Douglass Papers, Series One: Speeches, Debates, and Interviews*, 5 vols., ed. John Blassingame and others (New Haven, CT: Yale University Press, 1979), 4:240–59; Frederick Douglass, "The Claims of the Negro Ethnologically Considered," in *Frederick Douglass: Selected Speeches and Writings*, ed. Philip Foner, abridged and adapted by Yuval Taylor (Chicago: Lawrence Hill Books, 1999), 282–97.

16. For Haiti's impact on Douglass's political imagination, see Ifeoma Nwankwo, *Black Cosmopolitanism: Racial Consciousness and Transnational Identity in the Nineteenth-Century Americas* (Philadelphia: University of Pennsylvania Press, 2005); Millery Polyné, *From Douglass to Duvalier: U.S. African Americans, Haiti, and Pan Americanism, 1870–1964* (Gainesville: University Press of Florida, 2010); and Roberts, *Freedom as Marronage*. Douglass influenced, too, the political imaginary of nineteenth-century Haitian intellectuals, including the noted scholar and politician Joseph Anténor Firmin. See Firmin's portrayal of Douglass in his treatise from 1885, *The Equality of the Human Races: Positivist Anthropology* (Urbana: University of Illinois Press, 2002).

17. Frederick Douglass, *Life and Times of Frederick Douglass*, in *Autobiographies*, ed. Henry Louis Gates Jr. (New York: Library of America, 1994), 1026–45; "A Trip to Haiti," in *Frederick Douglass*, ed. Foner, 439–42; "Lecture on Haiti," in *Great Speeches by Frederick Douglass*, ed. James Daley (Mineola, NY: Dover, 2013), 105–24; "Toussaint L'Ouverture," Library of Congress, Washington, DC, at https://www.loc.gov/item/mfd.31034/ (folder 1) and https://www.loc.gov/item/mfd.31035/ (folder 2). Note as well Frederick Douglass, "Haiti and the United States: Inside History of the Negotiations for the Môle St. Nicholas," *North American Review* 153 (418) (1891): 337–45.

18. Douglass, *Life and Times*, 1045.

19. Douglass, "A Trip to Haiti," 440. For wider discourses on Haiti in the imagination of nineteenth-century blacks in the United States, see Maurice Jackson and Jacqueline Bacon, eds., *African Americans and the Haitian Revolution: Selected Essays and Historical Documents* (New York: Routledge, 2010).

20. Douglass, "Lecture on Haiti," 119–20.

21. Frederick Douglass, "West India Emancipation," in *Frederick Douglass*, ed. Foner, 367. In 1855, within the pages of the periodical *Frederick Douglass' Paper*, Douglass asserted, "The hour which shall witness *the final struggle*, is on the wing. Already we hear the *booming* of the bell which shall yet toll the death knell of human slavery. Liberty and Slavery cannot dwell together forever in the same country" ("The Final Struggle," in *Frederick Douglass*, ed. Foner, 335, original emphasis). The lessons of postemancipation British Caribbean polities reinforce Douglass's conviction here.

22. Juliet Hooker, "'A Black Sister to Massachusetts': Latin America and the Fugitive Democratic Ethos of Frederick Douglass," *American Political Science Review* 109 (4) (2015): 690–702, and *Theorizing Race in the Americas: Douglass, Sarmiento, Du Bois, and Vasconcelos* (Oxford: Oxford University Press, 2017).

23. Robert Gooding-Williams, *In the Shadow of Du Bois: Afro-Modern Political Thought in America* (Cambridge, MA: Harvard University Press, 2009). For the tradition of Afro-modern political thought, see also Cornel West, *Prophesy Deliverance! An Afro-American Revolutionary Christianity* (Louisville, KY: Westminster John Knox, 1982); Joy James, *Transcending the Talented Tenth: Black Leaders and American Intellectuals* (New York: Routledge, 1997); Hazel Carby, *Race Men* (Cambridge, MA: Harvard University Press, 1998); Michael Hanchard, "Afro-Modernity: Temporality, Politics, and the African Diaspora," *Public Culture* 11 (1) (1999): 245–68; Adolph Reed Jr., *Stirrings in the Jug: Black Politics in the Post-segregation Era* (Minneapolis: University of Minnesota Press, 1999); Patricia Hill Collins, *Black Feminist Thought: Knowledge, Consciousness, and the Politics of Empowerment* (New York: Routledge, 2000); Paget Henry, *Caliban's Reason: Introducing Afro-Caribbean Philosophy* (New York: Routledge, 2000); Cedric Robinson, *Black Marxism: The Making of the Black Radical Tradition* (Chapel Hill: University of North Carolina Press, 2000); Michael Dawson, *Black Visions: The Roots of Contemporary African-American Political Ideologies* (Chicago: University of Chicago Press, 2001); Fred Moten, *In the Break: The Aesthetics of the Black Radical Tradition* (Minneapolis: University of Minnesota Press, 2003); Hortense Spillers, *Black, White, and in Color: Essays on American Literature and Culture* (Chicago: University of Chicago Press, 2003); Ngũgĩ wa Thiong'o, *Something Torn and New: An African Renaissance* (New York: BasicCivitas, 2009); Paul Gilroy, *Darker Than Blue: On the Moral Economies of Black Atlantic Culture* (Cambridge, MA: Harvard University Press, 2011); Nick Bromell, *The Time Is Always Now: Black Thought and the Transformation of US Democracy* (Oxford: Oxford University Press, 2013); Martin Kilson, *Transformation of the African American Intelligentsia, 1880–2012* (Cambridge, MA: Harvard University Press, 2014); Katherine McKittrick, ed., *Sylvia Wynter:*

On Being Human as Praxis (Durham, NC: Duke University Press, 2015); Tommie Shelby, *Dark Ghettos: Injustice, Dissent, and Reform* (Cambridge, MA: Harvard University Press, 2016); Achille Mbembe, *Critique of Black Reason* (Durham, NC: Duke University Press, 2017); Keeanga-Yamahtta Taylor, ed., *How We Get Free: Black Feminism and the Combahee River Collective* (Chicago: Haymarket, 2017); Alex Zamalin, *Struggle on Their Minds: The Political Thought of African American Resistance* (New York: Columbia University Press, 2017).

24. Herbert Storing, ed., *What Country Have I? Political Writings by Black Americans* (New York: St. Martin's, 1970); Leslie Goldstein, "The Political Thought of Frederick Douglass," PhD diss., Cornell University, 1974, and "Morality and Prudence in the Statesmanship of Frederick Douglass: Radical as Reformer," *Polity* 16 (4) (1984): 606–23; Waldo Martin Jr., *The Mind of Frederick Douglass* (Chapel Hill: University of North Carolina Press, 1984); David Blight, *Frederick Douglass' Civil War: Keeping Faith in Jubilee* (Baton Rouge: Louisiana State University Press, 1989), *Frederick Douglass and Abraham Lincoln: A Relationship in Language, Politics, and Memory* (Milwaukee: Marquette University Press, 2001), "Frederick Douglass: Refugee," *The Atlantic,* February 7, 2017, at https://www.theatlantic.com/politics/archive/2017/02/frederick-douglass-refugee/515853/, and *Frederick Douglass: American Prophet* (forthcoming); Saidiya Hartman, *Scenes of Subjection: Terror, Slavery, and Self-Making in Nineteenth-Century America* (Oxford: Oxford University Press, 1997); Harold Cruse, *The Crisis of the Negro Intellectual: A Historical Analysis of the Failure of Black Leadership* (New York: New York Review of Books, 2005); Angela Y. Davis, *Abolition Democracy: Beyond Empire, Prisons, and Torture. Interviews with Angela Davis* (New York: Seven Stories, 2005), *The Meaning of Freedom* (San Francisco: City Lights, 2011), and *Freedom Is a Constant Struggle: Ferguson, Palestine, and the Foundations of a Movement* (Chicago: Haymarket, 2016); Peter Myers, *Frederick Douglass: Race and the Rebirth of Liberalism* (Lawrence: University Press of Kansas, 2008), "'A Good Work for Our Race To-Day': Interests, Virtues, and the Achievement of Justice in Frederick Douglass's Freedmen's Monument Speech," *American Political Science Review* 104 (2) (2010): 209–25, and "Frederick Douglass on Revolution and Integration: A Problem in Moral Psychology," *American Political Thought* 2 (1) (2013): 118–46; George Shulman, *American Prophecy: Race and Redemption in American Political Culture* (Minneapolis: University of Minnesota Press, 2008); Deborah McDowell, introduction to Frederick Douglass, *Narrative of the Life of Frederick Douglass* (Oxford: Oxford University Press, 2009); Michelle Alexander, *The New Jim Crow: Mass Incarceration in the Age of Colorblindness* (New York: New Press, 2010); Leigh Fought, *Women in the World of Frederick Douglass* (Oxford: Oxford University Press, 2017). See also Angela Davis's contribution to this volume (chapter 4).

25. W. E. B. Du Bois, *The Souls of Black Folk*, ed. David W. Blight and Robert Gooding-Williams (Boston: Bedford/St. Martin's, 1997), and *Black Reconstruction in America, 1860–1880* (New York: Free Press, 1992).

26. As a result of a publisher gaffe, Du Bois's intellectual adversary, Booker T. Washington, with the support of a ghostwriter, acquired the rights to compose the Douglass biography. Du Bois subsequently wrote instead a biography of John Brown. See W. E. B. Du Bois, *John Brown* (New York: Modern Library, 2001), and Booker T. Washington, *Frederick Douglass* (Honolulu: University Press of the Pacific, 2003).

27. Du Bois, *Souls of Black Folk*, 62, 67.

28. Hannah Arendt, *The Human Condition* (Chicago: University of Chicago Press, 1998).

29. Du Bois, *Souls of Black Folk*, 67–69.

30. Du Bois, *Black Reconstruction in America*, 670–708.

31. Ibid., 708.

32. Ibid., 13.

33. For the key tenets of BLM, see the website http://blacklivesmatter.com/. In *The Making of Black Lives Matter: A Brief History of an Idea* (Oxford: Oxford University Press, 2017) and *From #BlackLivesMatter to Black Liberation* (Chicago: Haymarket, 2016), respectively, Christopher Lebron and Keeanga-Yamahtta Taylor situate BLM in the context of modern black political thought and social movements. In addition, the actions of BLM involve what Christina Sharpe refers to as "wake work," or work that answers the following query: "In the midst of so much death and the fact of Black life as proximate to death, how do we attend to physical, social, and figurative death and also to the largeness that is Black life, Black life insisted from death?" (*In the Wake: On Blackness and Being* [Durham, NC: Duke University Press, 2016], 17). BLM, however, is, like Douglass, hopeful in a way Sharpe's Afro-pessimism is not.

34. Douglass, "West India Emancipation," 367.

35. Frederick Douglass, "What to the Slave Is the Fourth of July?" in *Great Speeches by Frederick Douglass*, ed. Daley, 46.

36. Frederick Douglass, "The Nation's Problem," in *Frederick Douglass*, ed. Foner, 726.

I

Slavery, Freedom, Agency

1

Masters, Mistresses, Slaves, and the Antinomies of Modernity

Paul Gilroy

Every Idea thrown into the mind of the Negro is caught up and realised with the whole energy of his will; but this realisation involves a wholesale destruction . . . it is manifest that want of self-control distinguishes the character of the Negroes. This condition is capable of no development or Culture, and as we see them at this day, such they have always been. The only essential connection between the Negroes and the Europeans is slavery . . . we may conclude slavery to have been the occasion of the increase in human feeling among the Negroes.

—G. W. F. Hegel

How man deals with man is seen, for example in Negro slavery, the ultimate object of which is sugar and coffee.

—Arthur Schopenhauer

You had better all die—die immediately, than live slaves and entail your wretchedness upon your prosperity. If you would be free in this generation, here is your only hope.

—Henry Highland Garnet

The free hills of old Scotland, where the ancient "Black Douglass" once met his foes . . . almost every hill, river, mountain and lake of which has been made classic by the heroic deeds of her noble sons. Scarcely a stream but has been poured into song, or a hill that is not associated with some fierce and bloody conflict between liberty and slavery.

—Frederick Douglass

For some years now, Euro-American social theory, philosophy, and cultural criticism have hosted bitter and politically charged debates into the scope and status of the concept of modernity and the related ideas of modernism and modernisation. These debates have not always been conducted explicitly, and their key concepts have been nuanced in a variety of ways according to the particular disciplinary context in which they have arisen, yet despite some lack of consistency in their application a surprisingly coherent series of exchanges has taken shape. These exchanges have been dominated by a constellation of formally opposed yet mutually reinforcing theoretical positions from many of the leading theorists of the Euro-American academic establishment. Jürgen Habermas, Jean François Lyotard, Fredric Jameson, and a host of other women and men have applied themselves to the task of examining these ideas and the distinctiveness of contemporary life in the West to which they point. Sometimes writers have been concerned to identify and account for recent decisive shifts in the cultural climate of the overdeveloped countries and in their relationship to the rest of the world. Many participants have constructed intellectual detours through modernity as a way of demarcating what is novel or historically original in the contemporary postmodern condition. Others have analysed the postmodern as if it had simply effaced or replaced the modern and, like Lyotard, have not delved deeply into the history of the postmodern, its emergence from modernity, or its relationship to the processes of modernisation.[1]

However they approach their task, these authors share a preoccupation with the impact of postwar changes on the cognitive and technological bases of social and cultural life in the overdeveloped world where they have been able to detect "a sort of sorrow in the Zeitgeist."[2] The concept of postmodernism is often introduced to emphasise the radical or even catastrophic nature of the break between contemporary conditions and the epoch of modernism. Thus there is little attention given to the possibility that much of what is identified as postmodern may have been foreshadowed, or prefigured, in the lineaments of modernity itself. Defenders and critics of modernity seem to be equally unconcerned that the history and expressive culture of the African diaspora, the practice of racial slavery, or the narratives of European imperial conquest may require all simple periodisations of the modern and the postmodern to be drastically rethought.[3]

The pivotal relationship between the modern and the postmodern raises a number of further issues not least because it constitutes a small part of wider enquiries into the continuing viability of what Habermas has called the Enlightenment project.[4] These discussions profess to be more than merely scholastic contributions to the intellectual history of the West. They have certainly acquired a broader political currency, particularly where they have pronounced upon the idea of progress and the view of civilisation guided steadily toward perfection by secular, rational principles that sustain that idea. Habermas and others have, for example, focused attention on the relationship between freedom and reason, which has been a fundamental feature of Western political discourses since the end of the eighteenth century. This has gained a special resonance during a period in which technological transformations and political upheavals appear to jeopardise both freedom and reason in equal measure. The contemporary restructuring of political and economic relations in the overdeveloped countries has called many of the historic assumptions of Western rationalism into question. Arguing against the defenders of modern rationalism, incredulous voices have drawn critical attention to the bold, universalist claims of occidental modernity and its hubristic confidence in its own infallibility. It is disappointing that the position of the sceptics has sometimes been undersold by a chorus of rhetorical commentary which draws its enthusiasm from the excesses of antipolitical poststructuralism in general and deconstructive literary criticism in particular.

I will not attempt to reconstruct the whole complexity of these exchanges here. A number of authors have already provided a valuable secondary literature on the principal positions involved.[5] I am, however, keen to emphasise that this extensive and unusual international debate is clearly tied both to the fate of the intellectual as a discrete, authoritative caste and to the future of the universities in which so many of its learned protagonists have acquired secure perches. In Europe at least, these institutions of higher learning are being ventilated by the chill breeze of downward mobility at a time when the autonomous cultural power and preeminence of their mandarin inhabitants as public intellectuals are also being severely reduced. This is only one of several reasons why it may be possible to argue that what is increasingly perceived as the crisis of modernity and modern values is perhaps better understood as the crisis of the intellectuals whose self-consciousness was once served by these terms.[6] Focusing on the role of intellectuals within modernity is an important way of drawing out the particularity that lurks beneath the universalist claims of the Enlightenment project, which was, in theory, valid for humanity as a whole even if humanity was to be rather restrictively defined. The meaning of being an intellectual in settings that have denied access to literacy and encouraged other forms of communication in its place is a recurring question in what follows.

Recent discussions of modernity and its possible eclipse are also inseparable from the currently bleak fortunes of expressly socialistic forces in the overdeveloped countries. It would therefore be wrong to suppose that the political importance of this debate is entirely diminished by its academic origins and special appeal to those dissident affiliates of the bourgeoisie who once, joyfully or regretfully, placed their weapons of criticism in alignment with the proletariat's criticism of weapons. Reformist and revolutionary leftist alike are now being challenged to defend the protocols of secular reason and the ideal of human and social perfectibility irrespective of whether it is carried out under the banner of working-class self-emancipation or the standard of more modest and avowedly realist political philosophies.

Though it may not contain the final verdict on the grand narrative of Euro-American progress and the infinite expansion of productive forces that is often seen by Left and Right alike as an essential precondition for the enhancement of social and political freedoms, this debate is important for several reasons which have not, so far, been noted from within it. It can be argued that much of the supposed novelty of the postmodern evaporates when it is viewed in the unforgiving historical light of the brutal encounters between Europeans and those they conquered, slaughtered, and enslaved. The periodisation of the modern and the postmodern is thus of the most profound importance for the history of blacks in the West and for chronicling the shifting relations of domination and subordination between Europeans and the rest of the world. It is essential for our understanding of the category of "race" itself and of the genesis and development of successive forms of racist ideology. It is relevant, above all, in elaborating an interpretation of the origins and evolution of black politics. This task requires careful attention to the complex intermixture of African and European philosophical and cultural systems and ideas. A concept of modernity that is worth its salt ought, for example, to have something to contribute to an analysis of how the particular varieties of radicalism articulated through the revolts of enslaved people made selective use of the ideologies of the Western Age of Revolution and then flowed into social movements of an anticolonial and decidedly anticapitalist type. Lastly, the overcoming of scientific racism (one of modernity's more durable intellectual products) and its postwar transmutation into newer, cultural forms that stress complex difference rather than simple biological hierarchy may provide a telling, concrete example of what scepticism toward the grand narratives of scientific reason adds up to.

To note the potential of this debate around modernity to address these pressing issues of race and racism is not to say that all the elements of its successful resolution are already in evidence. In what seems to be a step backward from what we can call the high-modern era, interest in the social and political subordination of blacks and other non-European peoples does not generally feature in contemporary debates around the philosophical, ideological, or cultural content and consequences of modernity. Instead, an innocent modernity emerges from the apparently happy social relations that graced post-Enlightenment life in Paris, Berlin, and London. These European locations are readily purged of any traces of the people without history whose degraded lives might raise awkward questions about the limits of bourgeois humanism. Montesquieu's famous question "How can one be Persian?"[7] remains stubbornly and wilfully unanswered. What might be labelled an easy postmodernism attacks both rationality and universality through an obvious and banal relativism, but such a position holds no promise for those who retreat from the suggestion that all modes of life are irreconcilable and the related idea that any ethical or political position is as valid as any other. The work of a number of black thinkers will be examined below as part of a general argument that there are other bases for ethics and aesthetics than those which appear immanent within the versions of modernity that these myopically Eurocentric theories construct. This chapter will examine some omissions and absences in these debates as well as some of the unacknowledged and frequently ethnocentric premises from which they have been conducted.

I want also to offer a critique of and a corrective to these exchanges, and my fundamental concern with the history of the African diaspora necessitates the specific starting point—the black Atlantic—that I set down in chapter 1 [of *The Black Atlantic*]. The distinctive historical experiences of this diaspora's populations have created a unique body of reflections on modernity and its discontents which is an enduring presence in the cultural and political struggles of their descendants today. I want to bring to the fore elements of this alternative sequence of enquiries into the politics of life in the West. This discontinuous "tradition" has been occluded by the dominance of European and American writing elites whose loud modernist voices have dominated the clamour of philosophical and political discourses that reaches out from the eighteenth century to haunt us now. However, I am suggesting something more than the corrective inclusion of those black commentaries on the modern which have so far been overlooked by Western intellectual history. I intend not only to question the credibility of a tidy, holistic conception of modernity but also to argue for the inversion of the relationship between margin and centre as it has appeared within the master discourses of the master race. In other words, I am seeking to contribute to some reconstructive intellectual labour which, through looking at the modern cultural history of blacks in the modern world, has a great bearing on ideas of what the West was and is today. This initially requires a return to and a rethinking of the characteristically modern relationship between the master and the slave. I see this work as complementing and extending the work of feminist philosophers who have opposed the figuration of woman as a sign for the repressed or irrational other of rationality identified as male. Their exposure of what Rosi Braidotti calls the "unacknowledged and camouflaged sexual distinction at the very heart of philosophy"[8] can be paralleled by an archaeology of the icons of the blacks that appear as signs of irrational disorder or as a means to celebrate the power of human nature uncorrupted by the decadence of the civilising process. In either guise, blacks enjoy a subordinate position in the dualistic system that reproduces the dominance of bonded whiteness, masculinity, and rationality.

Slavery and the Enlightenment Project

If popular writers like Jürgen Habermas and Marshall Berman are to be believed, the unfulfilled promise of modernity's Enlightenment project remains a beleaguered but nonetheless vibrant resource which may even now be able to guide the practice of contemporary social and political struggles.

In opposition to this view, I propose that the history of the African diaspora and a reassessment of the relationship between modernity and slavery may require a more complete revision of the terms in which the modernity debates have been constructed than any of its academic participants may be willing to concede.

Despite the many positive qualities of Berman's work, the persuasive generality of his argument leads him to speak rather hastily of the "intimate unity of the modern self and the modern environment." This is conveyed in an instinctive manner by "the first great wave of writers and thinkers about modernity—Goethe, Hegel, Marx, Stendhal and Baudelaire, Carlyle and Dickens, Herzen and Dostoevsky."[9] Their conspicuous European-centredness aside, remarks like this would seem not only to endorse the view of modernity as an absolute break with its past but also to deny the possibility that the distinctiveness of the modern self might reside in its being a necessarily fractured or compound entity. From Berman's perspective, the powerful impact of issues like "race" and gender on the formation and reproduction of modern selves can too easily be set aside. The possibility that the modern subject may be located in historically specific and unavoidably complex configurations of individualisation and embodiment—black and white, male and female, lord and bondsman—is not entertained. Berman compounds these difficulties by arguing that "modern environments and experiences cut across *all* boundaries of geography and ethnicity, of class and nationality, of religion and ideology: in this sense modernity can be said to unite all mankind."[10] This could be read as a suggestion that an all-encompassing modernity affects everyone in a uniform and essentially similar way. This approach therefore runs contrary to my own concern with the variations and discontinuities in modern experience and with the decentred and inescapably plural nature of modern subjectivity and identity.

Like Habermas, Berman makes some very bold claims for the Enlightenment's ideological and political bequest: "these images and ideas provide a rich legacy for modern political thought and form a sort of agenda for nearly all the radical movements of the past two centuries."[11] He notes perceptively, but rather ruefully, that Montesquieu and Rousseau "have given us an agenda, *but no utopia*."[12] We shall see below that the expressions of black Atlantic radicalism which are explored in subsequent chapters [of *The Black Atlantic*] have consistently acquired and sometimes even refined their utopian tones. One of my aims is to defend this choice and illuminate the occasional strengths with which it has endowed diaspora politics and aesthetics.

Elsewhere, in an interesting exchange with Perry Anderson,[13] Berman goes so far as to suggest that his own entirely laudable desire to remain as close as possible to the insinuating rhythms of everyday life and his admirable belief that left intellectuals should cultivate the capacity to read the signs in the street in defiance of contemporary pressures to retreat into a contemplative state are both valuable products of this special modernist perspective. Though not immune to the lure of the esoteric, for a variety of reasons black intellectuals, most of whom have not held academic positions, have tended to find it easier to remain in contact with the level of culture which Berman so rightly finds invigorating.

The same set of issues emerges in even sharper focus when, in another article, Berman describes a return to the area of the South Bronx where he spent his boyhood.[14] The breakdancers and graffitists that he observes moving across the shadows of that desolate urban landscape are not so easily to be claimed for the overarching modernism he seeks to affirm. Their history, which for all its appeal does not enter directly into Berman's accounts of the dizzying allure and the democratic potential of modern society, originates in distinctively modern institutions of the Western Hemisphere like the sugar plantation.[15] It constitutes the lineage of a variety of social thought—a movement or sequence of movements in cultural politics and political culture—which is an extremely ambiguous component of his modernist vision and has little to do with the innocent, European modernity that appears in the wider debates in which he is participating.

Later on we shall see in detail how specific groups of black intellectuals—again not simply writers—have analysed and sought to come to terms with their inherently ambivalent relationship to the West and its dubious political legacies. Here it is only necessary to note that the contemporary descendants and the protective cultural forms of black radicalism also raise queries about the assumption of symmetrical intersubjectivity which features in so much of this discourse on the nature of modernity and modernisation. In view of this, it is unsurprising that Berman speaks of those who make it out of the ruins of the South Bronx simply as "working-class heroes,"[16] as if their membership of or affiliation to an identifiable and cohesive working class is a self-evident fact that somehow confirms his sense of the centripetal effects of modernity.

I should emphasise that Berman is not being singled out for attack here and that I have a great deal of sympathy with his persuasive and stimulating account of modernity and its attendant political choices. Pointing to some of the lapses in his narrative of the modern should not lead one to overlook the fact that he, unlike many of his theoretical peers, does at least notice the black and Hispanic presence in the ruins of the modern city. He may not be concerned with the impact of racial categories and meanings in the work of "intuitive" modernists like Hegel, but he does recognise the contemporary cultural products of modern black history and seek to portray their positive value. Berman even appreciates that "not much of [their] art is produced in commodity form for sale."[17] However, none of these important insights interrupts his haste to annex the cultural forms of the black Atlantic for an image of the working class. In a small way, Berman's inability to give due weight to the plurality that I believe is integral to the modern raises further profound problems about his presentation of the continuity of modern identity and the totalising wholeness with which he invests his conception of modern experience.

Pointing out aspects of the particularity of modern black experiences should not be understood as an occasion for staging the confrontation between the regional values of a distinct sector or community and the supposed universalism of occidental rationality. I am not suggesting that the contemporary traces of black intellectual history comprise or even refer to a lifeworld that is incommensurable with that of the former slaveholders. That would be the easy way out, for in focusing on racial slavery and its aftermath we are required to consider a historical relationship in which dependency and antagonism are intimately associated and in which black critiques of modernity may also be, in some significant senses, its affirmation. The key to comprehending this lies not in the overhasty separation of the cultural forms particular to both groups into some ethnic typology but in a detailed and comprehensive grasp of their complex interpenetration.[18] The intellectual and cultural achievements of the black Atlantic populations exist partly inside and not always against the grand narrative of Enlightenment and its operational principles. Their stems have grown strong, supported by a lattice of Western politics and letters. Though African linguistic tropes and political and philosophical themes are still visible for those who wish to see them, they have often been transformed and adapted by their New World locations to a new point where the dangerous issues of purified essences and simple origins lose all meaning. These modern black political formations stand simultaneously both inside and outside the Western culture which has been their peculiar step-parent. This complex relationship points once again to the need to engage critically with the way in which modernity has been theorised and periodised by its most enthusiastic defenders and critics. Regrettably, both groups have been equally slow in perceiving the centrality of ideas of race and culture to their ongoing investigations.

Like Berman, whose work bears his influence, Jürgen Habermas's writings convey a deep faith in the democratic potential of modernity. Modernity is understood as a distinct configuration with its own spatial and temporal characteristics defined above all through the consciousness of novelty that surrounds the emergence of civil society, the modern state, and industrial capitalism. Neither writer would accept that the normative potential of this new era has been exhausted, but theirs is not a positivistic or naive enthusiasm. Modernity is apprehended through its counterdiscourses and often defended solely through its counterfactual elements, yet their analyses remain substantially unaffected by the histories of barbarity which appear to be such a prominent feature of the widening gap between modern experience and modern expectation. There is a scant sense, for example, that the universality and rationality of enlightened Europe and America were used to sustain and relocate rather than eradicate an order of racial difference inherited from the premodern era. The figure of Columbus does not appear to complement the standard pairing of Luther and Copernicus that is implicitly used to mark the limits of this particular understanding of modernity. Locke's colonial interests and the effect of the conquest of the Americas on Descartes and Rousseau are simply nonissues. In this setting, it is hardly surprising that, if it is perceived to be relevant at all, the history of slavery is somehow assigned to blacks. It becomes our special property rather than a part of the ethical and intellectual heritage of the West as a whole.[19] This is only just preferable to the conventional alternative response which views plantation slavery as a premodern residue that disappears once it is revealed to be fundamentally incompatible with enlightened rationality and capitalist industrial production.

Like a good many exslaves and abolitionists, Habermas is tenaciously committed to the course of making bourgeois civil society live up to its political and philosophical promises. Drawing his theory of modernity from the work of Kant and Hegel, he notes its contemporary crises but says that they can be resolved only from within modernity itself by the completion of the Enlightenment project. There is perhaps an irony in seeing the affiliates of historical materialism defending the very humanistic rationality which for many years was one of their major intellectual foes.

Habermas recognises the intimate ties between the idea of modernity and the development of European art which is able to act as a reconciler of the fragmented moments of reason. Using Weber and Nietzsche, he also defines modernity through its supercession of religious world views and the process of cultural rationalisation whereby science, morality, and art are separated into autonomous spheres, each governed by its own epistemological rules and procedures of validation. The differentiation of these spheres of value is characterised by an emphasis on decentration and reflexivity. Thus the modernisation of the lifeworld sees the concepts of authenticity, aesthetics, and ethics sharply differentiated, while the modern is identified in the rift between secular and sacred spheres of action opened up by the death of God and the consequent hole at the centre of the lifeworld. This divergence proceeds closely articulated with the reification of consciousness that can be apprehended in the severing of expert cultures from the lifeworld and the latter's "colonisation" by debased forms of pseudo-reason which serve only to integrate and functionalise the social system. Under these conditions, everyday consciousness becomes a "fragmented consciousness" divorced from the opportunity to engage in reflexive, self-critical practice or the chance to analyse experience in terms of distinct, cognitive, practical, and aesthetic standards.

Habermas does not follow Hegel in arguing that slavery is itself a modernising force in that it leads both master and servant first to self-consciousness and then to disillusion, forcing both to confront the unhappy realisation that the true, the good, and the beautiful do not have a single shared origin. This is probably because though Habermas's theory of modernity draws heavily on Hegel, its Kantian focus absolves it from exploring the dialectic of master and slave in which Hegel's allegory of consciousness and freedom is rooted. I will return to this point later on. It is interesting that when Habermas does finally touch on the master/slave relationship he is exclusively concerned with the psychological dimensions of the allegory. He cites Hegel's observation that it is only the "Wild Moguls" who have their Lords outside themselves whereas the authentic offspring of European modernity remain enslaved even as they carry their Lord inside themselves.[20]

It is particularly disappointing that he has not found the modern demand that European masters take their enslaved other seriously worthy of more detailed comment. Habermas is acute in appreciating that Hegel's account of the master/slave relationship is secreted inside many of the writings of contemporary theorists of modernity. He gives this account of the special significance of Hegel's work in initiating the debates over modernity which prefigure contemporary discussions: "Hegel is not the first philosopher to belong to the modern age but he is the first for whom modernity became a problem. In his theory the constellation among modernity, time consciousness and rationality becomes visible for the first time. Hegel himself explodes this constellation, because rationality puffed up into absolute spirit neutralizes the conditions under which modernity attained a consciousness of itself."[21] These words endorse the idea that a journey back to Hegel may be worth making. Struggling to specify the value of the same difficult passages, the historian David Brion Davis describes them thus:

> It was Hegel's genius to endow lordship and bondage with such a rich resonance of meanings that the model could be applied to every form of physical and psychological domination. . . . Above all, Hegel bequeathed a message that would have a profound impact on future thought[,] . . . [that] we can expect nothing from the mercy of God or from the mercy of those who exercise worldly lordship in His or other names; that man's true emancipation, whether physical or spiritual, must always depend on those who have endured and overcome some form of slavery.[22]

Brion Davis is not alone in seeking to defend a more directly social reading of Hegel's text than Habermas's own more strictly delimited and essentially psychological concerns would sanction. The writings of Alexandre Kojève have been particularly important in popularising an interpretation of the master/slave relationship which, without drifting toward a literal analysis, is both less psychological and more historically specific than is currently fashionable.[23] Kojève's identification of an existential impasse that develops out of the master's dependency on the slave is also interesting because it would seem to offer an interesting point of departure for the analysis of modern aesthetics. These passages in Hegel and Kojève's influential interpretation of them have been widely taken up in social and psychoanalytic theory, forming, for example, an important part of the background to Richard Wright's Parisian revisions of Marxism and appropriations of phenomenology and existentialism. They have also been of great interest to the feminist writers who have returned to Hegel's allegory (via the Lukács of *History and Class Consciousness*) as part of their clarifying the possibility of "standpoint epistemologies,"[24] particular sociological or experiential locations from which woman-centred knowledge about the world can proceed. This is a big debate and cannot be reconstructed in its entirety here. It has, however, been brought to bear on modern black history and political culture by a number of feminist authors, in particular Patricia Hill Collins, whose argument for the existence of a black women's standpoint epistemology is conducted in something of the same critical, reconstructive, and revisionist spirit that guides my thinking here.[25] Hill Collins argues that the Western traditions of thinking and thinking about thinking to which the human sciences are bound have systematically tried to separate these privileged activities from mere being. This insight is linked in her argument to criticism of the pernicious effects of the dualistic, binary thinking in which one partner in the cognitive couple is always dominated by its repressed and subjugated other half—male/female, rational/irrational, nature/culture, light/dark.

Though I concur with most of Hill Collins's diagnosis of this state of affairs, I disagree with her responses to it. Her answer to the Western separation of thinking (and thinking about thinking) from being is to collapse them back into each other so that they form a functional unity that can be uncritically celebrated. She utilises a feminist version of this reasoning as an analogy for understanding what black women can do to produce a critical theory capable of addressing their experiences of marginalisation from truth seeking and interpretive activities. This begins in an argument for the social construction of "race" and gender. There is no essential woman or woman in general that can focus the emancipatory project of feminist politics; therefore a feminist epistemology must proceed to construct its own standpoint addressed to that lack. This is done in a spirit disabused of the belief that essentially feminine experience can act as the guarantor of feminist knowledge claims. In the (nonblack) feminist discourse, the terms *woman* and *feminist* are distinguished and must remain separate for the critique to operate plausibly. There is no open counterargument from Hill Collins for the superior value of an essentialist understanding of black female subjectivity. However, another version of racial essentialism is smuggled in through the back porch even as Hill Collins loudly banishes it from her front door. In her transposition, the term *black* does a double duty. It covers the positions of knowing and being. Its epistemological and ontological dimensions are entirely congruent. Their simple expressive unity joins an act of political affirmation to this philosophical stance: "being black encompasses both experiencing white domination and individual and group valuation of an independent, long-standing Afrocentric consciousness."[26] Her inconsistent deployment of the term *Afrocentric,* sometimes appearing as a synonym for *black* and sometimes as equivalent to the sense of the word *feminist* that was opposed to the word *woman,* does little to solve the confusion that results from this: "Even though I will continue to use the term Afrocentric feminist thought interchangeably with the phrase Black feminist thought, I think they are conceptually distinct."[27]

Hill Collins repeatedly emphasises that the standpoint she is exploring is "self-defined." This formulation appears at the point where a classically "Leninist" version of vanguardism is imported into her writing. The mass of black women have experiences that open the way forward to unique forms of consciousness. However, they are incapable of "articulating" the standpoint and need to be helped to do this by an elite cadre of black female intellectuals who vaccinate ordinary folk with the products of their critical theorising, thereby generating resistance. This group also performs what appears to be a low-intensity disciplinary function in areas of black politics other than feminist struggles: "Black women intellectuals who articulate an autonomous, self-defined standpoint are in a position to examine the usefulness of coalitions with other groups, both scholarly and activist, in order to develop new models for social change."[28]

Whatever one thinks of the political strategies implied in all this, it is striking how the image of an integral, humanist, and thoroughly Cartesian racial subject underpins and animates the construct of self that has been situated at the core of this "Black women's standpoint—those experiences and ideas shared by African-American women that provide a unique angle of vision on self, community, and society."[29] The elision of black and African American in this passage is symptomatic of other problems that will be examined below. But what are we to make of the fact that self always comes first in this litany? What understanding of self is it to supply the subjectivity that can focus the subject of black politics?

Hill Collins's answers to these questions suggest that an embeddedness in Enlightenment assumptions continues despite the ostentatious gestures of disaffiliation. Experience-centred knowledge claims, mediated if at all by input from the intellectual vanguard, simply end up substituting the standpoint of black women for its forerunner rooted in the lives of white men. This may have some value as a short-term corrective, but it is less radical and less stimulating than the possibility that we might move beyond the desire to situate our claims about the world in the lives of these whole and stable, ideal subjects. For all its conspicuous masculinism and Eurocentrism, Hegel's allegory is relational. It can be used to point out the value of incorporating the problem of subject formation into both epistemology and political practice. This would also mean taking a cue from a politicised postmodernism and leaving the categories of enquiry open.[30]

My own interest in the famous section at the start of Hegel's *The Phenomenology of Mind*[31] is twofold: First, it can be used to initiate an analysis of modernity which is abjured by Habermas because it points directly to an approach which sees the intimate association of modernity and slavery as a fundamental conceptual issue. This is significant because it can be used to offer a firm rebuke to the mesmeric idea of history as progress and because it provides an opportunity to reperiodise and reaccentuate accounts of the dialectic of Enlightenment which have not always been concerned to look at modernity through the lenses of colonialism or scientific racism. Second, a return to Hegel's account of the conflict and the forms of dependency produced in the relationship between master and slave foregrounds the issues of brutality and terror which are also too frequently ignored. Taken together, these problems offer an opportunity to transcend the unproductive debate between a Eurocentric rationalism which banishes the slave experience from its accounts of modernity while arguing that the crises of modernity can be resolved from within and an equally occidental antihumanism which locates the origins of modernity's current crises in the shortcomings of the Enlightenment project.

Cornel West has pointed out that Hegel was the favourite philosopher of Dr. Martin Luther King Jr.[32] The point of entry into the discourse of modernity which Hegel affords is doubly significant because, as we shall see, a significant number of intellectuals formed by the black Atlantic have engaged in critical dialogues with his writings. Their difficult and deeply ambivalent relationship to his work and to the intellectual tradition in which it stands helps to locate their uncomfortable position relative to Western politics and letters and to identify the distinctive perspectives on the modern world that they have expressed. Amiri Baraka's 1963 poem "Hegel" captures this ambivalence and shows that the appropriation of Hegelian themes is by no means always negative:

> I scream for help. And none comes, has ever
> come. No single redeeming hand
> has ever been offered . . .
> no single redeeming word, has come
> wringing out of flesh
> with the imperfect beautiful resolution
> that would release me from this heavy contract
> of emptiness.[33]

In *Being and Nothingness* Sartre makes the point that Hegel's analysis does not deal with lateral relations between masters or within the caste of slaves let alone with the impact of a free, non-slave-owning population on the institution of slavery.[34] However, despite these contextual failings, its insights and view of slavery as, in a sense, the premise of modernity also give us the chance to reopen discussion of the origins of black politics in the Euro-American Age of Revolution and the consequent relationship between the contrasting varieties of radicalism which energised the slaves' struggles for emancipation and racial justice and which endure in the struggles of their dispersed descendants today. Plantation slavery was more than just a system of labour and a distinct mode of racial domination. Whether it encapsulates the inner essence of capitalism or was a vestigial, essentially precapitalist element in a dependant relationship to capitalism proper, it provided the foundations for a distinctive network of economic, social, and political relations. Above all, "its demise threw open the most fundamental questions of economy, society and polity,"[35] and it has retained a central place in the historical memories of the black Atlantic.

The way these populations continue to make creative, communicative use of the memory of slavery points constructively away from the twin positions that have overdetermined the debate on modernity so far— an uncritical and complacent rationalism and a self-conscious and rhetorical antihumanism which simply trivialises the potency of the negative.

Moving beyond these options requires consideration of what, following Walter Benjamin, can be called the primal history of modernity.[36] Although Benjamin was not attuned to the possibility that modern history could be seen as fractured along the axis that separates European masters and mistresses from their African slaves, there are elements of his thinking, particularly those which derive from his relationship to Jewish mysticism, which make it a valuable resource for my own critique.[37] The time has come for the primal history of modernity to be reconstructed from the slaves' points of view. These emerge in the especially acute consciousness of both life and freedom which is nurtured by the slave's "mortal terror of his sovereign master" and the continuing "trial by death" which slavery becomes for the male slave.[38] This primal history offers a unique perspective on many of the key intellectual and political issues in the modernity debates. I have already mentioned the idea of history as progress. Apart from that thorny perennial, the slaves' perspectives require a discrete view not just of the dynamics of power and domination in plantation societies dedicated to the pursuit of commercial profit but of such central categories of the Enlightenment project as the idea of universality, the fixity of meaning, the coherence of the subject, and, of course, the foundational ethnocentrism in which these have all tended to be anchored. Each of these issues has an impact on the formation of racial discourse and a relevance in understanding the development of racial politics. These problems aside, the slaves' perspectives necessitate a critical stance on the discourse of bourgeois humanism which several scholars have implicated in the rise and consolidation of scientific racism.[39] Using the memory of slavery as an interpretive device suggests that this humanism cannot simply be repaired by introducing the figures of black folks who had previously been confined to the intermediate category between animal and human that Du Bois identifies as a "tertium quid."[40]

In keeping with the spiritual components which also help to distinguish them from modern secular rationality, the slaves' perspectives deal only secondarily in the idea of a rationally pursued utopia. Their primary categories are steeped in the idea of a revolutionary or eschatological apocalypse—the Jubilee. They provocatively suggest that many of the advances of modernity are in fact insubstantial or pseudoadvances contingent on the power of the racially dominant grouping and that, as a result, the critique of modernity cannot be satisfactorily completed from within its own philosophical and political norms, that is, immanently. The representative figures whose work I shall explore below were all acutely aware of the promise and potential of the modern world. Nevertheless, their critical perspectives on it were only partly grounded in its own norms. However uneasily their work balanced its defences of modernity against its critiques, they drew deliberately and self-consciously on premodern images and symbols that gain an extra power in proportion to the brute facts of modern slavery. These have contributed to the formation of a vernacular variety of unhappy consciousness which demands that we rethink the meanings of rationality, autonomy, reflection, subjectivity, and power in the light of an extended meditation both on the condition of the slaves and on the suggestion that racial terror is not merely compatible with occidental rationality but cheerfully complicit with it. In terms of contemporary politics and social theory, the value of this project lies in its promise to uncover both an ethics of freedom to set alongside modernity's ethics of law and the new conceptions of selfhood and individuation that are waiting to be constructed from the slaves' standpoint—forever disassociated from the psychological and epistemic correlates of racial subordination. This unstable standpoint is to be understood in a different way from the clarion calls to epistemological narcissism and the absolute sovereignty of unmediated experience[41] which sometimes appear in association with the term. It can be summed up in Foucault's tentative extension of the idea of a *critical* self-inventory into the political field. This is made significantly in a commentary upon the Enlightenment: "The critical ontology of ourselves has to be considered not, certainly, as a theory, a doctrine, nor even as a permanent body of knowledge that is accumulating; it has to be conceived as an attitude, an ethos, a philosophical life in which the critique of what we are is at one and the same time the historical analysis of the limits that are imposed on us and an experiment with the possibility of going beyond them."[42]

Having recognised the cultural force of the term *modernity*, we must also be prepared to delve into the special traditions of artistic expression that emerge from slave culture. As we shall see in the next chapter [of *The Black Atlantic*], art, particularly in the form of music and dance, was offered to slaves as a substitute for the formal political freedoms they were denied under the plantation regime. The expressive cultures developed in slavery continue to preserve in artistic form needs and desires which go far beyond the mere satisfaction of material wants. In contradistinction to the Enlightenment assumption of a fundamental separation between art and life, these expressive forms reiterate the continuity of art and life. They celebrate the grounding of the aesthetic with other dimensions of social life. The particular aesthetic which the continuity of expressive culture preserves derives not from dispassionate and rational evaluation of the artistic object but from an inescapably subjective contemplation of the mimetic functions of artistic performance in the processes of struggles toward emancipation, citizenship, and eventually autonomy. Subjectivity is here connected with rationality in a contingent manner. It may be grounded in communication, but this form of interaction is not an equivalent and idealised exchange between equal citizens who reciprocate their regard for each other in grammatically unified speech. The extreme patterns of communication defined by the institution of plantation slavery dictate that we recognise the antidiscursive and extralinguistic ramifications of power at work in shaping communicative acts. There may, after all, be no reciprocity on the plantation outside of the possibilities of rebellion and suicide, flight and silent mourning, and there is certainly no grammatical unity of speech to mediate communicative reason. In many respects, the plantation's inhabitants live nonsynchronously. Their mode of communication is divided by the radically opposed political and economic interests that distinguish the master and mistress from their respective human chattels. Under these conditions, artistic practice retains its "cultic functions," while its superior claims to authenticity and historic witness may be actively preserved. It becomes diffuse throughout the subaltern racial collectivity where relations of cultural production and reception operate that are wholly different from those which define the public sphere of the slaveholders. In this severely restricted space, sacred or profane, art became the backbone of the slaves' political cultures and of their cultural history. It remains the means through which cultural activists even now engage in "rescuing critiques" of the present by both mobilising memories of the past and inventing an imaginary past-ness that can fuel their utopian hopes.

We can see now that the arts of darkness appear in the West at the point where modernity is revealed to be actively associated with the forms of terror legitimated by reference to the idea of "race." We must remember that however modern they may appear to be, the artistic practices of the slaves and their descendants are also grounded outside modernity. The invocation of anteriority as antimodernity is more than a consistent rhetorical flourish linking contemporary Africalogy and its nineteenth-century precursors. These gestures articulate a memory of preslave history that can, in turn, operate as a mechanism to distil and focus the counterpower of those held in bondage and their descendants. This artistic practice is therefore inescapably both inside and outside the dubious protection modernity offers. It can be examined in relation to modern forms, themes, and ideas but carries its own distinct critique of modernity, a critique forged out of the particular experiences involved in being a racial slave in a legitimate and avowedly rational system of unfree labour. To put it another way, this artistic and political formation has come to relish its measure of autonomy from the modern—an independent vitality that comes from the syncopated pulse of non-European philosophical and aesthetic outlooks and the fallout from their impact on Western norms. This autonomy developed further as slavery, colonialism, and the terror that attended them pitted the vital arts of the slaves against the characteristically modern conditions in which their oppression appeared—as a by-product of the coerced production of commodities for sale on a world market. This system produced an ungenteel modernity, decentred from the closed worlds of metropolitan Europe that have claimed the attention of theorists so far.

A preoccupation with the striking doubleness that results from this unique position—in an expanded West but not completely of it—is a definitive characteristic of the intellectual history of the black Atlantic. We will see that it can be traced through the works of a number of modern black thinkers. Frederick Douglass is the first of these representative figures, and his life is an exemplary one as far as this book is concerned. It spanned the Atlantic and involved a record of consistent activism and advocacy on behalf of the slave. There is no space here to discuss the impact of his travels in England and Scotland,[43] even though they help to map the spatial dimensions of the black Atlantic world. Unlike the other candidates for the role of progenitor of black nationalism—Martin Delany, Edward Wilmot Blyden, and Alexander Crummell—Douglass had been a slave himself. He is generally remembered for the quality and passion of his political oratory. His writings continue to be a rich resource in the cultural and political analysis of the black Atlantic.[44]

Lord and Bondsman in a Black Idiom

Douglass, who acquired his new postslave surname from the pages of Sir Walter Scott's *The Lady of the Lake*, published three autobiographies, rewriting his life story and reshaping his public persona at different stages of his life.[45] These texts present a range of important black perspectives on the problem of modernity. Their literary form also raises profound issues about the aesthetic dimensions and periodisation of black modernism. Both lines of enquiry can be extended by some intertextual consideration of the relationship between Douglass's autobiographies and his only venture into fiction, *The Heroic Slave.* His relationship to modernity was a complex and shifting one, particularly in that he retained and developed the religious convictions that lay at the core of his original opposition to the slave system. Yet Douglass would need no lessons from Habermas and his followers as to the incomplete nature of the Enlightenment project or the need for criticism of religion to precede other forms of social criticism. In his writings he repeatedly calls for greater enlightenment capable of bringing the illumination of reason to the ethical darkness of slavery. Unlike many of those who were to follow in his footsteps, Douglass conceived of the slave plantation as an archaic institution out of place in the modern world: "[The] plantation is a little nation of its own, having its own language, its own rules, regulations and customs. The laws and institutions of the state, apparently touch it nowhere. The troubles arising here, are not settled by the civil power of the state."[46] The state's lack of access to the plantation illustrated the plantation's general inaccessibility to the varieties of modern, secular political reason necessary to its reform. Douglass compared the slave plantation to the premodern, precapitalist relations of feudal Europe: "In its isolation, seclusion, and self-reliant independence [the] plantation resembles what the baronial domains were during the middle ages. . . . Grim, cold and unapproachable by all genial influences from communities without, there it stands; full three hundred years behind the age in all that relates to humanity and morals. . . . Civilization is shut out."[47] Douglass's own Christianity may have formed the centre of his political outlook, but he was emphatic that the best master he ever had was an atheist: "Were I again to be reduced to the condition of a slave, next to that calamity, I should regard the fact of being the slave of a religious slaveholder, the greatest that could befall me. For all the slaveholders with whom I have ever met, religious slaveholders are the worst."[48]

Douglass advocated the humanity of African slaves and attacked the exclusion of Africa from history in a celebrated ethnological lecture which he delivered in various venues from 1854 on. Later published as "The Claims of the Negro Ethnologically Considered,"[49] this piece offered a coherent challenge to the scientific racism of Douglass's own time. He discussed, among other things, the work of Samuel Morton.[50] It also conveyed the precision of Douglass's attack on the hellenomaniacal excision of Africa from the narrative of civilisation's development. This was an intensely contested issue at a time when scientific understanding was in motion toward a new version of the relationship among Ancient Greece, the Levant, and Egypt. As Martin Bernal has pointed out,[51] much of this debate turns on the analysis of the Nile Valley civilisations in general and Egypt in particular. Like many African Americans, Douglass visited Egypt. He travelled there with his second wife, Helen Pitts, during the late 1880s, making it clear that his journey was part of a long-term quest for the facts with which he could support his ethnological opinions.[52] It is obvious that the appeal of Egypt as evidence of the greatness of preslave African cultures, like the enduring symbol that Egypt supplies for black creativity and civilisation, has had a special significance within black Atlantic responses to modernity. At the very least, it helped to ground the cultural norms of diaspora politics outside the pathway marked out by the West's own progress from barbarism to civilisation and to show that the path began in Africa rather than Greece. Egypt also provided the symbolic means to locate the diaspora's critique of Enlightenment universals outside the philosophical repertoire of the West.[53] Though Douglass challenged the ethnological implications of Hegel's view of Africa and Africans from the platforms of numerous political meetings, his autobiographies provide a chance to construct critical revisions of Hegel in a rather different form. Douglass was certainly acquainted with the German idealist tradition. We are indebted to Douglass's biographer William McFeely for important details of his intimate relationship with Ottilie Assing, the translator of the German edition of *My Bondage and My Freedom* published in Hamburg in 1860. Assing came from a cultured and intellectual family background. She enjoyed close connections with her uncle's wife, Rahel Levin, an important figure in the Goethe cult. We know that Assing read both Goethe and Feuerbach to Douglass.[54] It would have been surprising if Hegel's name had not been raised in that illustrious company. Assing took her own life in the Bois de Boulogne in 1884 after Douglass's marriage to Helen Pitts.

With this suggestive connection in mind, I want to propose that we read a section of Douglass's narrative as an alternative to Hegel: a supplement if not exactly a transcoding of his account of the struggle between lord and bondsman. In a rich account of the bitter trial of strength with Edward Covey, the slave breaker to whom he has been sent, Douglass can be read as if he is systematically reworking the encounter between master and slave in a striking manner which inverts Hegel's own allegorical scheme. It is the slave rather than the master who emerges from Douglass's account possessed of "consciousness that exists *for itself*," while his master becomes the representative of a "consciousness that is repressed within itself." Douglass's transformation of Hegel's metanarrative of power into a metanarrative of emancipation is all the more striking as it is also the occasion for an attempt to specify the difference between a prerational, spiritual mode of African thought and his own compound outlook—an uneasy hybrid of the sacred and the secular, the African and the American, formed out of the debilitating experience of slavery and tailored to the requirements of his abolitionism.

In all three versions of the tale, this section of the narrative begins with Douglass being leased into Covey's care by Thomas Auld—his "real" master. Having broken up the Sabbath school that Douglass had organised for his fellow slaves, Auld desired his slave to be "well broken" lest he develop into "another Nat Turner." Unlike Auld, Covey was a poor man steeped in a variety of pseudopiety that Douglass viewed with special contempt. We are told, significantly, that he was a poor singer and relied mainly on Douglass for raising a hymn in the frequent acts of family worship to which his slaves were party. Douglass continually compares him to a serpent and tells us that his new master was as unreasonable as he was cruel. Without going into the detail of Covey's brutal regime or the nature of the confrontation that he engineered to break Douglass, [it can be said that] the conflict between them induced Douglass to flee. He describes the first six months of his stay with Covey in dramatic fashion: "A few months of his discipline tamed me. Mr Covey succeeded in breaking me. I was broken in body, soul and spirit. My natural elasticity was crushed; my intellect languished; the disposition to read departed; the cheerful spark that lingered about my eye died; the dark night of slavery closed in upon me; and behold a man transformed into a brute."[55]

After a particularly severe beating, Douglass returned to Auld to display his wounds and to appeal to him on the grounds that Covey's unjust and brutal regime had endangered a valuable piece of property, namely Douglass himself. Auld found excuses for Covey's behaviour and ordered Douglass to return to his custody. Hidden in the woods, "shut in with nature and nature's

God," Douglass prayed, like Madison Washington, the fictional hero of *The Heroic Slave*, for deliverance from slavery in general and from Covey in particular. Douglass concedes at this point that he experienced doubt about all religion and believed his prayers to be delusory. As night fell, he met another slave who was on his way to spend the Sabbath with his wife, who resided on a neighbouring plantation. Later in Douglass's narratives, readers learn that this man, Sandy, betrayed the slaves when they tried to escape. However, at this point in the tale Douglass looks upon him with respect. He was famous among local slaves for his good nature and his good sense: "He was not only a religious man, but he professed to believe in a system for which I have no name. He was a genuine African, and had inherited some of the so-called magical powers, said to be possessed by African and eastern nations."[56]

Douglass "pour[ed] his grief" into the conjurer's ears, and, after a meal, they discussed what strategy was most suitable in circumstances where out-and-out flight was impossible. Sandy's belief in the system of ancient African magic led him to offer Douglass a charmed magic root which, if worn on the right side of his body, would make him invulnerable to Covey's blows. Sandy answered Douglass's Christian scepticism by telling him that his book learning had not kept Covey off him. He begged the runaway to try the African—I am tempted to say Africentric—alternative, saying that it could certainly do no harm. Douglass took the root from Sandy and returned to the Covey household. He tells the eager reader, "A slight gleam or shadow of his superstition had fallen upon me."[57] In view of the fact that Douglass makes such great use of the symbolism of light and darkness, the construction "gleam or shadow" is an interesting evasion. Was it a gleam or a shadow? The two ideas are clear alternatives with strikingly different implications for our reading of the episode. The carefully deployed ambiguity may also be a cryptic acknowledgement of the different ways in which black and white readers were likely to respond to the tale.

On his return, Douglass met Covey and his wife en route to church dressed in their Sunday best. Covey had acquired the countenance of an Angel and smiled so broadly that Douglass began "to think that Sandy's herb had more virtue in it than I, in my pride, had been willing to allow."[58] All went well until Monday morning, when Covey, freed from his religious observance, returned to his customary and devious brutality. This was the moment when Douglass resolved, with devastating consequences, to stand up in his own defense. The Hegelian struggle ensued, but this time Douglass discovered an ideal speech situation at the very moment in which he held his tormentor by the throat: "I held him so firmly by the throat that his blood flowed through my nails. . . . 'Are you going to resist you scoundrel' said he. To which, I returned a polite 'Yes Sir.'"[59] The two men were locked together in the Hegelian impasse. Each was able to contain the strength of the other without vanquishing him. Enraged by Douglass's unexpected act of insubordination, Covey then sought to enlist the aid of the other people who were to hand, both slave and free. Covey's cousin Hughes was beaten off by Douglass; then Bill, the hired man, affected ignorance of what Covey wished him to do, and Caroline, the female slave in the Covey household, bravely declined her master's instruction to take hold of Douglass. In the text, each of these supporting characters is addressed by Douglass and Covey in turn. The mutual respect born in their tussle is conveyed by the manner in which they appealed to the others as equals. After two hours, Covey gave up the contest and let Douglass go. The narrator tells us that he was a changed man after that fight, which was "the turning point" in his career as a slave. The physical struggle is also the occasion on which a liberatory definition of masculinity is produced. "I was nothing before; I was a man now. It [the fight] recalled to life my crushed self-respect and my self confidence, and inspired me with a renewed determination to be a free man. A man without force is without the essential dignity of humanity. . . . I was no longer a servile coward, trembling under the frown of a brother worm of the dust, but my long-cowed spirit was roused to an attitude of manly independence. I had reached a point at which I was not afraid to die."[60] Douglass's tale can be used to reveal a great deal about the difference between the male slave's and the master's views of modern civilisation. In Hegel's allegory, which correctly places slavery at the natal core of modern sociality, we see that one solipsistic combatant in the elemental struggle prefers his conqueror's version of reality to death and submits. He becomes the slave, while the other achieves mastery. Douglass's version is quite different. For him, the slave actively prefers the possibility of death to the continuing condition of inhumanity on which plantation slavery depends. He anticipated a point made by Lacan some years later: "Death, precisely because it has been drawn into the function of stake in the game . . . shows at the same time how much of the prior rule, as well as of the concluding settlement, has been elided. For in the last analysis it is necessary for the loser not to perish, in order to become a slave. In other words, the pact everywhere precedes violence before perpetuating it."[61]

This turn toward death as a release from terror and bondage and a chance to find substantive freedom accords perfectly with Orlando Patterson's celebrated notion of slavery as a state of "social death."[62] It points to the value of seeing the consciousness of the slave as involving an extended act of mourning. Douglass's preference for death fits readily with archival material on the practice of slave suicide and needs also to be seen alongside other representations of death as agency that can be found in early African American fiction.[63] Ronald Takaki and others[64] have discussed these passages as part of a wider consideration of Douglass's changing view of the necessity of violence in the cause of black emancipation—a theme that Douglass developed further in *The Heroic Slave*. Douglass's departure from the pacifism that had marked his early work is directly relevant to his critical understanding of modernity. It underscored the complicity of civilisation and brutality while emphasising that the order of authority on which the slave plantation relied cannot be undone without recourse to the counterviolence of the oppressed. Douglass's description of his combat with Covey expresses this once again, offering an interesting though distinctly masculinist resolution of slavery's inner oppositions.

This idea of masculinity is largely defined against the experience of infantilism on which the institutions of plantation slavery rely rather than against women. However, it is interesting that this aspect of Douglass's political stance has been discussed elsewhere among the would-be savants and philosophes of the black Atlantic as a symptom of important differences in the philosophical and strategic orientations of black men and women. In his famous essay "On the Damnation of Women," Du Bois recounts a story told to him by Wendell Phillips which pinpoints the problem with precision:

Wendell Phillips says that he was once in Faneuil Hall, when Frederick Douglass was one of the chief speakers. Douglass had been describing the wrongs of the Negro race and as he proceeded he grew more and more excited and finally ended by saying that they had no hope of justice from whites, no possible hope except in their own right arms. It must come to blood! They must fight for themselves. Sojourner Truth was sitting, tall and dark, on the very front seat facing the platform, and in the hush of feeling when Douglass sat down she spoke out in her deep, peculiar voice, heard all over the hall: "Frederick, is God dead?"[65]

The question which Sojourner Truth detected in Douglass's fiery oratory and pessimistic political conclusion has an important place in philosophical debates over the value of modernity and the transvaluation of postsacral, modern values. In Germany at roughly the same time, another Frederick (Nietzsche) was pondering the philosophical and ethical implications of the same question. It remains implicit in the story of Douglass's struggles in and against slavery. It may also be a question that cannot be separated from the distinct mode of masculinity with which it has been articulated. To counter any ambiguity around this point in Douglass's tale, I want to pursue similar philosophical conclusions which appeared elsewhere in the history of the abolitionist movement as an important cipher for its emergent feminist sensibilities shortly after Douglass's own tale was published. The horrific story of Margaret Garner's attempted escape from slavery in Kentucky can usefully be read in conjunction with Douglass's autobiographical story. A version of this tale is still circulating, both as part of the African American literary tradition inaugurated by works like Douglass's *The Heroic Slave* and as part of what might be called the black feminist political project. This longevity is testimony not simply to Toni Morrison's conspicuous skill as a writer in reinventing this story in her novel *Beloved*[66] but to the continuing symbolic power of the tale and its importance as an element of the moral critique that anchors black antipathy to the forms of rationality and civilised conduct which made racial slavery and its brutality legitimate.

Contemporary newspaper reports, abolitionist material, and various biographical and autobiographical accounts provide the sources from which this episode can be reconstructed. The simplest details of the case shared by various accounts[67] seem to be as follows. Taking advantage of the winter which froze the Ohio River, which usually barred her way to freedom, Margaret Garner, a "mulatto, about five feet high, showing one fourth or one third white blood . . . [with] a high forehead . . . [and] bright and intelligent eyes,"[68] fled slavery on a horse-drawn sleigh in January 1856 with her husband, Simon Garner Jr., also known as Robert, his parents, Simon and Mary, their four children, and nine other slaves. On reaching Ohio, the family separated from the other slaves, but they were discovered after they had sought assistance at the home of a relative, Elijah Kite. Trapped in his house by the encircling slave catchers, Margaret killed her three-year-old daughter with a butcher's knife and attempted to kill the other children rather than let them be taken back into slavery by their master, Archibald K. Gaines, the owner of Margaret's husband and of the plantation adjacent to her own home. This case initiated a series of legal battles over the scope of the Fugitive Slave Act,[69] Margaret's extradition, her legal subjectivity, and the respective powers of court officers in the different states. Despite pleas that she be placed on trial for the murder of the little girl "whom she probably loved the best,"[70] Margaret's master eventually sent her to the slave market in New Orleans.

The contemporary reports of this episode are contradictory and burdened with the conflicting political interests that framed its central tragedy. One newspaper report suggested that the Garners' original decision to flee from bondage had, for example, been encouraged by a visit to the Gaines household by two English ladies.[71] The best-known account of the events is set down in the *Reminiscences of Levi Coffin*. Coffin was a local Quaker abolitionist and reputed president of the Underground Railroad who had been peripherally involved in the tragedy. A number of interesting points emerge from that authoritative source as well as from newspaper articles about the case; the American Anti-Slavery Society's annual report; an account given in the biography of Lucy Stone, the distinguished abolitionist and suffragist who visited Margaret Garner in prison and attended the court hearings; and a further version written for the *American Baptist* by one P. S. Bassett, who gave his address as the Fairmount Theological Seminary in Cincinnati.[72]

Hopelessly surrounded by a posse of slave catchers in the house of their kinsman Elijah Kite, Margaret's husband, Simon Garner Jr., fired several shots from a revolver at the pursuers. In a further struggle that took place after Gaines and his associates had succeeded in entering the house, one marshal had two fingers shot from his hand and lost several teeth from a ricocheting bullet. Coffin writes that "the slave men were armed and fought bravely," while the Anti-Slavery Society makes this resistance a matrimonial rather than gender-based phenomenon: "Robert and Margaret fought bravely and desperately to protect their parents, and their children, in their right to liberty, but were soon overpowered."[73] In this account Margaret's assault on the children takes place between two attacks on the house by Gaines and his henchmen. In Coffin's version of the story it is only *after* Margaret has appreciated the hopelessness of the slaves' besieged position and seen her husband overpowered that she begins her emancipatory assault on her children.

Some newspaper reports said that after almost decapitating the little girl's body in the act of cutting her throat, Margaret called out to her mother-in-law for assistance in slaying the other children, "Mother, help me to kill the children."[74] Bassett, who claimed to have interviewed both women, quoted Mary Garner as saying that she "neither encouraged nor discouraged her daughter-in-law,—for under similar circumstances she should probably have done the same." What mode of rational, moral calculation may have informed this appeal from one black woman to another? Other papers reported that the older woman could not endure the sight of her grandchildren being murdered and ran to take refuge under a bed. What are we to make of these contrasting forms of violence, one coded as male and outward, directed toward the oppressor, and the other coded as female, somehow internal, channelled toward a parent's most precious and intimate objects of love, pride, and desire? After her arrest, Margaret Garner is said to have sat in the Hammond Street Police Station House in a shocked and stupefied state. Archibald Gaines took the body of her dead daughter away so that he could bury it in Kentucky on land "consecrated to slavery."[75]

This tale was immediately repeated within the abolitionist movement as important proof of the venal menace posed by the unbridled appetites of the slave masters. From this perspective, much was to be made of the fact that the slain child had been female, killed by her mother lest she fall victim to this licentiousness. Lucy Stone emphasised this point to her biographer: "She was a beautiful woman, chestnut colored, with good features and wonderful eyes. It was no wild desperation that had impelled her, but a calm determination that, if she could not find freedom here, she would get it with the angels. . . . Margaret had tried to kill all her children, but she had made sure of the little girl. She had said that her daughter would never suffer as she had."[76]

Stone attended the courtroom deliberations over Margaret's fate and was accused of trying to pass a knife to her while visiting her in prison, so that she could finish the job she had begun. We are told by Coffin that Stone drew tears from many listeners when, in explaining her conduct before the court, she made this argument: "When I saw that poor fugitive, took her toil-hardened hand in mine, and read in her face deep suffering and an ardent longing for freedom, I could not help bid her be of good cheer. I told her that a thousand hearts were aching for her, and that they were glad one child of hers was safe with the angels. Her only reply was a look of deep despair, of anguish such that no words can speak."[77] Stone defended Margaret's conduct as a woman and a Christian, arguing that her infanticide sprung from the deepest and holiest feelings implanted alike in black and white women by their common divine father. Coffin quotes her [Stone] as likening Margaret's spirit to that of those ancestors to whom the monument at Bunker Hill had been erected. She made the proto-feminist interpretation of Margaret's actions quite explicit: "The faded faces of the Negro Children tell too plainly to what degradation female slaves submit. Rather than give her little daughter to that life, she killed it."[78]

Further indication of the power of this narrative in the development of a distinctly feminine abolitionist discourse comes from the lectures of Sarah Parker Remond, a black abolitionist and physician born free in Salem, Massachusetts, who eventually made her home in Italy.[79] Interestingly, we know that Lucy Stone had visited the Salem Female Anti-Slavery Society, to which Sarah belonged.[80] A version of Remond's account of the Garner story is given in a newspaper report of a packed public meeting that she addressed in the Music Hall, Warrington, England, three years after the incident.[81] Remond had discussed the case with John Jolliffe, Margaret Garner's attorney. Her concern throughout the one-and-a-half-hour lecture was to demonstrate the un-Christian and immoral character of slavery and to reveal its capacity to pervert both civilisation and the natural attributes of human beings. According to the conventions of abolitionist discourse, the image of abusive and coercive white male sexuality was prominently displayed. The perversion of maternity by the institution of slavery was a well-seasoned theme in abolitionist propaganda. Frederick Douglass had made this very point in his *Narrative,* recounting an incident in which a white woman, Mrs. Hicks, murdered her slave—a cousin of Douglass's—for failing to keep the baby she was charged with minding sufficiently quiet during the night. "The offence for which this girl was murdered was this:— She had been set that night to mind Mrs. Hick's baby and during the night she fell asleep and the baby cried. She having lost her rest for several nights previous, did not hear the crying. They were both in the room with Mrs. Hicks. Mrs. Hicks, finding the girl slow to move, jumped from her bed, seized an oak stick of wood by the fireplace, and with it broke the girl's nose and breastbone, and thus ended her life."[82] These stories raise complex questions about the mediating role of gender categories in racial politics and in particular about the psychological structures of identification facilitated by the idea of maternity. It is impossible to explore these important matters here. The Margaret Garner story corresponds most closely to Douglass's work in her refusal to concede any legitimacy to slavery and thereby to initiate the dialectic of intersubjective dependency and recognition that Hegel's allegory presents as modernity's precondition. Like Douglass's, her tale constructs a conception of the slave subject as an agent. What appears in both stories to be a positive preference for death rather than continued servitude can be read as a contribution toward slave discourse on the nature of freedom itself. It supplies a valuable clue toward answering the question of how the realm of freedom is conceptualised by those who have never been free. This inclination toward death and away from bondage is fundamental. It reminds us that in the revolutionary eschatology which helps to define this primal history of modernity, whether apocalyptic or redemptive, it is the moment of jubilee that has the upper hand over the pursuit of utopia by rational means. The discourse of black spirituality which legitimises these moments of violence possesses a utopian truth content that projects beyond the limits of the present. The repeated choice of death rather than bondage articulates a principle of negativity that is opposed to the formal logic and rational calculation characteristic of modern Western thinking and expressed in the Hegelian slave's preference for bondage rather than death. As part of his argument against her return to Kentucky, Margaret's lawyer, Mr. Jolliffe, told the court that she and the other fugitives "would all go singing to the gallows" rather than be returned to slavery. The association of this apparent preference for death with song is also highly significant. It joins a moral and political gesture to an act of cultural creation and affirmation. This should be borne in mind when we come to consider how intervention in the memories of slavery is routinely practised as a form of vernacular cultural history.

Douglass's writings and the popularity of the Garner narrative are also notable for marking out the process whereby the division of intellectual labour within the abolitionist movement was transformed. The philosophical material for the abolitionist cause was no longer to be exclusively generated by white commentators who articulated the metaphysical core of simple, factual slave narratives. It is also important to emphasise that these texts offer far more than the reworking and transformation of the familiar Hegelian allegory. They express in the most powerful way a tradition of writing in which autobiography becomes an act or process of simultaneous self-creation and self-emancipation.[83] The presentation of a public persona thus becomes a founding motif within the expressive culture of the African diaspora.[84] The implications that this has for the inner aesthetic character of black Atlantic modernity will be explored in greater detail below [in subsequent sections of *The Black Atlantic*]. It is important to note here that a new discursive economy emerges with the refusal to subordinate the particularity of the slave experience to the totalising power of universal reason held exclusively by white hands, pens, or publishing houses. Authority and autonomy emerge directly from the deliberately personal tone of this history. Eagerly received by the movement to which they were addressed, these tales helped to mark out a dissident space within the bourgeois public sphere which they aimed to suffuse with their utopian content. The autobiographical character of many statements like this is thus absolutely crucial. It appeals in special ways to the public opinion of the abolitionist movement against the arbitrary power intrinsic to a slave system which is both unreasonable and un-Christian. What Richard Wright would later identify as the aesthetics of personalism flows from these narratives and shows that in the hands of slaves the particular can wear the mantle of truth and reason as readily as the universal.

It is worth pausing for a moment to examine an especially significant passage at the end of the fifth chapter of Douglass's narrative which has been pointed out by William Andrews in his absorbing book *To Tell a Free Story*.[85] In this passage, Douglass is reflecting on a turning point in his life when, at the age of seven or eight, he was sent by his master to Baltimore to live with the Aulds. Looking back on this event, Douglass describes it as the first plain manifestation of a special providence which has attended him ever since. He acknowledges that the white reader is likely to respond sceptically to his claim to have been singled out for this special destiny: "I may be deemed superstitious, and even egotistical, in regarding this event as a special interposition of divine providence in my favour. But I should be false to the earliest sentiments of my soul if I suppressed the opinion. I prefer to be true to myself even at the hazard of incurring the ridicule of others, rather than to be false and incur my own abhorrence."[86] Andrews points out that Douglass does not appeal to *divine* authority to legitimate this declaration of independence in the interpretation of his own life. The passage underscores the link between autobiographical writing and the project of self-liberation. Its fundamental importance lies in the clarity of its announcement that truth to the self takes priority over what the readers may think is acceptable or appropriate to introduce into an abolitionist discourse. However, I believe that there is a deeper argument here concerning the status of truth and reason as universal concepts and the need to depart from absolute standards if the appropriate qualities of racial authenticity and personal witness are to be maintained. The distinctive pattern of self-creation evident in this text and many similar texts of the period is not, as some of the aspiring post-structuralist literary critics would have it, simply the inauguration of a new and vital literary genre. Douglass's conclusions direct the reader's attention to a distinct and compelling variety of metaphysical, philosophical commentary. They point to the initiation and reproduction of a distinctive political perspective in which autopoiesis articulates with poetics to form a stance, a style, and a philosophical mood that have been repeated and reworked in the political culture of the black Atlantic ever since. The vernacular components of black expressive culture are thus tied to the more explicitly philosophical writings of black modernist writers like Wright and Du Bois. They develop this line of enquiry by seeking to answer the metaphysical questions "Who am I?" and "When am I most myself?"

Some years later, Du Bois echoed Douglass with a disarming precision. He developed the argument implied in the earlier text, elevating it to a new level of abstraction: "This the American black man knows: his fight here is a fight to the finish. Either he dies or wins. If he wins it will be by no subterfuge or evasion of amalgamation. He will enter modern civilisation here in America as a black man on terms of perfect and unlimited equality with any white man, or he will not enter at all. Either extermination root and branch, or absolute equality. There can be no compromise. This is the last great battle of the West."[87]

Like Douglass, Du Bois wanted to establish that the history of blacks in the new world, particularly the experiences of the slave trade and the plantation, was a legitimate part of the moral history of the West as a whole. They were not unique events—discrete episodes in the history of a minority—that could be grasped through their exclusive impact on blacks themselves, nor were they aberrations from the spirit of modern culture that were likely to be overcome by inexorable progress toward a secular, rational utopia. The continuing existence of racism belied both these verdicts, and it requires us to look more deeply into the relationship of racial terror and subordination to the inner character of modernity. This is the path indicated by Wright, James, Du Bois, and a host of others who have contributed in a variety of ways to the hermeneutics which distinguishes the grounded aesthetics of the black Atlantic. This hermeneutics has two interrelated dimensions—it is both a hermeneutics of suspicion and a hermeneutics of memory. Together they have nurtured a redemptive critique.

In the period after slavery, the memory of the slave experience is itself recalled and used as an additional, supplementary instrument with which to construct a distinct interpretation of modernity. Whether or not these memories invoke the remembrance of a terror which has moved beyond the grasp of ideal, grammatical speech, they point out of the present toward a utopian transformation of racial subordination. We must enquire then whether a definition of modern rationality such as that employed by Habermas leaves room for a liberatory, aesthetic moment which is emphatically anti- or even prediscursive? In other words, in what follows, the critique of bourgeois ideology and the fulfilment of the Enlightenment project under the banner of working-class emancipation which goes hand in hand with it is being complemented by another struggle—the battle to represent a redemptive critique of the present in the light of the vital memories of the slave past. This critique is constructed only partly from within the normative structures provided by modernity itself. We can see this from the way it mobilises an idea of the ancient preslave past, often in the form of a concern with Egyptian history and culture, and uses this to anchor its dissident assessments of modernity's achievements.

Notes

First published as "Masters, Mistresses, Slaves, and the Antinomies of Modernity," in Paul Gilroy, *The Black Atlantic: Modernity and Double Consciousness* (Cambridge, MA: Harvard University Press, 1993), 41–71, 230–35. Copyright Paul Gilroy. Reprinted with the permission of the author.

1. Edward Said, "Representing the Colonised," *Critical Inquiry* 15 (2) (Winter 1989): 222.

2. Jean-François Lyotard, "Defining the Postmodern," in Lisa Appignanesi, ed., *Postmodernism* (London: ICA, 1986).

3. There are other possibilities signalled in Edward Said's pathbreaking work *Orientalism* (Harmondsworth, UK: Penguin, 1985) and in the work of other critics

and cultural historians who have followed the Foucauldian path in other directions. See Peter Hulme, *Colonial Encounters* (London: Methuen, 1986), and V. Y. Mudimbe, *The Invention of Africa* (Bloomington: Indiana University Press, 1988).

4. Jürgen Habermas, "Modernity: An Incomplete Project," in Hal Foster, ed., *Postmodern Culture* (London: Pluto Press, 1983), 3–15.

5. Marshall Berman, *All That Is Solid Melts into Air* (London: Verso, 1983); Peter Dews, ed., *Habermas: Autonomy and Solidarity* (London: Verso, 1986); Zygmunt Bauman, *Legislators and Interpreters* (Cambridge: Polity Press, 1987); Andreas Huyssen, *After the Great Divide* (Bloomington: Indiana University Press, 1986); David White, *The Recent Work of Jürgen Habermas: Reason, Justice, and Modernity* (Cambridge: Cambridge University Press, 1988); David Ingram, *Habermas and the Dialectic of Reason* (New Haven, CT: Yale University Press, 1987); Cornel West, "Fredric Jameson's Marxist Hermeneutic," in Jonathan Arac, ed., *Postmodernism and Politics* (Manchester: Manchester University Press, 1986); Alice A. Jardine, *Gynesis: Configurations of Women and Modernity* (Ithaca, NY: Cornell University Press, 1985); David Kolb, *The Critique of Pure Modernity* (Chicago: Chicago University Press, 1986); John McGowan, *Postmodernism and Its Critics* (Ithaca, NY: Cornell University Press, 1991); William E. Connolly, *Political Theory and Modernity* (Oxford: Basil Blackwell, 1988).

6. Bauman, *Legislators and Interpreters*. The specific attributes and locations of black intellectuals, who have rarely also been academics, have been usefully discussed by bell hooks and Cornel West in their collaboration *Breaking Bread* (Boston: South End Press, 1991).

7. Baron de Montesquieu, *Persian Letters* (Harmondsworth, UK: Penguin, 1986), 83.

8. Rosi Braidotti, *Patterns of Dissonance* (Cambridge: Polity Press, 1991), 193.

9. Berman, *All That Is Solid Melts into Air,* 132.

10. Ibid., 15, emphasis added.

11. Marshall Berman, *The Politics of Authenticity: Radical Individualism and the Emergence of Modern Society* (London: Allen and Unwin, 1971), 317.

12. Ibid., 317, emphasis added.

13. Marshall Berman, "The Signs in the Street: A Response to Perry Anderson," *New Left Review* 144 (1984): 114–23.

14. Marshall Berman, "Urbicide," *Village Voice*, September 4, 1984.

15. Manuel Moreno Fraginals, *The Sugar Mill: The Socioeconomic Complex of Sugar in Cuba* (New York: Monthly Review Press, 1976).

16. Berman, "Urbicide," 25.

17. Ibid., 17.

18. Studies of cultural syncretism in terms of day-to-day experiences have begun to appear: Mechal Sobel's *The World They Made Together: Black and White*

Values in Eighteenth-Century Virginia (Princeton, NJ: Princeton University Press, 1987) seems to me to be an exemplary text of this type.

19. The work of David Brion Davis is an important exception here, but he is an American and a historian.

20. Jürgen Habermas, *The Philosophical Discourse of Modernity* (Cambridge: Polity Press, 1987), 28.

21. Ibid., 43.

22. David Brion Davis, *The Problem of Slavery in the Age of Revolution, 1770–1823* (Ithaca, NY: Cornell University Press, 1975).

23. Alexandre Kojève, *Introduction to the Reading of Hegel* (New York: Basic Books, 1969); Hussein A. Bulhan, *Frantz Fanon and the Psychology of Oppression* (New York: Plenum Press, 1985). The division between those who, like Deleuze, argue that Hegel says the future belongs to the slave and those who interpret his words as pointing to a world beyond the master/slave relationship remains a deep one. See Gilles Deleuze, *Nietzsche and Philosophy* (London: Athlone Press, 1983).

24. Sandra Harding, *The Science Question in Feminism* (Milton Keynes, UK: Open University Press, 1986), 158; Nancy Hartsock, *Money, Sex, and Power* (Boston: Northeastern University Press, 1983), 240.

25. Hill Collins's emphasis on the outsider within could for example be readily assimilated to the notions of "double consciousness," "double vision," and "dreadful objectivity" discussed elsewhere in this book [*The Black Atlantic*]. It is interesting that she does not attempt to link this theme in her own work with the history of these ideas in African American political culture. See Patricia Hill Collins, "Learning from the Outsider Within: The Sociological Significance of Black Feminist Thought," *Social Problems* 33 (6) (1986): 14–32.

26. Patricia Hill Collins, *Black Feminist Thought: Knowledge, Consciousness, and the Politics of Empowerment* (New York: Routledge, 1991), 27. The deconstructive zeal with which Hill Collins urges her readers to take traditional epistemological assumptions apart is exhausted after tackling *woman* and *intellectual*. It runs out long before she reaches the key words *black* and *Afrocentric*, which appear to be immune to this critical operation (see p. 17).

27. Ibid., 40.

28. Ibid., 32–33.

29. Ibid., 23.

30. Jane Flax, *Thinking Fragments* (Berkeley: University of California Press, 1990).

31. G. W. F. Hegel, *The Phenomenology of Mind*, trans. J. B. Baillie (New York: Harper and Row, 1967), chap. 4.

32. Cornel West, "The Religious Foundations of the Thought of Martin Luther King, Jr.," in Peter J. Albert and Ronald Hoffman, eds., *We Shall Overcome: Martin Luther King and the Black Freedom Struggle* (New York: Pantheon, 1990).

33. Quoted in Kimberley Benston, *Baraka* (New Haven, CT: Yale University Press, 1976), 90. For a discussion of the relationship between Baraka and Hegel, see Esther M. Jackson, "LeRoi Jones (Imamu Amiri Baraka): Form and the Progression of Consciousness," in Kimberly W. Benston, ed., *Imamu Amiri Baraka (LeRoi Jones): Twentieth Century Views* (Englewood Cliffs, NJ: Prentice Hall, 1978).

34. Jean-Paul Sartre, *Being and Nothingness* (London: Methuen 1969), bk. 1, 157–58.

35. Eric Foner, *Nothing but Freedom* (Baton Rouge: Louisiana State University Press, 1983), 1.

36. Walter Benjamin, "Paris: The Capital of the Nineteenth Century," in *Charles Baudelaire: A Lyric Poet in the Era of High Capitalism* (London: Verso, 1976), 159. See also Richard Wolin, *Walter Benjamin: An Aesthetic of Redemption* (New York: Columbia University Press, 1982).

37. Andrew Benjamin, "Tradition and Experience," in Andrew Benjamin, ed., *The Problems of Modernity* (London: Routledge, 1989).

38. See Orlando Patterson's discussion of Hegel in *Slavery and Social Death: A Comparative Study* (Cambridge, MA: Harvard University Press, 1982), 97–101.

39. Dominique Lecourt, "On Marxism as a Critique of Sociological Theories," in Mary O'Callaghan, ed., *Sociological Theories: Race and Colonialism* (Paris: UNESCO, 1980), 267.

40. "Somewhere between men and cattle God had created a tertium quid, and called it Negro,—a clownish, simple creature, at times lovable within its limitations, but straitly foreordained to walk within the Veil" (W. E. B. Du Bois, *The Souls of Black Folk* [1903; reprint, New York: Bantam, 1989], 63).

41. For a critique of these appeals, see Joan Wallach Scott, "The Evidence of Experience," *Critical Inquiry* 17 (Summer 1991): 773–97.

42. Michel Foucault, "What Is Enlightenment?" in *The Foucault Reader,* ed. Paul Rabinow (Harmondsworth, UK: Peregrine, 1986), 50.

43. George Shepperson, "Frederick Douglass and Scotland," *Journal of Negro History* 38 (3) (1953): 307–21.

44. Waldo E. Martin, *The Mind of Frederick Douglass* (Durham: University of North Carolina Press, 1984); Leon Litwack and August Meier, *Black Leaders of the Nineteenth Century* (Urbana: University of Illinois Press, 1988); William S. McFeely, *Frederick Douglass* (New York: Norton, 1991).

45. Frederick Douglass, *The Life and Times of Frederick Douglass* (New York: Macmillan, 1962); *My Bondage and My Freedom* (New York: Miller, Orton and

Mulligan, 1855); and *Narrative of the Life of Frederick Douglass, an American Slave, Written by Himself* (Cambridge, MA: Harvard University Press, 1960). All quotations are taken from these editions.

46. Douglass, *Bondage*, 49.

47. Ibid., 50.

48. Ibid., 198. The antireligious theme is shared by a number of other narratives—for example, Henry Bibb's caustic comments on the complicity of Christianity with the institution of slavery. See also the remarks of Mr. Listwell in Douglass's novella *The Heroic Slave*, in Ronald Takaki, ed., *Violence in the Black Imagination: Essays and Documents* (New York: Putnam, 1972); and Robert B. Stepto, "Sharing the Thunder: The Literary Exchanges of Harriet Beecher Stowe, Henry Bibb, and Frederick Douglass," in Eric Sundquist, ed., *New Essays on Uncle Tom's Cabin* (Cambridge: Cambridge University Press, 1986).

49. Frederick Douglass, "The Claims of the Negro Ethnologically Considered," in *The Life and Writings of Frederick Douglass*, 5 vols., ed. Philip S. Foner (New York: International, 1950), 2:289–309.

50. Stephen Jay Gould, *The Mismeasure of Man* (Harmondsworth, UK: Pelican, 1984), chap. 2.

51. Martin Bernal, *Black Athena: The Afroasiatic Roots of Classical Civilization*, vol. 1: *The Fabrication of Ancient Greece, 1785–1985* (London: Free Association Books, 1987).

52. Martin, *The Mind of Frederick Douglass*, chap. 9.

53. George James, *Stolen Legacy: The Greeks Were Not the Authors of Greek Philosophy, but the People of North Africa, Commonly Called the Egyptians* (San Francisco: Julian Richardson, 1976).

54. McFeely, *Frederick Douglass*, 263.

55. Douglass, *Bondage*, 170.

56. Ibid., 184.

57. Ibid., 185.

58. Ibid., 185. The confrontation with Covey is a pivotal moment in all three versions of Douglass's autobiography.

59. Ibid., 187.

60. Ibid., 190.

61. Jacques Lacan, *Écrits: A Selection* (London: Tavistock, 1977), 308.

62. Patterson, *Slavery and Social Death*.

63. I am thinking in particular of the spectacular suicide of Clotel/Isabella (the tragic slave daughter of Thomas Jefferson) in the icy waters of the Potomac that can be found in William Wells Brown's novels *Clotel; or, The President's Daughter, a Narrative of Slave Life in the United States* (1853; reprint, New York: Collier

Books, 1970) and *Clotelle: A Tale of the Southern States* (Boston: Redpath, 1864). Chapter 16 of *Clotelle* is entitled "Death Is Freedom."

64. See also Ronald Takaki's discussion of this theme in the work of William Wells Brown and Martin Delany in *Violence in the Black Imagination;* and L. F. Goldstein, "Violence as an Instrument of Social Change: The Views of Frederick Douglass (1817–1895)," *Journal of Negro History* 61, pt. 1 (1976).

65. W. E. B. Du Bois, *Darkwater: Voices from within the Veil* (New York: Harcourt Brace, 1921), 176.

66. Toni Morrison's version of the story seems to have been prompted by a contemporary account reproduced in Harris Middleton, ed., with the assistance of Morris Levitt, Roger Furman, and Ernest Smith, *The Black Book* (New York: Random House, 1974), 10. Morrison would have been responsible for editing this volume during her employment at Random House.

67. *Annual Report Presented to the American Anti-Slavery Society* (New York, May 1856), 44–47; Levi Coffin, *Reminiscences of Levi Coffin, the Reputed President of the Underground Railroad* (1876; reprint, New York: Augustus Kelley, 1968), 560. Most of the references to newspapers are given by Julius Yanuck in "The Garner Fugitive Slave Case," *Mississippi Valley Historical Review* 40 (June 1953): 47–66. See also Herbert Aptheker, "The Negro Woman," *Masses and Mainstream* 2 (February1949): 10–17.

68. Coffin, *Reminiscences of Levi Coffin,* 562.

69. Stanley W. Campbell, *The Slave Catchers: Enforcement of the Fugitive Slave Law, 1850–1860* (Chapel Hill: University of North Carolina Press, 1968).

70. Coffin, *Reminiscences of Levi Coffin,* 560.

71. *New York Daily Times,* February 16, 1856.

72. This version is reprinted in Middleton, ed., *The Black Book.*

73. *Annual Report Presented to the American Anti-Slavery Society,* 45.

74. *New York Daily Times,* February 2, 1856; see also *Cincinnati Commercial,* January 30, 1856.

75. *Cincinnati Daily Gazette,* January 29, 1856.

76. Alice Stone Blackwell, *Lucy Stone: Pioneer of Women's Rights* (Boston: Little, Brown, 1930), 183–84.

77. Coffin claims to have been in the court when these words were spoken. This report is taken from his account, *Reminiscences of Levi Coffin.* A further version of this episode is given by Alice Stone Blackwell in *Lucy Stone:* "While visiting Margaret Garner in prison, Mrs. Stone asked her, in case she should be taken back into slavery, if she had a knife. In court, Mrs. Stone was asked if it was true that she had offered Margaret a knife. She answered, 'I did ask her if she had a knife. If I were a slave, as she is a slave, with the law against me, and the church against me,

and with no death dealing weapon at hand, I would with my own teeth tear open my veins, and send my soul back to God who gave it'" (184).

78. Coffin, *Reminiscences of Levi Coffin*, 565; *Cincinnati Daily Gazette*, February 14, 1856.

79. "A Coloured Lady Lecturer," *Englishwoman's Review* 7 (June 1861): 269–75; Mathew Davenport Hill, ed., *Our Exemplars, Poor and Rich* (London: Peter Cassell, 1861), 276–86 (I am grateful to Clare Midgeley for this reference); Ruth Bogin, "Sarah Parker Remond: Black Abolitionist from Salem," *Essex Institute Historical Collections* 110 (April 1974): 120–50; Dorothy Porter, "Sarah Parker Remond, Abolitionist and Physician," *Journal of Negro History* 20 (July 1935): 287–93.

80. Charlotte Forten Grimké, *Journals of Charlotte Forten Grimké*, ed. Brenda Stephenson (New York: Oxford University Press, 1988), 116–17 (entry for December 17, 1854). Partly because of their [Remond and Delany's] common vocation as physicians, Remond's odyssey from New England to Rome marks an interesting counterpoint to the life of Martin Delany discussed in chapter 1 [of *The Black Atlantic*].

81. *Warrington Times*, January 29, 1859; see also C. Peter Ripley, ed., *The Black Abolitionist Papers*, vol. 1 (Chapel Hill: University of North Carolina Press, 1985), 437–38.

82. Douglass, *Narrative*, 49.

83. William L. Andrews, *To Tell a Free Story: The First Century of Afro-American Autobiography, 1760–1865* (Urbana: University of Illinois Press, 1986).

84. Henry Louis Gates Jr., *Figures in Black: Words, Signs, and the "Racial" Self* (Oxford: Oxford University Press, 1987).

85. Andrews, *To Tell a Free Story*, 103.

86. Douglass, *Narrative*, 56.

87. W. E. B. Du Bois, *Black Reconstruction in America* (New York: Atheneum, 1977), 703.

2

The Fight with Covey

Bernard R. Boxill

I

Frederick Douglass's reflection on the results of his fight with Covey are something of a puzzle. In his *Narrative of the Life of Frederick Douglass,* he claims that the "battle with Mr. Covey" was the "turning-point" in his life as a slave, "recalled" his "departed self-confidence," and "inspired" him with "a determination to be free."[1] This was in 1845. Yet until at least 1849 he was a faithful Garrisonian pacifist warning of the counterproductive consequences of violent slave resistance and calling instead for the peaceful conversion of the slaveholders. Did he not sense the tension between this pacifist stance and his celebration of the psychological and moral consequences of fighting Covey?

Of course after 1849 Douglass became an uncompromising advocate of slave resistance. But this still leaves it a mystery why he was ever a pacifist, given his account of the benefits he gained from resistance. One explanation of his change from pacifist to advocate of violent slave resistance is that while he was always clear that the slaves had a right to resist their masters violently, before 1849 he warned against violent slave resistance because he believed it would delay the abolition of slavery and have bad consequences overall: after 1849 he changed his mind and began urging violent slave resistance because he believed it would hasten the end of slavery. This explanation is suggested by some of Douglass's own remarks on violence and pacifism. In 1847, for example, he declared that he would "suffer rather than do any action of violence—rather than that the glorious day of liberty might be postponed."[2] And when he began urging violent slave resistance in the 1850s, he did so on the ground that it was both right and wise, right because it was justified by the right of self-defense and wise because it would have the good consequence of discrediting the public's favorite justification of slavery and in this way help to end slavery.[3] But this explanation of Douglass's change from pacifist to advocate of violent resistance is not altogether satisfactory. In his account of his fight with Covey in the *Narrative*, Douglass extols the moral and psychological benefits he gained as a result of defending himself, claiming, in particular, that it inspired him with a "determination to be free."[4] Since this determination helped Douglass to win his freedom, and he gained it from fighting Covey, he should not have worried that slave resistance would "postpone" the day of liberty.

It may be argued that Douglass refrained from generalizing from his experience because he believed that his experience was exceptional and that he had gained the benefits of resistance only because of the unusual educational opportunities he had enjoyed while a slave. But this argument runs into difficulties. It is true that Douglass's educational achievements were unusual for a slave. He had learned to read and write, and he had studied the dialogues and speeches against slavery in *The Columbian Orator* by the time that he fell into Covey's hands. And it is also true that his education informed and increased his hatred of slavery. But he never cited his education as any part of the reason why resistance was beneficial for him. And he never suggested that it was his education that enabled him to see the injustice of slavery. On the contrary, he often insisted that he was aware of the injustice of slavery before consulting any books or laws or authorities.[5] Nor did he ever suggest that he was different from other slaves in this respect. He believed that all slaves came naturally to the conviction that they should be free. That was why the slaveholders tried to keep them from learning how to read and write and from getting an education. Lack of book learning would not prevent the slaves from coming to believe that they should be free, but it would at least prevent them from knowing how to free themselves and could therefore make them despair of ever gaining their freedom. The slaves' natural conviction that they should be free was also the reason why the slaveholders treated them so cruelly.[6]

These considerations lead me to believe that Douglass was willing to suppose that slaves in general would gain the benefits from resistance that he gained. But, until 1849, he failed to endorse slave resistance because he had become convinced, by the arguments of William Lloyd Garrison and others of Garrison's school, that nonviolent moral suasion was *morally* preferable to slave resistance as a means to freeing the slaves. As he wrote in a letter to Francis Jackson in 1846, emphasizing the advantages of nonviolent moral suasion, "Thank God liberty is no longer to be contended for and gained by instruments of death. A higher, a nobler, a mightier than carnal weapon is placed into our hands—one which hurls defiance at all the improvements of carnal warfare. It is the righteous appeal to the understanding and the heart."[7]

This was a reasonable position. Other things equal, the means that can reach its end without bloodshed is morally preferable to the means that requires or is likely to involve bloodshed. Further, even if violent slave resistance was morally defensible as a form of justifiable self-defense, moral suasion was not only morally defensible but also, its advocates claimed, likely to end slavery by converting the slaveholders to the truth and by making them into good citizens. If it could deliver what it promised, moral suasion would have more good consequences than slave resistance, which seemed likely to leave the slaveholders unregenerate, even if it forced them to give up their slaves.

As events unfolded, however, moral suasion failed both to free the slaves and to reform the slaveholders. Indeed it seemed to have the opposite effect, for following the period when it was most vigorously pursued, the slaveholders were emboldened to propose and managed to push through the infamous Fugitive Slave Law of 1850. Frustrated by the ineffectiveness of nonviolent moral suasion, Douglass turned to endorsing slave uprisings. But then he came to a further and more radical conclusion: it was not only that violent slave resistance was both morally defensible and likely to be more effective in ending slavery than nonviolent moral suasion. Violent slave resistance was also capable of producing the moral benefits that nonviolent moral suasion had promised but failed to deliver—moral reform of slaveholders.[8] And it was not only the slave masters who would benefit morally from slave resistance. The slave was also likely to grow in self-respect if he resisted his master. Of course, Douglass had already claimed in 1845 that he had benefited morally from fighting Covey. After 1850, however, when he became converted to slave resistance, his remarks broadened and hardened. Before 1850, he had not argued that the slave had to resist to gain his self-respect. After 1850, however, he began to make precisely that claim.

Evidence for this development of Douglass's views is the striking additions to the account of the fight with Covey in the *Narrative* that Douglass made in his two subsequent autobiographies, *My Bondage and My Freedom*, first published in 1855, and *The Life and Times of Frederick Douglass*, first published in 1893. It is only in the two later books, for example, that Douglass concludes his account of the fight with Covey with the lines from Byron,

> Hereditary bondman, know ye not
> Who would be free, themselves must strike the blow?

Byron did not intend to make the palpably false claim that the bondman would not be free of physical constraints unless he resisted his enslaver. He meant, and Douglass took him to mean, that the bondman would not be free of mental constraints, that he would not know himself to be the moral equal of others, unless he resisted his enslaver. And this view of the relationship between self-defense and self-respect informed Douglass's discussion of his fight with Covey in the two later autobiographies. For example, in *My Bondage and My Freedom* Douglass noted in a manner similar to the *Narrative* that the fight with Covey had renewed his determination to be free. But then he added—a point not in the *Narrative*—that the fight had recalled to life his "crushed self-respect" and then appended this further comment: "A man, without force, is without the essential dignity of humanity. Human nature is so constituted that it cannot honor a helpless man, although it can pity him; and even this it cannot do long, if the signs of power do not arise."[9] Since these claims reappear verbatim in *The Life and Times of Frederick Douglass* published forty years later, we are safe in assuming that Douglass meant them to be taken seriously. The general and uncompromising claim that human nature *cannot* honor a person without power or force implies that Douglass was expressing the view that human beings, including presumably slaves, cannot honor themselves unless they possess power or force. Taken in isolation, this can perhaps be read to mean that the slave need only be capable of defending himself against his master—not that he must actually do so—to be able to honor himself. I will undertake a detailed discussion of the point presently. For now, I note that Douglass broached it right after claiming that he had regained his self-respect from actually resisting Covey; that, and the fact that the lines he quoted from Byron say that the bondman "must" strike the blow, strongly suggest that Douglass meant that the power or force necessary to gain self-respect was not merely a capacity to defend oneself, but also a willingness to do so.

The analysis of Douglass's account of the results of his fight with Covey that follows focuses on what I take to be the more mature presentation in *My Bondage and My Freedom* and in *The Life and Times of Frederick Douglass*. It will also rely to some extent on his claim that violent slave resistance could help to reform the slaveholders.

II

According to Douglass, one of the results of his fight with Covey was that he "had reached the point, at which I *was not afraid to die*."[10] Douglass did not mean that Covey's mistreatment had made him weary of life, for then he should have attempted suicide instead of fighting Covey. His meaning is revealed by the immediately preceding comment that he "was no longer a coward trembling under the frown of a brother worm of the dust."[11] Since a coward fails to act as he ought to because he is afraid, and Douglass had just defended himself against Covey, I conclude that at least part of what Douglass meant by the claim that he had reached the point at which he was not afraid to die was that he had reached the point at which he would no longer fail to do his duty to defend himself because he was afraid to die. But we need to inquire more closely into the nature of the duty of self-defense than this discussion implies.

Douglass often suggested that slaves ought to be willing to imperil their lives for their freedom.[12] This argument suggests consequentialist considerations for resistance based on a nice weighing of the risks of attempts to escape against the great value of freedom. The slave should not throw away his life in a predictably vain attempt to gain freedom; life is too precious to justify that. Neither, on the other hand, should the slave play it altogether safe and refuse to take any chances to be free; freedom is too valuable for that. The slave should bide his time, but when the appropriate opportunity arises to gain his freedom, he ought to seize it even if it was not a sure thing; he ought to be willing to imperil his life for his freedom. And in his two attempts to escape Douglass showed his allegiance to that argument, giving vivid accounts of how he canvassed and weighed the risks these attempts to escape involved, but he did not appeal to it when he made the case for duty of self-defense under discussion.[13] When he defended himself against Covey, he was not imperiling his life for his liberty. He was not trying to escape. He was simply defending himself from physical abuse. "I had brought my mind to the firm resolve," he notes, "to obey every order, however unreasonable, if it were possible, and, if Mr. Covey should then undertake to beat me, to defend and protect myself to the best of my ability."[14] It is true that Douglass arguably won his freedom as a result of the determination to be free that he gained from fighting Covey. But he could not have foreseen that fighting Covey would result in such a determination and consequently could not have fought Covey in order to acquire it.

If Douglass's fight with Covey was not a calculated periling of his life to gain his liberty, it was equally not a calculated periling of his life to put an end to his physical abuse. It is true that one of the results of the fight was that he was never beaten by a master again. From the time of the fight, Douglass reports, "I was never fairly whipped."[15] This was because he came to have the reputation of being a slave who could only be whipped if he was also killed.[16] But, of course, Douglass had not anticipated this result when he undertook to fight Covey and consequently could not have fought Covey in order to gain it. It was not even the case that Douglass resisted Covey in order to avoid being whipped on that particular occasion. This would be a plausible possibility if he had anticipated *winning* the fight with Covey or if he had even calculated his chances of doing so. But he never reports that he engaged in such forecasts or calculations on that occasion.

The other consequentialist consideration for slave resistance that Douglass often suggested—that such resistance would help establish the "manhood" of the race by wiping out the reproach that blacks were unwilling to suffer and sacrifice for their liberty and were therefore fit for slavery—is even less applicable to his reasons for fighting Covey. Douglass was not trying to impress Covey or anyone else with his "manhood" or his unfitness for slavery when he defended himself. I doubt that when he resolved to defend himself he was even thinking about how others would interpret his actions. According to his own report, he resisted Covey because he had pledged to "stand up in my own defense."[17]

More generally, although Douglass insists that his fight with Covey restored his self-respect and manhood and helped him to gain eventually his freedom, he never said that he undertook it because he anticipated that doing so would help gain these good consequences. On the contrary, he seems to have anticipated bad consequences for fighting Covey. As he noted, he believed that he would "suffer for resistance."[18] This suggests that although Douglass came to the conclusion that self-defense in his circumstances was a duty, he did not come to this conclusion by considering the good consequences of self-defense. I do not mean that he did not welcome the good consequences of fighting Covey when he became aware of them after the fight; but even then he never said that they justified the fight. He seemed to have viewed them as a bonus on an act that was justifiable on independent grounds.

It may seem that the fact that Douglass did not fight Covey for the good consequences of doing so [meant] the fight must have been an act of desperation that happily turned out to have good consequences. But although Douglass's fight was certainly undertaken in desperate circumstances, it was not an act of desperation if this means it was undertaken unthinkingly. In the first place, the restrained manner in which he fought Covey did not have the typical earmarks of an unthinking conflict. He was, he said, "strictly on the defensive, preventing him from injuring me, rather than trying to injure him."[19] More important is the fact that the fight was undertaken only after the most careful consideration. The fight occurred on a Monday —that is, the day after the one day the slaves had time for reflection. And Douglass reports that he had spent the day pondering the situation and had resolved "during that Sunday's reflection" to defend himself if Covey tried to beat him.[20]

The fact that Douglass resolved to fight Covey only after careful consideration, though not in order to gain the good consequences of self-defense, suggests that he must have resolved to defend himself "on principle." In his circumstances, a principle supporting a resolution to fight Covey would probably involve the right not to be physically abused. But while such right justifies self-defense, it does not, by itself, *require* self-defense, especially if one has reason to believe that self-defense may lead to worse abuse and even death. Somehow we need to derive a duty to act on the right of self-defense, even in apparently hopeless circumstances. Douglass's views on this issue are suggested by his comment that he was "not only ashamed to be contented in slavery, but ashamed to *seem* to be contented."[21] Since shame necessarily involves a confession of failure, a fall from an acknowledged standard or duty, the clear implication is that the rights that slavery violates are so sacred and central a part of morality that one has a duty never to even *seem* to fail to be devoted to them and that one should therefore always be ready to show one's allegiance to them by standing up for them and fighting for them when they are violated or even impugned.

This conclusion is too strong as it stands. It may be both wise and right to seem contented with slavery in order to make good one's escape. And in general Douglass did not think that we could be moral without carefully weighing the consequences of our actions. Such an implication would be far indeed from his views. His whole career shows a keen appreciation of the fact that in most circumstances the consequences of our actions help determine whether they are morally obligatory or not. The careful plans he made for his own escape and his refusal to join John Brown in [Brown's] attack on Harper's Ferry are only two of many examples that show this attitude.

Why then did he suppose that the duty to defend oneself against physical abuse is absolute, at least when one is in the circumstances he was in when he was with Covey? Why is this duty different from the duty to secure one's freedom? The answer to this question lies partly in the consequences of severe physical abuse. These consequences are of a greater and different order than the consequences of restrictions on freedom.[22]

According to Douglass, a person who is subjected to severe and continuous or unpredictable physical violence is liable to be "humbled, degraded, broken down, enslaved, and brutalized." This is the way Douglass depicted his own condition as a result of Covey's mistreatment.[23] We need to get clearer on its exact nature to see why Douglass thought that avoiding it was so imperative. Describing the state of his mind when he was being brutalized by Covey, Douglass wrote, "When I was looking for the blow about to be inflicted on my head, I was not thinking of my liberty; it was my life." The implication is that severe and continuous pain is so imperious as to push all other thoughts out of one's mind, including thoughts of morality. It is not simply that one craves relief; one craves relief without indignation or resentment, without remembering that one's rights are being violated; one loses sight of, forgets, one's rights not to be physically abused and simply pleads for relief—or life. His "continual prayer," when he was with Covey, Douglass reports, was, "Spare my life."[24]

By comparison, the condition of one who, though deprived of his freedom, is not physically abused seems almost enviable. Such a person may, of course, long for freedom. But she is not degraded. She can think about her moral status, her rights and duties, and her moral equality to others. Douglass supposed this to be generally true. Slaves, in particular, would think about their liberty and moral equality if they were not brutalized. No particular book learning was necessary. Ordinary experience, even one so intellectually impoverished as a slave's, could convince anyone of average intelligence that she should be her own master. Douglass came to this conclusion by generalizing from his own experience. He wrote:

> When entombed at Covey's shrouded in darkness and physical wretchedness, temporal well-being was the grand desideratum; but temporal wants supplied, the spirit puts in its claim. Beat and cuff your slave, keep him hungry and spiritless, and he will follow the chain of his master like a dog; but, feed and clothe him well, work him moderately—surround him with physical comfort—and dreams of freedom intrude. Give him a bad master, and he aspires to a good master; give him a good master and he wishes to become his own master. Such is human nature. You may hurl a man so low, beneath the level of his kind, that he loses all just ideas of his natural position; but elevate him a little, and the clear conception of rights rises to life and power, and leads him onward.[25]

If the preceding paragraphs correctly describe the conditions of persons subjected to physical abuse and to a deprivation of freedom, Douglass's position on the relative urgency of the duty to avoid to stop these evils is understandable. The person subjected to continuous or unpredictable physical abuse is liable to be broken, humbled, brutalized—in a word, degraded. If resistance is the only way to avoid or stop continuous or unpredictable physical abuse, then perhaps we do have an absolute duty to resist such abuse. On the other hand, if Douglass is right that the consequences of being deprived of liberty are not as destructive to the soul as the consequence of severe and continuous physical abuse (though they are certainly serious), then the duty to resist deprivations of liberty probably need not be so unconditional.

It may be objected that the long passage from *My Bondage and My Freedom* just cited suggests that Douglass thought that severe physical abuse has its soul-destroying effects only while it lasts.[26] If this is indeed the case, then—even if resistance is the only way to stop physical abuse— it is not clear that we have a duty to resist such abuse without regard to the consequences. Degradation, it seems, is not permanent. Death on the other hand is permanent. Since resistance can mean death, it may therefore seem wiser to resist only when doing so is reasonably safe. But then the duty to defend oneself against severe and continuous physical abuse when in Covey-like circumstances does not seem absolute. This difficulty cannot be met by emphasizing the evil of degradation. Degradation is evil, and it may be worse than death, but if it is as impermanent as Douglass seems to suggest, if we recover from it as soon as the physical abuse that causes it ceases, perhaps it should be endured if resistance may mean death. A man who was being subjected to degrading torture would act irrationally if he resisted his torturers without regard to the possibility that they could kill him for resisting.

Despite his optimistic remarks suggesting that degradation is transient, Douglass had to know that it could outlast physical abuse. The assumption that it could was the reason why his master sent him to Covey. As Douglass noted, Covey "enjoyed the execrated reputation, of being a first rate hand at breaking young negroes." Slave masters sent Covey their "most fiery bloods" so as to get them back after a year or two, "well broken." All this would make no sense if the "fiery bloods" regained their fire as soon as they left Covey and returned to their masters. But if degradation can be permanent or even difficult to recover from once inculcated, the case for an absolute duty to resist physical abuse when in Covey-like circumstances seems more compelling. It may be irrational to choose death over impermanent degradation but rational to choose death over permanent degradation.

Reinforcing this argument is the consideration that a person being subjected to severe and continuous physical abuse is normally not in a position to know if or when he will be rescued. [Under the assumption] that his tormentors want to break or degrade him, they will want to keep him ignorant of his chances of being rescued and will usually be in a position to do so. Further, his ability to weigh the consequences of his actions is likely to be impaired by the distractions of the pain he is enduring, and once he is degraded, he will prefer even a permanently degraded life to resistance and death. These conditions seemed satisfied in Douglass's own case. He had been brutalized by Covey for six months, and there was no relief in sight. He had appealed to his master to no avail. Perhaps in a few more months he too would be returned to his master, "well broken." In such or like circumstances, his call for an absolute duty of self-defense seems plausible. To fail to resist, even to stop and weigh the consequences of resistance, could be to allow oneself to be reduced to a state in which one permanently lost a sense of one's equal moral standing.

These considerations indicate how important Douglass thought it was for a person to be self-consciously aware of her rights and her equal moral standing. But they do not quite show that we have an absolute duty to resist severe or continuous physical abuse. They rest on the assumption that resistance is the only way to avoid the abuse that leads to degradation. Is this assumption true? If it is not, then even if physical abuse has the soul-destroying effects that Douglass describes and for that reason must be stopped, why must it be stopped by resistance? Why not some other way? Even a slave in "Covey-like" circumstances, with no reason to expect that he will be rescued, seems to have options for seeking relief from abuse less dangerous than resistance.

Perhaps, for example, he could appeal to the pity or the humanity of his enslavers. Douglass knew from his own bitter experience that this was not a viable option. After a particularly vicious beating from Covey, he had appealed to his master for relief. "I presented," he wrote, "an appearance of wretchedness and woe, fitted to move any but a heart of stone. From the crown of my head to the sole of my feet, there were marks of blood. . . . In this unhappy plight, I appeared before my professedly Christian master, humbly to invoke the interposition of his power and authority, to protect me from further abuse and violence."[27] And he carefully made his appeal in terms of his master's interests rather than in terms of his own rights. He told his master that Covey was likely to kill him or "ruin" him "for future service."[28] But, as he reports, "I was disappointed." His master began by "finding excuses for Covey" and ended up "with a full justification of him, and a passionate condemnation of me."[29]

It is important not to misunderstand Douglass here. His rejection of appeals to the slaveholders' sense of pity was not meant as an indictment of pity per se. He did not believe that pity was inherently unreliable, nor did he hold, as many do, that it is suspect as a moral sentiment because the one who appeals for it necessarily demeans himself or because the one who feels it necessarily feels superior to the one he pities. Douglass esteemed pity as a decent and worthy sentiment that is a natural part of human nature. He spoke of the "pity" in a glance his mother gave him and recalled that he "pities" the slave woman Esther when he saw her severely whipped and that Miss Lucretia, his master's daughter, "pitied" him, clearly indicating in every instance that he felt that the sentiment reflected well both on those experiencing it and on those to whom it was directed.[30] Douglass rejected appeals to the slaveholders' sense of pity or humanity because he believed they were incapable of such sentiments. This is clear from his description of the way his master reacted to his appearance when he appealed to him for relief. As Douglass reports, "It was impossible—as I stood before him at the first—for him to seem indifferent. I distinctly saw his human nature asserting its conviction against the slave system, which made cases like mine possible; but, as I have said, humanity fell before the systematic tyranny of slavery."[31] There is no hint in this passage that it would have been inappropriate for his master to have feelings of pity or humanity for him. On the contrary, Douglass obviously felt that it was a failing on the part of his master that his humanity fell before the tyranny of slavery.

It may be objected that Douglass had an exceptionally hard-hearted master; if he did, his experience would not justify the conclusion that all appeals to the pity or humanity of slave masters are useless. But Douglass's own experience had taught him that most slaveholders were hard-hearted. He did not believe that they were naturally so; the passage just cited indicates that he believed that a capacity for humanity or pity was part of their human nature; it was having slaves that made them hard-hearted. He had observed the process firsthand. When he was ten years old, his master's sister-in-law Sophia, a naturally kind woman new to having slaves, had been almost a mother to him and had even undertaken to teach him how to read. But, Douglass reports, "the fatal poison of irresponsible power, and the natural influence of slavery customs, were not long in making a suitable impression on the gentle and loving disposition of my excellent mistress." Eventually, "her noble soul was overthrown. . ."[32] Not that Douglass ever put all slaveholders in one bag morally. For example, on one occasion Douglass came to his master's brother, Hugh, after a beating somewhat similar to the one he got from Covey. Hugh showed himself, Douglass says, in "every way more humane" than his brother and "gave many proofs of his strong indignation at what was done." On this occasion, too, he reports, the "heart" of his "once kind mistress, Sophia," was again "melted in pity" toward him.[33] But Douglass was under no illusions about Hugh and Sophia. Sophia's "affectionate heart" was "not yet dead," but it had been "hardened." And while Hugh's humanity might have been genuine, his indignation was not. As Douglass understood, "it resulted from the thought that his rights of property, in my person, had not been respected, more than from any sense of the outrage committed on me as man."[34] Had he believed, as his brother had, that "breaking" Douglass would improve him as property, he too would have suppressed his feelings of humanity.

It was therefore useless to appeal to the slaveholders' sense of pity and humanity as well as to their sense of justice. That too had been corrupted by having slaves.[35] But what of the option of appealing to the pity or sense of justice of those who were not slaveholders? Since they did not hold slaves, perhaps their capacity for pity and justice was still intact. Douglass could not dismiss this option altogether. Others had been touched by his condition and had helped him escape slavery, and, more generally, the abolitionists and those operating the Underground Railway seemed prepared to do what they could for the slave. But there were limits to the help that could be expected even from those who did not have slaves. Many of them had been corrupted by their proximity to slavery. And others, though opposed to slavery and perhaps as yet uncorrupted by it, could be frightened by the consequences of interfering. Douglass gave a vivid illustration of this point. On one occasion four men beat him bloody while fifty looked on, and "not a man of them all interposed a single word of mercy."[36] Douglass concedes that some of them might have "pitied" him. But if they did, he remarks, they "lacked the moral courage to come and volunteer their evidence. The slightest manifestation of sympathy or justice toward a person of color, was denounced as abolitionism; and the name of abolitionist, subjected its bearer to frightful liabilities."[37]

It seems then that Douglass felt that appeals to the pity or humanity or sense of justice of the enslavers or even uncorrupted bystanders were generally likely not to bring relief from the physical abuse slavery involved. But it does not follow that an absolute duty of self-defense in Covey-like circumstances can be derived from the good consequences of self-defense, for self-defense may be just as effective in bringing relief from physical abuse in such circumstances as appeals to pity, humanity, or the sense of justice. It may be objected that since self-defense necessarily involves the use of physical force, it is certain to end in either victory over the enslavers or escape or death. But self-defense may end in defeat and further abuse, not death or escape. There may, in fact, be no way to avoid abuse. In such circumstances the absolute duty of self-defense cannot depend on its consequences, but on the fact that it is a way to show allegiance to the principles of morality. A final objection is that we can show allegiance to the principles of morality by protesting injustice rather than by violently resisting it and consequently that there cannot be an absolute duty of self-defense even in Covey-like circumstances.[38] But this objection cannot be sustained. Some of the principles of morality entitle us to defend ourselves with force. We cannot show our allegiance to these principles if we steadfastly refuse to do what they entitle us to do.

I conclude that we if can have an absolute duty to defend ourselves against physical abuse in Covey-like circumstances, this duty must be based on the duty to show allegiance to the principles of morality, though acting on it can have good consequences, as is discussed in the next section.

III

Less obvious, and more philosophically interesting than the consequences of self-defense noted earlier (escape, victory, or death), is the possibility that Douglass describes. As we have seen, Douglass reports that his fight with Covey helped gain him the reputation of being a slave who could only be whipped if he were also killed, and *as* a result he was never again whipped. He also reports that the rewards he derived from resisting went well beyond being free of pain. No longer preoccupied with the thought of being beaten, he could again turn his thoughts to his liberty, his rights, and his moral equality with others. So important did Douglass consider this consequence of resistance that he claimed that when a slave "cannot be flogged he is more than half free."[39]

This claim must now be considered more closely. One difficulty is that Douglass seems to have overlooked that the slave who resisted only gained a qualified protection from physical abuse, for, of course, such a slave could still be beaten, even if beating him would require killing him. It is not an adequate answer to this objection that the master would not beat such a slave since this would mean that he would have to kill the slave and so destroy his own property. Killing slaves was not uncommon. They were valuable as property but not so valuable as to reliably stop the master from killing them. And a master could have a powerful motive to kill a defiant slave. If this made the other slaves more compliant, it would increase the value of the master's property. This difficulty is confirmed by Douglass's candid confession that he could not "fully explain" why Covey did not have him hanged for his defiance, as the law allowed, or at least publicly whipped as an example to other slaves.[40]

We should therefore remember that Douglass's experience with resistance was fortunate, though not altogether unprecedented or unique. Resistance was generally a very dangerous business. And this suggests a further difficulty. If continuous or unpredictable physical mistreatment can distract a man from thoughts of his moral status, degrade him, and make him incapable of acting morally, then surely the fear of being suddenly cut off can have the same result and perhaps even more effectively. But in that case resistance seems a bad bargain. Indeed it seems to be a way of jumping from the frying pan into the fire.

Douglass seems to have anticipated this difficulty. He had, he said, "reached the point at which he was not afraid to die."[41] Although life was precious to him and he did not wish his death, since he was not afraid to die, he was not agitated and distracted by the thought that he could be killed because of his resistance. It was a settled point for him that he would die rather than fail to resist physical abuse. His mind was therefore free to reflect on his equal moral status. As Douglass reported, the spirit of not being afraid to die made him "a freeman in *fact*," while he "remained a slave in *form*."[42]

But Douglass's claim that he had reached the point at which he was not afraid to die raises questions of its own. If reaching such a point is a necessary condition for enjoying the benefits of being a slave who cannot be whipped, perhaps most slaves will never be able to enjoy these benefits, for most people find it difficult not to be afraid to die. It may be suggested that this was why the early Douglass refrained from urging slave resistance; he was aware that only a few slaves could make themselves unafraid of death. But this suggestion runs into several difficulties. Douglass's claim that he had reached the point at which he was not afraid to die first appeared in *My Bondage and My Freedom* (1855) after Douglass had come out in favor of slave resistance. It does not appear in the *Narrative*, first published in 1845, when Douglass was still advising against slave resistance. In any case, the suggestion does not explain why Douglass changed his mind about slave resistance after 1849. Did he come to believe that most slaves would be able to overcome the fear of death? Douglass did seem to hold that belief. In *My Bondage and My Freedom* he wrote, "While slaves prefer their lives, with flogging, to instant death, they will always find Christians enough, like

unto Covey, to accommodate that preference."[43] The intimation in this passage that slaves who are flogged are somehow partly responsible for their
misfortune only makes sense if we suppose that such slaves have it in their
power to stop being afraid and to come to prefer instant death to lives with
flogging.[44] But is such a supposition at all plausible?

This question becomes more pressing when we notice that Douglass
records that he reached the point at which he was not afraid to die after
"resisting" Covey, as if his reaching that point was a result of his resisting
Covey. It seems to make more sense that he resisted Covey because he had
reached the point at which he was not afraid to die. The fact that Douglass
wrote that he had resolved to defend himself the day before the fight seems
to support this latter view. On the other hand, people often make apparently firm resolutions and then, when the moment to act arrives, fail to act
as they had resolved. And Douglass was aware that there was a significant
difference between making resolutions and acting on them. As he wrote, "I
was resolved to fight, and, what was better still, I was actually hard at it."[45]
We must therefore consider the possibility that Douglass reached the point
at which he was not afraid to die because he resisted Covey.

It would be unreasonable to take Douglass to be saying that any fight,
perhaps one undertaken on the spur of the moment or without good reason,
was "better" than resolving to fight. He meant that acting on his resolution
to fight was better than his bare resolution to fight. To understand why this
makes sense we must remember the nature of his resolution to defend himself. As I have argued, he resolved to defend himself because he believed
that his nature as a moral being required that he stand up for the principles
of morality. But as I have said, people commonly make apparently firm resolutions and then fail to act as they had resolved. Such a failure is always dis-
concerting, but it is likely to be devastating when the resolution was based
on principles that one had claimed to embrace as part of one's identity as a
moral being. It is, as Douglass indicates, an occasion for being ashamed, for
it is a kind of unmasking, showing that one's allegiance to morality is not as
firm as one had tried to deceive oneself into believing, that one is not the
person one claimed to be, and that one is a pretender and a hypocrite even
to oneself. But now it should be clear why acting on the resolution to fight
and defend oneself is better than the bare resolution to fight. It provides the
evidence that confirms that one is the person one claimed to be—one loyal
to morality—the more so when self-defense is likely to lead to one's death.

These considerations provide some support for Douglass's claim that one of the results of resisting Covey was that he was no longer afraid to die. Before the fight he could not be sure that he would fight if Covey tried to beat him; he had resolved to fight, but he knew that he could back down when Covey, whip in hand, confronted him. Given the importance he placed on being the kind of person who stood up for his rights, he could therefore be *afraid* that he would back down when that moment of truth arrived. However, after the fight, when he had the strongest possible evidence that he was the kind of person he wanted and claimed to be, the kind of person who stood up for his rights, he would no longer be afraid that he would back down if Covey tried to beat him.

It will be objected that this conclusion falls short of the claim that he was not afraid to die; no longer being afraid that he would back down if Covey tried to beat him and no longer being afraid to die seem different things. I argue, however, that Douglass could not have meant that resisting Covey made him unafraid to die, but that he must have meant instead that resisting Covey made him unafraid that he would fail to do his duty to stand up for the principles of morality if Covey tried to beat him.

Fear involves two parts: a wish that some harmful event not happen and an uncertainty whether it will happen or whether it will not happen.[46] Douglass accepts the first part of this account of fear. As I noted earlier, he says that life is "precious" to all human beings and not "lightly regarded by men of sane minds.[47] This suggests that all human beings wish not to die and that after the fight with Covey, Douglass, too, wished not to die, given that he did not think that at the time he was no longer of sane mind. Now consider the second part of the account of fear I proposed, that fear involves an uncertainty whether or not the harmful thing one wishes not to happen will happen. Supposing that Douglass accepts it implies that resisting Covey would have removed his fear of death only if it removed his uncertainty whether or not resisting Covey would lead to death. But it is difficult to see how resisting Covey could have had such an effect. Before the fight he was uncertain whether fighting Covey would mean his death or not. He compares his action to the act of someone who has "incurred something, hazarded something, to repel injustice."[48] I do not see how resisting Covey could remove all uncertainty about the consequences of resisting him a second or third time. Douglass got off easily the first time, but this could not have reasonably led him to believe that he had become invulnerable.

Douglass admits that he was never sure why Covey did not have him hanged. He could therefore not be certain that Covey would not have him hanged if he resisted again. I conclude that resisting Covey could not have made him unafraid to die. But, as I have indicated, it could have made him unafraid that he would back down if Covey tried to beat him.

This conclusion supports many of Douglass's claims about the results of his fight with Covey, most obviously that the fight gave him courage and confidence. With courage and confidence he would also, as he reported, be more determined to be a "freeman."[49] The conclusion also provides one interpretation of Douglass's claims about the relations between power and honor noted earlier. According to Douglass, the slave who cannot be flogged is "a power on earth."[50] If such a slave is as I have described him, someone with a demonstrated willingness to stand up for the principles of morality, then, by power, Douglass can only mean here the demonstrated willingness to stand up for the principles of morality. This account of power provides plausible readings of Douglass's claims that force (or power) is part of the "essential dignity of humanity" and that human nature cannot honor a helpless man. The claims mean that a demonstrated willingness to stand up for the principles of morality is part of the essential dignity of humanity and that human nature cannot honor a person who lacks such a willingness. Finally, if honor is close in meaning to respect, we have a justification of Douglass's claim that the fight restored his "crushed self-respect." Before the fight he had not demonstrated a willingness to stand up for the principles of morality and therefore could not honor or respect himself; his self-respect was crushed. But the fight demonstrated that he was willing to stand up for the principles of morality and therefore restored his crushed self-respect.

IV

These conclusions, though sound, have serious limitations. At best they can be generalized to apply to slaves who, like Douglass, defend themselves because of a firm resolution to act on the duty to show allegiance to the principles of morality. Such slaves, [these conclusions suggest], will grow in self-knowledge, confidence, courage, and self-respect. But is it reasonable to expect that all or most slaves can be persuaded to defend themselves on Douglass's high standard? Douglass certainly seemed to think so. And other black abolitionists like Henry Highland Garnet called for resistance on a similar standard.[51] Still, it is useful to see that self-defense could be morally beneficial for the slave even if it was not undertaken on the uncompromising ground of a duty to show allegiance to the principles of morality.

The argument is somewhat indirect, relying on the morally beneficial effects resistance could have on the enslaver. As I have already noted, Douglass often suggested that slaves ought to be willing to peril their lives for their liberty because this would wipe out the reproach that blacks were unwilling to make sacrifice for their liberty and were therefore fit for slavery. Although Douglass did not fight Covey for the reason this argument suggests, the argument could still be sound. If it is, slaves would not have to resist on the high ground that resistance showed allegiance to the principles of morality in order to derive moral benefits from resistance. If they resisted to gain their liberty, the public would look on them more favorably, and this could support their self-respect and eventually help them to gain their freedom.

Unfortunately the argument is not sound, though it does point to interesting possibilities. The most obvious failing of the argument is that it seems to rest on the false assumption that persons who are unwilling to make sacrifices for their liberty are fit for slavery. Such people are certainly more likely to be enslaved than other people and are also perhaps at fault, supposing that one ought to be willing to make sacrifices for one's liberty, but it does not follow that they are fittingly enslaved. It may be suggested that Douglass did not mean to endorse the assumption but was only pointing out that it was the basis of the public's toleration of slavery. But this lets the public off too easily. The public may have had some vague belief that persons ought to be willing to risk something for their liberty, but it did not believe that they must be willing to risk almost certain death and torture for liberty—at least it does not apply this standard to its own members. But this is the standard Douglass's argument suggests that the public applies to the slaves; it demands that they meet standards that it expects few to meet, and that they provide evidence for their humanity that it takes for granted in other people. This suggests that the public already had evidence of the slaves' humanity but that it ignores or misinterpreted this evidence. But in that case, what reason was there to believe that it would take notice of or correctly interpret any further evidence to that effect?

But slave resistance could have an effect on the public and the slaveholders, that would force them out of their dishonesty. That effect is fear. Douglass suggested this possibility in his "Speech on John Brown," where he claimed that the slaves could reach "the slaveholder's conscience through his fear of personal danger."[52] I have argued that the slaveholders ignore or overlook evidence of the slaves' rights to freedom. But, as Aristotle observes, "fear makes people inclined to deliberation."[53] Since we deliberate when we are not clear what we ought to do and are reconsidering and reexamining the evidence to determine how we ought to act, the effect that fear has on us that Aristotle points to may be sufficient to make the slaveholders acknowledge the slaves' humanity and consequently that they have rights to freedom. And fear has another effect that may make the deliberation it inclines us to especially effective: it tends to undermine the pride and avarice that can lead us to interpret evidence dishonestly and in a way that justifies or excuses our pride and avarice. If this is the case, then, as I have argued in another essay, slave resistance that arouses the fear of the public and the slaveholders could put them in a position to acknowledge the slaves' humanity and equal rights to be free.[54]

Douglass does not mention this argument in his discussion of his fight with Covey. But it is consistent with what he does say and indeed provides additional support for some of the good results he claimed to derive from the fight. First, Douglass reports that Covey was "frightened" by his resistance, "lost his usual strength and coolness," and "cried out lustily for help."[55] If fear has the effects I suggested, Covey's fear could have moved him to see Douglass in a new light, as a human being with rights, and Douglass might have seen this new respect in Covey's eyes. Since our conception of ourselves is supported by the conception of ourselves that we see in others' eyes, this could help explain why the fight with Covey helped Douglass regain his crushed self-respect.

There is a final, more speculative advantage of this line of argument. Douglass suggested that Covey did not have him hanged or publicly whipped because Covey was ashamed to admit that he had been "mastered by a boy of sixteen." Such an admission would also damage his reputation as a "negro breaker" and therefore hurt him financially because it was this reputation that enabled him to procure the use of other slaveholders' slaves for very trifling compensation.[56] But, as I have emphasized, Douglass only "ventured" this explanation and pointedly indicated that he was not fully satisfied with it. The present discussion may help fill it out. Perhaps Douglass reached Covey's conscience through arousing his fear of personal danger. Such fear could have, in the way I have suggested, led Covey to deliberate more honestly on the evidence of Douglass's humanity and consequently to see him as a human being with rights. This would not be a wholehearted respect, for in that case Covey would have released Douglass. But it could have been a kind of grudging respect that could combine with his pride and avarice and deter him from having Douglass hanged or publicly whipped.

If this discussion is sound, the good results Douglass claimed to have derived from his fight with Covey depended in part on his having won that fight. If he had resisted Covey but had been easily beaten or had not frightened him and had been easily beaten, perhaps he would have gained the important knowledge of himself as a man who would stand up for the principles of morality. This is no small matter. But if some people's consciences can only be revealed by arousing their fear, he would not have wrung any respect from Covey, and there would have been no respect in Covey's eyes to support [Douglass's] own self-respect. If this is true to Douglass's meaning, his remarks on power and its relation to honor and dignity bear a second interpretation. Power is not simply a demonstrated willingness to stand up for the principles of morality. It is also a capacity to arouse the fear of others. On this account Douglass would be an advocate of Black Power, though not perhaps in the manner of his great contemporary Martin Delany. For Delany, Black Power was necessary for blacks to avoid white oppression. For Douglass, Black Power was also necessary for blacks and whites to have any sense of morality.

Notes

1. Frederick Douglass, *Narrative of the Life of Frederick Douglass, an American Slave,* ed. B. Charles (Cambridge, MA: Harvard University Press, 1988), 104. All references to *Narrative* are to this edition unless otherwise noted.
2. Frederick Douglass, *The Life and Writings of Frederick Douglass,* 5 vols., ed. Philip Foner (New York: International Publishers, 1950–1975), 1:277.
3. Ibid., 2:284–89.
4. Douglass, *Narrative,* 104.
5. See, e.g., Frederick Douglass, *The Life and Times of Frederick Douglass* (New York: Gramercy, 1993), 50, 62, 138.
6. E.g., Douglass, *Life and Writings,* 2:157; Douglass, *Life and Times,* 128–33.

7. Douglass, *Life and Writings*, 1:136.

8. His argument that slave resistance would help to end slavery by discrediting the public's favorite argument for slavery suggests this view. It is made even more pointedly (in *Life and Writings*, 2:535) when he claimed that slave resistance would "reach the slaveholder's conscience through his fear of personal danger." See also his claim that the slave master has deprived "his victim of every means of reaching his sense of justice, except through his bodily fear" (*Life and Writings*, 5:213). I have tried to spell out the argument that slave violence could be morally persuasive in Bernard Boxill, "Fear and Shame as Forms of Moral Suasion in the Thought of Frederick Douglass," *Transactions of the Charles S. Pierce Society* 31 (4) (1995): 713–44.

9. Frederick Douglass, *My Bondage and My Freedom* (New York: Dover, 1969), 247.

10. Ibid., 247, emphasis in original.

11. Ibid.

12. E.g., Douglass, *Life and Writings*, 2:287, 534.

13. E.g., Douglass, *Bondage*, 281–90.

14. Ibid., 241.

15. Ibid., 247.

16. Douglass, *Narrative*, 105.

17. Douglass, *Bondage*, 242.

18. Ibid., 248.

19. Ibid., 242.

20. Ibid., 241.

21. Ibid., 273, emphasis in original.

22. This appeal to consequences does not contradict the position I have attributed to Douglass that the duty of self-defense when in Covey-like circumstances is absolute. The general rule justifying self-defense may be justified by its consequences, though the agent should follow the rule and defend herself without weighing the consequences. In other words, I am giving a rule-utilitarian interpretation of Douglass's deontological view of the duty of self-defense against physical abuse when in Covey-like circumstances. The agent should simply follow the rule without weighing the consequences when she is in Covey-like circumstances because people in such circumstances are very likely to weigh the relevant circumstances so as to justify the morally wrong conclusion.

23. Douglass, *Bondage*, 223.

24. Douglass, *Life and Writings*, 1:157.

25. Douglass, *Bondage*, 263, 264.

26. Consider also his claim that "as soon as the blow was not to be feared, then came the longing for liberty" (*Life and Writings*, 1:157).

27. Douglass, *Bondage,* 228.

28. Ibid., 230.

29. Ibid., 229.

30. Ibid., 36, 88, 130.

31. Ibid., 229.

32. Ibid., 144, 153.

33. Ibid., 315.

34. Ibid., 316.

35. Douglass, *Life and Writings,* 534.

36. Douglass, *Bondage,* 314.

37. Ibid., 317.

38. I have myself presented protest in this way in Bernard Boxill, "Self-Respect and Protest," in Leonard Harris, ed., *Philosophy Born of Struggle: An Anthology of Afro-American Philosophy from 1917* (Dubuque, IA: Kendall/Hunt, 1983), 190–98.

39. Douglass, *Narrative,* 247.

40. Ibid., 248. This was written more than twenty years after the incident. The same confession appears in *The Life and Times of Frederick Douglass,* published more than fifty years after the incident.

41. Douglass, *Narrative,* 247.

42. Douglass, *Bondage.*

43. Ibid.

44. This passage is deleted in the later biography.

45. Douglass, *Narrative,* 242.

46. Robert M. Gordon, "Fear," *Philosophical Review* 89 (4) (1980): 560–78.

47. Douglass, *Narrative,* 284.

48. Ibid., 247.

49. Ibid., 246.

50. Ibid., 247.

51. Herbert Aptheker, ed., *A Documentary History of the Negro People in the United States* (New York: Citadel, 1951), 227–32.

52. Douglass, *Life and Writings,* 2:535.

53. Aristotle, *On Rhetoric* (Oxford: Oxford University Press, 1991).

54. See Boxill, "Fear and Shame as Forms of Moral Suasion in the Thought of Frederick Douglass."

55. Douglass, *Narrative,* 243, 244.

56. I emphasize the tentative nature of Douglass's explanation. In the *Narrative,* he conceded that it did not "entirely satisfy him" (105).

Frederick Douglass's Master–Slave Dialectic

Margaret Kohn

Along with Plato's cave, Hegel's description of the struggle between master and slave in *The Phenomenology of Spirit* is one of the most powerful images in the history of philosophy. According to Hegel, each "self-consciousness" can attain certainty of himself only when another human being recognizes his reality as authoritative.[1] Each self-consciousness tries to force the other to recognize his point of view while withholding reciprocal recognition from the other. This violent struggle ends when one participant chooses submission and life over death, thereby establishing the relationship between master and slave.

In the late nineteenth century, American Hegelians interpreted this section of the *Phenomenology* to suggest that oppressive social relations and even slavery are essentially consensual since one party chooses bondage over death.[2] Most twentieth-century commentators, however, have reached the opposite conclusion. Influenced by Kojève's reading, they have tended to emphasize that for Hegel the truce between master and slave was merely the beginning of a dialectical process of emancipation driven forward by the slave qua worker.[3] These two conflicting interpretations reflect different theories of the relationship between freedom, domination, and violence. Although the master–slave dialectic has primarily been interpreted as an allegory illustrating the development of self-consciousness, Hegel was notoriously precise in his use of language. The use of the terminology of mastery and slavery (or lordship and bondage) draws attention to the issues of slavery, struggle, and liberation, issues that were not simply of historical interest in Hegel's day.

As Buck-Morss points out, Hegel recounted this highly abstract tale of struggle between lord and bondsman during a historical period when actually existing slaves had just begun to rise up against their masters. Hegel wrote the *Phenomenology of Spirit* in 1805–1806, shortly after the Haitian revolution, an event that was widely covered in the German-language press, including *Minerva*, an influential political journal read by Hegel. Buck-Morss concludes that Hegel "knew about real slaves revolting against real masters, and he elaborated his dialectic of lordship and bondage deliberately within this contemporary context."[4]

Forty years later Frederick Douglass told another version of the story of the struggle for recognition between master and slave. This time the medium was not the abstract language of German idealism but rather the powerful idiom of autobiography. Like Hegel, Douglass suggested that the "struggle to the death" was not simply about material comfort or physical domination but instead involved a transformative existential encounter. In a language quite similar to Hegel's, Douglass identified freedom as a kind of self-consciousness that is achieved when the individual chooses to risk death rather than endure bondage. This chapter reads these two nineteenth-century accounts of the struggle between master and slave in order to see how the texts illuminate, complicate, and challenge one another.

At first Douglass and Hegel might seem like an odd pairing: one's magnum opus was a first-person narrative of slavery, while the other aspired to tell the history of *Geist* from its emergence to the end of history. Despite their very different idioms and ambitions, they both attempted to describe the emergence of freedom and reason through the lives and struggles of particular men and movements. Reading Hegel provides help in discovering the philosophical depth of Douglass's reflections, and Douglass's text challenges the reader to foreground the politics in the *Phenomenology*.

The Fight with Covey

In the *Narrative of the Life of Frederick Douglass*,[5] Douglass highlights two pivotal events in his liberation, which we might call the Kantian and the

Hegelian moments: reading and rebelling against his master. The first step toward "enlightenment" was attaining literacy—a skill forbidden to slaves. Douglass was taught to read while working as a house slave in Baltimore. The wife of his master had never owned slaves and had not yet recognized the importance of keeping them in ignorance. After his master forbade any further instruction, Douglass continued to seek out books and teach himself until he became so adept that he was able to understand the arguments in *The Columbian Orator.* One of the texts was a dialogue between a master and a runaway slave. In the dialogue, the slave refuted the arguments in favor of slavery and was so persuasive that the master voluntarily emancipated him.[6] I call this the Kantian moment in the narrative because it reflects the enlightenment ideal that reason and persuasion can gradually bring about social improvement. It illustrates the doctrine of moral suasion that Douglass would come to hold in the early years of his work as an abolitionist lecturer, when he was employed by the Massachusetts Anti-Slavery Society and influenced by William Lloyd Garrison. It reflects his hope that persuasive arguments and compelling illustrations of the brutality of slavery could convert whites to the abolitionist cause.[7]

Throughout the *Narrative*, literacy, education, and reason are figured as crucial tools in the struggle for emancipation. After reading Sheridan's speeches on behalf of Catholic emancipation in *The Columbian Orator*, Douglass explained that "they gave tongue to interesting thoughts of [his] own soul, which had frequently flashed through [his] mind, and died away for want of utterance."[8] Douglass noted that slaveholders were right in forbidding their slaves from learning to read because literacy—and thus access to enlightenment humanism—would undermine the system by strengthening slaves' recognition of their own humanity and desire to be free.

The second pivotal event in Douglass's life as a slave was his fight with Covey. The details of the confrontation are already familiar to the many readers of Douglass's three autobiographies. Douglass had been hired out as a field slave on the farm of Edward Covey, a notorious slave breaker. The fight between master and slave took place after about six months of brutal treatment that had depleted him physically and spiritually. One afternoon in August 1833, after a long day of backbreaking labor in the hot sun, Douglass broke down from exhaustion. When he could not comply with Covey's command to rise, he was beaten and repeatedly kicked in the head. Bleeding profusely and fearing for his life, he decided to go to his owner (who had rented him to Covey for the year) to ask for his intervention. His owner, however, showed no sympathy for Douglass and ordered him to return to Covey to face his certain wrath. Douglass returned the next day but fled again when Covey greeted him with a cow skin, intending to give him another whipping. Douglass hid in the woods, despairing that he faced the choice between starving to death or being whipped to death.[9] In the woods he encountered Sandy Jenkins, a slave and the husband of a free woman, who gave him a meal and shelter before the night and convinced Douglass to take a root with protective powers that Jenkins claimed would protect him from any further beatings.

Returning to the farm, Douglass resolved to defend himself, and when Covey attempted to tie him up, "the fighting madness" came upon him, and he attached his fingers around the throat of his tormentor.[10] In *My Bondage and My Freedom*, Douglass's second autobiography, he suggested that this act of resistance reasserted a primal equality. He felt "as though we stood as equals before the law. The very color of the man was forgotten."[11] When Covey discovered that neither physical nor psychological means would crush Douglass's resistance, he called upon the other slaves and hired men for assistance. Only Covey's cousin came to his aid, and Douglass fought off both assailants. After several hours of struggle, Covey gave up, and, while claiming victory, he had not succeeded in beating Douglass and never tried to again.

The Paradox of Douglass's Pacifism

Given Douglass's pacifism, his reflections on the second pivotal event in the narrative—his fight with the slave breaker Edward Covey—are somewhat puzzling.[12] Douglass called the fight with Covey "the turning-point in [his] career as a slave."[13] This was not because it led directly to physical liberation; in fact, Douglass remained with Covey for six more months and did not flee slavery until four years later. Although the fight with Covey did bring about a cessation to the brutal beatings he had endured, the emancipatory consequences were primarily psychological in nature. Douglass emphasized this point when he introduced his description of the events with the statement, "You have seen how a man was made a slave; you shall see how a slave was made a man."[14] He seemed to be suggesting that his manhood—his dignity and humanity—emerged not through literacy or labor or leadership but through violence.

The fight with Covey is the dramatic climax of the *Narrative*. The conventional reading classifies this event as a classic case of the pursuit of masculine honor through violence as a way to contest the social death of slavery.[15] This reading suggests that violence, at least defensive violence, plays a crucial role in liberation. Douglass explained the psychological effects of violent struggle in terms strikingly similar to those of anticolonial theorist Fanon.[16] I quote Douglass's description of the existential significance of the fight at some length because his words powerfully convey the centrality of the event:

> [The battle] rekindled the few expiring embers of freedom, and revived within me a sense of my own manhood. It recalled the departed self-confidence, and inspired me again with a determination to be free. The gratification afforded by the triumph was a full compensation for whatever else might follow, even death itself. He only can understand the deep satisfaction which I experienced, who has himself repelled by force the bloody arm of slavery. I felt as I never felt before. It was a glorious resurrection, from the tomb of slavery to the heaven of freedom.[17]

Clearly Douglass is not simply arguing that a slave, like any person, has a natural right to defend his life. Instead, he makes the penetrating but controversial suggestion that the fight for ascendancy over an adversary can facilitate a psychological liberation, which is as powerful as physical freedom. This is a puzzling position to take for a pacifist.

Why did Frederick Douglass call the fight with Covey a turning point in his liberation in 1845, a time when he still retained his commitment to pacifism? To answer this question we must understand the nature of this commitment. Douglass's rejection of violence and embrace of moral suasion reflected his convictions as a Garrisonian. In 1845, the period when he wrote the *Narrative of the Life of Frederick Douglass*, the first of three autobiographies, he was allied with William Lloyd Garrison. Garrison is famous for his controversial argument that the United States Constitution was a slaveholding document and his conclusion that abolitionists should refrain from political participation in such a morally compromised polity.[18] Moreover, Douglass's mentor adhered to the doctrine of nonresistance, a kind of radical pacifism inspired by Christ's teaching to "turn the other cheek." Nonresistance required that people respond to wrongdoing with persuasion and avoid recourse to violence, even in self-defense. Strict adherents to the philosophy of nonresistance were even opposed to nonviolent uses of force such as government action.[19]

Douglass stated that he embraced nonresistance until he was attacked by a mob in Pendleton, Indiana, in 1843. He came to reject the doctrine after he concluded that the defense of his own life and that of his friends was justified.[20] Even after he no longer espoused the radical tenets of nonresistance, however, he still embraced pacifism, at least for strategic reasons. In 1848, he wrote in his newspaper the *North Star* that he was "inflexibly opposed to a resort of violence as a means of effecting reform" (May 5, 1848). Nor was this opposition to violence merely theoretical. At the Negro National Convention in 1843, Douglass entered into a controversial debate with Henry Highland Garnet, another black leader. Garnet did not advocate slave insurrection (a possibility feared by abolitionists and slaveholders alike) but instead proposed that slaves enact a general strike and, while not instigating violence, be prepared to defend themselves against the slaveholders' wrath. Douglass responded that there was "too much physical force" in Garnet's proposal and argued that they should try "the moral means a little longer."[21]

The tension between Douglass's account of the liberatory effects of violence and his ethical commitment to pacifism presents a problem for the reader. Surely Douglass, an acutely reflective chronicler of his own experience, did not simply fail to note the contradiction. There are several possible ways of reconciling the apparent inconsistency. Some commentators have suggested that Douglass never really embraced nonviolence as an ethical doctrine.[22] According to this position, his many statements condemning the use of violence were strategic not categorical; they merely reflected his conviction that slave revolts in the United States would be counterproductive and weaken rather than strengthen the emerging consensus in favor of abolition. After a decade in the abolitionist movement, he became increasingly pessimistic that moral suasion would convince Southerners and doubtful that peaceful abolition was likely. This was a different understanding of a tactical issue, not a transformation of his views on the legitimacy of violence.

A second explanation is that Douglass was a nonresistant until his meeting with John Brown in 1847. In the *Life and Times of Frederick Douglass*, Douglass emphasized the influence of John Brown, noting that after their meeting he became less hopeful about the peaceful abolition of slavery, and his "utterances became more tinged by the color of this man's strong impressions."[23] At an antislavery convention that year in Salem, Ohio, Douglass warned that "slavery could only be destroyed by blood-shed." In subsequent years, Douglass became more forthright in his defense of violence. In 1854 he wrote that violence against slaveholders was "wise as well as just."[24] In 1857 he stated that he hoped for a slave uprising in the South and praised the slave revolts in the West Indies.[25] By the outbreak of the Civil War, his transition had long been complete. It was not surprising that after having praised John Brown as a hero and martyr for his raid on Harpers Ferry, he strongly supported the Civil War and became active as an advocate of black enlistment in the union forces.

The are some difficulties, however, with this account of the way that a naive pacifist abolitionist became a reluctant advocate of slave insurrection and civil war. Even the modified version of this story, which suggests that Douglass changed his view of the efficacy of moral suasion not the legitimacy of violence, is problematic. The latter view fails to take into account Douglass's categorical statements against violence in the period before the 1847 meeting with Brown. For example, in a speech given in London in 1846, Douglass stated, "Such is my regard for the principle of peace; such is my deep firm conviction that nothing can be attained for liberty universally by war, that were I to be asked the question whether I would have my emancipation by the shedding of a single drop of blood, my answer would be the negative."[26] This seems to patently contradict his depiction of his fight with Covey, where he seemed immensely satisfied with the fact that he "caused blood to run where [he] touched him [Covey] with the ends of [his] fingers."[27] Given that the description of drawing blood was written just one year *before* the speech in England, the puzzle cannot be resolved by any simple story of change over time.

The most compelling interpretation of the contradictory evidence is a modified view of the periodization thesis. Before his gradual disillusionment with moral suasion, which culminated in the decisive meeting with John Brown, Douglass tried to formulate a position that justified self-defense while criticizing proactive violence. His texts, however, reveal his own difficulty in sustaining such a view. In the South, slaves were vulnerable to being beaten, raped, and even murdered at their masters' whim. Any perceived infraction—a slight decrease in effort or a wrong glance—could incite brutal and arbitrary punishment. Any attempt to resist the overseer—even a word of explanation or excuse—would often be met with violence. Under these conditions, where did the right to self-defense begin? Did the slave have the right to resist any unreasonable command? But what command would count as reasonable when it was based on treating another person as a piece of property? Was there a right to resist a whipping or only an assault that threatened his or her life? Henry Highland Garnet's proposal of a general strike successfully exploited this problem in the theory of self-defense. The slaves simply had to refuse to behave as other men's property in order to incite the slaveholders' violence and then legitimately use violence in self-defense.

Douglass's account of his fight with Covey reveals a second problem with the theory of defensive violence. Even if we accept that the fight could plausibly be described as self-defense, it is clear that its significance was not simply to avoid injury or death. In fact, Douglass stressed that it was precisely his own courage—his willingness to risk his life—that made the event so liberating.[28] In Douglass's second autobiography, written after ten years of additional reflection, he still emphasized the centrality of this event and its psychological significance. He described it as "a resurrection" that "revived a sense of [his] own manhood."[29] His repeated emphasis on manhood suggests that the fight was primarily about honor and dignity.

Why should physical resistance be crucial to a sense of honor, dignity, and humanity, given that violence, unlike, say, literacy, is something that we share with animals? Douglass himself posed this question by recounting an event that drew attention to the parallels between breaking animals and breaking men. Douglass, who had until recently worked as a house slave in Baltimore, was ordered to haul firewood using a team of unbroken oxen. Douglass was unable to control the oxen and took an entire day to complete the task; as punishment for this "laziness" Covey beat him severely.[30] In My Bondage and My Freedom Douglass noted how his own situation resembled that of the oxen. He reflected, "They were property, so was I; they were to be broken, so was I. Covey was to break me, I was to break them."[31] The similarity between men and animals is a motif that runs throughout Douglass's writing. Despite the ubiquity of animal imagery, the passage assimilating the breaking of oxen and men is troubling in light of the emphasis that Douglass subsequently places on physical resistance. He claimed that the fight with Covey showed "how a slave was made a man."[32] Yet animals, just like men, can physically resist their masters, and, in fact, Douglass fails to break the oxen, who overturn the cart again at the gate to the farm. Resisting their masters seems to be something that humans and animals share rather than something that separates them. As Franklin points out, many readers are troubled by the importance that Douglass places on the fight with Covey because it challenges assumptions about the priority of mind over body and suggests that power rather than knowledge may be key to personhood.[33]

For Douglass, however, the fight with Covey had a psychological as well as a physical dimension; it represented an existential crisis and rebirth. As indicated above, he described it as a "turning-point" that awoke his "self-respect" and "self-confidence."[34] According to Douglass, the fight "made [him] a freeman in *fact*, though [he] still remained a slave in *form*." There are two different reasons why the fight with Covey led to a certain kind of liberation. First, it had a very pragmatic benefit; Covey was no longer willing to risk beating him, and "when a slave cannot be flogged he is more than half free."[35] Second, it had a transformative effect. According to Douglass, no one respects a man without power; therefore, the willingness and ability to defend oneself is essential to human dignity. In all three accounts, he emphasized the fact that he had "reached the point where [he] was not afraid to die."[36] In *My Bondage and My Freedom* he quoted these lines from Byron:

> Hereditary bondman, know ye not
> Who would be free, themselves must strike the blow?[37]

In choosing to risk death rather than endure bondage, Douglass felt himself to be free, even though he had not yet escaped from slavery.

This decision to accept no alternative but liberty or death is the key to Douglass's transformation. It also distinguishes his resistance from that of the unbroken oxen he drove to fetch wood. Their actions were based on the instinct to follow natural desires. For Douglass, fighting back against Covey was not a matter of following natural desire but of triumphing over it. While no one wants to receive a beating, Douglass had every reason to believe that he would face worse suffering as a consequence of fighting back. The odds of victory—given that Covey had a white cousin, a slave, and a hired man to help him—were extremely small. Moreover, disobeying a master could be punished by a public flogging, and striking a master was a crime punishable by death. Douglass had no reason to believe that his physical condition would improve by fighting back, yet he nevertheless chose to risk his life rather than be subject to "brutification." Of course, the victory against

Covey did not win Douglass his freedom; he was still a slave. But he gained self-respect and recognition and thereby set in motion a process that culminated in his freedom.

Hegel's master–slave dialectic helps the reader understand the transformation that Douglass underwent during the fight with Covey. Like Hegel, Douglass understood that self-consciousness arises out of struggle. The fight became necessary when Douglass realized, "My book learning had not kept Covey off of me."[38] This statement suggests that the liberation that comes through literacy and reason is insufficient if it is not recognized by others. It reflects the Hegelian idea that man needs external affirmation of his reality. "If [man] is to be fully at home this reality must reflect back to him what he is."[39] Douglass felt himself to be the equal of Covey, but this reality was not reflected back to him. The fight with Covey changed this reality, establishing a sort of equality of physical force. Even though Douglass did not achieve physical freedom, he did have his internal conception of himself validated externally. Douglass explained, "When a slave cannot be flogged . . . [he] is really *a power on earth*."[40]

In his autobiographies, Douglass admitted that he had never figured out why Covey did not take advantage of his legal right to have Douglass publicly whipped by the authorities. The most likely reason was that Douglass had shown him that the man who would whip him must also kill him, and this was a cost that Covey was not prepared to pay. He needed Douglass's labor on his farm; he needed his reputation as a fierce slave breaker; and he could not afford to indemnify Douglass's owner. In other words, what emerged from the fight was that Covey was dependent on Douglass, whereas Douglass, who had faced death, was, in a sense, independent of these "particularistic" concerns. These are, of course, Hegelian themes. In both the *Phenomenology of Spirit* and the *Philosophy of Right,* Hegel suggests that the fear of death is necessary to free man from the narrow preoccupations of daily life and lead him to attain consciousness of the universal. Hegel also notes that the slave is the one who carries history forward because the master becomes dependent on the slave, while the slave, liberated from dependence on the material world, becomes capable of searching for a higher freedom. Douglass's story is the story of the enlightenment, but not one based on reason, consensus, and moral suasion. It is a story that foregrounds brutality and conflict in the struggle for freedom. The slave, who learned the meaning of liberty in the face of death and the darkness of bondage, was to be the bearer of progress.

Hegel: The Master–Slave Dialectic

Several commentators have thought about what it would mean to read Hegel's discussion of lordship and bondage as a commentary on modern slavery. In his pathbreaking study *Slavery and Social Death*, Patterson argued that Hegel's master–slave dialectic showed profound insight into the structure of inequality, but he criticized Hegel for mischaracterizing the significance of labor and the master's need for recognition by the slave.[41] In a more sympathetic vein, Buck-Morss suggested that the master–slave dialectic showed that "those who once acquiesced to slavery demonstrate their humanity when they are willing to risk death rather than remain subjugated."[42] Perhaps that is part of the reason why Hegel was the favorite philosopher of both Martin Luther King Jr. and W. E. B. Du Bois.[43]

Unlike subsequent black intellectuals, however, Frederick Douglass had not read Hegel before writing his account of the fight with Covey in *Narrative of the Life of Frederick Douglass*.[44] Nevertheless, there are important similarities between the two versions of the master–slave dialectic. Both are essentially struggles for recognition and meditations on the way that liberty emerges out of its own opposite. According to Gilroy, "Douglass can be read as if he is systematically reworking the encounter between master and slave in a striking manner which inverts Hegel's own allegorical scheme. It is the slave rather than the master who emerges from Douglass's account possessed of 'consciousness that exists for itself,' while the master becomes the representative of a 'consciousness that is repressed within itself.'"[45]

Gilroy is right to suggest that Douglass's text provides a provocative supplement to Hegel's master–slave dialectic. But there are several important dimensions of the relationship between the two accounts that previous commentators overlook. Most significant is the fact that in Hegel's version there is no fight between master and slave. There is a struggle between two self-consciousnesses who are independent of one another and exist in a state of primitive equality. The label "master–slave dialectic" makes it easy to overlook this crucial fact and turn the story into a struggle between a master and his slave rather than a struggle between equals that creates a master–slave relationship. Before it is possible to consider more fully the ways in which Hegel's and Douglass's texts illuminate one another, however, we must reconstruct some details of Hegel's master–slave dialectic.

The discussion of lordship and bondage comes in chapter 4 of the *Phenomenology of Spirit*. It is part of Hegel's answer to a dilemma that has preoccupied philosophers including Plato, Descartes, and Fichte: How is it possible to be certain that what we think we know is actually true? It is beyond the scope of this essay to explain the preliminary steps involved in answering this question, but the argument culminates in the following conclusion: the individual believes that self-certainty is possible only if his reality is confirmed as authoritative by another person.[46] This in turn requires a struggle because each person wants his reality, his point of view, to be recognized as authoritative. Each combatant would rather die than renounce his claim to recognition by the other. If this were the outcome, however, and the struggle ended in the death of one or both combatants, then the struggle would be in vain because a dead man cannot provide recognition. "One of those involved in the struggle prefers life . . . but gives up being recognized, while the other holds to its reference to itself and is recognized by the first who is his subject (*Unterworfenen*); the relation of master and servant."[47]

Initially, this outcome would seem to suggest that the impasse has been resolved and one party has achieved the certainty and recognition that she desired. But, according to Hegel, this apparent resolution proves unsatisfying because meaningful recognition can be provided only by an equal. At the end of the fight there is only a master and a servant,[48] and the latter, like a dead man, is incapable of satisfying the other's need for voluntary affirmation of his self-certainty. Furthermore, the master's desire for autonomy and control is actually undermined because he becomes dependent upon the servant. The servant, as a condition of servitude, is forced to control his own material desires and to work, in other words to transform the world according to a plan. The master, on the other hand, lives a life of indolent ease, and this life of indulgence does not provide the conditions for developing self-discipline or controlling desire, the basic components of reason. This is why history ultimately belongs to the servant, not the master. According to Hegel, true self-sufficiency or "freedom" is reached when the servant becomes conscious of reason, a capacity that emerges under servitude.[49] The *Phenomenology* tells the story of this self-consciousness as it developed through stoicism, skepticism, Christianity, and the French Revolution, eventually culminating in Hegel himself.

As Wood has argued, there are two different lessons that can be drawn from the master–slave dialectic. The first he calls a "doubtful platitude of authoritarian pedagogy"[50]: you learn to command by learning to obey. Only through subordination to the will of another can one control one's own desires. The alternative lesson is about self-realization rather than subordination. According to this interpretation, true freedom becomes possible after one has learned to detach oneself from selfish desires and can therefore reach decisions based on reason. The servant's consciousness is victorious because the master becomes slave to his desires and the servant learns to master his, thereby becoming a rational individual whose sense of self is confirmed by a community of equals. Hegel's story can be read as an analysis of the necessary failure of a social structure premised upon domination.

Several commentators have suggested that Hegel's theoretical analysis of domination is empirically flawed. Drawing upon the historical record of actual slave-owning societies, Patterson has argued that there is no existential impasse (and thus no need for dialectical *aufhebung*) because the master could attain recognition from other masters rather than from the slave.[51] The "existential impasse" refers to Hegel's claim that the master desires recognition, but such recognition is meaningless if it comes from a being incapable of independence: a slave.[52] According to Patterson, the social structure and culture of slavery was largely determined by the presence or absence of other free persons who recognized the honor conferred by mastery. While this is certainly true as a matter of historical record, it does not undermine Hegel's schema. The source of the master's failure is not only the inadequacy of the recognition offered by the slave but also his own complacency. It is easy to overlook this feature of the dialectic because it emerges implicitly, by way of contrast with the self-consciousness of the slave. For Hegel, the slave "acquires a mind of his own"—in other words, he becomes conscious of himself as a human being with rationality rather than just particularistic desires. This transformation occurs because of the negativity of "absolute fear."[53] Fear of death and subsequent service to the lord break the slave's connection to his natural desires. The absolute fear also makes the slave conscious of the abstract idea of freedom. The master, on the other hand, remains at a more primitive level of consciousness, merely seeking recognition of his particularistic self. Thus, to return to Patterson's criticism, the recognition conferred by other free persons presents no problem for Hegel since it recognizes mastery (particularistic desires) not the universal, rational side of man. It also increases the master's complacency and makes it less likely that he will seek universal self-consciousness. Even if the master attains recognition from other free persons, he is still dependent upon the slave and subject to his own base instincts.

Ultimately Hegel wants to show that the problem of self-certainty can be solved only by reciprocal recognition, and reciprocal recognition can be achieved only by agents who identify with their universal (rational) selves. If this interpretation is correct, then the *Phenomenology of Spirit* can be read as a critique of domination. But it is an ideal history as well as an abstract philosophy. The section on the master–slave dialectic does not end with a renewed contest between master and slave, in which the slave, now possessed of self-mastery and universal self-consciousness, once again risks death in order to realize the idea of freedom. Instead, Hegel abruptly shifts from a "timeless" rendering of lordship and bondage to a more historical register. He explains how stoicism, skepticism, Christianity, and science are attempts to work through the problem of self-certainty. The structure of the *Phenomenology,* which moves between intellectual histories and their social conditions, has encouraged some readers to place the discussion of lordship and bondage in historical time. Since it comes directly before Hegel's treatment of Stoicism, some commentators have understandably associated it with the issue of slavery in Greek society and the work of Aristotle or Plato (for example, Judith Shklar, "Self-Sufficient Man"[54]).

Slavery, however, was one of the foremost problems of the nineteenth century. The introduction of plantation slavery in the New World was one of the structures that generated vast economic resources in the *metropole,* which in turn facilitated the expansion and diffusion of European culture.[55] Flourishing in an age of ostensible liberalism and toleration, slavery became the often unacknowledged contradiction at the heart of Western civilization. While Hegel's text provides significant resources for thinking about structures of domination, I am not convinced that Hegel's master–slave dialectic was intended to expose the paradox of liberty and servitude, equality and exclusion at the heart of Enlightenment practice. The main reason for this conclusion is that the struggle he describes is between two self-consciousnesses (two unrelated individuals). Out of this struggle emerges lordship and bondage, a relationship that is inherently unstable because it fails to provide either party with the conditions for self-realization and universal freedom. This means that the opposition between the two must be overcome, but in Hegel's schema it is not overcome through a rematch between the master and slave, types that Hegel assumes have disappeared in modernity. The ideal to be realized in modernity is a synthesis of mastery and slavery, but a synthesis that emerges under transformed historical conditions. According to Kojève's influential reading of Hegel, in the modern world there are no masters and slaves, only the bourgeois, "who is neither Slave nor Master; . . . the Slave of Capital—his *own* slave."[56] The bourgeois—not the slave—must free himself by undergoing "the liberating risk of life" and thereby achieving the synthesis of theory (universal personhood, freedom) and actuality (the French Revolution).

While I do not believe that Hegel intended to explore the structure of slave revolt, this does not mean that the *Phenomenology* is irrelevant to a discussion of modern slavery. The author's intentions do not exhaust the range of possible interpretations of the text.[57] Hegel's discussion of lordship and bondage draws attention to the ubiquity of conflict and struggle that are an essential part of the story of freedom and rationality. It provides an alternative to the more popular Kantian-inspired view that social change can be a product of consensual agreement that does not leave behind unresolved remainders that fuel future conflict. While acknowledging the constitutive role of conflict in human relations, Hegel also explains why the attempt to resolve this conflict through domination inevitably fails. The master–slave dialectic also explores the existential dimensions of the struggle for recognition and identifies this struggle as part of the problem of freedom.

Despite these insights, Hegel's highly abstract rendering and the structure of the *Phenomenology* discourage the reader from connecting the master–slave dialectic to actual existing slavery. Reading slave narratives forces the student of Hegel to think about the fact that slavery did not disappear after the advent of Christian universalism but expanded and prospered in a period of supposed enlightenment and freedom. It poses the question of the philosophical, existential, and historical significance of a rematch between master and slave. Douglass's account of his fight with Covey, in part because of its numerous parallels with Hegel's story in chapter 4 of the *Phenomenology of Spirit,* provides some suggestions about how to think about this question. In the final section of this chapter I will bring the two strands of this story back together, first reconsidering how reading Douglass with Hegel in mind helps deepen our understanding of the existential dimensions of the encounter with Covey and then briefly explaining how Douglass's *Narrative* challenges and supplements Hegel's narrative.

The Fear of Death

At first it seems that we do not need Hegel's master–slave dialectic to help explain why Douglass felt the fight with Covey to be the fundamental turning point in his life as a slave, a "resurrection" that reawoke his confidence and desire for freedom. Above I suggested that Douglass's willingness to risk his life was critical to this existential transformation. This is not a novel interpretation; in fact, it is the lesson that Douglass explicitly encouraged his readers to draw. In *My Bondage and My Freedom* he insisted that during the fight with Covey he had reached a point where he was *"not afraid to die"* and this spirit made him "a freeman in *fact,* while [he] remained a slave in *form.*"[58] This statement is consistent with a theme that Douglass developed throughout his writing: a comparison between slaves and the pre-revolutionary American colonists. Both groups were heroic because they embraced Patrick Henry's slogan "Give me liberty or give me death."

Previous commentators have also noted Douglass's suggestion that one earns freedom by risking one's life. According to Gilroy, what distinguishes Hegel's master–slave dialectic from Douglass's version is that for Douglass "the slave actively prefers the possibility of death to the continuing condition of inhumanity on which plantation slavery depends."[59] This means that Douglass's account is an inversion of Hegel's. In Hegel's allegory one combatant decides that "he prefers his conqueror's version of reality to death and submits. He becomes the slave while the other achieves mastery."[60] In Douglass's version, the slave prefers death and thereby achieves freedom. Does this mean that Hegel has nothing to teach us about modern slavery, resistance, and freedom?

I want to suggest that Hegel helps answer a question that remains unresolved in Douglass's account, the issue of "from whence" the resolution to fight back came. In both versions, the slave is transformed by his confrontation with death, which deepens his understanding of freedom. Neither Douglass nor Hegel approaches freedom primarily in terms of negative freedom. Clearly, Douglass does not treat freedom exclusively as the absence of constraint. If this were the case, then he would not have been free until four years later when he finally made his way to the North. Yet Douglass tells his audience that the fight with Covey made him free. A careful reading of the three versions of the fight reveals that Douglass's freedom was not simply a matter of doing what he wanted, nor was it simply the sense of power that came from physical resistance. Remember that Douglass himself compared breaking slaves and oxen, which drew attention to the fact that resistance itself could be something instinctual. Douglass's existential transformation—and thus the key to his sense of freedom—came about *before* he fought Covey, during the night that he spent in the woods when he felt that "life, in itself, had almost become burdensome."[61]

After Douglass's master refused to protect him but before Douglass returned to Covey's farm, Douglass spent a day hidden in the forest, reflecting upon what to do. His physical condition was deplorable; he was covered in blood, exhausted, and had not eaten or rested. "Buried in [the wood's] somber gloom and hushed in its solemn silence,"[62] Douglass discovered that he could not pray. He felt that all of his "outward relations" were against him as he faced the choice between remaining in the wood and starving and returning to Covey's to have his "flesh torn to pieces."[63]

This portion of the story is less dramatic than the fight and has understandably received less attention. But there are indications that a transformation took place in the woods during that day when Douglass was cut off from all "outward relations" and was deeply shaken by the possibility of death. In the woods he experienced a kind of death and rebirth, but he was born again not as a believer but as a resolute opponent of slavery and all of its related institutions, including the Southern Christian church. There are two details from the text that suggest this fundamental transformation. First, there was Douglass's decision to accept an African talisman, a magical root from Sandy, which symbolized his recognition of the limits of Enlightenment rationalism (his "book learning" hadn't kept Covey off of him). The motif of religious transformation is underscored in his statement that upon returning to Covey's, he "soon had occasion to make his fallen state known"—an apparent allusion to Lucifer.[64] The Douglass who emerged from the woods was the antithesis of everything that slave society had trained him to be: a docile, obedient, ignorant, faithful slave. In the woods he experienced a dread so intense that he felt that life itself had almost become a burden.[65] The fear of death—not a remote abstract thought but an immediate, concrete possibility—severed his lingering connection to the worldview of slavery. It was this transformation that made it possible for him to violate the code of slave society and to fight Covey. He emerged from the woods ready to transgress the most profound norms of mastery and slavery, and it was this violation—not the violence itself—that made him free.

At least this is the interpretation that is suggested by Hegel's *Phenomenology of Spirit*. In Hegel's discussion of lordship and bondage, the fear of death liberates pure self-consciousness from the ego. This fear of death both liberates and enslaves the bondsman. It motivates one combatant to recognize the other and serve him, but simultaneously it frees him from his unreflective immersion in the banalities of daily life. In the fight for recognition, the one who emerges as master also risks his life, but he does not truly contemplate the meaning of nonbeing; thus he does not experience any transvaluation of values. The fear of death, however, is pivotal for the slave. "For this consciousness (the slave's) has been fearful, not of this or that particular thing or just at odd moments, but its whole being has been seized with dread, for it has experienced the fear of death, the absolute Lord. In that experience it has been quite unmanned, has trembled in every fiber of its being, and everything solid and stable has been shaken to its foundations. But this pure universal movement, the absolute melting-away of everything stable, is the simple, essential nature of self-consciousness, absolute negativity, pure being-for-itself."[66]

To call this "the fear of death" is somewhat misleading because Hegel's description indicates that the experience is the opposite of what we often associate with that phrase. Instead of making one more attached to mortal life—sensuous pleasures—it strips away these unessential elements and reveals the "pure universal moment." Understanding of the universal emerges out of "negativity"; in other words, it is produced by the fear of death, which severs the connection to the world of appearances. Through negativity the slave acquires the *idea* of freedom. Possessing the idea of freedom and not being free, the slave is led to transform the conditions of his existence, thereby realizing historical progress.[67]

According to Hegel, lordship showed itself to be the opposite of what it appeared to be.[68] It seemed to be autonomy but was actually dependence. Similarly, servitude turns into the opposite of what it immediately is; it becomes "a truly independent consciousness."[69] Under the influence of Kojève and Hegelian Marxism, many commentators have focused on the role of work—the fact that the slave must shape the objective world and control his own particular desires.[70] But the key moment of transformation comes from the experience of fear and trembling. It is a result of the "pure negativity" of the moment when the future slave confronts the possibility of his own death. This severs his connection to the contingent elements of existence and opens up the possibility of a deeper consciousness of freedom.[71]

A critic might respond that my attempt to draw parallels between the fight with Covey and the master–slave dialectic is ultimately unconvincing because the fear of death gave Douglass the courage to fight back, while it motivated Hegel's bondsman to serve the Lord, whom he feared. One response to this criticism would be that Douglass's decision to fight back was also an attempt to avoid death. In his autobiography he stated that he feared that he would be murdered if Covey's power over him remained unchecked, and we know that he believed that "[overseers] prefer to whip those who are most easily whipped."[72] But this solution is not wholly convincing because there is little in the text to suggest that Douglass approached the fight with Covey strategically, as a calculated attempt to minimize future harm.

It was the fear of death that cut Douglass off from all "outward relations"—relations of subordination and dependence. This liberation made him able to resist his master. The fear and trembling in the woods finally severed his connection with the ideologies and institutions of slavery and made him more deeply focused on his desire for freedom. He resisted Covey because he became conscious of the contradiction between his idea of his own freedom and its incomplete realization in the world. The same tension drives forward the development of self-consciousness in the *Phenomenology of Spirit*, except that its resolution becomes possible at the end of history rather than taking place in the life of one man.

Douglass's story provides an alternative to the historical periodization in Hegel's account. Douglass highlights the fact—overlooked in much of nineteenth-century political theory—that real not metaphorical slavery was not a relic of the ancient world but a distinctively modern phenomenon. It challenges the reader to think about domination and liberation in historical context and not to overlook the conflicts and cultures that do not fit so neatly into a progressive history of enlightenment. It reminds us of the situation of real slaves and recognizes them as the agents of their own emancipation and simultaneously bearers of social progress. Thus, Douglass's theoretically informed autobiographies serve as an important supplement and challenge to Hegel's understanding of modernity.

This Hegelian-inspired interpretation also leaves us with a different, more complex understanding of the series of events that, according to Douglass, made a slave a man. It is a version that adds fear and trembling to the triumphalist language of heroism and violence. It reexamines the slogan "Give me liberty or give me death" in order to recognize that liberty is often premised upon the death not of one's adversary but of an earlier version of oneself.

Notes

First published as "Frederick Douglass's Master–Slave Dialectic," *Journal of Politics* 67 (2) (May 2005): 497–514. Reprinted with the permission of the University of Chicago Press. Copyright © 2005, the University of Chicago Press.

Acknowledgment: I would like to thank Mark Reinhardt, Leslie Paul Thiele, and the anonymous reviewers for their comments on this chapter.

1. G. W. F. Hegel, *The Phenomenology of Spirit,* trans. A. V. Miller (Oxford: Oxford University Press, 1977), 104–10.

2. Shamoon Zamir, *Dark Voices: W. E. B. Du Bois and American Thought, 1888–1903* (Chicago: University of Chicago Press, 1995).

3. Alexandre Kojève, *Introduction to the Reading of Hegel,* ed. Allan Bloom (1947; reprint, New York: Basic Books, 1969).

4. Susan Buck-Morss, "Hegel and Haiti," *Critical Inquiry* 26 (4) (2000): 844.

5. Frederick Douglass, *Narrative of the Life of Frederick Douglass* (1845), in *Autobiographies,* ed. Henry Louis Gates Jr. (New York: Library of America, 1994), 1–102.

6. Ibid., 41–42.

7. Bernard Boxill, "Two Traditions in African-American Political Philosophy," *Philosophical Forum* 24 (1–3) (1992–1993): 125–28; Frank Kirkland, "Enslavement, Moral Suasion, and Struggles for Recognition: Frederick Douglass's Answer to the Question 'What Is Enlightenment?'" in Bill E. Lawson and Frank M. Kirkland, eds., *Frederick Douglass: A Critical Reader* (Malden, MA: Blackwell, 1999), 243–311.

8. Douglass, *Narrative,* 42.

9. Ibid., 62, 63.

10. Frederick Douglass, *My Bondage and My Freedom* (1855), in *Autobiographies,* 283.

11. Ibid.

12. Bernard Boxill, "The Fight with Covey," in Lewis R. Gordon, ed., *Existence in Black: An Anthology of Black Existential Philosophy* (New York: Routledge, 1997), 273–90. [*Volume editor's note:* See chapter 2 in this volume.]

13. Douglass, *Narrative*, 65.

14. Ibid., 60.

15. Orlando Patterson, *Slavery and Social Death: A Comparative Study* (Cambridge, MA: Harvard University Press, 1982). It is beyond the scope of this essay to focus on the interesting question of gender in Douglass's approach to liberation in particular and slave narrative in general. There is, however, an extensive literature on this topic. See, for example, Kristin Hoganson, "Garrisonian Abolitionists and the Rhetoric of Gender, 1850–1860,"*American Quarterly* 45 (4) (1993): 558–95; Kimberly Drake, "Rewriting the American Self: Race, Gender, and Identity in the Autobiographies of Frederick Douglass and Harriet Jacobs," *MELUS* 22 (4) (1997): 91–108; and Elizabeth Fox-Genovese, "To Write the Wrongs of Slavery," *Gettysburg Review*, Winter 1989, 63–76.

16. Frantz Fanon, *The Wretched of the Earth* (New York: Grove Press, 1963).

17. Douglass, *Narrative*, 65.

18. Carleton Mabee, *Black Freedom: The Nonviolent Abolitionists from 1830 through the Civil War* (New York: Macmillan, 1970).

19. Lewis Perry, *Radical Abolitionism: Anarchy and the Government in Antislavery Thought* (Ithaca, NY: Cornell University Press, 1973).

20. Leslie F. Goldstein, "Violence as an Instrument of Social Change: The Views of Frederick Douglass (1817–1895)," *Journal of Negro History* 61 (1) (1976): 61–72.

21. Mabee, *Black Freedom*, 59.

22. Goldstein, "Violence as an Instrument of Social Change."

23. Frederick Douglass, *Life and Times of Frederick Douglass*, in *Autobiographies*, 719.

24. Frederick Douglass, *The Life and Writings of Frederick Douglass*, 5 vols., ed. Philip S. Foner (New York: International Publishers, 1950–1975), 1:286.

25. Goldstein, "Violence as an Instrument of Social Change," 66.

26. Quoted in Booker T. Washington, *Frederick Douglass* (New York: Argosy Antiquarian, 1906), 110.

27. Douglass, *Narrative*, 64.

28. Ibid., 64–65.

29. Douglass, *Bondage*, 286.

30. Douglass, *Narrative*, 56.

31. Douglass, *Bondage*, 263.

32. Douglass, *Narrative*, 60.

33. H. Bruce Franklin, "Animal Farm Unbound," in Harold Bloom, ed., *Frederick Douglass's* Narrative of the Life of Frederick Douglass (New York: Chelsea House, 1988), 40.

34. Douglass, *Life and Times*, 591.

35. Ibid.

36. Ibid.

37. Douglass, *Bondage*, 297.

38. Ibid., 281.

39. Charles Taylor, *Hegel* (Cambridge: Cambridge University Press, 1975), 152.

40. Douglass, *Bondage*, 286, emphasis in original.

41. Patterson, *Slavery and Social Death*, 98–100.

42. Buck-Morss, "Hegel and Haiti," 844. I am familiar with several works that relate Hegel's master–slave dialectic to the historical reality of black slavery, but they differ from this essay in key respects. Cynthia Willett emphasizes the difference between the two versions of the story. She points out that Hegel's slave achieves self-mastery through stoicism and correctly notes that this is a form of asceticism that Douglass clearly rejects (*Maternal Ethics and Other Slave Moralities* [New York: Routledge, 1995], 103). Buck-Morss's work "Hegel and Haiti" is compelling because she draws attention to the paradox that opposition to slavery was a key metaphor in Western political thought at the same time that political theorists ignored the expansion of actually existing black slavery. She focuses on the historical plausibility of the connection between Hegel and Haiti rather than on the way that the *Phenomenology of Spirit* can serve as an interpretive resource. Paul Gilroy identifies similarities between the master–slave dialectic in Hegel and in slave narratives (including Douglass's) (*The Black Atlantic: Modernity and Double Consciousness* [London: Verso, 1993]), but his brief discussion overlooks the crucial fact that in Hegel's account there is never a fight between master and slave.

43. Gilroy, *The Black Atlantic*, 54.

44. According to his biographer William McFeely, in 1868 Douglass read Feuerbach, a famous Hegelian. He studied German idealism with Ottilie Assing, a friend who translated *My Bondage and My Freedom* into German. See William S. McFeely, *Frederick Douglass* (New York: Norton, 1991), 263.

45. Gilroy, *The Black Atlantic*, 60.

46. Terry Pinkard, *Hegel's* Phenomenology: *The Sociality of Reason* (Cambridge: Cambridge University Press, 1996), 46–53.

47. Hegel quoted in Allen Wood, *Hegel's Ethical Thought* (Cambridge: Cambridge University Press, 1990), 87.

48. In the German, Hegel uses both *Sklave* (slave) and *Knecht* (servant). I have followed his lead and used the two interchangeably.

49. Hegel, *Phenomenology of Spirit*, 197.

50. Wood, *Hegel's Ethical Thought*, 88.

51. Patterson, *Slavery and Social Death*. See also Jean-Paul Sartre, *Being and Nothingness: An Essay on Phenomenological Ontology* (London: Methuen, 1957).

52. Hegel, *Phenomenology of Spirit*, 116–17.

53. G. W. F. Hegel, *Elements of the Philosophy of Right,* ed. Allen W. Wood (Cambridge: Cambridge University Press), 196.

54. Judith Shklar, "Self-Sufficient Man: Dominion and Bondage," in John O'Neill, ed., *Hegel's Dialectic of Desire and Recognition: Texts and Commentary* (Albany: State University of New York Press, 1996), 189–303.

55. Buck-Morss, "Hegel and Haiti"; Eric Williams, *Capitalism and Slavery* (Chapel Hill: University of North Carolina Press, 1994).

56. Kojève, *Introduction to the Reading of Hegel,* 69, emphasis in original.

57. Jacques Derrida, *Writing and Difference,* trans. Alan Bass (Chicago: University of Chicago Press, 1978).

58. Douglass, *Bondage,* 286, emphasis in original.

59. Gilroy, *The Black Atlantic,* 63.

60. Ibid.

61. Douglass, *Bondage,* 278.

62. Ibid.

63. Ibid.

64. Douglass, *Life and Times,* 587; William L. Andrews, *To Tell a Free Story: The First Century of Afro-American Autobiography, 1760–1865* (Urbana: University of Illinois Press, 1986), 227.

65. Douglass, *Bondage,* 278.

66. Hegel, *Phenomenology of Spirit,* 117.

67. Kojève, *Introduction to the Reading of Hegel.*

68. Hegel, *Phenomenology of Spirit,* 117.

69. Ibid.

70. Ibid., 118; Kojève, *Introduction to the Reading of Hegel.*

71. One of the best recent works on Hegel is Pinkard, *Hegel's* Phenomenology. According to Pinkard, the slave who faced death "thus faces the contingency of everything, including his own deepest beliefs as to what he regarded as true. But this experience of the full contingency of everything is implicitly what puts him into the position to see the contingency of the master's dominance over him" (61). On the struggle for recognition more generally, see Axel Honneth, *The Struggle for Recognition: The Moral Grammar of Social Conflicts* (Cambridge, MA: MIT Press, 1996).

72. Douglass, *Bondage,* 182.

4

Lectures on Liberation

Angela Y. Davis

Introduction to the 1970 Pamphlet Published by the N.Y. Committee to Free Angela Davis

By UCLA Professors

Presented here are Professor Angela Davis's initial lectures for "Recurring Philosophical Themes in Black Literature," her first course at UCLA, taught during the fall quarter of 1969. At the time she was beginning a two-year appointment as acting assistant professor in philosophy, an appointment duly recommended by the Department of Philosophy and enthusiastically approved by the UCLA administration. The first of the two lectures was delivered in Royce Hall to an audience of over fifteen hundred students and interested colleagues. At the lecture's end Professor Davis was given a prolonged standing ovation by the audience. It was, we thought, a vindication of academic freedom and democratic education. For the lectures are a part of an attempt to bring to light the forbidden history of the enslavement and oppression of black people and to place that history in an illuminating philosophical context. At the same time, they are sensitive, original and incisive; the work of an excellent teacher and a truly fine scholar.

Now Professor Davis is a prisoner of the society that should have welcomed her talents, her honesty, and the contribution she was making toward understanding and resolving the most critical problem of that society—the division between its oppressors and its oppressed. First she was attacked by the regents of the University of California, who attempted to dismiss her from the university on the patently illegal ground of her membership in the Communist Party. When this attempt was overruled by the Superior Court of Los Angeles, the regents denied her the normal continuation of her appointment for a second year, in spite of recommendations from a host of review committees and the chancellor of UCLA that she be reappointed. During the summer of 1970, she was charged with kidnapping, murder, and unlawful flight to avoid prosecution and was placed on the FBI most wanted list. When apprehended, she was held on excessive bail, then denied bail, and subsequently has been kept in isolation from other prisoners.

In her first lecture Professor Davis points out that keeping an oppressed class in ignorance is one of the principal instruments of its oppression. Like Frederick Douglass, the black slave whose life and work she surveys here, Professor Davis is one of the educated oppressed. Like him, she has achieved full consciousness of what it is to be oppressed and has heightened this consciousness in her own people and in others. There can be little doubt that her effectiveness in blunting the oppressive weapon of ignorance was the chief motive for her removal from the University of California and a major motive in the harsh treatment she has since received.

These are lectures dealing with the phenomenology of oppression and liberation. It is one thing to make the elementary point that millions are still oppressed in what is advertised as the world's most free society. It is much more difficult to lay out the causes of that oppression and the ways in which it is perpetuated; its psychological meaning to the oppressor and the oppressed; the process by which the latter becomes conscious of it; and the way in which they triumph over it. This was the task Professor Davis set for herself. She brings to her work a rich philosophical background, a piercing intellect, and the knowledge born of experience.

It was perhaps inevitable that Professor Davis should become a symbol for conflicting groups and causes. But it is well to remember that behind the symbol lies the human being whose thoughts are recorded here and that when she stands trial, not only a human cause but also a human life will be tried. In the meantime, we take pride in presenting these two lectures by a distinguished colleague and friend. May they everywhere contribute to the defeat of oppression.

Signed,
Matthew Skulicz, English
Peter Orleans, Sociology
David Gillman, Mathematics
Sterling Robbins, Anthropology
Marie Brand, Nursing
J. C. Ries, Political Science
Jerome Rabow, Sociology
Donald Kalish, Philosophy
Evelyn Hatch, English
Kenneth Chapman, German
Laurence Morrissette, French
Temma Kaplan, History
Peter Ladefoged, Linguistics
D. R. Mccann, German
Robert Singleton, Business Administration
Richard Ashcraft, Political Science
John Horton, Sociology
Paul Koosis, Mathematics
Patrick Story, English
Alan E. Flanigan, Engineering
Roy L. Wolford, Medicine
Albert Schwartz, History
Wade Savage, Philosophy
Tom Robinson, Education
Barbara Partee, English
Carlos Otero, Spanish
Alex Norman, Urban Affairs
Henry McGee, School of Law
E. V. Wolfenstein, Political Science

First Lecture on Liberation

The idea of freedom has justifiably been a dominating theme in the history of Western ideas. Man has been repeatedly defined in terms of his inalienable freedom. One of the most acute paradoxes present in the history of Western society is that while on a philosophical plane freedom has been delineated in the most lofty and sublime fashion, concrete reality has always been permeated with the most brutal forms of unfreedom, of enslavement. In ancient Greece, where, so we are taught, democracy had its source, it cannot be overlooked that in spite of all the philosophical assertions of man's freedom, in spite of the demand that man realize himself through exercising his freedom as a citizen of the polis, the majority of the people in Athens were not free. Women were not citizens, and slavery was an accepted institution. Moreover, there was definitely a form of racism present in Greek society, for only Greeks were suited for the benefits of freedom: all non-Greeks were called barbarians and by their very nature could not be deserving or even capable of freedom.

In this context, one cannot fail to conjure up the image of Thomas Jefferson and the other so-called Founding Fathers formulating the noble concepts of the Constitution of the United States while their slaves were living in misery. In order not to mar the beauty of the Constitution and at the same time to protect the institution of slavery, they wrote about "persons held to service or labor," a euphemism for the word *slavery*, as being exceptional types of human beings, persons who do not merit the guarantees and rights of the Constitution.

Is man free or is he not? Ought he be free or ought not he be free? The history of Black literature provides, in my opinion, a much more illuminating account of the nature of freedom, its extent and limits, than all the philosophical discourses on this theme in the history of Western society. Why? For a number of reasons. First of all, because Black literature in this country and throughout the world projects the consciousness of a people who have been denied entrance into the real world of freedom. Black people have exposed, by their very existence, the inadequacies not only of the practice of freedom, but of its very theoretical formulation. Because if the theory of freedom remains isolated from the practice of freedom or rather is contradicted in reality, then this means that something must be wrong with the concept—that is, if we are thinking in a dialectical manner.

The pivotal theme of this course will thus be the idea of freedom as it is unfolded in the literary understanding of Black people. Starting with Frederick Douglass, we will explore the slave's experience of his bondage and thus the negative experience of freedom. Most important here will be the crucial transformation of the concept of freedom as a static, given principle into the concept of liberation, the dynamic, active struggle for freedom. We will move on to W. E. B. Du Bois, to Jean Toomer, Richard Wright, and John A. Williams. Interspersed will be poetry from the various periods of Black History in this country and theoretical analyses such as Fanon and Du Bois's *A. B. C. of Color.* Finally I would like to discuss a few pieces by African writers and poems by Nicolás Guillén, a Black Cuban poet, and compare them to the work of American Blacks.

Throughout the course, I have said, the notion of freedom will be the axis around which we will attempt to develop other philosophical concepts. We will encounter such metaphysical notions as identity, the problem of self-knowledge. The kind of philosophy of history that emerges out of the works we are studying will be crucial. The morality peculiar to an oppressed people is something we will have to come to grips with. As we progress along the path of the unfolding of freedom in Black literature, we should retrieve a whole host of related themes.

Before I get into the material, I would like to say a few words about the kinds of questions we ought to ask ourselves when we delve into the nature of human freedom. First of all, is freedom totally subjective, totally objective, or is it a synthesis of both poles? Let me try to explain what I mean. Is freedom to be conceived merely as an inherent, given characteristic of man, is it a freedom that is confined within the human mind, is freedom an internal experience? Or, on the other hand, is freedom only the liberty to move, to act in a way one chooses? Let us pose the original question as to the subjectivity or objectivity of freedom in the following manner: Is freedom the freedom of thought or the freedom of action? Or more important, is it possible to conceive of the one without the other?

This leads us directly to the problem of whether freedom is at all possible within the bounds of material bondage. Can the slave be said to be free in any way? This brings to mind one of the more notorious statements that the French existentialist Jean-Paul Sartre has made. Even the man in chains, he says, remains free, and for this reason: he is always at liberty to eliminate his condition of slavery even if this means his death. That is, his freedom is narrowly defined as the freedom to choose between his state of captivity and his death. This is extreme. But we have to decide whether or not this is the way in which we are going to define that concept. Certainly, this would not be compatible with the notion of liberation, for when the slave opts for death, he does much more than obliterate his condition of enslavement, for at the same time he is abolishing the very condition of freedom, life. Yet there is more to be said when we take the decision to die out of an abstract context and examine the dynamics of a real situation in which a slave meets his death in the fight for concrete freedom. That is to say, the choice, slavery or death, could either mean slavery or suicide or, on the other hand, slavery or liberation at all costs. The difference between the two situations is crucial.

The collective consciousness of an oppressed people entails an understanding of the conditions of oppression and the possibilities of abolishing these conditions. At the end of his journey toward understanding, the slave finds a real grasp of what freedom means. He knows that it means the destruction of the master–slave relationship. And in this sense, his knowledge of freedom is more profound than that of the master. For the master feels himself free, and he feels himself free because he is able to control the lives of others. He is free at the expense of the freedom of another. The slave experiences the freedom of the master in its true light. He understands that the master's freedom is abstract freedom to suppress other human beings. The slave understands that this is a pseudoconcept of freedom and at this point is more enlightened than his master, for he realizes that the master is a slave of his own misconceptions, his own misdeeds, his own brutality, his own effort to oppress.

Now I would like to go into the material. *Narrative of the Life of Frederick Douglass* constitutes a physical voyage from slavery to freedom that is both the conclusion and reflection of a philosophical voyage from slavery to freedom. We will see that neither voyage would have been possible alone; they are mutually determinant.

The point of departure for this voyage is the exclamation Frederick Douglass makes as a child, "O God, save me! God, deliver me! Let me be free! Is there any God? Why am I a slave? I will run away. I will not stand it. Get caught, or get clear, I'll try it. . . . It cannot be that I will live and die a slave."[1] His critical attitude when he fails to accept the usual answer—that God had made Black people to be slaves and white people to be masters—

is the basic condition that must be present before freedom can become a possibility in the mind of the slave. We must not forget that throughout the history of Western society there is an abundance of justifications for the existence of slavery. Both Plato and Aristotle felt that some men were born to be slaves, some men are not born into a state of freedom. Religious justifications for slavery are to be found at every turn.

Let's attempt to arrive at a philosophical definition of the slave. We have already stated the essence: he is a human being who, by some reason or another, is denied freedom. But is not the essence of the human being his freedom? Either the slave is not a man, or his very existence is a contradiction. We can rule out the first alternative, although we should not forget that the prevailing ideology defined the Black man as subhuman. The failure to deal with the contradictory nature of slavery, the imposed ignorance of reality is exemplified in the notion that the slave is not a man, for if he were a man, he should certainly be free.

We all know of the calculated attempts to rob the Black man of his humanity. We know that in order to maintain the institution of slavery, Black people were forced to live in conditions not fit for animals. The white slave owners were determined to mold Black people into the image of the subhuman being that they had contrived in order to justify their actions. A vicious circle emerges in which the slave owner loses all consciousness of himself.

The vicious circle continues to turn, but for the slave, there is a way out: Resistance. Frederick Douglass had one of his first experiences of this possibility of a slave becoming free upon resisting his own whipping:

Covey at length let me go, puffing and blowing at a great rate, saying that if I had not resisted, he would not have whipped me half so much. The truth was, that he had not whipped me at all. . . . This battle with Mr. Covey was the turning-point in my career as a slave. It rekindled the few expiring embers of freedom, and revived within me a sense of my own manhood. It recalled the departed self-confidence, and inspired me again with a determination to be free. The gratification afforded by the triumph was a full compensation for whatever else might follow, even death itself. He can only understand the deep satisfaction which I experienced, who has himself repelled by force the bloody arm of slavery. I felt as I never felt before. It was a glorious resurrection, from the tomb of slavery, to the heaven of freedom. My long-crushed spirit rose, cowardice departed, bold defiance took its place; and I now resolved that, however long I might remain a slave in form, the day passed forever when I could be a slave in fact. I did not hesitate to let it be known of me, that the white man who expected to succeed in whipping, must also succeed in killing me.[2]

Already we can begin to concretize the notion of freedom as it appeared to the slave. The first condition of freedom is the open act of resistance—physical resistance, violent resistance. In that act of resistance, the rudiments of freedom are already present. And the violent retaliation signifies much more than the physical act: it is refusal not only to submit to the flogging but refusal to accept the definitions of the slave master; it is implicitly a rejection of the institution of slavery, its standards, its morality, a microcosmic effort toward liberation. Douglass later wrote, "That slave who had the courage to stand up for himself against the overseer, although he might have hard stripes at first, became while legally a slave virtually a free man."[3]

The slave is actually conscious of the fact that freedom is not a fact, it is not a given, but rather something to be fought for; it can exist only through a process of struggle. The slave master, on the other hand, experiences his freedom as inalienable and thus as a fact: he is not aware that he too has been enslaved by his own system.

To begin to answer a question we posed earlier—Is it possible for a man to be in chains and at the same time be free?—we can now say that the path toward freedom can only be envisioned by the slave when he actively rejects his chains. The first phase of liberation is the decision to reject the image of himself that the slave owner has painted, to reject the conditions that the slave owner has created, to reject his own existence, to reject himself as slave.

Here the problem of freedom leads us directly into the question of identity. The condition of slavery is a condition of alienation. In a later autobiography he wrote, "Nature never intended that men and women should be either slaves or slaveholders, and nothing but rigid training long persisted in, can perfect the character of the one or the other." Slavery is an alienation from a natural condition; it is a violation of nature that distorts both parties—the slave and the slave owner. Alienation is the absence of authentic identity; in the case of the slave, he is alienated from his own freedom.

This nonidentity can exist on a number of levels: it can be unconscious—the slave accepts the master's definition, renders himself *unfree* in seeing himself as inherently unfit for freedom. Or it can be conscious; knowledge can strike a blow at it. We are most concerned with the second alternative, for it constitutes a stage in the voyage toward freedom.

The most extreme form of human alienation is the reduction to the status of property. This is how the slave was defined: something to be owned. "We were all ranked together at the valuation. Men and women, old and young, married and single, were ranked with horses, sheep, and swine. There were horses and men, cattle and women, pigs and children, all holding the same rank in the scale of being, and were all subjected to the same narrow examination. Silvery-headed age and sprightly youth, maids and matrons, had to undergo the same indelicate inspection. At this moment, I saw more clearly than ever the brutalizing effects of slavery upon both slave and slaveholder."[4]

Black people were treated as things, they were defined as objects. "The slave was a fixture," Douglass later remarked. His life must be lived within the limits of that abjectness, within the limits of the white man's definition of the Black man. Forced to live as if he were a fixture, the slave's perception of the world is inverted. Because his life is relegated to that of an object, he must forge his own humanity within those boundaries. "We had no more voice in that decision than the brutes among whom we were ranked."[5] The slave has no determination whatsoever over the external circumstances of his life. One day a woman could be living on a plantation among her children, their father—family, friends. The next day, she could be miles away with no hope of ever meeting them again. The idea of the journey loses its connotation of exploration; it loses the excitement of learning the unknown. The trip becomes a journey into hell, not away from the thingness of the slave's existence, but an even sharper accentuation of his nonhuman external existence. "A single word from the white men was enough—against all our wishes, prayers, and entreaties—to sunder forever the dearest friends, dearest kindred, and strongest ties known to human beings."[6] Frederick Douglass gives a moving account of the last days of his grandmother, who having faithfully served her master from his birth to his death, having had children and grandchildren for him, is looked upon in disdain by her then present owner—the original master's grandson. She is sent into the woods to die a solitary death.

Frederick Douglass's owner reveals to him unwittingly the path toward the consciousness of his alienation:

"If you give a nigger an inch, he will take an ell. A nigger should know nothing but to obey his master—to do as he is told to do. Learning would spoil the best nigger in the world. Now," said he, "if you teach that nigger (speaking of myself) how to read, there would be no keeping him. It would forever unfit him to be a slave. He would at once become unmanageable, and of no value to his master. As to himself, it could do him no good, but a great deal of harm. It would make him discontented and unhappy."[7]

The slave is alienated totally insofar as he accepts his master's will as the absolute authority over his life. The slave has no will, no desires, no being—his essence, his being he must find entirely in the will of his master. What does this mean? It is partly with the slave's consent that the white man is able to perpetuate slavery—when we say consent, however, it is not free consent, but consent under the most brutal force and pressure.

Frederick Douglass learns from his owner's observations precisely how he is to combat his own alienation: "I now understood what had been to me a most perplexing difficulty—to wit, the white man's power to enslave a black man. It was a grand achievement, and I prized it highly. From that moment, I understood the pathway from slavery to freedom."[8] If we look closely at the words of Frederick Douglass, we can detect the theme of resistance once again. His first concrete experience of the possibility of freedom within the limits of slavery comes when he observes a slave resist a whipping. Now he transforms this resistance into a resistance of the mind, a refusal to accept the will of the master, and a determination to find independent means of judging the world.

Just as the slave has used violence against the violence of the aggressor, Frederick Douglass uses the knowledge of his owner—i.e., that learning unfits a man to be a slave and turns it against him: he will set out to acquire knowledge precisely because it unfits a man to be a slave. Resistance, rejection, on every level, on every front, are integral elements of the voyage toward freedom. Alienation will become conscious through the process of knowledge.

In combating his ignorance, in resisting the will of his master, Frederick Douglass apprehends that all men should be free and thus deepens his knowledge of slavery, of what it means to be a slave, what it means to be the negative counterpart of freedom: "I would sometimes say to them,

I wished I could be as free as they would be when they got to be men. 'You will be free as soon as you are twenty-one, but I am a slave for life! Have not I as good a right to be free as you have?' These words used to trouble them; they would express for me the liveliest sympathy, and console me with the hope that something would occur by which I might be free. I was now about twelve years old, and the thought of being a slave for life began to bear heavily upon my heart."[9]

His alienation becomes real, it surfaces, and Frederick Douglass is going to existentially experience all that is entailed by being bound to a state of unfreedom materially, while mentally finding his way toward liberation. The tension between the subjective and the objective will eventually provide the impetus toward total liberation. But before that goal is reached, a whole series of phases must be traversed.

The slave, Frederick Douglass, thus mentally transcends his condition toward freedom. Herein lies the consciousness of alienation. He sees freedom concretely as the negation of his condition—it is present in the very air he breathes.

As I read and contemplated the subject, behold! That very discontentment which Master Hugh had predicted would follow my learning to read had already come, to torment and sting my soul to unutterable anguish. As I writhed under it, I would at times feel that learning to read had been a curse rather than a blessing. It had given me a view of my wretched condition, without the remedy. It opened my eyes to the horrible pit, but to no ladder upon which to get out. In moments of agony, I envied my fellow-slaves for their stupidity. I have often wished myself a beast. I preferred the condition of the meanest reptile to my own. Anything, no matter what, to get rid of thinking! It was this everlasting thinking of my condition that tormented me. There was no getting rid of it. It was pressed upon me by every object within sight or hearing, animate or inanimate. The silver trump of freedom had roused my soul to eternal wakefulness. Freedom now appeared, to disappear no more forever. It was heard in every sound, and seen in everything. It was ever present to torment me with a sense of my wretched condition. I saw nothing without seeing it, I heard nothing without hearing it, and felt nothing without feeling it. It looked from every star, it smiled in every calm, breathed in every wind, and moved in every storm.[10]

He has arrived at a true recognition of his condition. That recognition is at the same time the rejection of that condition. Consciousness of alienation entails the absolute refusal to accept that alienation. But the slave's predicament, by its very contradictory nature, is impossible: enlightenment does not bring happiness, nor does it bring real freedom—it brings desolation, misery, i.e., as long as the slave does not see a concrete path out of enslavement. In speaking of the slave owner's wife, Frederick Douglass says: "If I was in a separate room any considerable length of time, I was sure to be suspected of having a book, and was at once called to give an account of myself. Mistress, in teaching me the alphabet, had given me the *inch,* and no precaution could prevent me from taking the *ell.*"[11]

Moreover, it is not just his individual condition that the slave rejects, and thus his misery is not just a result of his individual unfreedom, his individual alienation. True consciousness is the rejection of the institution itself and everything that accompanies it. "It was slavery and not its mere incidents that I hated," he later wrote.[12] To foreshadow Frederick Douglass's path from slavery to freedom, even when he attains his own freedom, he does not see the real goal as having been attained. It is only with the total abolition of the *institution* of slavery that his misery, his desolation, his alienation will be eliminated. And not even then, for there will remain remnants, and there still remain in existence today the causes that gave rise to slavery.

On this road to freedom, Frederick Douglass experiences religion as a reinforcement and justification for his desire to be free. Out of the Christian doctrine, he deduces the equality of all men before God. If this is true, he infers, then slave masters must be defying the will of God by suppressing the will of human beings and should be dealt with in accordance with God's anger. Freedom, the abolition of slavery, liberation, the destruction of alienation—these notions receive a metaphysical justification and impetus through religion. A supernatural being wills the abolition of slavery: Frederick Douglass, slave and believer in God, must accomplish God's will by working toward the goal of liberation.

Douglass was not the only person to infer this from the Christian religion. Nat Turner received an important part of his inspiration from his faith in Christianity. John Brown was another example.

We all know that from the perspective of white, slave-owning society, Christianity was supposed to serve quite another function. The overriding idea behind exposing the slaves to religion was to provide a metaphysical justification not for freedom, but rather for slavery.

One of Karl Marx's more notorious statements is that religion is the opium of the people. That is—religion teaches men to be satisfied with their condition in this world—with their oppression—by directing their hopes and desires into a supernatural domain. A little suffering during a person's existence in this world means nothing compared to an eternity of bliss.

Marcuse likes to point out that we often ignore the fact that Karl Marx also said that religion is the wish-dream of an oppressed humanity. On the one hand, this statement means, of course, that wishes become dreams projected into an imaginary realm. But on the other hand, we have to ask ourselves: Is there anything else implied in Marx's statement about the notion of wish-dreams of an oppressed humanity? Think for a moment. Real wants, needs, and desires are transformed into wish-dreams via the process of religion because it seems so hopeless in this world: this is the perspective of an oppressed people. But what is important, what is crucial, is that those dreams are always on the verge of reverting to their original status—the real wishes and needs here on earth. There is always the possibility of redirecting those wish-dreams to the here-and-now.

Frederick Douglass redirected those dreams. Nat Turner placed them within the framework of the real world. So there can be a positive function of religion because its very nature is to satisfy very urgent needs of people who are oppressed. (We are speaking only of the relation of oppressed people to religion, not attempting to analyze the notion of religion in and for itself.) There can be a positive function of religion. All that need be done is to say: let's begin to create that eternity of bliss for human society here in this world. Let's convert eternity into history.

Why is it that more Black people did not shift the emphasis from the other world to concrete reality—to history? There was a calculated effort on the part of white, slave-owning society to create a special kind of religion that would serve their interests, that would serve to perpetuate the existence of slavery. Christianity was used for the purpose of brainwashing, indoctrinating, pacifying.

In his work *The Peculiar Institution,* Kenneth Stampp discusses extensively the role of religion in creating methods of appeasing Black people, of suppressing potential revolt. At first, Africans were not converted to Christianity because this may have given slaves a claim to freedom. However, the various slaveholding colonies passed laws to the effect that Black Christians would not automatically become free men by virtue of their baptism. Stampp formulates the reasons why it was finally decided to let slaves through the secret door of Christianity: "Through religious instruction, the bondman learned that slavery had divine sanction, that insolence was as much an offense against God as against the temporal master. They received the biblical command that servants should obey their masters and they heard of the punishments awaiting the disobedient slave in the hereafter. They heard, too, that eternal salvation would be their reward for faithful service and that on the day of judgment God would deal impartially with the poor and the rich, the black man and white."

Thus, those passages in the Bible that emphasized obedience, humility, pacifism, patience were presented to the slave as the essence of Christianity. Those passages, on the other hand, that talked about equality, freedom, the ones Frederick Douglass was able to discover because, unlike most slaves, he taught himself to read—these were eliminated from the sermons the slave heard. A very censored version of Christianity was developed especially for the slaves. A pious slave therefore would never hit a white man; his master was always right, even when he was by all human standards wrong. This use of religion was one of the most violent acts against humanity. It was used to teach a group of people that they were not human beings; it was used in an attempt to abolish the last remnant of identity that the slave possessed. But, in the long run, this project was not entirely successful, as can be witnessed by Frederick Douglass, Gabriel Prosser, Denmark Vesey, Nat Turner, and countless others who turned Christianity against the missionaries. The Old Testament was particularly helpful for those who planned revolts—Children of Israel were delivered out of bondage in Egypt by God—but they fought, they fought in order to carry out the will of God. Resistance was the lesson learned from the Bible. Christian spirituals created and sung by the masses of slaves were also powerful songs of freedom that demonstrate the extent to which Christianity could be rescued from the ideological context forged by the slaveholders and imbued with a revolutionary content of liberation.

Frederick Douglass's reaction to Nat Turner's revolt is revealing. In his later autobiography, *The Life and Times of Frederick Douglass*, he writes, "The insurrection of Nat Turner had been quelled, but the alarm and terror which it occasioned had not subsided. The cholera was then on its way to this country, and I remember thinking that God was angry with the white people because of their slaveholding wickedness, and therefore his judgments were abroad in the land. Of course it was impossible for me not to hope much for the abolition movement when I saw it supported by the Almighty and armed with death."

I'd like to end here by pointing to the essence of what I have been trying to get across today. The road toward freedom, the path of liberation, is marked by resistance at every crossroad: mental resistance, physical resistance, resistance directed to the concerted attempt to obstruct that path. I think we can learn from the experience of the slave. We have to debunk the myth that Black people were docile and accepting and the extreme myth, which by the way I read in my high school history texts in Birmingham, Alabama, that Black people actually preferred slavery to freedom. If you will begin to get into Frederick Douglass, at the next meeting we can try to continue our investigation into the philosophical themes of Black literature.

Second Lecture on Liberation

Before I continue the discussion of Frederick Douglass, I would like to say a few words about the course in general. Black Studies is a field that has long been neglected in the universities. We are just beginning to fill that vacuum. And we must be very careful because we do not want Black History, Black Literature, to be relegated to the same stagnant, innocuous, compartmentalized existence as, say, the history of the American Revolution. I could talk about Frederick Douglass as if he had the same relevance as, say, the so-called discovering of America by Columbus. History, Literature should not be pieces in a museum of antiquity, especially when they reveal to us problems that continue to exist today. The reasons underlying the demands for Black Studies programs are many, but the most important one is the necessity to establish a continuum from the past to the present, to discover the genesis of problems that continue to exist today, to discover how our ancestors dealt with them. We can learn from the philosophical as well as concrete experience of the slave. We can learn what methods of coming to grips with oppression were historically successful and what methods were failures. The failures are crucial because we do not want to be responsible for the repetition of history in its brutality. We learn what the mistakes were in order not to duplicate them.

We ought to approach the content in this course not as frozen facts, as static, as meaningful only in terms of understanding the past. We are talking about philosophical themes, recurring philosophical themes. Philosophy is supposed to perform the task of generalizing aspects of experience, and not just for the sake of formulating generalizations, of discovering formulas, as some of my colleagues in the discipline believe. My idea of philosophy is that if it is not relevant to human problems, if it does not tell us how we can go about eradicating some of the misery in this world, then it is not worth the name of philosophy. I think that Socrates made a very profound statement when he asserted that the raison d'être of philosophy is to teach us proper living. In this day and age "proper living" means liberation from the urgent problems of poverty, economic necessity and indoctrination, mental oppression.

Now—let me continue with the course. At our last meeting, I attempted to use the narrative of Frederick Douglass as the occasion for variations on the salient philosophical themes that we encounter in the existence of the slave. The transformation of the idea of freedom into the struggle for liberation via the concept of resistance, this sequence of interdependent themes—freedom, liberation, resistance—provides the groundwork for the course. Within this structure, we discussed last time the extent to which freedom is possible within the limits of slavery. We determined that the very existence of the slave is a contradiction: he is a man who is not a man—that is, a man who does not possess the essential attribute of humanity: freedom. White, slaveholding society defines him as an object, as an animal, as property. The alienation that is thereby produced as the reality of the slave's existence must surface—it must become conscious, if he is to forge a path toward liberation. He must recognize at first the contradictory nature of his existence, and out of the recognition, rejection emerges. We saw that recognition of alienation becomes a prerequisite of and entails rejection, resistance. Religion can play both a positive and a negative role in that road toward self-knowledge. It can thwart liberation—and this is the express purpose for converting the slave—or it can provide powerful assistance, as was the case in Frederick Douglass's first experience of religion.

I'd like to begin today by continuing that discussion of religion. Now, we will discover that Frederick Douglass's interest in and enthusiasm about religion wanes when he apprehends the hypocrisy that accompanied it in the thoughts and actions of the slaveholder. It is important to recognize that the transition from spiritual elevation to disillusionment is ushered in by an actual physical change in the conditions of Frederick Douglass, slave. During the time he developed fervent inclinations toward Christianity as a result of his learning to read, he lived in relatively comfortable circumstances—that is, if anything can be termed comfortable under slavery. His disenchantment occurs when he is forced to live under conditions of actual starvation—when he is given to Captain Thomas Auld.

A critical experience occurs when he observes his brutal and sadistic slave master's conversion to Christianity: "I indulged a faint hope that his conversion would lead him to emancipate his slaves, and that, if he did not do this, it would, at any rate, make him more kind and humane. I was disappointed in both these respects. It neither made him to be humane to his slaves, nor to emancipate them. If it had any effect on his character, it made him more cruel and hateful in all his ways; for I believe him to have been a much worse man after his conversion than before."[13]

These philosophical inferences from what Douglass took to be the essence of Christianity—the demonstration of Christian thoughts by Christian deeds—are refuted by the master's subsequent conduct. For the oppressed, for the slave, religion serves a quite positive purpose: it is a much needed medicine that helps to allay suffering, and at the same time it is an inverted consciousness of the world, projection of real needs and desires into supernatural domain. The slaveholder's experience of religion as it is exemplified in the behavior of Captain Auld has an entirely different texture. Religion, for him, is pure ideology that is totally contradictory to his real, day-to-day behavior. The slaveholder must constantly work to maintain that contradiction; his very existence is based on the rigid separation of his real life from his spiritual life. For if he takes the precepts of Christianity seriously, if he applies them to his daily life, then he would negate his own existence as an oppressor of humanity. Douglass explains: "Prior to his conversion, [Auld] relied upon his own depravity to shield and sustain him in his savage barbarity; but after his conversion, he found religious sanction and support for his slaveholding cruelty."[14]

At least on an unconscious level, there must be some awareness of these contradictions in the mind of the slaveholder. This is indicated by an actual sharpening of the contradictions by Auld himself. The more intense his religious involvement becomes, the more intense becomes his cruelty toward his slaves. An unrelatedness between his religious life and his real life becomes a predictable discontinuity. His increased practice of religion seems to be both an excuse and an expiation before the fact of his increased perpetration of misery among his slaves. Long and loud prayers and hymns justify long and hard flogging, justify outright starvation of the slaves.

What can we infer from this analysis of the slaveholder's relation to religion? As I stated in the last lecture, Western society and particularly the era of the rule of the bourgeoisie have been characterized by the gap between theory and practice, particularly between freedom as it is developed conceptually and the lack of freedom in the real world.

The fact that somewhere in one of the foundational documents of this country there is the statement that all men are created equal, and the fact that social and political inequality have never been eradicated cannot be regarded as unrelated to the relative nonchalance with which Master Auld discusses the gap between his religious ideas and his day-to-day precepts. The slaveholder's own words reveal to us the brutality that underlies not only his particular situation but that of society in general. We sometimes have to resort to the most extreme examples in order to uncover veiled meanings of the more subtle example.

Frederick Douglass's recognition of the contradictions between religious ideas and the behavior of his master brings him to a critical disposition toward the relevance of religion itself: "I assert most unhesitatingly, that the religion of the south is a mere covering for the most horrid crimes,—a justifier of the most appalling barbarity,—a sanctifier of the most hateful frauds,—and a dark shelter under which the darkest, foulest, grossest, and most infernal deeds of slaveholders find the strongest protection. Were I to be again reduced to the chains of slavery, next to that enslavement, I should regard being the slave of a religious master the greatest calamity that could befall me."[15]

Last time we pointed to Marx's interpretation of the role that religion plays in the society. I would like to point to some further observations he makes concerning religion in the *Contribution to the Critique of Hegel's Philosophy of Right*. I think that Marx's analysis of religion helps us to understand the state of Frederick Douglass when he begins to turn away from religion. I quote a passage from that work: "*Religious* suffering is at the same time an expression of real suffering and a *protest* against real suffering. Religion is the sigh of the oppressed creature, the sentiment of a heartless world, and the soul of soulless conditions. It is the opium of the people.

The abolition of religion as the illusory happiness of men, is a demand for their *real* happiness. The call to abandon their illusions about their condition is a *call to abandon a condition which requires illusions.*"

Frederick Douglass existentially experiences what Marx theoretically formulates. He sees through the veil of illusion in observing the rather schizophrenic behavior of his master relative to his religion and his daily life. It is not insignificant that this enlightenment emerges, as I have indicated before, at a time when his physical suffering becomes practically unbearable. We can infer that in seeing through the hypocrisy of his master, he attains a certain self-consciousness, self-knowledge. The master becomes a mirror of his own past escape. Situated in relative comfort, he had the luxury to think in metaphysical categories. Now he must come face to face with the absolute necessity to eradicate, to destroy his suffering. "Religion," Marx says, "is only the illusory sun about which man revolves so long as he does not revolve about himself."

Frederick Douglass gathers the courage to resist the slave breaker to whom he is sent for domestication, for taming—the slave breaker who is infinitely more brutal than any of his previous masters. He finds this courage when he is able to free himself of his religion. "I love the pure, peaceable, and impartial Christianity of Christ: I therefore hate the corrupt, slaveholding, women-whipping, cradle-plundering, partial and hypocritical Christianity of this land. Indeed, I can see no reason, but the most deceitful one, for calling the religion of this land Christianity."[16]

So we find that the role of religion during the era of slavery is not homogenous: it is extremely complex. The function of religion continually reverts from one extreme to the other. No one formula can suffice. If we saw at the last meeting that religion can play a positive role, now we are uncovering the detrimental aspects, how it suppressed the slave in the person of the slaveholder, how it provided internal control, and thus how it must often be transcended in order for real change to take place. Religious leaders of slave revolts found inspiration in religion; they found courage in it. Frederick Douglass, at this point in his life, as well as countless other people saw the necessity to cancel out illusions in order to transform the real world, in order to arrive at a total commitment to resist oppression.

I concur with Marx that one must overcome religion in order to regain one's reason, that the sigh of the oppressed creature in order to become an effective protest against oppression, must be articulated and acted upon in a political context. Yet I do not deny that to a certain extent the illusory nature of religion may well be transcended within the limits of religion— I gave Nat Turner, Denmark Vesey, Gabriel Prosser as examples last time. By the way, someone brought to my attention that I did not mention any women among these examples. I was not on my toes. The accomplishments of Harriet Tubman, Sojourner Truth, and many others can never be overestimated.

I would like to leave the discussion of religion now—perhaps we will take it up again at a further point in the life of Frederick Douglass. I would like to continue to develop the notion of alienation and how the slave experiences the world and history. We said that the extreme formulation of the slave's alienation is his existence as property, as capital, as money. There is a relatively long quotation from Douglass's later work, *The Life and Times of Frederick Douglass,* that I would like to take the time to read because I feel it epitomizes by its very concreteness the notion of alienation.

I am, thought I, but the sport of a power which makes no account either of my welfare or of my happiness. By a law which I can comprehend, but cannot evade or resist, I am ruthlessly snatched away from the hearth of a fond grandmother and hurried away to the home of a mysterious old master; again I am removed from there to a master in Baltimore; thence am I snatched away to the Eastern Shore to be valued with the beasts of the field, and with them divided and set apart for a possessor; then I am sent back to Baltimore, and by the time I have formed new attachments and have begun to hope that no more rude shocks shall touch me, a difference arises between brothers, and I am again broken up and sent to St. Michaels; and now from the latter place I am footing my way to the home of another master, where, I am given to understand, like a wild young working animal I am to be broken to the yoke of a bitter and lifelong bondage.

For the slave, the world appears as a hostile network of circumstances that continually are to his disadvantage. History is experienced as a cluster of chance events, accidental occurrences that, though far beyond his control, act in a way that is usually detrimental to his personal life. A trivial quarrel between brothers is enough to wreak and mutilate the slave's life—Frederick Douglass is brought back to the plantation of his real owner, one who is infinitely more sadistic than the brother with whom he had been living, as a result of such a banal disagreement.

Yesterday one of the white students in the class came to my office and wanted to know how I was going to conduct the course. He asked whether or not I was going to limit the course to the philosophical experiences of the slave, of the Black man in society, or whether I was going to talk about *people*. Now, aside from the fact that slaves and Black people are people, there is something in my mind that I think you should be aware of—and it is not unrelated to what I was just saying about alienation. Oppressed people are forced to come to grips with immediate problems every day, problems that have a philosophical status and are relevant to all people. One such problem is that of alienation. It is my opinion that most people living in Western society today are alienated, alienated from themselves, from society. To provide an objective demonstration of this would require some discussion, and if you like, we can take this up in one of the discussion periods. The point is that the slave, the Black man, the Chicano, and oppressed whites are much more aware of alienation, perhaps not as a philosophical concept, but as a fact of their daily existence. The slave, for example, experiences that alienation as the continual hostility of all his daily surroundings. During the era of slavery, I suppose it was common opinion that the slave was in bondage and the white man was free, the Black man was non- or subhuman and the white man was the apex of humanity. Again, let us take a look at the extreme example of the white man in slaveholding society—the slave breaker. There is something that I think we might call the concept of the slave breaker, and we can unfold this concept according to the concrete behavior of Covey, the Negro breaker under whose authority Frederick Douglass lives for a year.

Now, what do we mean by the concept of the slave breaker? His existence is the sine qua non of slavery, an indispensable fact for the perpetuation of slavery. At the same time, the slave breaker finds himself almost on the margin of slavery, the last barrier between physical enslavement and physical liberation. He is the one designated to tame impudent slaves, slaves who refuse to accept for themselves the definition that society has imposed upon them. He must break, destroy the human being in the slave before it succeeds in upsetting the whole balance present in the system of slavery. His instrument is violence. He does violence to the body in order to break the will. Not only continual whipping but work, labor not fit for a beast of burden, were the manifestations of that violence.

Just as I got into the woods, he came up and told me to stop my cart, and that he would teach me how to trifle away my time, and break gates. He then went to a large gum-tree, and with his axe cut three large switches, and, after trimming them up neatly with his pocket-knife, he ordered me to take off my clothes. I made him no answer, but stood with my clothes on. He repeated his order. I still made him no answer, nor did I move to strip myself. Upon this he rushed at me with the fierceness of a tiger, tore off my clothes, and lashed me till he had worn out his switches, cutting me so savagely as to leave the marks visible for a long time after. This whipping was the first of a number just like it, and for similar offences. I lived with Mr. Covey one year. During that first six months, of that year, scarce a week passed without his whipping me. I was seldom free from a sore back. My awkwardness was almost always his excuse for whipping me. We were worked fully up to the point of endurance. Long before day we were up, our horses fed, and by the first approach of day we were off to the field with our hoes and ploughing teams. Mr. Covey gave us enough to eat, but scarce time to eat it. We were often less than five minutes taking our meals. We were often in the field from the first approach of day till its last lingering ray had left us; and at saving-fodder time, midnight often caught us in the field binding blades.[17]

One of the lessons we can learn from the dialectical method is that in the process of functioning in the world, man undergoes changes himself that are consonant with his actions. That is, man cannot perform a task in the world without himself being affected by that performance. Now, what does this mean for Covey, the Negro breaker? His task is to mutilate the humanity of the slave. The question we must ask ourselves is whether he can perform that task without mutilating his own humanity. We ought to be able to infer, from the answer to this question, what happened to the humanity of the white man in general during the era of slavery.

We don't have to engage in any unnecessary philosophizing in order to answer that question. Frederick Douglass says it outright; he calls the slave breaker by his name.

There was no deceiving him. His work went on in his absence almost as well as in his presence; and he had the faculty of making us feel that he was ever present with us. This he did by surprising us. He seldom approached the spot where we were at work openly, if he could do it secretly. He always aimed at taking us by surprise. Such was his cunning, that we used to call him, among ourselves, "the snake." When we were at work in the cornfield, he would sometimes crawl on his hands and knees to avoid detection, and all at once he would rise nearly in our midst, and scream out. . . . His comings were like a thief in the night. He appeared to us as being ever at hand. He was under every tree, behind every stump, in every bush, and at every window, on the plantation.[18]

Who is the nonhuman here? Who lowers himself to the depths? Aside from the biblical imagery of the serpent as the representative of evil, the image of the snake, his very posture, crawling around on the ground, is symbolic and revealing. In order to induce the slaves to labor, the slave breaker lies; he is forced to lie, he is inhuman and is forced to be inhuman. He takes on the characteristics of the very task he sees himself as performing. I would go so far as to say that he is even more profoundly affected than the slave, for the slave can see what is occurring—he is aware of the fact that there is an external power dedicated to the suppression of the slave's basic human existence. He sees it, feels it, hears it in every act of the slave breaker.

The slave breaker on the other hand is unaware of the change he himself is undergoing as a result of his sadistic actions: "Mr. Covey's *forte* consisted in his power to deceive. His life was devoted to planning and perpetrating the grossest deceptions. Everything he possessed in the shape of learning or religion, he made conform to his disposition to deceive. He seemed to think himself equal to deceive the Almighty."[19]

This tendency toward unconscious self-annihilation was not confined to the slave breaker, to those who stood at the boundaries of slavery in order to maintain those boundaries. These characteristics were direct results of the system itself and could be attributed to slaveholders in general. As Douglass would later write, "Mean and contemptible as all this is, it is in keeping with the character which the life of a slaveholder was calculated to produce."[20]

And in referring to the naturalness of Mr. Covey's trickery and inclination to lie, Frederick Douglass later wrote, "It was an important system essential to the relation of master and slave."[21]

Let's continue to discuss this relation of master and slave and its effects on the master. As we were saying, the master is thought to be free, independent; the slave is thought to be unfree, dependent. The freedom and independence of the master, if we look at it philosophically, is a myth. It is one of those myths that, I was saying at the last session, we have to uncover in order to reach the real substance behind it. How could the master have been independent when it is the very institution of slavery that provided his wealth, that provided his means of sustenance? The master was dependent on the slave, dependent for his life on the slave.

In the *Phenomenology of Mind,* Hegel discusses the dialectical relationship between the slave and the master. He states, among other things, that the master, in reaching a consciousness of his own condition, must become aware that his very independence is based on his dependence on the slave. This might sound a bit contradictory, but then dialectics is based on discovering the contradictions in phenomena that can alone account for their existence. Reality is permeated through and through with contradictions. Without those contradictions, there would be no movement, no process, no activity. I don't want to go off on a theoretical tangent about dialectics, so let us get back to the slave and the master and see the dialectical relationship as it is actually practiced in reality. The independence of the master, we were saying, is based on his dependence on the slave. If the slave were not there to till the land, to build his estates, to serve him his meals, the master would not be free from the necessities of life. If he had to do all the things that the slave does for him, he would be just as much in a state of bondage as the slave. Only, the slave is the buffer zone, and in this sense the slave is somewhat of a master—it is the slave who possesses the power over the life of the master: if he does not work, when he ceases to follow orders, the master's means of sustaining himself has disappeared.

So, at this point we can make the following statement—and I hope it is clear. The master is always on the verge of becoming the slave, and the slave possesses the real, concrete power to make him always on the verge of becoming the master.

I don't want this to sound like a whole lot of philosophical word games. Sometimes, when one reads Hegel, one has the impression that this is what he is doing—playing with our minds: things are themselves, but they are constantly becoming other than themselves, they are constantly becoming their own contradictions.

I think I can demonstrate the truth of the proposition that the master is always on the verge of becoming the slave and the slave is always on the verge of becoming the master. Let's look at what I think is the most crucial passage in the *Narrative of the Life of Frederick Douglass.* It can be found in chapter 10. Frederick Douglass has just had the harrowing experience of being driven to work until the point when he physically collapses. At this point he has been broken—mentally his will is gone. Covey, refusing to accept his illness as a valid excuse for failure to continue, beats him while he is lying on the ground unable to move. Frederick Douglass decides to return to his master but, finding no form of compassion in the reaction of his master, returns. Fortunately, it is on a Sunday when he finally reaches the slave breaker's house, and because of his devoutness Mr. Covey does not beat him—or, as Sandy, a slave who has helped Frederick Douglass would like us to believe, Mr. Covey does not beat him as a result of the magical powers of a root that he has given to him. At any rate, the slave breaker does not enter into the person of Mr. Covey until after the Sabbath is over. Instinctively, unconsciously, Frederick Douglass fights back when the slave breaker attempts to beat him: "Mr. Covey seemed now to think he had me, and could do what he pleased; but at this moment—from whence came the spirit I don't know—I resolved to fight; and, suiting my action to the resolution, I seized Covey hard by the throat; and as I did so, I rose."[22]

What is the reaction of Mr. Covey? One would think that because, after all, he is the master, he is white, he would have no problems conquering a sixteen-year-old boy. The slave breaker, who has the reputation of being able to tame the wild-animal slaves from all around, trembles and calls for help: "Covey at length let me go, puffing and blowing at a great rate, saying that if I had not resisted, he would not have whipped me half so much. The truth was, that he had not whipped me at all."[23] He unsuccessfully calls upon a slave who is not under his authority for aid. He eventually attempts to command his own slave, a woman, to conquer Frederick. She refuses, and he is left helpless.

We have to ask ourselves what is happening here. Covey is certainly physically strong enough to overpower Frederick. Why is he unable to cope with that unexpected resistance? That act of open resistance challenges his very identity. He is no longer the recognized master; the slave no longer recognizes himself as slave. The roles have been reversed. And think about this as a concrete example of that proposition I put forth earlier—that the master is always on the verge of becoming the slave, and the slave is always

on the verge of becoming the master. Here, it has happened. Covey implicitly recognizes the fact that he is dependent on the slave not only in a material sense, not only for the production of wealth, but also for the affirmation
of his own identity. The fact that he appeals to all the slaves around him to
help him overpower Frederick indicates that he is dependent on that affirmation of his authority—they all reject it, and he is left in a vacuum—alienated from himself. This has the effect of sapping whatever physical strength
he may have needed in order to win the battle.

After having obviously lost the battle, with no substantial basis for his own
identity, his own role, he nonetheless attempts to reassert his authority: "Covey
at length let me go, puffing and blowing at a great rate, saying that if I had not
resisted, he would not have whipped me half so much. The truth was, that he
had not whipped me at all. I considered him as getting entirely the worst end
of the bargain; for he had drawn no blood from me, but I had from him."[24]

Covey never again attempted to whip him. Frederick Douglass describes this incident as the turning point in his life as a slave.

Notes

Previously published as Angela Y. Davis, "Lectures on Liberation" from *Narrative
of the Life of Frederick Douglass, an American Slave, Written by Himself: A New
Critical Edition* edited by Angela Y. Davis. Copyright © 2010 by Angela Y. Davis.
Reprinted with the permission of The Permissions Company, Inc., on behalf of
City Lights Books, www.citylights.com.

1. The original lecture quoted from *Life and Times of Frederick Douglass*: "O
God, save me! God, deliver me! Let me be free! Is there any God? Why am I a
slave?" [*Volume editor's note:* The notes given in this chapter were inserted by the
publisher, City Lights, in Davis's critical edition of *Narrative,* and they are silently
amended here for clarity.]

2. The original lecture quoted from *Life and Times:* "That slave who had the
courage to stand up for himself against the overseer, although he might have many
hard stripes at first, became while legally a slave virtually a free man. 'You can
shoot me,' said a slave to Rigby Hopkins, 'but you can't whip me,' and the result was
he was neither whipped nor shot."

3. From *Life and Times*.

4. The original lecture quoted from *Life and Times:* "Personality swallowed up
in the sordid idea of property! Manhood lost in chattelhood! . . . Our destiny was

to be fixed for life, and we had no more voice in the decision of the question than the oxen and cows that stood chewing at the haymow."

5. The original lecture quoted from *Life and Times:* "He had no choice, no goal, but was pegged down to one single spot, and must take root there or nowhere."

6. The original lecture quoted from *Life and Times:* "His going out into the world was like a living man going out of sight and hearing of wife, children, and friends of kindred tie."

7. The original lecture quoted from *Life and Times:* "'If you give a nigger an inch he will take an ell. Learning will spoil the best nigger in the world. If he learns to read the Bible it will forever unfit him to be a slave. He should know nothing but the will of his master, and learn to obey it.'"

8. The original lecture quoted from *Life and Times:* "'Very well,' thought I. 'Knowledge unfits a child to be a slave.' I instinctively assented to the proposition, and from that moment I understood the direct pathway from slavery to freedom."

9. The original lecture quoted from *Life and Times:* "When I was about thirteen years old, and had succeeded in learning to read, every increase of knowledge, especially anything respecting the free states, was an additional weight to the most intolerable burden of my thought—'I am a slave for life.' To my bondage I could see no end. It was a terrible reality, and I shall never be able to tell how sadly that thought chafed my young spirit."

10. The original lecture quoted from *Life and Times:* "Liberty, as the inestimable birthright of every man, converted every object into an asserter of this right. I heard it in every sound, and saw it in every object. It was ever present to torment me with a sense of my wretchedness, the more horrible and desolate was my condition. I saw nothing without seeing it, and I heard nothing without hearing it. I do not exaggerate when I say that it looked at me in every star, smiled in every calm, breathed in every wind and moved in every storm."

11. The original lecture quoted from *Life and Times:* "She aimed to keep me ignorant, and I resolved to know, although knowledge only increased my misery."

12. Quoted from *Life and Times.*

13. The original lecture quoted from *Life and Times:* "If he has got religion, thought I, he will emancipate the slaves. . . . Appealing to my own religious experience, and judging my master by what was true in my own case, I could not regard him as soundly converted, unless some such good results followed his profession of religion."

14. The original lecture quoted from *Life and Times:* "I will teach you, young man, that though I have parted with my sins, I have not parted with my sense. I shall hold my slaves and go to heaven, too."

15. The original lecture quoted from *Life and Times:* "Captain Auld could pray, I would fain pray; but doubts arising, partly from the sham religion which

everywhere prevailed, there was awakened in my mind a distrust of all religion and the conviction that prayers were unavailing and delusive."

16. [*Volume editor's note:* Davis cites this passage in the appendix to the *Narrative.*]

17. The original lecture quoted from *Life and Times:* "I was whipped, either with sticks or cowskins, every week. Aching bones and a sore back were my constant companions. Frequently as the lash was used, Mr. Covey thought less of it as a means of breaking down my spirit than that of hard and continued labor. He worked me steadily up to the point of my powers of endurance. From the dawn of day in the morning till the darkness was complete in the evening, I was kept hard at work in the fields or the woods."

18. The original lecture quoted from *Life and Times:* "His plan was never to approach in an open, manly and direct manner the spot where his hands were at work. No thief was ever more artful in his devices than this man Covey. He would creep and crawl in ditches and gullies, hide behind stumps and bushes, and practice so much of the cunning of the serpent, that Bill Smith and I, between ourselves, never called him by any other name than 'the snake.'"

19. The original lecture quoted from the *Life and Times:* "With Mr. Covey, trickery was natural. Everything in the shape of learning or religion which he possessed was made to conform to the semi-lying propensity. He did not seem conscious that the practice had anything unmanly, base or contemptible about it."

20. From *Life and Times.*

21. From *Life and Times.*

22. The original lecture quoted from *Life and Times:* "I do not know; at any rate, I was resolved to fight, and what was better still, I actually was hard at it. The fighting madness had come upon me, and I found my strong fingers firmly attached to the throat of the tyrant, as heedless of consequences, at that very moment, as if we stood as equals before the law. The very color of the man was forgotten."

23. The original lecture quoted from *Life and Times:* "He was frightened, and stood puffing, and blowing, seemingly unable to command words or blows."

24. The original lecture quoted from *Life and Times:* "'Now, you scoundrel, go to your work; I would not have whipped you half so hard if you had not resisted.' . . . The fact was, he had not whipped me at all. He had not, in all the scuffle, drawn a single drop of blood from me. I had drawn blood."

5

Douglass's Declarations of Independence and Practices of Politics

Robert Gooding-Williams

Hereditary bondsmen! Know ye not
Who would be free themselves must strike the blow?
　　—George Gordon, Lord Byron, *Childe
　　　　Harold's Pilgrimage*

Frederick Douglass one day hits back, he fights the slave-breaker with all his force, and the slave-breaker does not hit back; he stands trembling; he calls other slaves to help, and they refuse. The abstract philosophical concept of a freedom which can never be taken away suddenly comes to life and reveals its very concrete truth: freedom is not only the goal of liberation, it *begins* with liberation; it is there to be "practiced." This, I confess, I learned from you.

　　　　—Herbert Marcuse to Angela Davis

During the nineteenth century, African American political theorists time and again found reason to cite the lines appearing as the first epigraph to this chapter. Henry Highland Garnet invoked them in his incendiary

"Address to the Slaves of the United States" (1843), as did Martin R. Delany in his political novel *Blake; or, The Huts of America* (1861–1862). Frederick Douglass quoted them thrice: first in his short story "The Heroic Slave" (1853) and then again in two autobiographies, *My Bondage and My Freedom* (1855) and the *Life and Times of Frederick Douglass* (1881, 1892).[1] When, then, Du Bois adduced these lines as one of the epigraphs to "Of Mr. Booker T. Washington and Others," the third chapter of *Souls*, he was re-citing a text with a notable history in black political thought. Significantly, Du Bois's re-citation of Byron's militant exhortation prefaces and pairs it with a second epigraph drawn from the same poem: "From birth till death enslaved; in word, in deed, unmanned."[2] The two epigraphs present a stark choice: emasculating submission to slavery or insurrection. By counterposing the two options, Du Bois prefigures the chapter that follows, anticipating his critique of Washington's politics of unmanly submission and his expression of enthusiasm for the spirit that would "strike the blow."[3]

For Du Bois, Frederick Douglass was the preeminent representative of that spirit (the third chapter of *Souls* mentions neither Delany nor Garnet). Reserving his highest praise for Douglass's political leadership, Du Bois writes that

> after the war and emancipation, the great form of Frederick Douglass, the greatest of American Negro leaders, still led the host. Self assertion, especially in political lines, was the main programme. . . . Douglass, in his old age, still bravely stood for the ideals of his early manhood,— ultimate assimilation *through* self assertion, and on no other terms.[4]

The sentences quoted here include the only explicit references to Douglass in a chapter otherwise devoted to Booker T. Washington. And yet the spirit of Douglass, as Du Bois construes it, persistently haunts that chapter, so much so that we would be no less justified in reading it as an elegiac response to Douglass's passing than we have been in treating it as a forceful attack on the Wizard of Tuskegee. Du Bois, we know, wrote a series of elegies after hearing of Douglass's death. Chapter 3 of *Souls*, I am suggesting, was an addition to that series.

Three considerations argue for interpreting chapter 3 as a prose poem of lamentation. One pertains to the chapter's third epigraph (the first and second epigraphs having been provided by Byron), which comprises two lines of music drawn from the slave song "A Great Camp-meetin' in de Promised Land."[5] Specifically, this epigraph exhibits six and a half measures of treble clef music that "A Great Camp-meetin'" introduces to sound the theme of grief expressed in its first stanza choral lyrics—"Gwine to mourn an' nebber tire / Mourn an' nebber tire / Mourn an' nebber tire,"[6]—and that Du Bois has now introduced, arguably, to resound the same theme. The second consideration is that the chapter's first paragraph ties the "ascendancy of Mr. Booker T. Washington" to "the passing" of "war memories and ideals," thus suggesting that its mournful musical epigraph be heard as the death knell for the Civil War's grip on the American Negro's historical consciousness post-Reconstruction ("since 1876"), a finality that may well have been necessary for Washington's "leading" to begin.[7]

Chapter 3 also ties Washington's ascendancy to the passing of Frederick Douglass, for it precisely if tacitly relates that ascendancy to Douglass's demise in its final paragraph:

The black men of American have a duty to perform, a duty stern and delicate,—a forward movement to oppose a part of the work of their greatest leader. So far as Mr. Washington preaches Thrift, Patience, and Industrial Training for the masses, we must hold up his hands and strive with him, rejoicing in his honors and glorying in the strength of this Joshua called of God and of man to lead the headless host. But so far as Mr. Washington apologizes for injustice, North or South, does not rightly value the privilege and duty of voting, belittles the emasculating effects of caste distinctions, and opposes the higher training and ambition of our brighter minds,—so far as he, the South, or the Nation, does this,—we must unceasingly and firmly oppose them. By every civilized and peaceful method we must strive for the rights which the world accords to men, clinging unwaveringly to those great words which the sons of the Fathers would fain forget: "We hold these truths to be self-evident: That all men are created equal: that they are endowed by their Creator with certain unalienable rights; that among these are life, liberty, and the pursuit of happiness."[8]

A third reason, then, to read chapter 3 as prose elegy is Du Bois's subtle, analogical application of the story of Exodus to African American history and, specifically, to describe Washington's emergence as a political leader.[9] Du

Bois introduces the Exodus analogy in chapter 1 ("Of Our Spiritual Striv-
ings"), when he writes that forty years after emancipation "the Nation has
not yet found peace from its sins; the freedman has not yet found in freedom his promised land."[10] Twice more he draws on the figure of Canaan in
chapter 1 and then extends the analogy in the next chapter ("Of the Dawn
of Freedom") with a reference to the King's Highway, a road along which
the Israelites sought to travel on their way to the Promised Land.[11] In chapter 3, the portrait of Washington as a "Joshua called . . . to lead the headless
host" yet again invokes the Exodus tale and recalls the earlier allusion to
Douglass, "the greatest of American Negro leaders, [who] still led the host"
after the war and emancipation. Imagining Washington as Joshua, Du Bois
suggests that Douglass was the black Moses who previously led the host and
whose demise left the host headless. Having led his people out of the Egypt
of American slavery, Douglass, like Moses, died without leading them into
the Promised Land (for Du Bois, the promised land of assimilation). Called
to succeed Douglass, Washington, like Joshua, takes the place of his people's greatest leader (and, with Douglass gone, is now himself "their greatest
leader"), although his critics, Du Bois says, do not expect that in the manner
of Joshua fighting the battle of Jericho he will cause "the bias and prejudices
of years [to] disappear at the blast of a trumpet."[12] Du Bois discerns virtue
in Washington's politics but opposes it where it departs from the politics of
self-assertion that he sees as Douglass's legacy. When Du Bois complains
that Washington apologizes for injustice, does not rightly value the privilege
of voting, and so forth, he laments that Douglass is dead and that Washington has failed to preserve his spirit. Du Bois now mourns, but he "nebber
tires," for when he forcefully insists that "the black men of America" cling
to the words of the Declaration of Independence—"which the sons of the
Fathers would fain forget"—he echoes Douglass's famous July 5, 1852, exhortation to the sons of the Fathers to *"Cling to this day* [July 4] . . . and to
its principles."[13] Depicting himself as Douglass's remindful son and rightful
heir, Du Bois plays the trump of the countersublime, thereby prefiguring
his portrait of Alexander Crummell: aligning himself with the "the great
form" of Douglass, he suggests that Washington's politics, whatever its virtues, is but a diminished version of the politics that he, following Douglass,
embraces.

    In the introduction [to *In the Shadow of Du Bois*], I suggested several
reasons for bringing Douglass's *Bondage* into conversation with Du Bois's

Souls. One was to complicate our understanding of the history of African American political thought by interrogating Du Bois's reliance on Douglass's authority to promote his critique of Washington. When Du Bois affiliates himself with Douglass, he elides elements of Douglass's treatment of black politics that set it apart from the politics of expressive self-realization. For example, "Of Mr. Booker T. Washington and Others" lumps all opponents to separatism under the rubric of "assimilationism" and represents Du Bois and Douglass alike as assimilationists. Yet *Bondage* and in fact the July 5 speech present a Douglass who, if not a separatist, is certainly not an assimilationist in Du Bois's sense. *Bondage* evinces a Douglass whom I interpret as a radical reconstructionist *avant la lettre:* as a political theorist who thinks the possibility of refounding the Union on the basis of a reconstituted practice of citizenship. In the present chapter, then, I examine some underappreciated features of this Douglass's political thought, which differs in more than one way from the politics of expressive self-realization.

Another reason for bringing *Bondage* into conversation with *Souls,* I suggested, was to provide a critical perspective on the key claims supporting Du Bois's defense of a politics of expressive self-realization—a politics that is rule- and ruler-centered, expressivist, and predicated on an anomaly theory of white supremacy. In sharp contrast to *Souls, Bondage* sketches a picture of black politics that rejects the ruler model of leadership (which, ironically, Du Bois applies to Douglass when he figures him as a black Moses); is not expressivist; and regards white supremacy as a nonanomalous form of domination. By here elucidating that picture, I establish terms for putting into question Du Bois's key claims. (In the chapter that follows [in *In the Shadow of Du Bois*], I rely on and extend those terms to reconstruct and evaluate recent and contemporary debates about black politics in postsegregation America.)

While I focus here on *Bondage,* I do not claim that Douglass's second autobiography represents the substance of his thought as a whole or that it captures his "basic philosophy" as it evolves over the course of his long and complicated intellectual career.[14] *Bondage* is a unique contribution to Douglass's oeuvre. Comparing it with the other autobiographies, I agree with those scholars who have contrasted it to the 1845 *Narrative of the Life of Frederick Douglass* and would only add that it is equally easy to contrast it to the later *Life and Times.* Douglass's second autobiography exhibits a communitarian sensibility largely missing from the *Narrative,* while his third telling of his life's story—particularly in parts not already appearing in *Bondage*—through its emphases on the self-made man and economic self-help, recoups the *Narrative*'s individualism and suggests a stronger kinship with Booker T. Washington than is evident either in *Bondage* or in Du Bois's representation of Douglass in *Souls*.[15] And here, too, we should note that *Life and Times,* while it incorporates most of *Bondage,* likewise excises the book's preface and its appendix—including, for example, "The Nature of Slavery" and two excerpts from "What to the Slave Is the Fourth of July?"—which give *Bondage*'s readers reason to read it as a political theory of bondage and freedom and not simply as autobiography.[16] In a related vein, *Bondage* may also be compared to Douglass's nonautobiographical speeches and writings and with a similar result: despite the continuities that tempt us to seek out the overriding unity in Douglass's speech and writings, we notice that more than one mind, more than one voice, animate his intellectual career. For my purposes, then, *Bondage* is significant not because it illumines the ultimate integrity of Douglass's thought over the course of his lifetime, but because it uncovers often forgotten or unheeded conceptual possibilities for theorizing, with critical reference to Du Bois, the prospects for black politics in the postsegregation era.

It may be argued that Du Bois himself is a better resource than Douglass for thinking through these options. Or, to put the point somewhat differently, that Du Bois no more than Douglass was of one mind and that the later Marxist, Freudian Du Bois, can help to illuminate the limitations of the early Du Bois's thought better than Douglass. It is true that Du Bois's intellectual development is complex and differentiated. But with regard to two of the three questions in light of which I have been interrogating his early political theory, the "mature" Du Bois fails unambiguously to distinguish himself from the author of *Souls*. To be specific, Du Bois maintains his adherence to a rule-centered notion of political leadership well beyond the publication of *Souls*—in *Dark Princess* (1928) and *Dusk of Dawn* (1940), for example—and still relies on that notion during the last decade of his life.[17] Similarly, the political expressivist idea that effective and authoritative black politics must express a shared black spiritual identity continues to haunt both *Black Reconstruction* (1935), with its invocations of African folklore and slave music, and *Dusk of Dawn,* with its attempt to identify New World substitutes for African communalism.[18] Now it is true, arguably, that with his turn to Marxism Du Bois rejected anomaly theories of white supremacy.[19] But noting this difference between Du Bois's early and more mature thought is not enough to justify the claim that reading *Souls*, say, from the perspective of *Dusk of Dawn* or of some other mature work or works will prove more instructive than reading it from the perspective of *Bondage*. My argument, in any case, is that the latter strategy is likely to be the more instructive—at least as regards claims critical to Du Bois's defense of the politics of self-realization (as we have seen, claims relating to the nature of politics and political leadership, the importance of political expressivism, and the nature of white supremacy)—for *Bondage* marks a sharper break with those propositions than do any of Du Bois's post-*Souls* political theoretical writings.

Bondage highlights and elaborates two examples of black politics: a plantation politics enacted by enslaved, Southern blacks, and an extraplantation politics enacted by free, Northern blacks. In Douglass's narrative, declarations of independence pave the way for both politics. Before pledging himself to a plantation politics of subversive plotting, Douglass declares his independence from the system of slavery. Before dedicating himself to an extraplantation politics of print journalism, he declares his independence from the Garrisonian abolitionists. In each case Douglass's political action presupposes a declaration of freedom. Figuring black politics in terms of the deeds of the republic's founding fathers, Douglass depicts himself as, in the words of James McCune Smith's introduction to *Bondage*, a "Representative American Man"—not as a synecdoche for what the nation has become and is, but, in keeping with Emerson's notion of a representative man, as an *exemplar of the possibility of refounding and reconstructing the nation*.[20]

The True Nature of Slavery

In his introduction to *The Making of New World Slavery*, Robin Blackburn remarks that though New World "slave systems displayed something of the impersonality and functional logic of modern organization . . . the slave plantations themselves were based on the distinctive face-to-face relationship between overseer, driver and slave crew."[21] Like most other slave narratives, *Bondage* analyzes plantation-based, personal relationships, yet not without examining the "functional logic" of the slave plantation system. In fact, an important purpose of Douglass's book is to show just how personal relationships effectively serve the aims of that system. According to Douglass, the plantation regime is a form of domination the telos and function of which are "to reduce man to a level with the brute."[22] Douglass declares his independence from this regime, I shall argue, by fighting to enforce a limit to domination.

In a chapter entitled "A General Survey of the Slave Plantation," Douglass describes the plantation on which he lived as a boy:

> That plantation is a little nation of its own. . . . The laws and the institutions of the state, apparently touch it nowhere. The troubles arising here, are not settled by the civil power of the state. The overseer is generally accuser, judge, jury, advocate and executioner. The criminal is always dumb. The overseer attends to all sides of a case.[23]

Douglass's main point here, which he repeats throughout *Bondage,* is that to be a slave is to be subject to the unconstrained will of another human being. That human being is either the slave's master or the master's proxy—his overseer. Although a slave may find that he is directly subject to his master's will, he typically confronts that will in the person of his overseer, who "stand[s] between the slave and all civil constitutions—[the overseer's] . . . word is law, and is implicitly obeyed."[24] According to Douglass, the overseer, in his capacity as overseer, need not answer for his actions to a constitution or to any other body of law (his word "is law"). Neither need he take into account the slave's opinions because the slave, for all the overseer's intents and purposes, may as well be "dumb." In the rare case where the overseer's treatment of a slave appears to contravene the will of the master, the master tends ultimately to sanction the behavior of the overseer.[25] Analyzing the slaveholder's maxim "that it is better that a dozen slaves suffer, under the lash, without fault, than that the master or the overseer should *seem* to have been wrong in the presence of the slaves," Douglass remarks that *"Everything must be absolute here."*[26] He makes a similar point when he recounts Colonel Lloyd's treatment of Old Barney:

> Listening to complaints, however groundless, Barney must stand, hat in hand, lips sealed, never answering a word. He must make no reply, no explanation; the judgment of the master must be deemed infallible, for his power is absolute and irresponsible. In a free state, a master, thus complaining without cause, of his ostler, might be told—"Sir, I am

sorry I cannot please you, but, since I have done the best I can, your remedy is to dismiss me." Here, however, the ostler must stand, and listen and tremble. One of the most heart-saddening and humiliating scenes I ever witnessed, was the whipping of Old Barney.[27]

To the extent that the plantation nation places no restriction on a master's will as it applies to his slaves, it treats a master's power as unconditional, or absolute. The plantation has its "own rules and regulations," says Douglass, but there exist no rules or regulations to which a slave can appeal as a basis for demanding that his master show restraint in his conduct (for example, for demanding that her master forgo cruel and humiliating disciplinary "remedies"). For Douglass, the master is "ir-responsible," for he is not liable to account for his treatment of his slaves to a higher, public authority—as in fact he would be under the legal jurisdiction of a "free state."[28] Without recourse to some such authority, which could censure and constrain his master's will, a slave is everywhere and always vulnerable to his master's ability arbitrarily to interfere in his affairs. Douglass underlines the slave's vulnerability in this regard when he reports that "a slave-woman is at the mercy of the power, caprice, and passion of her owner."[29] He further explains that vulnerability when he asserts that the slave system requires that "there . . . be no force between the slave and the slave-holder, to restrain the power of the one, and protect the weakness of the other."[30]

I can summarize my analysis thus far of Douglass's account of the nature of slavery by saying that he conceptualizes the relationship of master to slave as, fundamentally, a form of domination. Following Philip Pettit's recent reconstruction of the republican tradition of political thought, we may say that one agent dominates another if, and only if, he possesses the power (the capacity) to interfere with that other on an arbitrary basis.[31] A person possesses that power when, through coercive or manipulative actions, he is able to worsen another person's choice situation (for example, if he can change her range of options, alter the expected payoffs to those options, or assume control over which outcomes will result from which options) at will or, more generally, without having to take account of the interests or opinions (pertaining, for example, to what her interests require) of that other person.[32] For Pettit, one person can dominate another even when she is not actually interfering with him because she still enjoys the power to interfere arbitrarily in his choices. With respect to those choices, then, the victim of domination lives at her mercy. It should be noted, finally, that Pettit, like republican political theorists before him, represents the relation of master to slave as a paradigmatic example of domination.

For Douglass, domination is a constitutive feature of plantation slavery, for the "plantation state," unlike the "free state," never compels slave masters to obey a constitutional, legal, or other public authority—let alone consider their "always dumb" slaves' interests or opinions—when deciding how to behave toward their slaves. As Douglass puts the point in one of the appendices to *Bondage* (called "The Nature of Slavery"), slavery subjects persons to "the arbitrary and despotic control of a frail, depraved, and sinful fellow-man."[33] The master dominates his slaves, for he is permitted to treat his slaves at his pleasure. The master's impulse, his whim, reigns because his treatment of his slaves suffers no limits.

> [Capt. Anthony] was not by nature worse than other men. Had he been brought up in a free state, surrounded by the just restraints of free society—restraints which are necessary to the freedom of all its members, alike and equally—Capt. Anthony might have been a humane man. . . . The slaveholder, as well as the slave, is the victim of the slave system. A man's character greatly takes its hue from the form and color of things around him. Under the whole heavens there is no relation more unfavorable to the development of honorable character, than that sustained by the slaveholder to the slave. Reason is imprisoned here, and the passions run wild. . . . Capt. Anthony could be kind, and, at times, he even showed an affectionate disposition. . . . But the pleasant moods of a slave-holder are remarkably brittle; they are easily snapped; they neither come often, nor remain long. His temper is subjected to perpetual trials; but, since these trials are never borne patiently, they add nothing to his natural stock of patience.[34]

A master's domination of his slaves, because it entails the power to interfere arbitrarily in his slaves' choices, provokes him to behave capriciously. Without "the just restraints of free society"—that is, without enforceable laws that secure the freedom of each member of society against the domination of others—human beings will indulge their passions and arbitrarily interfere in one another's choices for lack of compelling legal grounds not to do so. The absence of just restraints effectively bars reason from adducing such grounds (it "imprisons" reason) and, in a slave society, invites masters to exercise their dominion (their power of arbitrary interference) as their whims dictate.[35]

As indicated earlier, Douglass maintains that the telos and function of the plantation regime, or, as I may now put it, of masters' and overseers' domination of slaves, are to reduce men to the level of brutes. The plantation regime fulfills this function largely by two means: first, by disrupting slaves' social bonds and, second, by physically abusing individual slaves.[36] Domination is a feature of both tactics because the application of the power of arbitrary interference both breaks up social attachments and breaks individuals—physically and spiritually.

The disruption of social bonds is most keenly felt as an assault on the slave's feelings of family connectedness. Indeed, "the practice of separating children from their mothers, and hiring the latter out . . . is a successful method of obliterating from the mind and heart of the slave, all just ideas of the sacredness of *the family*."[37] In Douglass's view, slavery's violation of the mother–child relationship is but one feature of its general tendency to ignore slaves' kinship ties, a tendency he highlights when he claims that "slave law and practice" abolish the category of "father" and that the laws of slavery recognize neither fathers nor families "in the social arrangements of the plantation."[38] In the perspective of slave law, no normative significance attaches to the terms *mother, father, sister,* and *brother.* Biological parenthood, fraternity, and sorority exist among slaves, but the law no more treats these relations as a basis for attributing claims and obligations to slaves (inheritance rights, filial duties, and so forth) than it treats the same biological relations as a basis for attributing claims and obligations to cattle. For example, slave law omits to assign to slave mothers and fathers custodial rights pertaining to the interests of their children—rights the enforcement of which would constrain the power of slave masters arbitrarily to interfere in slave children's lives—and to that extent sanctions and supports the practice of separating children from their mothers. That practice helps to obliterate the idea that the family is a sacred institution, for it brutally concretizes the law's blindness to the slave's familial relationships.

In describing the consequences of the plantation regime's failure to acknowledge slave kinship, Douglass captures the substance of what Orlando Patterson terms "natal alienation," a condition defined by the slave's estrangement "from all formal, legally enforceable ties of 'blood,' and from any attachment to groups or localities other than those chosen for him by the master. . . . The slave was the ultimate human tool . . . as disposable as the master wished."[39] In essence, natal alienation is the exclusion of slave kinship from the sphere of legally protected kinship relations and the consequent subjection of slaves to the domination of masters. Oblivious to the slave's blood ties, slave law abandons the slave to her master's power of arbitrary interference and, specifically, as Douglass realizes when he recalls the first time he saw his siblings, to her master's power to transfer her from one plantation to another: "We were brothers and sisters, but what of that? Why should they be attached to me, or I to them? Brothers and sisters we were by blood; but *slavery* had made us strangers."[40] Observing that domination typically results in the disruption of the slave's social bonds (her attachment to groups other than those chosen by her master) and that slave law, by neglecting those bonds, facilitates and promotes that disruption, Douglass recognizes that natal alienation, *avant la lettre,* is a constituent element of slavery.

In a passage that recounts his travails from the time he first departed Maryland's Eastern Shore to his sojourn to the home of Edward Covey, "the Negro Breaker," Douglass suggests that the natally alienating disruption of his social attachments has been the unifying theme of his life:

Escape was impossible; so, heavy and sad, I paced the seven miles, which separated Covey's house from St. Michael's—thinking much by the solitary way—averse to my condition; but *thinking* was all I could do. Like a fish in a net, allowed to play for a time, I was now drawn rapidly to the shore, secured at all points. "I am," thought I, "but the sport of a power which makes no account, either of my welfare or of my happiness. By a law which I can clearly comprehend, but cannot evade nor resist, I am ruthlessly snatched from the hearth of a fond grandmother, and hurried away to the home of a mysterious 'old master'; again I am removed from there, to a master in Baltimore; thence am I snatched away to the Eastern Shore, to be valued with the beasts of the field and, with them, divided and set apart for a possessor; then am I sent back to Baltimore; and by the time I have formed new attachments and have begun to hope that no more rude shocks shall touch me, a difference arises between brothers, and I am again broken up, and sent to St. Michaels; and now, from the latter place, I am footing my way to the home of a new master, where, I am given to understand, that, like a wild young working animal, I am to be broken to the yoke of a bitter and life-long bondage."[41]

Snatched, removed, snatched again, set apart, sent back, and broken up, Douglass repeatedly relies on the passive voice to depict himself as the dupe of a fate he describes as "a law." A figure, perhaps, for the whole body of slave law, that law promotes the domination of the slave, for it ignores his family and community attachments (Douglass alludes to his ties to his grandmother and likewise to his "new attachments"), thereby letting him fall victim to his master's capacity to destroy those attachments through arbitrary interventions that treat his life as if it were naught but "sport" and that need not attend to his "welfare" or his "happiness." Domination leads to the treatment of human beings as animals, Douglass suggests, for the master's exertion of his power of arbitrary interference snatches the slave from one place to another, sunders his connections to kith and kin, and leaves him a "divided" and "broken up" fragment of the family and the community to which he once belonged, as if membership in a family or a community were no more meaningful to him than to "beasts of the field."[42]

The plantation regime reduces men to a level with brutes because slave law subjects slaves' human relationships to slave masters' domination and because the domination of slaves by masters gives rise to the regular (as if fated by a law) destruction of slaves' social attachments and thus to the treatment of slaves as if they were animals. In fine, the plantation regime serves its function through the practice of arbitrarily disrupting slaves' social bonds. But this is not the sole means with which it serves that function. A second means, again, is the physical abuse of individual slaves.[43] Douglass alludes to this means when he reports that, having been "broken up," he is headed to be "broken to the yoke of a bitter and life-long bondage." Covey's task, he implies, is to finish the task of breaking him—that is, of subduing him, just as he would subdue "a wild young working animal." Treating Douglass as an ornery brute, Covey will transform him into a compliant one.

Despite his natal alienation, Douglass retains an element of his humanity as he walks to Covey's home. That element, specifically, is thinking. Having fallen prey to a fate that secures him like a fish "at all points," Douglass demonstrates his capacity to act: thinking, he proclaims, was all he could do. Like Descartes, Douglass thinks and iterates "I am" (as well as "am I"), not to establish with certainty that he exists, but to express his aversion to the condition of his existence, a condition that is comparable to that of a trapped animal—a netted fish—and that therefore negates his humanity. By aversively thinking "I am," Douglass asserts and preserves his humanity despite a fate that would deny it. Yet even aversive thinking gives out when confronted with "Covey, the Negro breaker."[44] This, indeed, is the most important consequence of Covey's brutal and relentless tyranny. When all is said and done, Covey's domination of Douglass, as Douglass depicts it, destroys Douglass's aversive thinking and completes the process of humbling, degrading, and breaking him:

> Mr. Covey succeeded in breaking me. I was broken in body, soul and spirit. My natural elasticity was crushed; my intellect languished; the disposition to read departed; the cheerful spark that lingered about my eye died; the dark night of slavery closed in upon me; and behold a man transformed into a brute![45]

Covey exercises his power arbitrarily to interfere in Douglass's life through grueling work demands and "brutal chastisements"—including weekly floggings.[46] By physically abusing Douglass, he obliterates his thrall's mental engagement with the world around him. When Douglass is not working or otherwise submitting to Covey's command, he spends his time in a "beast-like stupor."[47] Physically and mentally subdued, he ceases to think aversively and becomes a perfect instance of the telos of slavery—man formed in the image of a stupid brute.

Douglass explains the true nature of slavery by showing how the plantation regime uses personal, face-to-face relationships—between masters and slaves and between overseers and slaves—to achieve its ultimate end. Because domination defines these relationships, and because masters and overseers repeatedly and relentlessly exert their power arbitrarily to disrupt slaves' social bonds and to beat them senseless, the plantation regime approximates the goal of reducing slaves to a level with the brute. But does it ever fully realize that goal? Perhaps not, and Douglass possibly exaggerates when he proclaims that he himself was literally reduced to a "beastlike stupor." Douglass's rhetorical performance of his degradation serves both aesthetic and moral ends. But it also serves a political theoretical end in that it illustrates vividly and so helps to explain the workings of the plantation regime. With his first declaration of independence Douglass rebels against that regime, picking Covey as his target. With his plantation politics he continues his defiance through a practice of politics that forges new social bonds and that threatens to upset the reproduction of domination.

First Declaration of Independence:
The Fight with Covey

In *Bondage,* Douglass depicts his fight with Covey as a drama with three scenes. He marks the transitions between these scenes by remarking that "now the scene was changed" and "the scene here, had something comic about it."[48] In the first scene, Covey attacks Douglass and Douglass defends himself, defeating Covey's attempt to "conquer" him.[49] In the scene that follows, Covey tries to strengthen his hand by enlisting the help of Hughes, his cousin, only to have Douglass severely injure Hughes and then drag Covey across the ground of a dung-covered cow yard. The final scene has Covey looking to a hired slave, Bill, and then to his own slave, Caroline, for assistance, but both refuse to aid him. The scene closes with Covey saying, "Now, you scoundrel, go to your work; I would not have whipped you half so much as I have had you not resisted." Reflecting on these remarks, Douglass proclaims that "the fact was, *he had not whipped me at all.*"[50]

Douglass claims that his battle with Covey was the "turning point" of his life as a slave.[51] Having shown how he was "humbled, degraded . . . and brutalized," he now describes "the *converse* of all this, and how it was brought about."[52] Peppering his narrative with Christian religious allusions (to Satan, when he depicts Covey as snakelike; to the persecuted Christ, when he describes himself as scarred by "briers and thorns"; and so on), Douglass relies on a traditional conversion narrative to establish the context of his transformation. It can be shown, however, that he deploys this narrative precisely to undermine its authority. Thus, in the view of one critic, Douglass secularizes the conversion narrative, "turning it from 'God's plot' into just one among many ways of structuring a narrative."[53] But Douglass also politicizes the traditional conversion narrative by representing his conversion-through-fighting as a "declaration of independence." Fighting with Covey transforms Douglass—"I was a changed being after that fight," he tells us—yielding a man where there was none ("I was *nothing* before; I WAS A MAN NOW") and a revival of "crushed self-respect and . . .

self-confidence."[54] Fighting has these consequences, Douglass suggests, because it declares and establishes his freedom.

In "Self-Reliance," Emerson proclaims that "the moment [a man] acts from himself, tossing the laws, the books, idolatries and customs out of the window, we pity him no more but thank and revere him."[55] Commenting on his fight with Covey, Douglass echoes but revises Emerson when he writes that "a man, without force, is without the essential dignity of humanity. Human nature is so constituted that it cannot *honor* a helpless man, although it can *pity* him; and even this it cannot do long, if the signs of power do not arise."[56] Our tendency to revere a man displaces our tendency to pity him just when he "acts from himself." Self-reliance, then, is antithetical to dependence on laws, books, customs, and the like. In rewriting Emerson, Douglass highlights a form of dependence that Emerson's great essay neglects: to wit, a slave's dependence on his master's power of arbitrary interference. Our tendency to revere or "honor" a slave (perhaps to honor any "man") will displace our tendency to pity him, Douglass implies, only if he embodies a force that resists domination. Where Emerson explains that self-reliance is aversion to conformity (which "loves . . . names and customs"), Douglass depicts it as aversion to domination.[57] Incarnating a force that expresses this aversion, Douglass, through his fight with Covey, achieves a measure of in-dependence, what he also calls "freedom."[58]

Douglass clarifies his notion of freedom in a paragraph that continues to describe the consequences of his fight with Covey:

> He only can understand the effect of this combat on my spirit, who has himself incurred something, hazarded something, in repelling the unjust and cruel aggressions of a tyrant. Covey was a tyrant, and a cowardly one withal. After resisting him, I felt as I had never felt before. It was a resurrection from the dark and pestiferous tomb of slavery, to the heaven of comparative freedom. I was no longer a servile coward, trembling under the frown of a brother worm of the dust, but, my long cowed spirit was roused to an attitude of manly independence. I had reached the point at which I was *not afraid to die.* This spirit made me a freeman in *fact,* while I remained a slave in *form.* When a slave cannot be flogged he is more than half free. He has a domain as broad as his own manly heart to defend, and he is really *"a power on earth."* While slaves prefer their lives, with flogging, to instant death, they will

always find christians enough, like Covey, to accommodate that preference. From this time, until that of my escape from slavery, I was never
fairly whipped. Several attempts were made to whip me, but they were
always unsuccessful. Bruises I did get, as I shall hereafter inform my
reader; but the case I have been describing, was the end of the brutification to which slavery had subjected me.[59]

In explaining the effects of combat on his spirit, Douglass emphasizes the
themes of freedom and independence. Specifically, he mentions "comparative freedom" and "manly independence," noting too that he has become
a "free man *in fact*" and "half free." By fighting Covey, Douglass prevents
Covey from whipping him. After he fights Covey, he never again is whipped.
Although masters and overseers will attempt to whip him, they will fail in
their efforts. Combat is the means Douglass deploys to assert his resolve
not to be whipped, the tactic he applies to curb Covey's power arbitrarily
to interfere in his life. Similarly, it is the means he will deploy to check the
arbitrary power of any master to whom he falls prey—the tactic he will use
to constrain that power from extending to and including the capacity to
whip him.[60] Because the power of arbitrary interference is the substance of
domination, curbing that power is tantamount to enforcing a limit to domination. And it is tantamount to imposing a limit on the degree to which an
otherwise dominated subject depends on the will of another—on the degree to which his ability to live as he wishes depends on another's decisions.
Combat brought Douglass ("manly") independence because it executed his
determination no longer to depend for his well-being on Covey's "merciful" decision not to whip him. His independence was a "comparative" or a
"half" freedom, for he remained subject to Covey's mercy in other respects.
In keeping with the republican tradition of political theory, Douglass represents independence as freedom and freedom as nondomination. As he
describes the fight with Covey, it secured him a limited freedom by establishing a limit to domination.[61]

Douglass's interpretation of freedom as nondomination is closely connected to his claims that the fight with Covey left him unafraid to die and
that his fearlessness toward death made him "a freeman in *fact*," even as he
"remained a slave in *form*." By battling Covey, Douglass discovers that he
is an individual who would rather die than not impose a limit to the domination he suffers at the hands of his masters and overseers. The prospect

of death ceases to cow the fighting Douglass—that is, to cause him fear—because he sees that his commitment to resist flogging is so very important to him, so fundamental to his view of himself, that he would welcome death before renouncing the struggle to enforce that commitment. Looking to the future, Douglass knows no fear of death, for he recognizes that sustaining this struggle matters deeply to him, while preserving his life does not.[62]

I turn now to the second claim, which turns on the distinction between fact and form. Douglass helps to clarify this distinction when he writes that "though I was, after my removal from Col. Lloyd's plantation, in *form* the slave of Master Hugh, I was in *fact*, and in *law*, the slave of my old master, Capt. Anthony."[63] Douglass was Master Hugh's slave "in form," I assume, because the *social* form of Master Hugh's relationship to him was that of a master to a slave. Put otherwise, Master Hugh's treatment of Douglass observed the day-to-day social conventions—the social forms—that generally governed a master's treatment of slaves. But Douglass was not Master Hugh's property; he did not belong to Master Hugh "in law." According to the law, Douglass belonged to Capt. Anthony. Due to Capt. Anthony's absence from Douglass's life, however (he remained on Col. Lloyd's plantation when Douglass went to live with Master Hugh), the day-to-day social conventions that normally qualify a master's relationship to his slaves did not qualify his relationship to Douglass. In form, Douglass was not Capt. Anthony's slave. How, then, could he have been his slave "in fact"?

A clue to grasping the distinction between form and fact is the distinction between fact and law. In the present context, law is written language that articulates the rules governing the distribution of property rights. According to the word of the law, Douglass belonged to Capt. Anthony. Douglass also belonged to Capt. Anthony "in fact," for Douglass, with his actions, never challenged Capt. Anthony's legally sanctioned power arbitrarily to interfere in Douglass's life. Here, then, I read "in fact" as "in deed," assuming that Douglass's now obsolete use of this expression was no different than Jane Austen's when, just forty years before the publication of *Bondage*, she described a character as "gracious in fact if not in word."[64] Following the death of Capt. Anthony, Douglass becomes the legal property of Thomas Auld, the master who sends him to Covey. After he fights Covey, Douglass is a free man "in fact," or "in deed," because henceforth he will persist through his deeds to enforce a limit to domination.[65] No matter to whom he subsequently belongs "in law," Douglass will not belong to that person "in fact," for in fact—that is, through his actions—he will relentlessly challenge his legal master's power to interfere in his life. Still a slave in law and in form—his treatment by his master or his master's proxies will still generally observe the social conventions for the treatment of slaves—Douglass will nonetheless have secured a limited freedom. His fearlessness toward death will have "made" him a free man because it will have displaced a fear that otherwise may have led him to abandon his commitment to resist flogging.[66]

"'You can shoot me but you can't whip me,' said a slave to Rigby Hopkins; and the result was that he was neither whipped nor shot. If the latter had been his fate, it would have been less deplorable than the living and lingering death to which cowardly and slavish souls are subjected."[67] With these remarks, Douglass claims that if a slave is cowed by the fear of death into succumbing to domination, then he submits to a living death that is worse than the death he fears. His insistence that this living death is deplorable prefigures his later contention—quoted earlier—that "a man, without force, is without the essential dignity of humanity. Human nature is so constituted that it cannot *honor* a helpless man." For Douglass, a person who is helpless in the face of domination—who thus succumbs to domination—is a dishonored person, someone whose life everyone with a "human nature," he himself included, will deplore rather than respect. Failing to resist domination, he will lack "the essential dignity of humanity." More exactly, he will not evince the dignity that he must evince to motivate himself and others to accord him the honor (the respect) that, Douglass elsewhere suggests, he deserves.[68] For Douglass, dignity expresses a slave's struggle to constrain the power of arbitrary interference. It is a display to others of a slave's ability to help himself, his ability to struggle. And dignity is "essential" not because a human being cannot be a human being without it, but because he cannot induce respect without it—either the respect of others or self-respect. In short, he cannot achieve his humanity in the eyes of others or in his own eyes. The essential dignity of humanity is an apparent, manifest dignity that human beings require—that all the members of humanity require—to acknowledge one another as human. By fighting Covey, Douglass evinces the essential dignity of humanity, thus motivating the rebirth of both his self-confidence (his trust in his ability to demonstrate dignity) and his theretofore "crushed self-respect."[69]

Douglass concludes his discussion of the fight with Covey by quoting the lines from Byron's *Childe Harold's Pilgrimage* that I have used as an epigraph for the present chapter. In Byron's poem, these lines begin a stanza that defends the claim that bondsmen must strike the blow that frees them ("By their right arms the conquest must be wrought?"), arguing that if they depend on other groups to strike that blow ("Will Gaul or Muscovite redress ye?"), they will fall prey to the domination of those groups.[70] In describing his fight with Covey, Douglass follows Byron in highlighting the role that physical force must play in establishing a limited freedom—that is, in securing a limited independence and nondomination. He suggests, moreover, that by establishing his freedom, he has declared his independence. In contrast to the founding fathers' written Declaration of Independence of July 4, 1776, Douglass's declaration takes the form of nonverbal deeds—it is, again, a declaration "in fact," not words.[71] Still, it remains a declaration, for acts of combat are the means through which Douglass makes apparent his limited independence. Douglass perhaps alludes to the founding fathers' declaration—and, specifically, to its claim to "assume among the powers of the earth the separate & equal station to which the laws of nature . . . entitle them"—when he claims that when a slave cannot be flogged, "he has a domain as broad as his own manly heart to defend, and he is really a '*power on earth*.'"[72] Echoing the words of the founders, who also rebelled against dependence and domination, Douglass suggests here that his rebellion has nullified his ties to the "slave power," thus transforming him into a separate and equal "power on earth" with a territory (a "domain") over which he is, as an individual, sovereign. Figuring his action with reference to the founders, Douglass presents his fight with Covey as the beginning of a revolution that aims to reconstitute the American nation.[73] In what follows, we shall see that he presents his plantation politics as a continuation of that revolution.

Plantation Politics

A week after his service to Covey ends, Douglass proceeds to the home of William Freeland (his new master "in form"), where he finds his situation much improved:

> The freedom from bodily torture and unceasing labor, had given my mind an increased sensibility, and imparted to it greater activity. . . . "How be it, that was not first which is spiritual, but that which is natural, and afterward that which is spiritual." When [I was] entombed at

Covey's, shrouded in darkness and physical wretchedness, temporal well-being was the grand *desideratum;* but temporal wants supplied, the spirit puts in its claims. Beat and cuff a slave, keep him hungry and spiritless, and he will follow the chain of his master like a dog; but feed and clothe him well . . . and dreams of freedom intrude . . . You may hurl a man so low, beneath the level of his kind, that he loses all just ideas of his natural position; but elevate him a little, and the clear conception of rights rises to life and power, and leads him onward. Thus elevated, a little, at Freeland's, the dreams called into being by that good man, Father Lawson[,] . . . began to visit me.[74]

By exercising his power of domination, Covey nullified Douglass's capacity to think aversively. Due to his declaration of independence and the beneficent treatment he received from Freeland, Douglass tells us, he regained that ability, his mind restored to an "increased sensibility," a "greater activity," former "dreams of freedom," and a "consciousness of rights." Douglass's renewed aversive thinking causally presupposes his declaration of independence, for without that declaration, which enforced a limit to domination, his ongoing subjection to Covey's whip would have kept him in a beastlike stupor. In other words, his physically expressed aversion to domination—his aversive fighting—was a precondition for the revival of his mentally expressed aversion to domination, that is, his aversive thinking. Again, whether or not Douglass rhetorically exaggerates features of the suffering he endured as Covey's thrall, his representation of that suffering, of his subsequent fight with Covey, and of his elevation at Freeland's conveys a plausible political theoretical insight: namely, that when oppressors cause the human beings they dominate extreme physical duress, it will be extraordinarily difficult and perhaps impossible for those human beings to perpetuate a critical, intellectual resistance to the conditions of their oppression. Only after relieving that physical duress will such resistance be possible.

Douglass's plantation politics is linked causally to his declaration of independence, for his plantation politics demands his renewed aversive thinking, which in turn presupposes his declaration of independence. As Douglass describes plantation politics, it is revolutionary politics fueled by rights-conscious thinking that is averse to the condition of slavery. But plantation politics requires more than aversive thinking. As we shall see, it additionally requires aversive speaking and acting.

For Douglass, plantation politics is unruly, aversively thinking African Americans concertedly engaged in nondominated speech and action that is not rule- or ruler-centered; not expressivist but still race conscious; and not aimed at assimilation. In this section I explicate Douglass's picture of plantation politics, focusing first on the theme of nondomination.[75]

Nondominated Speech and Action

In Douglass's narrative, slaves' collective political action is nondominated just to the extent that it is kept secret. When Douglass lived in St. Michaels, Master Thomas and two other white men broke up his efforts to help a "pious" young white man maintain a Sabbath school for slaves and free coloreds.[76] But when Douglass founds a Sabbath school on Mr. Freeland's plantation, no whites know about it. Slaves can subvert the slave regime (it being assumed that schooling in reading and writing is a form of subversion), he suggests, only if whites remain ignorant of slaves' subversive activities. For Douglass, secrecy is critical to "circumventing the tyrants," and while he claims that he hates secrecy, he adds that "where slavery is powerful, and liberty is weak, the latter is driven to concealment or to destruction."[77] On Douglass's account, slaves deploy secrecy to constrain their masters' capacities to interfere arbitrarily with their collective actions. Because masters cannot intervene in activities about which they remain ignorant, secrecy carves space for liberty—that is, for nondominated action. Whereas the fight with Covey enforced a limit to domination, the secreting of the Sabbath school's subversive activities effectively extends that limit. As we have seen, Douglass follows the republican tradition of political theory in understanding freedom as nondomination. When, then, he portrays insurgent plantation politics as a practice of collective, nondominated action, he conceptualizes that politics as a practice of freedom. Mr. Freeland's plantation is, indeed, free land, yet only "comparatively" free, for unlike the land of a "free state" its freedom is based not on the enforcement of law but on secrecy.

Politics without Rule

As we have seen, the plantation regime fulfills its function of reducing men to brutes largely by disrupting slaves' social bonds and physically abusing them. When Douglass fights Covey, he defends himself against the physical abuse, and by embracing plantation politics, he offsets the disruption of social bonds. As Douglass pictures it, plantation politics is a practice of freedom that establishes and sustains new social bonds—hence the title of the chapter he uses to introduce his troupe of subversives, "New Relations and Duties." In sharp contrast to the family attachments that Douglass emphasizes when discussing slavery's destruction of social bonds, these new relations result from voluntary consent, not biological descent.[78]

Douglass summarizes his experience of natal alienation when he writes that "there is not, beneath the sky, an enemy of filial affection so destructive as slavery. It had made my brothers and sisters strangers to me; it converted the mother that bore me, into a myth; it shrouded my father in mystery, and left me without an intelligible beginning in the world."[79] By neglecting the ties of biological paternity, fraternity, and sorority, slave law fosters the disruption of social bonds based on biological filiation—that is, on biological or "blood" descent. How, ultimately, does Douglass respond to the profoundly estranging consequences of this disruption? Not by embracing a version of European romanticism's myth that through a circuitous spiritual journey it is possible to regain, in a higher, "sublated" mode, his disrupted and lost ties to kin and home.[80] The *Bildungsreise* of the slave does not end with a redemptive return to the origin from which he departed:

A slave seldom thinks of bettering his condition by being sold, and hence he looks upon separation from his native place, with none of the enthusiasm which animates the bosoms of young freemen, when they contemplate a life in the far west, or in some distant country where they intend to rise to wealth and distinction. Nor can those from whom they separate, give them up with that cheerfulness with which friends and relations yield each other up, when they feel that it is for the good of the departing one that he is removed from his native place. Then, too, there is correspondence, and there is, at least, the hope of reunion, because reunion is *possible.* But, with the slave, all these mitigating circumstances are wanting. There is no improvement in his condition *probable,*—no correspondence *possible,*—no reunion attainable. His going out into the world, is like a living man going into the tomb, who, with open eyes, sees himself buried out of sight and hearing of wife, children, and friends of kindred tie.[81]

Sold and snatched from one place to another, the slave cannot go home again; he cannot reunite with kith and kin, and so he cannot restore the bonds that natal alienation has helped to sever. What, then, can he do to cope with the effects of his estrangement? If the slave renounces the romantic longing for return and reunion, how can he offset the plantation regime's dehumanizing ruination of family ties? With his portrait of his life on Mr. Freeland's plantation, Douglass answers these questions, suggesting, in essence, that the slave's practice of freedom (of nondominated action) can produce satisfying social attachments and potent political solidarities, even if the integrity of family and home cannot be restored.

> They were as true as steel, and no band of brothers could have been more loving. There were no mean advantages taken of each other . . . no tattling; no giving each other bad names to Mr. Freeland; and no elevating one at the expense of the other. We never undertook to do anything, of any importance, which was likely to affect each other, without mutual consultation. We were generally a unit, and moved together. Thoughts and sentiments were exchanged between us, which might well be called very incendiary, by oppressors and tyrants; and perhaps the time has not even now come, when it is safe to unfold all the flying suggestions which arise in the minds of intelligent slaves . . .
>
> The slaveholder, kind or cruel, is a slaveholder still—the every hour violator of the just and inalienable rights of man; and he is, therefore, every hour silently whetting the knife of vengeance for his own throat. He never lisps a syllable in commendation of the fathers of this republic, nor denounces any attempted oppression of himself, without inviting the knife to his own throat, and asserting the rights of rebellion for his own slaves.[82]

Although two of the six slaves belonging to Douglass's group were biological brothers (Henry and John Harris), the group as a whole was not united by biological bonds. Thrown together on Mr. Freeland's plantation, Douglass and his fellows find themselves working the same farmland. Soon, however, they begin to consult one another and, as Douglass suggests in the next chapter, to debate and deliberate the merits of different courses of action. Douglass and his friends act in concert (they move together), cultivate ties of loyalty, and form themselves into a band of subversive activists (a point I shall revisit in relation to Douglass's allusion to the "fathers of the republic"), consenting through their speech, action, and mutual commitments to resist slaveholder tyranny. Together they constitute a band of "brothers," not because they have filiative relationships to the same parent, but because they have affiliative relationships to one another—that is, because each has agreed to adopt as his own a mutually shaped sense of political purpose. "True as steel" and bound together by "hooks of steel" (an expression that Douglass later uses), Douglass and his cabal compensate for the loss of biologically based kinship ties by forging, through their collective action, consent- and affiliation-based political ties.[83]

By invoking the figure of a "band of brothers," Douglass points not only to his action-in-concert and affiliation-based conception of plantation politics but, likewise, to his rejection of the view, later embraced by Du Bois, that politics is exclusively a practice of rule. Douglass points to his rejection of this view by echoing a phrase—"We few, we happy few, we band of brothers"—that Shakespeare's King Henry V speaks specifically to set aside the status distinction between ruler and ruled and to endorse a sense of solidarity that is predicated not on obedience to a ruler but on mutual commitment and self-sacrifice.[84] In a similar vein, and in keeping with the spirit of King Henry's remarks, Douglass also asserts that among his affiliates there was "no elevating one at the expense of the other." In contrast to his ruler-centered vision of Garrisonian, abolitionist politics, which he figures as revolving around the directives of a sublime "hero," a "Moses raised up by God, to deliver his modern Israel from Bondage," Douglass portrays plantation politics as an enterprise of equals driven by a shared and discursively expressed concern to free the world of "tyrants and oppressors."[85] Neither Douglass nor any of his collaborators command their cabal, though Douglass, to be sure, is the "instigator"—the leader-as-initiative-taker rather than the leader-as-ruler—who spurs his fellows to meet, to deliberate, and to join him in planning the plot to run away.[86] And neither, finally, do they aspire to govern the actions of other slaves, as if they saw their band as forming an elite, a "talented tenth" that had been "raised up" to direct the uncalled along the path to freedom. The plantation politics that Douglass and his co-conspirators practice is the politics of a few (of six individuals) who pledge themselves to one another, not a politics geared to ruling the many.[87]

Political Race Consciousness without Political Expressivism

By highlighting the affiliation- and consent-based character of plantation politics, Douglass lets us see that African American politics need not be the expression of an antecedently given, kinship- and descent-based identity that the participants have in common. Indeed, he suggests that African American politics is possible where no such identity exists. Douglass similarly implies that African American politics is possible absent the existence of a black, biological, racial identity. If African American political solidarity is a function of concerted speech, action, and mutual commitment, then it does not require the existence of an antecedently given, biologically defined racial identity any more than it requires the existence of an antecedently given, biologically defined kinship identity. In Douglass's view, politics, not biology, dictates the common purposes and causes that generate and sustain political solidarity. African American politics, not African American biology, forges the purposes of African American politics.[88]

Notice that Douglass's refusal to biologize black politics did not require that he repudiate romantic political expressivism. Thus, without pain of contradiction, Douglass could well have rejected a biological conception of African American politics yet like Du Bois still sought to ground that politics in a spiritual-cultural conception of black racial identity. But Douglass declined to take this turn. To be precise, he declined to endorse the expressivist thesis that, to be effective and legitimate, black politics must avow and embody a racially specific and collectively shared spiritual or cultural orientation that antecedently unites all black Americans. That the Douglass of *Bondage* has no truck with political expressivism, thus understood, is evident in his portrait of Sandy Jenkins, one of his fellow slaves. After Douglass complains of Covey to Master Thomas, he returns to Covey's farm and encounters Sandy along the way. Responding to Douglass's tale of woe, Sandy, "a genuine African," gives him a root (an herb) "possessing all the powers required for . . . [his] protection."[89] A little later in his narrative, Douglass reports that he suspected that Sandy was the member of his band of brothers who betrayed the plot to escape.[90] Douglass's refusal of political expressivism is implicit, I shall argue, in his presentation of his involvement with Sandy and with what one critic describes as his "black heritage."[91]

To be sure, Douglass raises doubts as to whether the "authentic African experience" that Sandy represents defines a cultural identity that he can claim as his own.[92] Sandy tells Douglass that, with the root about his person, no white man could whip him. In effect, he maintains that the root will enable Douglass, or any slave, to thwart whites' efforts to whip him—as if to suggest that all blacks can count on African root and divination practices as a cultural resource. Douglass, however, reports that he has "no name" for Sandy's system of belief and that he has put Sandy's thoughts in his "own language," not in Sandy's. He also gives an explicitly Christian interpretation of Sandy's divination practices, calling them "dealings with the devil" but allowing, too, that they could express "the hand of the Lord."[93] In general, then, Douglass represents Sandy's divination practices as elements of a foreign culture that he cannot grasp in its own terms (hence, he is driven to a "Christianizing" interpretation of those practices). Still, when he later describes his reaction to Covey's attack (the fight begins when Covey tackles Douglass), Douglass writes, "I now forgot my *roots,* and remembered my pledge *to stand up in my own defense.*"[94] Here, by italicizing and playing on the word *roots,* Douglass recalls his reader to Sandy's belief in roots. And by relying on the phrase "my roots," he effectively intimates that, notwithstanding his earlier expressed skepticism, he retains some ties to Sandy's culture and spirituality. Note, however, that Douglass likewise claims that he forgot those ties when he began to fight Covey, but that he was not thereby left bereft of the solidarity of other slaves. When Covey demands that Bill and Caroline help him subdue Douglass, both slaves refuse, leading Douglass later to proclaim that "we [Douglass, Bill, and Caroline] were all in open rebellion, that morning."[95] As he later tells the tale, Bill and Caroline entered into solidarity with him, choosing to embrace his cause (to defend himself against Covey) as their own. Douglass wins his fight with Covey due in part to the aid of other slaves, who, on his account, were not supporting a cause that expressed an antecedently formed and racially specific spiritual or cultural orientation but a purpose that he remembers just as he forgets that he is tied to other slaves through some such common orientation. Here, then, Douglass implicitly denies that the efficacy of collective black political action in fighting racial oppression requires that the agents of that action acknowledge and express a previously established and distinctively black spiritual or cultural identity that unites them.[96]

It may go without saying that Douglass's description of Sandy's role in his life also discredits the thesis that avowing and embodying such an identity is essential to the legitimacy of black political action. For if Sandy is a figure for black political agency that reflects a peculiarly black spiritual ethos, then depicting him as a traitor suggests that the expression of some such ethos, far from helping to legitimize black political action, could spell its illegitimacy. But the language of "legitimacy" and "illegitimacy" may be out of place here because, and perhaps for good reason, it is not the language that Douglass uses. The discourse of legitimacy, I suggest, is closely and inextricably tied to a ruler-centered conception of politics.[97] Thus the shift to an action-in-concert conception may call for an alternative language for holding political actors accountable for what they do. And that language, Douglass suggests, is the language of fidelity and infidelity, of faithfulness and betrayal. For Douglass, then, holding Sandy accountable for his actions would be a matter of maintaining that he had betrayed his promises and pledges to his fellows, not of asserting that his actions had failed to satisfy some criterion of legitimate rule. Put otherwise, he suggests that Sandy is answerable not for a precept he issued—for the band of brothers never "elevated" its members to the status of ruler or commander—but for the deeds through which he, Sandy, avowed or disavowed his commitments to others. What validates and lends authority to a deed, Douglass implies, is its fidelity to such commitments, not its racial authenticity.[98]

Although I have been arguing that Douglass refuses political expressivism in his depiction of plantation politics, I do not take him to deny that African American politics can and sometimes should be a race-conscious enterprise that attributes significance to being black. Consider, for example, that when he and his cohort decide to keep their Freeland-plantation Sabbath school secret from whites—seeking help from a free colored man and not, as before, from a pious white man—they judge that black slaves and nonslaves can be trusted more than anyone classified as white. The condition of being black (of counting as black) has a salient significance for Douglass and his band, not because they derive their political purposes from that condition, but because those purposes—for example, resistance to slaveholder tyranny—and past experiences (the breakup of the Sabbath school at St. Michaels) prompt them to believe that reliability matters and that blacks are more reliable than whites.[99]

As Douglass describes it, African American plantation politics generated a race-conscious political solidarity because he and his fellow conspirators believed that the purposes around which they affiliated demanded the formation of a racially exclusive political cohort.[100] It is obvious, moreover, that they could have committed themselves to purposes contrary to the ones they did in fact endorse—for example, they might have decided not to resist slaveholder tyranny but to support it, perhaps on the grounds that the enslavement of blacks is God's will. Indeed, we can imagine a group of slaves, having fallen prey to what Douglass calls "the "slaveholding priest-craft," acting in concert to reinforce God's will by thwarting the likes of the band of brothers. For such men, being black would not mean being more reliable than whites but being subject to God's disfavor.[101]

Extrapolating, then, from the particulars of Douglass's narrative, I wish to suggest that, as he portrays it, consent- and affiliation-based African American politics can in principle take many directions, with each related to a different interpretation of the condition of being black. In effect, Douglass invites the thought that there can exist multiple and heterogeneous forms of race-conscious African American political solidarity characterized by diverse purposes and diverse understandings of the significance of that condition. As in Bonnie Honig's recent feminist reading of Hannah Arendt, the key idea here is that politics, rather than deriving from one identity, may produce many identities. For Honig, "Arendt's politics is agonistic because it always resists the attractions of expressivism, for the sake of her view of . . . identity as a performative production. . . . The strategy here is to proliferate difference . . . and the result might be the empowering discovery or insis-tence that there are . . . many ways to do one's gender. The homogenizing impulse of some (so-called) private identities would be weakened and that would allow for greater differentiation and contestability within the frame of these 'identities' themselves."[102]

In a similar vein, Douglass's view of plantation politics allows that there may be multiple and mutually contestable ways of "doing" or "forg-ing" race-conscious black solidarities. Resisting the attractions of political expressivism, which for the sake of political efficacy and legitimacy secures the purposes of black politics by appeal to an antecedently formed black spiritual or cultural identity, Douglass spurs us to regard black politics as the interplay of conflicting purposes and conflicting interpretations of the condition of being black.[103]

Radical Reconstruction versus Assimilation

A central aim of the present chapter is to highlight several features of Doug-lass's political thought that distinguish it from the politics of expressive self-realization. Thus far, I have focused on two of those features: namely, Douglass's non-ruler-centered depiction of plantation politics and his rejection of political expressivism. A third feature is what I have described as his radical reconstructionism.

As we have seen, Du Bois adapts some basic elements of Gustav Schmoller's social theory to argue that African American politics should attempt to solve the "Negro Problem"—that is, to bring African American life into conformity with the norms characteristic of America's basic social arrangements, which for Du Bois means the economic, moral, and perhaps aesthetic norms of modernity. In a nutshell, Du Bois holds that African American politics should aim to assimilate and normalize the black masses. But the aim of radical reconstruction is not the elimination of deviance; rather it is to reconstitute practices of citizenship and thereby to refound the American nation. With its emphasis on normative integration, Du Bois's politics of self-realization tends to prefigure a prominent strand of modern, American sociology that defines social "problems" and "disorganization" in terms of "deviation from norms," a theme that is still evident in the sociology of the black underclass.[104] In contrast to this tendency, Douglass's politics of radical reconstruction, which knows nothing of the sociology of the late nineteenth or twentieth centuries, more often appears to belong to a tradition of Roman and republican political theory.[105]

I have argued that Douglass presents the Covey fight as the beginning of a revolution (as a declaration of independence) that aims to reconstitute the American nation. Douglass presents his plantation politics as continuing that revolution when, after describing his insurgent band of brothers, he proclaims that the "slaveholder . . . the every hour violator of the just and inalienable rights of man . . . never lisps a syllable in commendation of the fathers of this republic . . . without inviting the knife to his own throat and asserting the rights of rebellion for his slaves." With these incendiary remarks, Douglass suggests that, in acting to assert their rights of rebellion, he and his fellow conspirators imitated the founding fathers. In other words, he suggests that they aspired to keep faith with the work of the founders (the men he also calls "the heroes of the revolution"), which was to establish a republic that respected "the just and inalienable rights of man."[106] By invoking the language of the Declaration of Independence ("inalienable rights"), Douglass implies that the seminal act of the founders was to commit themselves to the principles enshrined in the Declaration. In addition, he implies that this act fell short of the founders' wishes, for the reign of the slaveholder shows that that the nation it established no longer erects itself on and respects those principles. Douglass and his band emulate the founders by undertaking to refound the nation—that is, by performing insurgent acts (such as preparing to escape from Freeland's plantation) that reenact the founders' founding commitment to the principles of the Declaration, hoping thus to further the cause of transforming America into a nation that respects those principles.[107]

In his famous speech of July 5, 1852, excerpts of which he includes in *Bondage*, Douglass had already called for social reform that would echo the deeds of the founding fathers.[108] America, he says, is young and still "impressible." Indeed, "there is consolation that America is young," for "great streams are not easily turned from their channels." According to Douglass, youthful America's identity as a nation is available to be reformed. Here he charges the task of national reform to the (white) "sons" of the founding fathers: "Your fathers have lived, died, and have done their work, and have done much of it well. You live and must die, and you must do your work. You have no right to enjoy a child's share in the labor of your fathers, unless your children are to be blest by your labors." For Douglass, the work of the sons is to finish the work the fathers began—the work of founding a nation that respects the principles of the Declaration of Independence. "The principles contained in that instrument," he insists, "are saving principles." "Stand by those principles, be true to them on all occasions," he advises. Later in the speech Douglass suggests that the sons have forsaken these principles and that like the descendants of Abraham, who forsook Abraham's "faith and spirit," they have "repudiated the deeds" of their fathers: "Washington could not die till he had broken the chains of his slaves. Yet his monument is built up by the price of human blood, and the traders in the bodies and souls of men shout—'We have Washington as *our father.*'" It is no surprise, then, that Douglass finally denounces the sons' jubilee celebration as "mere bombast, fraud, deception, impiety, and hypocrisy," implying that their professed commitment to the ideals enshrined in the nation's founding document is insincere. In Douglass's view, there is a contradiction between the principles that the sons of the fathers purport to endorse—the principles of the Declaration—and the principles they do endorse. His main evidence for this contradiction is the "guilty practices" of slavery, which suggest that the principles of the Declaration mean nothing to the country's white citizenry, national anniversary celebrations notwithstanding: "Fellow citizens! I will not enlarge further on your national inconsistencies. The existence of slavery in this country brands your republicanism as a sham, your humanity as a base pretence, and your Christianity as a lie."[109]

I can summarize my reading of Douglass's July 5 speech by remarking that it relies on a narrative of decline.[110] Considering the present in the perspective of the past, Douglass describes the present as "degenerate times." The past to which he contrasts the present is marked by the "solid manhood" of the founders, for whom nothing was *"settled"* that was not right: "With them, justice, liberty and humanity were *'final'*; not slavery and oppression." Contemporary America is false to the past, Douglass argues, for while the founders unaffectedly embraced principles that opposed slavery (a controversial claim, to be sure)—even penning these principles into the Declaration and Constitution—their heirs, their deceptive and hypocritical sons, only pretend (profess) to embrace such principles.[111] And while Douglass has exhorted the sons to "cling" to the Fourth of July and to "cling" to its principles, he admits that they "cling" instead to the existence of slavery, "as if it were the sheet anchor of all [their] hopes." In his July 5 speech, Douglass envisions American history as the tale of a fall from grace: that is, as a decline from the time of the founding acts (the Declaration, the adoption of the Constitution) through which American leaders committed themselves to principles and purposes that opposed slavery—intending therein to found a nation that respected these principles—to the time of the speech, when the sons of the fathers harbor no commitment to these principles and purposes. In the main body of *Bondage,* Douglass presents the nation's black sons, men the July 5 speech describes as not sharing in the "inheritance of . . . liberty" bequeathed by the fathers, as imitating those heroes and as acting to refound the nation. In the July 5 speech, he calls on the nation's white sons to do the same—that is, to reenact their fathers' founding commitment to the principles of the Declaration (and thus to establish a nation without slavery)—even as he berates them for not having kept faith with that commitment.[112]

According to Hannah Arendt, the ancient Romans conceptualized acts of political innovation as acts of refounding the old institutions. Thus she writes that "all decisive political changes in the course of Roman history were reconstitutions, namely, reforms of the old institutions and the retrievance of the original act of foundation."[113] For the Romans, Arendt suggests, acts that radically transformed Roman institutions were deeds that reenacted and so revived the original act of founding Rome. Douglass develops a similar notion of political innovation based on the idea that the "original act" that founded the American nation was the founding fathers' committing themselves to the principles embodied in the Declaration. For Douglass, acts that could advance a radical reconstruction of American institutions—for example, the rebellious acts his band of brothers performs and the revolutionary acts he wishes the nation's white sons to undertake— were deeds that aimed to refound the American republic by reenacting the founding fathers' founding commitment to those principles. Like the Romans, Douglass interprets the path to radical political change—to change that would rid America of the "venomous creature" that is slavery—as the path of reestablishing the republic on the founding principles that the white sons of the founders have repudiated.[114] In sum, and reminiscent of Cicero and other writers in the tradition of republican political theory, he suggests that the decline of the republic is due to the moral failing of its sons and that the restoration of the republic will require their moral transformation.[115]

To begin to appreciate fully the nonassimilationist implications of Douglass's radical reconstructionism, we may recall Du Bois's suggestion that there was a "flat contradiction" between Southern whites' color prejudice, which helped to perpetuate the color line, and their "beliefs *and* professions," which expressed a commitment to the ideals evident in the "caste-levelling precepts of Christianity" and in the principle of "equality of opportunity for all men."[116] As I have argued in previous chapters, the early, Schmoller-inspired Du Bois was an anomaly theorist who both took the practice of racial prejudice to be extrinsically related to the prevailing "group" ideals and norms constituting modern American society and hoped to realize those ideals through (in part) a politics of self-assertion (one prong of the politics of self-realization) that combated racial prejudice with the aim, ultimately, of assimilating African American life to group norms. For Du Bois the core ideals were both professed and believed, which is to say that he declined to interpret the contradiction between the ideals and the practice of prejudice as an indication of hypocrisy. In this respect, Du Bois's thinking prefigured that of Gunnar Myrdal, who similarly declined to interpret the clash between the American creed and the practice of racism as a form of hypocrisy. Americans, Myrdal insisted, were truly committed to the creed: it was a "living reality" and a "living actuality" *that they did not merely profess.*[117] Like Du Bois, Myrdal was an anomaly theorist whose political prescriptions were geared to eliminate deviant practices through the promotion of widely and sincerely professed ideals.[118]

In the July 5 speech, Douglass writes neither as an anomaly theorist nor as an assimilationist (in Du Bois's sense), for unlike Du Bois and Myrdal he does not propose to bring group practices into conformity with norms of behavior or development corresponding to prevailing group ideals.[119] In Douglass's view, such a proposal would have been in error because the prevailing ideals were proslavery. In short, whether or not one agrees with Douglass that the founding fathers meant to found a nation wherein slavery had no place, it is critical to see that, formally speaking, his July 5 argument for reconstructing the American polity invoked the antislavery ideals to which he insists the founders were committed as a counterpoint to the prevailing, proslavery ideals of his hypocritical, insincere contemporaries.

In contrast to Du Bois and Myrdal, Douglass promotes a politics predicated on ideals that have ceased to be a living reality in the hearts and minds of the nation's white citizens. By recalling for those citizens the antislavery commitments of the founders, he hopes radically to transform their hearts and minds—thus, ultimately, to enlist them in the revolutionary project of refounding the American nation by renewing those commitments or, more exactly, the project of reconstituting the nation's prevailing group ideals by embracing the founders' ideals as their ideals. Were that project to have been fulfilled, it then would have made sense to demand that the nation's practices be brought into conformity with the norms corresponding to its prevailing ideals—but not otherwise.[120] For Douglass, the narrative of American history is the story of an ongoing contest between divergent ideals and commitments. The politics of radical reconstruction is the politics of contesting and displacing those prevailing ideals and commitments that signal the decay and decline of the republic.[121]

In chapter 4 of *Bondage,* Douglass writes,

> Public opinion in such a quarter [the slave plantation] is not likely to be very efficient in protecting the slave from cruelty. On the contrary, it must increase and intensify his wrongs. *Public opinion seldom differs very widely from public practice.* To be a restraint upon cruelty and vice, public opinion must emanate from a humane and virtuous community.[122]

Suggesting here that prevailing practices tend to track prevailing opinion, ideals, and the like, Douglass, I propose, prefigured Ralph Ellison's view that citizenship is a fabric of habits—of practices informed by opinions and beliefs and governed by norms—and that the elimination of racial subordination required the reconstitution of that fabric (here, as in the introduction, I follow Danielle Allen's reading of Ellison[123]). Writing in the early 1850s, Douglass sensed that satisfying the prevailing pro-slavery opinion and ideals of the white sons would entail the perpetuation of both the white sons' practices of domination, complicity with domination, and hypocrisy and the enslaved black sons' subjection to a system of domination that worked to reduce man to a level with the brute—that is, that assimilated black bondsmen to the norms of brutish behavior. For Douglass, the reconstruction of the nation required the reconstitution of the opinion, ideals, and practices constituting and intrinsic to the identity of the nation in its fall from grace. And for Douglass, as for Ellison, this meant transforming the habits of both the oppressors and the oppressed. Assimilating black behavior to the practices of domination, complicity with domination, and so on would no more reconstruct the nation than would assimilating black behavior to the behavior of brutes, for a nation of black and white masters and hypocrites would no more reflect the founding fathers' commitments than a nation of white masters and hypocrites. To reconstruct the nation and restore the republic, the enslaved black sons must repudiate the coerced habits of brute-like behavior and, imitating the fathers, declare their independence and rights to rebellion.[124] Similarly, to reconstruct the nation and restore the republic, the white sons must repudiate their habits of domination, complicity, and hypocrisy and, imitating the fathers, commit or recommit themselves to the Declaration's ideals. In Douglass's gendered, revolutionary imagination, the black sons and the white sons must conspire together to refound, reconstruct, and reconstitute the American nation.[125]

Second Declaration of Independence, Extraplantation Politics

It is well known that Douglass began to affiliate with William Lloyd Garrison just a few years after he escaped slavery. Here, I do not rehearse the story of his extensive activities as speaker for Garrison's organization. Rather I concentrate on one of the accounts he gives of his break with Garrison.

Douglass only completes that break in 1850–1851, when he announces his rejection of the theory that the Constitution is a pro-slavery document. In *Bondage*, however, he suggests that he had declared his independence from Garrison and his tutelage years earlier. Unifying Douglass's story is the proposition that texts, written and spoken, lend themselves to conflicting interpretations. Douglass introduces this proposition when discussing slave masters' opposition to teaching slaves to read. Thus he sets the stage for suggesting an important analogy between his treatment as a slave and his treatment by the white leaders of Garrison's movement.

When recounting the breakup of the St. Michaels Sabbath schools, Douglass seems to endorse a Protestant approach to biblical hermeneutics:

> These Christian class leaders were . . . consistent. They had settled the question, that slavery is *right,* and, by that standard, they determined that Sabbath schools are wrong. To be sure, they were Protestant, and held to the great Protestant right of every man to *"search the scriptures"* for himself; but, then, to all general rules, there are *exceptions.* How convenient! What crimes, may not be committed under the doctrine of the last remark.[126]

In the course of his later transactions with the Garrisonians, Douglass secularizes the Protestant approach to biblical interpretation. Specifically, he applies that approach to the problem of interpreting *the text of his life.* Douglass reports that when he was stumping for Garrison, Garrison would speak after Douglass, taking Douglass "as his text." Coming just a couple of pages after he describes Garrison as a man "raised up by God," who took the Bible as "his text book," Douglass's claim that he served Garrison as a text emphasizes the continuity between Garrison's appeal to the Bible and his appeal to Douglass—or, more precisely, to the text Douglass produced by narrating his life as a slave.[127] The problem that arises here is the one that arose at St. Michaels. Notwithstanding their professed Protestantism, the masters at St. Michaels behaved as if they were priests who alone enjoyed the authority to interpret the meaning of scripture. Similarly, the Garrisonians behaved toward Douglass as if they alone enjoyed the authority to interpret the meaning of his narrative of his life as a slave. "Give us the facts," the Garrisonians tell Douglass; "we will take care of the philosophy."[128] Douglass responded to this demand by declaring his independence from the hermeneutical authority of Garrisonian abolitionism:

> Just here there arose some embarrassment. It was impossible for me to repeat the same old story month after month, and to keep up my interest in it. . . . "Tell your story, Frederick," would whisper my then revered friend, William Lloyd Garrison. . . . I could not always obey, for I was now reading and thinking. New views of the subject were presented to my mind. It did not entirely satisfy me to *narrate* wrongs; I felt like *denouncing* them. I could not always curb my moral indignation for the perpetrators of slaveholding villainy, long enough for a circumstantial statement of the facts which I felt almost everybody must know. Besides, I was growing, and needed room. "People won't believe you ever was a slave, Frederick, if you keep on this way," said Friend Foster. "Be yourself," said Collins, "and tell your story." It was said to me, "Better have a *little* of the plantation manner of speech than not; 'tis not best that you seem too learned." These excellent friends were actuated by the best of motives, and were not altogether wrong in their advice; and still I must speak just the word that seemed to *me* the word to be spoken *by* me.[129]

When Douglass became a Garrisonian, he revered Garrison and fell prey to a "slavish" adoration of the members of Garrison's cohort.[130] And as we have seen, he later depicts Garrison's politics as ruler centered—that is, as revolving around his revered friend's directives. In keeping with this depiction, Douglass now presents Garrison as dictating the "story" Douglass should tell and as expecting that Douglass summarily "obey" his commands. In addition, Douglass suggests that the white members of Garrison's cohort dominated his activity as a public speaker and storyteller, exercising a power arbitrarily to interfere with—to censor and shape—his speech. They possessed a power of arbitrary interference, he implies, for they controlled his speech without taking into account his opinion of the words he would speak. Douglass declares his independence from the hermeneutical authority of the Garrisonian abolitionists by proclaiming that henceforth he will not submit to their rule and so permit them to dominate his speech; regardless of their judgment of the word he intends to speak, he will "speak . . . the word that seem[s] to [him] to be the word to be spoken *by* [him]."[131] Douglass will not only narrate his story; he will issue philosophical and moral interpretations of it, for he is no less entitled than the Garrisonians to search the scripture of his life for meaning.

Douglass's declaration of independence paves the way for an extraplantation politics of black print journalism, a politics that he initiates when he founds his newspaper the *North Star.* In *Bondage,* this politics comes into view as a practice of freedom: to wit, as a practice of collective action and speech that is not subject to the domination of the Garrisonian abolitionists. Like his plantation politics, the nondominated, extraplantation journalistic politics in which he joins with other free blacks illustrates a form of black political agency that is not captured by the politics-as-rule model exemplified by Garrison and later favored by Du Bois; is race conscious though not expressivist; and is geared to the project of radical reconstruction.

Reconstructionist, Race-Conscious Politics without Rule—Again!

By establishing an exclusively black newspaper "devoted to the interests of [his] enslaved and oppressed people," Douglass tried to advance the adoption of "abolition principles" by the citizens of the United States. Specifically, he argued that the low estimate of the "negro, as a man," had hindered the adoption of these principles and that the creation of a good black paper would help to alter this estimate by showing black people's "capacity for a more exalted civilization than slavery and prejudice had assigned to them."[132] When Douglass recounts his role as an instigator on Mr. Freeland's plantation, he remarks that "here began my *public* speaking."[133] When he recounts his establishment of a black newspaper, he shows himself to be continuing his public career by instituting a public forum that he and other free blacks can collectively deploy to combat racial oppression. Declining as before (as in his portrait of plantation politics) to adopt a rule- and ruler-centered notion of black politics, Douglass's representation of his extraplantation, journalistic politics pivots around the idea of public discourse and, *avant la lettre,* the notion of a black "counterpublic." It is worth noting, moreover, that Douglass initially invokes these concepts in the "Editor's Preface" to *Bondage,* most immediately to justify his decision to write *Bondage* but implicitly with the more general aim of justifying the public-sphere-centered politics to which both the *North Star* and *Bondage* contribute:

> Dear Friend: I have long entertained, as you very well know, a somewhat positive repugnance to writing or speaking anything for the *public,* which could, with any degree of plausibility, make me liable to the imputation of seeking personal notoriety, for its own sake. Entertaining that feeling very sincerely . . . I have often refused to narrate my personal experience in *public* anti-slavery meetings. . . . In my letters and speeches, I have generally aimed to discuss the question of Slavery in the light of fundamental principles, and upon facts, notorious and open to all. . . . I have never placed my opposition to slavery on a basis as narrow as my own enslavement. . . . I have also felt that it was best for those having histories worth the writing . . . to commit such work to hands other than their own. To write of one's self, in such a manner as not to incur the imputation of weakness, vanity, and egotism, is a work within the ability of but a few. . . .
>
> These considerations caused me to hesitate, when first you kindly urged me to prepare for *publication* a full account of my life as a slave, and my life as a freeman.
>
> Nevertheless, I see, with you, many reasons for regarding my autobiography as exceptional in its character, and as being, in some sense, naturally beyond those reproaches which honorable and sensitive minds dislike to incur. It is not to illustrate the heroic achievement of a man, but to vindicate a just and beneficent principle . . . by letting in the light of truth upon a system, esteemed by some as a blessing, and by others as a curse and a crime. I agree with you, that this system is now at the bar of *public opinion.* . . . Any facts . . . calculated to enlighten the *public mind,* by revealing the true nature, character and tendency of the slave system, are in order. . . .
>
> I see, too, that there are special reasons why I should write my own biography, in preference to employing another to do it. Not only is slavery on trial, but . . . the enslaved people are also on trial. It is alleged that they are naturally inferior; that they are so low in the scale of humanity, and so utterly stupid, that they are unconscious of their wrongs, and do not apprehend their rights. Looking, then, at your request, from this stand-point, and wishing everything of which you think me capable to go to the benefit of my afflicted people, I part

with my doubts and hesitation, and proceed to furnish you the desired manuscript; hoping that you may be able to make such arrangements for its *publication* as shall be best adapted to accomplish that good which you so enthusiastically anticipate.[134]

In *The Letters of the Republic,* Michael Warner argues that in eighteenth-century America the print ideology shaping the public sphere "valorized the general above the personal and construed the opposition between the two in the republican terms of virtue and interest."[135] According to Warner, republican print ideology saw print as the proper medium for public discourse, which it conceptualized as the rational, general, and impersonal expression of civic virtue. In short, it held that printed, public discourse should detach itself from private interest and concentrate on the common good. For Benjamin Franklin, Warner's ideal example of the republican "citizen-in-print," achieving this aim meant freeing public discourse from the "localization of the personal, the bodily, the corruptible."[136]

Douglass begins his "Editor's Preface" by relying on this rhetoric of republican print ideology. Adverting to the distinctions between writing (and speaking) for the public and seeking personal notoriety, between public meetings and personal experience, and between committing his story to others and risking the imputation of weakness, vanity, and egotism, he characterizes public discourse in terms that starkly oppose what is public and impartial to what is personal and corrupt. Douglass has hesitated to write his story because the genre of autobiography threatens to contaminate public discourse with personal vice. Were someone else to tell his tale, he implies—and here, it seems, he has in mind someone white—it would be possible to enlighten the public mind, influence public opinion, and still avoid that threat. Yet Douglass finally decides to tell his own tale, for enlightening the public entails more than an impartial description of the true nature of slavery. Specifically, it requires a demonstration of black people's humanity, of their awareness of their rights, and so on. Absent some such demonstration, a putatively virtuous public discourse that supposedly targets the common good is destined to convict black people of stupidity and inferiority. Douglass must write his own story to correct public discourse, but the narrative he presents will not reflect his personal interests. Rather he will write with an eye to the circumstances of black people generally, aspiring to a voice that is more general and impersonal than a personal voice, but less general and impersonal than public discourse is ordinarily. Speaking as if on behalf of a "black public," he will produce a public discourse about the common good of black people (slaves and free blacks included) that, through its very existence, criticizes the ruling public discourse, contesting its presumption of black inferiority and its pretension to speak for the common good of all. In effect, Douglass will project his voice as the agent of what contemporary political theorists would call a "subaltern counterpublic," a discursive arena wherein the members of a subordinated social group "invent and circulate counter-discourses, which in turn permit them to formulate oppositional interpretations of their identities, interests, and needs"—that is, interpretations that disrupt and challenge the interpretations advanced in "official public spheres."[137]

Douglass's argument for creating a black newspaper parallels his argument for writing his autobiography. In short, he defends both projects by appealing to their probable efficacy as means for countering the low estimation of blacks in the public mind. In his "Editor's Preface," Douglass conceptualizes the possibility of a subaltern, black counterpublic and represents *Bondage* as an attempt to shape a black counterpublic discourse. Near the end of his book, he represents his newspaper as the institutional embodiment of what he has conceptualized:

> My friends in England had resolved to raise a given sum to purchase for me a press and printing materials; and I already saw myself wielding my pen, as well as my voice, in the great work of renovating the public mind, and building up a public sentiment which should, at least, send slavery and oppression to the grave, and to restore to 'liberty and the pursuit of happiness' the people with whom I suffered, both as a slave and as a freeman.[138]

At a time when "there was not, in the United States, a single newspaper regularly published by the colored people," Douglass took the initiative to put "in the hands of persons of the despised race" a public forum in the form of a "tolerably well conducted press"—a vehicle for those persons to call out "the mental energies of the race," to make themselves acquainted with their "latent powers," and to enkindle "the hope that for them there is a future."[139] Depicting himself as resolving to collaborate with other freedmen to establish a collectively run black newspaper, he brings to a head his portrait of his political involvements with free blacks, which began when he participated in the debates of the East Baltimore Mental Improvement Society and continued when he attended the public meetings of the colored people of New Bedford. Like his description of his plantation politics, Douglass's treatment of his extraplantation politics imagines blacks acting and speaking in concert: to improve themselves, to pass and advance "resolutions," and to renovate the "public mind" of a wider public beyond their subaltern group.[140] And while Douglass represents extraplantation black politics as a race-conscious enterprise—that is, as an undertaking that is characteristically shaped by one or another view of the stakes and, more generally, the significance of being black—he never implies that its efficacy or legitimacy depends on the expression of a collective spiritual or cultural identity.

As we have seen, Douglass supposes that prevailing practices track predominant public opinion and ideals. And that supposition, I suggest, explains his interest in forming a black counterpublic to renovate the prevailing public mind. Douglass expects that a renovation of the white American public mind will help to engender new political practices and, ultimately, a radical transformation of the fabric of political habits constituting the nation in its fall from grace. In the closing pages of *Bondage*, Douglass recalls that he has used his newspaper to reshape the public mind on the matter of constitutional interpretation. Having repudiated the authority of Garrisonian hermeneutics as it applies to the text of his life, he also repudiates it as it applies to the text of the Constitution.[141] Declaring a politically "protestant" theory of constitutional interpretation, he insists that "every citizen has a right to form an opinion of the constitution [*sic*], and to propagate that opinion, and to use all honorable means to make his opinion the prevailing one."[142] Douglass defends an antislavery interpretation of the Constitution, hoping to make his interpretation prevail and thus to persuade fellow citizens both to commit themselves to the ideals he finds in the Constitution and to alter their practices accordingly. "All I ask of the American people," he writes, is "that they live up to the Constitution, adopt its principles, imbibe its spirit and enforce its provisions."[143] For Douglass, then, the black counterpublic's battle over constitutional interpretation is part of a radical reconstructionist battle to reconstitute the nation: first, by reconstituting citizens' prevailing interpretation (their public opinion) of the nation's constitution and, second, by urging them to bring their practices into accord with that re-constituted interpretation.[144]

Conclusion: Douglass, Du Bois, and the Negro Problem

In this final section I consider Douglass's speeches "The Negro Problem," delivered in 1890, and "Lessons of the Hour," which he gave in 1894.[145] Both speeches belong to the very same decade as Du Bois's "The Study of the Negro Problems" (1897), with "Lessons" coming fewer than ten years before the publication of *Souls* (1903). Because the elder Douglass's republican and radical-reconstructionist discussions of the "Negro problem" are nearly contemporary to the young Du Bois's writing on the topic, they offer a valuable reference point for evaluating Du Bois's assimilationism.

A thesis central to America's late nineteenth-century discourse about the "Negro problem" was that the Negro is, as Douglass put it, a "dangerous person."[146] In *Souls,* in the closing paragraphs of "Of the Sons of Master and Man," Du Bois responds to this thesis by contrasting the argument that Southern whites adduce to support it with a counterargument that he himself elaborates. The argument of the Southerners is "of great strength," he allows, but "not a whit stronger than the argument of thinking Negroes." Submitting that the social condition of the Negro is a danger or, as Du Bois writes, a "menace," Southern whites cite the Negro's "ignorance, shiftlessness, poverty, and crime" to justify the racial prejudice wherewith they hold the Negro at arm's length, thereby preventing him from infringing on and "sweep[ing] away the culture of [their] fathers [and] the hope of [their] children." Although Du Bois begins to counter this position with the recognition that "the condition of our masses is bad," he immediately adds that there is "adequate historical cause for this, and unmistakable evidence that no small number have, in spite of tremendous disadvantages, risen to the level of American civilization." Du Bois concludes his retort on a less defensive, more critical note:

When, by proscription and prejudice, these same Negroes [those who have risen to the level of American civilization] are classed with and treated like the lowest of their people, simply *because* they are Negroes, such a policy not only discourages thrift and intelligence among black men but puts a direct premium on the very things you complain of,— inefficiency and crime. Draw lines of crime, of incompetency, of vice,

as tightly and uncompromisingly as you will, for all these things must
be proscribed; but a color-line not only does not accomplish this purpose, but thwarts it.[147]

Du Bois can resolve the conflict between the two arguments he presents
because he interprets the discourse about the Negro problem and, specifically, the danger (menace) thesis set forth by Southern whites in terms
of the social theory he sketches in "The Study of the Negro Problems."
Each argument deserves the appreciation and sympathy of the "other's position" because each holds a grain of truth. The behavior of the black masses
presents a danger to American civilization (to the culture of the fathers
and so forth), Du Bois implicitly admits, but it need not do so, for it is possible and desirable to shape black lives to the norms of American civilization. Thus the Negro must "realize more deeply than he does at present the
need of uplifting the masses of his people." And while white people may
be justified in shunning incompetence, vice, and the like, they must admit
that not all blacks fall short of the norms of civilization and that treating
all as if they do will effectively thwart all attempts to transform the black
masses into assimilated, civilized Americans. Whites, then, must "realize
more vividly than they have yet done the deadening and disastrous effect
of a color-prejudice that classes Phillis Wheatley and Sam Hose in the same
despised class." For Du Bois, color-related prejudice and the backward social condition of the black masses "act as reciprocal cause and effect" such
that "a change in neither alone will bring the desired effect."[148] Applying the
social-theoretical framework of "The Study of the Negro Problems," he argues, in fine, that the danger the masses present can be eradicated through
assimilation and that eradicating that danger requires a two-pronged attack
on the mutually reinforcing obstacles to assimilation.

In chapter 3 of *Souls*, Du Bois describes [Booker T.] Washington's politics as one of compromise. Given the opportunity, Douglass, I conjecture,
would have similarly described the young Du Bois's politics, arguing that
Du Bois conceded too much in requiring sympathy and appreciation for the
white Southerner's thesis that the Negro is a menace. According to Douglass, the claim that the Negro presents a danger to society is a "red herring,"
a distraction that is nonetheless symptomatic of the "true problem," which
"is not the negro, but the nation." And this true, national problem, he insists, emanates from the dearth of civic virtue among the Southern, "white

ruffians" whose persecution, lawlessness, and corruption of the ballot box express a "moral depravity" that dishonors the nation. Assuming "to control the destiny of [the] Republic as well as the destiny of the negro," the very men "who led the nation in a dance of blood" now attempt to turn back the clock, asking that the polity "undo all that it did by the suppression of rebellion and in maintenance of the Union." Although the Negro poses no threat to the Union, the Union has begun to endanger the Negro due to sectional reconciliation and the new political power of the white Southerner. Discourse to the effect that there is a Negro problem hides the proper object of political concern, Douglass proclaims, which is the moral integrity of the nation.[149]

"There is nothing the matter with the negro," says Douglass, "he is all right."[150] But there may well be something the matter with the nation, as the elder Douglass no less than the Douglass of the 1850s is eager to proclaim:

> But let me say again, the South neither really fears the ignorance of the negro, nor the supremacy of the negro. It is not the ignorant negro, but the intelligent North that it fears; not the supremacy of a different race from itself, but the supremacy of the Republican party. It is not the men who are emancipated but the people who emancipated them that disturb its repose. In other words the trouble is not racial but political. It is not the race and color of the vote, *but the type of civilization represented by the vote.* Disguise this as it may, the real thing that troubles the south is the Republican party, its principles, and its ascendancy in the Southern States. When it talks of negro ignorance, and of negro supremacy, it means this, and simply this, and only this.[151]

For Douglass, the thesis that the Negro is a danger misrepresents a complaint about the nation as a complaint about the Negro. And the effect of that misrepresentation, he suggests, is to disguise a question about the type of civilization that should prevail in the United States—a political issue—as a question about the Negro's fitness for civilization per se, which is a racial issue. Douglass meets Southern discourse about the Negro problem with a hermeneutics of suspicion that unmasks its pretended attack on the Negro as an attack on the very principles (Republican Party principles) that have come to define the civilization of the nation in the wake of the Civil War. Put otherwise, Douglass interprets that discourse as an attempt to promote

Figure 2. Ball and chains wrapped around living-room curtains at the elder Frederick Douglass's Cedar Hill home, Anacostia, Washington, DC. Douglass kept them as a visual reminder of his enslaved past, the postemancipation specter of slavery, the promise of freedom, and judgment. (Photo by Neil Roberts.)

the reconstitution of the nation through the disavowal of principles that he presents as res adjudicata—as having settled the identity of the nation as a whole once and for all.[152]

From Douglass's perspective, Du Bois concedes too much to the white Southerner because he takes the danger thesis too seriously. To be sure, he responds critically to the thesis by proposing that the putative want of fit between the Negro and American civilization is due as much to white prejudice as it is to the backward social condition of the Negro. Still—and this is the critical point—Du Bois pursues the Southerner's bait, running after his red herring, precisely to the extent that he assumes that there is in fact a danger, a want of fit, that needs to be addressed. As I argue in chapter 4 [of *In the Shadow of Du Bois*], Du Bois too often neglects to question the validity of norms adduced in the name of American civilization: to borrow the words of a contemporary political theorist, he takes for granted "the unimpeachable desirability [and] estimability" of norms of this sort.[153] But Douglass puts such norms into question, suggesting that any decision to endorse them must await an interrogation as to whether they are norms of tyranny—norms that help to rationalize and reinforce the "dominion of whites [and] the . . . subjection of blacks"—or norms of republican freedom.[154] In short, he insists on the fundamental, political importance of asking whether the type of civilization that the danger ideologues and their sympathetic, appreciative interlocutors endorse and take for granted is a type of civilization that merits endorsement in the first place. From the standpoint of Douglass's republican and radical reconstructionist political thought, the question of whether the principles governing the polity are the right principles—whether they define appropriate standards of evaluation—must always take political priority over questions as to whether a particular group constitutes a danger to those principles or can be shaped to conform to them. And where these secondary questions do indeed obtain priority, it must immediately be suspected that they have been invoked to obscure a political struggle over the governing principles. Given these imperatives, Douglass's political thought could never pivot around the problem of the masses.

Notes

First published as "Douglass's Declarations of Independence and Practices of Politics," in Robert Gooding-Williams, *In the Shadow of Du Bois: Afro-Modern*

1. For discussion of the many references to Byron's *Childe Harold's Pilgrimage* in nineteenth-century African American letters, see Eric Sundquist, *To Wake the Nations: Race in the Making of American Literature* (Cambridge, MA: Harvard University Press, 1993), 124, 496.

2. Lord Byron, *Childe Harold's Pilgrimage*, canto 2, stanza 74, line 710, in *The Complete Poetical Works of Byron*, ed. Paul E. More (Boston: Houghton Mifflin, 1905).

3. In the text, Du Bois sharply separates the two epigraphs with a dotted line.

4. W. E. B. Du Bois, *The Souls of Black Folk*, ed. David W. Blight and Robert Gooding-Williams (Boston: Bedford Books, 1997), 66–67.

5. See ibid., 62, and M. F. Armstrong and Helen W. Ludlow, *Hampton and Its Students, with Fifty Cabin and Plantation Songs*, arranged by Thomas P. Fenner (New York: Putnam, 1874), 222–23. I follow Sundquist in assuming that the Hampton volume was the source of Du Bois's epigraphs; see Sundquist, *To Wake the Nations*, 497.

6. Armstrong and Ludlow, *Hampton and Its Students*, 222–23.

7. Du Bois, *Souls*, 62. The reading I give of the significance of Du Bois's placing of this epigraph differs from that given by Sundquist (cf. Sundquist, *To Wake the Nations*, 496–97), although I agree with Sundquist that the epigraph's allusion to mourning serves as a sort of ironic counterpoint to Du Bois's praise of Washington. It should be noted, also, that Fenner's arrangement of "A Great Camp-meetin'" indicates that the same six bars of music are meant to accompany different choral lyrics in each of the song's subsequent (second, third, fourth, and fifth) stanzas. But unlike the choral lyrics of the first stanza, none of these other lyrics seems to bear directly on Du Bois's engagement with Washington.

8. Du Bois, *Souls*, 72.

9. For an extensive discussion of African Americans' analogical use of the Exodus story to interpret African American history, politics, and so on, see Eddie S. Glaude Jr., *Exodus! Religion, Race, and Nation in Early Nineteenth-Century Black America* (Chicago: University of Chicago Press, 2000).

10. Du Bois, *Souls*, 40.

11. Ibid., 41, 61. Cf. Numbers 20:17, 21:22.

12. Du Bois, *Souls*, 70.

13. See Frederick Douglass, "What to the Slave Is the Fourth of July? An Address Delivered in Rochester, New York, on 5 July 1852," in *The Frederick Douglass Papers, Series One: Speeches, Debates, and Interviews*, 5 vols., ed. John W. Blassingame and others (New Haven, CT: Yale University Press, 1982), 2:359–88.

[*Volume editor's note:* In all quotations from Douglass that include italicized text, the emphasis is given in the original unless otherwise noted.]

14. Waldo E. Martin Jr., *The Mind of Frederick Douglass* (Chapel Hill: University of North Carolina Press, 1984), x.

15. For a good introduction to the 1845 *Narrative*, see, especially, Frederick Douglass, *Narrative of the Life of Frederick Douglass, an American Slave, Written by Himself,* ed. and introduced by David W. Blight (Boston: Bedford Books, 1993). Blight's introduction to this edition ("A Psalm of Freedom," 1–23) gives due emphasis to the heroic, individualistic character of the *Narrative.* For a detailed discussion of the communitarian turn in *Bondage,* see Williams L. Andrews, *To Tell a Free Story: The First Century of Afro-American Autobiography, 1760–1865* (Urbana: University of Illinois Press, 1988), 214–39, 280–91. For further discussion of the differences between the *Narrative* and *Bondage,* see Sundquist, *To Wake the Nations,* 83–112. For *Life and Times*'s emphasis on the doctrines of self-reliant individualism (compare Sundquist, *To Wake the Nations,* 92) and economic self-help, see Frederick Douglass, *Life and Times of Frederick Douglass: Written by Himself* (1892; reprint, New York: Collier Books, 1962), 360, 376, 466, 479–80, 505–6. See, too, Martin, *The Mind of Frederick Douglass,* chapter 10, for an extended account of the theme of the self-made man in Douglass's later speeches and writings. I do not want to suggest that there is nothing in *Bondage* that prefigures Washington's celebration of the spirit of economic self-help, for, as Robert S. Levine has shown, that spirit is explicitly evident in the opening pages of part 2 of *Bondage* ("Life as a Freeman"). See, on this point, Robert S. Levine, *Martin Delany, Frederick Douglass, and the Politics of Representative Identity* (Chapel Hill: University of North Carolina Press, 1997), 134–36.

16. Douglass's letter to the editor who invited him to write *Bondage* comprises more than half of the book's preface and indicates that *Bondage*'s purpose is to enlighten the public mind with respect to the "true nature, character, and tendency of the slave system" (*My Bondage and My Freedom,* ed. and introduced by William L. Andrews [Urbana: University of Illinois Press, 1987], 4). Both "The Nature of Slavery" and the excerpts from "What to the Slave Is the Fourth of July?" similarly contribute to this purpose. The preface and appendix also shed light on Douglass's understanding of the practice of freedom.

17. See my discussion of *Dusk of Dawn* in the main body of chapter 1 [of *In the Shadow of Du Bois*] and of *Dusk of Dawn, Dark Princess,* and the late "How United Are the Negroes?" in the notes to chapter 1 [of *In the Shadow of Du Bois*].

18. In *Black Reconstruction,* for example, Du Bois invokes the figure of John Henry to represent the political agency of the black worker (the "underlying cause" of the Civil War) as expressing "the philosophy of life and action which slavery bred

in the souls of black folk." See W. E. B. Du Bois, *Black Reconstruction in America*: *1860–1880* (New York: Atheneum, 1972), 14–15. For a similar interpretation of these pages, see Cedric J. Robinson, *Black Marxism: The Making of the Black Radical Tradition* (London: Zed Books, 1983), 322–23. For Du Bois on African communalism, see W. E. B. Du Bois, *Dusk of Dawn: An Essay toward an Autobiography of a Race Concept* (Piscataway, NJ: Transaction, 2000), 219.

19. For example, Charles Mills has suggested that Du Bois's discussion of the wages of whiteness in *Black Reconstruction* reflects a rejection of anomaly theories of white supremacy. See Charles Mills, *Blackness Visible: Essays on Philosophy and Race* (Ithaca, NY: Cornell University Press, 1998), 135.

20. See James McCune Smith, introduction to Douglass, *Bondage*, 17. In the first chapter of *Representative Men*, Emerson writes, "No man in all the procession of famous men is reason or illumination, or that essence we were looking for; but is an exhibition in some quarter of new possibilities." See Ralph Waldo Emerson, *Representative Men*, introduction by Andrew Delbanco (Cambridge, MA: Harvard University Press, 1996), 19. For an insightful discussion of Emerson's (and Nietzsche's) notion of the exemplar, see Stanley Cavell's essay "Aversive Thinking," the first chapter of his *Conditions Handsome and Unhandsome: The Constitution of Emersonian Perfectionism* (Chicago: University of Chicago Press, 1990), 10–11, 33–63.

21. Robin Blackburn, *The Making of New World Slavery: From the Baroque to the Modern, 1492–1800* (London: Verso, 1997), 10.

22. Douglass, *Bondage*, 29.

23. Ibid., 45.

24. Ibid., 48.

25. See, for example, Douglass's discussion of Colonel Lloyd's response to Mr. Gore's murder of Demby. See also his discussion of his appeal to Thomas Auld after Covey has abused him. Auld, Douglass tells us, offered a "full justification" of Covey in response to Douglass's appeal. See Douglass, *Bondage*, 79–80, 142.

26. Ibid., 78.

27. Ibid., 73–74.

28. For Douglass's suggestion that the plantation is a kind of "public," see ibid., 44. Compare, too, the following remarks, which help to set the stage for Douglass's description of Aaron Anthony's brutal beating of Esther: "What may have been mechanically and heartlessly done by the overseer, is now done with a will. The man [the slaveholder] who now wields the lash is irresponsible. *He may, if he pleases, cripple, or kill, without fear of consequences; except insofar as it may concern profit or loss*" (ibid., 57, emphasis mine). Significantly, Douglass acknowledges the existence of laws meant to protect the lives of slaves but notes that "the very parties who are nominally protected, are not permitted to give evidence, in courts of law,

against the only class of persons from whom abuse, outrage, and murder might be reasonably apprehended." See ibid., 81.

29. Ibid., 58.

30. Ibid., 95.

31. See Philip Pettit, *Republicanism: A Theory of Freedom and Government* (Oxford: Oxford University Press, 1997), esp. 31–79. See also Philip Pettit, "Keeping Republican Freedom Simple: On a Difference with Quentin Skinner," *Political Theory* 30 (June 2002): 339–56. Douglass's first exposure to republican notions of domination and of freedom as nondomination is likely to have been through his reading of *The Columbian Orator*—especially the speech by G. Cassius. The book also contains speeches by Cato and Cicero, which would also have contributed to Douglass's early introduction to republican political thought. See Caleb Binham, *The Columbian Orator*, ed. David W. Blight (New York: New York University Press, 1998), 15–16, 41–41, 125–27.

32. Here I follow Philip Pettit's formulation in his *A Theory of Freedom: From the Psychology to the Politics of Agency* (Oxford: Oxford University Press, 2001), 78–79. For enlightenment on these matters, especially as pertains to certain tensions in Pettit's formulation of his position (which I do not address here), I am indebted to conversations with Patchen Markell and to Markell's essay "The Insufficiency of Non-Domination," *Political Theory* 36 (1) (2008): 9–36.

33. Douglass, *Bondage*, 274.

34. Ibid., 54.

35. In at least one place (ibid., 77), Douglass suggests that overseers are tyrannical and masters "lawful." As I read him, his point here is that the members of the class of overseers are by nature tyrannical, while the members of the slaveholding gentry are by nature lawful. As the example of Aaron Anthony shows, the slave system tends to transform the character of the members of the slaveholding gentry and to provoke them to the sort of unrestrained, brutish behavior that comes naturally to overseers. When he discusses Sophia and Thomas Auld, Douglass likewise stresses the impact of the slave system on the character of slave masters (see ibid., 96–102, 142). For a similar line of argument relating to Douglass's comparison of masters and overseers, see Levine, *Martin Delany, Frederick Douglass, and the Politics of Representative Identity*, 122.

36. Here I write "largely" because I do not mean to imply that these are the only tactics the plantation regime uses to reduce human beings to a level with brutes (for example, using slaves as breeders, as Covey uses Caroline [see *Bondage*, 135] is another tactic). But I do think that Douglass emphasizes these tactics more than others, which is why I emphasize them.

37. Douglass, *Bondage*, 29.

38. Ibid., 28, 38.

39. Orlando Patterson, *Slavery and Social Death: A Comparative Study* (Cambridge, MA: Harvard University Press, 1982), 7.

40. Douglass, *Bondage,* 36.

41. Ibid., 128–29.

42. Domination leads to or gives rise to the treatment of human beings as animals, but not because masters must in principle dominate slaves by treating them as animals (indeed, masters can dominate their slaves without so treating them because they can dominate their slaves without ever exercising their power of arbitrary interference; on this point, see Pettit, *Republicanism,* 63–64). Rather, Douglass's view, again, is that the condition of domination—that is, the availability of the power of arbitrary interference—provokes masters to behave capriciously. More exactly, it provokes them regularly to indulge their whims and thus regularly to exercise their power of arbitrary interference in ways that lead them to treat their slaves as animals. Overseers likewise treat their slaves as animals, Douglass believes, because the brutal behavior to which masters must be provoked comes naturally to them and is not subject to constraint in situations where they enjoy the power arbitrarily to interfere in slaves' lives.

43. Douglass suggests that the city slave is less subject to physical abuse than the "whip-driven" plantation slave. Still, as the example of Mrs. Hamilton shows, the city slave is hardly immune to such abuse (see *Bondage,* 93–95).

44. This is the title of chapter 15 of *Bondage.*

45. Douglass, *Bondage,* 136.

46. Ibid., 137–38.

47. Ibid., 136.

48. Ibid., 149–50. For a compelling argument that *Bondage* narrates the fight with Covey in a low-mimetic, comic mode, see Andrews, *To Tell a Free Story,* 282–88.

49. Douglass, *Bondage,* 149.

50. Ibid., 151.

51. Ibid.

52. Ibid., 138.

53. See David Van Leer, "Reading Slavery: The Anxiety of Ethnicity in Douglass's *Narrative,*" in Eric Sundquist, ed., *Frederick Douglass: New Literary and Philosophical Essays* (Cambridge: Cambridge University Press, 1990), 121. Although Van Leer's essay focuses on Douglass's 1845 *Narrative,* much of his argument applies equally well to *Bondage.* I owe to Van Leer's essay my understanding of Douglass's use of the conversion narrative to depict the fight with Covey in *Bondage.*

54. Douglass, *Bondage,* 151.

55. Ralph Waldo Emerson, "Self-Reliance," in *Selections from Ralph Waldo Emerson,* ed. Stephen E. Whicher (Boston: Houghton Mifflin, 1957), 162.

56. Douglass, *Bondage*, 151.

57. See Emerson, "Self-Reliance," 149. Nathan Huggins has also stressed Douglass's affinity to Emerson. See Nathan Irvin Huggins, *Slave and Citizen: The Life of Frederick Douglass* (New York: HarperCollins, 1980), 44–46.

58. Here I differ with Bernard Boxill, whose most detailed discussion of the fight with Covey argues that Douglass was moved to fight Covey not by an aversion to domination but by the recognition of a duty to "to stand up for the principles of morality," specifically, to stand up "for his rights." Two considerations count against this interpretation. The first concerns the internal consistency of Boxill's account. Boxill takes seriously Douglass's claim that the fight with Covey revived his "crushed self-respect." But it is hard to see how Covey's abuse could have truly crushed Douglass's self-respect in the first place if, like Boxill, one holds that, despite such abuse, Douglass retained his belief that he was a human being with rights, a belief that would have yielded him some measure of self-respect (in his discussion of the impact of the fight on Covey, Boxill seems to maintain that seeing an individual—thus, seeing oneself—as a human being with rights is tantamount to according her at least a "grudging respect"). The second consideration is Douglass's suggestion, in the chapter after the one describing the fight with Covey, that Covey's abuse deprived him of "all just ideas of his natural position" and that he regained a "clear conception of rights" only after the fight. See Bernard R. Boxill, "The Fight with Covey," in Lewis Gordon, ed., *Existence in Black: An Anthology of Black Existential Philosophy* (New York: Routledge, 1997), 286–90 [and in chapter 2 of this volume], and Douglass, *Bondage*, 161–62. In a different essay, Boxill offers a briefer reading of the fight that is closer to my interpretation. For example, he argues that the ultimate cause of Douglass's decision to fight was his desire for liberty, a desire I have described as Douglass's aversion to domination (the immediate cause, claims Boxill, was the desire to avoid pain). Moreover, he now seems to recognize that, due to Covey's abuse, Douglass lost sight of his rights, only to regain that awareness after the fight. See Bernard R. Boxill, "Radical Implications of Locke's Moral Theory: The Views of Frederick Douglass," in Tommy L. Lott, ed., *Subjugation and Bondage: Critical Essays on Slavery and Social Philosophy* (Lanham, MD: Rowman and Littlefield, 1998), 39, 45–46.

59. Douglass, *Bondage*, 151–52.

60. Here I follow Pettit in using "arbitrary power" (of interference) and "power of arbitrary interference" synonymously. An act is arbitrary in this usage "by virtue of the controls—specifically, the lack of controls—under which it materializes, not by virtue of the particular consequences to which it gives rise." See Pettit, *Republicanism*, 55.

61. Douglass's strategy for effecting a limit to domination—in this case, Covey's power to interfere with him on an arbitrary basis—corresponds, roughly, to what

Pettit calls "the strategy of reciprocal power." It is a strategy of defending himself against a dominator's interference with his affairs in order to reduce what Pettit calls "the intensity of domination." On these points, see Pettit, *Republicanism*, 57–58, 67–68. For a detailed, historical introduction to and philosophical defense of the interpretation of freedom as nondomination, see Pettit, *Republicanism*. For a valuable analysis of the important connections between domination and dependence and implicitly between nondomination and independence, see Pettit, "Keeping Republican Freedom Simple," 341–42. See also Quentin Skinner, *Liberty before Liberalism* (Cambridge: Cambridge University Press, 1998), 70–77.

62. Here I reject Boxill's view that Douglass could not have meant what he says—namely, "that resisting Covey made him unafraid to die." As evidence for this view, Boxill cites Douglass's assertion that life is "precious" to all human beings and "not lightly regarded by men of sane minds" (Douglass, *Bondage*, 173). Assuming that the fear of death involves the wish not to die, Boxill holds that this assertion commits Douglass to the claim that, after the fight with Covey, he too wished not to die "given that he did not think that at the time he was no longer of sane mind." But is Boxill right about this? I agree that, after the fight, Douglass did not believe that he was no longer of sane mind. Even so, it is not absurd to suppose that he believed that human beings can have experiences that alter their sense of life's comparative worth and lead them to revalue their wish not to die. Even if, as a general rule, "sane minds" wish not to die, it remains plausible that extraordinary events, like the fight with Covey, will occasionally prompt them to recognize that other goods—in Douglass's case, enforcing his commitment to resist flogging—matter so much to them that the preciousness of life pales in comparison. Douglass arrives at this insight with no sacrifice of sanity, for fighting moves him to see that preserving his integrity—in essence, protecting the projects and attitudes with which he most closely and profoundly identifies—requires that he preserve his opposition to flogging, not that he preserve his life when it is subjected to flogging. In effect, he discovers that, relative to other considerations, his life and satisfying his wish not to die matter a good deal less to him than he thought they did. See Boxill, "Fight with Covey," 286–87. The notion of integrity I invoke here derives from Bernard Williams's essay "A Critique of Utilitarianism," in J. J. C. Smart and Bernard Williams, eds., *Utilitarianism: For and Against* (Cambridge: Cambridge University Press, 1973), 108–18.

63. Douglass, *Bondage*, 109.

64. See *The Compact Edition of the Oxford English Dictionary* (Oxford: Oxford University Press, 1971), first entry under "fact." Jane Austen's entire sentence is "Enscombe however was gracious, gracious in fact, if not in word" (*Emma*, vol. 2, chap. 12). Let me be clear that I do not suppose that Douglass's use of *fact* to refer to action is the only use of *fact* evident in his writing. I do suppose, however—here

and in the main body of the present chapter—that he, like Austen, relies on a conventional, English-language distinction between actions (deeds), on one hand, and speech and/or writing (words), on the other; see *The Compact Edition of the Oxford English Dictionary*, entry I.1.a., under "Action." Even so, I hardly wish to deny that he knew, in J. L. Austin's felicitous phrase, "how to do things with words." Having learned to read by studying *The Columbian Orator*, and having begun his abolitionist career as a Garrisonian moral suasionist, Douglass was all too aware of what, after Austin and John Searle, we have come to call "speech-acts." And he was especially and famously adept at the deployment of what Austin dubbed "perlocutionary utterance." In sum, I suppose that Douglass (again, like Jane Austen) believed that one could cogently speak of actions, or facts, as distinct from words, with the convention-based understanding that the actions one had in mind were nonverbal (as when he expresses concern about Lincoln's failure to limit the exposure of colored troops to capture by rebel soldiers: "[Lincoln] was silent . . . but charity suggested that being a man of action rather than words he only waited for a case in which he should be required to act" (see Douglass, *Life and Times*, 345)— and without in any way repudiating the moral suasionist's assumption that speech indeed does act and can bring about valuable moral effects.

65. In contrast to Willett, Boxill, and most other interpreters of *Bondage*, I deny that Douglass invokes the distinction between "fact" and "form" to describe the difference between "inside" and "outside" views of the self or between a mental and a physical freedom. As far as I can see, neither account can be easily squared with Douglass's earlier references to the differences among being someone's slave "in fact," being someone's slave "in form," and being someone's slave "in law." See Cynthia Willett, *Maternal Ethics and Other Slave Moralities* (New York: Routledge, 1995), 149, and Boxill, "Fight with Covey," 285. Support for my interpretation can also be found in *Life and Times*, when Douglass recounts his visit to one of his old masters, Thomas Auld, "after a period of more than forty years." Before he describes his meeting with Auld, Douglass writes at length of the "conduct" and the "deeds" through which "*to me* Captain Auld had sustained the relation of master" (emphasis mine). And he writes that "traveling the length and breadth of this country and England," he once upon a time had held up Auld's conduct to "the reprobation of all men who would listen to my words." But when Douglass recalls his feelings during his visit to Auld, he writes that "the conditions were favorable for remembrance of all his good deeds, and generous extenuation of all his evil ones. He was *to me* no longer a slaveholder either *in fact or in spirit*, and I regarded him as I did myself, a victim of the circumstances of birth, education, law, and custom" (emphasis mine). The last sentence I quote here is wholly consistent with and supports my interpretation of "in fact" in *Bondage*, for again it shows Douglass using that phrase to refer to deeds and, more precisely, to assert

that while Auld had long ago through his deeds (both good and evil) sustained the relation of master to him ("to me"), Douglass no longer through his deeds sustains that relation to him ("He was to me no longer a slaveholder"). I am assuming, of course, that because this last sentence comes at the end of a paragraph wherein Douglass represents the relation of master, or slaveholder, exclusively in terms of his master's deeds, it is natural to interpret "in fact" to mean "in deed"—in fact, it is quite difficult to see, in this context, how else plausibly to interpret it. Finally, because Douglass distinguishes between being a slaveholder in fact and being a slaveholder in spirit, it is quite reasonable to doubt Boxill's and Willett's assumption that when he uses the phrase "in fact," here or elsewhere, he has in mind an "inner" or "mental" state. See Douglass, *Life and Times*, 440–41.

66. Douglass, it seems, takes for granted that fighting to the point of risking one's life is sufficient to secure limited freedom. But as Derrick Darby has pointed out to me, this need not be the case. A slave could fight, risk his life, but then lose the fight, be bound by his overseer, and then flogged. Having been bound, he then would be powerless to resist the flogging.

67. Douglass, *Bondage*, 63.

68. I assume that Douglass uses *honor* and *respect* more or less synonymously. As I read Douglass, he held that all human beings deserve respect because all possess natural rights in virtue of which they deserve respect (for Douglass's reference to the just and inalienable rights of man, see *Bondage*, 165). Consistent with this belief, Douglass's discussion of dignity suggests that a slave will not receive the respect he or she is due (either from herself or from others) unless she manifests dignity through her resistance to domination. Douglass may have held that slaves' failure to resist domination and thus to demonstrate dignity explains the public's toleration of slavery. For a discussion and criticism of this view, see Boxill, "Fight with Covey," 288.

69. It may also be the case that Douglass motivates Covey to respect him, as Boxill suggests. Pace Willett, however, I see no evidence in the text for the claim that the desire for Covey's respect, or recognition, motivates Douglass to fight him. See Boxill, "Fight with Covey," 288–89; Willet, *Maternal Ethics*, 141–43, 174.

70. See Lord Byron, *Childe Harold's Pilgrimage*, canto 2, stanza 76. Pace Boxill, a reading of the entire stanza makes it clear that Byron has in mind physical, not mental, freedom (compare Boxill, "Fight with Covey," 276). In any case, Byron's assertion that hereditary bondsmen will not be free unless they themselves "strike the blow" is plausible if one assumes that slave masters will not voluntarily free their slaves and that slaves will be reenslaved by those (other than themselves) who free them. There may be exceptions to Byron's claim, but they are not so numerous as to render it obviously absurd.

71. I do not mean to deny here that the founding fathers saw nonverbal action as indispensable to their revolutionary endeavors or to claim that Douglass

regarded their revolutionary enterprise as wholly or even primarily "verbal." And by emphasizing the verbal character of the 1776 Declaration, I am not asserting that Douglass saw that document as "only" or "merely" words, as if to suggest somehow that the founding fathers did not regard their words as giving an important justificatory basis for nonverbal (e.g., military) actions. Rather, my point, simply, is that Douglass's declaration, though it is not a verbal declaration, may still be judged to be a declaration. I should add, finally, that recent philosophical discussions of declarations of independence have concerned the thesis that written declarations of independence seem to be at once "performative" and "constative"—see, e.g., Jacques Derrida, "Declarations of Independence," *New Political Science* 15 (1986): 7–15, and Bonnie Honig, *Political Theory and the Displacement of Politics* (Ithaca, NY: Cornell University Press, 1993), 104–9. Because Douglass's declaration is a declaration in deed, and not in word, I am suggesting that it is simply performative.

72. Here I cite the first paragraph of the 1776 American Declaration of Independence.

73. In *Bondage*, Douglass's narration of events preceding the fight with Covey—specifically, his appeal to Thomas Auld—also suggests a parallel to the founding fathers. Douglass's July 5 speech of 1852 emphasizes that the founding fathers rebelled after "they saw themselves treated with sovereign indifference, coldness, and scorn" (see Douglass, "What to the Slave Is the Fourth of July?" 362). Similarly, the presentation of the appeal to Auld in *Bondage*, in contrast to the presentation of that appeal in the 1845 autobiography, describes Auld as becoming "cold," suggests that he seemed "indifferent" after he repressed his feelings, and mentions that he abused Douglass with a "passionate condemnation" (see Douglass, *Bondage*, 142). By representing his travails as mirroring those of the founders, Douglass reinforces the suggestion that he aspires to refound and reconstitute the American nation.

74. Douglass, *Bondage*, 161–62.

75. In explicating Douglass's picture of plantation politics, I do not take myself to be explicating Douglass's intermittent use, or uses, of the term *politics*, as, for example, when he writes that from the slave plantation "religion and politics are alike excluded . . . [t]he politician keeps away, because people have no votes, and the preacher keeps away, because the people have no money" (ibid., 45–46). Rather, I take myself to be explicating an account, a concept, of politics that Douglass articulates through his narrative depictions of his life as a slave and a free man. Many thanks to Jack "Chip" Turner for directing my attention to the passage just cited. For a detailed discussion of the thesis that narratives can articulate concepts—that they can exhibit received concepts and even invent and present new ones (in the manner, say, of Kant's productive imagination in the formation of pure judgments of taste), see Robert Gooding-Williams, *Zarathustra's Dionysian Modernism* (Stanford: Stanford University Press, 2001), 10–14.

76. Douglass, *Bondage*, 124.

77. Ibid., 164, 171.

78. In this chapter, my use of the distinction between descent and consent draws inspiration from Werner Sollors's discussion of this distinction. The related distinction between filiation and affiliation draws inspiration from Edward Said. See Werner Sollors, *Beyond Ethnicity: Consent and Descent in American Culture* (New York: Oxford University Press, 1986), esp. 6, and Edward W. Said, *The World, the Text, and the Critic* (Cambridge, MA: Harvard University Press, 1983), 1–30.

79. Douglass, *Bondage*, 43.

80. For an excellent discussion of the figure of the circuitous journey in European literature and philosophy, see M. H. Abrams, *Natural Supernaturalism* (New York: Norton, 1971), esp. 169–95.

81. Douglass, *Bondage*, 111.

82. Ibid., 165.

83. Here and in much of what follows, my discussion of the "plantation politics" Douglass depicts in chapters 18 and 19 of *Bondage* owes a profound debt to the pathbreaking work of William Andrews and Eric Sundquist. Although my reading of these chapters differs in many significant respects from theirs, I am also, in many ways, building on their insights (see Andrews, *To Tell a Free Story*, 214–39, and Sundquist, *To Wake the Nations*, 112–34). I should like to stress, moreover, that in highlighting the consensual/affiliative character of Douglass's picture of collective action, or action-in-concert, I mean to be stressing its nonbiological, non-descent-based character and not at all to be suggesting that the property of being consensual is a property that suffices to distinguish action-in-concert from the practice of rule (as the example of representative government shows, rule can also be based on consent).

84. For Shakespeare, the bonds binding the band are also affiliative: "We few, we happy few, we band of brothers. / *For he today that sheds his blood with me / shall be my brother*" (*Henry V*, 4.3.60–62, emphasis mine). For my understanding of the political force of these lines, which derive from King Henry's famous Crispin Day Speech, I am indebted to Robert Lane's essay "'When Blood Is Their Argument': Class, Character, and Historymaking in Shakespeare's and Branaugh's *Henry V*," *ELH* 61 (1) (Spring 1994): 28–32.

85. Douglass, *Bondage*, 216. By emphasizing that he presents himself and his co-conspirators as discursively expressing their shared concern for the world they inhabit, I mean to suggest that Douglass, notwithstanding his reliance on the rhetoric of fraternity, depicts his involvement with his fellows as exhibiting the spirit of the political virtue that Hannah Arendt has called "friendship." See, in this connection, Hannah Arendt, *Men in Dark Times* (San Diego: Harcourt Brace, 1995), 3–31.

86. Here, then, my view is similar to that of William Andrews, who suggests that Douglass's leadership of his Freeland band grows out of a broader context of political activity characterized by mutual self-reliance and a lateral distribution of power. According to Andrews, "This fraternal instead of paternal relationship between leader and followers stuck in Douglass's mind as an unprecedented model of home. Paternalism tended to fragment the slaves' faith in their peers in favor of the cultivation of their immediate superiors and inferiors. But the fraternalism of Douglass's Freeland band distributed power laterally, not vertically, so that authority could not abuse community. The mutual self-reliance of these black men cemented them into a unity of identity and purpose that liberated Douglass from mere individuality." See William Andrews, "Introduction to the 1987 Edition," in Douglass, *Bondage*, xxi–xxii. It needs to be acknowledged, however, that Douglass did not always seem to adhere to a decentralized, fraternal conception of politics. In one version of the "Pictures and Progress" speech that he delivered in 1861, he contended that "the few think, the many feel. The few comprehend a principle, the many require illustration. The few lead, the many follow." Quoted in Martin, *The Mind of Frederick Douglass*, 264. For a brief account of the various versions of this speech that Douglass delivered in 1861, see *The Frederick Douglass Papers, Series One*, 3:452. For Douglass's description of his activities as an instigator, see *Bondage*, 168, 170–71. For the distinction between leaders-as-rulers and leaders-as-initiative-takers, see the introduction as well as Hannah Arendt, *Responsibility and Judgment*, ed. Jerome Kohn (New York: Schocken, 2003), 46–48.

87. My colleague John McCormick has suggested to me that Douglass's depiction of his transactions with his Freeland band of subversives illustrates a practice of democratic self-rule, not, as I interpret it, a practice of politics without rule. But I am not persuaded by this suggestion, for it seems to me that Douglass's explicit emphasis on mutual "commitment" and "pledging" (see, e.g., *Bondage*, 171, 176) better corresponds to what Hannah Arendt has described as a "'limited sovereignty" achievable through "the force of mutual promise" than to the idea of a group, or a people, that, having forged a collective or general will, exercises that will to command itself. On this point, see Hannah Arendt, *The Human Condition* (Chicago: University of Chicago Press, 1958), 221, 245. For the critically important insight that the distinction between politics as action-in-concert and politics as rule cuts across the distinction between the few and the many, see Hannah Arendt, *On Revolution* (New York: Viking, 1965), 279–80. I briefly touch on this point in chapter 1 [of *In the Shadow of Du Bois*].

88. Here I mean for the concept of political solidarity to capture identification between group members, shared values or goals, mutual trust, and mutual loyalty—thus all the features that Tommie Shelby mentions in his excellent

discussion of that concept. See Tommie Shelby, "Foundations of Black Solidarity: Collective Identity or Common Oppression," *Ethics* 112 (January 2002): 236–39.

89. Douglass, *Bondage,* 147.

90. See ibid., 181.

91. Van Leer, "Reading Slavery," 126. The argument I develop in the next few pages, that *Bondage* refuses romantic political expressivism, has strong affinities to Briallen Harper's argument that Harriet Beecher Stowe's romantic racialism comes under attack throughout the book. See Briallen Harper, "The Bondage of Race and the Freedom of Transcendence in Frederick Douglass's *My Bondage and My Freedom," Postgraduate English* 4 (September 2001): 1–12.

92. Van Leer, "Reading Slavery," 125.

93. Douglass, *Bondage,* 146–47.

94. Ibid., 149.

95. Ibid., 151. Cf. Andrews, *To Tell a Free Story,* 285–286, and John Pittman, "Douglass's Assimilationism and Anti-slavery," in Bill E. Lawson and Frank M. Kirkland, eds., *Frederick Douglass: A Critical Reader* (Malden, MA: Blackwell, 1999), 68.

96. Here it should also be noted that while Douglass, like Du Bois, acknowledges the power of the slave songs to express the suffering of the slave and to engender sympathy for that suffering, he declines to propose either (1) that they express the distinctive spiritual identity of the black slave (in fact, Douglass claims to have heard similar songs, characterized by the same *"wailing notes,"* in Ireland) or (2) that effective, emancipatory black political action must expressly heed and promote the message conveyed in those songs. See Douglass, *Bondage,* 65. For a general discussion of Douglass's ambivalence with respect to the political significance of slave culture generally and the slave songs specifically, see Sundquist, *To Wake the Nations,* 105, 127–30.

97. For the suggestion that the question of legitimacy is "concomitant" to the notion of rule, see Arendt, *Human Condition,* 228. It should be noted, however, that Arendt offers a rather different view in her essay "On Violence," where she writes that power, which she understands as action-in-concert, "needs no justification . . . what it does need is legitimacy." See Hannah Arendt, *Crises of the Republic* (New York: Harcourt Brace Jovanovich, 1972), 151.

98. The line of argument I develop in this paragraph is largely inspired by Hannah Arendt's discussion of promising as the source of a limited sovereignty corresponding to an action-centered notion of politics (see Arendt, *Human Condition,* 236–47, esp. 244–45). For Arendt, the faculties of promising and forgiveness are closely connected and establish for politics a "diametrically different set of guiding principles from the 'moral standards' inherent in the Platonic notion of rule" (ibid., 237). Douglass, too, seems to connect the two faculties, if only implicitly and all

too briefly, when, after suggesting that Sandy betrayed the band of brothers, he seems to forgive him, writing, "And yet, we could not suspect him. We all loved him too well to think it *possible* that he could have betrayed us" (Douglass, *Bondage*, 181). For a valuable treatment of Arendt's analysis of the faculties of forgiving and promising, see Susannah Young-ah Gottlieb, *Regions of Sorrow: Anxiety and Messianism in Hannah Arendt and W. H. Auden* (Stanford, CA: Stanford University Press, 2003), 151–56.

99. See, in a similar vein, Ronald Sundstrom's claim that "although Douglass disfavored racial organizations, he thought it was necessary for African Americans to organize and unify to fight against slavery and racial prejudice, and to struggle for justice . . . for Douglass, this political organizing and unification was not to be for reasons of race or culture, but strictly for political reasons." See Ronald Sundstrom, "Frederick Douglass's Longing for the End of Race," *Philosophia Africana* 8 (2) (August 2005): 152.

100. Although Douglass's defense of the formation of a racially exclusive cohort may well be taken to raise issues similar to those raised by his defense elsewhere of complexional institutions, I do not address those issues here. For an insightful discussion of Douglass's endorsement of complexional institutions and the suggestion that that endorsement sits uneasily with his "assimilationism," see Howard McGary, "Douglass on Racial Assimilation and Racial Institutions," in Lawson and Kirkland, eds., *Frederick Douglass*, 50–63. For a further discussion of assimilationism and the suggestion that in at least one significant sense of the term Douglass is not an assimilationist, see my interpretation of Douglass as a radical reconstructionist in the present chapter.

101. As bizarre as it may seem to suggest that black slaves could act together to support slaveholder tyranny, Douglass invites such speculation when he tells us that not even Sandy, who had strong ties to African beliefs and rites, had wholly freed himself from the slaveholding priestcraft (which Douglass represents as asserting that God is the author of slavery, that running away is an offense against God, and so on). In fact, by tying Sandy to the slaveholding priestcraft, Douglass suggests an interpretation of Sandy's political agency that is different than the one he suggests (and that I have emphasized in this chapter) when he connects Sandy to African divination practices. See Douglass, *Bondage*, 168.

102. See Bonnie Honig, "Towards an Agonistic Feminism: Hannah Arendt and the Politics of Identity," in Judith Butler and Joan W. Scott, eds., *Feminists Theorize the Political* (New York: Routledge, 1992), 226–32. For a similar line of argument, see Amy Allen, *The Power of Feminist Theory: Domination, Resistance, Solidarity* (Boulder, CO: Westview Press, 1999), 103–12.

103. For a more detailed discussion of the distinction between the condition of being black and the activity of interpreting and assigning significance to that

condition, see Robert Gooding-Williams, "Race, Multiculturalism, and Democracy," in Robert Gooding-Williams, *Look, A Negro! Philosophical Essays on Race, Culture, and Politics* (New York: Routledge, 2006), esp. 92–97.

104. See C. Wright Mills, "The Professional Ideology of Social Pathologists," *American Journal of Sociology* 49 (2) (September 1943): 165–80, esp. 169. For an account of the connection of the sociology of disorganization to contemporary discussions of the black underclass, see Adolph Reed, *Stirrings in the Jug: Black Politics in the Post-segregation Era* (Minneapolis: University of Minnesota Press, 1999), chap. 6, 187.

105. In stressing the republican dimensions of Douglass's political thought here and elsewhere, I intend neither to deny Douglass's "liberalism" nor to imply, as do some neorepublicans like Philip Pettit and Quentin Skinner, that republican and liberal political thought can always be clearly and sharply distinguished. An interesting symptom of the difficulties here, as Charles Larmore shows, is Pettit's placing of John Locke—a founder of the liberal tradition, who, like Douglass, conceptualizes freedom as nondomination—among the republicans (see Pettit, *Republicanism*, 40). For an important account of Douglass's political thought that places him within the American liberal tradition and that highlights both his affinities with and differences from Locke, see Peter C. Myers, *Frederick Douglass: Race and the Rebirth of American Liberalism* (Lawrence: University Press of Kansas, 2008). For Larmore's valuable discussion of Pettit, which emphasizes that "the liberal tradition is not all of a piece" and which disputes Pettit's claim to have broken with that tradition, see Charles Larmore, *The Autonomy of Morality* (Cambridge: Cambridge University Press, 2008), chap. 7.

106. Douglass, *Bondage*, 119.

107. Thus, refounding is a matter of reiterating the sort of action—in this case the founders' action of committing themselves to the principles embodied in the Declaration of Independence—that initially founded the nation. I develop this point further in my brief discussion of the Roman antecedents of Douglass's view.

108. The reading of Douglass's speech that follows [in the text] has been strongly influenced by David Blight's interpretation. See David W. Blight, *Frederick Douglass' Civil War: Keeping Faith in Jubilee* (Baton Rouge: Louisiana State University Press, 1989), 74–77.

109. For the passages cited in this paragraph, see Douglass, "What to the Slave Is the Fourth of July?" 360, 361, 366, 364, 367, 371, 383.

110. For a similar interpretation, see Priscilla Wald, *Constituting Americans: Cultural Anxiety and Narrative Form* (Durham, NC: Duke University Press, 1995), 90–92.

111. In *Life and Times* (389), Douglass similarly understands hypocrisy as a contradiction between what is professed and what is intended or wished.

112. For the passages cited in this paragraph, see Douglass, "What to the Slave Is the Fourth of July?" 365, 369, 364, 383, 368. According to Bernard Boxill, antislavery black moral suasionists held that the American nation's founding documents gave it a "common conscience" and so took their own task to be to persuade the nation to live up to its conscience. In Douglass's case, this meant persuading white slaveholding citizens to bring their (proslavery) professions into accord with the demands of their conscience. See Bernard R. Boxill, "Fear and Shame as Forms of Moral Suasion in the Thought of Frederick Douglass," *Transactions of the Charles S. Peirce Society* 31 (4) (Fall 1995): 714, 717. It seems to me, however, that Boxill's analysis cannot explain Douglass's speech of July 5, 1852, for, as I have been arguing, a central thesis of the speech is that the antislavery common conscience of the founding fathers is not the common conscience of his white contemporaries, their pretenses to the contrary notwithstanding. As I read him, Douglass invokes the authority of the founding fathers to persuade his white contemporaries to make the common conscience of the founding fathers their own (to exchange their proslavery conscience for the founding fathers' conscience) and thereby to acquire a conscience whose demands accord with the principles and ideals they profess.

113. Arendt, *On Revolution*, 209.

114. Here I conjecture that Douglass's notion of political innovation as refounding may be the key to explaining the paradox that Frank Kirkland interestingly identifies in his analysis of Douglass's political thought: namely, Douglass's apparent commitment to the view that there can be a form of morally informed political action that at once preserves an extant political culture and institutes a wholly *new* political culture. See Frank Kirkland, "Enslavement, Moral Suasion, and Struggles for Recognition: Frederick Douglass's Answer to the Question 'What Is Enlightenment?'" in Lawson and Kirkland, eds., *Frederick Douglass*, 283–84.

115. On the relation between moral failing (e.g., the collapse of *virtù*) and political decline in the tradition of republican political thought, see C. H. Wirszubski, *Libertas as a Political Idea at Rome during the Late Republic and Early Principate* (Cambridge: Cambridge University Press, 1960), 79–87, and Quentin Skinner, *The Foundations of Modern Political Thought*, vol. 1: *The Renaissance* (Cambridge: Cambridge University Press, 1978), 75–180. Douglass's Roman, republican thinking persists in *Life and Times* when, in explaining his escape from slavery to a former master (Captain Auld), he quotes Brutus's famous words from Shakespeare's *Julius Caesar* (3.3.21–22), writing that "I did not run away from *you*, but from *slavery;* it was not that I loved Caesar less, but Rome more." And explicitly invoking the Roman concept of political innovation, as Arendt analyzes it, he describes Lincoln's second Inaugural Address as the president's attempt to "restore [the republic] to its enduring foundations." See Douglass, *Life and Times*, 443, 362.

116. Du Bois, *Souls*, 146–47, emphasis mine. Here I take Du Bois to be suggesting that, with each generation, Southern white citizens come to feel more and more that there is such a contradiction and that they come to feel this because (1) there is in fact such a contradiction, and (2) their honesty and generosity lead them to see that there is in fact such a contradiction.

117. Gunnar Myrdal, *An American Dilemma: The Negro Problem and Modern Democracy* (New York: Harper and Brothers, 1944), 1–25.

118. For Myrdal as an anomaly theorist, see Mills, *Blackness Visible*, 132, 146.

119. Here, then, I am not denying that there are other senses of "'assimilationism" in which Douglass could correctly be judged to have been an assimilationist. According to Bernard Boxill, assimilationism is the thesis that a color-blind society is both possible and desirable in America. According to John Pittman, social assimilationism is the repudiation of an identity that is predominantly the effect of a system of oppression through the radical or revolutionary overthrow of that system (the sort of thing that Jean-Paul Sartre envisions for Jewish identity in *Anti-Semite and Jew*, trans. George J. Becker [New York: Schocken Books, 1948]). Douglass may well have been an assimilationist in Boxill's sense and an advocate of social assimilationism in Pittman's sense. See Bernard Boxill, "Two Traditions of African-American Political Philosophy," *Philosophical Forum* 24 (1–3) (Fall–Spring 1992–1993): 119, and Pittman, "Douglass's Assimilationism and Anti-slavery," 76–79.

120. But not otherwise, for otherwise the practices—specifically, the practice of slavery—would already have conformed to those norms. For a similar interpretation of Douglass's politics and, specifically, the July 5 speech, see George Shulman, *American Prophecy: Race and Redemption in American Political Culture* (Minneapolis: University of Minnesota Press, 2008), 9, 16–18.

121. By denying that Douglass's July 5, 1852, speech presents an "anomaly" account of American racism, I am taking issue with Charles Mills's interpretation of that speech. If I am right that Douglass implies that American history has harbored powerful but divergent ideals and commitments, then perhaps we should see him as anticipating the "multiple traditions" view of American political culture that is currently associated with the work of Rogers Smith. For Douglass, the existence of potent but conflicting ideals suggests that racial politics will be an ongoing struggle over the soul of the nation. See Charles Mills, "Whose Fourth of July? Frederick Douglass and 'Original Intent,'" in Mills, *Blackness Visible*, 167–200. For Smith's defense of the multiple traditions view, see Rogers Smith, *Civic Ideals: Conflicting Visions of Citizenship in U.S. History* (New Haven, CT: Yale University Press, 1997). For a more recent, programmatic statement in the same vein, see Desmond S. King and Rogers M. Smith, "Racial Orders in American Political Development," *American Political Science Review* 99 (1) (February 2005): 75–92.

122. Douglass, *Bondage*, 45, emphasis mine.

123. The argument I sketch in this paragraph is largely indebted to Danielle Allen's essay "Invisible Citizens: Political Exclusion and Domination in Arendt and Ellison," in Melissa S. Williams and Stephen Macedo, eds., *Political Exclusion and Domination* (New York: New York University Press, 2005), 29–76. See, too, Danielle S. Allen, *Talking to Strangers: Anxieties of Citizenship since* Brown v. Board of Education (Chicago: University of Chicago Press, 2004), 101–19.

124. Douglass's defense of the right to rebellion indicates his move away from his successful opposition to Henry Highland Garnet's call for an armed insurrection of slaves at the 1843 National Negro Convention and prefigures his defense of armed guerilla warfare geared to "drawing off the slaves to the mountains" in his conversation with John Brown and Shields Green on the eve of the Harpers Ferry raid. For Douglass's account of his initial encounter with Brown and of his later conversation with Brown and Green, see Douglass, *Life and Times*, 273–74, 319–20. For related commentary, see Michael G. Hanchard, "Racial Consciousness and Afro-Diasporic Experiences: Antonio Gramsci Reconsidered," *Socialism and Democracy* 7 (3) (1991): 83–106, and Michael C. Dawson, *Black Visions: The Roots of Contemporary African-American Political Ideologies* (Chicago: University of Chicago Press, 2001), 1–2.

125. Douglass's political thought is gendered, but I do not see that it is essentially gendered or patriarchal, at least with respect to the key themes I emphasize: the concept of black politics he illustrates, his rejection of political expressivism, and his radical reconstructionism. In other words, there is nothing in these notions to imply that black politics must be or must primarily be a male enterprise.

126. Douglass, *Bondage*, 163.

127. Ibid., 218, 216.

128. Ibid., 220.

129. Ibid., 220–21.

130. Ibid., 216, 241.

131. Nathan Huggins also characterizes Douglass's break with the Garrisonians as a declaration of independence. See Huggins, *Slave and Citizen*, 42–44.

132. Douglass, *Bondage*, 237.

133. Ibid., 168, emphasis mine.

134. Ibid., 3–4, emphasis mine.

135. Michael Warner, *The Letters of the Republic: Publication and the Public Sphere in Eighteenth-Century America* (Cambridge, MA: Harvard University Press, 1990), 76.

136. Ibid., 87.

137. Nancy Fraser, *Justice Interruptus: Critical Reflections on the "Postsocialist" Condition* (Routledge: New York, 1997), 81–82.

138. Douglass, *Bondage*, 240.

139. Ibid., 238, 237.

140. Ibid., 193, 213, 240.

141. Ibid., 242–43.

142. Douglass, "What to the Slave Is the Fourth of July?" 385.

143. See Frederick Douglass, "The *Dred Scott* Decision: An Address Delivered, in Part, in New York, New York, in May 1857," in *The Frederick Douglass Papers, Series One,* 3:183.

144. Here, then, my view is in accord with John Pittman's claim that, upon his break with the Garrisonians, Douglass "came to see the interpretation of the Constitution as a field of political contestation. This decisive move strengthened rather than compromised Douglass's sense of the anti-slavery struggle as one between social systems or civilizations, that is, as one whose successful conclusion would involve a radical and complete rupture with the fundamental structures and relations definitive of the social situation in America from the 1840s on." See Pittman, "Douglass's Assimilationism and Anti-slavery," 79.

145. See Frederick Douglass, "The Negro Problem: An Address Delivered in Washington, D.C., on 21 October 1890," and "Lessons of the Hour: An Address Delivered in Washington, D.C, on 9 January 1894," in *The Frederick Douglass Papers, Series One,* 5:436–56 and 575–607.

146. Douglass, "The Negro Problem," 443.

147. All the material cited in this paragraph derives from Du Bois, *Souls,* 146–47, emphasis in original.

148. All the material cited in this paragraph derives from ibid., 147.

149. For all the material cited in the paragraph, see Douglass, "The Negro Problem," 443–44.

150. Douglass, "Lessons of the Hour," 602.

151. Douglass, "The Negro Problem," 447, emphasis mine.

152. Ibid., 448.

153. Danielle Allen, "A Reply to Bader and Orwin," in Williams and Macedo, eds., *Political Exclusion and Domination,* 179.

154. Douglass, "The Negro Problem," 445. See, too, Douglass, "Lessons of the Hour," 607.

II

Judgment, Intersectionality, Human Nature

6

Douglass and Political Judgment

The Post-Reconstruction Years

Jack Turner

In the 2003 Supreme Court case *Grutter v. Bollinger*, upholding the limited use of affirmative action in higher education, Associate Justice Clarence Thomas opened his dissent with a long quotation from Frederick Douglass. Drawn from the address "What the Black Man Wants" (1865), the quotation reads: "In regard to the colored people, there is always more that is benevolent . . . than just, manifested toward us. What I ask for the negro is not benevolence, not pity, not sympathy, but simply *justice*. The American people have always been anxious to know what they shall do with us. . . . I have had but one answer from the beginning. Do nothing with us! . . . If the negro cannot stand on his own legs, let him fall. . . . Your interference is doing him positive injury."[1] Thomas enlists Douglass to oppose government efforts to offset white advantage in educational opportunity, giving the impression that Douglass is an unmitigated libertarian, even a social Darwinist. He exploits Douglass's luster as black America's most famous self-made man to suggest that government correction of material inequalities produced by slavery and Jim Crow is an offense against liberty and a paternalistic insult. Significant in its own right, Thomas's invocation of Douglass marks a larger trend in contemporary American conservatism: appropriation of Douglass to sanction laissez-faire individualism and color-blind constitutionalism.[2]

There is no doubt a libertarian Douglass. Slavery taught him the value of both negative liberty and self-ownership. Peter Myers observes that Douglass defended private property as "a basic natural right and an indispensable practical guarantor of property in one*self.*"³ Preaching self-help and delayed gratification, Douglass channeled the spirit of Benjamin Franklin in exhorting freedpeople, "You cannot make an empty sack stand on end. . . . Pardon me, therefore, for urging upon you, my people, the importance of saving your earnings, of denying yourselves in the present, that you may have something in the future."⁴ The conservative interpretation, in these respects, is accurate. But when one surveys Douglass's full corpus, one finds that the complexity of his thought exceeds the libertarian portrait and in many cases contradicts it. This is not to say that Douglass is a progressive or, preposterously, a socialist. His thought is not reducible to any contemporary partisan label. But it is to say that the conservative appropriation of Douglass must be scrutinized because it not only oversimplifies him but also—in crucial respects—betrays him.

In this chapter, I analyze Douglass's post-Reconstruction thought both because it most sharply opposes the conservative reading and because it deserves greater emphasis in its own right.⁵ It models an antiracist form of political judgment that can still help us identify forces of white supremacy that disguise themselves as fairness, virtue, and democracy.⁶ By "political judgment," I mean the interpretation and evaluation of political phenomena in the absence of criteria adequate to those phenomena. Deciding whether prevailing interpretive and evaluative criteria are adequate to political phenomena is itself an act of judgment, as is formulating judging principles of one's own. On the one hand, political judgment involves intensive attention to particularity, to the unique qualities of an act or situation, without assimilating those particulars into preexisting categories that may not adequately capture their uniqueness. On the other hand, political judgment may also involve inducing from the unprejudiced study of particulars new principles of interpretation and evaluation. Political judgment, in this respect, does not necessarily require interpreting and evaluating forever in the absence of principles; it may build new principles after it has jettisoned old ones. Crucial, however, are maintaining the critical capability that deconstructed the old as well as having the intellectual honesty and courage to turn that critical capability against the new. Only through such critical capability, intellectual honesty, and courage can one ensure that one does not become captive to any principles of judgment. Only through such critical capability, intellectual honesty, and courage, in other words, can one preserve one's ability to judge one's own principles inadequate when they become so.[7]

In judging post-Reconstruction American politics, Douglass works from a set of assumptions that challenge the prevailing interpretive and evaluative lenses of his time. He does not express these assumptions as principles of political judgment, but they are implicit in his interpretive and evaluative practices, and this chapter aims to draw them out. Most decisively, Douglass works from the assumption that there is a perpetual and fundamental conflict between two political spirits in American political culture—"the spirit of liberty" and "the spirit of slavery" or, more precisely, love of equal freedom and lust for domination (especially racial domination).[8] This conflict has its origins in the antebellum conflict between abolitionism and slavery and maps largely onto the conflict between North and South. But because the spirit of slavery sometimes seduces the North, and because the spirit of liberty sometimes springs up in the South, the conflict between the spirit of liberty and the spirit of slavery is the most basic and the more reliable guidepost for judgment.

Douglass's post-Reconstruction practice of political judgment involves scrutinizing political phenomena to see whether the spirit of liberty or the spirit of slavery animates them. Identifying the spirit of slavery is often challenging because it cloaks itself in liberty's garb. One task of political judgment is therefore to be alert to slavery's liberty-loving pretentions and prepared to expose them. When Southern states were disenfranchising African Americans in the late 1880s and early 1890s, for example, Douglass tore off the mask of those defending disfranchisement on account of "Negro ignorance": "To me this is the veriest affectation. When did we ever hear in any of these southern states of any alarm of this kind because of danger from the ignorant white voters of the south[?]"[9] He then set the "Negro ignorance" argument against a larger historical backdrop of antirepublican politics to help his audience recognize its corrupt and disingenuous nature: "They have taken up an idea which they seem to think quite new, but which in reality is as old as despotism. . . . It is the argument of the crowned heads and privileged classes of the world. It is as good against our Republican form of government as it [is] against the negro."[10] Douglass's critical reinterpretation of the movement to disenfranchise freedmen was necessary because many Northern whites—in their innocence—had been fooled by white Southern hysterics over "Negro supremacy."[11] Framing the movement as but one battle of the perennial war between freedom and slavery, Douglass demolished that movement's pretentions of innocence and encouraged his audience to share his evaluation of it. Appealing to that audience's general opposition to slavery and general identification with freedom, he cast the movement for disfranchisement as a continuation of not only racial slavery but also Old World antirepublican politics. The argument that freedmen were too ignorant to vote rested on the assumption that a popular majority or even a strong minority may decide who gets a say in political affairs. This idea could be deployed as readily against another class of the rulers' choosing as it could against freedmen. Working to mobilize general identification with republican principles into specific support for federal enforcement of the Fifteenth Amendment, Douglass portrayed the fight for black political equality as a fight for republicanism's general triumph. Such a move would be unnecessary if American republicanism were built on the assumption that the category "citizen" included more than white men. But given the racial circumscription of late-nineteenth-century American conceptions of citizenship, Douglass had to proclaim black equality imperatively and perform black excellence publicly to challenge that circumscription.[12] In doing so, he opened up a world of new meaning for republicanism, transforming it from a herrenvolk ideology into a black liberationist one.[13]

Perhaps the most powerful feature of Douglass's political judgment is its incorporation of both the perspectives of white citizens already secure in their enjoyment of freedom and the perspectives of black freedmen still struggling to make their freedom secure. Nick Bromell calls this Douglass's "perspectivalism"—his sensitivity to the ways "thinking and knowing [are] mediated by point-of-view."[14] Douglass's willingness to imagine and account for the perspectives of both opponents and allies enabled him to achieve what Hannah Arendt, echoing Immanuel Kant, called "enlarged mentality." "The power of judgment," Arendt explains,

> rests on a potential agreement with others, and the thinking process which is active in judging . . . finds itself always and primarily, even if I am quite alone in making up my mind, in an anticipated communication with others with whom I must come to some agreement. . . . This means . . . that such judgment must liberate itself from the "subjective

private conditions," that is, from the idiosyncrasies which naturally determine the outlook of each individual in his privacy. . . . This enlarged way of thinking, which as judgment, knows how to transcend its own individual limitations . . . needs the presence of others "in whose place" it must think.[15]

Douglass staked the validity of his judgments on enlarged mentality. In contrast to white interpreters, who took their own racial subject position as fully authoritative, he insisted, "No one man can tell the truth. Not even two men of the same complexion, sometimes, can tell it. It requires a white man and a black man—as black as he can be—to [tell] the whole truth."[16] Like Arendt, he encouraged the practice of multiple perspectivalism when formulating judgments; beyond Arendt, he specified that—in the postwar American context—multiple perspectivalism must account for racial subject position. This requires acknowledging that in societies so deeply based on racial slavery—such as the United States—social perspectives are racialized: standing on opposite sides of a major axis of power and powerlessness, white and black populations have sharply divergent understandings of their common world. The main failing of white political judgment during and after Reconstruction was that it insufficiently incorporated the perspective of black freedmen. Integrating the perspectives of both sides of the racial divide, Douglass's racially integrative enlarged mentality strengthened his judgments' claims to validity.[17] The abstraction from personal identity that Kant thought essential to good judgment[18] does not, in light of Douglass, mean abstraction into racelessness; instead, it means abstraction into the subject positions of racial others. This abstraction in turn requires research into the distinctive experiences of racial others. Racially integrative enlarged mentality opposes the conventional wisdom of white supremacist society, its taken-for-granted sense of how things are and how they ought to be. This practice of judgment is antiracist because it calls the invisible white bias of common sense to account and insists on forging a new common sense out of a truly representative sample of citizen experiences. Insofar, in Arendt's words, as "political thought is representative," because it consists in "considering a given issue from different viewpoints,"[19] the more representative quality of antiracist judgment means that it is also more political. Antiracist political judgment brings both the racialization of individuals and the structures and strategies of white supremacy into view and makes them the subject of political debate. It politically reveals the racial infrastructure of black and white citizens' "common world."[20]

My reconstruction of Douglass's practice of political judgment focuses on four principles of judgment that give that practice shape:

1. Sensitivity to power asymmetries
2. Skepticism toward formalistic arguments that obscure these asymmetries
3. A presumption of the spirit of slavery's continuity in American life
4. The subordination of constitutional forms to substantive political ends[21]

Those who insist that political judgment resists schematic formulation may oppose my attempt to enumerate these principles. Let me make a start at answering this objection. Principles (1) and (2) are fairly indeterminate. They identify self-reflexive interpretive dispositions, incapable of determining judgments but usefully guiding them in otherwise confusing contexts. Identifying such dispositions is hardly tantamount to trying to nail down judgment. Principles (3) and (4) are compensatory measures against countervailing prejudices that, in Douglass's America, hold undue sway. They prepare observers to resist ideological conditioning. Principle (3) especially helps citizens be on the lookout for phenomena that post–Civil War American ideology insists are not there. Principles (3) and (4) together steady the judgment in situations where it would otherwise be overwhelmed by prejudices of time and place. They are antidotes to racial innocence—to willful ignorance—as well as to constitutional idolatry.[22] To qualify as elements of judgment, all four of these principles must be subject to reevaluation and revision; otherwise, the judging faculty will become captive to its own guidelines. In Douglass's case, these principles of judgment fit his time; there is no evidence that they became dogmatic principles that corrupted his sense of reality; on the contrary, the evidence suggests that they enhanced his sense of reality.

Douglass's postwar performances of judgment discredited given framings of political issues and set them in new interpretive contexts to reveal larger historical forces of which they were a part. In this sense, Douglass "readjusted" American patterns of thought to make them responsive to the historical and political perspectives of freedmen. Such readjustment, according to Bryan Garsten, is a hallmark of judgment, "of responding to particular situations in a way that draws upon our sensations, beliefs, and emotions without being dictated by them in any way reducible to a simple rule."[23] There was a method to Douglass's practice of political judgment, but it was anything but simple: evaluating where a political phenomenon sat within the ongoing conflict between slavery and freedom in the American spirit. The judgment was all the more complex because the conflict unfolded unevenly: there were moments—such as the end of the Civil War—when liberty seemed triumphant; there were others—such as the Supreme Court's decision in 1883 to strike down the Civil Rights Act of 1875—when slavery seemed ascendant; there were still others when there was stalemate, the spirit of liberty ruling in some sectors of American life and the spirit of slavery in others.[24]

This chapter proceeds in two parts. First, it analyzes two speeches given by Douglass in the autumn of 1883 that exemplify his post-Reconstruction practice of political judgment; it distills that practice's four principles and illustrates them by reference to the larger whole of Douglass's post-Reconstruction political thought. Second, it discusses these principles and shows how together they constitute a general model of antiracist political judgment. The conclusion explains how that model may be useful in our own time.

Douglass in 1883: Fighting Formalism

The year 1883 marked a new nadir in postemancipation black experience. In October, the Supreme Court decided the *Civil Rights Cases*, striking down the Civil Rights Act of 1875, which had prohibited racial discrimination in public transportation and accommodation. In his opinion for the court, Associate Justice Joseph P. Bradley declared, "When a man has emerged from slavery . . . there must be some stage in the progress of his elevation when he takes the rank of a mere citizen and ceases to be the special favorite of the laws."[25] Bradley's remark captures the exasperation and moral fatigue felt by both Northern and Southern whites in the aftermath of the Civil War and Reconstruction and in the face of the ongoing struggle for racial justice. Applauding the Court's decision, the *New York Times* remarked that the Civil Rights Act had kept "alive a prejudice against negroes . . . which without it would have gradually died out."[26]

Just weeks before the decision, Douglass delivered an address entitled "Parties Were Made for Men, Not Men for Parties" before the National

Colored Convention in Louisville, Kentucky, laying bare his frustration with the nation's declining moral vigilance. In this address, Douglass first tackled the "seeming incongruity and contradiction" in a National Colored Convention. Impersonating his white interlocutors, he asked rhetorically, "'What more can the colored people of this country want than they now have?' . . . Why keep up this odious distinction between citizens of a common country and thus give countenance to the color line?" Douglass then responded, "The force of the objection is more in sound than in substance. No reasonable man will ever object to white men holding conventions in their own interests, when they are . . . in our condition and we in theirs."[27] He generally condemned popular movements for black cultural "race pride," stating in 1889: "What is the thing we are fighting against[?] . . . What is it, but American race pride; an assumption of superiority upon the ground of race and color? Do we not know that . . . every pretension we set up in favor of race pride is giving the enemy a stick to break our own heads? . . . Let us do away with this supercilious nonsense. If we are proud let it be because we have had some agency in producing that of which to be proud."[28]

But in "Parties Were Made for Men," Douglass defended pragmatic political forms of race consciousness and race solidarity, distinguishing them from biologically essentialist cultural nationalism: "The apology for observing the color line in the composition of our State and National conventions is in its necessity and in the fact that we must do this or nothing. . . . It has its foundation in the exceptional relation we sustain to the white people of the country."[29] The equivalency drawn between white racism and race-conscious solidarity against it, he suggested, is farcical. The exceptionally unequal relationship between African Americans and the general populace demanded consciousness raising and self-organizing measures adequate to it. African Americans had to become aware of themselves as a subordinated, racialized public and commit themselves to collective self-defense and self-assertion: "Why are we here in this National Convention? . . . Because there is a power in numbers and in union; because the many are more than the few; because the voice of a whole people, oppressed by common injustice is far more likely to command attention and exert an influence on the public mind than the voice of single individuals and isolated organizations."[30]

Douglass's defense of political race consciousness and solidarity gives us a glimpse into the first two principles of his political judgment: (1) sensitivity to power asymmetries and (2) skepticism toward formalistic arguments that obscure them. Moral equality between black and white Americans does not imply equality of political and economic power. The racial nature of African Americans' subordination requires them to cultivate forms of political consciousness and methods of political action that take that racial nature into account. This requirement justifies the use of race-conscious and race-solidaristic measures whose use by a domineering majority would be morally suspect. The test of these measures is whether they substantively reinforce or substantively oppose racial domination. When the color line "will cease to have any civil, political, or moral significance," Douglass argued, "colored conventions will then be dispensed with as anachronisms, wholly out of place, but not till then."[31] Douglass's analysis suggests that observers of racial conflict must judge race consciousness and solidarity not as decontextualized formal features of political institutions and action but in relation to the larger power structures of which they are a part. Race consciousness and solidarity likely to undo racial hierarchy, Douglass contended, is permissible in a way that race consciousness and solidarity likely to reinforce racial hierarchy is not.

We see Douglass's sensitivity to power asymmetries and skepticism toward formalistic arguments that obscure them in his response to the Supreme Court's decision in *Civil Rights Cases*. The Court reasoned that the Fourteenth Amendment empowered Congress to prohibit racial discrimination by the states but not by private corporations or individuals. The Civil Rights Act's barring of racial discrimination in commercial transportation, accommodation, and places of public amusement, the Court argued, was therefore unconstitutional.[32] Douglass lambasted this reasoning as formalistic absurdity. The decision presented the United States "before the world as a Nation utterly destitute of power to protect the rights of its own citizens upon its own soil." It gave "to a South Carolina, or Mississippi, Railroad Conductor, more power than . . . the National Government."[33] Douglass's reasoning coincided with that of the Court's lone dissenter, Associate Justice John Marshall Harlan. The text of the dissent was not yet available when Douglass made his speech,[34] so the two reached their conclusions independently. Said Harlan: "It was perfectly well known [at the time of the Fourteenth Amendment's ratification] that the great danger to the equal enjoyment by citizens of their rights as citizens was to be apprehended not altogether from unfriendly State legislation, but from the hostile action of corporations and individuals in the States. And it is to be presumed that it was intended by [section 5 of the Fourteenth Amendment] to clothe Congress with power and authority to meet that danger."[35]

The substance of citizenship rights, Harlan suggested, is realized not only in direct encounters between state and citizen but also in seemingly private commercial and civil societal spaces that still fall within the scope of the state's police power. Railroad companies' status as public corporations and inns' and theaters' subjection to state licensing requirements show that they are "*quasi*-public employments": "The innkeeper is not to select his guest. He has no right to say to one, you shall come to my inn, and to another, you shall not, as everyone coming and conducting himself in a proper manner has a right to be received, and, for this purpose innkeepers are a sort of public servants, they having, in return a kind of privilege of entertaining travelers and supplying them with what they want."[36]

This analysis of the public nature of much "private" commercial space led Harlan to conclude, "Discrimination practised by corporations and individuals in the exercise of their public or *quasi*-public functions is a badge of servitude the imposition of which Congress may prevent under its power, by appropriate legislation, to enforce the Thirteenth Amendment." The Fourteenth Amendment provided additional grounds for the Civil Rights Act: "In every material sense applicable to the practical enforcement of the Fourteenth Amendment, railroad corporations, keepers of inns, and managers of places of public amusement are agents or instrumentalities of the State, because they are charged with duties to the public and are amenable, in respect of their duties and functions, to governmental regulation." Harlan would allow Congress to prohibit racial discrimination in all public space ordinarily subject to regulation. "Exemption from race discrimination" was essential to equal citizenship.[37]

Douglass also believed strongly that equal citizenship meant equal standing, not just in the halls of government but also in the world of commerce.[38] Declaring that the Court's decision gave "joy to the heart of every man in the land who wishes to deny to others what he claims for himself," Douglass suggested that citizens' everyday public experiences of mutual respect were a test of civic equality.[39] In addition to a legal status, citizenship is an intersubjective condition of reciprocal recognition. Harlan's words may best capture the challenge of reciprocal recognition in post-Reconstruction America: "The difficulty has been to compel a recognition of the legal right of the black race to take the rank of citizens, and to secure the enjoyment of privileges belonging, under the law, to them as a component part of the people for whose welfare and happiness government is ordained."[40]

Douglass was generally unimpressed with the political philosophy of federalism behind the Court's decision. The majority portrayed itself as preventing Congress from exceeding the limits of its enumerated powers, from taking "the place of the State legislatures" and "supersed[ing]" them.[41] He contended, however, that American federalism's historical tendency to function as a shield for white supremacy should reduce—if not eliminate— our deference to it. Any institution that interferes with the national government's performance of the paramount duty of protecting freedmen's rights forfeits its claim to respect. "Whatever may have been the true theory of the organic law of the land before the late rebellion," Douglass said in 1889, "the suppression of that rebellion swept away, not only slavery, but the pretension of sovereignty of the individual states, and established a nation."[42] He was especially frustrated that after buttressing the federal government's power before the war to protect slaveholders' property rights, the Court now changed course and limited the federal government's power to protect freedmen's personal rights. "While slavery was the base line of American society, while it ruled the church and the state, while it was the interpreter of our law and the exponent of our religion, it admitted no quibbling, no narrow rules of legal or scriptural interpretations of Bible or Constitution. It sternly demanded its pound of flesh, no matter how much blood was shed in the taking of it." Now, however, the Court "has seen fit in this case, affecting a weak and much-persecuted people, to be guided by the narrowest rules of legal interpretation. It has viewed both the Constitution and the law with a strict regard to their letter, but without any generous recognition of their broad and liberal spirit."[43] The federal powers previously enlisted on behalf of slaveholders, Douglass believed, should now form the basis of federal protection of civil rights. He evaluated the Constitution from the point of view of the vulnerable freedman: "What does it matter to a colored citizen that a State may not insult and outrage him, if a citizen of a State may?"[44] Whatever got in the way of the protection of freedmen's rights was a new emanation of slavery's spirit, no matter how legalistically adorned.

Douglass characterized the Court's decision in the *Civil Rights Cases* "as one more shocking development of that moral weakness in high places which has attended the conflict between the spirit of liberty and the spirit of slavery from the beginning": "Liberty has supplanted slavery, but I fear it has not supplanted the spirit or power of slavery. Where slavery was strong, liberty is now weak."[45] Eighteen years after the Civil War, the victors were losing—in Lincoln's words—the "firmness in the right" required to achieve a "just" peace.[46] Douglass had been warning the North since the end of Reconstruction that it was squandering victory to a resurgent South still convinced of the justice of its cause.[47] Yet as David Blight has shown, Douglass assigned himself the task of keeping the memory of the moral conflict alive.[48] "I am not indifferent to the claims of a generous forgetfulness," he proclaimed in 1882, "but whatever else I may forget, I shall never forget the difference between those who fought for liberty and those who fought for slavery; those who fought to save the republic and those who fought to destroy it."[49]

Douglass believed that historical memory was an indispensable guide to political judgment: "Man is said to be an animal looking before and after. It is his distinction to improve the future by a wise consideration of the past."[50] Thucydides and Machiavelli made the idea that historical knowledge is essential to political judgment a commonplace of the Western tradition,[51] yet in the context of American racial conflict the idea of historical reflexivity is anything but commonplace; it is subversive, radical. After Reconstruction, the ascendant assumption of American political culture was that the war had engendered "a new birth of freedom"[52] and that postbellum America was discontinuous with the slaveholding republic that preceded it. This assumption made the celebration of sectional reconciliation increasingly appropriate and vigilance on behalf of African Americans decreasingly necessary. Call it the presumption of *discontinuity.* Douglass believed a presumption of *continuity* was more fitting. The presumption of continuity put the burden of proof on the South to show it had secured equality for African Americans and thus purged itself of the spirit of slavery. The presumption of continuity, he insisted, should form the baseline of our political judgment: "Though the rebellion is dead, though slavery is dead, both the rebellion and slavery have left behind influences which will remain with us, it may be, for generations to come."[53]

The presumption of continuity sharpened Douglass's political judgment and enabled him to discern the ways that slavery lived on in the South under freedom's forms. In "Parties Were Made for Men, Not Men for Parties," Douglass assessed the lived conditions of black Southern agricultural laborers and concluded that "there may be a slavery of wages only a little less galling and crushing in its effects than chattel slavery. . . . This slavery

of wages must go down with the other."[54] His analysis of Southern economic conditions and argument for a more just distribution of wealth echoed
nineteenth-century labor republicanism:[55] "The labor of a country is the
source of its wealth; without the colored laborer to-day the South would be
a howling wilderness. . . . This sharp contrast of wealth and poverty, as every
thoughtful man knows, can exist only in one way, and from one cause, and
that is by one getting more than its proper share of the reward of industry,
and the other side getting less."[56]

Douglass's standard for the "proper share of the reward of industry"
exceeds a formally negotiated wage. At the very least, the background conditions of negotiation must be such that the laborer has the wherewithal
to walk away. "He who can say to his fellow-man, 'You shall serve me or
starve,' is a master and his subject is a slave," Douglass insisted.[57] "It is hard
for labor, however fortunately and favorably surrounded, to cope with the
tremendous power of capital in any contest for higher wages."[58] He stopped
short of calling for the abolition of the wage-labor system—the aim of radical labor republican organizations such as the Knights of Labor.[59] It is nevertheless noteworthy how Douglass's assessment of power disparities is not
narrowly legalistic but economically realistic. Against the background of
economic power disparities, he condemned Southern labor contracts as, for
all intents and purposes, involuntary.

Douglass's increasing economic realism helps explain his support
for increasingly radical policy measures. Immediately after the Civil War,
Douglass's principled commitment to the sanctity of property—which he
saw as a corollary of the right of self-ownership—compelled him to oppose
proposals by Thaddeus Stevens to confiscate rebel land and redistribute it to
freedmen.[60] By 1883, however, Douglass voiced regret over his opposition
to these proposals and characterized Stevens as a "far-seeing" statesman
who recognized that leaving the freedmen without "a foot of ground from
which to get a crust of bread" effectually enslaved them to their former
owners.[61] He also hinted at the nation's obligation to provide reparations to
freedmen, in the same way that Pharaoh gave jewels to the Hebrews and
Russia land to the serfs.[62]

Although Douglass never put forward a new plan for land redistribution,[63] he did advocate a national system of public education: "The ignorance of any part of the American people so deeply concerns all the rest that
there can be no doubt of the right to pass a law compelling the attendance

of every child at school. . . . The National Government, with its immense resources, can carry the benefits of a sound common-school education to the door of every poor man from Maine to Texas."[64]

It is important to read Douglass's support of a national system of public education in conjunction with his support of strong federal enforcement of antidiscrimination law. Viewed together, they show the heavy weight he placed on the federal government's responsibility to make freedom effectual in every state and town. In 1888, he said that a government charged with securing liberty in its constitution must "have the power to protect liberty in its administration."[65] "For a nation historically accustomed to federalism," observes Peter Myers, Douglass's "proposals reflected an extraordinarily expansive conception of federal power."[66]

From these considerations, we can distill two additional principles of Douglass's political judgment: (3) a presumption of the spirit of slavery's continuity in American life and (4) the subordination of constitutional forms to substantive political ends. Most striking about Douglass's reaction to *Civil Rights Cases* is his interpretation of the decision as a symptom of the resurgence of the spirit of slavery. What drove the decision, he insisted, were not federalist scruples or concerns about the distinction between public and private but rather investment in racial domination and resentment of the limits imposed by racial equality. Personal habits of domination practiced in slave society and admired even by those who did not own slaves produced both this investment and this resentment. As Douglass explained in 1885, "Born, educated, and accustomed to the exercise of unlimited power over men, the slaveholder carried his habit of domination wherever he went."[67] The habit of domination persisted after abolition and searched for new legal forms to protect it. Finding new legal forms was, if not essential, then at least convenient because it allowed the spirit of slavery to use a cloak of principle to conceal itself. Ironically, the new principle was the same as the old: state sovereignty. Before the war, state sovereignty protected the right of whites to own blacks without federal interference (indeed, with federal protection); now, state sovereignty protected the right of whites to exclude blacks without congressional meddling. State sovereignty concealed the motive force of white supremacy from opponents and, perhaps just as importantly, from white supremacists themselves; it enabled them to say, "Our concern here is not race, but the forms of liberty." The drive to dominate disguised itself as federalist political philosophy. Wilson Carey McWilliams reminds us that for conservatives "order is precious and at least a little fragile. Conservatives treat it delicately, observing the forms."[68] Douglass, by contrast, saw constitutional forms not as ends but as means. Federalism had produced the crisis of slavery and war. As a political form, it deserved no deference.[69]

Douglass's Political Judgment

Let us review the four principles of Douglass's post-Reconstruction political judgment:

1. Sensitivity to power asymmetries
2. Skepticism toward formalistic arguments that obscure these asymmetries
3. A presumption of the spirit of slavery's continuity in American life
4. The subordination of constitutional forms to substantive political ends

These principles direct our attention to things that should strike us as obvious but fail to do so because of the ideological corruption of our perception. They specify differences to attend to, appearances to distrust, historical forces to look for, substantive considerations to remember. Sensitivity to power asymmetries requires *some* abstraction: after noting wealth and poverty, connections (or lack thereof) to the politically powerful, and access (or lack thereof) to means of production, the observer must make a synthetic assessment of the parties' strength and weakness. At the same time, as Douglass practiced it, political judgment incorporates information peripheral to the parties' legal status—land ownership, access to economic necessities, education, access to credit, geographical mobility—and is therefore more attuned to differences in the ability to enact one's will than axioms of legal equality can register. After Reconstruction's retreat and the emergence of new systems of racial repression in the Southern states, many white Northerners suggested that black Southerners "make an exodus to the Pacific slope." "With the best of intentions," Douglass noted, "they are told of the fertility of the soil and salubrity of the climate." Yet "if they should tell the same as existing in the moon the simple question, How shall they get there? would knock the life out of it at once. Without money, without friends, without knowledge, and only gaining enough by daily toil to keep them above the starvation point, where they are, how can such a people rise and cross the continent? The measure on its face is no remedy at all."[70]

Douglass's recognition of the social and financial capital required to migrate west—and freedmen's lack of that capital—enabled him to judge the celebrated promise of the American West as mythical in their case. His forthright acknowledgement of freedmen's abject poverty—and lack of economic mobility—also enabled him to judge the South's new system of wage labor as coercive despite its voluntary appearance: "The man who has it in his power to say to a man you must work the land for me, for such wages as I choose to give, has a power of slavery over him as real, if not as complete, as he who compels toil under the lash. All that a man hath he will give for his life."[71] Good political judgment privileges neither legal status nor formal contractual parity in power assessments; rather, it attends to the social and material prerequisites of free and effective action. Privileging legal status and formal contractual parity at the expense of examining the social and material prerequisites of free and effective action is a trick of both capitalism and white supremacy.[72]

Good political judgment also requires skepticism toward formalistic arguments that obscure power asymmetries. By "formalistic arguments," I mean those that treat moral, legal, and political conflicts as geometry problems or logic games, translating the contributing dynamics into mathematical variables that admit of a neat solution.[73] Formalism tends to impose symmetry upon asymmetry in a way satirized by Anatole France when he reflected, "The majestic equality of the law, forbids rich and poor alike to sleep under bridges, to beg in the streets, and to steal their bread."[74] Formalism flattens out distinctions that its purveyors deem irrelevant. In many conflicts, however, which distinctions are relevant is precisely the issue. When critics of the National Colored Convention of 1883 argued that such conventions were "odious" because they gave "countenance to the color line," they presumed (or pretended) that recognizing the color line was always reprehensible regardless of how precisely it was being recognized. The attendees of the National Colored Convention were recognizing the color line's political reality, yet they were accused of recognizing its biological significance. This conflation obscured the difference between believing in a racial biological fiction and organizing against oppression done in the name of that fiction. What cuts through such conflation is substantive judgment capable of identifying false equivalencies, of registering relevant differences, and of giving them proper weight. This is not to say that formalistic abstraction is never useful or appropriate; it is to say, however, that we subsume particulars under universals and reify concepts and categories at our peril. We must be reflexive in using such universals, concepts, and categories and remember that they are simplifications meant to clarify analysis, but always at the risk of banishing relevant information.

Because formalistic analysis always involves this risk, it is often a useful tool for power interests bent on excluding certain information from public consideration. The statement "The Negro is free" was true in 1866 in a formalistic legal sense. But stopping the analysis there would miss most of the story. For those who wanted to argue that the nation had done its duty by the Negro and owed him nothing more, the statement was politically convenient. In February 1866, for example, President Andrew Johnson invoked the Negro's formal freedom to defend his veto of a bill extending the life of the Freedmen's Bureau. He argued that the Second Freedmen's Bureau Bill insulted

the ability of the freedmen to protect and take care of themselves. . . . [A]s they have received their freedom with moderation and forbearance, so they will distinguish themselves by their industry and thrift, and soon show the world that in a condition of freedom they are self-sustaining, capable of selecting their own employment and their own places of abode, of insisting for themselves on a proper remuneration, and of establishing and maintaining their own asylums and schools. It is earnestly hoped that, instead of wasting away, they will, by their own efforts, establish for themselves a condition of respectability and prosperity. It is certain that they can attain to that condition only through their own merits and exertions.[75]

Johnson's analysis rested on background assumptions of economic mobility and fair competition that were willfully oblivious to power inequalities. Is it possible he was ignorant of facts on the ground? Johnson's lifelong familiarity with the South and experience from 1862 to 1865 as military governor of Tennessee make the plea of ignorance unconvincing. His amply demonstrated commitment to keeping America "a country for white men" renders an alternative explanation more likely: Johnson's aim was to keep the Freedmen's Bureau from relieving black economic desperation, thereby strengthening whites' ability to extort black agreement to exploitative labor contracts preserving white domination.[76] The path of least resistance to defending the veto was to portray the Freedmen's Bureau's assistance as unnecessary. Johnson used the cover of black Americans' formal freedom to deflect attention away from their social and economic subordination and to argue against government intervention on their behalf. One task of political judgment is to see through such half-truth. The point of formalistic argument is sometimes to clarify, but it is just as often used to deflect, to enchant, to obscure. Skepticism toward formalistic argument is essential to good judgment. In his quickness to distinguish "substance" from "sound,"[77] Douglass exemplified this skepticism.

Presuming the spirit of slavery's continuity in American life is the most controversial feature of Douglass's post-Reconstruction political judgment. Good judgment typically involves suspension of belief, the temporary surrender of standing assumptions in order to open the mind to novelty.[78] Presuming the spirit of slavery's continuity could block openness to countervailing evidence. How then was it consistent with good judgment? The answer lies in a twofold recognition of *(a)* that continuity's real existence and depth and *(b)* the overwhelming, all-encompassing force of the opposite presumption. The idea that slavery was not just history but *past* had become so popular in the 1880s that it required an act of will to perceive the continuity of its spirit. Presuming that continuity was an epistemic compensation against a furious zeitgeist of historical denial. As Douglass noted in 1888,

> Every northern man who visits the old master class . . . is told by the old slaveholders with a great show of virtue that they are glad that they are rid of slavery and would not have the slave system back if they could. . . . Thus northern men come home duped and go on a mission duping others by telling the same pleasing story. There are very good reasons why these people would not have slavery back if they could. . . . With slavery they had some care and responsibility for the physical well being of their slaves. Now they have as firm a grip on the freedman's labor as when he was a slave without any burden of caring for his children or himself.[79]

Notwithstanding differences in legal form, the intensities of exploitation between slavery and "freedom" were continuous. Presuming the general continuity of the spirit of slavery protected judgment from an unfounded and imperious presumption of discontinuity. In certain contexts, strong substantive presumptions are necessary to counterbalance their opposites' ideological aggression. Observers can guard against self-delusion by remembering that compensatory presumptions are precisely that—presumptions. One's commitment to them must be provisional, reflexive, and intellectually strategic. One must remain open to the possibility of their invalidity. But one should also be firm in holding them against corrupt attempts to displace them. As late as 1889, Douglass maintained: "It is still the battle between two opposite civilizations—the one created and sustained by slavery, and the other framed and fashioned in the spirit of liberty and humanity, and this conflict will not be ended until one or the other shall be completely adopted in every section of our common country."[80]

Subordinating constitutional forms to substantive political ends should be commonsensical, but constitutional idolatry runs so deep in US history that this precept must be made explicit.[81] The subject is complicated by the fact that Douglass exploited constitutional idolatry for his own purposes. Starting in the 1850s, he insisted that the US Constitution was an antislavery document.[82] After the war, he glorified the Thirteenth, Fourteenth, and Fifteenth Amendments, especially their strong enforcement clauses.[83] In 1886, he upheld the preamble to the Constitution as a general standard for judging national life.[84] On this occasion, Douglass explained that the Founders "set forth six definite and cardinal objects to be attained" by the Constitution: "These were: First. 'To form a more perfect union.' Second. 'To establish justice.' Third. 'To provide for the common defense.' Fourth. 'To insure domestic tranquility.' Fifth. 'To promote a general welfare.' And sixth. 'Secure the blessings of liberty to ourselves and our posterity.' Perhaps there never was an instrument framed by men at the beginning of any national career designed to accomplish nobler objects than those set forth in the preamble of this constitution."[85]

Notice Douglass's focus on the "objects" of the Constitution rather than on the "instruments" designed to realize those objects. In contrast to contemporary norms of constitutional interpretation—which treat the preamble as too vague to be helpful[86]—Douglass treated the preamble as a decisive interpretive compass that ought to orient our understanding of the Constitution's federal structure and institutional mechanisms.[87]

Douglass's response to *Civil Rights Cases* provides a specific example of this interpretive approach. The Court held that the Civil Rights Act of 1875 was invalid because in prohibiting private parties from engaging in racial discrimination, Congress exceeded its authority: the Fourteenth Amendment empowered Congress to prohibit states but not citizens or corporations within those states from engaging in racial discrimination. Strictly constructed, the language of the Fourteenth Amendment vindicates the Court's position. The language of section 1 focuses on states and no other entities: "No State shall make or enforce any law which shall abridge the privileges or immunities of citizens of the United States; nor shall any State deprive any person of life, liberty, or property, without due process of law; nor deny to any person within its jurisdiction the equal protection of the laws." Douglass, however, argued against strict construction: "Inasmuch as the law in question is a law in favor of liberty and justice, it ought to have had the benefit of any doubt which could arise as to its strict constitutionality."[88] Judgment of the law's favorability to liberty and justice should precede—and to a large extent direct—judgment of whether the law adheres to the Constitution. Douglass thus stood against the reverence for constitutional forms that McWilliams identifies as a hallmark of the conservative temperament. Reverence for constitutional objects must displace reverence for forms, even if—especially if—doing so opens up debate about substantive political ends. Such debate unavoidably threatens order, but it expresses liberty and is essential to justice.

The four principles of Douglass's political judgment interact in important ways. Sensitivity to power asymmetries helped Douglass discern the spirit of slavery's continuity, the pervasiveness of relationships in which one man can say to another, "You shall serve me or starve," rendering the former an effectual master and the latter an effectual slave. Skepticism toward formalistic arguments enabled Douglass to speak of postwar black economic life as a form of (neo)slavery. As he declared in 1889, "Slavery can as really exist without law as with it, and in some instances more securely, because less likely to be interfered with. . . . No man can point to any law in the United States by which slavery was originally established. The fact of slavery always precedes enactments making it legal. Men first make slaves and then make laws affirming the right of slavery."[89]

Sensitivity to power asymmetries also helped Douglass resist the charms of legal formalism. Because he judged laws from the perspective of freedmen vulnerable in their efforts to realize freedom, he recognized the hollowness of distinctions, say, between state and nonstate acts of racial discrimination. The "effect" on the freedman "is the same."[90] Douglass's practice of judging from the perspective of vulnerable citizens also bolstered his general disposition to prioritize moral and political substance over legal forms. What matters most is not the symmetry, harmony, and orderliness of the legal structure but rather that structure's effects on citizens' lives.

Douglass's post-Reconstruction political judgment was self-confident and intellectually self-reliant. His firsthand knowledge of slavery grounded his understanding of freedom's requirements: robust state protection of life and liberty as well as socially guaranteed opportunity for education and property accumulation, secured through equal citizenship.[91] Citizenship, for Douglass, names not only legal status but also equal standing. Routinized respect of citizens by all of a nation's civil and commercial institutions gives that standing meaning. Douglass's interpretation of freedom's requirements oriented his political judgment. Staying sensitive to power asymmetries, being vigilant against formalistic arguments that obscure them, acknowledging the spirit of slavery's continuity in American life, and subordinating constitutional form to political substance were essential to the larger work of universalizing freedom. The project of universalizing freedom thus also grounded Douglass's political judgment. That project rested on a prior moral judgment that all men and women deserve to be free.

Specifying the grounds of this moral judgment would require a chapter in its own right. But our identification of it reminds us of an important general lesson about political judgment: political judgment both formulates commitments and discloses them. In the act of judgment, we not only announce our own view but also reveal the basic commitments that constitute us. Here Arendt's words are apt: "Wherever people judge the things of the world that are common to them, there is more implied in their judgments than these things. By his manner of judging, the person discloses to an extent also himself."[92] Judging politically, she argues, lies at the heart of acting politically, of pronouncing positions on political things, of disclosing oneself before one's peers on behalf of principles one holds dear.[93]

Yet judgment for Douglass was more than an outlet for self-disclosure or an opportunity for exhilarating action; it was essential to claiming humanity. Born into a world that told him he was less than human, he had to judge that world mistaken, even corrupt, just to claim humanity. The political actors analyzed by Arendt were either born free (Athenian citizens, American colonists) or suffered oppression that fell short of racial slavery (the French Revolutionaries). Socrates, Adams, Jefferson, and the French Revolutionaries—all challenged their society's boundaries of political authority, but all could nevertheless assume that they shared with their oppressors if not a common status as citizen or Englishman, then at least a common humanity. Douglass's judgments challenged his society's boundaries of the human, requiring perhaps even more daring than Socrates's challenges to the Athenians, Adams's and Jefferson's challenges to the British, or the French Revolutionaries' challenges to the ancien régime. Douglass stared down racial slavery before the Civil War and called it a violation of his human dignity. After the Civil War, he stared down the spirit of slavery—even as it masqueraded as the spirit of freedom—and called it by its proper name. His identification of a general spirit of domination lurking in the heart of American political culture was essential to his effort to make sense of white supremacy's stubborn tenacity after emancipation. His identification of that spirit is essential for *us* because it pinpoints a truth we are reluctant to recognize: it is an open question whether love of freedom or lust for domination predominates our national life.[94]

Antiracist Political Judgment

In *Shelby County v. Holder* (2013), the Supreme Court invalidated section 4 of the Voting Rights Act of 1965, neutralizing the Justice Department's ability to prevent states and localities with a history of racial discrimination from infringing the right to vote. Despite a vast legislative record showing that black voter disfranchisement still abounds, predominantly in the states of the Old Confederacy,[95] Chief Justice John Roberts declared, "Our country has changed," making section 4 an unjust imposition on states' "equal sovereignty."[96] Roberts's opinion expresses a triumphalist narrative of racial progress that casts those still fighting for strong federal intervention on behalf of racial justice as overly invested in outdated racial grievance. "History," Roberts wrote, "did not end in 1965."[97]

Roberts's outlook in *Shelby County v. Holder* closely parallels that of Justice Bradley in *Civil Rights Cases*. Recall Bradley's statement, "When a man has emerged from slavery . . . there must be some stage in the progress of his elevation when he takes the rank of a mere citizen and ceases to be the special favorite of the laws." Both Roberts and Bradley see federal legislation specifically geared to counteract the legacies of slavery and the wrongs of racism as decreasingly necessary. Both assume that the harms of slavery and racism gradually diminish with time. Both pay greater heed to axioms of limited government than to recurring obstacles to black citizens' struggle for equal liberty. It is easy to see, in retrospect, that Bradley's prognosis was inaccurate and his prescription unfair. The history of Jim Crow exposes the error of his racial optimism. Bradley's example should be a warning to those today professing similar racial optimism. Is Roberts's racial optimism better warranted?

The distinguishing elements of Douglass's political judgment—which together constitute a compelling general model of antiracist political judgment—counsel against an affirmative response. In not only *Shelby* but also *Parents Involved v. Seattle* (2007), Roberts failed to attend to the asymmetrical racial power relations that diminish black civic equality. In the latter case, he held that state agencies may use race-conscious public policy to correct the aftereffects of de jure educational segregation but may not do so to combat de facto educational segregation, even when that segregation is a product of previously state-sanctioned residential segregation and even when it demonstrably harms nonwhite children. Consistency with the principle of color blindness—"The way to stop discrimination on the basis of race is to stop discriminating on the basis of race"[98]—trumps the imperative of dismantling a distribution of good public schooling still biased in favor of whites.

In *Shelby,* Roberts's opposition to section 4 of the Voting Rights Act on the grounds of states' equal sovereignty is—from the perspective of Douglass's writings—startling. Douglass argued that the principle of equal state sovereignty has historically functioned to give "the spirit of slavery" safe harbor. Roberts makes that principle the basis for insulating states and municipalities with deep and documented histories of disenfranchising black and brown voters from federal oversight. Roberts would, of course, reject any suggestion that his judicial actions accommodate the spirit of slavery, but Douglass would encourage us to judge those actions from the perspectives of America's most vulnerable, racialized citizens—many of whom justifiably see equal state sovereignty as a banner for domination.[99] Perhaps what accounts for Roberts's failure to give this viewpoint due weight is a failure to sufficiently incorporate African American worldviews into his own interpretive judgment. Compared to that of Frederick Douglass, the mentality of John Roberts is insufficiently enlarged.

The spirit of slavery may not today manifest itself in any actual effort to reestablish "the peculiar institution," but it does still manifest itself in the dismantlement of public policies that take direct aim at racial inequality; the net effect is to conserve the de facto white dominance born of slavery and Jim Crow. In using doctrines such as equal state sovereignty to restrain federal efforts to prevent racial injustice, Chief Justice Roberts extends the life of white supremacy under the cover of legal formalism. Such formalism permits the chief justice to project himself as a man of clarity, principle, and intellectual rigor even as he substantively reinforces racial hierarchy. "It is remarkable how rare in the history of tyrants is an immoral law," wrote Ralph Waldo Emerson. "Some color, some indirection was always used."[100] Roberts is a master of such "indirection." But hope is not lost so long as antiracist political judgment survives. Such judgment helps us see the "indirection" for what it is: the will of white supremacy to reproduce itself.

Notes

Earlier versions of this chapter were presented at research colloquia of Duke University's Program in American Values and Institutions, the University of Alabama's Department of Gender and Race Studies, Northwestern University's Political Theory Program, and Vanderbilt University's Social and Political Thought Program.

I am grateful to Michael Gillespie, Nora Hanagan, Utz McKnight, Alvin Tillery, and Emily Nacol for being such gracious hosts. Thanks also to Nolan Bennett, David Blight, Nick Bromell, Mary Dietz, James Farr, Megan Francis, Alex Gourevitch, George Kateb, Sharon Krause, Michael Lienesch, Alexander Livingston, Sara Monoson, Lucius Outlaw, Christopher Parker, Neil Roberts, Melvin Rogers, Sandra Skene, and Seth Trenchard for extensive feedback on earlier drafts of this chapter.

1. *Grutter v. Bollinger* 539 US 306 (2003), at 349–50. For the sake of brevity, I have condensed the quotation. The original can be found in Frederick Douglass, "What the Black Man Wants" (1865), in *Frederick Douglass Papers. Series One: Speeches, Debates, and Interviews*, 5 vols., ed. John W. Blassingame and others (New Haven, CT: Yale University Press, 1979–1992), 4:68. *Frederick Douglass Papers, Series One*, is hereafter cited as *FDP1*, followed by volume and page numbers.

2. Sean Coons, "Frederick Douglass: New Tea Party Hero?!" *Salon*, July 3, 2013, at http://www.salon.com/2013/07/03/frederick_douglass_new_tea_party_hero/.

3. Peter C. Myers, *Frederick Douglass: Race and the Rebirth of American Liberalism* (Lawrence: University Press of Kansas, 2008), 145, emphasis in original.

4. Frederick Douglass, "West India Emancipation: Extract from a Speech in Elmira, New York, 1 August 1880," in *Life and Times of Frederick Douglass, Written by Himself* (1893), in *Autobiographies*, ed. Henry Louis Gates Jr. (New York: Library of America, 1994), 935. "You cannot make an empty sack stand on end," echoes Franklin's literary persona "Poor Richard": *"'Tis hard for an empty Bag to stand upright"* (Benjamin Franklin, "Poor Richard Improved, 1758," in *Autobiography, Poor Richard, and Later Writings*, ed. J. A. Leo Lemay (New York: Library of America, 1987), 561, emphasis in original. See also Rafia Safar, "Franklinian Douglass: The Afro-American as Representative Man," in Eric J. Sundquist, ed., *Frederick Douglass: New Literary and Historical Essays* (Cambridge: Cambridge University Press, 1990), 99–117.

5. The literature on Douglass as a political thinker focuses preponderantly on his antebellum political thought. Exceptions are David W. Blight, *Frederick Douglass' Civil War: Keeping Faith in Jubilee* (Baton Rouge: Louisiana State University Press, 1989), chaps. 9 and 10; Tommy L. Lott, "Frederick Douglass and the Myth of the Black Rapist," in Bill E. Lawson and Frank M. Kirkland, eds., *Frederick Douglass: A Critical Reader* (Malden, MA: Blackwell, 1999), 313–38; Angela Y. Davis, "From the Prison of Slavery to the Slavery of Prison: Frederick Douglass and the Convict Lease System," in Lawson and Kirkland, eds., *Frederick Douglass*, 339–62; Peter C. Myers, "Frederick Douglass' Natural Rights Constitutionalism: The Postwar, Pre-Progressive Period," in John Marini and Ken Masugi, eds., *The Progressive Revolution in Politics and Political Science: Transforming the American Regime* (Lanham, MD: Rowman and Littlefield, 2005), 73–101; Gene Andrew Jarrett, "Douglass, Ideological Slavery, and Postbellum Racial Politics," in Maurice S. Lee, ed., *The Cambridge Companion to Frederick Douglass* (Cambridge: Cambridge University Press, 2009), 160–72; Jack Turner, *Awakening to Race: Individualism and Social Consciousness in America* (Chicago: University of Chicago Press, 2012), chap. 3. I limit my focus to the post-Reconstruction period because that is when Douglass's political judgment—the theme of this chapter—becomes sharpest. The retreat from Reconstruction forced him to look more deeply into the abyss of white supremacy than he had ever before. Coming to terms with white supremacy's power elicited his keenest insight into the ways it perpetuated itself under benign appearances.

6. Desmond Jagmohan also analyzes Douglass's political judgment in his impressive dissertation "Making Bricks without Straw: Booker T. Washington and the Politics of the Disfranchised," Cornell University, 2014. His interpretation focuses specifically on practical judgments relating to opportunities for political action. This chapter, however, focuses on interpretive and evaluative judgments relating to understanding political phenomena. For a powerful recent discussion of Douglass's

antebellum practices of denunciation as a form of political judgment, see Nolan Bennett, "To Narrate and Denounce: Frederick Douglass and the Politics of Personal Narrative," *Political Theory* 44 (2) (2016): 240–64.

7. My definition of political judgment is based on my readings of Hannah Arendt's, Jennifer Nedelsky's, and Linda M. G. Zerilli's astute analyses of the subject. See Hannah Arendt, "The Crisis in Culture: Its Social and Its Political Significance" and "Truth and Politics," in *Between Past and Future: Eight Exercises in Political Thought* (1961; reprint, New York: Penguin, 2006), 194–222, 223–59, and *Lectures on Kant's Political Philosophy*, ed. Ronald Beiner (Chicago: University of Chicago Press, 1992), 1–85; Jennifer Nedelsky, "Judgment, Diversity, and Relational Autonomy," in Ronald Beiner and Jennifer Nedelsky, eds., *Judgment, Imagination, and Politics: Themes from Kant and Arendt* (Lanham, MD: Rowman and Littlefield, 2001), 103–20; Linda M. G. Zerilli, *Feminism and the Abyss of Freedom* (Chicago: University of Chicago Press, 2005), chap. 4, and *A Democratic Theory of Judgment* (Chicago: University of Chicago Press, 2016). I have also benefitted from Seth Trenchard, "The Pleasure of Judgment and Its Use: Rethinking the Aesthetic Subject in Aesthetic Judgment," master's thesis, University of Washington, 2014. On the idea of interpretation, I am most indebted to Charles Taylor, "Interpretation and the Sciences of Man," *Review of Metaphysics* 25 (1) (1971): 3–51.

8. Douglass thus anticipates Desmond King and Rogers Smith's claim that "American politics has been historically constituted, in part, by two evolving but linked 'racial institutional orders': a set of 'white supremacist' orders and a competing set of 'transformative egalitarian' orders" ("Racial Orders in American Political Development," *American Political Science Review* 99 [1] [2005]: 75).

9. Frederick Douglass, "One Country, One Law, One Liberty for All Citizens: An Interview in Washington, D.C., in January 1889," in *FDP1*, 5:402.

10. Frederick Douglass, "Lessons of the Hour: An Address Delivered in Washington, D.C., on 9 January 1894," in *FDP1*, 5:593.

11. Frederick Douglass, "The Negro Problem: An Address Delivered in Washington, D.C., on 21 October 1890," in *FDP1*, 5:448.

12. On the racial circumscription, see Rogers Smith, *Civic Ideals: Conflicting Visions of Citizenship in U.S. History* (New Haven, CT: Yale University Press, 1997), chaps. 10 and 11. On performative speech as a claim to dignity, see Melvin L. Rogers, "David Walker and the Power of the Appeal," *Political Theory* 43 (2) (2015): 208–33.

13. On herrenvolk republicanism, see David Roediger, *The Wages of Whiteness: Race and the Making of the American Working Class*, new ed. (London: Verso, [1991] 2007). Both Jason Frank and Linda M. G. Zerilli note the way Douglass's rhetoric creatively reinterprets old political watchwords and infuses

them with new meaning. See Jason Frank, *Constituent Moments: Enacting the People in Postrevolutionary America* (Durham, NC: Duke University Press, 2010), chap. 7, and Zerilli, *Democratic Theory of Judgment*, 153–59. For Christopher S. Parker's interpretation of Douglass as an exemplar of a distinctive black republican tradition, see *Fighting for Democracy: Black Veterans and the Struggle against White Supremacy in the Postwar South* (Princeton, NJ: Princeton University Press, 2009), 86.

14. Nick Bromell, "A 'Voice from the Enslaved': The Origins of Frederick Douglass's Political Philosophy of Democracy," *American Literary History* 23 (4) (2011): 699, 698.

15. Arendt, "Crisis in Culture," 217. See also Arendt, *Lectures on Kant's Political Philosophy*, 42–43, 71, 73.

16. Frederick Douglass, "Good Men Are God in the Flesh: An Address Delivered in Boston, Massachusetts, on 22 September 1890," in *FDP1*, 5:432. See also Frederick Douglass, "Parties Were Made for Men, Not Men for Parties: An Address Delivered in Louisville, Kentucky, on 25 September 1883," in *FDP1*, 5:98, and Douglass, "Lessons of the Hour," 5:576.

17. Douglass's racially integrative enlarged mentality, in this sense, stands as a useful corrective to Arendt's own practice of political judgment. However valuable her general theoretical reflections on judgment, her failures to sufficiently integrate the perspectives of black citizens into her own judgments of American politics led to such misfires as "Reflections on Little Rock" (1959). On these misfires, see Danielle Allen, *Talking to Strangers: Anxieties of Citizenship since* Brown v. Board of Education (Chicago: University of Chicago Press, 2004), chap. 3; Jill Locke, "Little Rock's Social Question: Reading Arendt on School Desegregation and Social Climbing," *Political Theory* 41 (4) (2013): 533–61; and Kathryn T. Gines, *Hannah Arendt and the Negro Question* (Bloomington: Indiana University Press, 2014).

18. Arendt, *Lectures on Kant's Political Philosophy*, 71.

19. Arendt, "Truth and Politics," 237.

20. On judgment as a political faculty that brings the "common world" into view, see Zerilli, *Democratic Theory of Judgment*, 8–9.

21. In personal correspondence, Sharon Krause reminded me that there is a fifth major principle of Douglass's political judgment that works in tandem with these other four: the belief in natural right. Major elements of natural right include equality of persons, inalienable human rights, and individual self-ownership. Because the idea of natural right in Douglass has already been extensively analyzed, I bracket it in this essay and limit my focus to the qualities of judgment needed to respect natural right in a complex world of historical inheritance and power inequality. Excellent sources on Douglass and natural right include Myers, *Frederick Douglass*, chap. 2; Nicholas Buccola, *The Political Thought of Frederick Douglass:*

In Pursuit of American Liberty (New York: New York University Press, 2012), chap. 2; and Gregg Crane, "Human Law and Higher Law," in Lee, ed., *Cambridge Companion to Frederick Douglass,* 89–102. For Krause's dazzling interpretation of Douglass, see *Liberalism with Honor* (Cambridge, MA: Harvard University Press, 2002), 144–59.

22. On racial innocence, see Lawrie Balfour, *The Evidence of Things Not Said: James Baldwin and the Promise of American Democracy* (Ithaca, NY: Cornell University Press, 2001), chap. 4, and George Shulman, *American Prophecy: Race and Redemption in American Political Culture* (Minneapolis: University of Minnesota Press, 2008), chap. 4.

23. Bryan Garsten, *Saving Persuasion: A Defense of Rhetoric and Judgment* (Cambridge, MA: Harvard University Press, 2006), 7–8.

24. This is consistent with King and Smith's "racial orders" thesis (see "Racial Orders in American Political Development").

25. *Civil Rights Cases,* 109 US 3 (1883), at 25.

26. Quoted in Heather Cox Richardson, *The Death of Reconstruction: Race, Labor, and Politics in the Post–Civil War North, 1865–1901* (Cambridge, MA: Harvard University Press, 2001), 151.

27. Douglass, "Parties Were Made for Men," 5:88, 91.

28. Frederick Douglass, "The Nation's Problem: An Address Delivered in Washington, D.C. on 16 April 1889," in *FDP1,* 5:411–12.

29. Douglass, "Parties Were Made for Men," 5:91–92. In the final edition of *Life and Times,* Douglass characterized himself as a "race-man" in a distinctly political sense: "My cause first, midst, last, and always, whether in or out of office, was and is that of the black man; not because he is black, but because he is a man, and a man subjected in this country to peculiar wrongs and hardships" (954). For discussion, see Turner, *Awakening to Race,* 47–48, and Douglas A. Jones Jr., "Douglass' Impersonal," *ESQ: A Journal of the American Renaissance* 61 (1) (2015): 25.

30. Douglass, "Parties Were Made for Men," 5:90. On the idea of a racialized public becoming conscious of itself, see Eddie S. Glaude Jr., *In a Shade of Blue: Pragmatism and the Politics of Black America* (Chicago: University of Chicago Press, 2007), intro. and chap. 6.

31. Douglass, "Parties Were Made for Men," 5:94.

32. *Civil Rights Cases,* 109 US, at 3–26.

33. Frederick Douglass, "This Decision Has Humbled the Nation: An Address Delivered in Washington, D.C., on 22 October 1883," in *FDP1,* 5:120, 115–16.

34. Ibid., 5:111–12.

35. *Civil Rights Cases,* 109 US, at 54.

36. Ibid., at 41.

37. Ibid., at 43, 58–59, 56.

38. On citizenship as standing, see Judith N. Shklar, *American Citizenship: The Quest for Inclusion* (Cambridge, MA: Harvard University Press, 1991). Shklar also argues that Douglass conceived of citizenship as standing, but she roots her interpretation in Douglass's reflections on the franchise. I root my interpretation in his reflections on the need to prohibit racial discrimination in everyday commercial life.

39. Douglass, "This Decision Has Humbled the Nation," 5:122.

40. *Civil Rights Cases*, 109 US, at 61.

41. Ibid., at 13.

42. Douglass, "One Country, One Law, One Liberty," 5:400. Harlan did not go as far as to say that the Civil War eradicated any and all legislative prerogatives of individual states, but he did affirm that the Civil War amendments made "exemption from race discrimination in respect of the civil rights which are fundamental in *citizenship* in a republican government [into] a new right, created by the nation, with express power in Congress, by legislation, to enforce" (*Civil Rights Cases*, 109 US, at 56, emphasis in original).

43. Douglass, "This Decision Has Humbled the Nation," 5:120, 119. Harlan also remarked that the Court's opinion in *Civil Rights Cases* "proceeds, it seems to me, upon grounds entirely too narrow and artificial. I cannot resist the conclusion that the substance and spirit of the recent amendments of the Constitution have been sacrificed by a subtle and ingenious verbal criticism" (*Civil Rights Cases*, 109 US, at 26).

44. Douglass, "This Decision Has Humbled the Nation," 5:113, 120. On Douglass's expansive conception of federal power under the Constitution, see Myers, "Frederick Douglass's Natural Rights Constitutionalism," and *Frederick Douglass*, 144–45.

45. Douglass, "This Decision Has Humbled the Nation," 5:113, 120.

46. Abraham Lincoln, "Second Inaugural Address" (1865), in *Speeches and Writings, 1859–1865*, ed. Don E. Fehrenbacher (New York: Library of America, 1989), 687.

47. See Frederick Douglass, "There Was a Right Side in the Late War: An Address Delivered in New York, New York, on 30 May 1878," in *FDP1*, 4:480–92.

48. Blight, *Frederick Douglass' Civil War*, chap. 10; David W. Blight, *Race and Reunion: The Civil War in American Memory* (Cambridge, MA: Harvard University Press, 2001), 92–93, 316–17.

49. Frederick Douglass, "We Must Not Abandon the Observance of Decoration Day: An Address Delivered in Rochester, New York, on 30 May 1882," in *FDP1*, 5:47. See also Douglass, "There Was a Right Side in the Late War," 4:489.

50. Douglass, "There Was a Right Side in the Late War," 4:491. See also Douglass, "We Must Not Abandon the Observance of Decoration Day," 5:45–46, 48.

51. Thucydides, *The Peloponnesian War* (c. 400 BCE), trans. Richard Crawley, rev. T. E. Wick (New York: Modern Library, 1982), 1.22; Niccolò Machiavelli, *The Prince* (1532), in *The Portable Machiavelli*, ed. and trans. Peter Bondanella and Mark Musa (New York: Penguin, 1979), 78.

52. Abraham Lincoln, "Address at Gettysburg, Pennsylvania" (1863), in *Speeches and Writings*, 536.

53. Douglass, "We Must Not Abandon the Observance of Decoration Day," 5:46. See also Frederick Douglass, "We Are Confronted by a New Administration: An Address Delivered in Washington, D.C., on 16 April 1885," in *FDP1*, 5:178, and "Great Britain's Example Is High, Noble, and Grand: An Address Delivered in Rochester, New York, on 6 August 1885," in *FDP1*, 5:201. On presumptions of continuity and discontinuity in contemporary racial politics, see Robert C. Lieberman, "Legacies of Slavery? Race and Historical Causation in American Political Development," in Joseph Lowndes, Julie Novkov, and Dorian T. Warren, eds., *Race and American Political Development* (New York: Routledge, 2008), 206–33.

54. Douglass, "Parties Were Made for Men," 5:97.

55. On the labor republican tradition, see Alex Gourevitch, *From Slavery to the Cooperative Commonwealth: Labor and Republican Liberty in the Nineteenth Century* (Cambridge: Cambridge University Press, 2014).

56. Douglass, "Parties Were Made for Men," 5:98–99.

57. Douglass, "West India Emancipation," 932. See also Douglass, "Parties Were Made for Men," 5:100–101.

58. Douglass, "Parties Were Made for Men," 5:99.

59. Gourevitch, *From Slavery to the Cooperative Commonwealth*, chap. 4.

60. Waldo E. Martin Jr., *The Mind of Frederick Douglass* (Chapel Hill: University of North Carolina Press, 1984), 71–72; Myers, *Frederick Douglass*, 145–46. At the same time, Nicholas Buccola suggests that Douglass thought "the mode of holding" property and "the amount held" were properly subject to political regulation (*Political Thought of Frederick Douglass*, 53).

61. Douglass, "Parties Were Made for Men," 5:100–101. Douglass voiced regret for his previous opposition to Stevens's plan, in fact, as early as 1880 ("West India Emancipation," 932–33).

62. Douglass, "Parties Were Made for Men," 5:101.

63. In 1869, however, Douglass drew up a plan for the National Land and Loan Company, which would buy land throughout the South and lease or sell it to freedmen. Nothing, however, ever came of the proposal. See Frederick Douglass, "Plan to Buy Land to Be Sold to Freedmen," in Philip Foner, *Frederick Douglass: A Biography* (New York: Citadel Press, 1964), 254. For discussion, see Turner, *Awakening to Race*, 57–58.

64. Douglass, "Parties Were Made for Men," 5:103. Consult also Buccola, *Political Thought of Frederick Douglass*, 148–55.

65. Frederick Douglass, "Continue to Wave the Bloody Shirt: An Address Delivered in Chicago, Illinois, on 19 June 1888," in *FDP1*, 5:390.

66. Myers, "Frederick Douglass's Natural Rights Constitutionalism," 79.

67. Douglass, "Great Britain's Example," 5:205.

68. Wilson Carey McWilliams, "Ambiguities and Ironies: Conservatism and Liberalism in the American Political Tradition" (1995), in Patrick J. Deneen and Susan J. McWilliams, eds., *Redeeming Democracy in America* (Lawrence: University Press of Kansas, 2011), 178.

69. Douglass would probably recognize some devolution of power to the states as legitimate insofar as it enhanced public liberty and was administratively convenient. But he would understand such devolution as precisely that—the transfer of power from central authority to a subsidiary. This is the unavoidable implication of his contention that the Civil War abolished "sovereignty of the individual states" ("One Country, One Law, One Liberty," 5:400).

70. Frederick Douglass, "Strong to Suffer, and Yet Strong to Strive: An Address Delivered in Washington, D.C., on 16 April 1886," in *FDP1*, 5:232.

71. Douglass, "Parties Were Made for Men," 5:100.

72. Karl Marx, "On the Jewish Question" (1844), in *Selected Writings*, ed. Lawrence H. Simon (Indianapolis, IN: Hackett, 1994), 1–26; Kimberlé Williams Crenshaw, "Race, Reform, and Retrenchment," *Harvard Law Review* 101 (7) (1988): 1331–87.

73. For illuminating discussion of formalism, see Morton White, *Social Thought in America: The Revolt against Formalism*, new ed. (Boston: Beacon Press, [1947] 1957).

74. Quoted in *Parents Involved in Community Schools v. Seattle School District No. 1 et al.*, 551 US (2007), at 799 (Justice Stevens dissenting).

75. Andrew Johnson, "Veto of the Second Freedmen's Bureau Bill" (1866), in Bruce Frohnen, ed., *The American Nation: Primary Sources* (Indianapolis, IN: Liberty Fund, 2008), 97.

76. W. E. B. Du Bois, *Black Reconstruction in America, 1860–1880* (1935; reprint, New York: Free Press, 1992), chap. 8; Eric Foner, *Reconstruction: America's Unfinished Revolution, 1863–1877* (New York: Harper and Row, 1988), 176–84; Linda Faye Williams, *The Constraint of Race: Legacies of White Skin Privilege in America* (University Park: Pennsylvania State University Press, 2003), chap. 1.

77. Douglass, "Parties Were Made for Men," 5:91.

78. Dana R. Villa, "Thinking and Judging," in *Politics, Philosophy, Terror: Essays on the Thought of Hannah Arendt* (Princeton, NJ: Princeton University Press, 1999), 89.

79. Frederick Douglass, "In Law, Free; in Fact, a Slave: An Address Delivered in Washington, D.C., on 16 April 1888," in *FDP1*, 5:364.

80. Douglass, "The Nation's Problem," 5:423.

81. Jefferson anticipated this. See Thomas Jefferson to Samuel Kercheval, July 12, 1816, in *Jefferson: Political Writings*, ed. Joyce Appleby and Terence Ball (Cambridge: Cambridge University Press, 1999), 215–16.

82. Frederick Douglass, "The American Constitution and the Slave: An Address Delivered in Glasgow, Scotland, on 26 March 1860," in *FDP1*, 3:340–66.

83. Douglass, "Lessons of the Hour," 5:604; Frederick Douglass, "This Democratic Conversion Should Not Be Trusted: An Address Delivered in New York, New York, on 25 September 1872," *FDP1*, 4:341.

84. Douglass made similar interpretive moves with the preamble before the Civil War. See James A. Colaiaco, *Frederick Douglass and the Fourth of July* (New York: Palgrave MacMillan, 2006), 103–4; Frank, *Constituent Moments*, 222–23.

85. Douglass, "Strong to Suffer," 5:217–18.

86. Liav Orgard, "The Preamble in Constitutional Interpretation," *International Journal of Constitutional Law* 12 (2) (2014): 718–21.

87. In this respect, Douglass was far more radical than Harlan. See Harlan's opinion for the Court in *Jacobson v. Massachusetts*, 197 US 11 (1905): "Although the Preamble indicates the general purposes for which the people ordained and established the Constitution, it has never been regarded as the source of any substantive power conferred on the Government of the United States or on any of its Departments" (at 22).

88. Douglass, "This Decision Has Humbled the Nation," 5:114.

89. Douglass, "The Nation's Problem," 5:421.

90. Douglass, "This Decision Has Humbled the Nation," 5:121.

91. For Douglass's explanation of government's role in ensuring (substantive) equal opportunity, see "In Law, Free; in Fact, a Slave," 5:369, and "The Blessings of Liberty and Education: An Address Delivered in Manassas, Virginia, on 3 September 1894," in *FDP1*, 5:626.

92. Arendt, "Crisis in Culture," 220.

93. On the self-disclosing quality of political action, see Hannah Arendt, *On Revolution* (1963; reprint, New York: Penguin, 2006), 272–73.

94. For excellent discussion of this problem, see Jason Frank, "Pathologies of Freedom in Melville's America," in Romand Coles, Mark Reinhardt, and George Shulman, eds., *Radical Future Pasts: Untimely Political Theory* (Lexington: University Press of Kentucky, 2014), 435–58.

95. Ellen D. Katz, "What Was Wrong with the Record?" *Election Law Journal* 12 (3) (2013): 329–31; Keith G. Bentele and Erin E. O'Brien, "Jim Crow 2.0? Why

States Consider and Adopt Restrictive Voter Access Policies," *Perspectives on Politics* 11 (4) (2013): 1088–116.

96. *Shelby County v. Holder*, 570 US _____ (2013), at 24, 23, 15. See also Jack Turner, "The Racial Innocence of John Roberts," *The Contemporary Condition*, October 17, 2013, at http://contemporarycondition.blogspot.com/2013/10/the-racial-innocence-of-john-roberts.html.

97. *Shelby County v. Holder*, 570 US, at 20.

98. *Parents Involved v. Seattle*, 551 US, at 748.

99. Michael C. Dawson, *Black Visions: The Roots of Contemporary African-American Political Ideologies* (Chicago: University of Chicago Press, 2001), 258, 264.

100. Ralph Waldo Emerson, "Address to the Citizens of Concord" (1851), in *Emerson's Antislavery Writings*, ed. Len Gougeon and Joel Myerson (New Haven, CT: Yale University Press, 1995), 57.

7

Black Masculinity Achieves Nothing without Restorative Care

An Intersectional Rearticulation of Frederick Douglass

Ange-Marie Hancock Alfaro

The title of this chapter plays upon some of Frederick Douglass's most famous words, "Power concedes nothing without a demand," written as part of an address in 1857 regarding emancipation in the West Indies.[1] Much of Douglass's antislavery rhetoric has been characterized as quintessentially "American" in its rugged individualism, particularly regarding his conscientious presentation of himself as a self-made man in league with America's love affair with self-determination. Far too little attention, however, has been spent examining the political import of Douglass's relationships with other black men. This chapter explores his affection for and efforts to build community with his black male peers during slavery. Drawing upon *Narrative of the Life of Frederick Douglass* (1845) and *My Bondage and My Freedom* (1855), I contend that Douglass elucidates what I characterize as a black male ethic of care.

Uncovering this previously overlooked set of relationships expands our understanding of Douglass's political project. The restorative relationships he forged with black men creates a space for us to think about black men as capable of profoundly caring relationships that are distinct from traditional frames of care-ethic relationships—free of dependency and biological determinism[2] in liberating ways that enable us "to rethink humans as interdependent beings."[3] Rethinking the existence of black men as interdependent beings is a particularly relevant matter in this current era. Divergent narratives about them persist within black social movements—that black men are in need of particular protection and investment based on a long history of susceptibility to murderous violence and that they continue to reinscribe gender inequality in black communities through public–private programs such as My Brother's Keeper. Use of a novel framework such as a black male ethic of restorative care has an important role to play in elucidating an intersectional rearticulation of Frederick Douglass's understanding of the "self-made man."

In the Shadow of Douglass's Self-Made Man

Douglass is thought to have given his "Self-Made Men" speech more than fifty times after his dramatic escape from slavery.[4] This speech and allusions to this same trope in both *Narrative* and *Bondage* have been subjected to widespread critical scrutiny.[5] This interrogation most frequently turns on an analysis of the famed fight with slave breaker Edward Covey, which Douglass himself situates as a dramatic turning point along his path to freedom, manhood, and American self-determination.

Of the battle with Covey, Douglass contends, "From this time on I was never again what might fairly be called whipped, though I remained a slave for years afterwards. I had several fights but was never whipped."[6] This sentence can be read on two levels. First, there is the literal level, of course—historians have pored over every line of the *Narrative*, judging its historical veracity. I am more interested here in the second level: the sentence's symbolic meaning. Douglass is not claiming he was never again punished, but he wants to draw a clear distinction between being whipped (or what others consider his articulation of a uniquely "female slave" experience) and fighting. That he and Covey fought to a standoff serves as an important transition point. Many literary scholars have pointed out the fight's rhetorical and structural significance—it occurs at the halfway point between Douglass as slave and Douglass as fugitive/freedman.[7]

Jack Turner contends that Douglass's conception of freedom is simultaneously pragmatic and substantive rather than abstract.[8] However, like Nicholas Buccola and Wilson Moses, these interpretations of freedom in Douglass are focused on a liberal democratic notion of freedom, defined in large part by the thirst and willingness to die for freedom.[9] These interpretations lend even greater narrative weight to the battle with Covey and how we think of Douglass's construction of a liberated black masculinity.

Consistent with this reading of Douglass, the word *fight* connotes two subjects who battle on free and fair grounds. But the word *whipped* in Douglass's usage involves a subject and an object, one with agency and one without. Thus, his articulation of a fight that ends in a tie connotes one brand of equality with Covey—equality of brute power—and the stopping of the fight short of significant bodily harm, short of death, constitutes a more politically useful form of equality, allowing Douglass to be characterized as fully human as well as fully male—capable of stopping, of deciding not to allow such emotions to get the best of him. The meaning of the standoff—fighting to a "tie"—essentially creates a victory for Douglass in defining himself as fully human as well as fully male. The point was to get Covey to treat him as a human being, and beating Covey at his own game would seem to serve no more than an emotionally satisfying purpose rather than the broader political purpose of ending slavery. That Douglass could exercise such discipline, such bodily control, firmly establishes him as a legitimate candidate for liberal democratic citizenship in the classic Western sense.[10]

In a similar vein, Wilson Moses and Cynthia Willett contend that Douglass appropriates the European American trope of the "self-made man." For Moses, Douglass's strategic presentation of himself as an exceptional representative black man is attributable largely to his capacity for this appropriation.[11] Willett locates Douglass's theory of freedom in a particular experience of racial exclusion he encounters with his white abolitionist counterparts, suggesting that Douglass "countered alienation by usurping parts of white culture almost as though by right of conquest."[12]

All of these interpretations of the fight with Covey turn on liberal democratic assumptions about human nature grounded in individualism.[13] Douglass's pursuit of literacy, another site of frequent scholarly attention, is also grounded in these assumptions about the prequalifications for liberal democratic citizenship. An intersectional rearticulation of Douglass, however, is grounded in different epistemological assumptions about valid ways of producing and validating the knowledge that leads to political action.[14]

Intersectional Reconsiderations

For theorists of intersectionality, understanding a figure like Douglass must journey beyond questions of his fit into pre-existing canons of American political thought or into tropes such as the self-made man to explore the ways in which elements of his thought that *do not fit* these frameworks are rendered invisible. For example, Moses and others read *intra*racial relationships between Douglass and other black men with the same underlying conception of political relationships found in their reading of *inter*racial relationships between Douglass and white men such as William Lloyd Garrison.[15] An intersectional rearticulation, however, takes this assumption and turns it on its head in a search for evidence of connected (rather than atomized) ways of knowing. In other words, the assumption that the hypercompetitive context of interracial power struggles must also necessarily apply to intraracial relationships among black men seems too narrow to contain the full vision of Douglass because it limits the political utility of black masculinity to what is relevant for an aspiring liberal democratic citizen who has the misfortune of being born black.

In a similar vein, some scholars of African American thought focus on the traditional questions of liberal democracy concerning the relationship between an individual and society. Turner, for example, locates the origin of the "humility" and "interdependence" he reads in the connection Douglass has with the slave Sandy Jenkins, who gives him a talisman root before the landmark fight with Covey.[16] Turner limits his discussion of the political value of that connection to the self-confidence the root gives Douglass in the penultimate confrontation chronicled in the *Narrative*. But should we limit the political value of the connection between "Freddie" and Sandy to a hyperindividualist "self-confidence"?

An intersectional rearticulation asks different questions. For instance, one question emerges about the relationship between Sandy and the young Freddie in a way that potentially expands the discursive definition of black masculinity. I attend here to the politically relevant differences in how Douglass chronicles his friendships with other black men. In short, this intersectional rearticulation identifies a black male ethic of care in the interactions Douglass describes.

This intersectional rearticulation of Douglass also contrasts with prior black feminist engagements with Douglass as a self-made man. Deborah McDowell, Deborah Gray-White, Mary Helen Washington, and Helen Smith subject this trope to black feminist critique by seeking to "recover" the black feminine in Douglass's accounts of himself. For McDowell, Douglass's replacement of the subservient, bumbling "Sambo" with a hypermasculine "self-made man" renders both his mother, Harriet Bailey, and his first wife, Anna Douglass, invisible. More to the point, his self-presentation in this way obscures the fact that Anna, a free black woman, provided the economic engine for his escape from slavery.[17]

McDowell continues in this vein to compare Douglass's account of the battle with Covey in the *Narrative* with the repeated scenes of black women slaves being whipped while tied up. Douglass, as a sometimes hidden but other times in plain sight spectator to these episodes of torture, is catapulted, according to McDowell, from spectator to voyeur: "Douglass' repetition of the sexualized scene of whipping projects him into a voyeuristic relation to the violence against slave women, which he watches, and thus he enters into a symbolic complicity with the sexual crime he witnesses."[18] Somewhat ironically, both the black feminist and the liberal democratic engagements with Douglass are dependent on a distinction between the term *fight* and the term *whipping*. In these interrogations of Douglass as a self-made man, the black male ethic of restorative care is first and foremost invisible. When relationships between black men are explored at all, any black male care is contingent upon the appropriation of black female bodies.

Third and finally, interrogations of Douglass's fight with Covey (and the events that immediately precede it) serve as evidence of the tension in the self-made-man aspects of nineteenth-century American manhood that simultaneously divorces feelings and the human craving to act lovingly from the very definition of freedom itself. This more psychoanalytic engagement locates Douglass's presentation as a "self-made man" in the absence of his biological family, placing great significance on the absence of young Frederick Bailey's mother during his childhood. For David Blight, "Douglass was therefore, in the fullest sense, an orphan long in search of father and mother figures."[19] Willett contends that this separation, enforced by slavery as a system, causes a sort of spirit wound that only Douglass himself can heal. Indeed, she notes that Douglass, while briefly in the company of his maternal grandmother, feels himself to be a man by the age of seven or eight.[20] In other words, the normal evolution from birth to boyhood to manhood in a civic sense is interrupted first by the destruction of the bio-logical family and second by the transfer of Douglass to the slave breaker Covey.

Again, the liberal democratic assumptions underlying these engage-ments with Douglass assume only one possible source for the development of civic resources—the nuclear family.[21] Drawing from a vast literature that convincingly suggests slavery systematically destroyed nuclear families, these authors do not look elsewhere for possible contributions to Douglass's claims to freedom, citizenship, or equality.

What are we, then, to make of Douglass's actions immediately prior to the climactic confrontation with Covey? By this time in his teenage life, Douglass had become fully acquainted with the horrors of slavery, but he had also sought community and caring among other black males prior to this important event in his pursuit of self-made manhood.[22]

In his discussion of Douglass's oft-repeated "Self-Made Men" speech, Buccola identifies the caveat that Douglass's self-made man is in fact cog-nizant of the idea of interdependence.[23] Both Buccola and Turner argue for an understanding of Douglass where interdependence—specifically our responsibility to care for each other—plays a central role. Turner's notion focuses largely on the individual's obligation to provide for oneself and one's children, an obligation that coexists with society's obligation to ensure that its members have the prerequisites of freedom.[24]

My intersectional rearticulation suggests one location for growing the skill set for excellent execution of both dimensions of interdependence: an interpersonal space of choice, where the ethic of restorative care is freely exercised (at least by Douglass) as a type of expanded black masculinity in relationship to his black male friends. Let us now explore the roots of Douglass's interdependence because it has ramifications for a broader ethic of care that is restorative of black men's humanity as it coexists with the assertive masculinity identified by so many prior scholars. This exploration of an intersectional black male ethics of care is an important expansion of both black feminist and African American political thought's engagement with Douglass because it reveals a more multifaceted black masculinity in Douglass and a broader foundation for sustained political action over a life-time of obstacles.

Douglass's Experiences with Black Male Restorative Care

The black male ethic of care I describe here extends in a different direction from Patricia Hill Collins's original notion of an Afrocentric or black feminist epistemology.[25] Douglass, long a champion of women's rights and a vocal supporter of black women's rights,[26] is arguably a fascinating if untraditional subject for intersectional interrogation. I contend that his friendships with other black men, delivered in a register of "talking from the heart," provide a key part of what Collins describes as "developing the capacity for empathy,"[27] upon which political action can build. In particular, the heretofore invisible epistemology of connection, from which truth emerges through care,[28] teaches the self-educated Douglass a new way to know himself and others as well as right and wrong. Caregiver and care recipient are traditionally thought to be hierarchically arranged in a vertical power relationship. But one core element of this black male restorative-care framework is its attentiveness to a *horizontal* relationship between the presumed caregiver and the presumed recipient of care. If we return to the gift of the root Sandy Jenkins makes to young Freddie, this framework allows us to consider that it is neither the root itself nor the self-confidence the root supposedly confers that empowers Douglass; rather, it is the care relation—a specifically egalitarian care relation of friendship—that Douglass is able to draw upon for the penultimate struggle for his mental and later physical freedom.

Two early interactions in *Bondage* illustrate Douglass's ties to black men in a caring context that challenges both the notion of Douglass's self-made man as hyperindividualist and the traditional conceptualization of care ethics that presumes a vertical, unidirectional relationship of care provision. *Bondage* was written by a Douglass whom Blight calls "a more mature writer," a Douglass who was simultaneously more political and personally revealing ten years after *Narrative's* publication in 1845.[29] As the United States veered closer to the violent ruptures of the Civil War, Douglass expanded his autobiographical narrative to include more attention to the bonds of care among black men. Having been instructed to pray by the "good colored man" Charles Johnson, Douglass speaks in *Bondage* in a more detailed fashion about this religious and spiritual development. His introduction to this religious world "behind the veil" of a mostly but not exclusively enslaved race starts with the introduction he receives to "Lawson," another "good old colored man," while serving the Auld family in Baltimore when still a child.[30]

Douglass describes two important aspects of the relationship between himself and Lawson, one that challenges the conventional frame of care ethics as a vertical relationship. It is noteworthy that Douglass had genuine affection for Lawson, a free black man. Douglass spends several pages describing his relationship with Lawson as paternal but not exclusively vertical, which a more psychoanalytic framework might assume of such a quasi-parent–child relationship. Douglass describes his connection to "Uncle Lawson"[31] in the emotional terms of "becoming deeply attached to the old man." These times with Uncle Lawson are thus framed in horizontal rather than exclusively vertical terms: "The old man could read a little, and I was a great help to him, in making out the hard words, for I was a better reader than he. I could teach him *'the letter,'* but he could teach me *'the spirit.'"*[32] This horizontal aspect of the relationship calls into question the conventional aspects of care ethics that frame such relationships as unidirectional and vertical—one caregiver, one care recipient.

The esteem Douglass has for Lawson continues with a careful chronicling of all that Lawson gives him spiritually, in such a way as to avoid any confusion that his spiritual development is attributable to his mistress's white spiritual leader, Beverly Waugh. Calling Lawson "his spiritual father" whom he loved intensely, Douglass credits Lawson with instilling in him a destiny of greatness,[33] words to which he returned prior to his first serious attempt to escape slavery.[34] The type of care Lawson and Douglass offer each other is restorative as well as perhaps risky: it is care, not simply instruction, companionship, or exchange of resources. This type of emotional/ restorative care seems to emerge in Douglass's encounters with other black men later in his life as well.

Bondage features a compelling parallel story of Douglass's cousin, who appealed for mercy at the feet of her owner following a brutal beating by Mr. Plummer, an overseer. In dispassionate terms, Douglass relates the horrifying wounds she presented and the callous disregard that their shared master displayed for her injuries and her pleas for intervention.[35] Douglass's chronicle of this episode, articulated in hindsight decades later, suggests a long-term strategy of seeking relief from the overseer's lash despite the threat of an immediate beating from the master for daring to complain.[36]

Ironically, Douglass is obliged to pursue a similar remedy with his owner, Thomas Auld, following his own vicious beating by Covey prior to the legendary fight. Crucially, however, in neither *Bondage* nor *Narrative* does Douglass return to this rational, self-interested view of the dilemma facing him when rebuffed by Auld. He instead chronicles his despair—an emotional response. Most important for our purposes, he turns to another male slave, Sandy Jenkins, and to Sandy's free wife for restorative care of body and spirit.

In both *Narrative* and *Bondage,* Douglass gives broad attention to his encounter with the older male slave Sandy Jenkins. He illustrates a clear affection for Sandy in each work. In *Narrative,* he finds in Sandy "an old advisor," who "very kindly invited me to go home with him."[37] Here Sandy offers hospitality, a cherished value, but more importantly for our purposes here, he extends moral support, which Douglass eagerly avails himself of. In the longer autobiography, *Bondage,* Douglass points not only to his personal esteem for Sandy but also to Sandy's standing in the slave community as "the good-hearted Sandy—a man as famous among the slaves of the neighborhood for his good nature as for his good sense."[38]

Sandy's provision of health care, safe haven[39] (although the home is owned by his free wife, it is Sandy who offers it as a haven), and advice is again a multifaceted element of restorative care that can move Douglass to a stronger stand against the system of slavery and the power relations inherent in it. For example, although Douglass clearly acknowledges his skepticism of the efficacy of the root talisman for protection,[40] and many readers then and now would similarly doubt its force, Sandy's point in *Bondage* remains well taken, as Douglass readily agrees: "with all my precious learning— it was really precious little—Sandy was more than a match for me. 'My book learning,' he said, 'had not kept Covey off me,' (a powerful argument just then,) and he entreated me, with flashing eyes, to try this."[41] Douglass's willingness to take hold of Covey and to fight to a standoff are attributable to these care relationships—ones that tell Douglass of the great works in his future and that bind up his wounds—physical and emotional. Douglass admits as much: "Having, the previous night, poured my griefs into Sandy's ears, and got him enlisted in my behalf, having made his wife a sharer in my sorrows, and having, also, become well refreshed by sleep and food, I moved off, quite courageously, toward the much dreaded Covey's."[42] As with Uncle Lawson, Douglass receives care that goes beyond the liberal democratic formulation of an "exchange of resources," though a talisman root is indeed offered in this situation. I contend that Sandy sees Douglass in a way that Auld and Covey could not and that this perception, like Douglass's own perception of Lawson, is a critical resource for Douglass in his later political actions, including but not exclusively the fight with Covey.

The ethic of caring defined by Collins suggests that personal expressiveness, emotions, and empathy are central to development of the political analyses she calls a "black feminist standpoint."[43] The black male ethic of restorative care I find in Douglass has important lessons about civic friendships and the postslavery rivalries discussed by Moses and others. Douglass later travels with the black abolitionist Charles Remond and his sister, Sarah, developing a fondness for Remond that leads to his naming his second son "Charles Remond Douglass." In a similar vein, the introduction to *Bondage* is written by Douglass's friend James McCune Smith, who first identifies Douglass's capacity for "a deep and agonizing sympathy with his embruted, crushed and bleeding fellow slaves" and who later sees something that he, as a black male friend, could see but Douglass's white male friends—Wendell Phillips, Edmund Quincy, and William Lloyd Garrison—could not:

> Mr. Douglass enjoyed the high advantage of their assistance and counsel in the labor of self-culture, to which he now addressed himself with wonted energy. Yet, these gentlemen, although proud of Frederick Douglass, failed to fathom, and bring out to the light of day, the highest qualities of his mind; the force of their own education stood in their own way; they did not delve into the mind of a colored man for capacities which the pride of race led them to believe would be restricted to their own Saxon blood. Bitter and vindictive sarcasm, irresistible mimicry, and a pathetic narrative of his own experiences of slavery, were the intellectual manifestations which they encouraged him to exhibit on the platform or in the lecture desk.[44]

Smith, chosen by Douglass to provide the introduction to *Bondage*, speaks with an insight into Douglass's soul that leads to the revised version of the self-made man, who, although grateful for the tutelage these white men provided, has "the conviction of a truth which they [white men] had once promulged [*sic*], but now forgotten, to wit: that in their own elevation—self-elevation—colored men have a blow to strike 'on their own hook,' against slavery and caste."[45]

Attention to this ethic of care on its own terms has value independent of its instrumental value to later political relationships, not least because Douglass himself attributes great value to it. This is not to say that Douglass loved all black men or held them in friendship or to say that he agreed with all of his leading black male contemporaries, as he noted in a letter to Harriet Beecher Stowe:

> Hence, educated colored men, among the colored people, are at a very great discount. It would seem that education and emigration go together with us; for as soon as a man rises amongst us, capable, by his genius and learning, to do us great service, just so soon he finds that he can serve himself better by going elsewhere. In proof of this, I might instance the Russwurms—the Garnetts—the Wards—the Crummells and others—all men of superior ability and attainments, and capable of removing mountains of prejudice against their race, by their simple presence in the country; but these gentlemen, finding themselves embarrassed here by the peculiar disadvantages to which I have referred . . . have sought more congenial climes, where they can live more peaceable and quiet lives. I regret their election—but I cannot blame them; for, with an equal amount of education, and the hard lot which was theirs, I might follow their example.[46]

That said, it is clear that Douglass, like any other person, drew tremendous strength from being seen authentically by close friends and from both offering and receiving care in the spirit of reciprocity.

Douglass's Care Giving and Black Male Citizenship

In the guise of spiritual support, Sandy and Lawson provide something else more important to the young Douglass. Smith and Remond offer forms of civic friendship not otherwise available to Douglass. In short, both kinds of relationships provide restorative care, wherein one is seen as one authentically hopes to be seen within a political context where distortions of oneself abound. These horizontal relationships offer him a kind of care even Mrs. Auld, his "liberal" mistress, could not offer. In keeping with the horizontal orientation of these restorative-care relationships, Douglass the "care recipient" is also Douglass the "caregiver." He repeatedly illustrates his quest for knowledge and literacy as a man, not as a slave. Integral here are the "black man" aspects of the "representative black man" that Douglass very consciously constructs from the Euro-American myth of the "self-made man."

In a conversation about memoir and African American history, Toni Morrison suggests that Douglass's pursuit of literacy was an important part of his effort to humanize slaves/blacks. She contends that Douglass is emblematic of a larger slave narrative tradition: "These writers knew that literacy was power. Voting, after all, was inextricably connected to the ability to read; literacy was a way of assuming and proving the 'humanity' that the Constitution denied them. That is why the narratives carry the subtitle 'written by himself' or 'herself,' and include introductions and prefaces by white sympathizers to authenticate them. A literate slave was supposed to be a contradiction in terms."[47]

This notion of care between black men is underappreciated in our chronicles of Douglass. In getting the aforementioned restorative care, Douglass is reinforced in a way that allows him to form bonds later with Henry Harris, John Harris, Henry Bailey, and Charles Roberts, with whom he concocts a plan for all of them to run away. There are actual family ties among this group of men—Douglass is Bailey and Roberts's nephew. However, what is most interesting here is the development of a situational bond predicated upon their juridical status as slaves. This private (by necessity) formulation of a civic friendship excludes original caregivers Sandy Jenkins and Uncle Lawson but launches Douglass into a new phase of his quest for freedom. This transition moves him from the pursuit of physical protection from slavery's violence to social bonds among trusted black men in the risky pursuit of freedom from slavery altogether. As Douglass observes, "In coming to a fixed determination to run away, we did more than Patrick Henry, when he resolved upon liberty or death. With us it was a doubtful liberty at most, and almost certain death if we failed. For my part, I should prefer death to hopeless bondage."[48]

Although Douglass initially fails at escape from slavery, his response to the foiled attempt is instructive: "Immediately after the holidays were over, contrary to all our expectations, Mr. Hamilton and Mr. Freeland came up to Easton, and took Charles, the two Henrys, and John, out of jail and carried them home, leaving me alone. I regarded this separation as a final one. It caused me more pain than anything else in the whole transaction. I was ready for anything rather than separation."[49]

The emotional pain Douglass acknowledges here, of bonds broken, is far greater than any he experiences from the breaking of any other bond up to this point in the narrative. Certainly, it is understandable that Douglass, the ardent pursuer of freedom, is disappointed by his failed plan. But the despair over the loss of his black male friends is pointedly discussed as the worst part of the debacle—in terms of both the finality of that loss and the emotional pain it causes. This description deepens our sense of Douglass's humanity and points us in important directions for reconsidering black masculinity today—a masculinity that has yet to be fully plumbed or accepted by mainstream society.

The Potential of Restorative Care for Democracy

A long-standing line of feminist thought defines care ethics as including "values traditionally associated with women"[50] and vertical relationships between caregiver and care recipient. The black male ethic of restorative care that I have traced in the works of Frederick Douglass encourages us to rethink both notions of liberal democratic citizenship (exemplified by the trope of the "self-made man") and the site of black masculinity as a rich resource for civic friendship. This intersectional rearticulation of Douglass allows us to reexamine his friendships with black males over the course of his life and to expand what we know about his approach to interdependence, thus broadening our understanding of his political project. The capacity for connected knowing that he develops through restorative relationships with Lawson, Sandy Jenkins, his fellow escapees, Charles Remond, and James McCune Smith reshapes the bonds between political subjects. This care, in Douglass's own words, provides him with aspirations for greatness, willingness to risk physical and emotional retribution, and resiliency for the next "fight."

Moreover, in the contemporary era, when divergent narratives about black men persist, Frederick Douglass's commitment to restorative care in combination with unwavering commitment to women's rights (including those of black women) serves as a stark contrast to the binary gender politics of black America today. This intersectional rearticulation of Douglass, which has focused on recovering invisible aspects of interdependence, expands our vision, to be sure. More importantly, it transforms the entirety of our vision of a shared political future.

Notes

1. Frederick Douglass, "West India Emancipation," in *Frederick Douglass: Selected Speeches and Writings*, ed. Philip Foner, abridged and adapted by Yuval Taylor (Chicago: Lawrence Hill Books, 1999), 358–68.

2. In this regard, I follow Cynthia Willett's review of care ethics in *The Soul of Justice: Social Bonds and Racial Hubris* (Ithaca, NY: Cornell University Press, 2001).

3. Joan Tronto, *Moral Boundaries: A Political Argument for an Ethic of Care* (New York: Routledge, 2009), 21.

4. As determined by John Blassingame, cited in Nicholas Buccola, *The Political Thought of Frederick Douglass: In Pursuit of American Liberty* (New York: New York University Press, 2012), 115. See also Frederick Douglass, "Self-Made Men," in *The Essential Douglass: Selected Writings and Speeches*, ed. Nicholas Buccola (Indianapolis, IN: Hackett, 2016), 332–49.

5. Mary Helen Washington, "These Self-Invented Women: A Theoretical Framework for a Literary History of Black Women," *Radical Teacher* 17 (1980): 3–6; David Leverenz, "Frederick Douglass's Self-Fashioning," in *Manhood and the American Renaissance* (Ithaca, NY: Cornell University Press, 1989), 108–34; Deborah McDowell, "In the First Place: Making Frederick Douglass and the Afro-American Narrative Tradition," in Frederick Douglass, *Narrative of the Life of Frederick Douglass, an American Slave, Written by Himself*, ed. William L. Andrews and William S. McFeely, Norton Critical Editions (New York: Norton, 1997), 172–83; Willett, *Soul of Justice;* Wilson J. Moses, *Creative Conflict in African American Thought: Frederick Douglass, Alexander Crummell, Booker T. Washington, W. E. B. Du Bois, and Marcus Garvey* (Cambridge: Cambridge University Press, 2004); Buccola, *Political Thought of Frederick Douglass;* Jack Turner, *Awakening to Race: Individualism and Social Consciousness in America* (Chicago: University of Chicago Press, 2012).

6. Douglass, *Narrative*, 51.

7. Others contend that the slave narrative genre made a victory unfeasible because it would turn off many potential readers.

8. Turner, *Awakening to Race*, 58–59.

9. Ibid., 49. See also Buccola, *The Political Thought of Frederick Douglass*, and Moses, *Creative Conflict in African American Thought*.

10. The attenuation of that self-determined exercise of discipline emerges from what Douglass faced upon the conclusion of this standoff—return to his "place" as a slave under Covey's command for another six months, albeit without the vicious corporal punishment of the first six months.

11. Moses, *Creative Conflict in African American Thought*, 46–48.

12. Willett, *Soul of Justice*, 194.

13. Even for Turner and Buccola, who explore constructions of interdependence in Douglass, the obligations for such interdependence are built from an assumed atomistic individual and a liberal conception of government. I take this up more directly later in the chapter.

14. On intersectional knowledge, see Patricia Hill Collins, *Black Feminist Thought: Knowledge, Consciousness, and the Politics of Empowerment* (New York: Routledge, 1990), 202.

15. Here I do not mean to inject some facile assumption of racial solidarity among black men but rather refer to an openness to relationships that may not always feature hypercompetitive androcentric notions of masculinity. Following intersectionality theory, the idea here is that these relationships are fluid and can include both competition and restorative care in a contingent fashion.

16. Turner, *Awakening to Race*, 50; Douglass, *Narrative*, 51.

17. McDowell, "In the First Place," 175.

18. Ibid., 178.

19. David Blight, introduction to Frederick Douglass, *My Bondage and My Freedom* (New Haven, CT: Yale University Press, 2014), ix.

20. Willett, *Soul of Justice*, 197–98. Though Willett's care-ethics critique notably alerts us to the reductive tendency to collapse care into dependency (37) and a simplistic, unidimensional notion of trust (39), she does not extend this critique of care ethics to question how Douglass might seek care elsewhere, despite its absence in all the usual places.

21. It is also notable that both the source identified as liberal democratic—the nuclear family—and the care relationships I explore could be construed as "private." I address in a later section the civic potential of the care relationships I examine.

22. Wilson Moses notes that Douglass had deep, abiding, and complex friendships with black men throughout his life (*Creative Conflict in African American Thought*, 54–58).

23. Buccola, *Political Thought of Frederick Douglass*, 115.

24. Turner, *Awakening to Race*, 48.

25. Collins, *Black Feminist Thought*, 215.

26. Philip S. Foner, introduction to Frederick Douglass, *Frederick Douglass on Women's Rights*, ed. Philip S. Foner (Westport, CT: Greenwood Press, 1976), 11–12, 15, 18–19.

27. Collins, *Black Feminist Thought*, 216.

28. Ibid., 217.

29. Blight, introduction to Douglass, *Bondage*, ix.

30. Although scholars have debated the authenticity of Douglass's devotion to Christianity (e.g., Moses, *Creative Conflict in African American Thought*, 53,

71–72), I am decidedly more focused here on the relationship between Douglass and Lawson.

31. It is interesting to note that Douglass uses the term *uncle*, reserved for elder male slaves as a sign of respect, despite the fact that Lawson was a free colored man. See Douglass, *Bondage*, 57–58.

32. Ibid., 136, emphasis in original.

33. Ibid.

34. Ibid., 220.

35. Ibid., 67–68.

36. Ibid., 68–69.

37. Douglass, *Narrative*, 41.

38. Douglass, *Bondage*, 190.

39. Sandy's wife, as McDowell correctly notes, remains absent following a single mention.

40. Douglass is of course less sanguine about the talisman Sandy swears by for protection from Covey: "He told me, with great solemnity, I must go back to Covey; but that before I went, I must go with him into another part of the woods, where there was a certain root, which if I would take some of it with me, carrying it always on my right side, would render it impossible for Mr. Covey, or any other white man, to whip me. He said he carried it for years; and since he had done so, he had never received a blow, and never expected to while he carried it. I at first rejected the idea, that the simple carrying of a root in my pocket would have any such effect . . . but Sandy impressed the necessity with much earnestness. . . . To please him, I at length took the root" (*Narrative*, 49).

41. Douglass, *Bondage*, 190.

42. Ibid., 192.

43. Collins, *Black Feminist Thought*, 219.

44. James McCune Smith, introduction to Douglass, *Bondage*, 11, 15.

45. Ibid., 16.

46. Frederick Douglass, "Letter to Harriet Beecher Stowe," in Joseph Brotz, ed., *African American Social and Political Thought, 1850–1920* (New Brunswick, NJ: Transaction, 1993), 222.

47. Toni Morrison, "The Site of Memory," in William Zinsser, ed., *Inventing the Truth: The Art and Craft of Memoir* (New York: Houghton Mifflin, 1998), 189.

48. Douglass, *Narrative*, 57.

49. Ibid., 61.

50. Tronto, *Moral Boundaries*, 3.

8

"The Human Heart Is a Seat of Constant War"

Frederick Douglass on Human Nature

Nicholas Buccola

In *The Lincoln Persuasion,* J. David Greenstone demonstrates that although the mainstream of American political thought is marked by widespread commitment to "the basic [liberal] values of private property, individual freedom, and government based on popular consent," there remains significant dispute within liberalism over "broader social and philosophical" matters, perhaps the most important of which is "the nature of the human personality."[1] Greenstone argues that in order to make sense of a thinker's vision of "a good society," we must come to terms with what he or she thinks about human nature. In this chapter, I provide a detailed reconstruction of what one of America's greatest liberal thinkers, Frederick Douglass, thought about human nature.[2] Such a reconstruction is worthwhile not only because it can serve to deepen our understanding of the foundations of Douglass's political morality but also because it can serve to counter common criticisms of liberal views of human nature.

Criticisms of liberal theories of human nature tend to fall into three categories. First, there are those who claim that liberals ignore questions about human nature and replace them with a "formalistic preoccupation with rights, interests, and rational preferences."[3] Second, there are those who claim liberals offer a view of human nature that is overly optimistic because they overstate the sovereignty of the rational capacity, the tendency toward goodness, and the possibilities of improving men. Third, there are those who claim liberal views of human nature as far too pessimistic because they tend to overstate the sovereignty of human passions, man's selfishness, and his disregard for morality. Depending on whom you ask, then, liberalism lacks a theory of human nature or offers a theory of human nature that is overly optimistic or offers a theory of human nature that is overly pessimistic. In the face of these criticisms, we would do well to reconsider the ideas of the great thinkers such as Douglass to see just what liberals have actually said about human nature. I argue that none of these lines of criticism finds an easy target in Douglass, who did not ignore human nature or accept a one-sided view. He instead offered a nuanced theory that appreciates the competing tendencies within human beings. His nuanced theory of human nature was at the foundation of his morally robust formulation of liberal rights and duties.

Like thinkers within other ideological traditions, liberals are divided on questions about human nature. The liberal tradition has within it, to borrow Reinhold Niebuhr's felicitous language, "children of the light" and "children of the darkness."[4] Some liberals, such as John Stuart Mill and Thomas Jefferson, were on the whole optimistic about human nature.[5] They emphasized the rationality, progressivism, and capacity for good in man's nature. In contrast, liberals such as John Locke and Judith Shklar have highlighted man's inherent fearfulness and capacity for viciousness.[6] As noted earlier, critics are no less divided on the theory of human nature that animates liberalism. Several of liberalism's detractors, such as Sheldon Wolin, C. B. MacPherson, and Leo Strauss, have argued that liberal political theory is based on an excessively dark picture of human nature.[7] Other critics such as Niebuhr and Russell Kirk have described liberalism as a philosophy grounded in an undying faith in human goodness.[8]

Douglass's views of human nature, like so many other aspects of his thought, were shaped by his experiences. These experiences, I contend, led him to embrace a view somewhere in between that of the children of the light and that of the children of the darkness. On the one hand, his life as a slave made it impossible for him to fully embrace the optimistic, progressive view of human nature characteristic of the children of the light. On the other hand, through his work as a reformer Douglass came to see that human beings are capable of acting in humane, even heroic ways. This led him to see more light in human nature than the gloomy picture offered by the children of the darkness. Rather than fitting neatly into either the hopeful or fearful camps within liberal theory, Douglass offered a dualistic and dynamic view of human nature. In this essay, I argue that his theory of human nature can be reduced to four central dualities.

- **The Rational–Passionate Duality:** First, human beings are both rational *and* passionate creatures. Both reason and "feeling" influence human behavior, and these two capacities can come into conflict.
- **The Sociality–Individuality Duality:** Second, human beings are naturally drawn to sociality *and* individuality. They have a natural desire to interact with others and sometimes feel a sense of duty toward others. At the same time, they are naturally self-interested and long to be free from the coercion of others.
- **The Good–Evil Duality:** Third, human beings are naturally good, *but* they are constantly liable to do evil. On the one hand, reason allows them to recognize natural, moral laws, and they are endowed with a natural sense of affection for others. On the other hand, selfishness can trump natural goodness and lead them to act in antisocial ways.
- **The Malleability–Free Will Duality:** Fourth, human nature is malleable, *but* individuals retain control over their own wills. In other words, the character of individuals can be molded by external circumstances, but individuals are ultimately able to choose their own course of action and therefore retain personal moral responsibility for their choices.

Because Douglass's view is complex and nuanced, it contains within it many tensions. Rather than being a reason for dismissing his thoughts on human nature, this dynamism gives us reason to take them seriously. The tensions within Douglass's theory are a reflection of the tensions within his subject. I believe his appreciation for the complexity of human nature provided the foundation for his morally robust understanding of liberalism. Rather than embracing either an overly optimistic view that emphasizes human

rationality, sociality, and goodness *or* an overly pessimistic view that emphasizes human passion, individualism, and selfishness, Douglass identified all
of these elements as essential parts of human nature. This view makes him
less susceptible to the criticisms of liberal views of human nature described
earlier. Although Douglass saw the potential for human goodness, he cannot be cornered by the "realist" who accuses liberals of being committed
to an "excessively optimistic," "foolish," "fatuous," and "superficial view of
man."[9] His recognition of dark elements in human nature did not, however,
lead him to embrace a completely cynical view. This makes him less vulnerable to the criticisms offered by those who accuse liberals of overstating the
"asocial," "emotive," and "individualistic" nature of human beings.[10]

In what follows, I offer a fuller explanation of the four dualities that
make up the core of Douglass's view. In part I, I discuss Douglass's essay
"Is Civil Government Right?" in which he offered an outline of his theory
of human nature. This essay provides us with a vehicle to investigate his
views on the distinctive characteristics of human beings, such as rationality,
sociality, individuality, goodness, selfishness, free will, and malleability. I
explore in part II Douglass's views on natural goodness and depravity and
examine in part III his reflections on the malleability of human nature.
Finally, I conclude in part IV with some reflections on how his theory of
human nature informs his liberal political morality.

I. What Constitutes a Man: The Distinctive Characteristics of Human Beings

Although Douglass never offered a picture of "the state of nature," he often
spoke of man's "natural condition" in a way reminiscent of theorists such
as Thomas Hobbes, John Locke, and Jean-Jacques Rousseau.[11] His essay
"Is Civil Government Right?" (1851) begins with one such consideration of
man's natural condition and therefore is a fruitful starting point for this discussion.[12] The essay was written in response to the utopian thinker Henry
C. Wright, a Garrisonian abolitionist who rejected all forms of coercion as
equally illegitimate.[13] It starts with five claims about human nature.

- First, "that man is a social as well as an individual being; that he
  is endowed by his Creator with faculties and powers suited to his
  individuality and to society."

- Second, "that individual isolation is unnatural, unprogressive, and against the highest interests of man; and that society is required, by the natural wants and necessities inherent in human existence."
- Third, "that man is endowed with reason and understanding capable of discriminating between good and evil, right and wrong, justice and injustice."
- Fourth, "that while man is constantly liable to do evil, he is still capable of apprehending and pursuing that which is good; and that, upon the whole, his evil tendencies are quite outweighed by the powers within him, impelling him to good."
- Fifth, "that rewards and punishments are natural agents for restraining evil and for promoting good, man being endowed with faculties keenly alive to both."[14]

Douglass's first two claims describe the sociality–individuality duality in his theory of human nature. Man is a social being in the sense that his natural wants and necessities are best met through association with others. In making this claim, Douglass seems to have adopted the Aristotelian idea that a self-sufficient man would have to be either beastlike or godlike.[15] Society is, according to Douglass, natural in the sense that the survival and flourishing of individuals is best achieved through interaction with others. Almost half a century after Douglass penned the essay on civil government, he expressed this idea again in his famous speech "Self-Made Men":

> It must in truth be said though it may not accord well with self-conscious individuality and self-conceit, that no possible native force of character, and no depth or wealth of originality, can lift a man into absolute independence of his fellow-men, and no generation of men can be independent of the preceding generation. The brotherhood and interdependence of mankind are guarded and defended at all points. I believe in individuality, but individuals are, to the mass, like waves to the ocean. The highest order of genius is as dependent as is the lowest. . . . We differ as the waves, but are one as the sea.[16]

Unlike those forms of liberalism that critics claim are grounded in "asocial individualism," Douglass began his discussion of human nature with an explicit embrace of natural sociality and interdependence.[17] This appreciation for natural sociality led him to reject social Darwinist views that were ascendant in the late nineteenth century. Wilson Carey McWilliams has pointed out that Douglass's experience as a slave brought him "closer to a true recognition of human weakness and dependence" and to an understanding "that what is really to be feared in human affairs is isolation."[18]

This recognition of human sociality leads McWilliams to describe Douglass as a devotee of the ideas of "fraternity and humanity" as opposed to "individualism and self-reliance."[19] This interpretation, however, cannot be squared with Douglass's simultaneous recognition of human individuality. Although human beings are drawn to interact with others, Douglass argued, this attraction can come into tension with natural individuality. By "individuality," Douglass meant three things. First, he was pointing to the fact that human beings are created "separate" and "distinct" from one another.[20] Each individual has his or her own body, wants, faculties, powers, will, and so on.[21] This basic *ontological* claim had profound *moral* consequences for Douglass. The separateness and distinctness of persons provided the foundation of his case for human rights. Second, "individuality" refers to man's natural self-interest. Individuals are drawn to interact with others, but they have a particular concern for themselves, their family, and their friends.[22] Third, natural individuality refers to man's natural desire to be free. Douglass said there "is no impulse so strong as that of liberty" and described the desire to be free as "the deepest and strongest of all the powers of the human soul."[23] In a social context, the desire to be free moves men to rebel against excessive infringements on their autonomy.

Douglass's appreciation for natural sociality and individuality enabled him to avoid the extremes of radical individualism and radical communitarianism. On the one hand, because he believed individual isolation is not natural or progressive, he was not attracted by the morally questionable doctrine of social Darwinism. On the other hand, because he believed individuality is an essential part of human nature, he retained his core liberal commitment to individual freedom rather than embracing a collectivist view such as civic republicanism or utopian socialism.

The next claim made by Douglass in the essay on civil government is that human beings are rational creatures who can use their reason to discriminate between right and wrong. The rational capacity of human beings is important for several reasons. First, the rational capacity makes education possible because it enables individuals to acquire and retain knowledge.

Second, the rational capacity makes dialogue and collective deliberation possible because it enhances our ability to communicate with others.
Third, the rational capacity makes moral judgment possible because it enables individuals to contemplate abstract moral and religious ideas. Like
his predecessor in the liberal tradition, John Locke, Douglass made man's
"distinctive capacity" to contemplate moral and religious ideas central to his
case for human rights.[24] Man, Douglass said, possesses an eternal and inde-
structible soul and "is endowed with those mysterious powers by which [he]
soars above the things of time and sense, and grasps with undying tenacity,
the elevating and sublimely glorious idea of a God."[25] The rational capacity
separates man from the rest of creation and is, for Locke and Douglass, an
indication that he has a special dignity.

The ability to acquire and retain knowledge enables human beings to
think historically. Douglass repeatedly cited Shakespeare's *Hamlet* when
making this argument: "Man is said to be an animal looking before and
after. To him alone is given the prophetic vision enabling him to discern the
outline of his future through the mists and shadows of his past."[26] According
to Douglass, this capacity is another indication of man's distinctiveness and
dignity. By looking to the past, men are able to learn much about human nature through reflection upon examples of excellence in history: "We do well
to cultivate this sentiment. It is a distinguishing attribute of our Nature. It
separates us from all other creatures of earth and attests that man is, indeed, but 'made a little lower than the Angels.' It imparts dignity to human
nature, and makes the lives of the great and good, of all ages, contemporary
with our own, and co-workers with us."[27]

Conversely, he believed it is worthwhile to remember the deeds of evil
men. By recalling the omnipresence of evil in human history, we are reminded of the constant obstacles and threats to the achievement and security of a just social order.

Douglass argued that man's historical sense is important because it enables him to construct a narrative of his own past and to plan a narrative
for his future. The ability to reflect on the past enables human beings to
learn from their own and others' successes and failures. The ability to imagine what will happen in the future is an essential part of Douglass's argument for the natural right to liberty. He believed that it is precisely because
human beings are, in Loren Lomasky's helpful phrase, "project pursuers"
that excessive interference with personal liberty is illegitimate.[28]

Perhaps most importantly, Douglass contended that the rational capacity enables men to understand "right and wrong, good and evil, justice and injustice." He acknowledged that "feelings" play a part in our moral decision making, but he contended that reason ought to be the ultimate arbiter. "God has not left us," he wrote, "solely to the guidance of our feelings, having endowed us with reason, as well as with feeling, and it is in the light of reason that [moral questions] ought to be decided."[29] In making this argument, Douglass adopted what intellectual historian Daniel Walker Howe has argued was the dominant understanding of moral psychology in eighteenth- and nineteenth-century Europe and America. According to Howe, "faculty psychology" is both a descriptive view and a normative view. "First in order of precedence came the rational faculties of the will: conscience (or the moral sense) and prudence (or self-interest). Below them were the emotional springs of action, called either by the approving term 'affections' or the more derogatory word 'passions,' as the context might dictate. . . . The hierarchical structure of human nature . . . corresponded to humanity's intermediate position in the great chain of being, partly divine, partly animal."[30]

According to Douglass's view, our initial moral reaction to something is often emotive. He contended that it would be a mistake to follow our immediate emotive reaction because we are also endowed with a rational faculty that enables us to reflect more deeply on moral questions.

Douglass's embrace of faculty psychology is an indication that he does not fit into the strand of liberalism that accepts "the sovereignty of desires."[31] For proto-liberals such as Hobbes and utilitarian liberals such as Jeremy Bentham, desires "are essentially given and unalterable facts about human nature to which morality must accommodate itself."[32] According to this view, rationality is merely an instrumental faculty; it serves individuals by guiding them to the most efficient means of self-gratification.[33] It is evident that Douglass rejected this view. For him, rationality is to be used to deliberate about the rightness and wrongness of *ends,* not merely of means. Liberals who have accepted the sovereignty of desires as a fact about human nature have made it easy for critics to accuse liberalism of being a morally shabby political philosophy. Douglass's rejection of this view is an indication that liberals need not believe moral considerations are always trumped by human desires. He accepted an understanding of reason that transcends the instrumentalism posited by Hobbes and his intellectual heirs.

Douglass's claim was that the rational faculty enables men to "apprehend" that which is good and that which is evil. There is no guarantee,
however, that men will "pursue" the correct moral path. This is because
free moral agency is another essential aspect of Douglass's view of human
nature. The question of free will is the focus of part III, but it is worth
noting here that Douglass's belief that the rational capacity enables men
to understand natural law should *not* be interpreted as a claim that moral
understanding *necessarily* leads to just behavior. According to Douglass, it
is often the case that men reach the correct moral understanding of a situation but nevertheless proceed to act unjustly.

The human tendency to act unjustly is caused by selfishness in man's
nature. Douglass claimed that hope of reward and fear of punishment are
"natural agents" for "restraining evil" and "promoting good." This claim
is grounded in his belief in natural self-interest. Men are, on this view,
"pushed from behind" by fear of punishment and a desire to live comfortable lives.[34] Douglass did not, however, accept the "hardheaded cynicism"
of Hobbes.[35] He argued instead that human motivation is more complex.
Men are self-interested, but they have the capacity to act according to a
sense of moral obligation to others. "There is something greater," he said
late in life, "more potent, than ambition that sways the actions of conscientious men. It is duty."[36] Although the rational faculty directs men to act in
their own interest, it also provides men with the capacity to act conscientiously. Natural self-interest and conscience often come into conflict. When
this occurs, individuals are free to choose how they will act.

On the question of human motivation, then, Douglass charted a middle
course. Unlike the Garrisonian abolitionists, many of whom were attracted
to the ideas of utopian thinkers, Douglass maintained a chastened attitude
toward the possibility of human perfection.[37] Like other liberal thinkers, he
accepted the idea that human motivation is, at its core, inescapably imperfect. Unlike the more cynical liberal thinkers, however, he believed human
beings have the capacity to transcend their desire for personal comfort and
act from a sense of moral duty.

So far I have focused on the opening claims of Douglass's essay "Is
Civil Government Right?" to provide a sketch of his view of the "facts of
human nature."[38] According to Douglass, human beings are naturally social
and individualistic, rational and passionate, good and evil, self-interested
and conscientious. At its core, his picture of human nature emphasizes

human rationality, the capacity for moral judgment, and free will. Although he believed each of these attributes to be essential parts of human nature, he understood that none is absolute. The rational faculty is in constant competition with the passions; the capacity for moral goodness is constantly threatened by the blinding power of selfishness; and free agency is affected by external influences. It is to the tension between conscientiousness and selfishness that we now turn.

II. Our Divided Hearts: The Spirit of Humanity and the Spirit of Selfishness

Nature Makes Us Friends: The Powers within Man "Impelling Him to Good"

Douglass contended that man's rational and sentimental capacities enable him to understand and pursue that which is good.[39] He went on to make the even stronger claim that the forces "impelling him to good" are, generally speaking, stronger than his "evil tendencies."[40] According to Douglass, the forces "impelling [men] to good" have their roots in both sentiment and reason. Feelings provide men with natural affection for their fellow human beings. The rational faculty enables men to contemplate the reasons why they should behave humanely. Through reflection, Douglass argued, men are able to recognize the moral rules of natural law and apprehend the rightness of those rules. In this section, I point to some of Douglass's evidence for both of these claims, beginning with his belief in natural affection.

Douglass's autobiographical writings provide several examples of what he interpreted as the exhibition of the feeling of "natural love in our fellow creatures."[41] In *My Bondage and My Freedom,* for example, Douglass pointed to evidence for natural human goodness by drawing on his experiences with children. When he was a young boy, he refined his reading skills by bribing his white playmates with bread. During these sessions, he liked to discuss slavery with the white children. "I wish I could be free, as you will be when you get to be men," he would say to them. He described the scenes that followed:

> Words like these, I observed, always troubled them; and I had no small satisfaction in wringing from the boys, occasionally, that fresh and

bitter condemnation of slavery, that springs from nature, unseared and unperverted. Of all consciences, let me have those to deal with which have not been bewildered by the cares of life. I do not remember ever to have met with a *boy*, while I was in slavery, who defended the slave system; but I have often had boys to console me, with the hope that something would yet occur, by which I might be made free.[42]

Children provided Douglass with an image of human nature uncorrupted. The fact that the children he encountered had a natural abhorrence of slavery was evidence to him that human beings are endowed with a natural affection for others.

Although children are the most likely to embody natural affection, adults are able to exhibit this tendency as well. When Douglass was about ten years old, he was sent to live with Thomas and Sophia Auld in Baltimore. Sophia Auld, who had not been a slaveholder prior to Douglass's arrival, seemed to him to be the embodiment of innate human goodness: "She was, naturally, of an excellent disposition, kind, gentle, and cheerful." Although Mrs. Auld was eventually corrupted by "the natural influence of slavery customs," her initial reaction to Douglass's arrival was one of "natural sweetness." "At first," Douglass wrote, "Mrs. Auld regarded me simply as a child, like any other child; she had not come to regard me as *property*."[43] Her natural affection for Douglass led her to treat him much like one of her own children. She fed him well, treated him with respect, and even began teaching him to read before her husband forbade her from doing so. Although Sophia Auld ended up *becoming* cold and bitter toward Douglass, his initial experience with her contributed to his view that human beings have a natural tendency toward goodness.

Douglass also thought natural human goodness is evidenced by our tendency to shudder at the sight or thought of physical violence. In a speech given after John Brown's raid at Harper's Ferry, he offered these thoughts.

Every feeling of the human heart was naturally outraged at [the raid on Harper's Ferry], and hence at the moment the air was full of denunciation and execration. So intense was this feeling that few ventured to whisper a word of apology. . . . Let no word be said against this holy feeling; more than to law and government are we indebted to this tender sentiment of regard for human life for the safety with which we walk the streets by day and sleep secure in our beds at night. It is nature's grand police, vigilant and faithful, *sentineled* in the soul, guarding against violence to peace and life.[44]

Douglass made a similar argument in a speech after the killing of a man who was attempting to capture a runaway slave: "The shedding of human blood at first sight, and without explanation is, and must ever be, regarded with horror; and he who takes pleasure in human slaughter is very properly looked upon as a moral monster. . . . These tender feelings so susceptible to pain, are most wisely designed by the Creator, for the preservation of life. They are, especially, the affirmation of God, speaking through nature, and asserting man's right to live."[45] Rather than offering a dark picture of human beings as naturally depraved, wolflike creatures that enjoy doing violence to their fellows, Douglass argued that affection for human life is a part of our nature.

The three examples of natural human goodness offered thus far are rooted in "feelings" rather than in reason, but Douglass also believed that reason directs human beings to act morally. Indeed, he believed that, as a normative matter, reason, not feeling, ought to be the ultimate arbiter of moral questions. For example, in each of the cases described earlier, John Brown's raid and the killing of the "slave catcher," he argued that the initial response provided by feelings, though natural and "holy," do not lead to the correct moral conclusion.[46] It is clear, therefore, that more must be said about how reason impels men to act morally.

Douglass argued that the rational faculty enables human beings to understand the truths of natural law. According to his view, these truths are "easily rendered appreciable to the faculty of reason in man."[47] This perspective is reminiscent of that of his liberal predecessor, Locke, who argued that reason "teaches all mankind, who will but consult it," the obligations of natural law.[48] In the same vein, Douglass contended that the "human mind is so constructed as that, when left free from the blinding and hardening power of selfishness, it bows reverently to the mandates of truth and justice."[49] This belief provided him with some hope that a just social order might be achieved *if* "free discussion" were allowed.

Little hope would there be for this world covered with error as with a cloud of thick darkness, and studded with all abounding injustice,

wrong, oppression, intemperance, and monopolies, bigotry, superstition, King-craft, priest-craft, pride of race, prejudice of color, chattel-
slavery—the grand sum of all human woes and villainies—if there
were not in man, deep down, and it may be very deep down, in his soul
or in the truth itself, an elective power, or an attractive force, call it by
what name you will, which makes truth in her simple beauty and excellence, ever preferred to the grim and ghastly powers of error.[50]

Douglass seemed to think there is something mysterious about the human
attraction to truth. Whatever the source of this attraction, something in the
human constitution is drawn to it.

The key for both Locke and Douglass seems to be that human beings
are endowed with the capacity to recognize moral truth. Each thinker made
clear, however, that individuals retain the ability to choose whether they
will pursue the right moral path or not. Locke said natural law teaches men
"who will but consult it," and Douglass indicated that natural law would
direct the actions of those men who are "left free from the blinding and
hardening power of selfishness." Douglass recognized that this direction is
anything but a given because the dark side of human nature is prideful and
selfish. It is to that side of human nature that we now turn.

The Spirit of Selfishness: The Powers within Man Impelling Him to Evil

Douglass believed that although reason enables men to understand what is
morally right and feelings encourage men to care about the well-being of
others, the spirit of selfishness in human nature makes men "constantly liable to do evil."[51] He differentiated selfish behavior from other self-interested
behavior by saying that the former is unrestrained and licentious, whereas
the latter can often be quite reasonable and morally acceptable. In other
words, a selfish action is one that is committed without any regard to the
rights and interests of others. He believed that reason, conscience, nature,
and revelation direct man to respect the rights of others but that the spirit
of selfishness can morally blind men and make them unwilling to respect
any authority other than their own will. The omnipresence of selfishness in
human nature, he argued, is evident from both "the facts of human nature,
and by the experience of all men in all ages."[52] "From the earliest periods of

man's history, we are able to trace manifestations of that spirit of selfishness, which leads one man to prey upon the rights and interests of his fellow-man. Love of ease, love of power, a strong desire to control the will of others, lay deep-seated in the human heart. These elements of character, over-riding the better promptings of human nature, [have] cursed the world with Slavery and kindred crimes."[53]

Within human nature, then, there are tendencies toward sociality and justice *as well as* tendencies toward antisocial behavior and injustice. Human beings have the capacity to feel love for others and to understand natural law, but they also have a love of ease and a will to power.

The love of ease creates a temptation to exploit the labor of others rather than labor for oneself. For Douglass, the most nefarious manifestation of this tendency is the institution of slavery, under which the slave "toils that another may reap the fruit; he is industrious that another may live by idleness."[54] Slavery is not, however, the only avenue available for the exploitation of others. After the Civil War, Douglass continued to identify ways in which the love of ease led men to act unfairly. In the essay "The Labor Question" (1871), for example, he argued that it was the "selfishness" of economic elites rather than an inherent defect in capitalism that caused the vast disparity between rich and poor in "our industrial civilization."[55]

Douglass contended that human beings are also tempted by a love of power and a desire to control the will of others. Man, he argued, has a "disposition to trample upon the weak and play the tyrant."[56] Again, he said that one need not engage in abstract speculation to reach this conclusion because human history provides sufficient evidence. "No fact is more obvious," he said, "than the fact that there is a perpetual tendency of power to encroach upon weakness, and of the crafty to take advantage of the simple."[57] The facts of human history make clear that there will always be "hardened villains" who "will cheat, steal, rob, burn and murder their fellow creatures."[58] Although Douglass pointed to hardened villains as particularly blatant manifestations of the spirit of selfishness in human nature, he did not believe these habitual offenders have a monopoly on evil in humanity but rather that the capacity to do evil resides within every human heart.

In order to demonstrate the existence of the selfish tendency in human nature, Douglass pointed to what he thought were the most obvious manifestations of it in human behavior. "The very first element of Slavery," he said, "is selfishness, extreme and bitter selfishness—selfishness that destroys the happiness of one man, to increase that of another."[59] Douglass also argued that the American policy of "manifest destiny" was an example of "the low, the selfish, the ambitious and rapacious side of human nature" at work.[60] A third example of the spirit of selfishness operating in human nature was the resistance to Chinese immigration in the late nineteenth century. In 1882, Douglass said, "I have no sympathy for the narrow, selfish notion of economy which assumes that every crumb of bread which goes into the mouths of one class is so much taken from the mouths of another class; and hence, I can not join with those who would drive the Chinaman from our borders."[61]

Douglass believed the spirit of selfishness emanated from the human heart. By this, he meant that the will to power has its roots more in our feelings than in our reason. He referred to selfishness as a "tendency" and a "propensity."[62] However, those who desire to exploit, control, and dominate others also put reason to use. When we indulge the spirit of selfishness, we seldom act without rationalizing our evil deeds. Douglass pointed out, for example, that selfish individuals often attempt to justify their behavior by appealing to widely held prejudices. Racial, religious, ethnic, and gender prejudices have been ready weapons for those wishing to satisfy their selfish desires at the expense of others. Prejudice is, in Douglass's view, an *instrument*, not the *cause*, of subordination. The philosophical, political, economic, and pseudoscientific construction of racial hierarchy, for example, serves as a means by which individuals can satisfy their natural desire to dominate others. "Pride and selfishness," Douglass said, "combined with mental power, never want for a theory to justify them."[63]

The existence of selfish tendencies in human nature is, to Douglass, as obvious as it is regrettable. Selfishness can blind men to moral rules and make them capable of acting like hardened villains. The idea of selfishness in Douglass's theory is reminiscent of the idea of "corruption and viciousness" in Locke's state of nature.[64] For both thinkers, an idyllic state of perfect harmony is impossible because of the capacity for evil within all human beings.

"Nature's Two Voices"

Douglass's position on the natural goodness and depravity in human nature is somewhere in the middle of the spectrum of possibilities. His view was not entirely pessimistic; he believed that human beings have a natural affinity for one another and that they are able to recognize and feel bound by natural law. But his view was not entirely optimistic, either; he believed human beings have selfish, antisocial tendencies. His acceptance of the idea that men have a natural love of ease and a desire to control the will of others indicates that he had a dualistic rather than a completely optimistic view of human nature.[65] Within the human will, there are forces impelling men to respect natural law, but there are also forces tempting him to "[rush] upon his fellowman to gratify his own selfish propensities at the expense of the rights and liberties of his brother-man."[66] He summed up his view of human nature in this way: "Nature has two voices, one high, the other low: one is in sweet accord with reason and justice, and the other apparently at war with both."[67]

Although Douglass did not accept either extreme on the question of human goodness, he did make clear that he believed there is more goodness in humanity (individually and collectively) than there is evil. He often drew attention to this idea in his speeches in favor of universal suffrage. "If I believed," he said, "in the doctrine that human nature is totally depraved, that is in an evil nature unmixed with good, I should hold with Carlyle that it is better to restrict the right of suffrage among the masses of the people."[68] But he rejected this view in favor of a more optimistic outlook: "I believe that men are rather more disposed to truth, to goodness and to excellence, than to vice and wickedness."[69] This point is significant because he believed the basic goodness of human beings is essential to the claim that they are *capable* of exercising freedom in a responsible way. In a speech on women's suffrage in 1888, Douglass made this point clear, and he is worth quoting at length:

> Let me say in conclusion, if human nature is totally depraved, if men and women are incapable of thinking or doing anything but evil and that continually, if the character of this government will inevitably be the expression of this universal and innate depravity—then the less men and women have to do with government the better. We should abandon our Republican government, cease to elect men to office, and place ourselves squarely under the Czar of Russia, the Pope of Rome, or some other potentate who governs by divine right. But if, on the contrary, human nature is more virtuous than vicious, as I believe it is, if governments are best supported by the largest measure of

virtue within their reach, if women are equally virtuous with men, if
the whole is greater than a part, if the sense and sum of human goodness in man and woman combined is greater than in that of either
alone and separate, then the government that excluded women from all
participation in its creation, administration and perpetuation, maims
itself, deprives itself of one-half of all that is wisest and best for its usefulness, success and perfection.[70]

Douglass's basic idea is clear: A view of human nature that emphasizes depravity is easily used to justify authoritarian government. If human beings
are vicious creatures, then perhaps the best we can do is rely on a Hobbe-
sian sovereign to keep us from one another's throats. If, however, we believe
human beings are capable of good and, indeed, often prove themselves to
be capable of not only peace but also cooperation and virtue, we are better
able to defend the idea that individuals ought to be free.[71]

Douglass's view of human goodness, then, is best described as moderate optimism. Although he believed human beings are constantly liable to
do evil, he also thought they are more inclined to do good. His appreciation
for this duality in human nature had important consequences for his political thinking. His recognition of the selfishness of human beings led him to
reject utopian anarchism in favor of a limited liberal state that has the primary tasks of protecting individuals from the selfish propensities of others.
His belief in human goodness enabled him to envision a society in which
individuals can exercise personal and political freedoms in ways consistent
with relative peace and harmony. This appreciation for the human capacity
to reason with and feel for others allowed Douglass the wisdom to reject
illiberal theories that fear large spheres of individual freedom. His appreciation for the omnipresence of evil, though, also led him to offer a morally
demanding formulation of liberalism. A free society is not all about rights,
liberty, and interest; indeed, it cannot exist, Douglass thought, without a
heavy dose of responsibility, duty, and virtue.

Although Douglass thought it a waste of time to speculate on the *origin* of good and evil in the world, he did think it worthwhile to consider
the malleability of human nature in order to determine the extent to which
character and behavior can be modified by external forces such as law,
culture, and education. It is to the question of human malleability that we
now turn.

III. Nature and Nurture: Circumstances, Malleability, and Free Will

The struggles within men's souls between reason and feeling, sociality and individuality, and good and evil raise important questions about free will and the malleability of human nature. What impact do environmental factors or cultural circumstances have on the formation and development of an individual's moral character? Can social and political institutions "make men moral"? If external factors have a significant impact, how can it be legitimate to call men free agents who are morally responsible for their actions? Douglass reflected on these questions, and his responses are the focus of this section.

Douglass believed that environmental factors have a significant impact on the formation and development of an individual's nature. As noted in part I, he said that the moral nature of children is generally good before it is perverted and bewildered by "the cares of life."[72] He argued that we must distinguish between "human nature uncorrupted" and "human nature corrupted."[73] Uncorrupted human nature is embodied in innocents such as children. Corrupted human nature was embodied in Southern slaveholders and members of lynch mobs, whose moral capacities were "perverted by long abuse of irresponsible power."[74]

> We are not, in [the case of mob violence], dealing with men in their natural condition, but with men brought up in the exercise of arbitrary power. We are dealing with men whose ideas, habits and customs are entirely different from those of ordinary men. It is, therefore, quite gratuitous to assume that the principles that apply to other men apply to the Southern murderers of the negro, and just here is the mistake of the Northern people. They do not see that the rules resting upon the justice and benevolence of human nature do not apply to the mobocrats, or to those who were educated in the habits and customs of a slave-holding community.[75]

This passage suggests that Douglass believed environmental factors play a key role in the formation and development of moral character. In a letter to his former master, Thomas Auld, he made an even stronger statement in support of an "environmentalist" view of human nature:[76] "Born and brought up in the presence and under the influence of a system which at once strikes at the very foundation of morals, by denying—if not the existence of God—the equal brotherhood of mankind, by degrading one part of the human family to the condition of brutes, and by reversing all right ideas of justice and brotherly kindness, it is almost impossible that one so environed can greatly grow in virtuous rectitude."[77]

When discussing such morally depraved individuals, Douglass drew attention to the importance of cultural circumstances or what some contemporary thinkers have called "moral ecology."[78] He argued, for example, that the institution of slavery "pollutes our soil" and contaminates the moral nature of individuals who live in its presence. "It may be seen," he said, "corroding their vitals, their morals, and their politics."

> It destroys all the finer feelings of our nature—it renders the people less humane—leads them to regard cruelty with indifference, as the boy born and bred within the sound of the thundering roar of Niagara, feels nothing strange because he is used to the noise; while a stranger trembles with awe, and feels he is in the presence of God—in the midst of his mighty works. People reared in the midst of slavery become indifferent to human wrongs, indifferent to entreaties, the tears, the agonies of the slave under the lash; all of which appear to be music to the ears of slaveholders.[79]

In language reminiscent of Karl Marx's base–superstructure concept, Douglass argued: "Like any other embodiment of social and material interest peculiar to a given community, slavery generated its own sentiments, its own morals, manners, and religion; and begot a character all around it in favor of its own existence."[80]

If embodiments of social and material interest are able to beget the moral character of individuals in a community, is there any room for free will and moral responsibility? Douglass's contention that it is "almost impossible" for individuals in certain circumstances to live virtuously seems to leave little room for the latter concepts. It would be a mistake, however, to interpret this understanding of moral ecology as a rejection of free will.

From the beginning of Douglass's career to the end, one can find evidence that he rejected deterministic theories of human agency. One piece of evidence against reading Douglass as a strong environmentalist is provided by his foray into the Scottish Free Church Controversy during the 1840s. According to Douglass's description, the Free Church of Scotland was composed of individuals who broke off from the Established Church in "defense of Christian liberty."[81] During the 1840s, abolitionists criticized the Free Church for accepting money from American slaveholders. Douglass described the charge against the Free Church in this way:

> The Free Church stands charged with fellowshipping slaveholders as followers of Christ, and of taking the wages of unrighteousness to build her churches and to pay her ministers. Are those charges true, or are they false? The Free Church admits these truths, but denies she has done wrong. Then the question between us is as to the rightfulness of holding Christian fellowship with slaveholders, and taking the results of slaveholding to build churches and pay ministers. The Free Church says it is right; I say it is wrong; and you shall judge between us.[82]

Douglass's assessment of the Free Church controversy indicates that he believed in the inescapability of free will and moral responsibility.

The leader of the Free Church, Dr. Thomas Chalmers, defended his willingness to take money from slaveholders by saying that "DISTINCTION *ought to be made between the character of a system and the character of the person whom CIRCUMSTANCES have implicated therewith.*"[83] Douglass called this distinction the "doctrine of circumstances" and said its chief defender was the utopian socialist Robert Owen. Owen had gained prominence for his industrial experiments in New Lanark, Scotland, and the founding of a utopian community in New Harmony, Indiana, in the first quarter of the nineteenth century. According to Owen, "facts prove" that "character is universally formed *for,* not *by,* the individual" and that "the affections are *not* under the control of the individual."[84] The leaders of the Free Church believed that because the character of slaveholders was completely determined by their cultural circumstances, it was defensible to associate with them and to accept their donations.

Douglass could not have been more adamant in his denunciation of the doctrine of circumstances. "This doctrine carried out," he said, "does away with moral responsibility. All that a thief has to do in justification of his theft is to plead that circumstances have implicated him in theft, and he has Dr. Chalmers to apologize for him, and recognize him as a Christian."[85] Although he did accept the idea that cultural circumstances have a deep impact on moral character, he believed that free choice is an inescapable part of human nature and that no individual can escape ultimate responsibility for his actions. "All attempts to remove the responsibility of the slaveholder from the individual to the nation, is erroneous, fallacious, false. All attempts to make it exclusively an individual matter are equally wrong—however it is more of an individual matter than a national one. The slaveholder holds his slave from *choice*—he trades in the bodies and souls of his fellow-men, because it is convenient for him to do so."[86]

Douglass believed that though various forms of socialization leave their mark and cultural pressures can be very strong, individuals remain capable of recognizing right from wrong and making choices accordingly. In the context of the Civil War, he described the idea of free moral agency in the starkest of terms: "Men have their choice in this world. They can be angels, or they may be demons."[87]

Later in Douglass's career, we find additional statements in support of a strong view of moral agency. In an editorial urging free blacks to enlist in the Union army during the Civil War, he said the following about the inescapability of free will and moral responsibility:

If you were only a horse or an ox, incapable of deciding whether the rebels are right or wrong, you would have no responsibility, and might like the horse or the ox go on eating your corn or grass, in total indifference, as to which side is victorious or vanquished in the conflict. You are however no horse, and no ox, but a man, and whatever concerns man should interest you. He who looks upon a conflict between right and wrong, and does not help the right against the wrong, despises and insults his own nature, and invites the contempt of mankind. . . . In the presence of [the Civil War] there is no neutrality for man. Manhood requires you to take sides, and you are mean or noble according to how you choose between action and inaction.[88]

After the war, he made clear that he rejected all deterministic explanations of the conflict and its outcome in favor of a view that placed human agency at the center of the moral and political universe. In a speech on his philosophy of reform given in 1883, Douglass said this: "It seems to me that a true philosophy of reform is not found in the clouds, or in the stars, or any where else outside humanity itself. So far as the laws of the universe have been discovered and understood, they seem to teach that the mission of man's improvement and perfection has been wholly committed to man himself. So he is to be his own savior or his own destroyer. He has neither angels to help him nor devils to hinder him."[89]

Douglass believed the human capacity to contemplate and understand moral truth imposes upon all individuals a heavy burden of responsibility. This agent-centered understanding views history as an "eternal conflict between right and wrong, good and evil, liberty and slavery, truth and falsehood, the glorious light of love, and the appalling darkness of selfishness and sin"[90]—a conflict in which the choices each of us makes can be of tremendous practical importance.

So where do these two strands of argument leave us? On the one hand, we find Douglass saying that human nature can be "corrupted and perverted by long abuse of irresponsible power," and so it is of little surprise that some individuals behave in immoral ways. On the other hand, we find Douglass defending a strong theory of moral agency. As with other aspects of his view of human nature, he occupied a middle ground. He acknowledged the importance of cultural and political institutions in promoting moral behavior and discouraging immoral behavior. He called the improvability of man "the grand distinguishing attribute of humanity," an attribute that "separates man from all other animals."[91] In an essay entitled "The Prospect in the Future," published in 1860, he expressed hope that "several generations of humanitarian culture" might make men more disposed to act according to the "higher and better elements of human nature."[92] The fact that men's natures can be subject to external influences does not mean, however, that individuals lack the capacity to choose. There was little question in Douglass's mind, for example, that growing up in the culture of slavery, where one group of people is permitted to exercise license toward another group of people, left deep scars on the moral psyche of individuals. No matter how clouded these individuals' moral vision became, however, Douglass still believed their actions were a matter of choice.

Where does Douglass's moderate view of free will and the malleability of human nature fit into his liberal political morality? The idea of environmentalism was a central piece of his argument against those who defended slavery on the basis of "natural" inequality. For him, there was no better way to respond to these arguments than by pointing to the environmental *causes* of black degradation. "When they tell the world that the Negro is ignorant, and naturally and intellectually incapacitated to appreciate and enjoy freedom, they also publish their own condemnation, by bringing to light those infamous Laws by which the Slave is compelled to live in grossest ignorance. When they tell the world that the Slave is immoral, vicious and degraded, they but invite attention to their own depravity; for the world sees the Slave stripped, *by his accusers*, of every safeguard to virtue, even of that purest and most sacred institution of marriage."[93]

Douglass's use of environmentalism as an argument for liberation is reminiscent of the use by the Jeffersonians of the early republic, who, according to historian Joyce Appleby, made "authoritarian institutions the cause rather than the consequence of human waywardness" and in so doing "turned the traditional justification for them on its head."[94] It is clear that Douglass believed authoritarian institutions have a negative impact on the moral nature of both the possessors of power and their victims, but he also considered the opposite to be true. He was confident that sound institutions could promote a healthy moral atmosphere in which individuals would be more likely to make morally responsible choices.

Douglass coupled this belief in environmentalism with a claim that individuals retain ultimate control over the choices they make. Given his ideological commitments and cultural context, it is not surprising that he retained this belief. The liberal commitments to individual freedom and personal responsibility follow from a basic belief in free will. This belief had clear practical implications for the political struggles of which Douglass was a part. A strong view of free will bolstered the case for abolition and other progressive causes by providing a basis for the natural rights of the oppressed as well as a basis for this-worldly punishment of the oppressors. Furthermore, as historian Eric Foner has pointed out, the revivals of the Second Great Awakening placed free will back at the center of religious salvation and connected the promise of eternal life to the individual's willingness to commit himself to "eliminating sin from society and paving the way for the Second Coming."[95] Operating within a context in which these individualistic religious ideas were ascendant, Douglass relied on them to urge his audiences to devote time and energy to progressive politics.

IV. Conclusion: The Dualities of Human Nature and Douglass's Liberal Politics

Douglass identified at least four struggles that occur within human beings. First, he drew attention to the fact that both reason and passion influence human behavior. Rational and passionate faculties are not, prima facie, good or evil. Each can be the cause or instrument of good or evil, which is a second duality within human nature. Human beings have the capacity to act conscientiously or selfishly. The third duality within human nature is the tension between sociality and individuality. Although human beings are drawn to interact with each other, they are also born with a natural desire to be free. Finally, Douglass contended that human beings are influenced by their cultural circumstances, but they retain ultimate control over their own wills.

Douglass's unwillingness to adopt extreme positions on human nature may create some frustration for contemporary interpreters seeking to categorize him. It is clear, however, that the complexities of the political problems he faced made it difficult for him to embrace a one-sided view. I believe the complexity and moderation of his theory of human nature enhance rather than detract from its attractiveness. On the one hand, because he recognized the human capacity for selfish, antisocial, and irrational behavior, he did not adopt an excessively optimistic view of man's nature. On the other hand, because he believed human beings are naturally social and endowed with a rational faculty that enables them to achieve moral understanding, he did not adopt an overly cynical view. Although those who emphasize the dark side of human nature like to call themselves "realists," I think a view such as Douglass's that appreciates the duality and dynamism of man's nature is far closer to reality.

Over the course of his long public career, Douglass developed a liberal political theory that constitutes one of the great chapters in the American political tradition. His liberalism cannot be fully understood without an appreciation of his thoughts on human nature. His recognition of the human being's constant liability to do evil led him to an appreciation of the precariousness of human freedom and the need to protect it with strong institutions *and* with a moral atmosphere that will make individuals more likely to respect and protect the rights of others. Douglass's belief in the natural sociality of human beings and his confidence that there is

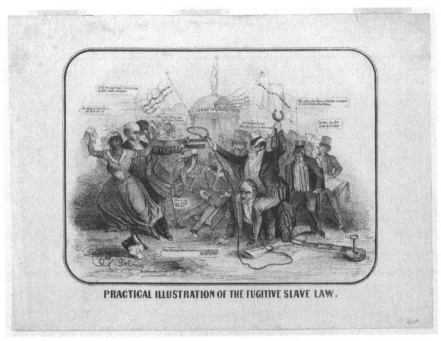

Figure 3. Practical Illustration of the Fugitive Slave Law, 1851. This satirical work highlights the implications of the Fugitive Slave Law of 1850 and the responses to it by supporters and critics after its passage. Represented in the illustration are a slave woman, slave driver, black man with a pistol, federal marshals, William Lloyd Garrison, Secretary of State Daniel Webster, Temple of Liberty, the Constitution, and volumes of law and gospel. (Reproduction number: LC-DIG-ppmsca-34495, Library of Congress.)

more good than evil in human nature led him to believe that a free society can be achieved and maintained. He was especially hopeful about the prospect of good triumphing over evil because he was attentive to the fact that circumstances shape human beings in important ways. Although these circumstances do not free us from moral responsibility, they can play a powerful role in shaping our habits of heart (our passions) and our cast of mind (our reason). A free society is more likely to be achieved if individuals are shaped by a "humanitarian culture" that teaches not only the rights of man but also the duties and virtues that are necessary to secure those rights.

Notes

Portions of section III of this chapter have been adapted from Nicholas Buccola, *The Political Thought of Frederick Douglass: In Pursuit of American Liberty* (New York: New York University Press, 2012), with the permission of New York University Press. Copyright © by New York University.

1. J. David Greenstone, *The Lincoln Persuasion* (Princeton, NJ: Princeton University Press, 1994), 48, 53.

2. In this chapter, I do not offer much of a defense of the claim that Douglass is best understood as a liberal. Scholars have coalesced around this interpretation, and suffice it to say that Douglass shared basic liberal commitments to individual rights, private property, democratic government limited by minority rights, and religious toleration. The major debate within Douglass studies is not about whether he was a liberal or not, but about just what kind of liberalism best captures his political philosophy. See, for example, Peter C. Myers, *Frederick Douglass: Race and the Rebirth of American Liberalism* (Lawrence: University Press of Kansas, 2008), and Nicholas Buccola, *The Political Thought of Frederick Douglass: In Pursuit of American Liberty* (New York: New York University Press, 2012). Greenstone himself had intended to write a chapter on Douglass's liberalism for *The Lincoln Persuasion*, but he passed away before he was able to do so.

3. Ronald Beiner, *What's the Matter with Liberalism?* (Berkeley: University of California Press, 1992), 7.

4. Reinhold Niebuhr, *The Children of the Light and the Children of the Darkness* (New York: Scribner's, 1960).

5. For a discussion of Mill's optimism about human nature, see Wendy Donner, *The Liberal Self: John Stuart Mill's Moral and Political Thought* (Ithaca, NY: Cornell University Press, 2001), 123. For a discussion of Jefferson's optimism, see David N. Mayer, *The Constitutional Thought of Thomas Jefferson* (Charlottesville: University of Virginia, 1994), 104.

6. For this interpretation of Locke, see Sheldon Wolin, *Politics and Vision: Continuity and Innovation in American Political Thought* (Princeton, NJ: Princeton University Press, 1960), and Leo Strauss, *Natural Right and History* (Chicago: University of Chicago Press, 1953). For Shklar's views, see Judith Shklar, *Ordinary Vices* (Cambridge, MA: Belknap Press of Harvard University Press, 1984).

7. See, for example, Wolin, *Politics and Vision;* C. B. MacPherson, *The Political Theory of Possessive Individualism: From Hobbes to Locke* (New York: Oxford University Press, 1964); Strauss, *Natural Right and History.*

8. See, for example, Reinhold Niebuhr, *The Nature and Destiny of Man*, vol. 1 (New York: Prentice Hall, 1980), and Russell Kirk, *The Conservative Mind* (New York: Regnery, 2001).

9. Niebuhr, *Children of the Light and Children of the Darkness*, xii, 10, 11.

10. For versions of this critique, see Michael Sandel, *Liberalism and the Limits of Justice* (Cambridge: Cambridge University Press, 1998), and Alasdair MacIntyre, *After Virtue* (South Bend, IN: Notre Dame University Press, 1984).

11. See, for example, Frederick Douglass, "Letter to Thomas Auld, My Former Master," in *The Life and Writings of Frederick Douglass*, 5 vols., ed. Philip S. Foner (New York: International Publishers, 1950–1975), 1:339.

12. Frederick Douglass, "Is Civil Government Right?" (1851), in *Life and Writings of Frederick Douglass*, 5:208.

13. For a discussion of the context of Douglass's essay, see Buccola, *Political Thought of Frederick Douglass*, 61–63.

14. Douglass, "Is Civil Government Right?" 5:209.

15. Aristotle, *The Politics*, bk. I, chap. 2.

16. Frederick Douglass, "Self-Made Men," in *The Frederick Douglass Papers, Series One: Speeches, Debates, and Interviews*, 5 vols., ed. John Blassingame and others (New Haven, CT: Yale University Press, 1979–1992), 5:549. Hereafter, citations to *The Frederick Douglass Papers* refer to *Series One*.

17. Stephen Mulhall and Adam Swift, *Liberals and Communitarians* (Oxford: Blackwell, 2000), 158.

18. Wilson Carey McWilliams, *The Idea of Fraternity in America* (Berkeley: University of California Press, 1973), 582.

19. Ibid.

20. Douglass, "Letter to Thomas Auld, My Former Master," 1:339.

21. Ibid.

22. Consult, for example, Douglass's discussion of what motivates human beings to work in "The Meaning of the Fourth of July for the Negro," in *Life and Writings of Frederick Douglass*, 2:200–201.

23. Frederick Douglass, "The Late Election" and "The Claims of Our Common Cause," in *Life and Writings of Frederick Douglass*, 2:528, 2:261–62. For more discussion of the importance of this idea in Douglass's thought, see Leslie Goldstein, "The Political Thought of Frederick Douglass," Ph.D. diss., Cornell University, 1974, 33–34.

24. Jeremy Waldron, *God, Locke, and Equality: Christian Foundations in Locke's Political Thought* (New York: Cambridge University Press, 2002), 87.

25. Douglass, "The Claims of Our Common Cause," 2:255.

26. Frederick Douglass, "Freedom Has Brought Duties," in *The Frederick Douglass Papers*, 5:56.

27. Frederick Douglass, "In Honor of Asa S. Wing," in *The Frederick Douglass Papers*, 3:109.

28. Loren E. Lomasky, *Persons, Rights, and the Moral Community* (New York: Oxford University Press, 1987), 26.

29. Frederick Douglass, "Is It Right and Wise to Kill a Kidnapper?" in *Life and Writings of Frederick Douglass*, 2:285.

30. Daniel Walker Howe, *Making the American Self: Jonathan Edwards to Abraham Lincoln* (Cambridge, MA: Harvard University Press, 1997), 21.

31. Anthony Arblaster, *The Rise and Decline of Western Liberalism* (Oxford: Blackwell, 1987), 28.

32. Ibid., 28.

33. Greenstone has argued that in the context of American political thought this instrumental rationality has manifested itself in what he calls "humanist liberalism," which has been "concerned primarily with the satisfaction of the preferences of individuals." The "concern with satisfying preferences," Greenstone states, "also implies a commitment to instrumental reasoning" (*The Lincoln Persuasion*, 36, 54).

34. Strauss, *Natural Right and History*, 199–201. For this reading of liberalism, see also Wolin, *Politics and Vision*, 257–65.

35. James T. Kloppenberg, *The Virtues of Liberalism* (New York: Oxford University Press, 2000), 25.

36. Frederick Douglass, "Duty Has Been the Moving Power of My Life," in *The Frederick Douglass Papers*, 5:458.

37. John A. Collins was a prominent Garrisonian who was attracted to utopian socialism. See, generally, Carl J. Guarneri, *The Utopian Alternative* (Ithaca, NY: Cornell University Press, 1991).

38. Douglass, "Is Civil Government Right?" 5:213.

39. This section is adapted from Buccola, *The Political Thought of Frederick Douglass*, 80–83. The section title paraphrases Douglass. In *My Bondage and My Freedom* (New York: Miller, Orton, and Mulligan, 1855), he wrote: "Nature had made us friends, slavery made us *enemies*" (161). In this quotation and in subsequent quotations from Douglass in the text, emphasis is given in the original unless otherwise noted.

40. Douglass, "Is Civil Government Right?" 5:209.

41. Douglass, *My Bondage and My Freedom*, 113. Goldstein calls this feeling the "divinely or naturally implanted sentiment of human brotherly love" ("The Political Thought of Frederick Douglass," 60–61).

42. Douglass, *My Bondage and My Freedom*, 115–16.

43. Ibid., 105, 107.

44. Frederick Douglass, "Did John Brown Fail?" in *The Frederick Douglass Papers*, 5:10.

45. Douglass, "Is It Right and Wise to Kill a Kidnapper?" 2:285.

46. In the case of Brown's raid, Douglass argued that Brown's actions, viewed in context, were not only defensible but praiseworthy. He acknowledged that moral feeling caused people to shudder at Brown's actions, but "happily reason has her voice as well as feeling, and though slower in deciding, her judgments are broader, deeper, clearer and more enduring" ("Did John Brown Fail?" 5:10). In the case of the runaway-slave kidnapper, Douglass said: "Contemplated in the light warmth of these feelings, it is in all cases, a crime to deprive human life: but God has not left us solely to the guidance of our feelings, having endowed us with reason, as well as with feeling, and it is in the light of reason that this question ought to be decided" ("Is It Right and Wise to Kill a Kidnapper?" 2:285).

47. Frederick Douglass, "The Antislavery Movement," in *The Frederick Douglass Papers*, 3:46. See also Goldstein, "The Political Thought of Frederick Douglass," 41.

48. John Locke, *Second Treatise of Government* (Indianapolis, IN: Hackett, 1980), 9.

49. Frederick Douglass, "The American Apocalypse," in *The Frederick Douglass Papers*, 3:437.

50. Frederick Douglass, "The Proclamation and a Negro Army," in *The Frederick Douglass Papers*, 3:553.

51. Douglass, "Is Civil Government Right?" 5:209. This section is adapted from Buccola, *The Political Thought of Frederick Douglass*, 19–22.

52. Douglass, "Is Civil Government Right?" 5:213.

53. Frederick Douglass, "The Proclamation and the Negro Army," in *The Frederick Douglass Papers*, 2:73.

54. Frederick Douglass, "Slavery and the Slave Power," in *The Frederick Douglass Papers*, 2:255.

55. Frederick Douglass, "The Labor Question," in *Life and Writings of Frederick Douglass*, 4:282.

56. Frederick Douglass, "Who and What Is Woman?" in *The Frederick Douglass Papers*, 5:252.

57. Frederick Douglass, "In Law, Free, in Fact, a Slave," in *The Frederick Douglass Papers*, 5:360.

58. Douglass, "Is Civil Government Right?" 5:212–13.

59. Frederick Douglass, "Aggressions of the Slave Power," in *Life and Writings of Frederick Douglass*, 3:127.

60. Frederick Douglass, "The Color Line," in *Life and Writings of Frederick Douglass*, 4:344.

61. Frederick Douglass, "We Must Not Abandon the Observance of Decoration Day," in *Life and Writings of Frederick Douglass*, 5:51.

62. Frederick Douglass, "Strong to Suffer and Yet Strong to Survive," in *Frederick Douglass Papers*, 5:360.

63. Frederick Douglass, "The Presidential Campaign of 1860," in *Life and Writings of Frederick Douglass*, 2:507.

64. Locke, *Second Treatise on Civil Government*, chap. 9, sec. 128.

65. For an interpretation that overstates Douglass's optimism, see Waldo E. Martin Jr., *The Mind of Frederick Douglass* (Chapel Hill: University of North Carolina Press, 1984), 20, 22, 118.

66. Douglass, "Is Civil Government Right?" 5:213–14.

67. Frederick Douglass, "The Southern Convention," in *Life and Writings of Frederick Douglass*, 4:251.

68. Frederick Douglass, "Letter to W. J. Wilson," in *Life and Writings of Frederick Douglass*, 4:173.

69. Ibid. Douglass wrote elsewhere: "I am so free in my religious opinions, so entirely free from that notion of the total depravity of man, and such a believer in the preponderating good in human nature that I believe that all the bad can be trusted with all the good, that all ignorance can be trusted with all the intelligence, and that this government will never be what it ought to be until all the people who live under it have some method of diffusing or infusing themselves into the government" ("The Civil Rights Cases," in *Life and Writings of Frederick Douglass*, 4:396).

70. Frederick Douglass, "I Am a Radical Woman Suffrage Man," in *The Frederick Douglass Papers*, 5:387.

71. I recognize that I am referring to several different types of freedom—for example, political freedom and personal freedom—without acknowledging the important differences and possible tensions between these types. I am doing so because, for Douglass, these arguments from human nature apply to all of the different types being discussed. Due to space constraints, I am unable to explore possible tensions between these conceptions of freedom, but I hope to address the complexities of Douglass's views of freedom in a future project.

72. Douglass, *My Bondage and My Freedom*, 115–16.

73. Frederick Douglass, "Lessons of the Hour," in *The Frederick Douglass Papers*, 5:589–90.

74. Ibid.

75. Ibid., 5:590.

76. By "strong environmentalist," I mean the view that individuals' moral character is formed entirely or almost entirely by the environments in which they find themselves.

77. Frederick Douglass, "Letter to Capt. Thomas Auld, Formerly My Master," in *Life and Writings of Frederick Douglass*, 1:404.

78. See, for example, Allen D. Hertzke and Chris McRorie, "The Concept of Moral Ecology," in Peter Augustine Lawler and Dale McConkey, eds., *Community and Political Thought Today* (Westport, CT: Praeger, 1998), 1–26.

79. Frederick Douglass, "America's Compromise with Slavery and the Abolitionists' Work," in *The Frederick Douglass Papers*, 1:210.

80. Frederick Douglass, "We Are Confronted by a New Administration," in *The Frederick Douglass Papers*, 5:174. Douglass offered a similar argument in an earlier speech: "Slavery, like all other gross and powerful forms of wrong which appeal directly to human pride and selfishness, when once admitted into the framework of society, has the ability and tendency to beget a character in the whole network of society surrounding it, favorable to its continuance" ("The American Apocalypse," 3:444).

81. Frederick Douglass, "The Free Church Connection with the Slave Church," in *The Frederick Douglass Papers*, 1:161.

82. Ibid.

83. As given in ibid.

84. Robert Owen, "Address to the Inhabitants of New Lanark," in Terence Ball and Richard Dagger, eds., *Ideals and Ideologies* (New York: Pearson, 2004), 205.

85. Douglass, "The Free Church Connection with the Slave Church," 1:163–64.

86. Frederick Douglass, "Emancipation Is an Individual, a National, and an International Responsibility," in *The Frederick Douglass Papers*, 1:253, emphasis added.

87. Douglass, "The American Apocalypse," 3:437–38.

88. Frederick Douglass, "The American Constitution and the Slave," in *Life and Writings of Frederick Douglass*, 3:341.

89. Frederick Douglass, "It Moves, or The Philosophy of Reform," in *The Frederick Douglass Papers*, 5:137.

90. Douglass, "The American Apocalypse," 3:437–38.

91. Frederick Douglass, "Our Composite Nationality," in *The Frederick Douglass Papers*, 4:255.

92. Frederick Douglass, "The Prospect in the Future," in *Life and Writings of Frederick Douglass*, 2:497.

93. Frederick Douglass, "The Folly of Our Opponents," in *Life and Writings of Frederick Douglass*, 1:114.

94. Joyce Appleby, *Capitalism and a New Social Order* (New York: New York University Press, 1984), 82.

95. Eric Foner, *Politics and Ideology in the Age of Civil War* (New York: Oxford University Press, 1981), 65.

III

Law

9

Seed-Time and Harvest-Time

Natural Law and Rational Hopefulness in Frederick Douglass's Life and Times

Peter C. Myers

"It will be seen in these pages," Frederick Douglass writes in the concluding chapter of his third and what he meant at the time to be his culminating autobiography, *Life and Times of Frederick Douglass,* "that I have lived several lives in one."[1] Just so, one might say that *Life and Times* comprises several books in one, and one might question how well those several books and several lives cohere with one another. In their introduction to the *Douglass Papers'* splendid new edition, Robin L. Condon and Peter P. Hinks suggest an answer. The work reveals at one level "a pastiche of inconsistencies and interpolations" and at another an encompassing coherence: "Douglass's last autobiography preserved and accommodated each of his former identities even as it enunciated new ones."[2]

To this sound judgment I would add that the coherence of Douglass's design in *Life and Times* appears also and most fundamentally at the level of principles. Douglass's reconciling of his various narrative "selves" signifies also a coherence in pedagogy, grounded in the principles of moral and political philosophy that he meant his story to convey. More specifically, I suggest that Douglass's design in this work, as in his moral and political thought as a whole, derives its basic coherence from his distinctive understanding of the law of nature. In this essay I consider Douglass's general idea of the law of nature and then consider the ways in which that idea informed his understandings of major events in various stages of his life. Douglass applied his conception of natural law in particularly interesting and sometimes problematic ways, first to the events leading up to slavery's abolition; second, to the initially promising period of Reconstruction; and finally, to the much gloomier period following Reconstruction and continuing to the end of his story.

Douglass's Idea of Natural Law

Frederick Douglass frequently invoked this venerable idea in Western political thought, and he did so with emphasis in the concluding chapter of the earlier *Life and Times*, "Retrospection." In that chapter's final paragraph, he summarized the moral lessons that he meant his life and work to convey in particular to his fellow African Americans. "I have aimed to assure them . . . that all the prayers of Christendom cannot stop the force of a single bullet, divest arsenic of poison, or suspend any law of nature . . . that the universe is governed by laws which are unchangeable and eternal, that what men sow they will reap, and that there is no way to dodge or circumvent the consequences of any act or deed."[3]

One sees in that brief summation the main elements of an understanding of natural law that fundamentally accords with traditional accounts yet also incorporates a significant modification distinctive to certain nineteenth-century thinkers. In keeping with the tradition of medieval and modern moral thought that developed out of the works of St. Thomas Aquinas, Grotius, and John Locke, among others, Douglass held that human actions are subject to laws that are at once *moral, rational,* and *universal* in scope. The natural laws are *moral* in that they outline the rights and obligations proper to human beings and thus direct us toward our proper happiness. They are *rational* in that they are accessible to natural human reason, grounded in a proper understanding of human nature and the natural human condition; they are not dictates of mere human will, and our knowledge of them is independent of divine positive revelation. And they are *universal* in that they apply to all human beings and human actions as such; their application is not confined by particularities of time, place, culture, or ethnic identification. For Douglass, the fundamentals of the moral law of nature were epitomized in the Declaration of Independence—"that glorious document which can never be referred to too often," whose affirmation of the equal natural rights of all human persons stood as history's most powerful expression of "the eternal principles of truth, justice, and humanity."[4]

Douglass frequently invoked the law of nature both because he was convinced of its profound truth and also by virtue of its utility in various practical applications. The natural law of human rights as epitomized in the Declaration served as an indispensable weapon in the philosophical and rhetorical arsenal that he brought to bear against slavery and for equal civil and political rights for all. The Declaration's principles "would release every slave in the world," as he remarked in an important speech on July 4, 1862.[5] Those principles also assisted Douglass in his efforts to remind abolitionists that the foundations of antislavery arguments are natural and rational, not only theological or scriptural, and likewise in his admonitions to his fellow African Americans, as in the conclusion to the 1881 *Life and Times,* against an excessive reliance on divine providential agency to deliver them from the evils of slavery and racial subordination. The principles fortified his arguments still further as he urged legislators to enact strong and clear guarantees of liberty in the postemancipation era. "Let your Government be what all governments should be," he advised the people of the United States on behalf of the black national convention in 1864, "a copy of the eternal laws of the universe."[6]

The law of nature was useful to Douglass in all these particular applications as a source of moral prescription, supplying guidance as to how to judge the rightness or wrongness of actions. But a further dimension of its usefulness to him reflects the distinctiveness of his idea. Douglass spoke of natural law not only as prescriptive but also as *predictive,* capable of informing not only our judgments of right and wrong but also our expectations concerning the *consequences* of particular courses of action. In other words, Douglass agreed with traditional accounts that the law of nature, to qualify as law in the strict sense, must carry effective sanctions—rewards for right and punishments for wrong actions—but he diverged from that tradition in his understanding of the nature and proximate source of those sanctions. Restating the traditional view, John Locke observed, "We must, where-ever we suppose a Law, suppose also some Reward or Punishment annexed to that Law"; and "the only true touchstone of *moral Rectitude,*" Locke continued, is "the *Divine* law . . . which God has set to the actions of

Men . . . [enforced] by Rewards and Punishments, of infinite weight and du-
ration, in another Life."[7] But when Douglass declared it a natural-law truth
that "what men sow they will reap," he did not refer to sanctions in another
life; he referred instead to the natural, this-worldly consequences of virtues
and vices, just and unjust actions.

The notion of a moral law carrying effective natural sanctions was not
original to Douglass. It was propounded in his day by widely renowned
thinkers in both the United States and Britain. In his essay "Compensation,"
Ralph Waldo Emerson objected to "the immense concession that the bad are
successful; that justice is not done now." To the contrary, Emerson insisted,
"All things are moral. . . . Justice is not postponed. . . . Every crime is punished, every virtue rewarded. . . . Cause and effect, means and ends, seed
and fruit, cannot be severed."[8] Likewise according to the abolitionist minister Theodore Parker, friend and colleague to both Emerson and Douglass,
"justice is the constitution or fundamental law of the moral universe," and
"the proverbs of the nations tell us this. . . . 'Ill got ill spent,' 'The triumphing
of the wicked is but for a moment.'" Such sayings may "have a little ethical ex-
aggeration about them," Parker allowed, "but yet more often they represent
the world's experience of facts more than its consciousness of ideas."[9]

Douglass was familiar with and influenced by both Emerson's and
Parker's works, but by his own testimony the primary influence on this
dimension of his thinking was the Scottish phrenologist and natural-law
theorist George Combe, an author widely read in mid-nineteenth-century
America. In his book *The Constitution of Man Considered in Relation to
External Objects* (1829), Combe affirmed the close conformity of physical
and moral laws, which to him constituted "parts of one connected system."
Moral laws are immanent in nature, Combe argued, so that "obedience to
each of [those laws] is attended with its own reward, and disobedience with
its own punishment." Combe contended further that "nations are under the
moral and intellectual law, as much as individuals," and are thus exposed
to grievous potential consequences for transgressing it.[10] In *Life and Times,*
Douglass described Combe as a "singularly clear-headed man," whose book
"had relieved [his] path of many shadows." During a visit to Scotland in
1846, Douglass's "very intense desire" was gratified as he received the opportunity to meet and converse with Combe over breakfast.[11]

In his repeated references to the "moral government of the universe"
constituted by "self-acting," "self-executing," or "inexorable" moral laws,

Douglass drew upon the argument of Combe.[12] This is the moral vision informing his hortative conclusion to the first *Life and Times,* which he expressed with equally striking confidence in his retrospective on John Brown, delivered at Harpers Ferry the same year that edition of *Life and Times* was published.

> There is, in the world's government, a force which has in all ages been recognized, sometimes as Nemesis, sometimes as the judgment of God and sometimes as retributive justice. . . . The universe, of which we are a part, is continually proving itself a stupendous whole, a system of law and order, eternal and perfect. Every seed bears fruit after its kind, and nothing is reaped which was not sowed. The distance between seed time and harvest, in the moral world, may not be quite so well defined or as clearly intelligible as in the physical, but there is a seed time, and there is a harvest time, and though ages may intervene . . . yet the harvest nevertheless will surely come. . . . The bloody harvest of Harper's Ferry was ripened by the heat and moisture of merciless bondage of more than two hundred years.[13]

Douglass maintained that so far as the law's natural sanctions were palpably evident and human beings remained rational beings, attentive and responsive to rewards and punishments, the moral law held significant predictive force. This was a crucially important point. On the premise that the moral law was effectively sanctioned, Douglass could make use of it not only as a source of prescriptive guidance but also as a motivational tool. The toil required to overcome injustice and to improve the condition of its victims could only be sustained by some amalgam of hope and fear; and it could be a powerful source of both to believe, as Douglass declared in the "West Indies Emancipation" speech (1880) that he appended to *Life and Times,* that in the end "the nation or people which shall comply with [the moral law] will rise, and those which violate [it] will fall." As he explained in concluding *Life and Times*'s first edition, he wrote in part "for the encouragement of a class whose aspirations need the stimulus of success."[14]

Allowing that "ages may intervene" between seed and harvest times, Douglass acknowledged the imperfect predictive power of his natural-law vision. In contrast to physical laws of nature, the moral laws were not instantly or perfectly effective, the history of chronic injustices—most notably slavery—readily attested. But this fact, along with Douglass's cognizance of it, raises difficult questions for his argument. Most pointedly, in view of his acknowledgment of the variable, uncertain schedule by which natural moral sanctions operate, one may question whether Douglass's *Life and Times* in the end yields discouragement rather than the encouragement its author intended for the antiracist, pro-equality cause. Upon reading the book's third part in particular, which finds Douglass coming to terms with the failure of Reconstruction as he extends his story through the disappointments of the 1880s and early 1890s, one is forced to consider how far even Douglass himself had come to doubt his long-held convictions concerning the moral design of nature and the progressive trajectory of US and human history.

To assess properly his case for the efficacy of the moral law and the rational basis for hopefulness—and therewith the coherence of *Life and Times*—we need to take a closer look at the specific argument that Douglass adumbrated through part 2, highlighted by his accounts of emancipation and racial reconciliation, and then to consider how much of that argument survived, or could survive, the account of racial reaction that he supplied in part 3.

Natural Law in Action: the Abolition of Slavery

The most impressive specific application of Douglass's general argument for rationally grounded hopefulness and the efficacy of the natural moral law appears in his predictions and explanations of slavery's abolition. So great a crime as slavery, in Douglass's reasoning, must be not only wrong but also, because of its very wrongness, inherently self-destructive. To say this is not to disregard the doubts that occasionally troubled him during the abolitionist stage of his career. But those doubts were exceptional; the salient fact is Douglass's steadfastness in maintaining his argument for hopefulness through what must have seemed to most of slavery's opponents the extraordinarily bleak and foreboding decade of the 1850s. In response to the *Dred Scott* ruling of 1857, which might well have been viewed (as slavery's defenders and many Northern Democrats did view it) as a crushing defeat for the political-abolitionist cause, Douglass insisted: "My hopes were never brighter than now. . . . By all the laws of nature, civilization, and of progress, slavery is a doomed system."[15] The following is an abbreviated summary of the argument that Douglass put forward in support of this optimism.[16]

The premise from which all else followed in Douglass's argument is that slavery is naturally wrong and human beings naturally know it. Everyone knows slavery is wrong for himself, and everyone without an interest knows that slavery is wrong for others. From this follow three crucial implications, involving natural, predictable responses on the part of three groups of actors: (1) the primary victims of slavery, those who were themselves enslaved; (2) nonslaveholding observers; and (3) slaveholders and their political supporters. The various responses of these groups would collaborate in bringing about slavery's downfall.

Among those enslaved, the awareness of slavery's wrongness naturally generated an extreme dissatisfaction, issuing in acts of resistance. Recalling his own dissatisfaction as slaveholder Hugh Auld expropriated his earnings as a ship caulker in Baltimore, Douglass presented that dissatisfaction as "proof of the same human nature which every reader of this chapter in [his] life is conscious of possessing."[17] The resulting acts of resistance varied according to circumstances and opportunities. In everyday instances, they took the forms of dilatory, grudging responses to slaveholders' commands to labor and of acts of petty theft or what slaveholders regarded as theft. In less frequent but more meaningful instances, they appeared in plots and attempts to escape—from the time he was seven or eight years old, Douglass reported that he cherished thoughts of fleeing slavery, inspired by the successful escape of his aunt Jennie and uncle Noah—and still more dramatically in their acts of violent resistance to slaveholders' cruelties.[18]

Slaveholders, despite their public professions of their institution's paternalism, were acutely aware of the volatile discontent among their victims. "It was the interest and business of slaveholders to study human nature," Douglass observed, "and the slave nature in particular. . . . Their safety depended on their vigilance. Conscious of the injustice and wrong they were every hour perpetrating . . . they were constantly looking out for the first signs of the dread retribution." That slaveholders could have no peace was in the very nature of things.[19]

In Douglass's argument, the causes of slaveholders' troubled sleep extended well beyond their fears of vengeance by their primary victims. The stories concerning acts of courageous resistance that he told in his earlier autobiographies and retold in *Life and Times* were predicated upon his expectation that such stories would help elicit readers' admiration and activate their antislavery sympathies. Douglass was convinced that the rise of a determined abolitionist sentiment at least among a minority of Americans was a natural inevitability. In *Life and Times*, evidence of the vitality of the cause and of the potential power of the movement appears once again in the testimony supplied by slaveholders. Noticing as an adolescent boy "the vindictive bitterness, the marked caution, the studied reserve, and the ambiguity practiced by our white folks in alluding to abolitionism," Douglass realized "that there was fear as well as rage" animating their discussions of the subject, and "from this [he] inferred that [the abolitionists] must have some power in the country."[20]

Whatever the overestimation in this youthful inference, in his mature argument Douglass reasonably assigned to abolitionism a very substantial, if mostly indirect, reason for slavery's demise. Urgently aware both of slaves' own discontentment and of the subterranean antislavery sentiment liable to emerge among nonslaveholding citizens in the North, slaveholders predictably regarded the suppression of abolitionist speech and, more broadly, the expansion of slavery's political hegemony at both federal and state levels as vital imperatives. Accordingly, they adopted a course of action that would quickly prove fatal to their own designs. In his chapter entitled "Increasing Demands of the Slave-Power," Douglass recounted a long train of specific slave-power aggressions and then summarized their effect. "In a word, whatever was done or attempted, with a view to the support and security of slavery, only served as fuel to the fire, and heated the furnace of agitation to a higher degree than any before attained. This was true up to the moment when the nation found it necessary to gird on the sword for the salvation of the country and the destruction of slavery." Granted, Douglass lost confidence in Northern resolve for a brief season after Abraham Lincoln's election; but it [Douglass's stance] was in keeping with his own broader argument that "the South was mad," as he put it, determined to dissolve the Union itself to secure slavery, and that Northerners would go to war rather than allow the slaveholding South to destroy the constitutional union that secured their rights as free people.[21]

In Douglass's interpretation, then, slavery's abolition appears as a singularly momentous instance of the operation of self-executing, naturally sanctioned moral laws of nature. In his 1869 commemoration of West Indies emancipation, he declared, "I contemplate the termination of slavery simply as a natural and logical event. The evil contained the seeds of its own destruction."[22] To reconstitute the erstwhile enslaved as freedpeople, however, was one thing, and to make them full citizens quite another. What remained to be seen was whether Douglass's natural-law argument and the optimism it yielded, solidly vindicated by the events of the 1860s, could be sustained in the difficult decades to come.

Natural Law in Action: The Reconstruction Era

The Emancipation Proclamation "changed everything," Douglass wrote, and from that point through the conclusion of *Life and Times*'s second part, his narrative followed an upward trajectory. Chapters 13 through 19 contain celebratory, even triumphalist, accounts of the enactment of the Reconstruction Amendments and of Douglass's various personal struggles for social as well as civil and political equality. The high point occurs in chapter 16, though, with stories of his reunions in the 1870s with Amanda Auld Sears and Thomas Auld, his return to the Lloyd plantation, and his speaking engagement in 1881 at Harpers Ferry. The kindness with which the Lloyds received him moved him to summarize the theme of this entire section of *Life and Times* with the affirmation that "a new dispensation of justice, kindness, and human brotherhood was dawning not only in the North, but in the South. . . . [T]he war and the slavery that caused the war were things of the past, and . . . the rising generation are turning their eyes from the sunset of decayed institutions to the grand possibilities of a glorious future." In chapter 19, the concluding chapter of this edition of *Life and Times*, he summarized this portion of his story as "the life of victory, if not complete at least assured."[23]

   Amid the edifying theme of reconciliation that Douglass sounds throughout this section of the work may also be heard a discordant note or two. The most significant of these arises in his lengthy discussion of his position on the "black Exodus" movement in the late 1870s in which large numbers of black Southerners left their homes to resettle in Kansas and other locations. Any large-scale interest in such a movement would cast serious doubt, of course, on his sunny assurances that a new, egalitarian dispensation was dawning in the South. Douglass initially opposed efforts to promote the exodus, and in doing so, as he commented shortly after the fact in *Life and Times*, he found himself "more widely and painfully at variance with leading colored men of the country" than ever before. In explaining his opposition, he noted "the outrages committed in some parts of the Southern

States against the Negro" and even declared that "the time for conciliation and trusting to the honor of the late rebels and slaveholders has passed." Yet he maintained, "the situation at the moment is exceptional and transient."[24] Like his stories of reconciliation, Douglass's insistence that African Americans stand their ground and fight for their rights in the South rested on his unsupported optimism that the forces of justice were winning and would soon enough complete their victory in the larger battle for equal rights in the United States.

Soon enough, of course, that optimistic outlook would encounter grave disappointment. But my purpose in reflecting critically on this portion of Douglass's argument is not to rehearse the evidence, by now well known, that undermines his Reconstruction-era faith that white racism was fading and that Republican officeholders could be relied upon to enforce a new constitutional regime of equal rights. For the present purposes, the question is whether Douglass's mistaken optimism in *Life and Times*'s second part represents a legitimate corollary of his notion of an efficacious natural moral law, so that the exposure of his optimism in this period as unfounded must also discredit his broader, natural-law argument. Does Douglass's error here indicate a defect in his natural-law principles themselves, or did he merely misjudge how those principles would apply to conditions in the Reconstruction era?

Whatever might be the true or final answer to this complex and difficult question, Douglass's own answer is indicated by the fact that in *Life and Times*'s third part (published in 1892), he seems clearly to renounce the near-term optimism characteristic of the second part, but he does not renounce his natural-law argument. To see why he did not need to renounce that argument, let us consider more closely the weaknesses in his case for optimism in the second part.

The optimism he expressed there was perhaps fueled by his contention that in "the logic of events," one advance in the pursuance of justice "prepares and makes easy the way to another."[25] In Douglass's abolitionist-era argument, the mechanism by which the natural law operates is that injustice tends to produce over time a convergence of interests in opposition to it, and in turn that convergence of interests tends, again over time, to expand moral sympathies and reform moral convictions.[26] Slavery became vulnerable when it endangered the rights of Northern whites; and it fell into extreme peril when it threatened the survival of the Union. At that point, abolition became an imperative of interest, or what Douglass called the "low motive of military necessity" in the war to preserve the Union. This lower motive of interest lent much-needed force to the higher motives of moral sentiment and principle to which abolitionists had long appealed. In the postwar period, the questions as framed by Douglass's natural-law argument then became: Would the convergence of interests between African Americans and whites continue, so that the latter would regard resurgent white supremacy in the former Confederate states as a similar danger to their rights or a similarly destabilizing force within their constitutional union? Or better still, would the convergence of interests that, by enormous mutual sacrifice, defeated chattel slavery expand into strong, enduring bonds of moral sympathy and conviction between African Americans and all whites, in the Southern as well as the Northern states?

The main thrust of Douglass's discussion in *Life and Times*'s second part is to show that both these sets of events, but especially the latter, were in fact occurring in the 1870s. The evidence that he supplies clearly fails to establish his claims, and it does so for reasons knowable and perhaps known to Douglass at the time. Space constraints do not permit an examination of the particulars here, but a common shortcoming of the anecdotes that he presents in chapter 16 is that he fails to demonstrate that these likely unrepresentative cases are actually representative of societal reforms in racial sentiments. Perhaps this failure was simply an error on Douglass's part. Perhaps in the excitement of the near-term aftermath of emancipation and the Union victory, he was overeager to conclude that white supremacy was doomed just as chattel slavery had been, so that he allowed his optimistic forecasts to rest on thinner evidence and weaker reasoning than he had marshaled in the more clear-sighted realism of his abolitionist argument. Or perhaps, as I believe more likely, Douglass by strategic design placed the most optimistic gloss on evidence he knew to be ambiguous. In other words, Douglass was mindful as ever that the moral law of nature is not instantly effective, and he was painfully aware, too, that the convergence of interests between African Americans and whites might well prove fleeting, that evidence of postwar retreat was accumulating, and that the larger meaning of the war was no less sharply contested in its aftermath than it had been prior to Emancipation. In his awareness of all these facts he judged it a prudential imperative to lend such rhetorical force as he was able to the proposition that racial reconciliation was the war's true meaning and consequence.

In this way we might shed additional light on Douglass's meaning when he disclosed in concluding the second part that he had written "for the encouragement of a class whose aspirations need the stimulus of success."[27] But whatever Douglass's intention in this respect, the decisive point for present purposes is that his fundamental conception of the naturally sanctioned law of nature survived, even in the face of his failed attempts in this part of *Life and Times* to sustain and expand the reformist energy of the wartime period. As our reading of the third part will show, however, it survived in a refined, or perhaps usefully clarified, form.

Natural Law in Action: The 1880s and Beyond

By the time Douglass came to add a third part to *Life and Times,* his tone had changed dramatically. If the preponderant sentiment of the second part is a somewhat triumphalist optimism, that of the third part is a chastened, though still resolute, realism. The story of progress told in the second part gave way to a story of reaction, written in a spirit of renewed agitation, in the third part. Whereas the theme of the second part was Douglass's hopeful observation and expectation of republican gratitude, the theme of the third part was republican ingratitude or forgetfulness on the part of the American republic in general and of the Republican Party in particular. In this context his conception of the natural law reappears, but in a more cautious, clear-sighted expression than it had received eleven years earlier. One striking indication of the third part's change in tone and focus appears in the harshness of Douglass's review of the presidency of Rutherford B. Hayes—a denunciation that, according to some critics, Douglass was culpably late in issuing.[28] However that might be, with the aid of hindsight he was unsparing in his judgment of the Hayes presidency. "The whole four years of this administration were, to the loyal colored citizen, full of darkness and dismal terror." Hayes was a "well-meaning" man, Douglass observed, who had "persuaded himself and others to believe that [a] conciliation policy would arrest the hand of violence, put a stop to outrage and murder, and restore peace and prosperity to the rebel States. The results of this policy were no less ruinous and damning because of [his] good intention."[29] With this judgment, Douglass repudiated not only the "sickly conciliation" policy of President Hayes but also his own chapters on the postwar years in *Life and Times*'s second part.

A further indication of the reactionary trend of the post-Reconstruction years, in Douglass's view, was the 1884 election to the presidency of Grover Cleveland, the first Democrat elected to that office since before the Civil War. To Douglass, Cleveland's election was assignable mainly to the moral decline of the Republican Party in the post-Reconstruction era, and in his analysis of the outcome one again sees elements of his natural-law perspective. "The life of the Republican party lay in its devotion to justice, liberty and humanity," he maintained, and in defeat it suffered the natural consequence of its abandonment of those principles. "There never was yet, and there never will be, an instance of permanent success where a party abandons its righteous principles to win favor of the opposing party."[30]

It is striking enough that Douglass's invocation of a naturally sanctioned moral law of nature does not disappear in this final addition to his story. It is all the more striking, however, that it reappears amid his discussion of what he regarded as the single "most flagrant example of this national [postwar] deterioration."[31] That example came in the form of a singularly demoralizing ruling by the US Supreme Court. The year was 1883, and the ruling came in the *Civil Rights Cases,* a set of five cases consolidated into one. The issue was whether the 1875 Civil Rights Act, which prohibited discrimination on grounds of race, color, or previous condition of servitude by the owners of various public accommodations, was a proper exercise of Congress's authority under the Fourteenth Amendment. The Court's answer was an emphatic no. According to the Court, only the states, not the US Congress, had the constitutional authority to legislate against private acts of discrimination.[32]

Douglass thought that this ruling was incorrectly decided as a matter of constitutional interpretation, and he also thought it a disgrace to American nationhood. The fact that all the justices were Republican appointees made it a signal act of betrayal. But what is most interesting for present purposes is the fact that at the heart of his speech on the *Civil Rights Cases,* the full text of which he inserted into *Life and Times,* appears the most forceful, concentrated, and revealing invocation of the natural law in the third part. His statement is worth quoting at length:

No man can put a chain about the ankle of his fellow man, without at last finding the other end of it about his own neck. . . . A wrong done to one man is a wrong done to all men. . . . The evil may be long delayed, but so sure as there is a moral Government of the universe, so sure as there is a God of the Universe, so sure will the harvest of evil come. . . . [In] Ireland, persecution has at last reached a point where it reacts terribly upon her persecutors. England is today reaping the bitter consequences of her own injustice and oppression. Ask any man of intelligence, 'What is the chief source of England's weakness? What has reduced her to the rank of a second class power?' and . . . the answer will be 'Ireland!' . . . Fellow Citizens! We want no black Ireland in America. We want no aggrieved class in America. . . . The power and friendship of seven millions of people . . . are not to be despised.[33]

Several points are significant. First, in contrast to *Life and Times*'s second part, Douglass here invoked the naturally sanctioned law of nature only as an admonition—not to explain, encourage, or predict moral progress but instead only to warn of the consequences of continuing injustices. In this respect his appeal to the law of nature in the third part signifies a return to the emphasis of his corresponding appeals in his abolitionist period, when he warned of the insecurity of slaveholders and the instability of the Union as natural consequences of the broadly shared crimes of slavery.

Second, when he warned of the dangerous effects of African Americans' disaffection from the United States, he had in mind more than the danger of possible disloyalty in wartime. A speech that he gave barely a month before his *Civil Rights Cases* speech in which he also invoked Ireland made clear that he was thinking also about the domestic ill effects of such disaffection.[34] The specter of a "black Ireland" was the prospect of a chronically aggrieved and demoralized class of millions who feel unprotected by law and disrespected by the larger community and who are convinced that efforts at self-improvement on their part are doomed to end in futility. The heavy costs to the nation's security, prosperity, and prestige, Douglass insisted, should have been obvious to all.

Third, his warning illustrates the complexity of his idea of the law of nature. The natural law might be sanctioned with punishments, but those punishments might or might not have the effect of moving transgressors to reform. The emergence of an alienated, demoralized "black Ireland" in the United States would certainly be damaging to the interests of white Americans, but it might very well be no less damaging to the interests of African Americans, and the vices attendant upon a spirit of moral and civic alienation among African Americans would be at least as likely to reinforce whites' racism as to induce any spirit of sympathy or penitence among them. The logic of Douglass's natural-law argument in this instance reveals the possibility of a downward spiral in which chronic injustice engenders vice among its victims, and the vices of victims are taken in turn to justify the continuation of the injustice. An observation from the second part is pertinent here: "The way of transgression is a bottomless pit."[35]

As in any speech or writing by the irrepressibly hopeful Douglass, glimmers of hopefulness appear even in *Life and Times*'s third part. His account of the election cycle of 1888 highlights his exhortations to the Republicans and to the nation, evidence of his undying faith that the United States could not become deaf to appeals to its sense of justice and honor.[36] He closed the work with a characteristic expression of "warmest gratitude" for "the respect and confidence of my fellow men" and for "the many honors" bestowed upon him in the course of his public life.[37] Those closing words may seem narrowly personalized. To that one might say that such honors convey at least something hopeful about the republic that bestowed them upon the most prominent representative of a dishonored class. But on the whole, *Life and Times*'s third part leaves the reader with a decidedly grim near-term outlook for the cause of racial equality.

Conclusion

As Douglass updated *Life and Times* with the addition of its third part, his conception of a naturally sanctioned natural law returned to a closer conformity with teachings predominant in the tradition of classical liberal political philosophy. Despotism is odious, observes the Baron de Montesquieu, but it also has a substantial basis in human nature; it is indeed the most common of governmental forms. The law of nature is intelligible to all rational creatures, John Locke argued, but its natural sanctions are at best imperfect; the "great Robbers" are often "too big for the weak hands of justice in this world," and popular resistance to transgressors is unlikely until the evil extends to or threatens the majority.[38]

Properly understood, Douglass's account of the operation of natural law in the abolitionist period yielded a similarly cautious conclusion; this was not the manifestly false optimism that nature's sanctions must promptly stamp out injustices where they arise, nor was it the millennialist interpretation of the Civil War that seems to inform *Life and Times*'s second part. Instead it was the more realistic expectation that great wrongs, *generally felt,* are in the nature of things powerfully sanctioned. In this more traditional insight there is cause for sobriety, but also a rational basis for hopefulness.

"I do not pretend to understand the moral universe," said Theodore Parker in an 1853 sermon; "the arc is a long one, my eye reaches but little ways," but "from what I see I am sure it bends toward justice."[39] As the decades passed in the postwar era, Douglass saw with renewed clarity that the confounding power of bigotry is greater and more durable than he had allowed himself, for a time, to say or even to think. Yet his recognition of the length of the arc or of the often maddening distance between seed-time and harvest-time in the moral universe did not require him to relinquish his conviction that that arc indeed somehow bends toward justice. Saying that there is a naturally sanctioned moral law of nature did not commit Douglass to the claim that injustice is weak or ephemeral in human affairs. It committed him only to the reasonable propositions that tyranny carries its own costs; that tyranny by its nature breeds arrogance and insecurity among tyrants and provokes resistance among those subject to them; and that such resistance tends over time to destabilize regimes that perpetrate it. So understood, Douglass's natural-law argument yields expectations broadly in keeping with the evidence of US history. Where resistance to injustice is guided by a prudent leadership that combines appeals to moral principle, enlightened patriotism, and practical interest—and where it is sustained by the rational faith in the arc of the moral universe that sustained Douglass and his fellow abolitionists, along with their successors in the civil rights movement—in time it produces profound and durable reforms.

Notes

First published as "Seed-Time and Harvest-Time: Natural Law and Rational Hopefulness in Frederick Douglass's *Life and Times,*" *Journal of African American History* 99 (1–2) (Winter-Spring 2014): 56–70. Reprinted with the permission of the University of Chicago Press. Copyright © 2014, the University of Chicago Press.

1. Frederick Douglass, *Life and Times of Frederick Douglass,* in *The Frederick Douglass Papers, Series Two: Autobiographical Writings,* 3 vols., ed. John Blassingame and others (New Haven, CT: Yale University Press, 1999–2012), 3:372.

2. Robin L. Condon and Peter P. Hinks, "Introduction to Volume Three," in Douglass, *Douglass Papers, Series Two,* 3:xliv.

3. Douglass, *Life and Times*, 3:373, cf. 479.

4. Frederick Douglass, *The Frederick Douglass Papers, Series One: Speeches, Debates, and Interviews*, 5 vols. (New Haven, CT: Yale University Press, 1979–1992), 4:126; Frederick Douglass, *The Life and Writings of Frederick Douglass*, 5 vols., ed. Philip S. Foner (New York: International Publishers, 1950–1975), 4:523.

5. Douglass, *Life and Writings*, 3:248.

6. Ibid., 3:421.

7. John Locke, *An Essay Concerning Human Understanding*, ed. Peter Nidditch (Oxford: Oxford University Press, 1976), 351–52, emphasis original.

8. Ralph Waldo Emerson, *The Works of Ralph Waldo Emerson* (New York: n.p., 1925), 1:115, 117, 118.

9. Theodore Parker, "Of Justice and the Conscience," in *The Collected Works of Theodore Parker*, ed. Francis Power Cobbe (London: n.p., 1879), 2:40, 48.

10. George Combe, *The Constitution of Man Considered in Relation to External Objects* (Boston: Boston, Carter and Hendee, 1829), vii–viii, 130–31, 23, 234.

11. Douglass, *Life and Times*, 3:187–88.

12. Ibid., 3:480; Frederick Douglass, *My Bondage and My Freedom*, in *Autobiographies*, ed. Henry Louis Gates Jr. (New York: Library of America, 1994), 189; Douglass, *Douglass Papers, Series One*, 5:137.

13. Douglass, *Douglass Papers, Series One*, 5:10–11.

14. Douglass, *Life and Times*, 3:373, 479.

15. Douglass, *Life and Writings*, 2:411, 414. On the reaction to *Dred Scott*, see Don E. Fehrenbacher, *The* Dred Scott *Case: Its Significance in American Law and Politics* (New York: Oxford University Press, 1978), 417–48.

16. I discuss it relatively briefly here because I have discussed it at greater length elsewhere. See Peter C. Myers, *Frederick Douglass: Race and the Rebirth of American Liberalism* (Lawrence: University Press of Kansas, 2008), esp. 47–82.

17. Douglass, *Life and Times*, 3:146.

18. Ibid., 3:41, 81–83.

19. Ibid., 3:123–24, 234.

20. Ibid., 3:69–70. See also Douglass, *Life and Writings*, 2:354.

21. Douglass, *Life and Times*, 3:228–29, 259.

22. Douglass, *Douglass Papers, Series One*, 4:230.

23. Douglass, *Life and Times*, 3:352, 372.

24. Ibid., 3:335–44.

25. Ibid., 3:267, 299.

26. For a lately influential, more pessimistic interpretation of the convergence of interests as a mechanism of reform, see Derrick A. Bell Jr., "*Brown v. Board of Education* and the Interest–Convergence Dilemma," *Harvard Law Review* 93 (January 1980): 518–33.

27. Douglass, *Life and Times*, 3:373.

28. Douglass, *Life and Writings*, 4:99–101; William S. McFeely, *Frederick Douglass* (New York: Norton, 1991), 289–95; John Stauffer, *Giants: The Parallel Lives of Frederick Douglass and Abraham Lincoln* (New York: Twelve, 2008), 310.

29. Douglass, *Life and Times*, 3:393, 384.

30. Ibid., 3:407–8.

31. Ibid., 3:395.

32. *Civil Rights Cases*, 109 US 3 (1883).

33. Douglass, *Life and Times*, 3:401. Ireland was a career-long concern of Douglass's, tracing to his first sojourn in Great Britain in 1845–1847. Upon visiting Ireland and meeting Irish politician and "liberator" Daniel O'Connell, Douglass readily saw an analogy between English subordination of the Irish and white Americans' subordination of blacks in the United States. Douglass discusses his early experience in Ireland and with O'Connell in *Life and Times;* see *Life and Times*, 3:182–86.

34. Douglass, *Douglass Papers, Series One*, 5:101. This speech may reveal the otherwise uncertain object of his reference to "black Ireland" in his "Civil Rights Cases" speech. In this September 1883 speech, Douglass warned, "Out of the misery of Ireland comes [*sic*] murder, assassination, fire, and sword." The reference seems to be to the "Phoenix Park murders"—the May 1882 assassination in Dublin of the British government's chief secretary for Ireland and his undersecretary, evidently by members of a secret society named the Irish Invincibles, a violent faction of the pro-independence Irish Republican Brotherhood. See Douglass, *Douglass Papers, Series One*, 5:89 n. 3.

35. Douglass, *Life and Times*, 3:299.

36. Ibid., 3:436–38.

37. Ibid., 3:457.

38. Baron de Montesquieu, *The Spirit of the Laws*, ed. Ann M. Cohler et al. (Cambridge: Cambridge University Press, 1989), bk. V, chap. 14; John Locke, *Second Treatise of Government*, in *Two Treatises of Government*, ed. Peter Laslett (Cambridge: Cambridge University Press, 1988), sec. 12, 168, 176, 208–9.

39. Parker, "Of Justice and the Conscience," 2:48.

10

The Affect of God's Law

Vincent Lloyd

The language of God's law appears throughout the varied and storied career of Frederick Douglass. It is language that was in the air, used by William Lloyd Garrison and many abolitionists.[1] At one extreme, some abolitionists argued for theocracy, that the United States ought to be governed directly on divine (biblical) principles and that the current constitution and government were illegitimate. Douglass famously broke with Garrison, both personally and intellectually—though the views of Douglass and Garrison were never as synchronized as the latter would have had their audiences believe. It was after this break that Douglass evinced a more complicated relationship with the US Constitution, acknowledging its potential while also decrying its misuses.

Publishing his own newspaper in Rochester, Douglass deepened his links with the intellectual traditions of African America. This followed three years in Britain and Ireland, where he made new connections and solidified his identification with the international temperance movement and the women's rights movements. In the years leading up to the Civil War, Douglass endorsed increasingly radical positions, praising John Brown and suggesting that violence against slave owners and their agents was justified. Throughout this period, Douglass continued making speeches, distinguishing himself with his oratorical skill. And throughout, he continued talking about God's law.

It was during the 1850s that reflection on God's law appears most frequently and robustly in Douglass's speeches. This was also the period of his most famous orations, including his Fourth of July speech. The year 1850 saw the passage of the Fugitive Slave Act, requiring citizens in the North to assist in the capture and return of escaped slaves. The year 1855 saw US senator Charles Sumner, an abolitionist, severely beaten at his Senate desk by slavery supporter Preston Brooks, a member of the US House of Representatives. Events accelerated in the years before the opening shots of the Civil War. The *Dred Scott* decision was handed down by the Supreme Court in 1857, and John Brown's raid occurred in 1859. It was in this volatile context, in which the federal government's position was as precarious as ever, that Douglass spoke frequently on such topics as "the eternal truth" and "God's law outlawed."

In these speeches, Douglass presented truth, all truth, as timeless; he presented error, in contrast, as having a starting point and an ending point. In the Declaration of Independence, he argued, certain truths are recorded: eternal truths. They include "the great truth of man's right to liberty," which "was born with us; and no laws, constitutions, compacts, agreements, or combinations can ever abrogate or destroy it. It is so simple a truth that we have no occasion to look into the mouldy records of the past, in order to demonstrate it; it is written on all the powers and faculties of the human soul; the record of it is in the heart of God."[2] The eternal truth is God's, but it is also accessible through man. Not only is eternal truth accessible through man, but it is also crystal clear. There is no need to dig through the records of the past or the conventions of society to find it. Quite the opposite: the more one looks to the past or to social conventions, the more God's law is obscured.

Human Nature and God's Law

What are the "powers and faculties of the human soul" of which Douglass writes? In a speech at Western Reserve College entitled "The Claims of the Negro Ethnologically Considered" in July 1854, the first graduation address ever delivered by a black person at a major American university, Douglass described what this phrase might mean.[3] He atypically spent many hours preparing this speech, consulting with academic friends and reading ethnographical scholarship. The resulting oration, however, was not burdened

by an aspiration to the scholarly. It repackaged Douglass's standard moral
and political points in conversation with the scholarly queries of the day. He
addressed the argument that "inalienable rights" do not accompany blacks
because blacks are not men by considering what it means to be a man:

> Man is distinguished from all other animals, by the possession of cer-
> tain definite faculties and powers, as well as by physical organization
> and proportions. He is the only two-handed animal on the earth—
> the only one that laughs, and nearly the only one that weeps. Men in-
> stinctively distinguish between men and brutes. Common sense itself
> is scarcely needed to detect the absence of manhood in a monkey, or
> to recognize its presence in a negro. His speech, his reason, his power
> to acquire and to retain knowledge, his heaven-erected face, his
> habitudes, his hopes, his fears, his aspirations, his prophecies, plant
> between him and the brute creation, a distinction as eternal as it is
> palpable. . . . Tried by all the usual, and all the *un*usual tests, wheth-
> er mental, moral, physical, or psychological, the negro is a MAN—
> considering him as possessing knowledge, or needing knowledge, his
> elevation or his degradation, his virtues, or his vices—whichever road
> you take, you reach the same conclusion, the negro is a MAN. His good
> and his bad, his innocence and his guilt, his joys and his sorrows, pro-
> claim his manhood in speech that all mankind practically and readily
> understand[s]."[4]

In this wonderfully rich passage, Douglass steps aside from direct engagement with the science of the day. In fact, the quotation is interrupted—
marked by the ellipses in the passage quoted—by a dismissal of evolutionary
theory. He instead appeals to the self-evident, to precisely that which is obscured when the human is theorized scientifically or historically or socially.
He appeals to joys and sorrows, virtues and vices, innocence and guilt—all
of which simultaneously, paradoxically, characterize "MAN." The "powers
and faculties of the human soul" cannot be reduced to the capacity to reason. That is not the way in which humans reflect God's image, though that
is part of it, an obvious part. Douglass speaks of reason in a sentence that
progresses from the superficially to the subtly obvious: from "speech" and
"reason" to "fears" and "aspirations" and, ultimately, "prophecies," which
once again link the human and the divine.

The secularist would turn away at talk of the divine or dismiss it as mere rhetoric. But if we work through this language rather than dismiss it, we can see that something more interesting appears. The divine, reflected in the human and sometimes articulated by a human in prophecy, is that which cannot be reduced to human description—historical, social, or scientific. Douglass has little more to say about God than this. He called himself a Christian and spoke of his faith, yet he was also consistently and pointedly critical of the American Christian churches.[5] In the South, churches offered a justification for slavery. In the North, churches tacitly or explicitly endorsed segregation, a phenomenon Douglass was shocked to encounter above the Mason–Dixon line. Douglass's faith was a faith in paradox, in humans' incapacity to perfectly describe their worlds and themselves. And it was a faith that raged against those who made such attempts: they were the sinners; they did the work of Satan.

There has been a significant amount of scholarly literature produced about Douglass's natural-law language and concepts, and there has also been a significant amount of discussion of his use of affect, including his "sentimentalist" style.[6] Many scholars investigating Douglass and natural law have sought to locate him within the abolitionists' debates concerning these issues, paying particular attention to his relationship with the Declaration of Independence and the US Constitution. They ask questions about Douglass's interpretation of these documents, in what cases natural law can or cannot be ignored, and whether Douglass's position changed as he moved from context to context—from association with abolitionists to exile in Britain and then to an American return that thrust him into the midst of a Northern African American community from which he had previously kept a distance. Scholars investigating his use of affect have asked questions about how his evocations of affect changed over the course of his life and literary output, about how his prose relates to the burgeoning genre of sentimentalist fiction in the 1840s and 1850s, and about whether the sentimentalism of his prose is in tension with its ostensible political message.

Some scholars have recently approached both sets of questions together. Nick Bromell and Nicholas Buccola have suggested, against the standard reading of Douglass as firmly located within the liberal political tradition, that Douglass in fact has affinities with certain critics of liberalism because of his willingness to offer a political role to affect.[7] Bernard Boxill has deftly made the case that Douglass uses emotions to increase moral sensitivity.[8]

Even Douglass's most militant speeches take this tactic, according to Box-ill, because he believed that fear (in a general rather than acute sense) can make us aware of moral problems and choices that we would otherwise overlook. The slave owner confronted with the possibility of destitution if John Browns were to proliferate—as Douglass hoped—was prompted to reflect more deeply on the justice or injustice of his lifestyle. In this way, questions concerning the affect produced by Douglass's prose are tied to questions concerning morality, not just law or politics.

Responses to both types of questions, the first on Douglass's natural-law language and the second about his sentimentalism, start from the secularist assumption that Douglass cannot *really* mean anything substantial when he talks about religion. For it is religion, or more broadly the theological, that links affect and natural law in Douglass's writings and speeches. In spite of his subtle analysis, Boxill does not elevate the moral above the human plane, as it were. His argument is compelling, to the extent that it is, because we can recognize increased moral sensitivity. Implicitly, what counts as moral is what a sufficiently (or perfectly) reflective person would treat as moral. Box-ill is, after all, an analytic philosopher, and his argument proceeds through ordinary language analysis. Fear, for Boxill, is an exceptional case, a sort of supplement to reason that performs the work of reason through an alterna-tive means—but that is ultimately verified through reason.

If we take the theological seriously, it becomes clear how invoking God's law holds the promise of trumping worldly authorities. A law sanctioned by God clearly stands above a law sanctioned only by humans. The problem, of course, is that knowing God's law is much more difficult than knowing the law of the land. Access to God's law not only supposes that God exists but also supposes that we humans can have specific knowledge about God—knowledge of facts about God and how they translate into norms applicable in the world. From a political perspective, it is thus tempting to reduce away invocations of God's law either as rhetoric or as ethics or as both. Given that belief in God is not universal—and even if it were universal, there would be disagreement over specific facts about God—there would seem to be two ways to understand appeals to God's law. They could be appeals on the one hand to a specific community that shares specific beliefs about God or on the other hand to a broader public that is motivated by the phrase "God's law," just as that public might be motivated by the phrase "four score and seven years ago"—because it is part of a shared cultural heritage that continues to resonate, even in a relatively secular world. In neither case is God's law substantially connected with an account of collective life or the common good that would be relevant to all.

In response to such criticism, those who support the political relevance of God's law argue that, at least in the Judeo-Christian tradition, all human beings have access to God's law because we have been created in the image of God. That we image God is what makes humans distinct from other animals, on this account. By reflecting on those aspects of ourselves that are distinctively human, we may be able to reach conclusions about the content of God's law. This method would not necessarily provide an exhaustive account of that law. The portion of God's law that is accessible in this manner is often referred to as "natural law." What scholars who take this approach generally conclude is that the distinctive feature of our humanity is that we have the capacity to reason. Indeed, recent accounts of natural law have simply identified it with practical rationality. These accounts often rely on a distinctive understanding of practical reason, drawn from a reading of Thomas Aquinas, that views reasons as responsive to goods. We can reflect on these goods, identifying certain basic goods (such as friendship, appreciation of beauty, recreation, and family), and reach conclusions about laws that respect or do not respect these basic goods.[9] For adherents of such a view, belief in God is not required. We all can reach natural-law conclusions by reflecting on our own human nature. Moreover, it seems quite plausible that politics should start from the good rather than from the right. Natural law provides a way to envision such a politics. The conservative Catholic public intellectual Robert P. George has associated this tradition with African American invocations of God's law and specifically with Frederick Douglass.[10]

Just as it is troubling for some critics to deflate invocations of God's law into mere rhetoric, it seems equally troubling for other critics to inflate such invocations into an elaborate theory about practical reason. This essay proposes that Frederick Douglass's invocations of God's law are both rhetorical and substantive; indeed, the two interpretations cannot be detached from one another. Such an account is necessary if we want political theorizing and the practice of politics to be closely connected: if we think political theory is implicit in political practice and if we think political practice turns into action the commitments of political theory. Moreover, if our conception of politics includes not only state institutions but social movements, not only authority and legitimacy but also ideology critique, alternatives must be sought to the terms of contemporary natural-law theory. Indeed, natural-law theory has moved so close to liberal political theory, with its focus on offering an account of the rational actor who legitimates laws, that the more radical, more critical potential of invoking God's law is forgotten. Put another way, contemporary natural-law theory has secularized, carefully managing the disturbing invocation of the otherworldly that might force us to question the status quo and catalyze social movements of the disenfranchised. Yet such questioning and catalyzing are precisely the work done by Frederick Douglass's invocations of God's law.

Normative Affect

Let us approach Douglass's invocations of God's law using the structure but not the content of current natural-law theory. Specifically, let us see how Douglass's account of human nature does not identify rationality as its essential characteristic but instead gives affect a central role in defining what is distinctively human. As we have begun to see, it is affect, not reason, that reflects the image of God in humans, and it is affect, not reason, that results in normative conclusions with political implications. In a sense, these claims return to the central Christian claim that God is, most essentially, love— the best metaphor for God has to do with affect, not with reasoning. But just as contemporary natural-law theory presents itself as equally legible to believers and atheists, this reading of Douglass is not dependent on Christian commitments—though it is compatible with those commitments. Most importantly, the shift from an account of God's law that hinges on reason to an account of God's law that hinges on affect moves away from the individualism of reason to the sociality of affect. As recent theorists have shown, affect can be shared; it circulates, and it has, in a sense, a life of its own. Affect is elicited by rhetoric, and this is how rhetoric persuades. This sociality adds a new dimension to natural-law theory, connecting the individual human's ability to discern justice with the collective movement toward a more just world. As such, the affective approach to natural law provides resources that are particularly valuable when considering Frederick Douglass.

Douglass was an orator, an organizer, and a political thinker. It is important to understand these three vocations together to appreciate his gifts and his place in American political history. Against recent accounts of charismatic black leadership that emphasize the male, heteronormative, and ultimately regressive nature of such modes of political engagement, Douglass is an example of how one may perform radical politics without contradiction.[11] Oratory need not be paternalistic or condescending—such a view already supposes the autonomy of reasoning actors rather than the circulation of affect across semipermeable bodies. Such oratory primes listeners for organizing: not top-down organizing but self-organizing because the listeners, through listening, have become aware of their own capacity for affect, and that is their source of normativity. They can now see and challenge those laws and social norms that run counter to the normativity that they themselves can access—normativity that is self-evident to them. This self-evidence is a principle tenet of natural-law theory, and part of the appeal of natural-law theory is that it is accessible to all, requiring no expert knowledge. Put differently, the critique of charismatic leadership relies on the notion that affect can deceive and be organized by ideological forces invested in maintaining the status quo—if not with respect to race, then with respect to gender and sexuality. Simplified to a slogan of popular psychology, this critique goes as follows: you feel toward the charismatic speaker how you feel toward your father. But such an analysis ignores the potential for affect to lead to norms and for affect itself to propel movements that affirm those new norms. Affect, like reason, cannot be entirely reduced to being an instrument of ideology.

Whereas on Boxill's account the affect produced by Douglass's rhetoric sharpens the human capacity to reason about norms, on the natural-law view I am developing affect is not subordinate to reason. The affect produced by Douglass's rhetoric displays performatively the falsity of certain norms as it displays the sanctity of human nature. In explicitly theological terms, it shows how God is imaged in human nature. This is a point developed in both secular and theological terms in the work of phenomenologist Michel Henry's account of "auto-affection."[12] We are individuated, according to Henry, when we feel ourselves feeling—that is, when we become aware of our essential humanity, which is simply this capacity. Henry demonstrates how various aspects of modernity, in particular rationalism and scientism as institutionalized in the state, the media, and culture more broadly, disguise or distort our human nature. This disguise or distortion he calls "barbarism." Modernity, he charges, prevents us from becoming aware of our own affect; from this claim, we can draw the conclusion that certain norms and laws ought to be changed—for example, laws that apply scientific or technical reasoning to social life. For Henry, the normative potential of auto-affection is primarily negative: it offers critique rather than constructive alternatives.[13] Henry does not explicitly consider race, but the fact that racialization developed along with the rest of modernity's suite of rationalistic, scientistic managerial projects makes his account highly suggestive—not of commending race-blind norms and laws but of critiquing racist norms and laws.

Reading Douglass in light of the natural-law tradition and in light of Michel Henry's account of auto-affection provides a way to link his rhetoric, argument, and organizing. Douglass is committed to an account of "the human soul" with affect at its center, standing as a bridge to the divine. He evokes affect in his rhetoric, reminding his listeners that each of them has the capacity for affect in himself or herself and that this capacity generates normative conclusions. The affect generated in Douglass's oratorical performances circulates and resonates, catalyzing a social movement that implements those normative conclusions (most basically, the conclusion that laws denying the humanity of blacks ought to be overturned). Obviously, I am making a lofty claim, too lofty. Many listeners and readers were not affected in this way by Douglass's texts, and Douglass's texts do not strike the perfect balance of analysis and affect to do what I attribute to them. But my claim is simply that Douglass's work tends in these directions and that natural law and affect provide a way of understanding Douglass as a part of and a critic of the American political tradition.

The Rhetoric of God's Law

Contemporaneous accounts of Douglass's own oratorical performance confirm the affective power of his words. As he spoke, Douglass was "filled with energy," and his words came "spontaneously."[14] Could it be that Douglass's words were spontaneous because in his case the cliché that they came "from the heart," from his humanity as such, was true? A reporter admired "his talent, his good sense, and his zeal in a cause,"[15] suggesting the obviousness, the self-evidence, of his spontaneous performance. Douglass began his first reported speech, given in Lynn, Massachusetts, in October 1841, "I have come to tell you something about slavery—what *I know* of it, as I have *felt* it,"[16] mixing reason and emotion from the very start. As a listener of a later speech recalled, Douglass's performance "was not what you could describe as oratory or eloquence. It was sterner—darker—deeper than these. It was the volcanic outbreak of human nature."[17] From the earliest descriptions of Douglass's speeches, it is clear that observers noted the effect he had on his audiences. As one newspaper wrote, his speech "thrilled through every one present, and compelled them to feel for the Wrongs he had endured."[18] The raw humanity unleashed by Douglass's oratory was contagious: the audience knew and felt along with the speaker.[19]

These connections between affect and natural law become especially clear in Douglass's speech following the Supreme Court's *Dred Scott* decision in 1857 as well as in Douglass's open letter to his former master published as an appendix to his second autobiography, *My Bondage and My Freedom*. The *Dred Scott* speech is particularly notable, coming five years after Douglass's most famous address, "What to a Slave Is the Fourth of July?" In the latter, much analyzed speech, Douglass at once embraced American ideals and distanced himself from them.[20] He began by lauding "your National Independence," speaking of the bravery and greatness of the Founding Fathers, only later to interject himself as someone present but uncounted within the American nation. "What have I, or those I represent, to do with your national independence?" he asked.[21] By affirming the equal manhood of slaves, Douglass saw potential to reconcile the conflict. There is talk of God and Christianity in "What to the Slave Is the Fourth of July?" but it is primarily in terms of slavery's affront to Christian liberty. In the face of the *Dred Scott* decision, Douglass's hope in American ideals was dimming. The hope that remained was provided by God, and in certain ways this view echoed Douglass's position from earlier speeches.

Douglass was not inclined to describe God (much less Christ or the Holy Spirit), except to affirm God's power and eternity, which he did in the *Dred Scott* speech:

> The Supreme Court of the United States is not the only power in this world. It is very great, but the Supreme Court of the Almighty is greater. Judge Taney can do many things, but he cannot perform impossibilities. He cannot bale out the ocean, annihilate the firm old earth, or pluck the silvery star of liberty from our Northern sky. He may decide, and decide again; but he cannot reverse the decision of the Most High. He cannot change the essential nature of things—making evil good, and good evil. Happily for the whole human family, their rights

have been defined, declared, and decided in a court higher than the Supreme Court.[22]

Here Douglass presented a very standard natural-law position. Indeed, it would almost seem like an "ontological" view of God's law, positing the existence of two realms of being, one earthly and one heavenly, each with its own law, and the law of the "higher" trumping the law of the "lower." But Douglass quickly proceeded:

> Your fathers have said that man's right to liberty is self-evident. There is no need of argument to make it clear. The voices of nature, of conscience, of reason, and of revelation, proclaim it as the right of all rights, the foundation of all trust, and of all responsibility. Man was born with it. It was his before he comprehended it. The deed conveying it to him is written in the center of his soul, and is recorded in Heaven. The sun in the sky is not more palpable to the sight than man's right to liberty is to the moral vision.[23]

He later continued, "We can appeal from this hell-black judgment of the Supreme Court, to the court of common sense and common humanity. We can appeal from man to God. If there is no justice on earth, there is yet justice in heaven."[24] At first, Douglass's thoughts seem incoherent. How can he be appealing beyond man to God but also be appealing to man's soul and to common sense? We can resolve this apparent tension if we realize that Douglass had in mind something quite different than an ontological view of God's law. God's law is revealed through both "nature" and "revelation." It is revealed but also familiar: it is "self-evident," accessible simply through "common sense." The means of accessing the "higher" realm is through our undistorted (which is to say always already distorted: paradoxical) humanity—the center of the soul provides a trapdoor to the heavens. This is why Douglass had hope, why he did not "feel gloomy and sad." All individuals have the capacity to know for themselves—when they allow themselves to access their souls, when they work through the difficult mix of analysis and affect that neither rationalizes nor sentimentalizes—that slavery is evil.

Douglass presented the case for this higher law in a relatively straightforward, relatively analytical tone. And yet these passages are embedded in a speech that is highly evocative of the senses. Consider the first and the last sentences of the *Dred Scott* oration: "While four millions of our fellow countrymen are in chains—while men, women, and children are bought and sold on the auction-block with horses, sheep, and swine—while the remorseless slave-whip draws the warm blood of our common humanity—it is meet that we assemble as we have done to-day, and lift up our hearts and voices in earnest denunciation of the vile and shocking abomination," and "When this is done, the wounds of my bleeding people will be healed, the chain will no longer rust on their ankles, their backs will no longer be torn by the bloody lash, and liberty, the glorious birthright of our common humanity, will become the inheritance of all the inhabitants of this highly favored country."[25]

At first, it seems as though Douglass was simply using graphic, shocking imagery to gain the sympathy of his audience. But woven into these opening and closing lines is precisely the same theme that he develops analytically in the passages from the middle of the speech: "our common humanity." These emotional passages that frame the speech and the analytical discussion at the speech's center are doing the same work: evoking a humanity that cannot be sufficiently described either way, either as rational or affective, but only with the two forever together, forever in tension. We *feel* the ache of our common humanity sundered when slaves are described in chains, treated like animals; we *think* our common humanity with common sense, providing access to something more trustworthy and eternal than any court. When both are performed at the same time, we do more than either feel or think; we hold them together, impossibly.

"To My Old Master, Thomas Auld" (1848) is a peculiar text. It takes the form of an open letter and purports to be written on the anniversary of Douglass's emancipation, but it was not mailed, nor is it likely that it was written when Douglass asserts it was.[26] Indeed, Douglass carefully crafted and revised it to suit his purposes. Scholars have shown that he included hearsay anecdotes that he knew to be false, and he continued reprinting the letter without qualification even after he knew that Auld had emancipated his slaves,[27] despite the letter's extended introductory remarks reflecting on the advantages and disadvantages of such a public exposure. In short, Douglass's text is a work of rhetoric, not aiming at descriptive accuracy and not crafted to persuade Auld but rather aiming to persuade a broader public audience, particularly those sympathetic with the perceived innocence of white slave owners.

The backbone of Douglass's text is again the theme of common human-ity, a humanity shared by both slave and slave owner. The letter begins, "The long and intimate, though by no means friendly, relation which unhap-pily subsisted between you and myself . . . ." As strange as it may seem, slave and slave owner were two human beings living in proximity to each other and so developing an intimate relation, no matter how much the slave owner would want to deny it. The letter ends ambiguously, as Douglass writes that he intends "to make use of you as a weapon with which to assail the system of slavery" but also that "I entertain no malice toward you personally." In a tone that does not even hint at irony, Douglass says that Auld is more than welcome to visit him and stay at his house, concluding in the penultimate line, "I should esteem it a privilege to set you an example as to how mankind ought to treat each other." In the final line, the salutation, Douglass writes, "I am your fellow-man, but not your slave."[28] As we saw earlier, Douglass emphasizes how humans are complicated, contradictory creatures, both virtuous and vicious, capable of both elevation and degradation. To rec-ognize common humanity is both to praise and to chastise, but underlying both such acts is a sense of hospitality.

In the text of the letter, Douglass shares his reasoning and his feel-ings with Auld, another mark of hospitality and common humanity. "I have often thought I should like to explain to you the grounds upon which I have justified myself in running away from you," he writes. Significantly, he continues, "I am almost ashamed to do so now, for by this time you may have discovered them yourself."[29] How could Auld discover these reasons? Presumably Douglass does not think Auld took to reading abolitionist news-papers (banned in the South). According to Douglass, what makes Auld ca-pable of this discovery is that the two men share a common humanity with Douglass. Auld and Douglass share the "powers and faculties of the human soul," which provide access to a higher law. Acknowledging this shared hu-manity, through performing this shared humanity, allows all to see that slavery is an injustice. To believe in a common humanity is to have faith that each person may also come to believe in a common humanity.

Douglass proceeds to lay out his justification for escape:

When yet but a child about six years old, I imbibed the determina-tion to run away. The very first mental effort that I now remember on my part, was an attempt to solve the mystery—why am I a slave?

And with this question my youthful mind was troubled for many days, pressing upon me more heavily at times than others. When I saw the slave-driver whip a slave-woman, cut the blood out of her neck, and heard her piteous cries, I went away into the corner of the fence, wept and pondered over the mystery. I had, through some medium, I know not what, got some idea of God, the Creator of all mankind, the black and the white, and that he had made the blacks to serve the whites as slaves. How he could do this and be *good*, I could not tell. I was not satisfied with this theory, which made God responsible for slavery, for it pained me greatly, and I have wept over it long and often. . . . I resolved that I would some day run away. The morality of the act I dispose of as follows: I am myself; you are yourself; we are two distinct persons, equal persons. What you are, I am. You are a man, and so am I. God created both, and made us separate beings. I am not by nature bound to you, or you to me.[30]

This is not at all what one would expect when one is told to anticipate a justification. Douglass does not offer reasons. This is an emotionally charged story, and it is the affect described in and produced by the story that creates a reason, that provides the justification. Douglass is clear about this: an affective experience allowed him to "solve the mystery" of his enslavement. He tried to solve this problem rationally, thinking really hard about it, but without success. Then he saw the whipping of a female slave, saw the blood, heard her cries, and meditated. His meditation was not rational reflection: he "wept and pondered over the mystery"—where the mystery now was both the whipping and his own enslavement. This meditation involved the rejection of theory (in this case positive theology): the rational account of God smoothing over the difficulties of the world by ordaining different positions for blacks and whites no longer made sense. Douglass wept, and he pondered, and the only intellectual conclusion he reached was the obvious: he was a human just like his master. This is not exclusively an intellectual conclusion; it is inextricably tied to a practical conclusion. "I resolved that I would some day run away." The justification that the reader anticipates is not presented as a logical progression: *here* are the premises, and *here* are the conclusions. Quite the contrary, the critical moment when justification happens is opaque: it occurs as Douglass "wept and pondered," and "The whole mystery was solved at once."

Broadening God's Law

Others have questioned the hegemony of the conservative Catholic natural-law tradition, attempting to make room for additional perspectives and voices. Jeffrey Stout, for example, has suggested a deflationary account of natural-law theory that is motivated by the desire to make sense of both Thomas Aquinas and Martin Luther King Jr. as natural-law theorists.[31] Stout takes his lead from philosophers of science who imagine the laws of nature as an ideal system of equations governing the behavior of the universe, only a portion of which we now know but all of which we can aspire to learn at the "end of inquiry." Perhaps, he suggests, natural law is similarly what obtains at the end of moral inquiry. We may catch only glimpses of natural law now, but a commitment to natural law is a commitment to the possibility of an "end of inquiry"—and this possibility motivates inquiry itself. Or, less strongly and in an idiom Stout would prefer, this possibility is a commitment implicit in the practice of inquiry.

Stout's account of natural law is deflationary insofar as it provides a framework for talking about natural-law language without entailing any problematic (or perhaps even debatable) metaphysical commitments. God and all his avatars are gone. But are we left with anything more than mere rhetoric, the phrase "higher law" providing extra force to certain moral claims? It is unclear whether Stout takes natural law to be mere rhetoric: he is redescribing a certain morally efficacious rhetorical trope in palatable philosophical terms (as a pragmatist, he can aspire to little more). But in the deflationary move that Stout makes, the robust intellectual work that someone like Douglass developed gets lost. Douglass's performances are *critical:* they humble rationalists and sentimentalists of all stripes. Even though one could say that Douglass, like Stout, eschews robust metaphysical commitments, Douglass does not tacitly accept the starting point of the discussion. Moreover, commitment to an "end of inquiry" is not entailed by Douglass's practice. He identifies the telos of his critical practice as paradox (the paradox at the heart of the human), with the result that Douglass is just committed to critical practice itself: the imagined goal of the performance, as with the words of the Lacanian analyst, is a tantalizing void simply motivating further performance.

In *Feminist Ethics and Natural Law*, Cristina Traina argues not only that the two projects named in her title are compatible but also that they need each other.[32] Natural law is not a certain set of conclusions or precepts but rather a process of reasoning that takes account of "the innate rational inclination to the good." To begin that process of reasoning necessarily involves examining local circumstances and varying capacities. "The good" that we all innately pursue, according to Traina, is not the same for everyone, or, rather, it is always named in the local idiom. Traina suggests that her synthesis "accounts for historical and cross-cultural diversity in experience and even in norms without relinquishing its prophetic edge." Moreover, her position is one in which "centripetal and centrifugal forces are balanced, so that diverse ethics move in orbits rather than collapsing indistinguishably into a common center or spinning off wildly and randomly to the far reaches of the universe."[33]

Interpreting Douglass or other African American natural-law theorists in the way Traina suggests would mean articulating certain "black" (rather than, as in Traina's case, "female") capacities and circumstances that need to be taken into account for African Americans to make sense of their innate inclination toward the good. Phrased in this way, however, Traina's account seems much less plausible in the case of race than in the case of gender. The radical potential that the natural-law tradition invoked by Douglass or King holds—the potential to overturn a deeply entrenched cultural system—is lost once natural law is understood as a style of reasoning that takes as its starting point the circumstances and capacities of a community. Traina wants to avoid saying that there are certain circumstances and capacities that all humans share, but Douglass makes an even more radical move. He contends the one thing that all humans share, at the core of their humanity, is an essential contradiction or paradox. The process of reasoning about natural law is a process of working that paradox indefinitely, always failing, trying to fail better. Traina, in contrast, supposes that circumstances and capacities can be named accurately and so can provide a firm starting point for reasoning about the (undefined) good. Like Stout's deflationary approach, Traina's alternative account of natural law lacks the capacity for ideology critique found in Douglass's work.

Natural Law and Social Change

This critical potential is not only in theory. Its materialization is demonstrated in perhaps the most famous passage of Douglass's prose: his fight

with Covey as described in each of his autobiographies. Douglass performed natural law in his speeches, but he also performed it in his own
actions as he describes them in these autobiographical texts. In each case,
the smoothing functions of reason and affect are removed as their tension is
revealed. In Douglass's speeches, the result was contagious commitment to
humanity through abolitionist politics that spread through his audience. In
the climactic moment of Douglass's autobiographical narratives, the result
is commitment to his own humanity through physical confrontation.

In *My Bondage and My Freedom,* Douglass writes, "Whence came the
daring spirit necessary to grapple with a man who, eight-and-forty hours
before, could, with his slightest order have made me tremble like a leaf in a
storm, I do not know; at any rate, *I was resolved to fight,* and, what was better still, I was actually hard at it."[34] Commitment arises out of nowhere—not
out of reasoning or out of feeling but out of their contradictory mixture
(Douglass had spent the previous days, after being whipped by Covey, in
hiding, angry and pensive). And it arises in a flash: as soon as Douglass
becomes aware of his situation, becomes aware of his commitment, he is
already struggling, already fighting.

The text continues, "The fighting madness had come upon me, and I
found my strong fingers firmly attached to the throat of my cowardly tormentor; as heedless of consequences, at the moment, as though we stood
as equals before the law. The very color of the man was forgotten."[35] In the
critical performance, the natural law is revealed. All are equal—or rather, it
is *as if* all are equal before the law. It is as if the higher law has descended to
the world, as if bodies are transparent to the souls within. It is not a moment
of madness, but of "fighting madness," a moment of commitment, of struggle,
grounded not in anger or in reason but in contradiction, in paradox. There is
no positive content of humanity revealed beyond humanity itself—humanity
as void, as paradox. Douglass does not fight to win. He does not strike blows.
His actions are negative, defensive. He blocks Covey's blows: "Every blow of
his was parried, though I dealt no blows in turn. I was strictly on the *defensive,* preventing him from injuring me, rather than trying to injure him."[36]

The fight with Covey is the crucial, transformative moment in Douglass's story of himself. "I was a changed being after that fight. I was *nothing*
before; I WAS A MAN NOW." Douglass also observes, "It was a resurrection
from the dark and pestiferous tomb of slavery, to the heaven of comparative
freedom. I was no longer a servile coward trembling under the frown of a

brother worn of the dust, but, my long-cowed spirit was roused to an attitude of manly independence."[37] He had simply echoed the regimes of thinking and feeling in which he lived. Douglass had understood himself as a slave, saw the world from the perspective of a slave, felt the world from the perspective of a slave (his feelings distorted, alienated). Now, as a man, he is capable of grappling with his peculiar contradictions, his peculiar virtues and vices, humors and sorrows, memories and hopes. To grapple with them is a continuation of grappling with Covey: commitment to struggle born when it is recognized that we are alienated from our affect by social norms. How is it that Douglass can conclude, at the end of his description of the fight, "I had reached the point, at which I was *not afraid to die*"?[38] Is he a philosopher of existence foreshadowing the twentieth-century existentialist movement, as some have claimed, acknowledging the absurdity of life?[39] Not at all.

Douglass's earlier fear of death was a result of the illusory comforts in which he once partook: affective commitment to a system that alienated him from his own affect. Such alienating affect necessarily produced a remainder, as alienation always does. In this case, that remainder is fear of his own death, affect attached to the only thing not controllable by the slave system's management of affect. In struggle, Douglass can acknowledge his own affect, for he is no longer alienated from his "soul." And from one moment of struggle, he transforms his life into one of perpetual struggle. In theological terms, after Douglass's "resurrection," his life is sacralized.[40] It begins to image God, to allow the divine to shine through the human. He is aware of his "soul," his capacity for affect; he becomes aware of the normative conclusions that follow, and he catalyzes a social movement to implement those conclusions. For Douglass, God's law names this possibility: that affect can make the world more just.[41]

Notes

1. See Lewis Perry, *Radical Abolitionism: Anarchy and the Government of God in Antislavery Thought* (Ithaca, NY: Cornell University Press, 1973); John Stauffer, *The Black Hearts of Men: Radical Abolitionists and the Transformation of Race* (Cambridge, MA: Harvard University Press, 2001).

2. Frederick Douglass, "God's Law Outlawed," in *The Frederick Douglass Papers, Series One: Speeches, Debates, and Interviews*, 5 vols., ed. John W.

Blassingame and others (New Haven, CT: Yale University Press, 1979–1992), 2:454–55; see also *Series Two: Autobiographical Writings*, 3 vols., ed. John Blassingame and others (New Haven, CT: Yale University Press, 1999–2012). Subsequent citations to *The Frederick Douglass Papers* include the series, volume, and page numbers in the following format: series.volume:page (e.g., 1.2:498).

3. On the historical importance of Douglass's speech, see the editors' preface in Frederick Douglass, "The Claims of the Negro Ethnologically Considered," in *The Frederick Douglass Papers*, 1.2.498–99.

4. Douglass, "The Claims of the Negro Ethnologically Considered," 1.2:502, emphasis in the original.

5. For an overview of Douglass's religiosity, see John Ernest, "Crisis and Faith in Douglass' Work," in Maurice Lee, ed., *The Cambridge Companion to Frederick Douglass* (Cambridge: Cambridge University Press, 2009), 60–72; Scott C. Williamson, *The Narrative Life: The Moral and Religious Thought of Frederick Douglass* (Macon, GA: Mercer University Press, 2002); Reginald F. Davis, *Frederick Douglass: A Precursor of Liberation Theology* (Macon, GA: Mercer University Press, 2005). For a particularly astute reconsideration, see Jared Hickman, "Douglass Unbound," *Nineteenth-Century Literature* 68 (3) (2013): 323–62.

6. For an overview of the literature on Douglass and sentimentalism, see Arthur Riss, "Sentimental Douglass," in Lee, ed., *The Cambridge Companion to Frederick Douglass*, 103–17. See especially Stephanie A. Smith, "Heart Attacks: Frederick Douglass's Strategic Sentimentality," *Criticism* 34 (1992): 193–216; P. Gabrielle Foreman, "Sentimental Abolition in Douglass's Decade: Revision, Erotic Conversion, and the Politics of Witnessing in 'The Heroic Slave' and *My Bondage and My Freedom*," in Mary Chapman and Glenn Hendler, eds., *Sentimental Men: Masculinity and the Politics of Affect in American Culture* (Berkeley: University of California Press, 1999), 149–62; and Eric J. Sundquist, *To Wake the Nations: Race in the Making of American Literature* (Cambridge, MA: Harvard University Press, 1993), chap. 1.

7. Nick Bromell, "The Liberal Imagination of Frederick Douglass," *The American Scholar* 77 (2) (2008): 34–45, and *The Time Is Always Now: Black Political Thought and the Transformation of US Democracy* (Oxford: Oxford University Press, 2013); Nicholas Buccola, "'Each for All and All for Each': The Liberal Statesmanship of Frederick Douglass," *Review of Politics* 70 (2008): 400–19, and *The Political Thought of Frederick Douglass: In Pursuit of American Liberty* (New York: New York University Press, 2012).

8. Bernard R. Boxill, "Fear and Shame as Forms of Moral Suasion in the Thought of Frederick Douglass," *Transactions of the Charles S. Peirce Society* 31 (4) (1995): 713–44.

9. John Finnis, *Aquinas: Moral, Political, and Legal Theory* (Oxford: Oxford University Press, 1998); Mark C. Murphy, *Natural Law in Jurisprudence and Politics* (Cambridge: Cambridge University Press, 2006).

10. Robert P. George, *The Clash of Orthodoxies: Law, Religion, and Morality in Crisis* (Wilmington, DE: ISI Books, 2001), chap. 9.

11. Erica R. Edwards, *Charisma and the Fictions of Black Leadership* (Minneapolis: University of Minnesota Press, 2012). Compare Vincent W. Lloyd, *In Defense of Charisma* (New York: Columbia University Press, 2018).

12. For a theological development, see Michel Henry, *I Am the Truth: Toward a Philosophy of Christianity* (Stanford, CA: Stanford University Press, 2003). For Henry's development of auto-affection in secular terms, see, for example, *Material Phenomenology* (New York: Fordham University Press, 2008). On Henry's uses of auto-affection for cultural and political critique, see especially *Barbarism* (London: Continuum, 2012).

13. Henry is, however, committed to protecting the sanctity of life, and this commitment has constructive potential (for example, regarding the protection of fetuses and the prohibition on euthanasia).

14. As given with Frederick Douglass, "I Have Come to Tell You Something about Slavery," in *The Frederick Douglass Papers*, 1.1:3.

15. As given with Frederick Douglass, "The Anti-Slavery Movement, the Slave's Only Earthly Hope," in *The Frederick Douglass Papers*, 1.1:20.

16. Douglass, "I Have Come to Tell You Something about Slavery," 1.1:3.

17. As given with Frederick Douglass, "Southern Slavery and Northern Religion," in *The Frederick Douglass Papers*, 1.1:25.

18. As given with Douglass, "I have Come to Tell You Something about Slavery," 1.1:3.

19. Although drawing on a somewhat different theoretical framework, I have found helpful Teresa Brennan's book *The Transmission of Affect* (Ithaca, NY: Cornell University Press, 2004).

20. Jason Frank's reading of this speech also brings together its rhetoric and its politics, analyzing its function as ideology critique. See Jason Frank, *Constituent Moments: Enacting the People in Postrevolutionary America* (Durham, NC: Duke University Press, 2010), chap. 7. See also James A. Colaiaco, *Frederick Douglass and the Fourth of July* (New York: Palgrave Macmillan, 2006).

21. Frederick Douglass, "What to a Slave Is the Fourth of July?" in *The Frederick Douglass Papers*, 1.2:367.

22. Frederick Douglass, "Speech on the *Dred Scott* Decision," in *The Frederick Douglass Papers*, 1.3:167–68.

23. Ibid., 1.3:168.

24. Ibid.

25. Ibid., 1.3:163, 183.

26. Riss, "Sentimental Douglass," 109.

27. In addition to Riss, "Sentimental Douglass," see Sundquist, *To Wake the Nations*, 97–100.

28. Frederick Douglass, "To My Old Master, Thomas Auld," in *The Frederick Douglass Papers*, 2.2:247, 253–54, 254.

29. Ibid., 2.2:249.

30. Ibid., emphasis in original.

31. Jeffrey Stout, "Truth, Natural Law, and Ethical Theory," in Robert P. George, ed., *Natural Law: Contemporary Essays* (Oxford: Clarendon Press, 1992), 71–102.

32. Cristina L. H. Traina, *Feminist Ethics and Natural Law: The End of Anathemas* (Washington, DC: Georgetown University Press, 1999). Pamela M. Hall makes a related point in *Narrative and the Natural Law: An Interpretation of Thomistic Ethics* (Notre Dame, IN: University of Notre Dame Press, 1994).

33. Traina, *Feminist Ethics and Natural Law*, 8.

34. Frederick Douglass, *My Bondage and My Freedom*, in *The Frederick Douglass Papers*, 2.2:138, emphasis in original. In *Race, Slavery, and Liberalism in Nineteenth-Century American Literature* (Cambridge: Cambridge University Press, 2006), Arthur Riss makes a related point about this passage with regard to "the irreducibility of [Douglass's] 'personhood'" (176–77). Here I also have in mind the analysis in Alain Badiou, *Ethics: An Essay on the Understanding of Evil*, trans. Peter Hallward (London: Verso, 2001).

35. Douglass, *My Bondage and My Freedom*, 2.2:138.

36. Ibid., emphasis in original.

37. Ibid., 2.2:141, emphasis in original.

38. Ibid., emphasis in original.

39. See, for example, Lewis R. Gordon, *Existentia Africana: Understanding African Existential Thought* (New York: Routledge, 2000), chap. 3.

40. For a more extensive theological reading of this "resurrection," see J. Kameron Carter, "Race, Religion, and the Contradictions of Identity: A Theological Engagement with Douglass's 1845 *Narrative*," *Modern Theology* 21 (1) (2005): 37–65. Carter places his reading of Douglass in broader theological context in *Race: A Theological Account* (Oxford: Oxford University Press, 2008).

41. I develop the themes of this chapter further in Vincent W. Lloyd, *Black Natural Law* (New York: Oxford University Press, 2016).

11

Law-breaker

Frederick Douglass and the Rule of Law

Anne Norton

Uncertainty

Maryland's Eastern Shore is an indefinite, uncertain place. The earth gives way to water and to marsh, which is neither earth nor water, but both at once. There is no easy division here between the land and the sea, between freshwater and salt. The rivers pour freshwater into the sea and bear the salt of the ocean in their currents. In the day, marsh grass hides the place where land gives way to water. In the night, it is still harder to see the boundary between land and sea.

It was in this uncertain place that Frederick Douglass, born a slave, raised his hand to the man who broke him. It was in this uncertain place that Frederick Douglass learned to read and was forbidden to read. It was in this uncertain place that Frederick Douglass was sold, inherited, traded, and traded again only to become a man without price. Once set in circulation as a commodity, he would set himself in motion and escape the system of exchange that set a value on a man and made him something that could be bought and sold. It was in this uncertain place that Frederick Douglass was broken and in this place that Frederick Douglass broke his chains.

In Douglass's account of his journey to freedom, each moment away is anchored to a place. Each place orients a precise relation to freedom and to slavery. Slavery and freedom are given not as abstract but as material conditions: in a body, in a place. Douglass narrates not slavery but slavery in America. He begins with a location. "In Talbot county, Eastern Shore, Maryland, near Easton," there is a dilapidated, "wornout" place known for "the sandy, desert-like appearance of its soil." A river runs through it. This place of "ague and fever," poor and "truly famine stricken," is called "Tuckahoe." The first paragraph of Douglass's narrative describes the place; the second gives it meaning. The name "Tuckahoe" marks a theft. Someone, Douglass says, "was guilty of the petty meanness of taking a hoe."[1] The opening of his account is anchored at the confluence of a place and a crime. The place is the "Eastern shore, Maryland, near Easton." The crime is slavery.[2]

Tuckahoe—or, more precisely, his grandmother's cabin—is poverty stricken but it is also beautiful in Douglass's memory. His description is loving and precise: the cabin with its clay floor and ladder stairway, the cleverly crafted well where a small child could draw water without effort, the trees, the loft made of Virginia fence rails, his oyster-shell spoon. This is the place apart from the master's house, before the knowledge of slavery. The cabin is Eden before the Fall. But no ground is firm, no place is safe, in this uncertain land.

This is the place where Frederick Douglass found the way from slavery to freedom. This way, too, is uncertain terrain. Douglass's narrative reveals that slavery and freedom are indefinite, uncertain places. The free man is present in the slave, the slave in the free. Slavery binds the free with the slave. Law serves injustice as well as justice. Appeals to rights secure both freedom and property and in securing property make freedom elusive. The order of slavery is abstract, national and institutionalized, but it is made real in particular places, by and on and in the bodies of men and women. These are not abstract bodies. Douglass gives them to us as people, the distinctive bodies of individuals: "More than one gray hair which peeped from the ample and graceful folds of her newly ironed bandanna turban," "sable," "yellow," "Indian," "elastic and muscular," "a haggard aspect," "muttering to himself," "her neck and shoulders covered with scars," "his wolfish face with his greenish eyes," "lame," "a virago."[3]

Knowledge of slavery comes with the movement to Wye, though it had shadowed his life before. Douglass links that knowledge to a hard journey, "full twelve miles," some of it on his grandmother's strong back. Learning comes in Miss Sophia's parlor in Baltimore and stops there as well when

Hugh Auld forbids his wife to teach the newly lettered Frederick any further. In Douglass's accounts, slavery is never abstract; it is always personal, material, embodied in the slave and the slaveholder, enacted through the lash, experienced hung from a hook near the hearth, fighting in a cow yard, even in the comparative safety of a cabin.

The fundamental materiality of slavery is critical, for it is in that materiality—learning to read in a parlor, being lashed by the fireside, buying a book, grappling with the overseer—that slavery is enacted, evaded, and escaped. Douglass's careful recognition of the particularities of his slavery "in Talbot county, Eastern Shore, near Easton," and how he overcame it mirrors the work of Harriet Tubman. Douglass gave high praise to Tubman. He wrote, "You ask for what you do not need when you call upon me for a word of commendation. I need such words from you far more than you can need them from me." Tubman confronted slavery and freedom at their most physical, their most immediate, their most material. She returned again and again to the land of slavery. "The difference between us is very marked," Douglass wrote. "Most that I have done and suffered in the service of our cause has been in public, and I have received much encouragement at every step of the way. You, on the other hand, have labored in a private way. I have wrought in the day—you in the night. . . . The midnight sky and the silent stars have been the witnesses of your devotion to freedom and of your heroism."[4]

Tubman and Douglass were people of the Eastern Shore. Tubman, "the Moses of her people," guided them through the marshes, along the rivers, to the Underground Railroad and freedom. Her knowledge of the land and the practices of the place enabled her to conceal herself and her charges and ensured that she was praised as a conductor who had never lost a passenger. She worked in the land, with the living bodies of men and women. Douglass worked in writing, on a national—indeed, an international—stage. He worked to change, to free minds. Yet he, too, depended on local knowledge, on the examined experience of embodied enslavement. His autobiographical work, articles, and speeches used his local, situated knowledge of slavery to guide people to freedom.

Slavery has ended now, but freedom is not yet achieved. Robert Gooding-Williams observes that the inclusion of the essay "The Nature of Slavery" and excerpts from the speech "What to the Slave Is the Fourth of July?" mark Douglass's second autobiography, *My Bondage and My Freedom*, as "a political theory of bondage and freedom." Gooding-Williams also observes that Douglass was "Moses" in the political understanding of W. E. B. Du Bois.[5] Douglass gives an account of the knowledge he acquired in slavery, about slavery, in order to survive slavery. He uses the knowledge of slavery against slavery. He used what he learned in slavery and freedom for survival after slavery, in the experience of a partial and imperfect freedom, and to advance the freedom of others. The North Star can still orient a journey. Douglass's observations still furnish a guide from slavery to freedom on uncertain, changeable terrain.

By his own account, Douglass recognized the inadequacy of theories of slavery in his childhood. Neither divine ordination nor theories of color hierarchy held up to the child Frederick's scrutiny. There were always problems and "puzzling exceptions." Slavery was, as the child recognized, simply a "*crime*," but the order that crime secured was neither simple nor readily discerned. The child Frederick saw that "there were blacks who were *not* slaves" and "whites who were *not* slaveholders."[6] The adult Douglass recognizes the involvement of slaves in the order of slavery. It was his beloved grandmother who carried him to his master's house—and who spoke of the Old Master "with every mark of reverence."[7] There were slave tyrants, Aunt Katy "fiendish in her brutality" and Doctor Isaac Copper with his "praying and flogging."[8] Douglass suspected his slave and fellow conspirator Sandy of betraying an attempt at escape. Though all whites were corrupted by the order of slavery, there were degrees of evil among them: the sadistic murderer Mrs. Hicks, the limited kindness of Miss Lucretia. "Though Freeland was a slaveholder, and shared many of the vices of his class, he seemed alive to the sentiment of honor." The white children of Baltimore "and the good Irishman" so affected by learning that Douglass was "a slave and a slave for life" were at some distance from the overseers Covey and Gore and even from Miss Sophia, whose deference to her husband corrupted and degraded her.[9]

Douglass's ultimate success in escaping slavery—and his success in surviving it—depends on his ability to learn who can be trusted, in what, when, and how far. He has to learn who can teach him, what they can teach him, where it will be safe to learn, and how reluctant teachers can be coaxed to instruction.

The child Frederick learned to find oysters and catch crab to supplement a meager ration of cornmeal. He learned to read and thereafter learned how to hunt: knowledge that was both forbidden and elusive. He learned certain skills (notably caulking) that seemed to offer a way out of slavery.

Though that way failed, the local knowledge Douglass acquired made his escape possible. Armed with the borrowed papers of a free seaman, Douglass, "rigged out in sailor style," chose a train he knew would be crowded, and depended on his ability to "talk sailor like an old salt" to disguise himself.[10] He succeeded.

Local knowledge ensures Douglass's escape. Local practices, local beliefs delay him. The greatest bar to escape was neither distance nor the threat of violence. Douglass writes: "To look at the map and observe the proximity of Eastern Shore, Maryland, to Delaware and Pennsylvania, it may seem to the reader quite absurd to regard the proposed escape as a formidable undertaking. But to *understand,* some one has said, a man must *stand under.* The real distance was great enough, but the imagined distance was, to our ignorance, much greater."[11]

Ignorance, Douglass argues, is one of the main supports of the slave system. Another is that combination of fear, acceptance, and self-doubt that weighs down the already burdened. The poor fear that they will lose the little they have. They fear that they do not deserve the little they have. They fear that what is said about them is true. Douglass's journey from slavery to freedom depends on overcoming force, law, custom, and the burdens that weigh upon the soul. Legal, social, and psychic obstacles remain after slavery. They remain with us now. Douglass remains our guide.

Douglass's confrontation with Covey is one of the most honored, studied, and loved moments in African American—indeed, American— political thought. It is in this moment that Douglass confronts slavery as force and overcomes it. The slave Frederick is sent to Covey *"to be broken,"* and Covey breaks him. "Mr. Covey succeeded in breaking me," Douglass writes. "I was broken in body, soul and spirit."[12] Covey breaks Douglass's will by violence, and it is by violence that Douglass overcomes him. Equality, Hobbes argued, is grounded in a common mortal vulnerability. Men are, he declared, *"by nature equal . . .* [f]or as to strength of body, the weakest has strength enough to kill the strongest."[13] Douglass's fight with Covey proceeds on a similar principle. Once he had committed to fight, with his hands at Covey's throat, Douglass was "as heedless of consequences, at the moment, as though we stood as equals before the law. The very color of the man was forgotten." Legal inequality and social inequality were abandoned in the struggle of man against man. Though they would be reinstalled at the close of the fight, something of this understanding remained in Douglass.

"I was a changed being after that fight. I was *nothing* before; I WAS A MAN NOW."[14]

If the underlying logic of this experience of equality is akin to Hobbes's logic, both the language and the sentiments anticipate Frantz Fanon.[15] Reading Fanon in light of Douglass illuminates the liberatory effects of violence. Douglass's experience of equality does not depend on killing Covey. There are no bombs, no guns. Indeed, it is the immediacy of grappling skin to skin with Covey in the dirt of the cow yard that seems to bring equality home. Douglass does not need to defeat Covey decisively to become a changed being. Douglass writes, "A man without force is without the essential dignity of humanity," but the next paragraph alters the direction of the argument. Douglass moves from the use of force to quite different elements in the fight with Covey. The experience, he writes, can be understood only by someone "who has himself incurred something, hazarded something, in repelling the unjust aggressions of a tyrant."[16]

Douglass's more precise account of his experience points toward suffering, risk, and opposition to injustice. Martin Luther King Jr. would later argue, as Christians often have, that "unearned suffering is redemptive."[17] This argument sounds hollow apart from the Christian cosmology. One sees incalculable suffering and an apparent absence of redemption. Gandhi, however, gave the argument force when he observed that the translation "nonviolence" was a misunderstanding of the term *satyagraha*. The practice of *satyagraha* often involves a confrontation with violence, the experience of violence: as Douglass puts it, one "incur[s] something, hazard[s] something."[18] Douglass knows that the consequence of his resistance can be death. Maryland law "assigns hanging to the slave who resists his master."[19] The choice to resist presents a challenge to the economy of slavery. Insofar as Douglass's decision makes him subject to a death sentence, it takes him out of slave economics. The slave who is subject to a sentence of death under the law is no longer the property of the master but of the state, which will not compensate the master for his death. Slave economics thus offers a complex calculus to the master faced with a rebellious slave. Because the decision to resist belongs to Douglass, he is, in the moment of that decision, one who disposes of himself, who takes ownership of his body from the master. The perversity of the idea of self-ownership reveals itself vividly in these circumstances. The one who owns himself is still bound in an economy where a man can be property: alienable and exchangeable. To own oneself is no perfect victory: it reaffirms the system it appears to defeat. Recognizing Douglass's resistance as self-ownership does, however, illuminate both the strategic limits and the strategic possibilities of his resistance under Maryland law.

It is not, however, the calculable effects of the decision to resistance that have the most liberating effects. The economic logic of Douglass's position diminishes the possibility that resistance will bring death. Yet it is the confrontation with death, the risk of death, that Douglass finds liberating. "I had reached the point at which I *was not afraid to die.* This spirit made me a freeman in *fact,* while I remained a slave in *form.*"[20] Douglass becomes free in facing death, in putting himself at risk. That decision, I have argued elsewhere, is at the heart of the democratic subject.[21] Democracy requires that we risk great things and small, every day. Democracy requires us to put ourselves constantly at risk. Douglass's resistance makes him a free man for a moment, gives him a fugitive freedom, but he remains a slave in form, a slave under the law.[22]

Douglass knows that he is not altogether free. When Covey gives up the fight with Douglass, he says, "Now scoundrel, go to your work; I would not have whipped you half so much as I have had you not resisted." Douglass writes, "The fact was, *he had not whipped me at all.*"[23]

This confrontation is often seen as Douglass's defeat of Covey and his first moment of freedom. That is not how Douglass sees it. He writes that the fight with Covey is "the turning point in my *life as a slave.*"[24] He knows that he is not yet free. In resisting Covey, he breaks the man who broke him; yet after the fight, when Covey says, "Go to your work," Douglass does exactly that. He goes to his work. He remains with Covey for another six months, and though Covey never lays hands on him in anger again, neither does Douglass rebel. He continues to work until that Christmas, when he returns to St. Michaels. He submits to the law.

Douglass's defeat of Covey is a rupture, but it is temporary and incomplete. What is changed is the mind of the rebel, not the mind of the master. The individual is changed, but not the order. The moment when Douglass defies Covey anticipates and clarifies Fanon. Douglass recognizes the power and the limits of violence.

Douglass also recognizes the power and limits of solidarity. His victory over Covey (for it is a victory, albeit a limited one) depends on solidarity. Covey calls on other slaves to help him. Bill refuses, saying that his master has hired him out to work, not to whip Frederick. Covey then calls on Caroline, "a powerful woman" who could have easily mastered the already tired Douglass.[25] She, too, refuses, but at greater cost. Douglass recognizes that Bill can refuse Covey without running the risk of being flogged because "Samuel Harris, to whom Bill belonged, would not let his slaves be beaten, unless they were guilty of some crime, which the law would punish." Caroline is not so protected. She is Covey's slave woman, "and he could do what he pleased with her."[26]

Douglass's freedom from flogging, his partial freedom from Covey, depend on Bill and Caroline. This is not one man's struggle. "We were all in open rebellion that morning." Without Bill and Caroline, Douglass would have been lost. Gooding-Williams observes that Douglass's narrative of the unplanned, unanticipated acts of solidarity by Bill and Caroline "implicitly denies that the efficacy of collective black political action in fighting racial oppression requires that the agents of that action acknowledge and express a previously established and distinctively black spiritual or cultural identity that unites them."[27] He might go further. Douglass does: his account indeed shows solidarity in rebellion as something that is the gift of a common oppression, that may be called up in the absence of prior planning. He also recognizes the significance of Bill's and Caroline's differing positions at Covey's.

Bill's solidarity is the work of his own courage, but its efficacy is increased by his knowledge of his precise position in the order of slavery. His master enslaves Bill but makes the law bind the punishment another can give him.[28] The law enslaves Bill, but it provides limits to the punishment he can be given. Covey and Bill know Bill's place in the order of slavery and the strategic possibilities it offers and forecloses. Caroline's act, however, makes visible another set of strategic possibilities and limits. Because Caroline is "the slave of Covey," she lacks the limited protections Bill's position gives him. Caroline's defiance is more costly. In joining in the open rebellion, she risks a harsher punishment—a punishment limited only by her owner's economic interest. She may also have had to overcome a complex series of resentments at her sexual exploitation not only by Covey but also by Bill. Caroline was bought, Douglass narrates, *"as a breeder.* But the worst is not told in that naked statement." Caroline was "virtually compelled" by Covey to have sex with Bill. "Mr. Covey himself had locked the two up together every night." Douglass does not reproach Bill directly, but in the paragraph that follows this explanation he castigates Covey for the act and repeats, in harsher terms, his judgment that the woman was forced.[29] Caroline is not only called on to bear heavier costs of rebellion but also faced with more complex questions of loyalty and solidarity.

Bill and Caroline's "open rebellion" shows the power of solidarity, but it also shows its limits. Covey is not able to defeat—or to punish—Douglass. Yet he is able to keep the hierarchies of the slave system in place. The law that protects Bill aids Douglass, but it keeps both men enslaved.

Knowing that Douglass will not submit, seeing the other slaves stand with him, Covey does not simply retreat. He lies. He acts as if he has whipped Douglass and gives him an order. Douglass obeys. Bill and Caroline, witnesses to "the fact" that Covey does not whip Douglass, witness the lie and witness Douglass's submission as well. They shelter the truth within themselves, but the lie is sufficient—at least for the moment—to maintain the order of slavery. Douglass may have defeated Covey's dominion, but slavery—the law—maintains its dominion over him.

Hierarchies belong not to individuals but to orders. When they are codified and secured by law, law must be broken. When they are secured by custom, the observance of those customs must cease. When they depend on fear and self-doubt, these feelings must be overcome. All of these obstacles—especially fear and self-doubt—are almost insurmountable. The journey to freedom requires an incalculable judgment and courage. Douglass's account testifies to these requirements. He also reminds us that the journey depends for its success not on one person alone but on many.

Gooding-Williams notes that Douglass acts within and gives an account of both plantation politics and politics beyond the plantation. As Gooding-Williams observes, Douglass's account of his life and politics in the nominally free states illuminates both the limits of the law and the entanglement of the psychic and social with the legal order.[30]

Throughout his narratives, Douglass observes the power exercised by custom and belief. He suggests that the power exercised by the "old master" over his grandmother was not exacted by force or law but commanded by subtler means. She called him "old master" "with every mark of reverence."[31] And, Douglass notes, there are "colored men weak enough to believe" that "God requires them to submit to slavery."[32] Miss Sophia, Mrs. Hugh Auld, abandons her humanity "like an obedient wife."[33] In speculating on why Covey "did not have me taken in hand by the authorities," whipped, or hung, Douglass recognizes that Covey, too, is constrained by social forces and his own amour propre: "Covey was, probably, ashamed to have it known and confessed that he had been mastered by a boy of sixteen." He "enjoyed the unbounded and very valuable reputation of being a first rate overseer and *negro-breaker*."[34] Douglass's successful resistance may cost Covey personal pride, social reputation, and economic gain. Children, however, are not yet drawn into the web of custom, economic gain, social propriety, and silence that supports slavery. Although slavery is "a delicate subject, and very cautiously talked about" among adults, "I frequently talked about it—and that very freely—with the white boys." They could be talked with, reasoned with, and the young Frederick could "wring from the boys, occasionally, that fresh and bitter condemnation of slavery that springs from nature, unseared and unperverted."[35] Although they might be slow to condemn slavery, not one would defend the slave system.

Douglass is most discerning with regard to his own experiences of slavery in the soul and the social order. He tells how "a shade of disquiet" rested on him in his earliest years and "haunted" his childhood. In his account of his slavery under Hugh Auld, he shows how economic gain informed Auld's calculations and his own consciousness of slavery. He shows how the social requirements of the slave system and subjection to the duties of a wife alter the conduct and the character of Sophia Auld. "Nature had made us *friends,* slavery made us *enemies.*"[36] Douglass details how religion, both Christianity and the animism of "the root man," frustrate rebellion and resistance. He tells us of his own religious journey. Christianity alternately consoles and disappoints him. In a speech given at Finsbury Chapel in England in 1846, Douglass defended both his own Christianity and his critical remarks on the failures of religion in America: "I hate the slaveholding, the woman-whipping, the mind-darkening, the soul-destroying religion that exists in the southern states of America."[37] His experiences with religion in the North indicate that though it was generally kinder, it was not free from white supremacy, even among the Friends.

Douglass arrives in a free state feeling the long arm of the slave system. He knows he remains a commodity from which an enterprising slave catcher can profit. He is still haunted by fear. He is also utterly destitute. He seeks out allies and is sent to New Bedford. Here, he feels safe, but he is soon to discover that custom will subject him where the law does not. He finds work as a caulker only to learn "that every white man would leave the ship if I struck a blow upon her."[38] He is confronted, from New York to Boston, with the attitude *"We don't allow niggers in here."*[39] As Douglass rises as an orator, he faces a subtler but more degrading form of discrimination among the abolitionists. The abolitionists were, as Douglass notes, not free from color prejudice, though many were "nobly struggling against it." "In their eagerness, sometimes, to show their contempt for the feeling, they proved that they had not entirely recovered from it."[40] Their prejudices were most visible in their unconscious efforts to bind Douglass. As Gooding-Williams writes, "The Garrisonians behaved toward Douglass as if they alone enjoyed the authority to interpret the meaning of his narrative of his life as a slave."[41] Douglass might have been harsher. Not only the Garrisonians but also Garrison himself obliged Douglass to act the slave, to have "a *little* of the plantation manner of speech," not to "seem too learned," and to confine himself solely to the autobiographical. Philosophy and politics were to be left to others. When Douglass returns from England with the plan to start a newspaper, he is met not, as he expected, with enthusiasm but with the suspicion that his abilities are not up to the challenge.[42] Douglass is magnanimous to Garrison and his colleagues. They are "actuated by the best of motives" and "not altogether wrong" in anticipating disbelief that so eloquent an orator could have been a slave.[43] They seem, however, to be sublimely unconscious of both the support they are providing the slave system and the cruelty they are committing to an ally and a friend. Here, Douglass provides an invaluable account of how the opponents of injustice can inadvertently serve it.

Douglass has to escape not only his enemies but also his allies.

Lincoln's "House Divided" speech, arguing that the nation cannot continue to exist "half slave and half free," presumes a legal and political clarity in the status of free and slave and hence grants a moral clarity to the Civil War. The years of African American subjection afterward unsettle that. Jim Crow, segregation, lynching, and above all the transformation of the Fourteenth Amendment from the recognition of a common humanity to a support for corporate personhood and a burgeoning capitalism force the recognition that emancipation requires more than law, more than the state can give. Freedom is realized in and through the resources law provides, but it is also dependent on force, on the negotiation of a complex social and economic order, and, finally, on face-to-face relations between human beings. Douglass is invaluable for understanding postsegregation politics because the impediments of freedom persisted well beyond the removal of (at least the most conspicuous) legal supports for slavery and white supremacy. His autobiographical works provide an account of how he negotiated the obstacles to each of these. His attention to sexual as well as racial hierarchies and their strategic effects is intersectionality *avant la lettre.* His reflections on property command our attention still.

Douglass's descriptions of women are one of the most remarkable aspects of his autobiographical narratives. In a time when women are seen as fragile and dependent, Douglass describes them as strong and powerful. In a time when beauty seems confined in the prison of whiteness, Douglass sees that black is beautiful. In a time when women are thought to be dependent, he shows them as clever, enterprising, independent, and respected. His grandmother "was held in high esteem"; she could make nets, catch fish, grow more and better sweet potatoes, and preserve the seedlings. She was "a woman of power and spirit . . . marvelously straight in figure, elastic and muscular." Douglass's mother was "tall and finely proportioned; of deep black, glossy complexion." She was a field hand, strong enough to walk twenty-four miles in a night to see her child. Against the odds, she had somehow learned to read, the only slave in Tuckahoe to do so, and Douglass rightly honors the "native genius of my sable, unprotected and uncultivated mother."[44]

Douglass's recognition of the strength of women is paralleled by a recognition of the care black men give to one another. Douglass is sheltered by Sandy, joined in rebellion by Bill, and freed by the generosity of the black seaman who lends him his papers.[45]

Douglass's views on property are another, very powerful instance of the forgotten or unheeded conceptual possibilities of his work for "politics in the post-segregation era."[46] In *My Bondage and My Freedom* and throughout his work, Douglass puts the "sacred right of property" in question. Appeals to that right are rendered suspect the moment it is applied to property in men. Douglass questions that right further, distinguishing theft of food by the hungry from other thefts and then establishing the "clear right" of the slave to steal not only from the slaveholder but also from "society at large."[47] At the opening of this autobiography, he identifies the crime of slavery with the crime of theft. He recognizes the inadequacy of self-ownership, learning in freedom that he remains a commodity, subject to theft, a source of profit. With these recognitions, he gestures toward an approach to democracy's uncertain relations to equality, property, and the commons.

Douglass recognizes the power of poverty, the lessons of a precarious life, in shaping the citizen. As Judith Butler has so eloquently observed, the recognition of a precarious life may bring forth solidarity.[48] Douglass teaches that it can make democrats.[49] *My Bondage and My Freedom* is an account of the making of a democrat. Douglass's struggle from bondage to freedom is not only the story of a man who achieves freedom, citizenship, political influence, and moral eminence. Douglass's teaching concerns the grounding of democracy. Born with rights to a world in which those rights are neither honored nor recognized, the democrat must find dignity outside law, custom, and wealth. The democrat must find dignity in poverty. Without this, there is no true recognition of rights. In that state of hunger and danger, the subject may come to seek security. Recognition of a common vulnerability can teach solidarity and self-reliance. Douglass's anger at the denial of rights gives him courage: the courage to wrestle skin to skin with Covey in the dirt; the courage to plan an escape; the courage, when that first plan fails, to carry through another. Courage makes his freedom possible; courage maintains it. Douglass finds the courage to defy friends as well as enemies, to escape the bonds of patronage as well as those of slavery.

Freedom, Douglass learns, is precarious. One may be born to freedom or to slavery. Through courage, the slave can become free: "I had reached the point at which *I was not afraid to die.* This spirit made me a freeman in *fact."*

One may lose one's freedom to the law, in poverty, to patrons. Courage, the willingness to hazard "something, in repelling the unjust aggressions of a tyrant"[50]—even the most benign of tyrants—maintains that freedom.

Law-breaker

Liberal democracy is commonly thought to rest on a familiar set of institutions: the rule of law, representation, constitutionalism, rights. Democrats are granted only the unassuming virtues proper to these institutions. They are said to be—ideally—law abiding, deferential to expertise, responsible in their obligations, committed to constitutional government, and confident in the law as the defender of their rights. Conservatives claim that democracy survives not because of but despite democracy. The democratic imperative that "the earth belongs to the living" falls before the demands of the dead and the unborn. Deference to the customs, hierarchies, and traditions of the past as well as duty to posterity can produce chastened and reverential democrats who will restrain themselves. Their respect for established law and institutions secures what law and institutions alone cannot. Liberals claim that democracy survives where democrats submit to the rule of law, defer to the rights of others, and seek the security of their own rights in the courts. For all their differences, both liberals and conservatives regard democrats and democracy as a problem. Both seek a chastened and subject democracy, restrained by law.

Most people, especially in established democracies, come to democracy as an inheritance or as a given. Others, defeated in war, receive democratic institutions as the gift of a conqueror. Those who found democracies come to them in the furor of conflict, as a people bound together by the shape of events and their own collective will. In other times, they might be liberals or conservatives, but in the moment—in the acts—of revolution they refuse the governance of the past and set themselves beyond the law.

Frederick Douglass came to democracy as a fugitive and a law-breaker. Perhaps this made him particularly acute in his vision of democrats and democratic mores. His experience of coming to democracy as a slave, a fugitive, a man without place or possessions, friends, or family make his experience revelatory. Perhaps it is as a chronicle of Douglass's flight to democracy and as an account of his democratic education that generations of Americans have read his autobiographies.

Douglass shows us a set of virtues—and a democratic education—that departs from the democratic virtues we have come to take for granted. The making of citizen Douglass involved rebellion, lawbreaking, courage, and daring. It also turned on poverty. Douglass is important not only because he provides an account of his own political education but also because he made himself a particularly good citizen: one whose work advanced the democracy he sought as a fugitive. He became a good citizen not because he obeyed the law but (like the American revolutionaries who took the Declaration as their creed) because he refused to obey it. The shape of his automachia, his writing, and his theoretical and practical work teaches us that the democratic enterprise depends not only on the rule of law but also on lawbreaking, not on the conservative virtues of deference and acquiescence but on daring and the courage to rebel.

Describing an unsuccessful attempt at escape with a number of his fellow slaves, Douglass writes, "These meetings must have resembled, on a small scale, the meetings of revolutionary conspirators . . . we were plotting against our (so-called) lawful rulers."[51] Douglass, as Gooding-Williams observes, was fully conscious of the likeness of his rebellions to those of the American Revolution, of his declarations of independence to the Declaration of Independence.[52] Like the revolutionaries, Douglass was a rebel, a fugitive, and a law-breaker. Like them, he made the world new.

Lawbreaking must be not for the one but for the many. Lawbreaking will not serve the many for long. The defiance of law can free both one slave and the multitude, for a moment. The prolonged absence of law exposes the weak to the strong, the temperate to the greedy, the restrained to the ambitious, the disciplined to the barbarous. The rule of law is often posed as the answer to this. That has merit, but not in the way it is usually understood. The answer is not simple submission to the rule of law. People must learn to rule law.

Ruling the Law

Douglass's constitutional theory is often linked to Lysander Spooner's defense of the Constitution against the Garrisonian rejection. I find it more resonant with Langston Hughes. In "Freedom's Plow," Hughes writes:

A long time ago, but not too long ago, a man said:
ALL MEN ARE CREATED EQUAL—
ENDOWED BY THEIR CREATOR
WITH CERTAIN INALIENABLE RIGHTS—
AMONG THESE LIFE, LIBERTY
AND THE PURSUIT OF HAPPINESS.
His name was Jefferson. There were slaves then,
But in their hearts the slaves believed him, too,
And silently took for granted
That what he said was also meant for them.[53]

For Hughes, preeminent interpretive authority belongs not to the Founders but to the slaves. If Americans are to be the people of the Declaration, then the presence of slavery is a wound that must be healed, a sin that must be recompensed, a shame that must be overcome. If the Constitution is to constitute the people of the Declaration, it cannot be held within the limits of practice at the time of the founding. If it is to have substantive integrity, the institutional provisions that structure an accommodation with slavery must be amended and the text held to the principles of the preamble. Original intent is corrupt. The meaning of the words is to be found not in the moment of their writing or publication or ratification but in the future, when the promise they held might be realized. The slaves' silent ratification redeems the words written by a slaveholder. If those words are to be fulfilled, it will not be from the vantage of the slaveholder, but from that of the slave. The slaves know "what he said must be meant for every human being." It is the slaves who are "guarding in their hearts the seed of freedom."[54] The slaves know what is at the heart of America, the evil that is and has been, the good that is not yet achieved.

Double consciousness not only illuminates the position of African Americans or, more broadly, the subaltern. Where constitutions are aspirational or mark a distance between what is and what should be, it is the subaltern whose placement in the social order enables them to measure the distance and confirm when and where it has been overcome. Double consciousness confers a particular capacity for constitutional interpretation.

That preeminent interpretive capacity is not only confined to the constitutional text but also extends to all constitutional texts, to the judgment of the nation. Douglass's speech "What to the Slave Is the Fourth of the July?" measures the distance between "the declarations of the past, or the professions of the present" and the claimed commitment to liberty. "Would you have me argue that man is entitled to liberty, that he is the rightful owner of his own body? You have already declared it." To fail to remember the slaves on the Fourth of July would be, Douglass declares, "treason most scandalous and shocking."[55] It is not simply that slavery is wrong and the endorsement of slavery a sin and a shame in any human being. Slavery is not simply a crime and a wrong in America; it is treason to America. To fail in that judgment is, Douglass declares, a betrayal of the fundamental principles of the nation and so a betrayal of the nation itself. As Douglass writes, it is treason.

Douglass's position on constitutional interpretation recognizes that a constitution, if it is to be constitutional, must be constantly shaping the people and shaped by them.[56] This conception of the constitutional dialectic accords with the texts of American constitutional documents. It accords with the demands of democracy. Tom Paine declared that the earth belongs to those who live upon it, to living men. He, like Jefferson, protested against life under the dead hand of the past. They must rule themselves. They must rule the law. They must remain revolutionaries.

The slave, or anyone unjustly deprived of equal citizenship, stands in relation to the law that democracy must reject. If we are to rejoice in the blessings of liberty, we hold them in common. Democracy requires that the citizens rule and are ruled in turn, that they are both sovereign and subject. The slave is subject alone. It is only by seizing sovereignty that the slave can become the citizen. The slave must become law's sovereign: breaker and maker of the nation's laws. That alone will remedy a double fault: transforming the merely subject into citizens and securing for the people the rights held in common upon which democracy depends. Rule of law alone is mere subjection. The Constitution's "We, the People" is fulfilled only when the people rule the law. Douglass recognizes interpretive authority as the rule of law by lawmakers: by the sovereign people and by each citizen as sovereign. Interpretive authority is not and cannot be the special province of the judiciary. It is properly *democratic* interpretive authority, disseminated, with sovereignty, through the people.

Uncertainty

Water still hides beneath the marsh grass of the Eastern Shore. The sea still runs into the sky, land into water, water into land. Salt and fresh still mix in the bays and rivers. This is an uncanny place still. The rich are hidden in the marshes here. The poor are seen along the roads. This is the place before freedom, where freedom was seized in defiance of the law. This place was settled in the time before the revolution. That settlement was ruptured in the revolution, settled again in accommodation with slavery, unsettled by Douglass and Tubman, the Moses of her people. There is another settlement now. The unspeakable rich hide behind the unacknowledged poor. The wealthy and privileged live out of sight, hidden on vast estates. Farmworkers labor along the roads. Once again, the law secures white privilege and permits the hunting of young black men. This is the time before the revolution.

Figure 4. "Portrait of Frederick Douglass, Intellectual and Statesman, April 1870." This image captures Douglass during the period of Reconstruction when he began contemplating more systematically the efficacy of rhetoric and the meanings of citizenship and democracy for the nation, the hemisphere, and the increasingly interconnected world. (Photographer: George Francis Schreiber. Reproduction number: LC-USZ62-15887, Library of Congress.)

Notes

1. Frederick Douglass, *My Bondage and My Freedom*, in *Autobiographies*, ed. Henry Louis Gates Jr. (New York: Library of America, 1994), 1.

2. "Slaveholders," Douglass would come to recognize, "are only a band of successful robbers" (ibid., 227).

3. Ibid., 165, 148, 172, 173, 263, 165, 155.

4. Frederick Douglass to Harriet Tubman, n.d., quoted in Sarah Bradford, *Harriet Tubman: The Moses of Her People* (New York: Corinth Books, 1961), 134–35.

5. Robert Gooding-Williams, *In the Shadow of Du Bois: Afro-Modern Political Thought in America* (Cambridge, MA: Harvard University Press, 2009), 164–65.

6. Douglass, *My Bondage and My Freedom*, 179; emphasis is as given in the original in all quotations from Douglass.

7. Ibid., 143.

8. Ibid., 167, 166.

9. Ibid., 293, 224, 233.

10. Ibid., 310; Frederick Douglass, *Life and Times of Frederick Douglass*, in *Autobiographies*, 644–45.

11. Douglass, *My Bondage and My Freedom*, 609.

12. Ibid., 256; Frederick Douglass, *Narrative of the Life of Frederick Douglass, an American Slave*, in *Autobiographies*, 58, also quoted in *My Bondage and My Freedom*, 268.

13. Thomas Hobbes, *Leviathan*, ed. Michael Oakshott (New York: Collier Books 1971), 98, emphasis in original.

14. Douglass, *My Bondage and My Freedom*, 283, 286. Douglass's account of the struggle in *Narrative* is sparer and less analytic but testifies to the same liberatory effect of violent struggle.

15. In saying this, I am far from endorsing the crude reading Jean-Paul Sartre gave Frantz Fanon, which recent work by Homi Bhabha has done something to overcome (Homi Bhabha, foreword to Frantz Fanon, *The Wretched of the Earth*, trans. Richard Philcox [New York: Grove Press 2004], vii–xli; see also Anne Norton, "Sacrifice," in *Bloodrites of the Poststructuralists: Word, Flesh, and Revolution* [New Brunswick, NJ: Routledge 2002]).

16. Douglass, *My Bondage and My Freedom*, 286.

17. *Christian Century* 77 (April 27, 1960): 510.

18. Douglass, *My Bondage and My Freedom*, 286.

19. Ibid., 287.

20. Ibid., 286.

21. Anne Norton, "Evening Land," in Aryeh Botwinick and William Connolly, eds., *Democracy and Vision: Sheldon Wolin and the Vicissitudes of the Political* (Princeton, NJ: Princeton University Press, 2001), 161–72.

22. In *In the Shadow of Du Bois*, Robert Gooding-Williams provides a discerning discussion of the distinction between form and fact in Douglass and their relation to law. His reading is consonant with mine but refers to a different theoretical literature and has a different inflection, which is valuable indeed.

23. Douglass, *My Bondage and My Freedom*, 285.

24. Ibid., 286.

25. Ibid., 156.

26. Ibid., 285.

27. Gooding-Williams, *In the Shadow of Du Bois*, 189.

28. Douglass, *Narrative*, 64, and *My Bondage and My Freedom*, 285.

29. Douglass, *My Bondage and My Freedom*, 267. This is yet another of those moments that testify to Douglass's profound recognition of sexual as well as racial oppression. In the former, as in the latter, he is able to name brute force and to discern oppression's subtler forms.

30. Gooding-Williams, *In the Shadow of Du Bois*, 189.

31. Douglass, *My Bondage and My Freedom*, 143.

32. Ibid., 226–27.

33. Ibid., 217. Douglass's critical eye toward sexual hierarchy is at work here as well.

34. Ibid., 287.

35. Ibid., 224.

36. Ibid., 228. Douglass shows his characteristic magnanimity to Sophia Auld. "We were both victims to the same over-shadowing evil—*she* as mistress, *I* as slave."

37. Frederick Douglass, "Speech at Finsbury Chapel, Moorfields, England, May 22, 1846," appendix to *My Bondage and My Freedom*, 407.

38. Douglass, *My Bondage and My Freedom*, 358–59.

39. Ibid., 375.

40. Ibid., 393. I blush for the abolitionists as I write this, fearing I have done the same. If I have, I have met with the same magnanimity that Douglass showed.

41. Gooding-Williams, *In the Shadow of Du Bois*, 198–99.

42. Douglass, *My Bondage and My Freedom*, 390–91.

43. Ibid., 366–67, also quoted in Gooding-Williams, *In the Shadow of Du Bois*, 199.

44. Douglass, *My Bondage and My Freedom*, 156.

45. I am indebted to Stephen Marshall for this point, which deserves a fuller account than I have given here.

46. Gooding-Williams, *In the Shadow of Du Bois,* 167. I have edited Gooding-Williams to expand both his praise of Douglass and the invitation he offers. It is not only "with critical reference to Du Bois" that Douglass should be read, though that is useful and illuminating for both thinkers, nor is that theorizing valuable only with regard to "black politics," though that may be where fundamental democratic issues appear first and most sharply. Douglass's work, as Gooding-Williams demonstrates, addresses the most fundamental political issues and illuminates subtle structures and stratagems maintaining injustice.

47. Douglass, *My Bondage and My Freedom,* 247–48.

48. Judith Butler, *Precarious Life: The Powers of Mourning and Violence* (London: Verso, 2004).

49. I am indebted to Juliet Hooker, whose comments and questions on an earlier version of this chapter taught me how Douglass illuminates the importance of precarity to democratic life. Her insights have taken me far beyond this essay, and I am grateful.

50. Douglass, *My Bondage and My Freedom,* 286.

51. Ibid., 309.

52. Gooding-Williams, *In the Shadow of Du Bois,* chap. 5: "Douglass's Declarations of Independence and Practices of Politics," 162–209.

53. Langston Hughes, "Freedom's Plow" (1943), at https://www.poemhunter.com/best-poems/langston-hughes/freedom-s-plow/.

54. Ibid.

55. Frederick Douglass, "What to the Slave Is the Fourth of July?" in *My Bondage and My Freedom,* 432, 433.

56. The US Constitution, as William F. Harris II observed, is written in the present tense. The language of the text marks the constitutional dialectic (*The Interpretable Constitution* [Baltimore: Johns Hopkins University Press, 1993]; see also Anne Norton, "Transubstantiation: The Dialectic of Constitutional Authority," *University of Chicago Law Review* 55 [2] [1988]: 455–72).

IV

Rhetoric, Citizenship, Democracy

12

Frederick Douglass

Herbert J. Storing

One of the major themes of American statesmanship and political thought is the indelible impression made upon the American polity by the institution of slavery. Few men understood that institution so well as Frederick Douglass. Few men labored so wisely and effectively to destroy it. Few men saw so deeply into its implications. Douglass never abandoned the perspective of the black American. He was always and deliberately a partisan, in the sense that he adopted the stance and the duties of one who speaks for only a part (though in this case a uniquely important part) of the political whole. Yet few men deserve so fully the rank of American statesman.

Douglass began his public career when, not three years after his escape from slavery and while leading the hard life of a common laborer in New Bedford, Massachusetts, he accepted an invitation to speak a few words at an 1841 antislavery convention on his experiences as a slave. He spoke so well that he was invited by the Massachusetts Anti-Slavery Society to become one of its agents, telling of his experiences throughout the eastern states. But it was not enough for him to follow the advice of his white abolitionist friends: "Give us the facts," they said, "we will take care of the philosophy." Douglass's mind was always working; he could not talk about slavery without thinking about it. "It did not entirely satisfy me to *narrate* wrongs—I felt like *denouncing* them."[1]

Inevitably doubts were expressed whether a man who reasoned so well and in such fine and eloquent language could ever have been a slave. Partly in response to these doubts Douglass wrote the first of his several autobiographical works, *A Narrative of the Life of Frederick Douglass, an American Slave*, published in 1845.[2] The facts were established—at considerable risk to Douglass, for his whereabouts thereby became known in Maryland—but the small volume is a good deal more than a narrative. It is, in fact, an excellent treatise, in narrative form, on the inner workings and principles of the institution of American slavery. Like Harriet Beecher Stowe, who drew on his volume, Douglass showed how the best in slavery is implicated in the worst and pulled down to it. He described how his kind and tenderhearted Baltimore mistress, who first taught him to read, painfully learned "that I sustained to her the relation of a mere chattel, and that for her to treat me as a human being was not only wrong, but dangerously so"; and he described the evil effects upon her of the lesson. He described the slave breaker, Covey, who could rent slaves cheaply because of his reputation for restoring them to their masters chastened and dispirited. But at what a cost! Covey lurked around his own plantation, spying on the slaves, sometimes crawling on his hands and knees to surprise them—utterly degrading himself in the exercise of his miserable mastership. Though Douglass spent his rare moments of rest with Covey "in a sort of beast-like stupor," the natural human desire for liberty continued to burn fitfully. It burst into flame when, unjustly attacked by Covey, Douglass successfully defended himself in a two-hour struggle. From that time on, he ceased being a slave "in *fact*," though he might "remain a slave in *form*";[3] for he determined that in the future no one should succeed in beating him without succeeding in killing him.

Covey represented the depths of slavery; and Douglass's condition improved thereafter, but the improvements only made the slave less contented with his bonds. Hired by his master to a fair and kind man who treated him well, Douglass responded by making an unsuccessful attempt to escape. Instead of selling him south, his master permitted him to return to Baltimore, where he was hired out and later permitted to hire his own time. Yet the experience only flaunted the robbery of slavery before Douglass's eyes and made him more anxious to escape. The more slavery adopted the characteristics of freedom, the more intolerable it became. Douglass experienced the contradiction of the house divided against itself, and he understood it fully:

I have observed this in my experience of slavery,—that whenever my condition was improved, instead of its increasing my contentment, it only increased my desire to be free, and set me to thinking of plans to gain my freedom. I have found that, to make a contented slave, it is necessary to make a thoughtless one. It is necessary to darken his moral and mental vision, and, as far as possible, to annihilate the power of reason. He must be able to detect no inconsistencies in slavery; he must be made to feel that slavery is right; and he can be brought to that only when he ceases to be a man.[4]

Moral Reform and Political Action

During his first years as a public man Douglass was a devoted disciple of William Lloyd Garrison, fully accepting his argument that the Constitution was a pro-slavery document and his doctrine of nonvoting. "With him, I held it to be the first duty of the non-slaveholding states to dissolve the union with the slaveholding states, and hence my cry, like his, was 'No union with slaveholders.'"[5] Douglass liked "radical measures," whether by the abolitionists or the slaveholders. "I like to gaze upon these two contending armies, for I believe it will hasten the dissolution of the present unholy Union, which has been justly stigmatized as 'a covenant with death, an agreement with hell.'"[6] He held the Constitution to be "radically and essentially slave-holding." "For my part I had rather that my right hand should wither by my side than cast a ballot under the Constitution of the United States."[7]

Douglass carried these views with him when he moved to Rochester, New York, and established his own abolitionist newspaper. "Slavery will be attacked in its stronghold—the compromises of the Constitution, and the cry of disunion shall be more fearlessly proclaimed, till slavery be abolished, the Union dissolved, or the sun of this guilty nation must go down in blood."[8] The Constitution and government of the United States are "a most foul and bloody conspiracy" against the rights of the slaves. "Down with both, for it is not fit that either should exist!"[9] The oath to support the Constitution "requires that which is morally impossible."[10] As for the Free Soilers, who attempted to justify their support of the Constitution as a way of promoting beneficial measures, "they have our sympathies, but not our judgment." Douglass rejected their "theory of human government, which makes it necessary to do evil, that good may come." A Constitution at war with itself cannot be lived up to, and therefore "the platform for us to occupy, is outside that piece of parchment."[11]

As he exercised his always strong and independent judgment, Douglass became increasingly doubtful of the Garrisonian position, and in 1851 he announced his break with it.[12] He adhered to the opinion that the basic problem was a moral one and that the abolition of slavery depended upon a moral regeneration. But he concluded that the Garrisonians had no adequate answer to the question of how this was to be done. Moreover, he came to see that the Garrisonian position was not only politically but morally defective. For all their righteousness, the Garrisonians needed to learn morality in the politics of a free (though imperfect) republic. "As a mere expression of abhorrence of slavery," the Garrisonian sentiment of no union with slaveholders was a good one, "but it expresses no intelligible principle of action, and throws no light on the pathway of duty. Defined, as its authors define it, it leads to false doctrines, and mischievous results."[13] It amounted, in fact, to an abandonment of the great idea with which the antislavery movement began: "It started to free the slave. It ends by leaving the slave to free himself."[14]

Douglass adopted the position of the political abolitionists that slavery was "a system of lawless violence; that it *never was lawful, and never can be made so.*"[15] He was "sick and tired of arguing on the slaveholders' side of this question,"[16] and he came to the conclusion that the slaveholders not only were wrong about slavery but were also wrong about the Constitution. He adopted the view "that the Constitution, construed in the light of well established rules of legal interpretation, might be made consistent in its details with the noble purposes avowed in its preamble; and that hereafter we should insist upon the application of such rules to that instrument, and demand that it be wielded in behalf of emancipation."[17] Douglass came to understand the design of the Framers of the Constitution, who tried, while making necessary provision for the existing institution of slavery, to leave no principle in the Constitution that would sanction slavery and no word that would defile the constitution of a free people. Once he penetrated this design, Douglass seized the opportunity it provided. The black could now speak fully the language of the law, the language of defense of the Constitution. He could now call upon the country to return not only to the fundamental political principles of the republic as expressed in the Declaration of Independence but to its fundamental legal principles as expressed in the Constitution.

Under his new persuasion Douglass held that "it is the first duty of every American citizen, whose conscience permits him so to do, to use his *political* as well as his *moral* power for its overthrow."[18] "Men should not, under the guidance of a false philosophy, be led to fling from them such powerful instrumentalities against Slavery as the Constitution and the ballot."[19] Thus Douglass embarked upon a course of political activity that sought to maintain the moral purity and therefore the moral power of abolition, while at the same time finding ways of making it politically effective. Defending his support of the Free Soil candidate in 1852, Douglass stated the following rule of political action.

> It is evident that all reforms have their beginning with ideas, and that for a time they have to rely solely on the tongue and pen for progress, until they gain a sufficient number of adherents to make themselves felt at the ballot-box. . . . We ask no man to lose sight of any of his aims and objects. We only ask that they may be allowed to serve out their natural probation. Our rule of political action is this: the voter ought to see to it that his vote shall secure the highest good possible, at the same time that it does no harm.[20]

With his tongue and pen Douglass continued to fight for uncompromising abolition; but when the time came to go to the polls he focused on the good that he could do in the immediate future rather than on the good he was aiming for in the long run. "The mission of the political abolitionists of this country is to abolish slavery. The means to accomplish this great end is, first, to disseminate anti-slavery sentiment; and, secondly, to combine that sentiment and render it a political force which shall, for a time, operate as a check on violent measures for supporting slavery; and, finally, overthrow the great evil of slavery itself."[21]

Douglass's problems well illustrate the apparent dilemma of the reformer in politics. In 1856, for example, writing "What Is My Duty as an Anti-Slavery Voter?" Douglass argued that "the purity of the cause is the success of the cause." While he might participate in politics, "the first duty of the Reformer is to be right. If right, he may go forward; but if wrong, or partly wrong, he is as an house divided against itself, and will fall." Since the Republican Party did "not occupy this high Anti-Slavery ground, (and what is worse, does not mean to occupy it)," Douglass urged his readers to vote for the presidential candidate of the Radical Abolitionists, even at the risk of throwing the election to the Democrats and losing Kansas to slavery. "We deliberately prefer the loss of Kansas to the loss of our Anti-Slavery integrity."[22] Yet four months later, in August 1856, Douglass abandoned the Abolitionist candidate, Gerrit Smith, and announced his support of Republicans John Fremont and William Dayton. The purity of the cause was subordinate, even for the partisan reformer, to a higher morality.

> The time has passed for an honest man to attempt any defence of a right to change his opinion as to political methods of opposing Slavery. Anti-Slavery consistency itself, in our view, requires of the Anti-Slavery voter that disposition of his vote and his influence, which, in all the circumstances and likelihoods of the case tend most to the triumph of Free Principles in the Councils and Government of the nation. It is not to be consistent to pursue a course politically this year, merely because that course seemed the best last year, or at any previous time. Right Anti-Slavery action is that which deals the severest deadliest blow upon Slavery that can be given at that particular time. Such action is always consistent, however different may be the forms through which it expresses itself.[23]

On this basis, Douglass later supported Abraham Lincoln, although often with grave doubts and usually with impatience and exasperation. His criticisms of Lincoln, especially during the years prior to the Emancipation Proclamation, were often cutting and even harsh. He found Lincoln's first Inaugural Address a "double-tongued document"; he accused him of being destitute of antislavery principle; he contended that he was "active, decided, and brave" for the support of slavery, "and passive, cowardly, and treacherous to the very cause of liberty to which he owes his election"; he questioned his honesty.[24] He found the Emancipation Proclamation itself disappointing, making a burden of what should have been a joy, touching neither justice nor mercy.[25] "Abraham Lincoln, President of the United States, Commander-in-Chief of the army and navy, in his own peculiar, cautious, forbearing and hesitating way, slow, but we hope sure, has, while the loyal heart was near breaking with despair, proclaimed and declared" the Emancipation Proclamation.[26]

As circumstances drew the black leader and the white statesman closer together, Douglass grew in his understanding of Lincoln. This is not to say that their relations were ever smooth or that Douglass saw matters as Lincoln saw them. Regarding the use by the Union of black troops, for example, they were constantly at odds. After months of urging that black troops should be used and long negotiations about how they would be used, Douglass reluctantly agreed to support a system that was in some respects unfair to black troops because he thought that the cause of black freedom was served by cooperation even on such terms.

Douglass met in Lincoln true statesmanship and came to understand his own and his people's place in relation to it. While Charles Sumner was "to me and to my oppressed race . . . higher than the highest, better than the best of all our statesmen," Lincoln was simply "the greatest statesman that ever presided over the destinies of this Republic."[27] Douglass gave expression to this understanding in 1876 on the occasion of the unveiling of the Freedmen's Monument in Washington, DC.[28] Lincoln was not, he said, "in the fullest sense of the word, either our man or our model. In his interests, in his associations, in his habits of thought, and in his prejudices, he was a white man." He came to office on the principle of opposition to the extension of slavery, but he was prepared to defend and perpetuate slavery where it existed, and his whole policy was motivated by "his patriotic devotion to the interests of his own race." Yet "while Abraham Lincoln saved for you a country, he delivered us from a bondage, according to Jefferson, one hour of which was worse than ages of the oppression your fathers rose in rebellion to oppose." Lincoln's very prejudices were an element of his success in preparing the American people for the great conflict and bringing them safely through it. "Viewed from the genuine abolition ground, Mr. Lincoln seemed tardy, cold, dull, and indifferent; but measuring him by the sentiment of his country, a sentiment he was bound as a statesman to consult, he was swift, zealous, radical, and determined."

The blacks believed in Lincoln, despite acts and words that tried the faith and taxed the understanding.

When he tarried long in the mountain; when he strangely told us that we were the cause of the war; when he still more strangely told us that we were to leave the land in which we were born; when he refused to employ our arms in defence of the Union; when, after accepting our service as colored soldiers, he refused to retaliate our murder and torture as colored prisoners; when he told us he would save the Union if he could with slavery; when he revoked the Proclamation of Emancipation of General Freemont; when he refused to remove the popular commander of the Army of the Potomac, in the days of its inaction and defeat, who was more zealous in his efforts to protect slavery than to suppress rebellion; when we saw all this, and more, we were at times grieved, stunned, and greatly bewildered; but our hearts believed while they ached and bled.

Nor was this merely a blind, unreasoning faith. "Despite the mist and haze that surrounded him; despite the tumult, the hurry, and confusion of the hour, we were able to take a comprehensive view of Abraham Lincoln." Douglass never abandoned his point of view as a black spokesman and leader, but he did come to understand the deeper harmony of black and white of which Lincoln was the guardian. "It mattered little to us what language he might employ on special occasions; it mattered little to us, when we fully knew him, whether he was swift or slow in his movements; it was enough for us that Abraham Lincoln was at the head of a great movement, and was in living and earnest sympathy with that movement, which, in the nature of things, must go on until slavery should be utterly and forever abolished in the United States."[29]

"What Country Have I?"

In England between 1845 and 1847, where he had fled to prevent recapture and to preach abolitionism, Douglass often explained that he was "an outcast from the society of my childhood, and an outlaw in the land of my birth." "That men should be patriotic is to me perfectly natural; and as a philosophical fact, I am able to give it an *intellectual* recognition. But no further can I go."[30] "I have no love for America, as such; I have no patriotism. I have no country. What country have I? The institutions of this country do not know me, do not recognize me as a man. . . . I have not, I cannot have, any love for this country, as such, or for its Constitution. I desire to see its overthrow as speedily as possible, and its Constitution shivered in a thousand fragments, rather than this foul curse should continue to remain as now."[31]

When Douglass abandoned Garrisonianism, he no longer saw the black as, strictly speaking, an "outlaw" because he now held that slavery was not lawful under the Constitution. The black was still an "outcast" because he was in fact held a slave, but he had a moral and a legal claim to the protection of "his" country. This is the theme of one of Douglass's major prewar statements, an oration given in Rochester, New York, in 1852, "The Meaning of July Fourth for the Negro."

> Fellow-citizens, pardon me, allow me to ask, why am I called upon to speak here to-day? What have I, or those I represent, to do with your national independence? Are the great principles of political freedom and of natural justice, embodied in that Declaration of Independence extended to us? . . .
>
> Would to God, both for your sakes and ours, that an affirmative answer could be truthfully returned to these questions. . . .
>
> . . . This Fourth July is *yours* not *mine*. You may rejoice, I must mourn. To drag a man in fetters into the grand illuminated temple of liberty, and call upon him to join you in joyous anthems, were inhuman mockery and sacrilegious irony. Do you mean, citizens, to mock me, by asking me to speak to-day?[32]

In return for mockery, Douglass gave his audience the whip of America's self-betrayal. Looking at the day from the slave's point of view, he declared that the character and conduct of the nation had never looked blacker. "America is false to the past, false to the present, and solemnly binds herself to be false to the future." To those who said that the abolitionists denounce when they ought to persuade, Douglass asked, What is it that needs argument? That the slave is a man? That a man is entitled to liberty? That slavery is wrong? That slavery is not divine? Words are valuable now only as they move to action.

> At a time like this, scorching irony, not convincing argument, is needed. O! had I the ability, and could reach the nation's ear, I would to-day pour out a fiery stream of biting ridicule, blasting reproach, withering sarcasm, and stern rebuke. For it is not light that is needed, but fire; it is not the gentle shower, but thunder. We need the storm, the whirlwind, and the earthquake. The feeling of the nation must be quickened; the

conscience of the nation must be roused; the propriety of the nation must be startled; the hypocrisy of the nation must be exposed; and its crimes against God and man must be proclaimed and denounced.[33]

And so Douglass flayed his fellow citizens:

Fellow-citizens, I will not enlarge further on your national inconsistencies. The existence of slavery in this country brands your republicanism as a sham, your humanity as a base pretense, and your Christianity as a lie. It destroys your moral power abroad: it corrupts your politicians at home. It saps the foundation of religion; it makes your name a hissing and a bye-word to a mocking earth. It is the antagonistic force in your government, the only thing that seriously disturbs and endangers your *Union*. It fetters your progress; it is the enemy of improvement; the deadly foe of education; it fosters pride; it breeds insolence; it promotes vice; it shelters crime; it is a curse to the earth that supports it; and yet you cling to it as if it were the sheet anchor of all your hopes.[34]

Strong words, yet words directed to "fellow-citizens," as Douglass repeatedly addressed his audience. Five years later, however, the Supreme Court in the *Dred Scott* decision denied Douglass's interpretation of the Constitution, holding that blacks could claim none of the rights and privileges secured by the Constitution to citizens of the United States. In his speech on this decision Douglass was not scorching fellow-citizens (a term he used here only once, and that in the formal salutation) but defending himself against an enemy. The decision was "infamous," "devilish," "the judicial incarnation of wolfishness," "an open, glaring, and scandalous tissue of lies." Douglass appealed against "this hell-black judgment of the Supreme Court, to the court of common sense and common humanity." He declared that "all that is merciful and just, on earth and in Heaven, will execrate and despise this edict of Taney."[35] On most occasions, as Douglass gave ample evidence of understanding, such an unqualified partisan attack on the supreme instrument of lawfulness would be utterly irresponsible and self-defeating. But the Court's decision in *Dred Scott* amounted to an act of outright war against the black, excluding him from participation in the American political community, and the black had to defend himself in like manner, even at the risk of seriously damaging that very political community in which he sought to secure his rightful place. Thus, Douglass confessed in his autobiography to a feeling allied to satisfaction at the prospect of a war between North and South. "Standing outside the pale of American humanity, denied citizenship, unable to call the land of my birth my country, and adjudged by the Supreme Court of the United States to have no rights which white men were bound to respect, and longing for the end of the bondage of my people, I was ready for any political upheaval which should bring about a change in the existing condition of things."[36]

It is instructive in this connection to compare Douglass's speech on the *Dred Scott* decision with his speech in 1883 on the *Civil Rights* case, striking down federal legislation prohibiting discrimination against blacks. The war was over, for the country and for the black, and the character of the speech was determined by that great fact. This is not to suggest that the *Civil Rights* case was not a serious blow. Douglass saw it as standing in a line that included the forcing of slavery into Kansas, the enactment of the Fugitive Slave Act, the repeal of the Missouri Compromise, and the *Dred Scott* decision. "We have been, as a class, grievously wounded, wounded in the house of our friends," he said at the mass meeting called to protest the *Civil Rights* decision.[37] But although wounded, the blacks were not turned out of their political house, as they had been in *Dred Scott;* and Douglass's rhetoric was governed by that difference. Here there was none of the violence of his attack on the Taney decision. He began by noting that he had taken the trouble to write out his remarks, that they might be "well-chosen, and not liable to be misunderstood, distorted, or misrepresented." He suggested that it may be that "the hour calls more loudly for silence than for speech," and he exhibited an unusual reluctance to enter into the criticism he had to utter. He aimed to achieve a certain kind of silence while speaking. He contended that the most serious evil in the land, "which threatens to undermine and destroy the foundations of our free institutions," is not race prejudice or injustice to blacks, as one might have expected, but "the great and apparently increasing want of respect entertained for those to whom are committed the responsibility and the duty of administering our government." Douglass urged his partisan audience never to forget that "whatever may be the incidental mistakes or misconduct of rulers, government is better than anarchy, and patient reform is better than violent revolution." While not interfering with fair criticism, he would give "the emphasis of a voice from heaven" to the repugnance felt by all good citizens to any disrespect for governors.[38]

Coming "a little nearer to the case now before us," he began his criticism but again interrupted himself to caution that "if any man has come here tonight with his breast heaving with passion, his heart flooded with acrimony, wishing and expecting to hear violent denunciation of the Supreme Court, on account of this decision, he has mistaken the object of this meeting and the character of the men by whom it is called."[39] Douglass then entered into a vigorous criticism, but he did so only after having introduced the subject with the greatest circumspection and concern for maintaining the dignity and authority of the Court and the law for which it spoke. This was now the blacks' Court as well as the whites'. Better to have a Court that does serious harm to blacks than to have none at all.

Indeed, the privilege of having a part in the American political institutions was a precious victory that Douglass had helped to win. This privilege did not, as Douglass clearly understood, necessarily accompany emancipation. Emancipation could justly be claimed on the basis of the fundamental principles of the American Declaration of Independence and Constitution, and it could therefore be justly argued that in this respect the black's interest was fundamentally identical with the interest of the rest of the nation. Even in his speech on *Dred Scott,* Douglass concluded, "All I ask of the American people is, that they live up to the Constitution, adopt its principles, imbibe its spirit, and enforce its provisions."[40] But while the black fought to be a free man, he also fought to be a free *American.* And while the best American statesmen had always agreed that American principles demanded freedom for the black, there was much less agreement about whether they demanded freedom for the black *in the United States.* With respect to this question—whether the blacks, once freed, should stay in the United States or go elsewhere—it was not so clear that the good of the black and the good of the country were identical. It is of some interest to note that the first official reception by any president of a group of blacks came in 1862 when Abraham Lincoln invited a committee of blacks to lend their support to a plan for colonizing blacks in Central America.[41]

The colonization issue was, of course, an old one. The first printed notice of Frederick Douglass, indeed, was a report in the Garrisonian *Liberator* of March 29, 1839, that the young exslave had addressed an anticolonization meeting, arguing "that the inordinate and intolerable scheme of the American Colonization Society shall never entice or drive *us* from our native soil."[42] From this time until the very end of his long career Douglass fought the numerous schemes of colonization put forward as solutions to the "Negro problem."[43]

Douglass argued the civilizing effect of a permanent location, which the American blacks were just beginning to experience. "We say to every colored man, *be a man where you are*. . . . You must be a man here, and force your way to intelligence, wealth and respectability. If you can't do that here, you can't do it there. By changing your place, you don't change your character." The argument was not simply directed against restless nomadism, although that is part of it. "We believe that contact with the white race, even under the many unjust and painful restrictions to which we are subjected, does more toward our elevation and improvement, than the mere circumstance of being separated from them could do."[44] Although he despised many who made the argument, Douglass nevertheless saw "that the condition of our race has been improved by their situation as slaves, since it has brought them into contact with a superior people, and afforded them facilities for acquiring knowledge,"[45] and he fought to keep the blacks in contact with that superior people—superior, it is hardly necessary to add, not in nature but in fact. Douglass saw that the contact was not of equal advantage to the two sides. Speaking of the profit to himself of association with the son of his former master, he said, "The law of compensation holds here as well as elsewhere. While this lad could not associate with ignorance without sharing its shade, he could not give his black playmates his company without giving them his superior intelligence as well."[46]

Whatever the whites might think was best for America, the blacks knew what was best for them, and, according to Douglass, they would fight to stay. "Our minds are made up to live here if we can, or die here if we must; so every attempt to remove us, will be, as it ought to be, labor lost. Here we are, and here we shall remain."[47] The black has stayed despite his great differences from the European, despite "greater hardships, injuries and insults than those to which the Indians have been subjected," and despite cunning schemes to teach his children that this is not his home. "It is idle—worse than idle, ever to think of our expatriation, or removal. . . . *We are here*, and here we are likely to be. To imagine that we shall ever be eradicated is absurd and ridiculous. We can be remodified, changed, and assimilated, but never extinguished. We repeat, therefore, that *we are here;* and that this is *our* country; and the question for the philosophers and statesmen of the land ought to be, what principles should dictate the policy of the action toward us?"[48]

Douglass did argue that there was no ineradicable prejudice against blacks and that the proper response to prejudice is to root it out rather than to pander to it. He argued that the South had a positive need for the blacks' labor. He argued on the basis of human brotherhood, and he sometimes suggested that greater intercommunication of the races was historically necessary and morally desirable. But he never formed these various suggestions into a comprehensive argument that colonization would be, like slavery, as bad for the country as for the black. Douglass's argument here might be paraphrased as follows. "I think that the United States has a duty to keep her black stepchildren; I think that she will be enriched by so doing, and that the problems involved in it can be solved. However, the cost to the country of retaining the freedman and its possible damage to the fabric of American political life are not questions that it is my duty to ponder deeply. The black is willing—must be willing—to see the American polity pay almost any price, run almost any risk, to admit him. For him it is a matter, not, it is true, of life or death or freedom or slavery, but of that for the sake of which life and freedom are sought; and he will resist any attempt, however reasonable to others, to loosen his grip on the white man's civilization."

The colonization issue was the last great battle in the black's paradoxical war with America to become part of America, and it was in principle his most difficult battle, more difficult than emancipation, on the one side, or the securing of civil and political rights, on the other. The black's victory in this struggle was commemorated in Douglass's oration at the unveiling of the Freedmen's Monument in 1876, from which we have already quoted.[49] This speech contains one of the most profound statements ever made of the relations between the American blacks and the American polity. Douglass described, in stately terms, the setting in the capital of the nation and the audience drawn from all the segments of the government, present to give witness to the blacks' entry into the American community through their praise of America's greatest statesman. He did not succumb to the temptation of shallow praise; he did not claim Lincoln for the blacks; he felt no need to blur the truth. "We fully comprehend the relation of Abraham Lincoln both to ourselves and to the whole people of the United States." Lincoln was a white man, an American of the Americans.

He was preeminently the white man's President, entirely devoted to the welfare of white men. He was ready and willing at any time during the first years of his administration to deny, postpone, and sacrifice the rights of humanity in the colored people to promote the welfare of the white people of this country. In all his education and feeling he was an American of the Americans. . . . The race to which we belong were not the special objects of his consideration. . . . We are at best only his step-children; children by adoption, children by forces of circumstances and necessity.

But the circumstances were such that Lincoln could not promote the welfare of whites without promoting the welfare of blacks, for both rested on the same principle, individual freedom, and their destinies were too entwined ever to be separated. The Freedmen's Monument stood for the blacks' praise of Lincoln but also for their *title* to praise him—stepchildren, indeed, but, for better or worse, his and the country's children. "Fellow-citizens, I end, as I began, with congratulations. We have done a good work for our race today. In doing honor to the memory of our friend and liberator, we have been doing highest honors to ourselves and those who come after us; we have been fastening ourselves to a name and fame imperishable and immortal."

What Shall We Do with the Black?

If, then, the blacks were to stay in the United States, the question was asked, What shall we do with them? Douglass answered, "Do nothing with them; mind your business, and let them mind theirs. Your *doing* with them is their greatest misfortune." The question implies "that slavery is the natural order of human relations, and that liberty is an experiment." But the reverse is true, and consequently human duties are mostly negative. "If men were born in need of crutches, instead of having legs, the fact would be otherwise. We should then be in need of help, and would require outside aid; but according to the wiser and better arrangement of nature, our duty is done better by not hindering than by helping our fellow-men; or, in other words, the best way to help them is just to let them help themselves."[50] While not wishing to check any benevolent concern, Douglass suggested pointedly, "Let the American people, who have thus far only kept the colored race staggering between partial philanthropy and cruel force, be induced to try what virtue there is in justice." The black's misfortune is precisely that "he is everywhere treated as an exception to all the general rules which should operate in the relations of other men."[51] "[I]f the Negro cannot stand on his own legs, let him fall. . . . All I ask is, give him a chance to stand on his own legs! Let him alone!"[52]

Let the Negro alone. This was the touchstone; obviously it was not exhaustive. Douglass was well aware that the black did need crutches, for his limbs were stiff from the shackles of slavery. "Time, education, and training will restore him to natural proportions, for, though bruised and blasted, he is yet a man."[53] Douglass knew the debt owed the black, but he did not harp on it. He knew and in various ways presented the black's need for generous help as well as his demand for justice; but there was never any question about the priority of the black's demand to be allowed to stand or fall as he is capable of standing or falling.

The demand to be let alone is, however, not so negative as it might sound due to the scope and character of the whites' "doing" for the blacks in the past. Douglass demanded "the most perfect civil and political equality, and . . . all the rights, privileges and immunities enjoyed by any other members of the body politic." "Save the Negro and you save the nation, destroy the Negro and you destroy the nation, and to save both you must have but one great law of Liberty, Equality and Fraternity for all Americans without respect to color."[54]

The two main objectives of Douglass's campaign to have the blacks "left alone," in this fundamental sense of being subject only to the one great law for all Americans, were the right to vote and freedom from color prejudice. The former need not detain us here. Blacks wanted the vote, as Douglass repeatedly explained, because it was their right, because it was a means of education, because its denial was "to brand us with the stigma of inferiority," because it was a means of self-defense in a hostile South, and because it was an instrument for maintaining federal authority in the South.[55]

Douglass's concern with prejudice against the black requires more attention. From the beginning he saw this prejudice as arising from and contributing to the black's enslavement, his proposed expatriation, and his actual degradation. "This prejudice must be removed; and the way for abolitionists and colored persons to remove it, is to act as though it did not exist, and to associate with their fellow creatures irrespective of all complexional differences." Douglass marked out this path for himself and pursued it "at all hazards."[56] He spoke and acted against any form of public discrimination whatsoever against blacks. On trains and ships, in hotels and restaurants, in meetings and other public places, he resisted the conventional expressions of race prejudice. He described what might in modern parlance be called a "stroll-in" when he passed the time waiting for a steamer in New York City walking with two white ladies and had to beat off the attentions of several ruffians as a result. He engaged in such behavior, he said, "with no purpose to inflame the public mind; not to provoke the popular violence; not to make a display of my contempt for public opinion; but simply as a matter of course, and because it was right to do so."[57] Douglass certainly had that love of sheer combat that is necessary to the good politician-—"I glory in the fight as well as in the victory"[58]—but he rarely did something that was right unless he thought it was also politic. This was certainly true of his persistent testing and challenging of conventions of race discrimination.

"The question is not can there be social equality?" for that does not exist anywhere. The question is rather, "Can the white and colored people of this country be blended into a common nationality, and enjoy together, in the same country, under the same flag, the inestimable blessings of life, liberty and the pursuit of happiness, as neighborly citizens of a common country?" This is not simply a matter of public behavior. It is true that Douglass argued that "men who travel should leave their prejudices at home,"[59] but fundamentally Douglass believed that men should not *have* any color prejudice that needs to be left at home. For blacks and whites to live together as fellow citizens, color prejudice must be eradicated. In an essay in 1866, "The Future of the Colored Race," Douglass stated as his "strongest conviction" that the black would neither be expatriated nor exterminated nor forever remain a separate and distinct race, "but that he will be absorbed, assimilated, and will only appear finally . . . in the features of a blended race."[60] He emphasized that this would not happen quickly or by any forced process or "out of any theory of the wisdom of such blending of the two races." He did not, he said, advocate intermarriage between the two races; neither did he deprecate it. But seeing this as the only condition finally in which the Negro could survive and flourish in the United States, he naturally advocated a course of action that would prepare for it.

Douglass often displayed the concern with the psychological effects of segregation with which we are today so familiar. Thus an aspect of his campaign to get blacks into the army during the Civil War was the effect that this would have on the blacks' own self-regard, both directly and indirectly through an enhanced regard in the eyes of others. He had a similar concern in other areas, such as voting, but the psychological consideration was never the only reason for Douglass's policy and seldom a major one.

Such considerations were of more than usual importance in the education of the young. Douglass indignantly described how he withdrew his nine-year-old daughter from a private school when it was proposed to teach her separately, "as allowing her to remain there in such circumstances, could only serve to degrade her in her own eyes, and those of the other scholars attending the school."[61] More than twenty years later he urged passage of a bill providing for mixed schools in the District of Columbia "in order that the mad current of prejudice against the Negro may be checked; and also that the baleful influence upon the children of the colored race of being taught by separation from the whites that the whites are superior to them may be destroyed." "Educate the poor white children and the colored children together; let them grow up to know that color makes no difference as to the rights of a man; that both the black man and the white man are at home; that the country is as much the country of one as of the other, and that both together must make it a valuable country." "We want mixed schools not because our colored schools are inferior to white schools—not because colored instructors are inferior to white instructors, but because we want to do away with a system that exalts one class and debases another."[62]

There is, then, a connection between the views of Douglass and those of today's integrationists with regard to race prejudice and segregation. But the main lesson lies in the differences. First, although all such segregation carries an implication of black inferiority in the opinion of the white segregators, not all segregation is equally harmful merely on that account. The harm is great in the case of black children, Douglass thought, but it is small as more mature blacks are the objects of segregation. Unlike Martin Luther King Jr., Douglass did not see segregation as doing any harm *to himself*.[63] Describing harassment by a Syracuse mob in 1861, Douglass said that the aim was to humble and mortify him. "Just as if a man could feel himself insulted by the kick of a jackass, or the barking of a bull-dog. It is, to be sure, neither pleasant to be kicked nor to be barked at, but no man need to think less of himself on account of either."[64] At the same time that he fought to prevent the damage that segregation can do to the self-respect of black children and to childlike adults, Douglass held himself forward as an example of the man who has risen above that kind of harm.

Douglass fought prejudice and all its manifestations fundamentally not because of its psychological effect, but because of the objective harm to which prejudice leads. He did express the belief that "the tendency of the age is unification, not isolation; not to clans and classes, but to human brotherhood"; but he did not rest his political case on it. Indeed he expressed this belief in the context of the deep and firm moral and political hold the black has upon *this* country.[65] Douglass's political concern was to free the black from very clear and objective oppression, provide him with the platform of equal opportunity, and show him how to use his opportunity to live a decent, independent, civilized life. "Having despised us, it is not strange that Americans should seek to render us despicable; . . . having denounced us as indolent, it is not strange that they should cripple our enterprise; having assumed our inferiority, it would be extraordinary if they sought to surround us with circumstances which would serve to make us direct contradictions to their assumption."[66]

What concerned Douglass was not fundamentally the whites' despising, denouncing, or assuming, but their rendering despicable, their crippling of enterprise, their imposition of degrading circumstances. The black's fight against prejudice was not, in Douglass's view, fundamentally a fight for "integration"; it was a fight to establish the outworks of his claim to be left alone. "The spirit which would deny a man shelter in a public house, needs but little change to deny him shelter, even in his own house."[67] Douglass was concerned mainly with the shelter, not the spirit.

Consistently with this view, Douglass linked almost every one of his criticisms of social and other forms of segregation with observations on the black's duty to exert himself. "It is too true, that as a People, our aspirations have not been sufficiently elevated; and it is also equally true, that we have been and still are the victims of an ostracism as relentless as the grave." Yet "our elevation as a race, is almost wholly dependent upon our own exertions."[68] "He who would be free must strike the first blow," Douglass repeated again and again. But this is not enough—at least in Douglass's opinion. Not all restrictions on freedom are imposed by others. Not all prejudice has its source simply in the mind of the bigot. While striking off his shackles, the black also had to take a responsibility for the good use of his freed limbs and mind.

What Shall the Black Man Do with Himself?

Douglass was acutely aware of the extremely limited means for self-improvement available to the blacks. Speaking of Southern blacks in 1886, he said, "They are asked to make bricks without straw. Their hands are tied, and they are asked to work. They are forced to be poor, and laughed at for their destitution."[69] Nevertheless, every major part of Douglass's argument—whether dealing with abolition, black troops, the vote, color prejudice, or anything else—was accompanied by stern calls to the black man to exert himself. "We have but to toil and trust, throw away whiskey and tobacco, improve the opportunities that we have, put away all extravagance, learn to live within our means, lay up our earnings, educate our children, live industrious and virtuous lives, establish a character for sobriety, punctuality, and general uprightness, and we shall raise up powerful friends who shall stand by us in our struggle for an equal chance in the race of life. The white people of this country are asleep, but not dead."[70]

Again and again, Douglass asked, as he did, for example, in his newspaper in 1848, "What is the use of standing a man on his feet, if, when we let him go, his head is again brought to the pavement?" No matter how much we beg and pray our white friends for assistance, he said, and no matter how generously they provide it, "unless we, the colored people of America, shall set about the work of our own regeneration and improvement, we are doomed to drag on in our present miserable and degraded condition for ages."

> What we, the colored people, want is *character*, and this nobody can give us. It is a thing we must get for ourselves. We must labor for it. It is gained by toil—hard toil. Neither the sympathy nor the generosity of our friends can give it to us. . . . It is attainable; but we must attain it, and attain it each for himself. I cannot for you, and you cannot for me. . . . We must get character for ourselves, as a people. A change in our political condition would do very little for us without this. . . . Industry, sobriety, honesty, combined with intelligence and a due self-respect, find them where you will, among black and white, must be *looked up* to—can never be *looked down upon*. In their presence, prejudice is abashed, confused and mortified.[71]

Here, as usual, Douglass speaks of what he clearly regards as good in itself, regeneration and character, as means to the end of removing prejudice. Douglass's argument is, "Be a man and you will, in time, be treated as a man." In a comprehensive view, as Douglass saw, the end is to be a man. While we urge that Congress and the country perform their duties toward the black, "we must never forget that any race worth living will live, and whether Congress heeds our request in these and other particulars or not, we must demonstrate our capacity to live by living. We must acquire property and educate the hands and hearts and heads of our children whether we are helped or not. Races that fail to do these things die politically and socially, and are only fit to die."[72]

Nevertheless, from the point of view of the black, hampered and oppressed by the effects of prejudice, the immediate end is to be treated like a man, to which being one is a means. Douglass's statements typically contain the more comprehensive view but focus on the more particular one. The following is one further example, taken from dozens, written in 1883.

> After all, our destiny is largely in our own hands. If we find, we shall have to seek. If we succeed in the race of life, it must be by our own energies, and our own exertions. Others may clear the road, but we must go forward, or be left behind in the race of life.
>
> If we remain poor and dependent, the riches of other men will not avail us. If we are ignorant, the intelligence of other men will do but little for us. If we are foolish, the wisdom of other men will not guide us. If we are wasteful of time and money, the economy of other men will make our destitution the more disgraceful and hurtful. If we are vicious and lawless, the virtues and good behavior of others will not save us from our vices and our crimes.
>
> We are now free, and though we have many of the consequences of our past condition to contend against, by union, effort, co-operation, and by a wise policy in the direction and the employment of our mental, moral, industrial and political powers, it is the faith of my soul, that we can blot out the handwriting of popular prejudice, remove the stumbling-blocks left in our way by slavery, rise to an honorable place in the estimation of our fellow-citizens of all classes, and make a comfortable way for ourselves in the world.[73]

Conclusion

In Frederick Douglass we find a deep understanding of the dependence of the partial good, the good of blacks, on the good of the whole American community. It is well that there are leaders who take upon themselves the duty of promoting the good of the part, but that duty includes a recognition of and participation in a higher statesmanship. A Douglass knows the horizons of a Lincoln, although he does not himself need often to climb so high and scan so widely. The partisan and the statesman have ultimately the same end, but they begin from different points. They meet, in our system of government, in the political arena, where the parts take (at least implicitly) some responsibility for the whole, while they make demands on the whole—as Douglass did when he supported Fremont for the presidency in 1858 and when he criticized and defended the Supreme Court in 1883.

Douglass argued that the black's greatest struggle was the struggle to become a part of the American political community and that the reason for that struggle was his creditable desire to keep his grip on the civilization that the white man possessed. Douglass was not assailed by refined doubts about "identity" or about the meaning of "civilization." For the time being, at any rate, the matter seemed clear enough. Speaking in 1868 at the inauguration of the Douglass Institute in Baltimore, Douglass elaborated on the grounds and the structure of civilization:

> Now, what are those elemental and original powers of civilization about which men speak and write so earnestly, and which white men claim for themselves and deny to the Negro? I answer that they are simply consciousness of wants and ability to gratify them. Here the whole machinery of civilization, whether moral, intellectual or physical, is set in motion.
>
> We who have been long debarred the privileges of culture may assemble and have our souls thrilled with heavenly music, lifted to the skies on the wings of poetry and song. Here we can assemble and have our minds enlightened upon the whole circle of social, moral, political and educational duties. Here we can come and learn true politeness and refinements. Here the loftiest and best eloquence which the country has produced, whether of Anglo-Saxon or of African descent, shall flow as a river, enriching, ennobling, strengthening and purifying all

who will lave in its waters. Here may come all who have a new and unpopular truth to unfold and enforce, against which old and respectable bars and bolts are iron gates.[74]

Douglass saw, moreover, that if the object is to share in this civilization, the means of securing that share must be designed so as to do no damage, or as little as possible, to that civilization.

Above all Douglass taught that the black, like every man, must walk the road of opportunity himself. As the black makes good use of the opportunities he has, more opportunities will open up; as he gives less reason for prejudice, prejudice will decline.

> Without pretending to have exerted ourselves as we ought, in view of an intelligent understanding of our interest, to avert from us the unfavorable opinions and unfriendly action of the American people, we feel that the imputations cast upon us, for our want of intelligence, morality and exalted character, may be mainly accounted for by the injustice we have received at your hands. What stone has been left unturned to degrade us? What hand has refused to fan the flame of popular prejudice against us? What American artist has not caricatured us? What wit has not laughed at us in our wretchedness? What songster has not made merry over our depressed spirits? What press has not ridiculed and condemned us? What pulpit has withheld from our devoted heads its angry lightning, or its sanctimonious hate? Few, few, very few; and that we have borne up with it all—that we have tried to be wise, though denounced by all to be fools that we have tried to be upright, when all around us have esteemed us knaves—that we have striven to be gentlemen, although all around us have been teaching us its impossibility—that we have remained here, when all our neighbors have advised us to leave, proves that we possess qualities of head and heart, such as cannot but be commended by impartial men.[75]

It is said that in 1895 a young man asked Frederick Douglass's advice about what the young black just starting out should do. "The patriarch lifted his head and replied, 'Agitate! Agitate! Agitate!'" Four years later the same youth asked the same question of Booker T. Washington, "who answered, 'Work! Work! Work! Be patient and win by superior service.'"[76] The contrast is full of significance, but for the present it is sufficient to reiterate that this agitator laid a striking amount of emphasis upon work. Some tell you to go to Africa or Canada or to go to school, Douglass told his readers in 1853. "We tell you to go to work; and to work you must go or die. Men are not valued in this country, or in any country, for what they *are;* they are valued for what they can *do.* It is vain that we talk about being men, if we do not do the work of men."[77]

"Agitate!" but at the same time "Work!" Work because that is a good form of agitation, and work because the opportunity to work is what you are agitating *for.* External obstacles are not, after all, decisive. Obviously that is no reason placidly to accept them. Douglass in fact spent most of his energy and most of his words in trying to remove them. But while he was concerned, partly by chance and partly by deliberate choice, mainly with helping to provide the conditions of the good life for the black, Douglass did not lose sight of the fact that possession of the opportunity to live well is not living well. Concluding his autobiography, Douglass described what he had tried to teach:

> That knowledge can be obtained under difficulties—that poverty may give place to competency—that obscurity is not an absolute bar to distinction, and that a way is open to welfare and happiness to all who will resolutely and wisely pursue that way—that neither slavery, stripes, imprisonment, nor proscription need extinguish self-respect, crush manly ambition, or paralyze effort—that no power outside of himself can prevent a man from sustaining an honorable character and a useful relation to his day and generation—that neither institutions nor friends can make a race to stand unless it has strength in its own legs—that there is no power in the world which can be relied upon to help the weak against the strong or the simple against the wise—that races, like individuals, must stand or fall by their own merits.[78]

Selected Suggested Readings

Life and Times of Frederick Douglass: The Complete Autobiography. New York: Collier Books, 1962.

The Life and Writings of Frederick Douglass. Edited by Philip Foner. 4 vols. New York: International Publishers, 1950.

See especially the following selections:

"What Are the Colored People Doing for Themselves?" (1848). In *Life and Writings*, 1:314–20.

"The Destiny of Colored Americans" (1849). In *Life and Writings*, 1:416–18.

"The Meaning of July Fourth for the Negro" (1852). In *Life and Writings*, 1:181–204.

"Oration in Memory of Abraham Lincoln" (1876). In *Life and Writings*, 4:309–19.

Storing, Herbert J., ed. *What Country Have I? Political Writings by Black Americans.* New York: St. Martin's Press, 1970.

Notes

1. Frederick Douglass, *Life and Times of Frederick Douglass: The Complete Autobiography* (New York: Collier Books, 1962), 217. [*Volume editor's note:* In quotations from Douglass, the emphasis is always in the original.]

2. Frederick Douglass, *A Narrative of the Life of Frederick Douglass, an American Slave* (Garden City, NY: Doubleday, 1963).

3. [Frederick Douglass, *My Bondage and My Freedom*, ed. John David Smith (New York: Penguin, 2003), 181.]

4. Douglass, *Narrative*, 98. See Douglass, *Life and Times*, 150.

5. Douglass, *Life and Times*, 260.

6. Frederick Douglass, *The Life and Writings of Frederick Douglass*, 5 vols., ed. Philip S. Foner (New York: International Publishers, 1950–1975), 1:269–70.

7. Ibid., 1:274–75.

8. Ibid., 1:347.

9. Ibid., 1:379.

10. Ibid., 2:117.

11. Ibid., 2:119.

12. Douglass, *Life and Times*, 260–61.

13. Douglass, *Life and Writings*, 2:351.

14. Ibid., 2:350.

15. Ibid., 2:156.

16. Ibid., 2:149.

17. Ibid., 2:155.

18. Ibid., 2:156.

19. Ibid., 2:177.

20. Ibid., 2:213–14.

21. Ibid., 2:220.

22. Ibid., 2:391–94.

23. Ibid., 2:397.

24. Ibid., 3:72, 186, 268, 127, 267.

25. Ibid., 3:309.

26. Ibid., 3:273.

27. Ibid., 4:239, 368.

28. Ibid., 4:309 ff.

29. Ibid., 4:314.

30. Ibid., 1:126.

31. Ibid., 1:236.

32. Ibid., 2:188–89.

33. Ibid., 2:192.

34. Ibid., 2:201.

35. Ibid., 2:410–12.

36. Douglass, *Life and Times,* 329.

37. Douglass, *Life and Writings,* 4:392 ff.

38. Ibid., 4:394.

39. Ibid., 4:395–96.

40. Ibid., 2:424.

41. Abraham Lincoln, *The Collected Works of Abraham Lincoln,* 9 vols., ed. Roy P. Basler (New Brunswick, NJ: Rutgers University Press, 1953), 5:370–75.

42. Douglass, *Life and Writings,* 1:25.

43. The last two substantive pieces in Foner's [collection of Douglass's works,] *Life and Writings,* are "Lecture on Haiti" (1895, 4:478) and a long essay, "Why the Negro Is Lynched" (1894, 4:491), both of which contain substantial discussions of the colonization issue.

44. Douglass, *Life and Writings,* 2:173.

45. Ibid.

46. Douglass, *Life and Times,* 44.

47. Douglass, *Life and Writings,* 1:351.

48. Ibid., 1:417.

49. Ibid., 4:309 ff.

50. Ibid., 3:188–90.

51. Ibid., 3:190.

52. Ibid., 4:164.

53. Ibid., 4:435.

54. Ibid., 3:348–49.

55. Ibid., 4:159–60.

56. Ibid., 1:387.

57. Ibid., 2:126.

58. Ibid., 1:137.

59. Ibid., 2:450.

60. Ibid., 4:195.

61. Ibid., 1:372.

62. Ibid., 4:288–89.

63. Martin Luther King Jr., *Stride toward Freedom: The Montgomery Story* (New York: Harper, 1958), 20–21.

64. Douglass, *Life and Writings*, 3:182.

65. Ibid., 4:412.

66. Ibid., 2:268.

67. Ibid., 4:295.

68. Ibid., 2:373, 360.

69. Ibid., 4:436.

70. Ibid., 4:441.

71. Ibid., 1:316–18.

72. Ibid., 4:388.

73. Ibid., 4:366–67.

74. Ibid., 4:181–82.

75. Ibid., 2:266–67.

76. Philip S. Foner, "Frederick Douglass," in Douglass, *Life and Writings*, 4:149.

77. Douglass, *Life and Writings*, 2:224.

78. Douglass, *Life and Times*, 479.

13

Staging Dissensus

Frederick Douglass and "We the People"

Jason Frank

Any interpretation of the political meaning of the term *people* ought to start from the peculiar fact that in modern European languages this term always indicates also the poor, the underprivileged, and the excluded. The same term names the constitutive political subject as well as the class that is excluded—de facto if not de jure—from politics.
> —Giorgio Agamben, "What Is a People?" in *Means without End: Notes on Politics*

The aporia of ordinary language that Agamben positions at the heart of "the political meaning of the term *people*" goes strangely unacknowledged in most theoretical discussions of popular sovereignty, even though the people are generally construed as the basis of attempts to grasp the meaning of democratic legitimacy. In the familiar oppositions that govern most discussions in contemporary democratic theory—will and reason, legitimacy and legality, democracy and constitutionalism, majoritarianism and individual rights, the liberty of the ancients and the liberty of the moderns—the people are equated with the first half of each pairing, and the theoretical difficulty is taken to be how to best reconcile or resolve the opposing logics.

Democratic theorists who resist the governing imperatives of this framework and instead attempt to conceptualize a political role for the people
outside the institutions that legally organize them or who embrace the productivity of paradox in democratic politics are sometimes accused of "democratic mysticism."[1]

In this chapter I build on the foregoing account of the postrevolutionary
double inscription of the people. Through an exploration of select speeches
and essays by the radical American abolitionist Frederick Douglass, I argue
that we can learn important lessons about the peculiarities of democratic
claims making from an understanding of the people not as a unified subject,
or what Ernesto Laclau calls a "social datum," or as a "legitimating fiction"
or as "impersonal networks of intersubjective communication."[2] Rather,
here I propose an understanding of the people as a form of political subjectification enacted through the simultaneous claiming of the two poles that
Agamben describes: the people as at one and the same time the legitimating "fount of all political power" and that which lies beyond the pale of its
authorizing claims. Unlike Agamben, however, I do not believe that this
internal division need culminate in a "biopolitical plan to produce a people
without fracture."[3] To the contrary, Douglass's speeches transmit an understanding of the people as a form of political subjectification enacted by what
Jacques Rancière describes as "the part that has no part in the name of the
whole."[4] My reading of Douglass is therefore inspired by Rancière's insight
that "the fact that the people are internally divided is not . . . a scandal to be
deplored . . . [so much as] the primary condition of the exercise of politics."[5]

I will initially focus my discussion on Douglass's most celebrated address, "The Meaning of July Fourth for the Negro," delivered on July 5,
1852, before a largely white antislavery society in Rochester, New York.[6] In
this address Douglass exemplified the form of political subjectification that
I call a constituent moment. As previously described [in *Constituent Moments*], constituent moments enact felicitous claims to speak in the people's
name, even though those claims explicitly break from the authorized procedures or norms for representing popular voice. The dilemmas of authorization that spring from these moments appear, as we have seen, in the formal
political settings of constitutional conventions and political associations as
well as in the relatively informal political contexts of crowd actions, political oratory, and literature. While having no authorization to speak for the
people, Douglass—an escaped slave, one sans part—nonetheless claimed

to speak on their behalf. Douglass made this claim from an indeterminate or paradoxical position, insofar as he spoke at once as a slave—representing in his words "a people long dumb, not allowed to speak for themselves"— and as part of a political collectivity still without social determination.[7] This rhetorical positioning extracted Douglass from dominant categories of identification and classification (escaped African slave, racially determined or historically monumental invocations of the American people) while simultaneously setting the stage for a new political subject's emergence. In his Fourth of July address Douglass both spoke from outside the people to whom his speech was addressed and claimed to speak in their higher name.[8]

In doing so Douglass reveals in his Fourth of July address how democratic claims made by the part that has no part in the name of the whole reiterate in everyday rhetorical contexts dilemmas of popular authorization that democratic theorists have typically associated with and isolated in founding moments. "How can a people give birth to itself as a political subject?" becomes "Who are they—the uncounted, the subordinate, the low—to make claims at once *against and on the part of* the whole?" In both instances the grounds of authorization are absent, and the contingency underlying the existing system of rule is revealed. In both cases authorization arrives too late, after the fact of its proclamation. Throughout his work Douglass claims a continuity between the revolutionary events memorialized by the Fourth of July holiday—the events enacted by what he describes as "agitators and rebels, dangerous men"—and his own struggle against the organization of slave power.[9] Yet he establishes this connection in a manner generally overlooked by scholars who focus solely on analyzing the manifest content of Douglass's speech—emphasizing, for example, his appeal to natural law, liberalism, antislavery constitutionalism, or millennial providentialism—while neglecting the dramatic *staging* of the address itself.[10] Widely accepted interpretations of Douglass that turn on his unparalleled use of historically situated immanent critique, his rhetorical appeal to commonly held principles—"that all men are created equal" or "that they are endowed by their creator with certain unalienable rights"—to critique existing political practice overlook the break implied by the prior staging of these (only then) recognizable claims. Rancière's recent work on aesthetics and politics rigorously attends to this problem of staging. He describes this intervention into the political distribution of the sensible as a political poetics.[11]

I contend that an approach paying attention to this poetics or conflictual staging better captures the historical efficacy and challenge of Douglass's celebrated forms of public address than do interpretations that subsume his speeches into one ideological paradigm or another. Such attempts wrongly presume an equality of the speaking subject or a unified space of representation in assessing the meaning of Douglass's address. This presumption not only is theoretically problematic, in that it neglects the underlying dilemmas of authorization entailed by the "peculiar situation" of Douglass's speech, but also contributes to a misunderstanding of the speech's historical effectivity.[12] By emphasizing the *absence* of such an equal space of communicative exchange, Rancière's work helps to illuminate aspects of Douglass's famous speech that most attempts to slot it into familiar ideological paradigms have obscured. The Douglass that emerges from this encounter offers important insights into the fraught dynamics of democratic claims making.

In the Fourth of July address Douglass staged what Rancière characterizes as the "*demonstration* proper to politics," which "is always both argument and opening up the world where argument can be received and have an impact—argument about every existence of such a world."[13] One of Douglass's contemporaries, the poet James Russell Lowell, indicated this demonstrative dimension of Douglass's "argument," its prior "opening up the world," when he wrote that "the very look and bearing of Douglass are an irresistible logic against the oppression of his race."[14] Such staging precedes and enables Douglass's argument; it enacts a prior demonstration that is necessary for the audience to properly "hear" the arguments of Douglass's speech as arguments that have a claim on them. The demonstration must first *convert* them into the kind of people who could themselves retrospectively authorize such a claim. This staging first "makes visible that which had no reason to be seen"; it "lodges one world into another."[15]

The emphasis on staging shifts the narrative focus of revolutionary commemoration invoked in Douglass's address from juridical rights incompletely applied to the people incompletely enacted, from legal recognition to the democratic struggles that demand them. Thus understood, Douglass's claims are much more radical and less easily assimilable than familiar retrospective narratives of constitutional development allow—that is, those narratives emphasizing the historical overcoming of contradictions that purportedly existed between the universality of the rights declared in the Declaration of Independence or the preamble to the Constitution and the particularity of their historical application to "white, propertied, Christian, North American male heads of household."[16] Taking orientation from Douglass's example does not mean retrospectively confirming an underlying (or overlapping) liberal consensus but being more receptive to the emergent claims that fall outside this consensus. Douglass was deeply suspicious of retrospective appeals to common principle that animated the forces of reconciliation and solace, noting for example how the "cause of liberty may be stabbed by the men who glory in the deeds of [the] fathers."[17] In contrast to self-congratulatory narratives of historical reconciliation, Douglass offers a narrative of the American past that equates its full comprehension with ever-emergent forms of transformative democratic action and "unsettlement." Unlike familiar, dialectical narratives of unfolding universal rights, the enactment and reenactment of the people as presented by Douglass are not uniformly linear but rather a punctuated and unpredictable history of democratic claims making—a changed emphasis with distinct theoretical consequences explored below.

Finally, this chapter's focus on staging also illuminates the connections between the formal and constitutional dimensions of Douglass's speeches—the dissensus that they enact within the representational space of political remembrance and constitutional law—and the contentions enacted in daily life over the reigning distribution of places and roles. In Rancière's words, staging "decomposes and recomposes the relationships between ways of *doing*, of *being*, of *saying* that define the perceptible organization of the community."[18] The concept of the staging of dissensus illuminates the interdependence of the macropolitical and micropolitical dimensions of Douglass's abolitionist politics. This chapter therefore explores Douglass's consideration of the power of claims enacted through practice as well as speech, through the transgressive occupation of different places and roles. It concludes by reflecting on how the civil rights activist and novelist James Baldwin—one of Douglass's great twentieth-century admirers—both extended and reiterated this conflictual staging in his own writing on America's ambivalent revolutionary inheritance.

I

Douglass's Fourth of July address, commonly celebrated as the greatest of abolition speeches, was delivered before five to six hundred people in Corinthian Hall, a neoclassical theater built in 1849 and Rochester's premier lecture hall; Susan B. Anthony, Ralph Waldo Emerson, Charles Dickens, William H. Seward, and William Lloyd Garrison all addressed audiences there. Douglass was asked to deliver the address by the Rochester Ladies' Anti-Slavery Society, and he was prominently billed as the featured speaker in the placards advertising the event. His address was preceded by an opening prayer and the customary reading of the Declaration of Independence by the Syracuse preacher Robert R. Raymond. What followed Raymond's somber invocation of the nation's founding principles was an unexpected break from the established protocols of epideictic Fourth of July address. Douglass—the era's most prominent black abolitionist—radically reappropriated America's revolutionary topoi.[19] He tapped a rhetorical countertradition that positioned the insurgent or escaped slave as the inheritor of America's "unfinished revolution."

Douglass navigated this speech situation's peculiar demands through a careful—and to his audience no doubt unexpected and shocking—series of rhetorical maneuvers.[20] His address enacted a powerful evasion of his audience's doctrine of assumptions, refusing the rhetorical commonplace and the obligatory commemoration of the "nation's jubilee." Rather than monumentalize the revolutionary generation's deeds, Douglass provocatively suggested that these deeds had been drained of their significance through the very acts of ceremonial repetition he was called on to perform: "The causes which led to the separation of the colonies from the British crown," Douglass remarked in his opening, "have never lacked for a tongue. They have been taught in your common schools, narrated at your firesides, unfolded from your pulpits, and thundered from your legislative halls, and are as familiar to you as household words. . . . [T]he American side of any question may be safely left in American hands."[21] Douglass's provocative separation of his own perspective from "the American side" marked a clear break from traditional Fourth of July oratory while also, eventually, claiming his own inheritance of the revolution and of the people it declares. Through this rhetorical doubling Douglass transformed the revolution from a "rational, orderly, natural, conservative," and, most importantly, completed event to one "demanding sacrifice, unfinished."[22]

Douglass broke with the anticipated repertoires of Fourth of July address most dramatically by refusing the traditional identification of speaker and audience in a rhetorical invocation of a national and unified "we." His use of apostrophe, moreover, took this denial beyond the scope of his assembled audience to a wider if undefined public. Although he opened his speech with an appeal to his "fellow citizens," Douglass quickly proceeded to remark on the injustice hidden in this falsely unifying gesture. By establishing his own exclusion from the nation's annual festival of self-regard, by establishing a sharp boundary between "you" and "me," Douglass set himself apart from his audience. He thus rejected the self-celebration of the "good people" and struck an unexpectedly discordant note: "The purpose of this celebration is the Fourth of July. It is the birthday of your National Independence, and of your political freedom. This, to you, is what the Passover was to the emancipated people of God. It carries your minds back to the day, and to the act of your great deliverance."[23] Douglass's repeated *disidentification* creates a rhetorical perspective from which the audience can see itself anew—as a chosen people, yes, but internally divided, haunted by disavowed violence or injustice. Douglass not only emphasizes his inability to partake in the national celebration but suggests that the very cause and animating principles celebrated by his audience are the basis of his exclusion: "The sunlight that brought life and healing to you, has brought stripes and death to me. This Fourth of July is *yours,* not *mine. You* may rejoice, *I* must mourn."[24]

In refusing the anticipated assertion of a rhetorical commonplace, common principles, or a unitary "we," Douglass also called attention to the power organizing the speech situation itself, thereby staging the absence of a space of equal communicative exchange. Douglass elaborated on his understanding of "the peculiar relation subsisting" between him and the audience he was about to address in an oration given the following year to another largely white antislavery audience in New York. "I am a colored man, and this is a white audience. No colored man . . . can stand before an American audience without an intense and painful sense of the immense disadvantage under which he labors. . . . The ground which a colored man occupies in this country is every inch of it sternly disputed. . . . It is, perhaps, creditable to the American people . . . that they listen eagerly to the report of wrongs endured by distant nations. . . . But for my poor people enslaved— blasted and ruined—it would appear that America had neither justice, mercy nor religion. *She has no scales in which to weigh our wrongs—she has no standard by which to measure our rights.* Just here lies the difficulty of my cause. It is found in the fact that . . . we may not avail ourselves of admitted American principles. . . . Our position is anomalous, unequal, and extraordinary."[25] Douglass connects this immeasurable and extraordinary injustice to an incapacity of speaking and hearing. The absence of "scales" and "standard" to measure the wrongs of a "blasted and ruined" people, while facilitating the moral orientation toward *other* peoples, places these extraordinary anomalies below the threshold of recognition and justice and renders African Americans incapable of having their claims heard as claims. They have *phônê* but no logos.[26] There are no common standards here capable of adjudicating between competing claims, no unitary space of representation; their wrongs cannot be resolved through judicial procedures. The "peculiar relation," the "anomalous, unequal, and extraordinary" position described in Douglass's address, is a consequence of being denied a place from which a claim can be made on behalf of "admitted American principles." If Douglass cannot avail himself of these principles, if he cannot speak from within or among the unified position of "we the people," then from where does he speak? What is the necessary supplement for registering his claims as claims?

The most obvious answer would be to say—and Douglass himself at times *does* say—that Douglass speaks on behalf of the enslaved, advocating "for a people long dumb, not allowed to speak for themselves." Douglass was widely proclaimed, as stated in the *New York Times* in 1872, "the representative orator of the colored race."[27] But Douglass's understanding of race—a lively and controversial topic in the scholarship—is inseparable from the relationship of the part with no part in relation to the whole. Douglass refused to speak from a racially unmarked position and railed against those who did: "I utterly abhor and spurn with all contempt possible that cowardly meanness . . . which leads any colored man to repudiate his connection with his race. . . . [A]s a colored man I do speak—as a colored man I was invited here to speak—and as a colored man there are peculiar reasons for my speaking. The man struck is the man to cry out. I would place myself—nay, I am placed among the victims of American oppression. I view the subject from their standpoint—and scan the moral and political horizon of the country with their hopes, their fears, and their intense solicitude."[28] For Douglass race was a consequence of shared experiences of oppression and of shared struggle *against* oppression: "*The man struck is the man to cry out.*" Douglass claimed to speak from a particular position or perspective, but the position could only be understood as a relation to the whole that excluded it. For Douglass there was no speaking position wholly removed from the hegemonic, white "we the people" that oppressed and defined him, but neither could he speak from within this position. Although Douglass clearly rejected the "mystic racial chauvinism" that emerged alongside racialized nineteenth-century conceptions of the nation, it is misleading simply to ascribe to him a universalist position. Scholarly attempts to position Douglass as the principal representative of the "assimilationist" tradition in African American political thought or that criticize him as nineteenth-century America's greatest example of "racial liberalism" elide the complexity of Douglass's rhetorical claims, reducing them to a set of "positions."[29] That complexity and the source of those claims' power lay in Douglass's *refusal* of the opposition between racial particularism (a standpoint epistemology) and the supposed unmarked universalism of racial liberalism. Douglass's staging of dissensus refuses the terms of what Bernard Boxill has called the "two traditions in African American political philosophy."[30]

The staging of Douglass's "we the people" is revealed in what Eddie S. Glaude has described as Douglass's "ambiguously rich notion of we'ness."[31] Douglass's rhetorical "we the people" highlights its politically constructed character. He denies his public the captivating self-certitude of a falsely unifying we, highlighting the we as a fragile and highly contested political achievement. Douglass refused to simply proclaim a we on behalf of an already constituted political identity, whether the black or the constitutionally organized white people. Douglass spoke on behalf of a people that was not . . . yet. Doing so, he illuminated the politically performative dimension of any claim to speak on behalf of a "we." The "we," as Émile Benveniste argues, never speaks in its own name—a we can never say we. The "we" is always a question of "drawing a line" and "summoning a collective."[32] The political valence of this "summoning" is all the more acute when the "we" invoked is understood, as it was for Douglass, as "an original supreme Sovereign, [an] absolute and uncontrollable, earthly power," and when the claimant has no place within its authorizing claims.

Douglass's attachment to the authority of "we the people," along with his regular invocation of the tropes of American exceptionalism, has led many readers to contain the radicalism of his claims within a consensual or dialectically unfolding liberalism. Along with Martin Luther King's "Letter from the Birmingham City Jail" (1963), Douglass's Fourth of July address is commonly invoked as a paradigmatic instance of immanent critique in the dissenting traditions of American political thought.[33] The address is held up as a powerful example of what Michael Walzer calls "connected criticism." A connected critic, Walzer explains, "starts, say, from the views of justice embedded in the covenantal code . . . on the assumption that what is actual in consciousness is possible in practice, and then he challenges the practices that fall short of these possibilities."[34] According to this approach, Douglass exposes a *contradiction* between the universality of the principle and the historical particularity of its application. He affirms the underlying principles that are said to animate the "nation's jubilee"—the Declaration's "all men were created equal," for example, or the righteous morality of a humanistic Christianity—and then exposes the hypocrisy of declaring these principles in a country that accepted the conversion of black men, women, and children into slaveholder's property. Some find in this a reason to celebrate Douglass; others find in it reason to critique how his speeches reaffirmed an ideological hegemony even as they called for dissent—how, in Sacvan Bercovitch's words, they "enlisted radicalism itself in the cause of institutional stability."[35]

There is much textual support for this interpretation. As Douglass declares in the Fourth of July address, to the slave "your celebration is a sham; . . . your shouts of liberty and equality, hollow mockery; your prayers and hymns mere bombast, fraud, deception, impiety and hypocrisy—a thin veil to cover up crimes which would disgrace a nation of savages. There is not a nation on the earth guilty of practices, more shocking and bloody, than are the people of these United States, at this very hour."[36] After experiencing the force and precision of such devastating claims, it seems all too delicate to reduce these hypocrisies to mere "national inconsistencies," but Douglass repeatedly affirms the proclaimed principles of white Americans as the basis of his critique of their failure to live up to these principles. As he writes in his second autobiography, *My Bondage and My Freedom* (1855), "The slaveholder . . . never lisps a syllable in commendation of the fathers of this republic . . . without inviting the knife to his own throat, and asserting the right of rebellion for his own slaves."[37] However, he also emphasizes the absence of *"scales in which to weigh our wrongs"* and "the fact that . . . we may not avail ourselves of admitted American principles."

While the emphasis on immanent critique is true as far as it goes, and it surely explains some of the persuasive power of Douglass's rhetoric, it also overlooks the underauthorized performativity of his claims. The assimilationist or "racial liberal" interpretation of Douglass neglects the extent to which his enactment of the people would radically change the very people in whose name it is enacted. It neglects the complicated position from which Douglass spoke as well as the explicitly thematized (in)audibility of his speech. Not only does Douglass return to the contested and constructed character of the authorizing "we," but he also emphasizes that before any substantive appeal to principle can be claimed, the claim must first be heard as a claim. Douglass insists time and again that he is not asking for "mercy" or "pity," but to be heard as one with a claim—that is, one making "an *inconsiderate, impertinent and absurd claim to citizenship.*"[38] As he said in 1853 in an address on behalf of the "Colored Convention": "Notwithstanding the impositions and deprivations which have fettered us— notwithstanding the disabilities and liabilities, pending and impending— notwithstanding the cunning, cruel, and scandalous efforts to blot out that right, we declare that we are, and of right ought to be *American citizens.* We claim this right, and we claim all the rights and privileges, and duties which, properly, attach to it."[39]

Approaches that focus solely on the substance of Douglass's claims (for example, his invocation of natural law) pay insufficient heed to the position from which he was making them or on the staging of the claims.[40] Who is *he*, after all, to be speaking for *them?* In the Fourth of July address Douglass acted as both a subject who lacked the rights that he had (his division between *you* and *me*) and one who had the rights that he lacked (in his very speaking of these claims). Doing so, he staged the logic of dissensus: he "put two worlds in one and the same world."[41] In the Fourth of July address and in many of Douglass's other speeches and texts from this volatile period leading up to the Civil War, the centrally reiterated, radical, and unavoidable claim is that Douglass *better* represents the destiny of the people he at once addresses and is excluded from than do their official representatives in Congress, their spokesmen in political parties, or the constitutional authority of the Supreme Court. It is in this sense that Douglass's address exemplifies a constituent moment.

II

The dilemma of popular authorization navigated in Douglass's rhetorical invocation of the "we" is also central to his understanding of constitutional authorization, or what I will characterize as Douglass's popular constitutionalism. Douglass addressed this dilemma most explicitly in a speech that he gave shortly after Chief Justice Roger B. Taney's infamous *Dred Scott* decision in 1857, which stated that all people of African descent, both free and slave, were not and could never be fully enfranchised citizens of the United States. The decision effectively overturned the Missouri Compromise of 1820, which had prevented the further spread of slavery into northern and western states and legitimated the extension of slavery throughout the (soon to be divided) union. It was therefore not only the constitutionality of the Missouri Compromise that was at issue but also the threatened nationalization of slavery itself.

Douglass's response to this disastrous decision not only took issue with the particulars of Taney's constitutional interpretation (in particular his narrowly juridical understanding of the preamble's invocation of "We the People") but also, and relatedly, questioned the judicial supremacy of the Supreme Court. Tapping revolutionary traditions of popular constitutionalism, Douglass refused to acknowledge the final authority of this latest judicial attempt to "settle" the slavery question. Douglass, like many black abolitionists who resisted William Lloyd Garrison's anticonstitutionalism, fully understood the invariant *politics* of constitutional interpretation. As Donald G. Nieman writes, many nineteenth-century "black leaders understood that the general language of the constitution made it a malleable document whose meaning was subject to redefinition through political and legal processes, that the polity was, in a sense, an ongoing constitutional convention."[42] The failure of settlement and the perpetuation of political contest over the issue rested for Douglass in the incomplete enactment of the people declared by the "RING-BOLT" of the nation's destiny, by the self-creating constituent power of the people. "Loud and exultingly have we been told that the slavery question is settled, and settled forever. You remember it was settled thirty-seven years ago, when Missouri was admitted into the Union. . . . Just fifteen years afterwards, it was settled again. . . . Ten years after this it was settled again by the annexation of Texas. . . . In 1850 [with the Fugitive Slave Law] it was again settled. This was called the final settlement. By it slavery was virtually declared to be the equal of Liberty. . . . Four years after this settlement, the whole question was once more settled, and settled by a settlement which unsettled all the former settlements."[43]

In sharp contrast to Garrisonian abolitionists, who construed the United States Constitution as a "covenant with death, and agreement with hell,"

Douglass had faith in a democratic politics of unsettlement that he believed the Constitution authorized. This faith emerged from a belief that the interpretive authority of the Constitution rested not with governmental agencies or in the balanced relationship between them, but ultimately with "the people themselves."[44] Douglass's occasional invocation of the work of radical antislavery constitutionalists such as Lysander Spooner, William Goodell, Beriah Green, and Gerrit Smith situates him within this broad tradition of constitutional radicalism. Robert Cover, Wayne D. Moore, and William M. Wiecek have traced these traditions of popular constitutionalism within the abolitionist movement, and each has singled out the particular importance of Douglass.[45] "The collected writings of Frederick Douglass," David E. Schrader summarizes, "give us a kind of record of the dispute on constitutional interpretation within the abolitionist movement."[46] Douglass's reliance on the people's interpretive authority poses difficulties for scholars who have either admired or criticized his invocation of "original intent" as a basis of constitutional interpretation. As Douglass announced in his Fourth of July address, "I hold that every American citizen has a right to form an opinion of the constitution, and to propagate that opinion, and to use all honorable means to make his opinions the prevailing one"[47] The constitutional politics that Douglass advocated often revolved around what constituted such "honorable means," but the redemptive model of the revolution and its clear resonance with Douglass's struggle for independence as an escaped slave highlighted the fraught nature of Douglass's political claims. "Douglass's greatest need," Robert Cover writes, "was for a vision of law that both validated his freedom and integrated norms with a future redemptive possibility for his people. . . . [He embraced] a vision of an alternative world in which the entire order of American slavery would be without foundation in law."[48] For Douglass the Garrisonian refusal to make a constitutional claim in the people's name was ultimately an abdication of political responsibility. "Dissolve the Union, on this issue, and you delude the people of the free States with the false notion that their responsibilities have ceased, though the slaves remain in bondage."[49]

Douglass's popular constitutionalism led him not only to reject the judicial supremacy implied by Taney's decision; it was also the central objection that he made to the *substance* of the decision. Of particular importance to Douglass's argument was his rejection of Taney's basis for the denial of citizenship rights—that is, African ancestry. As Taney wrote in his decision,

"The words 'people of the United States' and 'citizens' are synonymous terms. . . . They both describe the political body who . . . form the sovereignty. . . . The question before us is, whether the class of persons described in the plea in abatement [people of African ancestry] compose a portion of this people, and are constituent members of this sovereignty? We think they are not, and that they are not included . . . under the word 'citizens' in the Constitution, and can therefore claim none of the rights and privileges which that instrument provides for . . . citizens."[50] Douglass refuses this foundational equation of "the people" with "citizen," juridically defined (and, for Taney, also racially defined). Turning to the preamble's invocation of "We the People," Douglass writes in response: "We the people—not we the white people—not we, the citizens, or the legal voters—not we, the privileged class, and excluding all other classes but we the people; not we, the horses and cattle, but we the people—the men and women, the human inhabitants of the United States, do ordain and establish this Constitution, &c."[51] Douglass believed that the preamble to the Constitution provided sufficient legal basis to eradicate slavery. As James A. Colaiaco writes, "Douglass considered the Preamble, like the Declaration of Independence, as a part of the nation's fundamental law. For him, the key to interpreting all sections and clauses of the constitution lay in comprehending its purpose in light of the language of the Preamble, which reveals the moral aspirations of the framers."[52] However, what Douglass emphasizes here is not simply "moral aspirations" but the people's political capacity for democratic self-creation. Douglass's faith in popular sovereignty has to be emphasized, particularly when considered alongside the period's usual invocation of popular sovereignty as a way of justifying slavery and the inviolability of states' rights (consider the popular-sovereignty positions staked out by John Calhoun or Stephen Douglas). By locating constitutional authorship in "the human inhabitants of the United States," Douglass may seem to give the "people" a seemingly unambiguous referent in the territory's population, but the argument actually works to reveal again the always partial nature of any claim to speak in the people's name. In basing its authority in the people, Douglass's democratic constitutionalism continually condemned its own inevitable denial of inclusion and equality; it revealed the contestability of any boundary around the authorizing "we." "By claiming membership among 'the people,'" Wayne D. Moore has written, Douglass "*presumed* to be among those able to maintain (reauthorize) constitutional forms to represent the people's collective and separate political identities."[53] Douglass enacted the very popular and nonjuridical claiming that he argued for in the substance of his claim.

III

The language of presumption and claim highlights another important aspect of Douglass's work—and its connection to the form of political subjectification I am exploring here—in that it indicates his persistent refusal to *justify* his claim to speak in the name of "We the People." As noted above, Douglass frequently thematized the conditions required to hear of his claims *as claims*. He broke "the logic of expression" and refused to apply words "to their assigned mode of speaking."[54] This refusal is explicit in his Fourth of July address. Like many abolitionist writers—constitutionalists and anticonstitutionalists alike—Douglass was occasionally compelled to respond to critics who, while admiring the goals and principles of abolitionism, were nonetheless shocked by its manner and style. "I fancy I hear some one of my audience say," Douglass says in the Fourth of July address, "that you and your brother abolitionists fail to make a favorable impression on the public mind. Would you argue more, and denounce less . . . your cause would be much more likely to succeed."[55] The voices of deliberative moderation—then as now—tend to presume a speech situation of communicative parity. Yet, as already discussed, according to Douglass it is the very parity of the speaking situation that cannot be presumed, its absence marking the "peculiarity" of his situation in relation to his audience. Because of this situation, appeals to reasoned argument are misplaced. Douglass continues: "At a time like this, scorching irony, not convincing argument, is needed. O! had I the ability, and could I reach the nation's ear, I would, to-day, pour out a fiery stream of biting ridicule, blasting reproach, withering sarcasm, and stern rebuke. For it is not the light that is needed, but fire. . . . The feeling of the nation must be quickened; the conscience of the nation must be roused; the propriety of the nation must be startled."[56] Quickened, roused, startled: Douglass's insights into the democratic importance of nondeliberative discourse and claims-making practices were not unique to him but a central component of abolition's public sphere.[57]

The distance between the abolitionist public sphere and the deliberative publics celebrated by recent theorists of political liberalism is further demonstrated in the radical Garrisonian Wendell Phillips's *Philosophy of the Abolition Movement* (1854), which explored the manner and language of abolitionist claims. Like Douglass in the Fourth of July address, Phillips responded to common charges that "in dealing with slaveholders and their apologists, we indulge in fierce denunciations, instead of appealing to their reason and common sense by plain statement and fair argument."[58] Also like Douglass, Phillips emphasized the importance of these radical denunciations to piercing the "crust of . . . prejudice or indifference."[59] Such claims, he writes, were essential not to "convincing" their public of the rightness of their cause but to "converting" them to it. "How else," Phillips asks, "shall a feeble minority . . . with no jury of millions to appeal to—denounced, vilified, and contemned—how shall we make way against the overwhelming weight of some colossal reputation?"[60] As with Douglass's claim to a people that was not . . . yet, Phillips engages here in an explicitly prophetic mode of speech: "We are weak here—out-talked, out-voted. You load our names with infamy, and shout us down. But our words bide their time. We warn the living that we have terrible memories, and that their sins are to never be forgotten."[61] Both men stake their claims on an authority that was to be realized only in the future; both enact through their address a prospective orientation to time.

Because of this fiery invocation of the divine and the fierce denunciation of the injustice of existing law, liberal theorists have, in William Rogers's words, traditionally "display[ed] a certain uneasiness and awkwardness in their treatment of antebellum reform movements like abolition."[62] Considering abolitionists' sensitivity to power in their acts of claims making, their refusal to engage in common deliberation or dwell on public justifications, and their insistence on prophetic speech, it is curious that a number of contemporary democratic theorists, and particularly those taken with the reigning deliberative paradigm, have returned to the abolitionists as a case study. A particularly relevant example can be found in John Rawls's discussion of public reason in *Political Liberalism*. Rawls asks whether the abolitionists went against "the ideal of public reason." He then urges that readers view this important question "conceptually" and not "historically." When the question is so viewed, according to Rawls, abolitionists like Phillips and Douglass "did not go against the ideal of public reason; or rather they did not provided they thought, or on reflection would have thought (as they certainly could have thought), . . . that the comprehensive reasons they appealed to were required to give sufficient strength to the political conception to be subsequently realized."[63] In other words, given the particularity of their historical conditions, it was not *unreasonable* for the abolitionists to appeal to comprehensive moral views and to refuse to subject them to the bar of public reason. Such unreasonable participation in the public sphere is, Rawls suggests, sometimes necessary to better establish the conditions for a more just and well-ordered society (in which such unreasonable political enactments would presumably no longer be necessary). As Amy Gutmann and Dennis Thompson similarly argue, "Some issues cannot even reach the political agenda unless some citizens are willing to act with passion, making statements and declarations rather than developing arguments and responses. When nondeliberative politics . . . are necessary to achieve deliberative ends, deliberative theory consistently suspends the requirements for deliberation."[64] In revisiting his arguments about public reason, Rawls argues even further that "new variations" of public reason must be allowed "from time to time" so that "claims of groups or interests arising from social change" will not be "repressed and fail to gain their appropriate political voice."[65] These claims, he avers, may even be based in particular comprehensive doctrines, with the "proviso" that "in due course proper political reasons . . . are presented" to justify or support their claim.[66]

The problem with these eminently reasonable arguments is that they confidently presume the possibility of easily assessing "deliberative ends" or "proper political reasons" in advance of the claims themselves. In contrast to Rawls, I think that these important questions should be viewed historically as well as conceptually. Viewed historically, the theoretical confidence of contemporary political liberals seems misplaced, and abolition provides a particularly acute example of the burdens of historical judgment. The conceptual confidence that these writers evince in a liberal political culture's ability to distinguish the temporarily unreasonable (but justified) from the simply unreasonable (and therefore illegitimate) depends on the ability to identify a kernel of justice, a "trace of reasonableness," within these claims. On this basis Rawls can argue that abolitionists like Douglass and Phillips *could* have argued according to the protocols of public reason and that given the opportunities for proper reflection they *would* have argued in this way. But the confident identification of such claims' justice tends to be retrospective.

In *retrospect*, the liberal political philosopher can see that these actions were easily subsumed within an unfolding and self-correcting constitutional tradition. This retrospection often does very little to support emerging political struggles. As William Connolly has argued, the dialectic of unfolding justice "always functions best as a retrospective description of movements that have already migrated from a place under-justice to a place on the register of justice/injustice."[67] The abolitionists certainly would not have passed the heuristic test that Rawls offers—"How would our arguments strike us presented in the form of a Supreme Court opinion? Reasonable? Outrageous?"[68] The abolitionist case in general and Douglass's life and work in particular suggest that such criteria not only fail to assist newly emergent democratic claims but may actively inhibit them. Robert Cover's analysis of how the legal order of slavery and its appeal to the rule of law undermined the legitimacy of claims for abolition is a powerful case study in this general dynamic.[69] Douglass himself was fully aware of it.

At several moments in Douglass's speeches he speaks out against the tendency to recall the principles of the past to reanimate reconciliation and inhibit the enactment of democratic "unsettlement." As Robert Fanuzzi has argued in his study of abolition's public sphere, Douglass and Garrison portrayed the movement as prophetically discordant with its own time. Abolition portrayed itself "as a rupture in the fabric of time, and as a suspension of orderly succession."[70] For Douglass this orientation was secured through a particular understanding of democratic "struggle" and "unsettlement" and his belief that contradictions of principle would not resolve themselves over time but that liberties would have to be presumptuously claimed. This is what he means, I think, when in a lecture titled "The Do-Nothing Policy" (1856) he writes: "The open sesame for the colored man is action! action! action!"[71] Or when in [the] speech "West India Emancipation" he says:

If there is no struggle there is no progress. Those who profess to favor freedom yet depreciate agitation, are men who want crops without plowing up the ground. . . . They want the ocean without the awful roar of its many waters. . . . *Power concedes nothing without demand.* It never did and it never will. Find out just what any people will quietly submit to and you have found out the exact measure of injustice and wrong that will be imposed upon them and these will continue until they are resisted with either words or blow, or with both. The limits of tyrants are prescribed by the endurance of those whom they oppress.[72]

This theme is central to *My Bondage and My Freedom.* In that text Douglass envisions an African American politics that rejects racial essentialism and that is born of agonistic political struggle. Douglass aspires not to bring African American life into conformity with the constitutive norms of the polity but to radically reimagine those norms. Douglass calls for neither recognition nor separation, but mutual transformation. It was moreover a transformative political struggle that he believed took place not only in the rhetorical contexts of political oration or in the formal contexts of legal interpretation but also on the conflicted terrain of everyday life.

IV

Douglass's Fourth of July address, like Rancière's theory of political dissensus, emphasizes the continuity between the constitutional and the everyday, between formal, juridical power and politics and their more quotidian manifestations, between the macropolitical and the micropolitical. The struggle and "unsettlement" that Douglass called for in the 1850s were not simply directed at laws or government policies or even at values, but at everyday activities, what Rancière describes as the "distribution of the sensible"—the regime of bodies, affects, and perceptions. Abolitionists commonly took this approach, directing reform efforts not just at citizens' opinion or policy reform. As Garrison put it in the prospectus to his newspaper the *Liberator,* to "abolitionize" is to engage "the people, the whole people in the work; every man, woman and every child."[73] The abolitionists' opponents also recognized this attempt to link legal reform with a more thoroughgoing reform of the social body. Russell Sullivan, author of the widely read *Letters against the Immediate Abolition of Slavery* (1835), wrote that Garrison and the Anti-Slavery Society had "commenced the agitation of a legal, constitutional, and political reform . . . by measures adopted to inflame the passions of the multitude, inducing the women and children, the boarding school misses and factory girls . . . upon the avowed plan of turning the current of popular opinion."[74]

    Among abolitionist writers Douglass may have had the most fully developed account of how slavery perpetuated itself not only through legal mechanisms, state power, and force but through a fully spiritualized despotism: "The whole relationship [of slavery] must not only demonstrate to [the slave's] mind its necessity, but also its absolute rightfulness."[75] At times

Douglass's sophisticated account of the "organization of slave power" is reminiscent of a Gramscian theory of hegemony. The slaveholding powers, he writes in his essay on the *Dred Scott* decision, enjoy "the advantage of complete organization":

> They are organized; and yet were not at the pains of creating their organizations. The State governments, where the system of slavery exists, are complete slavery organizations. The church organizations in those States are equally at the service of slavery; while the Federal Government, with its army and navy, from the chief magistracy in Washington, to the Supreme Court, and thence to the chief marshalship at New York, is pledged to support, defend, and propagate the crying curse of human bondage. The pen, the purse, and the sword are united against the simple truth, preached by humble men in obscure places.[76]

Just as Douglass's constitutional claim to a "We the People" transcends the state's constituted authority and the Supreme Court's decision-making power, so did he call to combat the "organization of slave power" at the informal level of daily life by resisting the various roles and social practices that perpetuated it. Douglass returns often to the question of how the "organization of slavery" may be daily resisted. If, as Pierre Bourdieu quips, what is essential about the "objective consensus on the sense of the world *goes without saying because it comes without saying*,"[77] enacted challenges to the regime of the visible or the sayable—to Douglass's "complete organization of power"—occur not just through explicit invocations of an impossible authorization (claiming to speak in the name of a people that is not . . . yet) or a competing set of values or principles but also in practical activity or staging that works to bring that world into being.

Thus in addition to embracing the democratic value of sarcasm, irony, and denunciation, Douglass suggested that the claims made on behalf of those who have no part are also practically enacted and in many ways acknowledged by their opponents in everyday life. In a moving passage revealing how the "organization of slave power" is based in myriad daily acknowledgments that undermine the slave owners' claim of natural white supremacy, Douglass offers a powerful example of how implied equality inhabits the very structure of hierarchical rule, thereby exposing the unsupportability of its claims and the contingency of its order: "Is it not astonishing that, while we are ploughing, planting, and reaping, using all kinds of mechanical tools, erecting houses, constructing bridges, building ships, working in metals of brass, iron, copper, silver, and gold; that while we are reading writing and ciphering, acting as clerks, merchants and secretaries, having among us law-yers, doctors, ministers, poets, authors, editors, orators, and teachers; that, while we are engaged in all manner of enterprises common to other men, digging gold in California, capturing the whale in the Pacific, feeding cattle on the hill side, living, moving, acting, thinking, planning, living in families as husbands, wives, and children, and, above all, confessing and worship-ping the Christian's God, and looking hopefully for life and immortality be-yond the grave, we are called upon to prove that we are men!"[78] This is not argument so much as it is showing. The "proof" of slave equality, denied in ideology and speech, may be nonetheless detected in everyday acts of acknowledgment that may implicitly corrode these discursive justifications. In a perceptive comment on this passage, Patchen Markell has argued that Douglass here is not calling for recognition or simply the debunking of the "false belief in the nonhumanity of the slave." Instead the passage reveals "a contradiction within the actual, a disavowal on the part of the slaveholder of part of the meaning of their [*sic*] own practices."[79] The implicit equality of making the command to comprehending subjects undermines the com-mand's self-evident legitimacy.

That former slaves could also be "lawyers, doctors, ministers, poets, authors, editors, orators, and teachers" unsettled the functional distribution of proper roles, eschewing sociological reductionism and highlighting the constructed quality of place. Douglass appreciated the power of enacting suspensions of these assigned modes of speaking and being, even those "as-signed" to him by his erstwhile white abolitionist supporters. In *My Bond-age and My Freedom* Douglass describes his painful break with Garrison and other advocates of moral suasion in just this way. While Garrison and others initially lionized Douglass and relied heavily on his personal experi-ence in slavery to mobilize support for their cause, they actively resisted his attempts to do more than speak from personal experience, his attempts not to be reduced to "experience" and "testimony." Douglass described white abolitionist attempts to pin him down to his "simple narrative" as yet an-other effort to keep blacks in their place. "Give us the facts," said one of his white abolitionist supporters, "we will take care of the philosophy."[80] For Douglass this well-meaning advice from white abolitionists relying on the sentimental authenticity of his experience was all too reminiscent of the meticulous orchestration of subservience and place under the "organization of slave power."

Already in his first autobiography, the *Narrative of the Life of Frederick Douglass* (1845), Douglass emphasized at some length how the cruel slave owner the Rev. Rigby Hopkins demanded and violently enforced small and daily acts of subservience and groveling deference from his slaves. "A mere look, word, or motion—a mistake, accident, or want of power—are all matters for which a slave may be whipped at any time."[81] Of course the Jim Crow laws quickly established throughout the American South in the wake of emancipation and failed Reconstruction also recognized the quotidian dimensions of domination and worked to more carefully legislate the micropolitical segregation of races, further insinuating white supremacy into the fabric of everyday life. This quotidian domination became a central site for the staged confrontations of the civil rights movements in the following century, when claims to enact a people that is not yet took the form of proliferating acts of civil disobedience aimed to intervene at this micropolitical level as well as at the level of the formal institutions of government and law.

Just over a century after Douglass's Fourth of July address, James Baldwin, in an essay titled "They Can't Turn Back" (1960), elegantly captured the quotidian dimensions of what Rancière calls the order of the "police," which "stems as much from the assumed spontaneity of social relations as from the rigidity of state functions," while also suggesting how this order might be challenged and transformed (an enacted "redistribution of the sensible") through political activity that "shifts a body from the place assigned to it or changes a place's destination."[82] Baldwin did so by recounting the intricate orchestration of power through gesture and manner in the postwar South:

I am the only Negro passenger at Tallahassee's shambles of an airport. It is an oppressively sunny day. A black chauffeur, leading a small dog on a leash, is meeting his white employer. He is attentive to the dog, covertly very aware of me and respectful of her in a curiously watchful, waiting way. She is middle aged, beaming and powdery faced, delighted to see both the beings who make her life agreeable. I am sure that it has never occurred to her that either of them has the ability to judge her or would judge her harshly. She might almost, as she goes toward her chauffeur, be greeting a friend. No friend could make her face brighter. If she were smiling at me that way I would expect to shake her hand. But if I should put out my hand, panic, bafflement, and horror would then overtake that face, the atmosphere would darken, and danger, even the threat of death, would immediately fill the air.

On such small signs and symbols does the southern cabbala depend. . . . The system of signs and nuances covers the mined terrain of the *unspoken—the forever unspeakable—and everyone in the region knows his way across* the field. This knowledge that a gesture can blow up a town is what the South refers to when it speaks of its "folkways."[83]

Baldwin's imagined outstretched hand may be construed as a claim made by those without part, a claim of equal reciprocity, a claim threatening the practical choreography of gesture and movement that reproduces the reigning order of places and roles; by Baldwin's account the simple act of outstretching a hand could have the effect of speaking the unspoken, revealing the contingency underlying the "mined terrain" of the social "field" as it threatens to "blow up" the town. It is notable that the darkening of the atmosphere described by Baldwin is occasioned not by an enemy who sets out to threaten or destroy but by a friend of sorts—a loyal servant who makes life "agreeable." Baldwin imagines not a direct challenge to the order that comes from without—a challenge much more easily legible and therefore combatable—but one that comes uncannily from within the "terrain of the unspoken." Like Douglass's invocation a century earlier of the "anomalous, unequal, and extraordinary" position of blacks in America, for whom there is no available "scale" or "standard," Baldwin's imagined action allows us to glimpse the "evidence of things not said."[84]

In *The Fire Next Time* (1963), Baldwin made clear that the stakes of the civil rights movement and its ultimate claims lay in bringing into being a new people, a new political subject, and it is here that I think the continuities between Baldwin and Douglass are most striking and that their work is most productive when viewed from the perspective of constituent moments. Baldwin, writing a century after the emancipation of the slaves failed to overturn the system of white supremacy, had a much greater appreciation than Douglass of the difficulties and the resistance to what he described as "history's strangest metamorphosis"; there is a tragic dimension in Baldwin's writing rarely present in Douglass's redemptive prose. Baldwin suggests that the mutually transformative dimension of the civil rights movement—its prophetic invocation of a people yet to come—explained the depth of southern white horror and resistance to the movement. For Baldwin the movement's ultimate claims were not simply about recognizing a formally excluded social group but a vertiginous challenge to the identities of both groups and the staging of the possible emergence of a new political subject (what Rancière calls a "third people"[85]). In the preface to *The Fire Next Time,* Baldwin writes, "The danger in the minds of most white Americans, is the loss of their identity. Try to imagine how you would feel if you woke up one morning to find the sun shining and all the stars aflame. You would be frightened because it is out of the order of nature. Any upheaval in the universe is terrifying because it so profoundly attack's one's sense of one's own reality. Well, the black man has functioned in the white man's world as a fixed star, as an immovable pillar: and as he moves out of his place, heaven and earth are shaken to their foundations."[86] Baldwin's invocation of how the black man's moving out of his place shakes the foundations of the order of nature is at once figurative and literal; he suggests the close correlation between social and literal place and how challenges to the former often imply reorganizing the latter. It is the vertigo produced by the exposure of the contingency of the order, on Baldwin's account, that helps to explain the fury elicited to sustain it.

African American college students who began sitting in at segregated lunch counters in Greensboro, North Carolina, in February 1960 and soon thereafter in Nashville and throughout the South shattered the prevailing southern myth of "good race relations" and dramatized the shifting of the "fixed star" of race through the occupation of places where they should not be seen. As the historian Jason Sokol has recently written, the system of southern racial segregation, codified in Jim Crow laws and buttressed by everyday behavior, was directly confronted by the spatial tactics of the movement's acts of civil disobedience. The occupation of different spaces in the movement's quest to reorganize social roles so scrambled prevailing white southern understandings of the affectionate relations between the races that most white southerners immediately attributed the activism to the influence of outside agitators—Communists, the NAACP, northern liberals, and so on—seeking comfort in the idea that this challenge came from outside rather than from within. Sokol suggests that this physical occupation and the interruption of the choreography of power in the South brought home to white southerners their world's fraying fabric. Sokol quotes one white woman as saying, "The Negroes I now knew bore little resemblance to the Negro I had envisaged since childhood. . . . No greater dislocation of my thought and emotion could have resulted if I had been catapulted to another planet."[87] Rancière theorizes this dynamic when he writes, "Political subjectification redefines the field of experience that gave to each their identity with their lot. It decomposes and recomposes the relationships between ways of *doing,* of *being,* of *saying* that define the perceptible organization of the community, the relationship between where one does one thing and those where one does something else, the capacities associated with this particular *doing* and those required for another."[88] The redistribution of the sensible that Rancière associates with this form of political subjectification sets a condition for the emergence of a new political subject, and it is just this political subject, this "strangest metamorphosis" into a "third people," that Baldwin invokes in his account of "liberation." Baldwin expressly did not mean by that term the emancipation of a given identity but the struggle to be free from the grip of inherited identities, the enactment of a new identity through mutually transformative political struggle.[89] "The possibility of liberation which is always real is also always painful, since it involves such an overhauling of all that gave us our identity. The Negro who will emerge out of this present struggle—whoever, indeed, this dark stranger may prove to be—will not be dependent, in any way at all, on any of the props and crutches which help form our identity now. And neither will the white man. We will need every ounce of moral stamina we can find. For everything is changing from our notion of politics to our notion of ourselves, and we are certain, as we begin history's strangest metamorphosis, to undergo the torment of being forced to surrender far more than we ever realized we had accepted."[90] In denying that this transformative process can be achieved without effecting the transformation of all parties to this shared inheritance of racial injustice, Baldwin, like Douglass before him, invoked a key political dilemma whose authority can only ever be prospective. Rather than base his claims in already constituted identities and subjects or simply on behalf of underlying principles on which existing parties can seemingly agree, he makes his claims in the name of the people that is not . . . yet. In his famous call to "achieve our country," Baldwin, too, remains firmly within the mythos of American exceptionalism, as his thought limns what Emerson called "this new yet unapproachable America" and what Langston Hughes invoked when he wrote, "let America be America again / the land that has never been yet."[91] Far from being a sign of ritualized consensus, in which such dissenting claims surreptitiously reinforce the reigning distribution of places and roles, these claims ask their audience not to simply reconfirm and reapply their existing moral commitments—to affirm the grounds of an overlapping consensus—but to abandon a part of themselves, to be besides themselves, to become subject of a collective transformation and to "undergo the torment of being forced to surrender far more than we ever realized we had accepted."[92] This is not to reaffirm a consensual rite of assent so much as to confront, time and again, that rite's inevitable failure.

As mentioned above, Douglass's Fourth of July address was actually delivered on the fifth of July. In the nineteenth century, black Americans celebrated a number of holidays and commemorations—New Year's Day festivals, West Indies Emancipation Day, New York Abolition Day, and others—that both marked their isolation from white America and hopefully commemorated unfulfilled movements of slave insurrection and emancipation.[93] These "freedom celebrations" quite literally staged a dissensus within the prevailing order of commemoration. On July 4, 1827, the State of New York outlawed slavery, and beginning in the following year numerous black communities began holding festive public celebrations to commemorate the event. To dramatize the "fundamental contradiction between the nation's commitment to democratic ideals and the practices of racial exclusion,"[94] most of these communities celebrated the holiday on July 5. Doing so, they drew attention to a time out of joint. Douglass's Fourth of July address, like the "holiday" on which it was performed, was an unusual commemoration insofar as it did not monumentalize the past or celebrate the already achieved independence of "we the people." Instead, it set the stage for the emergence of another people, a "third people."[95] Douglass offered a monument not to the past but to the future; his speech and the holiday on which it was delivered provided his audience—a virtual people—with a paradoxical commemoration of what will have been.

In the concluding sentence of *Invisible Man,* Ralph Ellison's nameless narrator asks the reader: "Who knows, but that on the lower frequencies I speak for you?"[96] From the perspective of constituent moments we might understand this question as an elementary or inaugurating political gesture, particularly when the claim is made by the invisible and the uncounted. Ellison's question dramatizes how in democratic contexts we are always caught taking the risk of speaking in one another's names, as well as [dramatizing] our inability to know if these claims are authorized until we make them, until we attempt to tap the "lower frequencies" of the audience of our address. We can never know in advance who is implicated by our claims to community.[97] That Ellison's questioning narrator is known only by his invisibility also dramatizes the peculiarity of the position from which such claims are made: the Invisible Man asks his question from an obscure hole in a basement, one flooded with the stolen energy of "Monopolated Light & Power."

Democracy may require us to imagine ourselves as speaking for others, to base our claims in an authority that always comes after the fact, but it does not provide rules to adjudicate impartially between those claims or definitively to determine their legitimacy before the fact of their enunciation. The people never emerge to speak in their own name. As Danielle Allen has written, "The people exists finally only in the imagination of democratic citizens who must think [and feel] themselves into this body in order to believe that they act through it."[98] Douglass's Fourth of July address suggests that to speak for others on the "lower frequencies" is not simply to tap a system of shared values, much less to speak from a position of delegated authority, but to stage a strange scene of interlocution, to stage a dissensus. Ellison's Invisible Man also claims to speak for an audience that cannot hear him, to stand for an audience that cannot see him. Although the political meaning of the people has always carried the double valence of the unified political subject and those excluded from politics, the term also contains another double meaning. The people has meant both the ordinary folk and a source of political redemption and renewal. The uncanny persistence of these founding dilemmas, these constituent moments, in the democratic scenarios of everyday life may enliven a sense not only of their precariousness but of their still untapped potentials. On the lower frequencies, we may still have it in our power to begin the world anew.

Notes

First published as "Staging Dissensus: Frederick Douglass and 'We the People,'" in Jason Frank, *Constituent Moments: Enacting the People in Postrevolutionary America* (Durham, NC: Duke University Press, 2010), 209–36, 292–97. Reprinted by permission of the copyright holder. www.dukeupress.edu.

1. Stephen Holmes, *Passions and Constraint: On the Theory of Liberal Democracy* (Chicago: University of Chicago Press, 1995), 167. Good examples of

contemporary democratic theorists who affirm the productivity of paradox are Emilios Christodoulidis, "The Aporia of Sovereignty," *King's College Law Journal* 12 (1) (2001): 111–33; William Connolly, *Political Theory and Modernity* (New York: Blackwell, 1988); and Alan Keenan, *Democracy in Question* (Stanford, CA: Stanford University Press, 2003).

2. For a canonical treatment of the people as a unified subject, see Jules Michelet, *The People* (Urbana: University of Illinois, 1973). By "social datum" Laclau refers to both the people as a sociological entity and the variety of social scientific attempts to empirically quantify the people through voting procedures, opinion polls, demographic studies, and so on. See Ernesto Laclau, *On Populist Reason* (New York: Verso, 2005), 224. Edmund Morgan shows how during the seventeenth century political "representatives invented the sovereignty of the people in order to claim it for themselves." In treating the people as a political fiction used to further expand the reach of state power, Morgan offers a one-sided account of the governmental logics of this fiction, neglecting how it enabled and inspired forms of popular contention against the state. See Edmund Morgan, *Inventing the People* (New York: Norton, 1989), 49–50. Habermas offers a picture of "desubstantialized" popular sovereignty: "Subjectless and anonymous, an intersubjectively dissolved popular sovereignty withdraws into democratic procedures and the demanding communicative presuppositions of their implementation." This democratic theory transubstantiates the people into a quite different form of democratic mysticism. See Jürgen Habermas, "Popular Sovereignty as Procedure," in *Between Facts and Norms: Contributions to a Discourse Theory of Law and Democracy* (Cambridge, MA: MIT Press, 1996), 466–81, 486.

3. Giorgio Agamben, "What Is a People?" in *Means without End: Notes on Politics*, ed. C. Casarino (Minneapolis: University of Minnesota Press, 2000), 33.

4. Jacques Rancière, *Dis-agreement: Politics and Philosophy* (Minneapolis: University of Minnesota Press, 1999), 1–19. Laclau's recent work positions his theory of articulation and the political logic of the empty signifier on very similar terrain as Rancière. "It is in the contamination of the universality of the *populus* by the partiality of the *plebs*," Laclau writes, "that the peculiarity of the 'people' as a historical actor lies." See Laclau, *On Populist Reason,* 224.

5. Jacques Rancière, "Who Is the Subject of the Rights of Man?" *South Atlantic Quarterly* 103 (2–3) (2004): 7.

6. Frederick Douglass, "What to the Slave Is the Fourth of July?" in David Hollinger and Charles Capper, eds., *The American Intellectual Tradition*, vol. 1: *1630–1865* (New York: Oxford University Press, 1993), 492–506.

7. Frederick Douglass, *Life and Times of Frederick Douglass* (New York: Collier, 1962), 375.

8. Alan Keenan has identified the paradoxical dimension of this task: "To lay the conditions for the people to become a people, one must appeal to the sense of

the people *as* a people; yet the success of that appeal depends on those conditions already being in place, or at the very least being imaginable. The paradoxical task of the legislator—or rather, of all democratic political actors—then, is to make an appeal that sets the conditions for its own proper reception; one must appeal to the political community in such a way that its members will accept the regulations that will make them into the kind of (general) people able to 'hear' such an appeal." See Keenan, *Democracy in Question*, 52.

9. Douglass, "What to the Slave Is the Fourth of July?" 494. [*Volume editor's note:* Where italics are used in quotations from Douglass and other authors in this chapter, the emphasis is given in the original unless otherwise noted.] Douglass makes this connection frequently in his writings, as when he writes that if the slave "kills his master, he imitates only the heroes of the revolution." See Frederick Douglass, *My Bondage and My Freedom*, ed. John David Smith (New York: Penguin, 2003), 283.

10. For an interpretation of Douglass that emphasizes natural law and "Lockean liberalism," see Bernard Boxill, "Two Traditions in African American Political Philosophy," *Philosophical Forum* 24 (1–3) (1992–1993): 119–35. On antislavery constitutionalism, see Wayne Moore, *Constitutional Rights and Powers of the People* (Princeton, NJ: Princeton University Press, 1996). On prophecy and millennial providentialism, see Eddie Glaude, *Exodus! Religion, Race, and Nation in Early Nineteenth-Century America* (Chicago: University of Chicago Press, 2000); William Rogers, *"We Are All Together Now": Frederick Douglass, William Lloyd Garrison, and the Prophetic Tradition* (New York: Routledge, 1995); and George Shulman, *American Prophecy: Race and Redemption in American Political Culture* (Minneapolis: University of Minnesota Press, 2008).

11. In his insistence on the inescapably "poetic" or aesthetic dimensions of politics, Rancière critiques Habermas's attempt in *The Philosophical Discourse of Modernity* to deflate the literary, poetic, metaphorical, or "world-disclosive" dimensions of language as secondary to the inherent telos of speech (mutual understanding). In addition to *Dis-agreement*, 43–60, see Jacques Rancière, "Dissenting Words," *Diacritics* 30 (2) (2000): 113–26; Jürgen Habermas, *The Philosophical Discourse of Modernity* (Cambridge, MA: MIT Press, 1987), 185–210. Nikolas Kompridis has brilliantly elaborated on Habermas's politically disabling neglect of "world disclosive" speech in *Critique and Disclosure* (Cambridge, MA: MIT Press, 2006).

12. The presence of the body inflects the meaning of the oration and the dissensus that it stages, something lost in most interpretations. For an interesting discussion of this issue, see Robert Fanuzzi, "Frederick Douglass's Public Body," in *Abolition's Public Sphere* (Minneapolis: University of Minnesota Press, 2003), 83–128.

13. Rancière, *Dis-agreement*, 56. Rancière offers the example of the plebeian secession at Aventine to explain this point: "The patricians at Aventine do not understand what the plebeians say; they do not understand the noises that come out of the plebeians' mouths, so that, in order to be audibly understood and visibly recognized as legitimate speaking subjects, the plebeians must not only argue their position but must also construct the scene of argumentation in such a manner that the patricians must recognize it as a world in common. It is necessary to 'invent a scene.'" See Rancière, "Dissenting Words," 125, 116.

14. Cited in James A. Colaiaco, *Frederick Douglass and the Fourth of July* (New York: Palgrave Macmillan, 2006), 24.

15. Jacques Rancière, "Ten Theses on Politics," *Theory and Event* 5 (3) (2001): 11 [available online at Project MUSE].

16. Seyla Benhabib, "Democracy and Difference," *Journal of Political Philosophy* 2 (1) (1994): 12.

17. Douglass, "What to the Slave Is the Fourth of July?" 494.

18. Rancière, *Dis-agreement*, 40.

19. Jacqueline Bacon, "'Do You Understand Your Own Language?': Revolutionary Topoi in the Rhetoric of African-American Abolitionists," *Rhetoric Society Quarterly* 28 (2) (1998): 55–75.

20. For an elaboration of the established repertoires and topoi of the nineteenth-century Fourth of July address, see John E. Bodnar, "Public Memory in Nineteenth-Century America: Background and Context," in *Remaking America: Public Memory, Commemoration, and Patriotism in the Twentieth Century* (Princeton, NJ: Princeton University Press, 1992), 21–38, and Howard H. Martin, "The Fourth of July Oration," *Quarterly Journal of Speech* 44 (4) (1958): 393–401.

21. Douglass, "What to the Slave Is the Fourth of July?" 494–95.

22. See James Jasinsky, "Rearticulating History in Epideictic Discourse: Frederick Douglass's 'The Meaning of the Fourth of July to the Negro,'" in Thomas W. Benson, ed., *Rhetoric and Political Culture in Nineteenth-Century America* (East Lansing: Michigan State University Press, 1997), 78.

23. Douglass, "What to the Slave Is the Fourth of July?" 496.

24. Ibid.

25. Frederick Douglass, "A Nation in the Midst of a Nation: An Address Delivered in New York, New York, on 11 May 1853," in *The Frederick Douglass Papers, Series One: Speeches, Debates, and Interviews*, 5 vols., ed. John Blassingame and others (New Haven, CT: Yale University Press, 1979–1992), 2:423–40, 424–25.

26. Rancière, *Dis-agreement*, 21–42.

27. Cited in Colaiaco, *Frederick Douglass and the Fourth of July*, 5.

28. Douglass, "A Nation in the Midst of a Nation," 2:427–28.

29. This familiar interpretation of Douglass is elaborated in Boxill, "Two Traditions in African American Political Philosophy." Charles W. Mills takes a similar approach in his savaging of Douglass's "inspiring" but "naive" view of American racial politics in "Whose Fourth of July? Frederick Douglass and 'Original Intent,'" in Bill E. Lawson and Frank M. Kirkland, eds., *Frederick Douglass: A Critical Reader* (Malden, MA: Blackwell, 1999), 100–142, 105. The familiar binary of assimilationism and separatism obscures much of the nuance in writers like Douglass, Du Bois, Ellison, and Baldwin.

30. Boxill, "Two Traditions of African American Political Philosophy."

31. Glaude, *Exodus!* 115. Consider the following passage: "We are Americans, and as Americans, we would speak to Americans. We address you not as aliens nor as exiles, humbly asking to be permitted to dwell among you in peace; but we address you as American citizens asserting their rights on their own native soil." See Frederick Douglass, "The Claims of Our Common Cause," in *Frederick Douglass: Selected Speeches and Writings,* ed. Philip S. Foner, abridged and adapted by Yuval Taylor (Chicago: Lawrence Hill Books, 1999), 260–71, 261.

32. Or, as Robert Musil puts it, "We are a we to which reality does not correspond." Cited in Pierre Rosanvallon, *Democracy Past and Future* (New York: Columbia University Press, 2006), 91. I am grateful to Emilios Christodoulidis for drawing my attention to Benveniste's work on this question. See Emilios Christodoulidis, "Against Substitution: The Constitutional Thinking of Dissensus," in Martin Loughlin and Neil Walker, eds., *The Paradox of Constitutionalism: Constituent Power and Constitutional Form* (Oxford: Oxford University Press, 2007), 189–210, 200–206. On the political dilemmas of "we," see also Carrol Clarkson, "Who Are 'We'? Don't Make Me Laugh," *Law and Critique* 18 (3) (2007): 361–74, and Bert Van Roermund, "First-Person Plural Legislature: Political Reflexivity and Representation," *Philosophical Explorations* 6 (3) (2003): 235–50.

33. I agree with Nikhil Pal Singh's recent critique of familiar attempts to retrospectively assimilate black political thinkers like Douglass and King into an unbroken tradition of "shared national identity across time," as the "fulfillment of a project" and the "completion of a destiny." What Singh says of King and his legacy is also true of Douglass: their "black freedom dreams had a habit of exceeding the sanctioned boundaries and brokered compromises of the established political order." See Nikhil Pal Singh, *Black Is a Country: Race and the Unfinished Struggle for Democracy* (Cambridge, MA: Harvard University Press, 2004), 5.

34. Michael Walzer, *The Company of Critics: Social Criticism and Political Commitment in the Twentieth Century* (New York: Basic, 1988), 19.

35. Sacvan Bercovitch, *The Rites of Assent: Transformations in the Symbolic Construction of America* (New York: Routledge, 1993), 50.

36. Douglass, "What to the Slave Is the Fourth of July?" 498.

37. Douglass, *Bondage*, 65.

38. Douglass, "The Claims of Our Common Cause," 264.

39. Ibid.

40. Frank M. Kirkland also urges readers of Douglass to pay more attention to the "rhetorical and communicative settings in which Douglass is engaged." See Frank M. Kirkland, "Enslavement, Moral Suasion, and the Struggles for Recognition," in Lawson and Kirkland, eds., *Frederick Douglass*, 243–310, 244.

41. Rancière, "Who Is the Subject of the Rights of Man?" 6.

42. Donald G. Nieman, *Promises to Keep: African-Americans and the Constitutional Order, 1776 to the Present* (New York: Oxford University Press, 1991), viii.

43. Frederick Douglass "The *Dred Scott* Decision," in *Frederick Douglass*, ed. Foner, 344–58, 347.

44. [The Garrisonians'] motto was printed on the masthead of Garrison's radical abolitionist newspaper the *Liberator.*

45. Robert M. Cover, *Justice Accused: Antislavery and the Judicial Process* (New Haven, CT: Yale University Press, 1975); Moore, *Constitutional Rights and Powers of the People;* William M. Wiecek, *The Sources of Antislavery Constitutionalism in America, 1760–1848* (Ithaca, NY: Cornell University Press, 1977).

46. See David E. Schrader, "Natural Law in the Constitutional Thought of Frederick Douglass," in Lawson and Kirkland, eds., *Frederick Douglass*, 85–99, 85.

47. Douglass, "What to the Slave Is the Fourth of July?" 505.

48. Robert M. Cover, "Nomos and Narrative," in *Narrative, Violence, and the Law: The Essays of Robert Cover,* ed. Martha Minow (Ann Arbor: University of Michigan Press, 1995), 137.

49. Douglass, "The *Dred Scott* Decision," 352.

50. An unabridged version of Chief Justice Taney's *Dred Scott* decision may be found on the website of the Library of Congress. The most definitive discussion of the *Dred Scott* case is Don E. Fehrenbacher, *The* Dred Scott *Case: Its Significance in American Law and Politics* (Oxford: Oxford University Press, 1978).

51. Douglass, "The *Dred Scott* Decision," 354.

52. Colaiaco, *Frederick Douglass and the Fourth of July*, 103.

53. Moore, *Constitutional Rights and Powers of the People*, 63–64, my emphasis.

54. Jacques Rancière, "Jacques Rancière: Literature, Politics, Aesthetics," *SubStance* 92 (2000): 5.

55. Douglass, "What to the Slave Is the Fourth of July?" 497.

56. Ibid., 498.

57. See Fanuzzi, *Abolition's Public Sphere*, and Joel Olson, "The Freshness of Fanaticism: The Abolitionist Defense of Zealotry," *Perspectives on Politics* 5 (4) (2007): 685–701.

58. Wendell Phillips, *Philosophy of the Abolition Movement,* in Mason Lowance, ed., *Against Slavery: An Abolitionist Reader* (New York: Penguin, 2000), 246.

59. Ibid., 249.

60. Ibid., 247.

61. Ibid., 248. For a broader treatment of the central role of prophetic discourse in the dissenting traditions of American political thought, especially as those traditions bear on questions of race, see Shulman, *American Prophecy.*

62. Rogers, *"We Are All Together Now,"* 17.

63. John Rawls, *Political Liberalism* (New York: Columbia University Press, 1993), 251.

64. Amy Gutmann and Dennis Thompson, *Why Deliberative Democracy?* (Princeton, NJ: Princeton University Press, 2004), 51. See also Amy Gutmann and Dennis Thompson, *Democracy and Disagreement* (Cambridge, MA: Harvard University Press, 1996), 133–37.

65. John Rawls, "The Idea of Public Reason Revisited," in *Law of Peoples* (Cambridge, MA: Harvard University Press, 2001), 129–80, 142–43.

66. Ibid., 152.

67. William Connolly, *The Ethos of Pluralization* (Minneapolis: University of Minnesota Press, 1995), 186.

68. Rawls, *Political Liberalism,* 254.

69. Cover, *Justice Accused.*

70. Fanuzzi, *Abolition's Public Sphere,* xix.

71. Frederick Douglass, "The Do-Nothing Policy," in *Frederick Douglass,* ed. Foner, 342–44, 355.

72. Frederick Douglass, "West India Emancipation," in *Frederick Douglass,* ed. Foner, 358–68, 367, emphasis added. Douglass's insistence that quiescence does not in any way indicate the absence of domination clearly resonates with the "power debates" and the critique of pluralism that preoccupied American political scientists in the 1970s. The best study to emerge from these debates and the one that provides the clearest sense of the stakes of these debates for democratic theory and for democratic politics is John Gaventa, *Power and Powerlessness: Quiescence and Rebellion in an Appalachian Community* (1980; reprint, Urbana: University of Illinois Press, 1982).

73. Cited in Fanuzzi, *Abolition's Public Sphere,* xii–xiii.

74. Cited in ibid., xiv.

75. Douglass, *Bondage,* 337.

76. Douglass, "The *Dred Scott* Decision," 345–46.

77. Pierre Bourdieu, *Outline of a Theory of Practice* (Cambridge: Cambridge University Press, 1977), 167.

78. Douglass, "What to the Slave Is the Fourth of July?" 497.

79. Patchen Markell, "The Potential and the Actual," in Bert van der Brink and David Owen, eds., *Recognition and Power* (New York: Cambridge University Press, 2007), 36.

80. Douglass, *Bondage*, 266.

81. Frederick Douglass, *Narrative of the Life of Frederick Douglass* (New York: Penguin, 1982), 111.

82. Rancière, *Dis-agreement*, 29–30. "The police is thus first an order of bodies that defines the allocation of ways of doing, ways of being, ways of saying, and sees that those bodies are assigned by name to a particular place and task; it is an order of the visible and the sayable that sees that a particular activity is visible and another is not, that this speech is understood as discourse and another as noise" (29).

83. James Baldwin, "They Can't Turn Back," in *Collected Essays* (New York: Library of America, 1998), 622–37, 623.

84. For a wonderful exploration of this theme in Baldwin's work as it relates to debates in contemporary democratic theory, see Lawrie Balfour, *The Evidence of Things Not Said* (Ithaca, NY: Cornell University Press, 2001).

85. Rancière, *Dis-agreement*, 88.

86. James Baldwin, *The Fire Next Time*, in *Collected Essays*, 291–348, 294.

87. Jason Sokol, *There Goes My Everything* (New York: Knopf, 2006), 63.

88. Rancière, *Dis-agreement*, 40.

89. See Balfour, *The Evidence of Things Not Said*, 135–39.

90. James Baldwin, "The Dangerous Road before Martin Luther King," in *Collected Essays*, 638–58, 658.

91. "Achieving our country" comes from the final sentence of Baldwin's *The Fire Next Time*, 346; Ralph Waldo Emerson, "Experience," in *Essays: First and Second Series* (New York: Library of America, 1990), 241–62, 255; Langston Hughes, "Let America Be America Again," in *Collected Poems of Langston Hughes* (New York: Knopf, 1994), 189.

92. Sacvan Bercovitch has made the strongest case for the all-absorbing hegemony of the figure of the "unfinished mission" in American political cultures from the seventeenth century through the revolution and to the present day, claiming that through the ubiquitous Jeremiadic imperatives of the chosen people all varieties of political dissent and resistance are invariably enlisted in the forces of a narrow cultural continuity. It is a provocative thesis. However, the formalism of Bercovitch's approach, his presumption that such a ritualized identity exists apart from competing claims to speak on its behalf, too quickly enfolds these different historical enactments within a largely undifferentiated "ritual" of collective belonging. He is insufficiently attentive to how "the" ritualized invocation gets refigured and contested through these claims, that no ritual exists independently of

these alternative claimings. The possible failure of the ritual is its own condition of possibility. See Bercovitch, *Rites of Assent.*

93. William B. Gravely, "The Dialectic of Double-Consciousness in Black American Freedom Celebrations," *Journal of Negro History* 67 (Winter 1982): 302–17; Shane White, "It Was a Proud Day: African Americans, Festivals, and Parades in the North, 1741–1834," *Journal of American History* 81 (1) (1994): 13–50.

94. Glaude, *Exodus!* 86.

95. Rancière, *Dis-agreement,* 88.

96. Ralph Ellison, *Invisible Man* (New York: Vintage, 1995), 581.

97. I take this formulation from the work of Stanley Cavell. See his *The Claim of Reason* (New York: Oxford University Press, 1979), 22.

98. Danielle Allen, *Talking to Strangers: Anxiety of Citizenship since* Brown v. Board of Education (Chicago: University of Chicago Press, 2004), 68.

14

"A Blending of Opposite Qualities"

Frederick Douglass and the Demands of Democratic Citizenship

Nick Bromell

In the fall of 1886, three years before his death and twenty-three years after Lincoln's Emancipation Proclamation, Frederick Douglass and his wife left the United States for a European tour. Unlike his earlier voyages abroad, this trip was about pleasure, not business. Yet as Douglass recounts the journey in the fourth version of his autobiography, *Life and Times of Frederick Douglass* (1893),[1] virtually every place he visited spoke to him of his abolitionist labors and lifelong struggle against prejudice and injustice. Arriving in England, Douglass made a point of revisiting Parliament, where he heard "Mr. William E. Gladstone, the great Liberal leader," speak against the Irish Force Bill. Douglass tells us that while Gladstone sat waiting to debate the Tory leader, Arthur Balfour, his face exhibited "a blending of opposite qualities. There were the peace and gentleness of the lamb, with the strength and determination of the lion." Douglass witnessed such a blending also when Gladstone rose to speak. He began "in a tone conciliatory and persuasive" and then, "after marshaling his facts and figures . . . , raising his voice and pointing his finger directly at Mr. Balfour, he exclaimed, in a tone almost menacing and tragic, 'What are you fighting for?' The effect," Douglass concludes, "was thrilling."[2]

In this essay, I unpack the political theory embedded in this anecdote, which is just one of a number of parables of democracy (as I call them) that Douglass included in *Life and Times of Frederick Douglass*. As we shall see, as a political theorist and activist Douglass occupied two distinct and virtually "opposite" standpoints that he blended in one outlook.[3] (This is one reason why he identified so strongly with Gladstone's "blending of opposites.") The first perspective was that of an enslaved black person, the second that of a free man. Because the first was so radically unknown to the entire tradition of Western philosophy—and, indeed, as Charles Mills and others have argued,[3] had been systematically excluded from it—he could not express it easily in the conceptual language of that tradition. As a consequence, when we try today to give an account of Douglass's political thought, we have to listen very carefully to hear both aspects of what I am calling his blended standpoint, not allowing the one we are more familiar with (that of the free mind speaking to other free minds) to occlude the other (that of an unfree mind discovering and conceptualizing a distinctive version of "the political").[4]

Douglass himself quickly became aware of the imperfect "fit" between his blended angles of vision and the political language he learned to speak so well when he became an abolitionist and writer. In his writing, he sometimes deliberately calls his readers' attention to the gap or the slippage between his own distinctive perspective and the political language he must perforce use to express it. In *My Bondage and My Freedom*, for example, he introduces his radical perspectivalism through a simple story. He recounts walking as a child through the woods on the way to his master's planation for the first time and being terrified of monstrous apparitions in the gloom until they turned out to be just tree stumps and branches. He concludes the story with the wryly understated philosophical observation: "Thus early I learned that the point from which a thing is viewed is of some importance."[5] Douglass more explicitly acknowledges the illegibility of his own "point" to most white abolitionists when he writes of their response to his plans to start his own newspaper: "My American friends looked at me with astonishment. 'A wood-sawyer' offering himself up to the public as an editor! A slave, brought up in the very depths of ignorance, assuming to instruct the highly civilized people of the north in the principles of liberty, justice, and humanity! The thing looked absurd."[6]

But perhaps the most famous instance of such metacommentary on perspectival epistemology is Douglass's meditation on "slave songs," where he concludes that their true meaning can be grasped only by someone who, like himself, has stood both "within the circle" of enslavement and "without" it. Familiar as this scene is to all readers of Douglass, I would like to begin this essay by examining the microrevisions Douglass made to it over the course of writing his autobiographies. The passage as a whole and his subtle revisions to it highlight his struggle against the terminology in which he perforce had to express himself; they also help us identify some of the persisting key terms around which his thought took form.

In the *Narrative of the Life of Frederick Douglass, an American Slave*, of 1845, Douglass wrote that "the mere hearing of those songs would do more to impress some minds with the horrible character of slavery, than the reading of whole volumes of philosophy on the subject could do."[7] Ten years later, in *My Bondage and My Freedom*, Douglass changed this passage to read: "I have sometimes thought that, the mere hearing of those songs would do more to impress truly spiritually-minded men and women with the soul-crushing and death-dealing character of slavery, than the reading of whole volumes of its mere physical cruelties."[8] Observe, then, that "some minds" has become "truly spiritually-minded men and women"; "horrible character" has become "soul-crushing and death-dealing character"; and "philosophy" has been replaced with "volumes of its mere physical cruelties."[9] Why?

I would argue that, taken together, these changes reflect Douglass's growing sense of himself as a philosopher of power and politics, not just a witness and critic of slavery. By 1855, he had become interested in tracing the phenomenology of enslavement's injuries and their implications for the political per se, so he no longer wished to disparage "whole volumes of philosophy." Indeed, he found himself wanting to give a more precise account of the particular kind of "mind" required to understand slavery and its implications. One must have, he suggests, a mind that sees things "spiritually," which perhaps means infusing knowing or cognition with a moral sensibility rather than thinking of them as distinct.

We discover a further deepening of Douglass's philosophical interests when we look closely at the revisions he incorporated in the final version of this passage in the second edition of *Life and Times* (1893). In *My Bondage and My Freedom*, he had written (quoting the *Narrative*), "I did not, when a slave, understand the deep meanings of those rude, and apparently incoherent songs. I was myself within the circle, so that I neither saw nor heard as those without might see and hear. " Now in *Life and Times* he wrote: "I did not, when a slave, *fully* understand the deep *meaning* of those rude, and apparently incoherent songs. I was, myself, within the circle. So that I could *then* neither see nor hear as those without might see and hear."[10] By adding the word *fully* and changing "meanings" to "meaning," Douglass gave a more precise account of his own work: it was to understand in a fuller, broader way or within an enlarged framework because the object of understanding now presented itself to him as a complex but unitary manifold rather than as a set of distinct and alternative possibilities. That is, he more accurately saw the songs' full meaning as residing more in a complex, blended, perhaps inconsistent or self-contradictory unity than in a range of different possibilities. Finally, by adding "then," he emphasized the passage of time between the event and his writing about it, time in which his thinking had changed along with his temporal location and standpoint.

All of these revisions carry forward what was implied by an observation that he had inserted in *My Bondage and My Freedom* and that he revised slightly but significantly in *Life and Times.* In 1855, he had written that the slaves' songs might seem self-contradictory, but "such is the constitution of the human mind that, when pressed to extremes, it often avails itself of the most opposite methods. Extremes meet in mind as in matter."[11] In the later autobiography of 1881 (and revised in 1893), he wrote: "It is not inconsistent with the constitution of the human mind that it avails itself of one and the same method for expressing opposite emotions."[12] Both versions express his belief that the human "mind" may sometimes appear to be self-contradictory when in fact it is not. That is, the "opposites" through which binary thinking has shaped its vision of the world do not always do justice to the ways reality itself may be a compound, or blending, of these opposites. In the first passage, he identifies the seeming contradiction as one between "opposite methods," and in the second he identifies it as one between "opposite emotions." Again, why would he make such a change?

I would suggest that when he wrote *Life and Times,* he believed that the contradiction lay not so much in the methods used as in the mind itself, where the opposite emotions of a person vie for expression. Moreover, by the 1880s he found himself very far from the "extreme" conditions of enslavement in which the slave songs had been sung. Now he was less interested in the means ("methods") by which persons try to deal with extreme conditions than in the conflicting feelings they experience within more or-dinary conditions of democratic citizenship. Thus, as I hope will become increasingly clear, a direct line of thought connects his identification of his standpoint in 1855 as one that fuses the opposites of "within" *and* "without," his titling of his second book *My Bondage and My Freedom,* his reflections in 1855 and 1893 on the ways the "mind" both contains *and* expresses "op-posites," and his admiration in 1893 for Gladstone as a political figure in whose words and countenance he witnessed a "blending of opposites."

These examples of Douglass's careful, almost obsessive revisions to his autobiographies should suffice to indicate that throughout his long career as an activist thinker he identified himself as a distinctive kind of politi-cal philosopher and struggled to give adequate expression to his thinking in a language not perfectly suited to it.[13] Trying to remain sensitive to this struggle, I focus in this essay on a topic that scholars and critics of Dou-glass have largely bypassed: his reflections on the nature and challenges of democratic citizenship. As is well known, Douglass began to articulate his political thought in his speeches of the late 1840s and in *My Bondage and My Freedom,* where it revolves most energetically around questions of constitutional interpretation and the relation of higher law to politics and history. In this chapter, I continue to draw on this familiar period of Dou-glass's life and work, but I focus as well on the still relatively neglected *Life and Times,* which is the richest repository of his reflections on the de-mands of democratic citizenship. And little wonder: by 1881, Douglass had been a citizen of the United States for several decades, and throughout that time he had worked not to emancipate enslaved persons into citizenship but to gain for them the full citizenship that they had been formally granted. Whereas the earlier task had called for arguments that slavery was incom-patible both with higher law and with the US Constitution, his later work called for rhetoric that persuaded white citizens to disinvest in whiteness and enlarge their conception of citizenship to include African Americans.

Underlying both of these political projects were two interlocking sets of questions familiar to political theorists today. First, to what degree (if any) does democracy require some conception of eternal or higher law in order to justify itself, adjudicate deep disagreement among its citizens, and guide its actions? That is, does democracy require foundations? Second, on what basis or by what criteria does a democracy decide who is a citizen entitled to the rights and responsibilities of citizenship? When and how should a conception of who belongs to "we the people" make room for others who seem not to meet it? Viewed as problems or challenges of democratic citizenship (which is how Douglass tended to see them), these problems take a slightly different form: What stance toward the tension between obedience to higher law and commitments to pluralism and historical action should citizens adopt? And what forms of intersubjective communication or what practices of recognition, regard, and respect should citizens develop in order to acknowledge and work through significant differences among themselves?

Sustaining the Tension between Higher Law and History

The relation of democracy to eternal principles or foundations troubled citizens of the antebellum period as much as it does political theorists today. Starting around the middle of the 1830s, many textbooks produced for secondary schools and colleges felt obliged to come to grips with this problem. In particular, they felt obliged to explain how a constitution founded on eternal and "self-evident" principles could allow itself to be subject to change through the constitutional amendment process. Answers to this question reflected their authors' own political positions and thus tended to vary.

In *The Political Class Book: Intended to Instruct the Higher Classes in the Origin, Nature, and Use of Political Power* (1832), for example, Democrat William Sullivan encouraged his readers to understand that because "we the people" are the ultimate sovereigns, the people have the right to change their political order as often and as much as they choose. Anticipating political theorists Sheldon Wolin and Benjamin Barber, among others, he asserted that political "authority resides, always, in those who compose the political community. This community has not only the exclusive right to judge whether power, established for its benefit, is constitutionally exercised but also the absolute right to amend, and even to abolish, the existing system, and substitute any other."[14] But even as Sullivan emphasized the citizens' right "to amend, and even to abolish, the existing system," including the Constitution, he wrote that there is a limit to such changes, a limit established by the immutable and universal truths discoverable by "reason," which he defines as "that power whereby the mind comprehends truths, which are necessary and universal in their application . . . ; as that two things, each of which is equal to a third, must be equal to one another." Thus, even as citizens of democracy have an absolute right to revolution, they are also obliged to use their reason to discover the immutable laws to which they must submit: "Our first duty . . . is to use the gift of reason in learning the laws which are prescribed to us."[15]

In *The Constitutional Class Book: Being a Brief Exposition of the Constitution of the United States Designed for the Use of the Higher Classes in Common Schools* (1834), Federalist Joseph Story took a very different view of the matter. He set forth the philosophical and existential challenges of constitutional democracy quite explicitly: "A Government, which has no mode prescribed for any changes, will in the lapse of time become utterly unfit for the nation. . . . But at the same time, it is equally important to guard against too easy and frequent changes; and to secure due deliberation and caution in making them." The solution Story proposed is "to follow experience, rather than speculation and theory": "it cannot escape notice, how exceedingly difficult it is to settle the foundations of any government upon principles, which do not admit of controversy or question. The very elements, out of which it is to be built, are susceptible of infinite modifications. . . . Whatever, then, has been found to work well in experience, should rarely be hazarded upon conjectural improvements. . . . To be of any value, they [the "improvements"] must become cemented with the habits, the feelings, and the pursuits of the people."[16]

Story gave due place to "reason" in his conception of citizenship but also warned explicitly against "speculation," "theory," and conjecture. In his view, the principles of democratic government should definitely *not* be conceived of as abstract truths such as "two things, each of which is equal to a third, must be equal to one another." Unlike the axioms of geometry, the principles of democratic government are by definition controversial and revisable, dangerously so. Therefore, civic education should train citizens to accept change but not to seek it. Story believed that the safest hedge against "too frequent and easy changes" is "experience," which becomes sedimented in the citizenry as "habits," "feelings," and "pursuits."[17]

These problems continue to vex both theorists and citizens of US democracy today. For example, when Story wrote that "it cannot escape notice, how exceedingly difficult it is to settle the foundations of any government upon principles, which do not admit of controversy or question," he was anticipating the words of John Rawls, who would argue 150 years later that "as a practical political matter no general moral conception can provide the basis for a public conception of justice in a modern democratic society. . . . [S]uch a [public] conception [of justice] must allow for a diversity of doctrines and the plurality of conflicting, and indeed incommensurable conceptions of the good affirmed by the members of existing democratic societies."[18] Rawls believed that liberalism—in particular his own conception of justice as fairness—could provide Americans with a way to accommodate themselves to this dilemma of democratic citizenship. But, of course, many political theorists have contested Rawls's arguments, and most Americans at the turn of the twenty-first century are still holding fast to the belief, or hope, that a public conception of justice can be anchored to a shared public conception of what is good, not just to procedures that may be just.

Throughout his life, Douglass was a firm believer in higher law and universal, eternal truths. When he first joined the abolitionist movement, he was a loyal Garrisonian who adopted William Lloyd Garrison's view of the Constitution: it was a "covenant with hell" (the Garrisonians' motto) because it was the product of historical compromises between slaveholding and free states, and one should never compromise with the principles of higher law. Moreover, Garrison also believed that because antebellum democratic politics were convened under this fatally flawed document, they should be rejected entirely, and abolitionists should work primarily through moral suasion instead. But as the pro-slavery forces skillfully worked the political system to grow stronger, triumphing with the passage of the Fugitive Slave Act in the Compromise of 1850, Douglass was drawn to another wing of the abolitionist movement—the "political abolitionists," who were willing to use all the mechanisms of democratic action to defeat the law and the slavery system. They, too, claimed to believe in higher law. But they saw no inconsistency between the higher law and the Constitution because the word *slavery* is not ever used in the Constitution. Douglass was very reluctant to accept the political abolitionists' logic-chopping sophistry over the mass of historical evidence Wendell Phillips had compiled to demonstrate that the Founders had knowingly compromised their principles. But pressured by the growing power and the relentless spread of the slavery system, he at last converted to political abolitionism.[19]

There is no way to be certain, but I believe Douglass was only partially convinced by the political abolitionists' argument and accepted it only because he wanted more scope to act in history—even within a morally compromised political system. His explanation of his conversion to political abolitionism at the eighteenth annual meeting of American Anti-Slavery Society in May 1851 shows him taking a nuanced position that does not quite map onto either Garrisonian or political abolitionism's view of the Constitution's relation to higher law. He had "arrived," he announced, "at the firm conviction that the Constitution, construed in the light of well-established rules of legal interpretation, might be made consistent in its details with the noble purposes in its preamble" and that the Constitution could "be wielded in behalf of emancipation."[20] Alert to how careful he often was with his wording, we might take note that he stated that the founding document can "be made" consistent, not that it "is" consistent. He suggested that the challenge for democratic citizenship is to *make* the "details" of the Constitution, by which he meant the compromised historical forms in which the framers cast their new democracy, consistent with its "noble purposes and the eternal truths expressed in the Constitution's preamble." Both contingent historical "details" and eternal truths—seeming opposites—must be kept in play. As he had realized when reflecting upon the meaning of slave songs, the interpreting mind must sometimes avail "itself of the most opposite methods."

Douglass's former colleagues in the American Anti-Slavery Society did not buy his new position. They instantly attacked him for having abandoned his principles and joined with the compromisers and hypocrites. They demanded to know how he could uphold one interpretation of the Constitution so fervently one day and then switch to the opposite view so quickly. Clearly, they thought, he was an unprincipled opportunist. Most historians have subsequently confirmed this judgment, noting that even after Douglass changed sides and joined the political abolitionists, he continued to shift his allegiances in response to his analysis of what was possible or, likely, politically expedient. "Throughout the 1850s," Waldo Martin observes, "Douglass followed a pattern in which at first he would align himself primarily with the Liberty Party and Radical Abolitionists in principle. Come election time, however, he would opt for expediency."[21] David Blight calls Douglass's inconsistency a struggle between "pragmatism" on the one hand and "moral principle" on the other.[22] Wilson Moses is even more critical: "Douglass' ideology was thoroughly inconsistent, usually opportunistic, and always self-serving."[23]

But perhaps the assertion of this binary opposition between principle and pragmatism is an example of the ways we are not hearing Douglass speak from both of his standpoints—that of an enslaved person and that of a free man—as he blends these dual perspectives of bondage and freedom into a single "method." He was not as troubled as his critics were (and are) by his alleged inconsistency, for he understood that the committed political actor must try to honor eternal, higher-law principles in a historical setting or in what George Yancy describes as "the concrete muck and mire" of human existence;[24] one's strategy might change, while one's allegiance to fixed principles remains constant. Attempting to explain this novel conception of "consistency," Douglass declared that "the only truly consistent man is he who will, for the sake of being right today, contradict what he said wrong yesterday."[25] He attempted to clarify this position when he wrote that "true stability consists not of being of the same opinion now as formerly, but in a fixed principle of honesty, ever urging us to the adoption or rejection of that which may seem to us true or false at the ever-present now."[26]

We should take special note of three details in the latter statement. The first is the phrase "fixed principle of honesty": it blends two ideas in a startling synthesis, for the "fixed principles" that are usually imagined as standing outside history and beyond humankind are here placed within a human character trait or, more precisely, within a human disposition—that of being honest. The second is Douglass's careful choice of the word *seem* (not *is*): it expresses his belief that we human beings often cannot know for certain what is true or false and that we must therefore act on the basis of what *seems to us* to be true or false. Here again, in other words, we find Douglass's attunement to standpoint standing side by side with its seeming opposite: fixed principles. Finally, the phrase "ever-present now" underscores Douglass's deep belief that we always act and think in the present moment. We may try to act in accordance with a higher law we take to be eternal, but in our moment of action we work in and through history, not eternity.

Where had Douglass acquired this twofold perspective? As I have argued at length elsewhere, while living in conditions of radical unfreedom he had acquired a sense of the radical difference between his perspective as a racially embodied slave and the perspective of his free white masters. This slave perspective gave him a sharp sense of the standpoint contingency of "truth" even as it underscored for him the necessity of truths that reside outside and beyond all contingency standpoints. When Douglass escaped from slavery, he brought this perspective with him. Upon joining the Garrisonians, he found his belief in higher law powerfully confirmed by his abolitionist colleagues, but at the same time he saw that they did not quite see things as he did—that standpoint contingency operated in the free states, too, only less visibly. This imperfect fit between his views and those of his fellow abolitionists surfaced whenever he tried to actualize his blended standpoint.

Douglass's famous speech "What to the Slave Is the Fourth of July?" (1852) powerfully demonstrates his commitment to this blended standpoint. On the one hand, he says that he "stands identified" with the American slave; on the other, he addresses his audience of abolitionists as "fellow citizens" no fewer than eight times. On the one hand, he denounces US democracy as a fraud, while on the other he urges his audience to "cling fast" to the principles of the Declaration of Independence. These seeming inconsistencies are clear expressions of his distinctive perspective.

Consider, as another example of Douglass's negotiation of seeming opposites, his editorial "The Republican Party—Our Position," published in 1855. Here he defended himself *not* from Garrison's accusations of having sacrificed principle for expediency but from charges of sacrificing expediency to principle. The abolitionist newspaper *Oneida Sachem* had argued that by lending his continued support to the Liberty Party instead of to the new Republican Party, Douglass was "indulging in what he conceives to be an abstract proposition" rather than working pragmatically for the eventual abolition of slavery.[27] In reply, Douglass began by countering the *Oneida Sachem*'s argument that no one in "'his sober senses'" could possibly maintain that Congress could abolish slavery if it so chose. He pointed out that in fact he "has never asserted" that "it is the duty or prerogative of Congress to enact a specific law, in order to *make* Slavery illegal"; that cannot be done, he observed, for the simple reason that slavery was never legal under the Constitution in the first place. After all, the Constitution itself declares that "'no person shall be deprived of liberty, without due process of Law,' and that 'the right of all people to be secure in their persons shall not be violated.'" Therefore, *"Congress is bound, constitutionally bound, to provide all necessary means in having this principle [of slavery's illegality] carried out in practice."* Douglass went on to argue that although Congress could not logically accomplish this end through legislation that *made* slavery illegal, it did have a range of other methods at its disposal to abolish slavery in the

individual states. Above all, it had the constitutional prerogative and obligation to secure the basic rights guaranteed by the Constitution when these
rights were denied by the institutions of the individual states. "We must
ever remember that if the Constitution calls upon the federal Government,
to 'secure the blessings of liberty'—'to establish justice'—'insure domestic tranquility'— . . . and [that when] the powers of the General Government are too limited to 'interfere' with a State institution' which is a fruitful
source of all manner of Despotism, of injustice, of wars, etc. etc., the State
Governments virtually abolish the General Government, as their powers
are supreme, and the General government is a nullity."[28]

Douglass's aim, then, was to carve out space between principle
and pragmatism, a position that looked unprincipled to Garrisonians
and unpragmatic to the *Oneida Sachem.* The Liberty Party did indeed
cling fast to its principles, but this commitment did not mean that it was
abstaining from democratic practice; on the contrary, his editorial insisted,
the Liberty Party was deeply immersed in the practical democratic
actions of urging Congress to "exercise its legitimate powers" to secure
rights guaranteed by the Constitution. How, he asked, "can we accept
the invitation of the *Sachem,* to join the Republican Party, conceding,
as it does, to the slaveholder the 'Constitutional Right' to rob his present
and future victims, in the slave States? We can endorse no such Principle.
Nor can we 'forsake' our own principles, on the ground of their alleged
impracticability . . . ."[29]

Was Douglass being an inconsistent, unprincipled pragmatist when just
a few months later (as Waldo Martin notes) he switched his allegiance from
the Liberty Party and backed Republican candidate John C. Fremont? Not
if we regard "consistency" as "a fixed principle of honesty, ever urging us to
the adoption or rejection of that which may seem to us true or false at the
ever-present now." Perfect consistency might be possible in realms where
citizens act unburdened by historical pressures and contingencies—that is,
in realms of perfect freedom, such as logic and mathematics. But in the
realm of actual democratic action, citizens are less "free" than they usually
suppose themselves to be.

This is the key insight that Douglass tried to bring to nineteenth-century American political theory and practice. He saw more clearly than free
citizens that even they must submit to and cling to the "ringbolt" of higher
law, which they are "bound" to serve. Their freedom is thus limited by duty

and necessity. Yet he knew just as well that democratic citizens are morally obligated to act in the present, this "ever-present now"; their democratic duty does not allow them to preserve their sense of perfect moral integrity by standing to one side in the expectation that progress will roll in on wheels of inevitability (to paraphrase Martin Luther King Jr.). In short, in Douglass's view democratic citizenship presents citizens with several dilemmas that can never be resolved. According to Douglass, it is endemic to democracy that although we must believe that democracy is sanctioned by immutable eternal principles (e.g., that "all men are created equal"), as citizens we must also dare to act in ways that challenge or reject conventional, majoritarian understandings of those principles (e.g., by claiming, historical evidence to the contrary notwithstanding, that the word *men* in the Declaration of Independence includes black men as well as white men, women as well as men, homosexuals as well as heterosexuals, and so on). Yet citizens must be careful not to take this freedom to revise the Constitution as license to suppose that they no longer need to "cling fast" to certain eternal principles of what is true and what is right. Citizens of a democracy must somehow hold these contradictory obligations in tension with each other.

We might more clearly see what is distinctive about Douglass's political theory of citizenship—in which consistency is taken from the sphere of freedom and redefined by someone who has known unfreedom as well— by bringing it to bear on current debates over whether democracy gains or loses by thinking of itself as needing "foundations." Antifoundationalist Benjamin Barber, for example, argues that "foundationalism, even where it represents an authoritative establishing of the credentials of democracy [as, for example, in the work of the Founders], tends . . . to undermine democracy, and democracy both requires and entails an immunity to its own foundations if it is to flourish." That is, democratic action in the present should not be curtailed by decisions made in the past; all decisions should be arrived at through a thoroughly open-ended process of contestation and argument. Foundationalists, Barber claims, tend to enter into this process with their minds made up. Indeed, they "may be said to be ineducable and thus immune to democracy for they know their truths up front and have nothing to learn from the democratic process."[30]

Frederick Douglass was certainly a foundationalist all his life, but he does not quite fit Barber's description of one.[31] As we chart his changing political positions throughout the 1850s, we repeatedly encounter his openness to change, his continuing commitment to keeping the democratic process alive. Douglass would share Barber's commitment to a democratic field of action that is not hampered by the past: as he stated more than once, "We have to do with the past only as we can make it useful to the present and to the future."[32] But Douglass's blended perspective also remains attentive to an aspect of the issue that Barber and many other antifoundationalists dismiss too easily. Yes, "the free must freely choose (rechoose) their principles to make them their own," as Barber puts it.[33] But, as Douglass's work makes clear, the "free" are not nearly as free as they (and Barber) suppose themselves to be. Only their complacent security in their freedom allows them to suppose that they are. If they had ever occupied the standpoint of an enslaved person, they would have a much keener sense of freedom's contingency and fragility, which would encourage them to perceive and value (as Douglass did) "the just restraints of free society—*restraints which are necessary to the freedom of all its members, alike and equally.*"[34] That is, free citizens who believe in the eternal truth of their right to be free must also bear in mind the historical contingency of their actual possession of freedom and therefore must often freely choose *not* to consider themselves to be free to choose. That is, they must understand that their historical, contingent freedom depends, to a degree, on their being less than completely free, because only through persistent faithfulness to their democratic duties can they remain free. One of their duties is to observe a "fixed principle of honesty" as they wrestle with such dilemmas inherent in democracy. This is a key part of the knowledge Douglass brought into the constitutional debates of the 1850s, and it is why he figured the principles of the Declaration as a "ringbolt" in the "chain" of the nation's errant history—a metaphor surely intended to evoke the chains that also bound persons in slavery. The "free," too, are bound, though they know it not.

So although Barber is correct that "in America the revolutionary spirit founded a constitution that in time came to be at odds with that spirit,"[35] the conflict or inconsistency he names takes one form in the realm of theory and another in the realm of democratic practice. In the realm of theory, the conflict appears to be a negative: the Constitution appears to "betray" the "spirit" that brought it into being. But in democratic practice or in the realm of democratic citizenship, the conflict takes the form of a daunting but enabling challenge. It lodges an irreducible instability in democracy, one that requires citizens to continually wrestle with a paradox: democracy requires them not only to grasp a "ringbolt" of eternal, ahistorical truths but also to continually debate the meaning of those truths and revise them in the light of changing historical circumstances and needs. Instead of being dismayed by this inherent inconsistency, advocates of strong democracy should be encouraged by it. The instability it generates is a strong assurance that democracy will retain its revolutionary vigor.

Citizenship beyond Whiteness

In the postbellum decades, Douglass confronted a related but different problem endemic to US democracy. As white racism worked tirelessly to deprive African American citizens of their rights enshrined in higher law and actualized historically in the Fourteenth and Fifteenth Amendments, the theoretical issue that came to the fore was the problem of democratic inclusion: Who constitutes "the people," and how much difference can "the people" accommodate before they cease to feel the sense of unity and community the very phrase "we the people" is meant to express? Facing this problem and struggling with it, Douglass again drew on his experience in both slavery and freedom and again looked for a solution that was more dispositional than theoretical, one that took up the challenge of articulating a style or stance of citizenship that could sustain a perpetual tension between opposites.

As sociologist Orlando Patterson and historian Steven Hahn have argued, enslaved persons in the United States experienced politics in large part as a struggle conducted through and over personal relationships.[36] Hahn writes: "Slavery . . . was a system of extreme personal domination in which a slave had no relationship that achieved legal sanction or recognition other than with the master, or with someone specifically designated by the master. . . . Consequently, the slaves' struggles to form relations among themselves and to give those relations customary standing in the eyes of masters and slaves alike was [sic] the most basic and the most profound of political acts in which they engaged."[37] This may explain why when Douglass turned to the problem of redescribing citizenship, he did so by narrating personal encounters across racial divisions. In *Life and Times*, he tells a series of stories meant to serve as parables of democratic citizenship. In them, the former slave and his former masters relinquish their resentments, recognize each other's vulnerabilities, and behave with empathic compassion.[38] Apprehensive that some of my readers might find such a way of doing political theory naive or sentimental, I end this section by suggesting that Douglass's approach remains valuable if it is complemented by historical and structural analyses of racism; I hope to show also that his approach anticipates and gives concrete instantiation of recent political theory by Danielle S. Allen and William Connolly.

In 1861, Douglass was elected by the city of Rochester to represent it at the National Loyalist's Convention for the enfranchisement of "the colored population," which was to meet in Philadelphia. Ironically, the organizers of the convention were dismayed by Douglass's presence as a black man; they feared that his visible association with their work—especially in the parade they had organized—would spark outrage against them. When they approached Douglass and asked him to quit the convention, he characteristically refused. Thereafter, they ostracized him so ruthlessly that on the morning of the parade he faced acute embarrassment. As he writes in *Life and Times,*

> The members of the convention were to walk two abreast, and as I was the only colored member of the convention, the question was, as to who of my brother members would consent to walk with me? The answer was not long in coming. There was *one man* present who was broad enough to take in the whole situation, and brave enough to meet the duty of the hour; one who was neither afraid nor ashamed to own me as a man and a brother; one man of the purest Caucasian type . . . and that man was *Mr. Theodore Tilton.* He came to me in my isolation, seized me by the hand, and in a most brotherly way, and proposed to walk with me in the procession.[39]

When Douglass says that Tilton was "broad" enough to set aside his racial prejudice and privilege, he is signaling a personality type, or a disposition, the opposite of which is "narrow" (or, as we shall see, "strict" or "restrictive"). Such a disposition is also "generous": "I never appreciated an act of courage and generous sentiment more highly than I did that of this brave young man."[40] Significantly, Douglass does not represent Tilton as acting on principle—for example, on a firm conviction in the equality of all men. Nor does he suggest that Tilton's act is reasoned or rational; indeed, because it flies in the face of public opinion and sets aside self-interest, it is highly irrational. Rather, Douglass emphasizes the degree to which this behavior is a matter of disposition; it is an expression of Tilton's "broad" character.

Such dispositional qualities are held up for readers' approval and imitation in a sequence of anecdotes Douglass narrates in *Life and Times*. The first is about his return in 1881 to the Great House Farm, where he had been inducted into slavery sixty-three years earlier. This vast estate owned by Colonel Lloyd was once a "dark domain . . . stamped with its own peculiar iron-like individuality," where "crimes, high-handed and atrocious, could be committed with strange and shocking impunity!" Now, Douglass planned to return there—and he even called it "home." He had been told by friends that the current Colonel Lloyd was "a liberal-minded gentleman" who "would take a visit" from Douglass "very kindly."[41] Still, he was uneasy: Would this Colonel Lloyd really be willing to greet a runaway slave, one who had unsparingly criticized his grandfather?

When the steamship pulled up at the Lloyds' jetty, Douglass learned that Colonel Lloyd himself had been called away, but his son Howard was there to greet him. This young man escorted Douglass around the estate. Douglass writes: "I found the buildings, which gave it the appearance of a village, nearly all standing, and I was astonished to find that I had carried their appearance so accurately in my mind for so many years." He noticed that "the little closet in which I slept in a bag . . . had been taken into the room," and "the dirt floor, too, had disappeared under a plank."[42] Douglass surely knew that these words would call to his readers' minds the most famous scene in all three versions of his autobiography—the one in which he peeps out of this closet and sees his own aunt Esther being whipped. As he wrote in 1845, "I shall never forget it whilst I remember anything. It was the blood-stained gate through which I was about to pass . . . , the entrance to the hell of slavery."[43]

Howard Lloyd and Douglass also toured the Lloyds' family cemetery, and while Douglass walked among the headstones, Lloyd gathered "a bouquet of flowers and evergreens" and then presented it to him. Douglass tells us that he was so moved by this gesture that he took the bouquet back to his new home in the Washington suburb of Uniontown and kept it in memory of this visit. Finally, Lloyd took Douglass into the Great House itself and onto "its stately old verandah, where we could have a full view of its garden, with its broad walks, hedged with box and adorned with fruit trees and flowers of almost every variety. A more tranquil and tranquilizing scene I have seldom met in this or any other country."[44]

What Douglass is doing here is portraying for his readers what a "liberal-minded" gentleman might be. It is someone who, like the young Howard Lloyd, is willing to set aside any identification of citizenship with whiteness and to try to stand in the shoes of a former slave and empathize with his feelings. Through his courteous words and gestures, Lloyd tried to convey that he recognized and respected Douglass's complex feelings of rage and grief. Why else would Douglass have kept the wreath if it did not hold some such meanings?

Another of Douglass's parables of democratic citizenship recounts his visit in 1881 to Captain Thomas Auld, the man who had been his master. When Auld heard that Douglass was in the area of St. Michaels, Maryland, he sent word inviting Douglass to come see him. Douglass was shocked. "To me, Captain Auld had sustained the relation of master—a relation which I held in extremest abhorrence. . . . He had struck down my personality, had subjected me to his will, had made property of my body and soul. . . . I, on my part, had traveled through the length and breadth of this country and of England, holding up this conduct of his . . . to the reprobation of all men who would hear my words."[45]

Douglass relates that when the two men met, they "addressed each other simultaneously, he calling me 'Marshal Douglass' and I, as I had always called him, 'Captain Auld.'" Douglass was deeply moved by the captain's generous gesture of calling him "marshal" (Douglass at this time held the position of marshal of the District of Columbia), and he instantly demonstrated a reciprocal generosity: "Hearing myself called by him 'Marshal Douglass,' I instantly broke up the formal nature of the meeting by saying, 'not Marshal, but Frederick to you as formerly.' . . . We shook hands cordially," Douglass writes, "and he, having been long stricken with palsy, shed tears as men thus deeply afflicted will do when excited by any deep emotion. The sight of him[,] . . . his tremulous hands constantly in motion, and all the circumstances of his condition affected me deeply, and for a time choked my voice and made me speechless." Douglass was afterward strongly criticized by some in the African American community for having paid this visit, but in *Life and Times* he is unapologetic: "Now that slavery was destroyed, and the slave and master stood upon equal ground, I was not only willing to meet him, but very glad to do so. . . . He was to me no longer a slaveholder either in fact or in spirit, and I regarded him as I did myself, a victim of the circumstances of birth, education, law, and custom."[46]

This story, then, like the portraits of Theodore Tilton and Howard Lloyd, offers an account of what it is to be a "broad," "liberal-minded" citizen: it means regarding oneself and others as being in significant part shaped by "the circumstances."[47] In other words, it is to view a person's identity as produced in significant measure by historical and cultural contingencies. Such a view predisposes one to understand that whiteness and blackness are not essences of identity but historically created signifiers whose meaning is subject to revision and even rejection. We thus find ourselves back on the side of Douglass's thinking that sees truth as perspectival and contingent, not eternal and universal.

To appreciate what was at stake in Douglass's parables, it helps to place them in the context of his writings about postbellum Reconstruction and reconciliation. Far from being ready to forgive the South and forget the crimes committed by the slavery system, Douglass frequently opposed the nation's growing tendency to leave the past behind and rush toward reunion. "The South has a past not to be contemplated with pleasure, but with a shudder," he wrote in 1870, when the nation was already beginning to succumb to nostalgia for Dixie and its plantation life. "She has been selling agony, trading in blood and in the souls of men. If her past has any lesson, it is one of repentance and thorough reformation."[48] "I am no minister of malice," he told an audience in 1871, "but . . . may my tongue cleave to the roof of my mouth if I forget the difference between the parties to that . . . bloody conflict. . . . I may say if this war is to be forgotten, I ask in the name of all things sacred what shall men remember?"[49] Douglass was infuriated by the nation's adulation of Robert E. Lee and by its rush to forget the past in the spirit of sectional reconciliation. "Fellow citizens," he declared in a speech in 1882, "I am not indifferent to the claims of a generous forgetfulness, but whatever else I may forget, I shall never forget the difference between those who fought for liberty and those who fought for slavery, between those who fought to save the republic and those who fought to destroy it."[50]

Repentance and reformation, however, were exactly what most leading citizens of the South refused to demonstrate as they resisted radical Reconstruction and fought hard to reinstate their power by imposing their narrow, restrictive, and racist conception of democratic citizenship on emancipated blacks. In Douglass's portrayal of young Lloyd and old Auld, his readers beheld the possibility of a very different style of white Southern leadership. Both Lloyd with his flowers and Auld with his tears indicated to Douglass that they recognized the evils of slavery and sought his forgiveness. Both paid tribute to Douglass's dignity without fearing that by doing so they compromised their own. And Auld even identified with his former slave, telling Douglass that "'had I been in your place, I should have done as you did.'"[51] Doubtless, Douglass would have been more pleased if they had given more explicit signs of reformation and repentance. Nevertheless, he was willing to meet them halfway because, by his account, he, too, had a generous, courageous, and "liberal-minded" spirit.[52]

Given Douglass's well-established political ambition, we might reasonably ask whether his parables of citizenship were not, in fact, merely thinly disguised self-promotion conveying that white persons took him, a black man, seriously. I think there is some truth to such a view, but it is an incomplete and far too cynical reading of Douglass's character. By 1850, Douglass had come to regard himself as the shrewdest black advocate for African American rights and citizenship. It becomes nearly impossible to peel apart his principled motives from his political ones from the mid-1850s on. Yet from his own blended standpoint, perhaps, this very distinction was false. In the introduction to *My Bondage and My Freedom,* his friend and mentor James McCune Smith tried to capture Douglass's unusual fusion of bondage and freedom, action and thought, body and mind in his coinage of *"work-*able, *do-*able words." After arguing at some length that for Douglass's "special mission" of abolitionism, his "plantation education was better than any he could have acquired in any lettered school," Smith writes that "his were not mere words of eloquence . . . that delight the ear and then pass away. No! They were *work-*able, *do-*able words that brought forth fruits in the revolution in Illinois, and in the passage of the franchise resolutions by the Assembly of New York."[53]

The *"work-*able, *do-*able" thrust of Douglass's parables of citizenship emerges clearly in his response to the Supreme Court's decision in 1883 to overturn the Civil Rights Act of 1875. "There are tongues in trees," he wrote, "sermons in stones, and books in the running brooks. This law [the Fourteenth Amendment] . . . did speak. It expressed the sentiment of justice and fair play common to every honest heart. Its voice was against popular prejudice and meanness. It appealed to all the noble and patriotic instincts of the American people. It told the American people that they were all equal before the law; that they belonged to a common country and were equal citizens."[54]

Note that Douglass does not here ground the Fourteenth Amendment in something like self-evident truth, much less in reason, but in "sentiment," in the "heart," and in the "instincts" of "patriotic . . . Americans." The amendment is a "moral standard" that expresses "the sentiment of justice and fair play common to every honest heart." It is a defense of "American liberty" by the "American people." Douglass explicitly contrasts these "sentiments" with the feelings of "prejudice and meanness" animating the Supreme Court, which "has seen fit in this case affecting a weak and much persecuted people, to be guided by the *narrowest* and most *restricted* rules of legal interpretation. It has viewed both the Constitution and the law with a strict regard to their letter, but without any *generous* recognition and application of their *broad* and *liberal* spirit."[55] Thus, the language Douglass's uses to affirm the value of the Fourteenth Amendment and to criticize the Supreme Court's ruling is precisely the language he uses to recount his private meetings with his former masters. In both public and private realms, he contrasts conservatism's strictness, meanness, and prejudice with the "broad and liberal spirit" and its "sentiment of justice and play." His point is that democratic citizenship requires precisely the "spirit" expressed in the amendment and, conversely, that the amendment itself expresses the "spirit" properly found in democratic citizenship.

In *Life and Times,* then, Douglass's principal mode of doing political theory is to portray exemplary democratic citizens and their intersubjective exchanges across racial lines. This mode of doing political philosophy plainly differs from that of most political theorists working today, and it has the obvious shortcoming of slighting—or seeming to slight—the importance of structural racism. As literary historian John Ernest has written, "What is white about white people . . . is not the color of their skin (which is not, after all, white) but rather the historical situation that has made 'white' bodies such able predictors of experience, understanding, and access to privilege and cultural authority—a whiteness, in other words, that cannot be transcended merely by good intentions or by the reach of an individual's consciousness."[56] The risk that accompanies Douglass's dramatizing of individuals' behavior as a model of democratic comportment, then, is that it implies that whiteness can "be transcended merely by good intentions or by the reach of an individual's consciousness." However, this danger is not necessarily or logically entailed by an assignment of individual responsibility for racism. Indeed, I would argue that the challenge facing whites in a white supremacist society is to take personal responsibility for racism while also understanding that admission of such personal accountability is neither fully achievable nor sufficient to the task of dismantling racism.

In any case, a number of notable political theorists today continue to call attention to the ways white racism must be addressed in part by individual white persons holding themselves accountable for it and changing their behavior and disposition. For example, Danielle S. Allen has taken note of the nation's failure to actualize even the formal mandates of the *Brown* decision of 1954, which she suggests reflects its even deeper failure to construct an understanding and practice of citizenship that militates against the formation of racist dispositions. Observing that the citizenship instruction most commonly given to citizens is "don't talk with strangers," she argues on behalf of "a new mode of citizenship in friendship understood not as an emotion but [as] a practice." "Political friendship consists finally of trying to be like friends. Its payoff is rarely intimate, or genuine friendship, but it is often trustworthiness and, issuing from that, political trust. Its art, trust production, has long gone by the abused name of rhetoric. Properly understood, rhetoric is not a list of stylistic rules but an outline of the radical commitment to other citizens that is needed for a just democratic politics."[57]

Surely Douglass is trying to dramatize and model a conception of citizenship as "trust production" that closely resembles what Allen has called for. Like Allen, he does not suggest that he and young Lloyd or that he and Captain Auld became lifelong friends and intimates. Rather, he precisely choreographs an exchange of simultaneous and reciprocal gestures that build trust across immeasurably deep chasms of experience and outlook. Like Allen, therefore, he is interested in a "rhetoric" of citizenship, one in which citizens communicate with each other through styles of deportment and shared commitments to a particular disposition. Of course, Allen produces argument in a form recognizable to political theorists today, but, like Douglass, she is more concerned with theory that helps produce a new practice of citizenship than with theory that focuses exclusively on relationships among ideas (e.g., justice, race, equality, and the like).

Similarly, toward the end of his book *A World of Becoming,* William Connolly turns his attention from ideas, forces, and other such abstractions to the persons who are his readers and who constitute at least a part of "the people" of a democracy. Connolly urges them to recognize that their subjectivity consists of the multiple "roles" they play and to exploit this performativity by redefining and recombining these roles:

> The accumulation of rapid shifts in role performance might introduce new pressures into the world. . . . The possibilities are endless. The point of individual and group experimentation with role assignments is simultaneously to make a direct difference through our conduct, to open us to new experiences that might alter our relational sensibilities even further, to unscramble role assumptions assumed by others, to form operational connections with others from which larger political movements might be generated, and to make connections with noble role warriors in other regions and walks of life to enlarge the space and visibility of positive action.[58]

These words, I would argue, offer a recognizably "theoretical" account of what Douglass is attempting to convey through the concrete, intersubjective exchanges dramatized in his parables of citizenship. Douglass's stories present his readers white and black with vivid instances of "rapid role shifts" as masters and formerly enslaved persons meet; they show persons in the very act of altering "their relational sensibilities"; and they also work to "unscramble role assumptions" held by his white readers that their citizenship and dignity depend in large measure on a contemptuous attitude toward blacks. Connolly's phrase "noble role warriors" is an apt description of the way Douglass portrays himself, Tilton, and Gladstone, suggesting that the "operational connections" among such persons is an effective way to build "larger political movements." Finally, by inviting his readers to view the private words spoken by young Lloyd and Captain Auld as admirable "experimentation with role assignment," Douglass works to "enlarge the space" of the political and make more visible the various forms that "positive action" might take—a greeting, a proffered bouquet, a handshake.

One of the last places Douglass visited on his European tour in 1886 was the cemetery in Florence where the abolitionist and social reformer Theodore Parker had been buried. And Douglass explains why: Parker's disposition was "broad as the land in his sympathy with mankind," he writes. "The liberal thought which he had taught" was marked by a sympathetic flexibility that welcomed rather than repelled difference. "He loved Mr. Garrison, but was not a Garrisonian. He worked with the sects, but was not sectarian. His character was cast in a mold too large to be pressed into a form or reform less broad than humanity. . . . He was the large and generous brother of all men."[59] Encountered toward the close of Douglass's last book, Parker serves formally and rhetorically as the American equivalent of William Gladstone. The "blending of opposites" Douglass admired in Gladstone takes the form here of the "liberal thought" of Theodore Parker: Parker "loved Mr. Garrison, but was not a Garrisonian"; "he worked with sects, but was not sectarian." In praising Parker's ability to hold opposites in tension with each other and his insistence on occupying a space that might not always be legible to others, Douglass is also limning his own self-portrait. And by identifying his own blended perspectives with the temperament of a free, white man, Douglass is again holding up a disposition of democratic citizenship for all his readers to emulate. A citizen so disposed is "broad" enough to be able to bear the tension of standing between two seemingly contradictory imperatives, between fidelity to eternal truths and obligations to historical action now. Such a citizen is "generous" enough not to acquire his or her own dignity at the expense of others but rather feels his or her own sense of self-worth enlarged by encounters with fellow citizens who are different. Such a citizen meets the dilemmas inherent in democracy not by simply trying to reason through them but by developing a disposition "large" enough to contain and "brave" enough to sustain them.

Notes

1. Douglass published four versions of his autobiography: *Narrative of the Life of Frederick Douglass, an American Slave* (1845), *My Bondage and My Freedom* (1855), and then two versions of *Life and Times of Frederick Douglass*, the first published in 1881 and then the second a revised and expanded edition published in 1893.

2. Frederick Douglass, *Life and Times of Frederick Douglass*, in *Autobiographies*, ed. Henry Louis Gates Jr. (New York: Library of America, 1994), 986–87; Gates used the expanded edition of *Life and Times* published in 1893. All of my references to Douglass's autobiographies are to the Gates edition.

3. Charles W. Mills, "Racial Liberalism," *PMLA* 23 (5) (October 2008): 1380–97.

4. I argue this point at some length in "A 'Voice from the Enslaved': The Origins of Frederick Douglass's Political Philosophy of Democracy," *American Literary History* 23 (4) (2011): 697–723. In my essay here, I draw upon arguments first published in "The Liberal Imagination of Frederick Douglass: Honoring the Emotions That Give Life to Liberal Principles," *American Scholar* 77 (2) (Spring

2008): 34–45, and in *The Time Is Always Now: Black Thought and the Transformation of US Democracy* (Oxford: Oxford University Press, 2013).

5. Frederick Douglass, *My Bondage and My Freedom*, in *Autobiographies*, 148.

6. Ibid., 390. Note the humor, especially irony, in Douglass—one way that he marked the slippage.

7. Frederick Douglass, *Narrative of the Life of Frederick Douglass, an American Slave*, in *Autobiographies*, 24. Douglass's implied disparagement of "philosophy" might have been provoked by his fellow (white) abolitionist John A. Collins saying to him, "'Give us the facts, we will take care of the philosophy'" (Douglass, *Life and Times*, 663, 662).

8. Douglass, *My Bondage and My Freedom*, 184.

9. For a fuller account of Douglass's revisions of *Narrative* in *My Bondage and My Freedom*, see Nicholas Bromell, *By the Sweat of the Brow: Labor and Literature in Antebellum America* (Chicago: University of Chicago Press, 1993), 193–205. See also Neil Roberts, *Freedom as Marronage* (Chicago: University of Chicago Press, 2015), 71–76.

10. Douglass, *Life and Times*, 502–3, emphasis added.

11. Douglass, *My Bondage and My Freedom*, 185.

12. Douglass, *Life and Times*, 503.

13. John Stauffer notes these struggles when he observes that, "for Douglass, representations of slavery brought feelings of freedom and degrees of power. But representations of freedom created in him a crisis of language and aesthetics" ("Frederick Douglass and the Aesthetic of Freedom," *Raritan: A Quarterly Review* 25 [1] [Summer 2005]: 114). One explanation for this seeming paradox inheres, as Stauffer observes, in the genre of the slave narrative itself: it was designed to represent bondage, not freedom. My complementary explanation here points to Douglass's sense that his experience of enslavement had given him a certain philosophical authority different from that which he acquired as a free man. This would explain why, as Stauffer puts it, "long after he had escaped from bondage in 1838, Douglass insisted that he was still a slave" (115). Douglass valued the slave's standpoint—more precisely, the aspect of his blended standpoint he had acquired within slavery—and he was determined to keep trying to give voice to it no matter how challenging that might be.

14. William Sullivan, *The Political Class Book: Intended to Instruct the Higher Classes in the Origin, Nature, and Use of Political Power* (Boston: Carter, Hendee, 1832), unpaginated first page of the introduction.

15. Ibid., 10, 12.

16. Joseph Story, *The Constitutional Class Book: Being a Brief Exposition of the Constitution of the United States Designed for the Use of the Higher Classes in Common Schools* (Boston: Hilliard, Gray, 1834), 142–43, 153.

17. Ibid., 153.

18. John Rawls, "Justice as Fairness: Political Not Metaphysical," *Philosophy and Public Affairs* 14 (1985): 225.

19. On Douglass's changing views on the constitutionality of slavery, see especially David W. Blight, *Frederick Douglass' Civil War: Keeping Faith in Jubilee* (Baton Rouge: Louisiana State University Press 1989), 30–35; Gregg D. Crane, *Race, Citizenship, and Law in American Literature* (Cambridge: Cambridge University Press, 2002), 104–30; Philip S. Foner, *Frederick Douglass: A Biography* (New York: Citadel Press, 1964), 136–54; Waldo E. Martin Jr., *The Mind of Frederick Douglass* (Chapel Hill: University of North Carolina Press, 1984), 31–40; Charles W. Mills, "Whose Fourth of July? Frederick Douglass and 'Original Intent,'" in Bill E. Lawson and Frank M. Kirkland, eds., *Frederick Douglass: A Critical Reader* (Malden, MA: Blackwell, 1999), 100–142.

20. Frederick Douglass, "Change of Opinion Announced," *North Star*, reprinted in *The Liberator*, May 22, 1851, and in *The Life and Writings of Frederick Douglass*, 5 vols., ed. Philip S. Foner (New York: International Publishers, 1950–1975), 2:155–56.

21. Martin, *The Mind of Frederick Douglass*, 33.

22. Blight, *Frederick Douglass' Civil War*, 50.

23. Wilson Moses, *Creative Conflict in African American Thought: Frederick Douglass, Alexander Crummell, Booker T. Washington, W. E. B. Du Bois, and Marcus Garvey* (Cambridge: Cambridge University Press, 2004), 48.

24. George Yancy, "African-American Philosophy: Through the Lens of Socio-existential Struggle," *Philosophy and Social Criticism* 37 (5) (2011): 552.

25. Frederick Douglass, "The Constitution and Slavery," in *Life and Writings of Frederick Douglass*, 1:361.

26. Ibid.

27. "The Position of Parties," *Oneida Sachem*, in Douglass, *Life and Writings of Frederick Douglass*, 2:379.

28. Frederick Douglass, "The Republican Party—Our Position," in *Life and Writings of Frederick Douglass*, 2:380, 381.

29. Ibid., 382–83.

30. Benjamin R. Barber, "Foundationalism and Democracy," in Seyla Benhabib, ed., *Democracy and Difference: Contesting the Boundaries of the Political* (Princeton, NJ: Princeton University Press, 1996), 352.

31. In 1893, Douglass remained as committed to higher law as the foundation of democracy as he had been in 1845: "Schooled as I have been among the abolitionists of New England," he writes in *Life and Times*, "I recognize that the universe is governed by laws which are unchangeable and eternal" (914).

32. Frederick Douglass. *The Frederick Douglass Papers, Series One: Speeches, Debates, and Interviews*, 5 vols., ed. John W. Blassingame and others (New Haven, CT: Yale University Press, 1979–1992), 2:366.

33. Barber, "Foundationalism and Democracy," 353.

34. Douglass, *My Bondage and My Freedom*, 171, emphasis added.

35. Barber, "Foundationalism and Democracy," 351.

36. Orlando Patterson, *Slavery and Social Death: A Comparative Study* (Cambridge, MA: Harvard University Press, 1982); Steven Hahn, *A Nation under Our Feet: Black Political Struggles in the Rural South from Slavery to the Great Migration* (Cambridge, MA: Harvard University Press, 2003).

37. Hahn, *A Nation under Our Feet*, 16–17.

38. It seems likely that Douglass derived the idea of these staged dialogues between master and slave from a dialogue he had read many years earlier in *The Columbian Orator*. See *Narrative*, 41–42.

39. Douglass, *Life and Times*, 828, original emphasis.

40. Ibid.

41. Ibid., 879, 880.

42. Ibid., 881.

43. Douglass, *Narrative*, 18.

44. Douglass, *Life and Times*, 883.

45. Ibid., 875.

46. Ibid.

47. Note that there are other such parables in *Life and Times*.

48. Quoted in Blight, *Frederick Douglass' Civil War*, 229–30.

49. Frederick Douglass, "The Unknown Dead: An Address Delivered in Arlington, Virginia, 30 May 1871," in *The Frederick Douglass Papers, Series One: Speeches, Debates, and Interviews*, 5 vols., ed. John W. Blassingame and others (New Haven, CT: Yale University Press, 1979–1992), 4:290–91.

50. Frederick Douglass, "We Must Not Abandon the Observance of Decoration Day: An Address Delivered in Rochester, New York, 30 May 1882," in *The Frederick Douglass Papers. Series One*, 5:47.

51. Douglass, *Life and Times*, 463, 874.

52. The word *liberal* has a history that lets us see even further into what Douglass is doing here. In the eighteenth and early nineteenth centuries, *liberal* simply meant "generous." A liberal person gave unstintingly, and his opposite was a person who was mean—grasping and slow to give. This distinction shaded gradually into another, and liberal generosity began to imply an open stance toward life and a broad-minded attitude toward other people's ideas and values. Meanness, by contrast, suggested a strict, close-minded disposition that could become mean-

spirited—prejudiced, unkind, or even cruel. The semantic thread that winds its way through these first meanings of liberalism originates in the ancient Greek word *luw*, meaning "to let loose," "to let go." Liberal generosity and broadmindedness are at bottom a kind of looseness and self-abandonment.

53. James McCune Smith, introduction to Douglass, *My Bondage and My Freedom*, 126, 132.

54. Douglass, *Life and Times*, 978.

55. Ibid., 974, emphasis added.

56. John Ernest, *Chaotic Justice: Rethinking African American Literary History* (Chapel Hill, NC: University of North Carolina Press, 2009), 41.

57. Danielle S. Allen, *Talking to Strangers: Anxieties of Citizenship since Brown v. Board of Education* (Chicago: University of Chicago Press, 2004), 156, 157.

58. William Connolly, *A World of Becoming* (Durham, NC: Duke University Press, 2011), 144–45.

59. Douglass, *Life and Times*, 1015–16.

Acknowledgments

I am thankful to many people for their invaluable help, feedback, and encouragement throughout the process of completing this volume. Stephen Wrinn and Patrick J. Deneen kindly invited me to submit a book proposal on Frederick Douglass's political thought for the University Press of Kentucky's series Political Companions to Great American Authors. Wrinn and Allison Webster periodically checked in with me to see how the volume was coming together. They never imposed an ultimatum deadline but instead, prior to their respective departure and retirement from the press, underscored that I should assemble the best book possible and finish it at that highest-quality level. I appreciate that advice. My editor, Melissa Hammer, inherited this project yet nonetheless shepherded the book from manuscript review to publication with timeliness and precision. It has been a delight working with her.

I thank the authors of both newly commissioned and previously published chapters for their wonderful works on Douglass's thought, which I hope will be beneficial to readers well into the future. Some contributors' original essays were first presented at the roundtable "Frederick Douglass and the Power of Persuasion" at an annual meeting of the American Political Science Association in Chicago. Many thanks to the publishers and copyright holders for reprint permissions. Acknowledgment of reprinted works appears in the chapter endnotes.

The anonymous reviewers of the book proposal and subsequent manuscript strengthened the book's architecture and content through their painstaking constructive criticism. So, too, did the incisive comments by students in my course "Frederick Douglass and the Idea of Freedom," which led me to revise points posited in the book's introduction. Nneka Dennie and Hari Ramesh, brilliant former undergraduate students of mine who are now PhD candidates, provided stellar research assistance at integral stages of the project. In addition to intellectual contributions, there were financial ones. I am grateful to the Office of the Dean of Faculty at Williams College for essential funding that enabled preparation and publication of the final version of the book.

My wife, Karima Barrow, and eldest son, Kofi Roberts, constantly inspire me, and their feedback on Douglass, from across generations, demonstrates the manifold ways Douglass's ideas live on as we approach the two hundredth anniversary of his birth. I dedicate this volume to my youngest child, Santiago Roberts, and to the memory of my two late grandmothers, Olive Gordon and Hyacinth Roberts, who recently became ancestors. Santiago's happy demeanor and indomitable spirit amid life's early challenges highlight why, as Douglass also understood, hope is more than a slogan. My grandmothers set the standards for how I understand and respect humanity. Their ethics of living, respecting, loving, and imagining showed me that other future worlds are indeed possible, however improbable.

Neil Roberts
Williamstown, Massachusetts
August 2017

Selected Bibliography

Primary Works

Douglass, Frederick. *Autobiographies*. Edited by Henry Louis Gates Jr. New York: Library of America, 1994.

———. *Escape from Slavery: The Boyhood of Frederick Douglass in His Own Words*. Edited by Michael McCurdy. New York: Knopf, 1994.

———. *The Essential Douglass: Selected Writings and Speeches*. Edited by Nicholas Buccola. Indianapolis, IN: Hackett, 2016.

———. *Frederick Douglass on Women's Rights*. Edited by Philip S. Foner. Boston: Da Capo, 1992.

———. The Frederick Douglass Papers. Library of Congress. At https://www.loc. gov/collection/frederick-douglass-papers/about-this-collection/.

———. *The Frederick Douglass Papers. Series One: Speeches, Debates, and Interviews*. 5 vols. Edited by John Blassingame and others. New Haven, CT: Yale University Press, 1979–1992.

———. *The Frederick Douglass Papers. Series Two: Autobiographical Writings*. 3 vols. Edited by John Blassingame and others. New Haven, CT: Yale University Press, 1999–2012.

———. Frederick Douglass Project. University of Rochester. At http://rbscp.lib. rochester.edu/2494.

———. *Frederick Douglass: Selected Speeches and Writings*. Edited by Philip S. Foner. Abridged and adapted by Yuval Taylor. Chicago: Lawrence Hill Books, 1999.

———. *Great Speeches by Frederick Douglass*. Edited by James Daley. Mineola, NY: Dover, 2013.

———. *Life and Times of Frederick Douglass, Written by Himself*. Edited by Rayford Logan. Mineola, NY: Dover, 2003.

———. *The Life and Writings of Frederick Douglass*. 5 vols. Edited by Philip S. Foner. New York: International Publishers, 1950–1975.

———. *My Bondage and My Freedom*. Edited by William L. Andrews. Urbana: University of Illinois Press, 1987.

———. *My Bondage and My Freedom*. Edited by John David Smith. New York: Penguin, 2003.

———. *Narrative of the Life of Frederick Douglass, an American Slave, Written by Himself*. Edited by Angela Y. Davis. San Francisco: City Lights, 2010.

———. *Narrative of the Life of Frederick Douglass, an American Slave, Written by Himself*. Edited by Robert B. Stepto. Cambridge, MA: Harvard University Press, 2009.

———. *The Oxford Frederick Douglass Reader*. Edited by William L. Andrews. Oxford: Oxford University Press, 1996.

———. *The Portable Frederick Douglass*. Edited by John Stauffer and Henry Louis Gates Jr. New York: Penguin, 2016.

Biographies

Blight, David W. *Frederick Douglass: Prophet of Freedom*. New York: Simon & Schuster, 2018.

Bontemps, Arna. *Free at Last: The Life of Frederick Douglass*. New York: Dodd Mead, 1971.

Foner, Philip. *Frederick Douglass: A Biography*. New York: Citadel Press, 1964.

McFeely, William S. *Frederick Douglass*. New York: Norton, 1991.

Preston, Dickson. *Young Frederick Douglass: The Maryland Years*. Baltimore: Johns Hopkins University Press, 1980.

Quarles, Benjamin. *Frederick Douglass*. New York: Atheneum, 1968.

Sandefur, Timothy. *Frederick Douglass: Self-Made Man*. Washington, DC: Cato Institute, 2018.

Edited Collections

Andrews, William L., ed. *Critical Essays on Frederick Douglass*. Boston: Hall, 1991.

Brotz, Howard, ed. *African-American Social and Political Thought, 1850–1920*. Piscataway, NJ: Transaction, 1991.

Brown, Wesley, ed. *The Teachers and Writers Guide to Frederick Douglass*. New York: Teachers and Writers Collaborative, 1996.

Fisch, Audrey, ed. *The Cambridge Companion to the African American Slave Narrative*. Cambridge: Cambridge University Press, 2007.

Follett, Richard, Eric Foner, and Walter Johnson, eds. *Slavery's Ghost: The Problem of Freedom in the Age of Emancipation*. Baltimore: Johns Hopkins University Press, 2011.

Frisch, Morton, and Richard Stevens, eds. *American Political Thought: The Philosophic Dimensions of American Statesmanship*. Itasca, IL: Peacock, 1983.

Hall, Stuart, ed. *Representation: Cultural Representations and Signifying Practices.* Thousand Oaks, CA: Sage, 1997.

Hamm, Theodore, ed. *Frederick Douglass in Brooklyn.* New York: Akashic, 2017.

Harris, Leonard, ed. *Philosophy Born of Struggle: Anthology of Afro-American Philosophy from 1917.* Dubuque, IA: Kendall/Hunt, 1983.

Jaffa, Harry, ed. *Original Intent and the Framers of the Constitution: A Disputed Question.* Washington, DC: Regnery Gateway, 1994.

James, Joy, ed. *The New Abolitionists: (Neo)Slave Narratives and Contemporary Prison Writings.* Albany: State University of New York Press, 2005.

Lawson, Bill E., and Frank M. Kirkland, eds. *Frederick Douglass: A Critical Reader.* Malden, MA: Blackwell, 1999.

Lee, Maurice S., ed. *The Cambridge Companion to Frederick Douglass.* Cambridge: Cambridge University Press, 2009.

Leone, Mark, and Lee Jenkins, eds. *Atlantic Crossings in the Wake of Frederick Douglass: Archaeology, Literature, and Spatial Culture.* Boston: Brill, 2017.

Levine, Robert S., ed. *Martin R. Delany: A Documentary Reader.* Chapel Hill: University of North Carolina Press, 2003.

Levine, Robert S., and Samuel Otter, eds. *Frederick Douglass and Herman Melville: Essays in Relation.* Chapel Hill: University of North Carolina Press, 2008.

Litwack, Leon, and August Meier, eds. *Black Leaders of the Nineteenth Century.* Urbana: University of Illinois Press, 1988.

Lott, Tommy, ed. *Subjugation and Bondage: Critical Essays in Slavery and Social Philosophy.* Lanham, MD: Rowman and Littlefield, 1998.

McKivigan, John, and Heather Kaufman, eds. *In the Words of Frederick Douglass: Quotations from Liberty's Champion.* Ithaca, NY: Cornell University Press, 2012.

Pittman, John, ed. *African-American Perspectives and Philosophical Traditions.* New York: Routledge, 1997.

Pitts, Helen, ed. *In Memoriam: Frederick Douglass.* Philadelphia: Yorston, 1897.

Rice, Alan, and Martin Crawford, eds. *Liberating Sojourn: Frederick Douglass and Transatlantic Reform.* Athens: University of Georgia Press, 1999.

Sekora, John, and Darwin Turner, eds. *The Art of the Slave Narrative: Original Essays in Criticism and Theory.* Macomb: Western Illinois University Press, 1982.

Storing, Herbert, ed. *What Country Have I? Political Writings by Black Americans.* New York: St. Martin's, 1970.

Sundquist, Eric, ed. *Frederick Douglass: New Literary and Historical Essays.* Cambridge: Cambridge University Press, 1990.

Thompson, Julius, James Conyers Jr., and Nancy Dawson, eds. *The Frederick Douglass Encyclopedia.* Santa Barbara, CA: ABC-CLIO, 2010.

Wallace, Maurice, and Shawn Smith, eds. *Pictures and Progress: Early Photography and the Making of African American Identity.* Durham, NC: Duke University Press, 2012.

Articles and Monographs

Alexander, Michelle. *The New Jim Crow: Mass Incarceration in the Age of Colorblindness.* New York: New Press, 2010.

Allen, Danielle. *Our Declaration: A Reading of the Declaration of Independence in Defense of Equality.* New York: Liveright, 2014.

———. *Talking to Strangers: Anxieties of Citizenship since* Brown v. Board of Education. Chicago: University of Chicago Press, 2004.

Andrews, William L. *To Tell a Free Story: The First Century of Afro-American Autobiography, 1760–1865.* Urbana: University of Illinois Press, 1986.

Aptheker, Herbert. *Abolitionism: A Revolutionary Movement.* Boston: Twayne, 1989.

———. "Du Bois on Douglass." *Journal of Negro History* 49 (4) (1964): 264–68.

Arendt, Hannah. *Men in Dark Times.* New York: Harcourt, Brace and World, 1968.

Barnes, L. Diane. *Frederick Douglass: Reformer and Statesman.* New York: Routledge, 2013.

Baxter, Terry. *Frederick Douglass's Curious Audiences: Ethos in the Age of the Consumable Subject.* New York: Routledge, 2004.

Bennett, Nolan. "To Narrate and Denounce: Frederick Douglass and the Politics of Personal Narrative." *Political Theory* 44 (2) (2016): 240–64.

Bernier, Celeste-Marie. *Characters of Blood: Black Heroism in the Transatlantic Imagination.* Athens: University of Georgia Press, 2012.

———. "A 'Typical Negro' or a 'Work of Art'? The 'Inner' via the 'Outer' Man in Frederick Douglass's Manuscripts and Daguerreotypes." *Slavery and Abolition* 33 (2) (2012): 287–303.

Berry, Diana. *The Price for Their Pound of Flesh: The Value of the Enslaved, from Womb to Grave, in the Building of a Nation.* Boston: Beacon, 2017.

Best, Stephen. *The Fugitive's Properties: Law and the Poetics of Possession.* Chicago: University of Chicago Press, 2004.

Best, Stephen, and Saidiya Hartman. "Fugitive Justice." *Representations* 92 (1) (2005): 1–15.

Blight, David. "'The Civil War Lies on Us Like a Sleeping Dragon': America's Deadly Divide—and Why It Has Returned." *Guardian,* August 20, 2017. At https://amp. theguardian.com/us-news/2017/aug/20/civil-war-american-history-trump.

————. *Frederick Douglass and Abraham Lincoln: A Relationship in Language, Politics, and Memory*. Milwaukee: Marquette University Press, 2001.

————. *Frederick Douglass' Civil War: Keeping Faith in Jubilee*. Baton Rouge: Louisiana State University Press, 1989.

————. *Race and Reunion: The Civil War in American Memory*. Cambridge, MA: Harvard University Press, 2001.

Boxill, Bernard. *Blacks and Social Justice*. Lanham, MD: Rowman and Littlefield, 1992.

————. "Fear and Shame as Forms of Moral Suasion in the Thought of Frederick Douglass." *Transactions of the Charles S. Pierce Society* 31 (4) (1995): 713–44.

————. "Two Traditions in African-American Political Philosophy." *Philosophical Forum* 24 (1–3) (1992–1993): 119–35.

Bromell, Nick. *The Time Is Always Now: Black Thought and the Transformation of US Democracy*. Oxford: Oxford University Press, 2013.

————. "A 'Voice from the Enslaved': The Origins of Frederick Douglass's Political Philosophy of Democracy." *American Literary History* 23 (4) (2011): 697–723.

Buccola, Nicholas. *The Political Thought of Frederick Douglass: In Pursuit of American Liberty*. New York: New York University Press, 2012.

Byrd, Brandon. "Frederick Douglass, Haiti, and Diplomacy." *Black Perspectives*, February 11, 2017. At http://www.aaihs.org/frederick-douglass-haiti-and-diplomacy/.

Carby, Hazel. *Race Men*. Cambridge, MA: Harvard University Press, 1998.

Chaffin, Tom. *Giant's Causeway: Frederick Douglass's Irish Odyssey and the Making of an American Visionary*. Charlottesville: University of Virginia Press, 2014.

Chesebrough, David. *Frederick Douglass: Oratory from Slavery*. Westport, CT: Greenwood Press, 1998.

Chestnutt, Charles. *Frederick Douglass*. Mineola, NY: Dover, 2002.

Coates, Ta-Nehisi. *Between the World and Me*. New York: Spiegel & Grau, 2015.

Colaiaco, James. *Frederick Douglass and the Fourth of July*. New York: Palgrave Macmillan, 2006.

Cooper, Anna Julia. *A Voice from the South*. Oxford: Oxford University Press, 1988.

Crane, Gregg. *Race, Citizenship, and Law in American Literature*. Cambridge: Cambridge University Press, 2002.

Darby, Derrick. *Race, Rights, and Recognition*. Cambridge: Cambridge University Press, 2009.

Davis, Angela Y. *Abolition Democracy: Beyond Empire, Prisons, and Torture. Interviews with Angela Davis*. New York: Seven Stories, 2005.

————. *Freedom Is a Constant Struggle: Ferguson, Palestine, and the Foundations of a Movement*. Chicago: Haymarket, 2016.

————. *The Meaning of Freedom*. San Francisco: City Lights, 2011.

Davis, David Brion. *Inhuman Bondage: The Rise and Fall of Slavery in the New World*. Oxford: Oxford University Press, 2006.

————. *The Slave Power Conspiracy and the Paranoid Style*. Baton Rouge: Louisiana State University Press, 1969.

Davis, Reginald F. *Frederick Douglass: A Precursor to Liberation Theology*. Macon, GA: Mercer University Press, 2005.

Dawson, Michael C. *Black Visions: The Roots of Contemporary African-American Political Ideologies*. Chicago: University of Chicago Press, 2001.

Diedrich, Maria. *Love across the Color Lines: Ottilie Assing and Frederick Douglass*. New York: Hill and Wang, 1999.

Du Bois, W. E. B. *Black Reconstruction in America, 1860–1880*. New York: Free Press, 1992.

————. *John Brown*. New York: Modern Library, 2001.

————. *The Souls of Black Folk*. Edited by David W. Blight and Robert Gooding-Williams. Boston: Bedford/St. Martin's, 1997.

Fanuzzi, Robert. *Abolition's Public Sphere*. Minneapolis: University of Minnesota Press, 2003.

Foner, Eric. *Forever Free: The Story of Emancipation and Reconstruction*. New York: Vintage, 2005.

————. *The Story of American Freedom*. New York: Norton, 1998.

Fought, Leigh. *Women in the World of Frederick Douglass*. Oxford: Oxford University Press, 2017.

Frederickson, George. *The Black Image in the White Mind: The Debate on Afro-American Character and Destiny, 1871–1914*. Middletown, CT: Wesleyan University Press, 1987.

Gates, Henry Louis, Jr. *Figures in Black: Words, Signs, and the "Racial" Self*. Oxford: Oxford University Press, 1987.

Giddings, Paula. *Ida: A Sword among Lions*. New York: HarperCollins, 2008.

Glaude, Eddie, Jr. *Exodus! Religion, Race, and Nation in Early Nineteenth-Century America*. Chicago: University of Chicago Press, 2000.

Goldstein, Leslie F. "Morality and Prudence in the Statesmanship of Frederick Douglass: Radical as Reformer." *Polity* 16 (4) (1984): 606–23.

————. "The Political Thought of Frederick Douglass." Ph.D. diss., Cornell University, 1974.

Gooding-Williams, Robert. *Look, a Negro! Philosophical Essays on Race, Culture, and Politics*. New York: Routledge, 2006.

Gordon, Lewis R. *Existentia Africana: Understanding Africana Existential Thought.* New York: Routledge, 2000.

Gregory, James. *Frederick Douglass the Orator.* Springfield, MA: Wiley, 1893.

Habermas, Jürgen. *Between Facts and Norms: Contributions to a Discourse Theory of Law and Democracy.* Cambridge, MA: MIT Press, 1996.

Hack, Daniel. *Reaping Something New: African American Transformations of Victorian Literature.* Princeton, NJ: Princeton University Press, 2017.

Hacker, Andrew. *Two Nations: Black and White, Separate, Hostile, Unequal.* New York: Ballantine, 1992.

Hahn, Steven. *A Nation under Our Feet: Black Political Struggles in the Rural South from Slavery to the Great Migration.* Cambridge, MA: Harvard University Press, 2003.

Hamilton, Cynthia. "Models of Agency: Frederick Douglass and 'The Heroic Slave.'" *Proceedings of the Antiquarian Society* 114 (2005): 87–136.

Hanchard, Michael. "Afro-Modernity: Temporality, Politics, and the African Diaspora." *Public Culture* 11 (1) (1999): 245–68.

———. "Contours of Black Political Thought: An Introduction and Perspective." *Political Theory* 38 (4) (2010): 510–36.

———. *Party/Politics: Horizons in Black Political Thought.* Oxford: Oxford University Press, 2006.

———. *The Spectre of Race: How Discrimination Haunts Western Democracy.* Princeton, NJ: Princeton University Press, 2018.

Harding, Vincent. *There Is a River: The Black Struggle for Freedom in America.* New York: Vintage Books, 1981.

Hartman, Saidiya V. *Lose Your Mother: A Journey along the Atlantic Slave Route.* New York: Farrar, Straus, and Giroux, 2007.

———. *Scenes of Subjection: Terror, Slavery, and Self-Making in Nineteenth-Century America.* Oxford: Oxford University Press, 1997.

Hickman, Jared. *Black Prometheus: Race and Radicalism in the Age of Atlantic Slavery.* Oxford: Oxford University Press, 2017.

Hooker, Juliet. "'A Black Sister to Massachusetts': Latin America and the Fugitive Democratic Ethos of Frederick Douglass." *American Political Science Review* 109 (4) (2015): 690–702.

———. *Theorizing Race in the Americas: Douglass, Sarmiento, Du Bois, and Vasconcelos.* Oxford: Oxford University Press, 2017.

Huggins, Nathan. *Slave and Citizen: The Life of Frederick Douglass.* New York: HarperCollins, 1980.

Jacobs, Harriet. *Incidents in the Life of a Slave Girl, Written by Herself.* Cambridge, MA: Harvard University Press, 1987.

James, Joy. *Shadowboxing: Representations of Black Feminist Politics.* New York: St. Martin's Press, 1999.

Kateb, George. *Lincoln's Political Thought.* Cambridge, MA: Harvard University Press, 2015.

Kawash, Samira. *Dislocating the Color Line: Identity, Hybridity, and Singularity in African-American Narrative.* Stanford, CA: Stanford University Press, 1997.

Kelley, Robin. *Freedom Dreams: The Black Radical Imagination.* Boston: Beacon, 2002.

Kendi, Ibram. *Stamped from the Beginning: The Definitive History of Racist Ideas in America.* New York: Nation Books, 2016.

Kendrick, Paul, and Stephen Kendrick. *Douglass and Lincoln: How a Revolutionary Black Leader and a Reluctant Liberator Struggled to End Slavery and Save the Union.* New York: Walker, 2008.

King, Richard. *Civil Rights and the Idea of Freedom.* Oxford: Oxford University Press, 1992.

Kirkland, Frank. "Is an Existential Reading of the Fight with Covey Sufficient to Explain Frederick Douglass's Critique of Slavery?" *Critical Philosophy of Race* 3 (1) (2015): 124–51.

Krause, Sharon. *Liberalism with Honor.* Cambridge, MA: Harvard University Press, 2002.

Lebron, Christopher. *The Color of Shame: Race and Justice in Our Time.* Oxford: Oxford University Press, 2013.

———. *The Making of Black Lives Matter: A Brief History of an Idea.* Oxford: Oxford University Press, 2017.

Lemons, Gary. *Womanist Forefathers: Frederick Douglass and W. E. B. Du Bois.* Albany: State University of New York Press, 2009.

Levine, Robert S. *Dislocating Race and Nation: Episodes in Nineteenth-Century American Literary Nationalism.* Chapel Hill: University of North Carolina Press, 2008.

———. *The Lives of Frederick Douglass.* Cambridge, MA: Harvard University Press, 2016.

———. *Martin Delany, Frederick Douglass, and the Politics of Representative Identity.* Chapel Hill: University of North Carolina Press, 1997.

Lloyd, Vincent. *Black Natural Law.* Oxford: Oxford University Press, 2016.

Marshall, Stephen. *The City on the Hill from Below: The Crisis of Prophetic Black Politics.* Philadelphia: Temple University Press, 2011.

Martin, Waldo E., Jr. *The Mind of Frederick Douglass.* Chapel Hill: University of North Carolina Press, 1984.

Mbembe, Achille. *Critique of Black Reason.* Durham, NC: Duke University Press, 2017.

McCartney, John. *Black Power Ideologies: An Essay in African-American Political Thought*. Philadelphia: Temple University Press, 1992.

Meier, August. *Negro Thought in America, 1880–1915: Racial Ideologies in the Age of Booker T. Washington*. Ann Arbor: University of Michigan Press, 1963.

Miller, Branford. *Returning to Seneca Falls: The First Women's Rights Convention and Its Meaning for Men and Women Today*. Hudson, UK: Lindisfarne, 1995.

Mills, Charles W. *Blackness Visible: Essays on Philosophy and Race*. Ithaca, NY: Cornell University Press, 1998.

———. *Black Rights/White Wrongs: The Critique of Racial Liberalism*. Oxford: Oxford University Press, 2017.

Moses, Wilson J. *Creative Conflict in African American Thought: Frederick Douglass, Alexander Crummell, Booker T. Washington, W. E. B. Du Bois, and Marcus Garvey*. Cambridge: Cambridge University Press, 2004.

Moten, Fred. *In the Break: The Aesthetics of the Black Radical Tradition*. Minneapolis: University of Minnesota Press, 2003.

Muller, John. *Frederick Douglass in Washington, D.C.: The Lion of Anacostia*. Charleston, SC: History Press, 2012.

Myers, Peter C. "Frederick Douglass on Revolution and Integration: A Problem in Moral Psychology." *American Political Thought* 2 (1) (2013): 118–46.

———. *Frederick Douglass: Race and the Rebirth of Liberalism*. Lawrence: University Press of Kansas, 2008.

———. "'A Good Work for Our Race To-Day': Interests, Virtues, and the Achievement of Justice in Frederick Douglass's Freedmen's Monument Speech." *American Political Science Review* 104 (2) (2010): 209–25.

Nielson, Cynthia. *Foucault, Douglass, Fanon, and Scotus in Dialogue: On Social Construction and Freedom*. New York: Palgrave, 2013.

Nwankwo, Ifeoma. *Black Cosmopolitanism: Racial Consciousness and Transnational Identity in the Nineteenth-Century Americas*. Philadelphia: University of Pennsylvania Press, 2005.

Oakes, James. *The Radical and the Republican: Frederick Douglass, Abraham Lincoln, and the Triumph of Antislavery Politics*. New York: Norton, 2007.

Obama, Barack. *The Audacity of Hope: Thoughts on Reclaiming the American Dream*. New York: Random House, 2006.

———. *Dreams from My Father: A Story of Race and Inheritance*. New York: Three Rivers, 2004.

Patterson, Orlando. *Rituals of Blood: Consequences of Slavery in Two American Centuries*. New York: Basic Civitas, 1998.

———. *Slavery and Social Death: A Comparative Study*. Cambridge, MA: Harvard University Press, 1982.

Pocock, J. G. A. *Politics, Language, and Time: Essays on Political Thought and History.* New York: Atheneum, 1973.

Polyné, Millery. *From Douglass to Duvalier: U.S. African Americans, Haiti, and Pan Americanism, 1870–1964.* Gainesville: University Press of Florida, 2010.

Prince, April. *Who Was Frederick Douglass?* New York: Grosset and Dunlap, 2014.

Rankine, Claudia. *Citizen: An American Lyric.* Minneapolis: Graywolf, 2014.

Reed, Adolph, Jr. *Stirrings in the Jug: Black Politics in the Post-segregation Era.* Minneapolis: University of Minnesota Press, 1999.

Reinhardt, Mark. *Who Speaks for Margaret Garner?* Minneapolis: University of Minnesota Press, 2010.

Roberts, Dorothy. *Killing the Black Body: Race, Reproduction, and the Meaning of Liberty.* New York: Vintage, 1997.

Roberts, Neil. *Freedom as Marronage.* Chicago: University of Chicago Press, 2015.

Robinson, Cedric. *Black Movements in America.* New York: Routledge, 1997.

Rogers, William. *"We Are All Together Now": Frederick Douglass, William Lloyd Garrison, and the Prophetic Tradition.* New York: Routledge, 1995.

Sharpe, Christina. *In the Wake: On Blackness and Being.* Durham, NC: Duke University Press, 2016.

Shelby, Tommie. *Dark Ghettos: Injustice, Dissent, and Reform.* Cambridge, MA: Harvard University Press, 2016.

———. *We Who Are Dark: Philosophical Foundations of Black Solidarity.* Cambridge, MA: Harvard University Press, 2005.

Shklar, Judith. *American Citizenship: The Quest for Inclusion.* Cambridge, MA: Harvard University Press, 1991.

———. *Redeeming American Political Thought.* Chicago: University of Chicago Press, 1998.

Shulman, George. *American Prophecy: Race and Redemption in American Political Culture.* Minneapolis: University of Minnesota Press, 2008.

Sinha, Manisha. *The Slave's Cause: A History of Abolition.* New Haven, CT: Yale University Press, 2016.

Smith, K. Carl. *Frederick Douglass Republicans: The Movement to Re-ignite America's Passion for Liberty.* Birmingham, AL: AuthorHouse, 2011.

Smith, Kimberly. *African American Environmental Thought: Foundations.* Lawrence: University Press of Kansas, 2007.

Smith, Rogers. *Civic Ideals: Conflicting Visions of Citizenship in U.S. History.* New Haven, CT: Yale University Press, 1997.

———. *Political Peoplehood: The Roles of Values, Interests, and Identities.* Chicago: University of Chicago Press, 2015.

Smith, Valerie. *Self-Discovery and Authority in Afro-American Narrative.* Cambridge, MA: Harvard University Press, 1991.

Spillers, Hortense. *Black, White, and in Color: Essays on American Literature and Culture.* Chicago: University of Chicago Press, 2003.

Stauffer, John. *The Black Hearts of Men: Radical Abolitionists and the Transformation of Race.* Cambridge, MA: Harvard University Press, 2001.

———. *Giants: The Parallel Lives of Frederick Douglass and Abraham Lincoln.* New York: Twelve, 2008.

Stauffer, John, Zoe Trodd, and Celeste-Marie Bernier. *Picturing Frederick Douglass: An Illustrated Biography of the Nineteenth Century's Most Photographed American.* New York: Liveright, 2015.

Stephens, Gregory. *On Racial Frontiers: The New Culture of Frederick Douglass, Ralph Ellison, and Bob Marley.* Cambridge: Cambridge University Press, 1999.

Stepto, Robert. *From Behind the Veil: A Study of Afro-American Narrative.* Urbana: University of Illinois Press, 1979.

Storing, Herbert. *What the Anti-Federalists Were For: The Political Thought of the Opponents of the Constitution.* Chicago: University of Chicago Press, 1981.

Stow, Simon. "Agonistic Homegoing: Frederick Douglass, Joseph Lowery, and the Democratic Value of African American Public Mourning." *American Political Science Review* 104 (4) (2010): 681–97.

———. *American Mourning: Tragedy, Democracy, Resilience.* Cambridge: Cambridge University Press, 2017.

Sundquist, Eric. *To Wake the Nations: Race in the Making of American Literature.* Cambridge, MA: Harvard University Press, 1993.

Sundstrom, Ronald. *The Browning of America and the Evasion of Social Justice.* Albany: State University of New York Press, 2008.

Sweeney, Fionnghuala. *Frederick Douglass and the Atlantic World.* Liverpool: Liverpool University Press, 2007.

Taylor, Keeanga-Yamahtta. *From #BlackLivesMatter to Black Liberation.* Chicago: Haymarket, 2016.

Turner, Jack. *Awakening to Race: Individualism and Social Consciousness in America.* Chicago: University of Chicago Press, 2012.

Walker, Peter. *Moral Choices: Memory, Desire, and Imagination in Nineteenth-Century Narrative.* Baton Rouge: Louisiana State University Press, 1978.

Wallace, Maurice. *Constructing the Black Masculine: Identity and Ideality in African American Men's Literature and Culture, 1775–1995.* Durham, NC: Duke University Press, 2002.

Warren, James. *Culture of Eloquence: Oratory and Reform in Antebellum America.* University Park: Pennsylvania State University Press, 1999.

Washington, Booker T. *Frederick Douglass.* Honolulu: University Press of the Pacific, 2003.

West, Cornel. *Black Prophetic Fire.* Boston: Beacon, 2014.

————. *Prophesy Deliverance! An Afro-American Revolutionary Christianity.* Louisville, KY: Westminster John Knox, 1982.

Whitehead, Colson. *Underground Railroad.* New York: Doubleday, 2016.

Willett, Cynthia. *Maternal Ethics and Other Slave Moralities.* New York: Routledge, 1995.

————. *The Soul of Justice: Social Bonds and Racial Hubris.* Ithaca, NY: Cornell University Press, 2001.

Wilson, Ivy. *Specters of Democracy: Blackness and the Aesthetics of Politics in the Antebellum U.S.* Oxford: Oxford University Press, 2011.

Wolin, Sheldon. *Democracy Incorporated: Managed Democracy and the Specter of Inverted Totalitarianism.* Princeton, NJ: Princeton University Press, 2008.

————. *Fugitive Democracy and Other Essays.* Princeton, NJ: Princeton University Press, 2016.

Wu, Jin-Ping. *Frederick Douglass and the Black Liberation Movement: The North Star of American Blacks.* New York: Garland, 2000.

Yancy, George. *Black Bodies, White Gazes: The Continuing Significance of Race in America.* Lanham, MD: Rowman and Littlefield, 2017.

Yothers, Brian. *Reading Abolition: The Critical Reception of Harriet Beecher Stowe and Frederick Douglass.* Rochester, NY: Camden House, 2016.

Zamalin, Alex. *Struggle on Their Minds: The Political Thought of African American Resistance.* New York: Columbia University Press, 2017.

Contributors

Ange-Marie Hancock Alfaro is professor and chair of gender studies at the University of Southern California. Prior to graduate school, Alfaro worked for the National Basketball Association and wrote the original business plan for the Women's National Basketball Association. She is the author of the award-winning book *The Politics of Disgust and the Public Identity of the Welfare Queen* (2004). Alfaro's other works include the widely cited article on the study of intersectionality "When Multiplication Doesn't Equal Quick Addition" (2007) and the books *Solidarity Politics for Millennials* (2011) and *Intersectionality: An Intellectual History* (2016). With Nira Yuval-Davis, she is coeditor of the Palgrave-Macmillan Politics of Intersectionality book series.

Bernard R. Boxill is professor emeritus of philosophy at the University of North Carolina, Chapel Hill. He works in the areas of social and political theory, ethics, and African American thought. Boxill is author of the critically acclaimed book *Blacks and Social Justice* (1984), editor of *Race and Racism* (2001), and contributor of numerous journal articles and book chapters, including a series of essays on Frederick Douglass's political thought. He is currently completing two book manuscripts: "A History of African American Political Thought: From Martin Delany to the Present" and "Boundaries and Justice: On International Ethics and Distributive Justice."

Nick Bromell is professor of English at the University of Massachusetts, Amherst. He is the author of several books, including *By the Sweat of the Brow: Literature and Labor in Antebellum America* (1993), *The Time Is Always Now: Black Thought and the Transformations of US Democracy* (2013), and *A Political Companion to W. E. B. Du Bois* (University Press of Kentucky). He is currently completing a book on the political philosophy of Frederick Douglass.

Nicholas Buccola is professor of political science and the founding director of the Frederick Douglass Forum on Law, Rights, and Justice at Linfield College. He is the author of *The Political Thought of Frederick Douglass* (2012) as well as the editor of *The Essential Douglass: Selected Writings and Speeches* (2016) and *Abraham Lincoln and Liberal Democracy* (2016). His scholarly essays have appeared in a wide range of journals, including *Review of Politics* and *American Political Thought*.

Angela Y. Davis is professor emerita of history of consciousness at the University of California, Santa Cruz. An internationally noted scholar-activist, black feminist, theorist of the prison-industrial complex, Davis is the author of such books as *Angela Y. Davis: An Autobiography* (1974), *Women, Race, & Class* (1981), *Women, Culture, & Politics* (1990), *The Angela Y. Davis Reader* (edited by Joy James, 1998), *Blues Legacies and Black Feminism* (1999), *Are Prisons Obsolete?* (2003), *Abolition Democracy* (2005), *The Meaning of Freedom* (2012), and *Freedom Is a Constant Struggle* (2016).

Jason Frank is associate professor of government at Cornell University. His work historically situates approaches to democratic theory, with an emphasis on early American political thought and culture. Frank's books include *Vocations of Political Theory* (2000), *Constituent Moments* (2010), *A Political Companion to Herman Melville* (University Press of Kentucky, 2013), and *Publius and Political Imagination* (2013), and his articles and reviews have appeared in such journals as *Political Theory, Modern Intellectual History, Theory & Event, Public Culture, Constellations, Perspectives on Politics*, and *Review of Politics* as well as in several anthologies.

Paul Gilroy is professor of American and English literature at King's College, London. One of the most widely cited scholars in the humanities and social sciences, his intellectual background is multidisciplinary, and he has extensive interests in literature, art, music, cultural history, and modern political theory. Gilroy is best known for his work on racism, nationalism, and ethnicity and for his original approach to the history of the African diaspora into the Western Hemisphere. He is the author of *"There Ain't No Black in the Union Jack": The Cultural Politics of Race and Nation* (1987), *The Black Atlantic: Modernity and Double Consciousness* (1993), *Small Acts: Thoughts on the Politics of Black Cultures* (1993), *Against Race* (2000),

Postcolonial Melancholia (2005), *Black Britain* (2007), and *Darker Than Blue: On the Moral Economies of Black Atlantic Culture* (2010).

Robert Gooding-Williams is professor of philosophy at Columbia University. His areas of interest include Friedrich Nietzsche, W. E. B. Du Bois, critical race theory, African American political thought, nineteenth-century continental philosophy, existentialism, and philosophy in literature. Gooding-Williams is the author of *Zarathustra's Dionysian Modernism* (2001), *Look, A Negro! Philosophical Essays on Race, Culture, and Politics* (2005), and the award-winning work *In the Shadow of Du Bois* (2009). His edited and coedited volumes include *Reading Rodney King/Reading Urban Uprising* (1993), the Bedford Books edition of *The Souls of Black Folk* (1997), and a special issue of the *Du Bois Review* titled "Race in the 'Postracial' Epoch" (2014).

Margaret Kohn is associate professor of political science at the University of Toronto. Her primary research interests are in the areas of colonialism, democratic theory, critical theory, and urbanism. Kohn's articles have appeared in such journals as *Political Theory, Polity, Dissent, Constellations,* and the *Journal of Politics.* She is author of *Radical Space: Building the House of the People* (2003), *Brave New Neighborhoods: The Privatization of Public Space* (2004), *Political Theories of Decolonization* (with Keally McBride, 2011), and *The Death and Life of the Urban Commonwealth* (2016).

Vincent Lloyd is associate professor of theology and religious studies at Villanova University. He is author of several books, such as *The Problem with Grace* (2011), *Black Natural Law* (2016), and *Is Charisma Moral?* (2017), and his edited and coedited volumes include *Race and Secularism in America* (2012), *Sainthood and Race* (2016), and *Anti-blackness and Christian Ethics* (2017). Lloyd coedits the journal *Political Theology.*

Peter C. Myers is professor of political science at the University of Wisconsin, Eau Claire. He is the author of journal articles such as "'A Good Work for Our Race To-Day': Interests, Virtues, and the Achievement of Justice in Frederick Douglass's Freedmen's Monument Speech" in the *American Political Science Review* (2010). His books include *Our Only*

Star and Compass: Locke and the Struggle for Political Rationality (1999) and *Frederick Douglass: Race and the Rebirth of Liberalism* (2008). Myers is currently completing a book on the idea of color blindness in American political thought.

Anne Norton is professor of political science at the University of Pennsylvania. Educated at the University of Chicago, Norton is the author of the critically acclaimed books *Alternative Americas: A Reading of Antebellum Political Culture* (1986), *Reflections on Political Identity* (1988), *Republic of Signs: Liberal Theory and American Popular Culture* (1993), *Bloodrites of the Poststructuralists* (2002), *95 Theses on Politics, Culture, and Method* (2004), *Leo Strauss and the Politics of American Empire* (2004), and *On the Muslim Question* (2013). She is part of the Bridge Initiative against Islamophobia and founding coeditor of the journal *Theory & Event*. Norton has working projects on radical democracy, the problem of property, and racial inequality.

Neil Roberts is associate professor of Africana studies, political theory, and the philosophy of religion at Williams College. He is the author of articles in periodicals such as *Caribbean Studies, Daily Nous, New Political Science, Perspectives on Politics, Philosophia Africana, Political Theory, Small Axe,* and *Society for U.S. Intellectual History,* and he is coeditor of the collections *Creolizing Rousseau* (2015) and *Journeys in Caribbean Thought* (2016). He has also served as editor and coeditor for special issues of *Theory & Event* and the *C. L. R. James Journal.* His book *Freedom as Marronage* (2015) is the recipient of awards from the American Political Science Association Foundations of Political Theory section and *Choice* magazine, and the Association for College and Research Libraries selected it as a top-twenty-five book for 2015. Roberts is president of the Caribbean Philosophical Association.

Herbert J. Storing was at the time of his death Robert K. Gooch Professor of Government at the University of Virginia and the director of the Program on the Presidency at the White Burkett Miller Center of Public Affairs. Storing had previously taught at the University of Chicago. His publications include *Essays on the Scientific Study of Politics* (1962), *The State and the Farmer* (with Peter Self, 1962), and the posthumous texts *What the*

Anti-Federalists Were For: The Political Thought of the Opponents of the Constitution (1981) and *Toward a More Perfect Union* (1995).

Jack Turner is associate professor of political science at the University of Washington and director of the Washington Institute for the Study of Inequality and Race. He specializes in American political thought, race in American politics, critical race theory, and democratic theory. He is the author of *Awakening to Race: Individualism and Social Consciousness in America* (2012) and the editor of *A Political Companion to Henry David Thoreau* (University Press of Kentucky, 2009). His most recent article is "Thinking Historically" (2016).

Index

Page numbers in *italics* refer to photographs.

Political Companions to Great American Authors

Series Editor

Patrick J. Deneen, University of Notre Dame

Books in the Series

A Political Companion to Ralph Waldo Emerson
Edited by Alan M. Levine and Daniel S. Malachuk

A Political Companion to Marilynne Robinson
Edited by Shannon L. Mariotti and Joseph H. Lane Jr.

A Political Companion to James Baldwin
Edited by Susan J. McWilliams

A Political Companion to Frederick Douglass
Edited by Neil Roberts

A Political Companion to Walt Whitman
Edited by John E. Seery

A Political Companion to Henry Adams
Edited by Natalie Fuehrer Taylor

A Political Companion to Henry David Thoreau
Edited by Jack Turner

A Political Companion to John Steinbeck
Edited by Cyrus Ernesto Zirakzadeh and Simon Stow